S0-BIM-764

POLITICS AND RITUAL IN EARLY MEDIEVAL EUROPE

The Judgement of Solomon, as described in I Kings, iii, verses 16-28 (centre). Solomon being led to his royal consecration (top left); his anointment (I Kings, i, verses 39-40) (top right).
(Bible of San Paolo Fuori le Mura, fol. 188^{V}; Frontispiece to Proverbs)

POLITICS AND RITUAL IN EARLY MEDIEVAL EUROPE

JANET L. NELSON

THE HAMBLEDON PRESS
LONDON AND RONCEVERTE

Published by The Hambledon Press, 1986

35 Gloucester Avenue, London NW1 7AX (U.K.)

309 Greenbrier Avenue, Ronceverte
West Virginia 24970 (U.S.A.)

ISBN 0 907628 59 1

History Series 42

British Library Cataloguing in Publication Data

Nelson, Janet
Politics and ritual in early medieval Europe.
– (History series; 42)
1. Europe – History – 476-1492
I. Title II. Series
940.1'4 D102

Library of Congress Cataloging-in-Publication Data

Nelson, Janet (Janet L.)
Politics and ritual in early medieval Europe.

Includes index.
1. Franks – France – Kings and rulers.
2. France – Kings and rulers.
3. France – Politics and government – To 987.
4. Great Britain – Kings and rulers.
5. Great Britain – Politics and government – 449-1066.
I. Title.
DC64. N45 1986 941.01 86–15016

Printed and bound in Great Britain by
WBC (Printers), Bristol and WBC (Bookbinders), Maesteg

CONTENTS

ACKNOWLEDGEMENTS

The articles reprinted here first appeared in the following places and are reprinted by the kind permission of the original publishers.

1 *Medieval Women: Essays Dedicated and Presented to Professor Rosalind M.T. Hill*, edited by D. Baker. *Studies in Church History: Subsidia*, vol. 1 (Blackwell, Oxford, 1978), pp. 31-77.

2 *Studies in Church History*, 14 (1977), pp. 51-67.

3 *Studies in Church History*, 10 (1973), pp. 39-44.

4 *Studies in Church History*, 16 (1979), pp. 103-18.

5 *Ideal and Reality. Studies in Frankish and Anglo-Saxon Society Presented to J.M. Wallace-Hadrill*, edited by P. Wormald (Blackwell, Oxford, 1983), pp. 202-27.

6 *Studies in Church History*, 20 (1983), pp. 15-30.

7 *English Historical Review*, 92 (1977), pp. 241-79.

8 *Charles the Bald: Court and Kingdom*, edited by M. Gibson and J.L. Nelson, BAR International Series, 101 (Oxford, 1981), pp. 15-36.

9 *Speculum*, 60 (1985), pp. 251-93.

10 *Studies in Church History*, 7 (1971), pp. 41-59.

11 *Studies in Church History*, 13 (1976), pp. 97-119.

12 *Early Medieval Kingship*, edited by P.H. Sawyer and I.N. Wood (School of History, University of Leeds, 1977), pp. 50-71.

13 *Journal of Ecclesiastical History*, 18 (1967), pp. 145-63.

14 *Studies in Church History*, 11 (1975), pp. 41-51.

15 *Authority and Power: Studies in Medieval Law and Government Presented to Walter Ullmann*, edited by B. Tierney and P. Linehan (Cambridge, 1980), pp. 29-48.

16 This appears here for the first time.

17 *Proceedings of the Fourth Battle Conference on Anglo-Norman Studies* (Boydell Press, Woodbridge, 1982), pp. 117-32, 210-21.

PREFACE

Anyone who studies early medieval history is aware of the difficulties and gaps in the evidence: conclusions have to be provisional. The essays in this book span nearly twenty years, and I make no apology for having sometimes changed my mind. But readers will be aware of a larger shift in perspective, and for this I owe an explanation.

I will put it in terms of three debts. The first is to the late Walter Ullmann who taught me as an undergraduate and supervised my research. My Cambridge Ph.D. thesis, *Rituals of Royal Inauguration in Early Medieval Europe* (1967), and the publications that came out of it, were very strongly influenced by his teaching. It was he who first directed my attention to the coronation *Ordines* as important evidence for ideas about kingship in the early Middle Ages. The second debt is to the historians of my own generation with whom I came into contact after becoming a university teacher myself in 1970, especially Tim Reuter, Pauline Stafford, Ian Wood, and my colleagues in the University of London, John Gillingham and Wendy Davies. Their published work, and their willingness to discuss and criticise mine, sharpened my interest in political history and in the source-criticism on which it must depend. The third debt is to the undergraduates and research students I have taught, and learned from, over the years. They have shared my fascination in the early Middle Ages, in kingship and queenship, and in the sources of Carolingian history. Their commitment, and their questioning, have contributed constantly to my own research. I envisage them, and their successors, as the sort of audience this book may have: I hope that they will find its varying views, and its omissions, a spur to working out their own views and criticisms.

Nine of the seventeen papers that follow arose out of the work on my Ph.D. The one previously unpublished paper (no. 16) is a revision of the final chapter of my thesis: the impetus to write it came from an invitation to the International Conference on Medieval Coronations at the University of Toronto in February 1985. There I had the pleasure of meeting Paul L. Ward whose articles, over forty years ago, set the study of the early English *Ordines* on firm foundations. It has taken far too long for the building to go up – though Dr. Ward was nice enough not to complain about this! The plans I had in 1967 to prepare an edition of the Anglo-Saxon *Ordines* have long since been shelved. The last four papers in the present collection are a contribution on that subject. Others, I hope, will soon write the full history of medieval English king-makings and produce the long-desired edition of the *Ordines*.[1]

My own interests, as the remaining papers in this book show, have increasingly moved towards Merovingian and Carolingian history. Several of the papers are prolegomena to the study of the reign of Charles the Bald on which I am currently engaged. Though coronations have ceased to be the focus of my work, I am more than ever convinced of the importance of ritual to an understanding of early medieval politics. King-making rituals themselves are one segment of a large terrain for which modern maps scarcely exist. The title of this book suggests not just two subjects but an interaction between them, which I and others are only now beginning to explore.[2] I want to forestall disappointed expectations: the papers in this book do not deal systematically with the problem of connecting politics and ritual. But anyone determined enough to read on should feel encouraged to make connections of his or her own.

The picture used as a frontispiece to this book illustrates its twin themes. This complex piece of Carolingian ruler-iconography comes from a Bible made on the orders of Charles the Bald *c.*875 and presented to the pope.[3] In the central scene, Solomon sits enthroned giving the famous judgement described in I Kings (III *Reg.*) iii:16–28. On either side, and slightly below, warriors hear and approve, while beneath them, the judgement is carried out. The two smaller scenes above the throne show how Solomon got there: in the first, Solomon is led on David's mule to Gihon, and in the second Zadoch the priest and Nathan the prophet anoint him king:

> And they blew the trumpet; and all the people
> said, God save king Solomon.
> And all the people came up after him, and the
> people piped with pipes, and rejoiced with great
> joy, so that the earth rent with the sound of them.
>
> (I Kings, i:39–40.)

In the consecration scene, the king is recognisably a Carolingian; priest and prophet evoke their 'successors' the bishops, and the people the 'new Israel' – the Franks.

A book is the place to acknowledge, in this case belatedly, the help and

[1] George Garnett of St. John's College, Cambridge, and Richard Jackson of the University of Houston, Texas, have these projects well in hand.

[2] A paper of mine on broader aspects of Carolingian royal ritual is forthcoming in *Rituals of Royalty*, edd. D. Cannadine and S. Price (CUP 1986). Important new work can be looked forward to from such scholars as Stuart Airlie and Nikolaus Staubach.

[3] Frontispiece to the Book of Proverbs, Bible of San Paolo fuori le Mura: F. Mutherich and J. Gaehde, *Carolingian Painting* (London, 1977), plate 44.

patience of library staff: I am very grateful to those of the British Library, the London Library, and the libraries of King's College, the Warburg Institute, the University of London, and especially that most congenial of workplaces, the Institute of Historical Research. My special thanks are due to Martin Sheppard without whom this book would never have been conceived or produced. Finally, I want to thank my family for a lot of moral support, and Lizzie, Billy and Helen, in particular, for help with the index.

ABBREVIATIONS

AAWL	*Abhandlungen der Akademie der Wissenschaften und der Literatur*
AASS	*Acta Sanctorum*
AJ	*Ampleforth Journal*
Annales	*Annales: Economies, Sociétés, Civilisations*
ASC	*Anglo-Saxon Chronicle*
BEC	*Bibliothèque de l'École des Chartes*
BL	British Library, London
BS	*Byzantinoslavica*
BT	*The Bayeux Tapestry*, ed. F.M. Stenton, 2nd ed. (London, (1965)
BZ	*Byzantinische Zeitschrift*
CC	*Corpus Christianorum*
CCM	*Cahiers de Civilisation Médiévale*
CHJ	*Cambridge Historical Journal* (subsequently *Historical Journal*)
DA	*Deutsches Archiv*
DOP	*Dumbarton Oaks Papers*
DTC	*Dictionnaire de Théologie Catholique*
EHR	*English Historical Review*
HBS	Henry Bradshaw Society
HE	*Historia Ecclesiastica*
HJch	*Historisches Jahrbuch*
HZ	*Historische Zeitschrift*
JEH	*Journal of Ecclesiastical History*
JRS	*Journal of Roman Studies*
JTS	*Journal of Theological Studies*
LThK	*Lexicon für Theologie und Kirche*
Mansi	J.D. Mansi, *Sacrorum conciliorum nova et amplissima collectio*, 31 vols. (Florence/Venice, 1757-98)

MGH	*Monumenta Germaniae Historica*
	–, *AA* *Auctores Antiquissimi*
	–, *DD* *Diplomata*
	–, *Epp* *Epistolae*
	–, *SSRM* *Scriptores rerum merovingicarum*
	–, *SSRL* *Scriptores rerum langobardicarum*
MIÖG	*Mitteilungen des Instituts für österreichische Geschichtsforschung*
MStn	*Mittelalterliche Studien*
NA	*Neues Archiv*
PhK	Philosophisch-historisch Klasse
PL	*Patrologia Latina*
PP	*Past and Present*
RBPH	*Revue Belge de Philologie et d'Histoire*
REB	*Revue des Études Byzantines*
RGG	*Die Religionen in Geschichte und Gegenwart*
RH	*Revue Historique*
RHE	*Revue d'Histoire Ecclésiastique*
SBAW	*Sitzungsberichte der bayerischen Akademie der Wissenschaften*
SCH	*Studies in Church History*
SS Spoleto	*Settimane di Studio sull' alto medioevo*, Centro sull' alto medioevo, Spoleto

To my mother, Leila Muir (*née* Laughland),

and in memory

of my father, Billy Muir

1

QUEENS AS JEZEBELS: BRUNHILD AND BALTHILD IN MEROVINGIAN HISTORY[1]

SINCE they got a toe-hold in universities, the achievement of women in the field of medieval history has been high. Some female historiography may have been justly criticised for a certain breathlessness of style, a narrowness of concern, a subjectivity, even romanticism, of approach: faults produced, no doubt by the pressures of most women's early socialisation.[2] But the work of Rosalind Hill has shown an exemplary freedom from the faults and contributed substantially to the achievement. The combination of good sense and judgement with breadth of vision might perhaps have been expected from that rare person (of either sex) who can combine scholarly excellence with prowess in mountaineering. And so, despite its title, the paper that follows, in which I deal with the careers of two very active and intelligent women who commanded both the respect and the affection of many contemporaries (however unfairly posterity has treated them) will not, I hope, be thought a wholly inapt tribute.

That women played a 'large role' in Merovingian society is a commonplace of the historiography of the period. Queens Brunhild and Balthild[3] have been cited as cases in point. But if it is important to stress at the outset the obvious point that queens are not typical of women in this or any other period, it is also worth pursuing a little further the banal observation about the 'large role' of women to inquire *which* women appear as significant actors in the later sixth and seventh centuries, and why they do so. Some women sometimes found

[1] I am very grateful to Ian Wood, John Gillingham and Pauline Stafford for friendly criticism, and to Paul Fouracre for keen discussion of Merovingian matters.

[2] On some problems (if not the faults) of historical work by and about women, see the comments of [Susan Mosher] Stuard in her introduction to *Women* [*in Medieval Society*] (University of Pennsylvania Press 1976) pp 1–12. For some lively criticisms of the male-dominated historiography of women, see the remarks of Ria Lemaire in *CCM* 20 (1977) pp 261–3.

[3] For the sake of simplicity I have used anglicised spellings of these and other familiar names.

themselves in positions of wealth and potential power: they were those who belonged to a land-based aristocracy whose members generally married within their own ranks.[4] These women—as wives, bringers of dowries and receivers of bride-wealth, as widows and mothers (or stepmothers) custodians of family estates, as daughters heiresses to some or all of their parents' wealth—shared the status of their male kin, and had to be protected and provided for. If women loom so large in the history of Columbanan monasticism in seventh-century Gaul, this was not, I think, because 'women, especially, were seduced by the rigours of Columban's teachings',[5] but because, rather, these were new monastic structures eminently adapted to, and thus adopted by the managers of, land-based familial structures in which women already and necessarily occupied key positions. The number of sixth-century women's houses had remained low partly because monasticism on an

[4] This statement seems to me essentially true both for the Gallo-Roman and barbarian aristocracies in the period covered in this paper. On the former, see [K. F.] Stroheker, [*Der senatorische*] *Adel* [*im spätantiken Gallien*] (Tübingen 1948); on the latter, [R.] Sprandel, [*Der*] *merovingische Adel* [*und die Gebiete ostlich des Rheins*], *Forschungen zur oberrheinischen Landesgeschichte,* 5 (Freiburg-im-Breisgau 1957), and 'Struktur und Geschichte des merovingischen Adels', *HZ,* 193 (1961) pp 33–71; K. F. Werner, 'Bedeutende Adelsfamilien im Reich Karls des Grossen', in *Karl der Grosse, Lebenswerk und Nachleben,* ed W. Braunfels, 5 vols (Düsseldorf 1965–8) 1 pp 83–142, with full bibliography. The jural status of women differed as between Roman and various barbarian laws, but the long-term trend was towards heavy influence on the latter by the former and by canon law. Changes from the second half of the sixth century onwards made for an improvement in the status of women under the Salic law, especially in the matter of inheritance of ancestral land in which females could now share under certain circumstances, and in the women's control of her own *dos* or bride-price. On all this see [F. L.] Ganshof, '[Le] statut [de la femme dans la monarchie franque]', *Recueils Jean Bodin,* 12 (1962) pp 5–58, esp 15–17, 25–35. The specific political and social developments which, as Ganshof observes, (p 57) lie behind these legal changes have yet to be thoroughly examined. But see meanwhile F. Beyerle, 'Das legislative Werk Chilperics I', *ZRG GAbt* 78 (1961) esp pp 30–8. For particular aspects of women's legal position see K. F. Drew, 'The Germanic Family of the *Leges Burgundionum*', *Medievalia et Humanistica* 15 (1963) pp 5–14 and [J.-A.] McNamara and [S. F.] Wemple, '[Marriage and] Divorce [in the Frankish kingdom]', in Stuard, *Women,* pp 95–124. For a broader comparative view see two recent works of J. Goody: *Production and Reproduction* (Cambridge 1976), and his introductory chapter to *Family and Inheritance: Rural Society in Western Europe, 1200–1800,* ed J. Goody, J. Thirsk and E. P. Thompson (Cambridge 1976), both offering characteristically stimulating insights and analysis for historians as well as social scientists. See also his *Succession* [*to High Office*] (Cambridge 1966) esp pp 1–56.

[5] [P.] Riché, *Education* [*and Culture in the Barbarian West, Sixth through Eighth Centuries,*] trans J. J. Contreni (University of North Carolina Press 1976) p 329. For details of women's participation in monasticism, see [F.] Prinz, [*Frühes*] *Mönchtum* [*im Frankenreich*] (Munich/Vienna 1965); the good short survey in the first chapter of [G. A. de Rohan Chabot, marquise de] Maillé, [*Les Cryptes de*] *Jouarre* (Paris 1971). There remains, however, a basic problem of explanation.

urban, or suburban, episcopally-directed model could not readily be accommodated to the requirements (for solidarity and biological continuity) of aristocratic families: witness the complaint of the mother of Rusticula, her only child, who had entered the convent of St John at Arles: 'I look at the possessions of our house, the innumerable multitude of our *familia* and whom I shall leave it all to, I don't know . . . Who will look after me in my old age, now that the one daughter I had is lost?'[6] In the seventh century, Sadalberga, whose hagiographer writes glowingly of contemporary foundations *per heremi vastitatem* established her first convent *in hereditate paterna* having first conveniently converted husband and children to the monastic life;[7] while Moda, widow of the magnate Autharius, moved in with her own kin to take over control of her stepson Ado's recent foundation at Jouarre.[8] The importance of such family connexions is equally, and poignantly, shown in the case of Wulftrude, daughter of Grimoald and abbess of the Pippinid foundation at Nivelles, whose removal from office was attempted by Merovingian *reges* and *reginae* 'out of hatred for her late father', their family's enemy.[9]

No *Frauenfrage* of the deprived or alienated arises, then, in reference to the seventh-century nuns and abbesses of Gaul. It is rather a matter of families' deployment of their personnel. The one function that critically distinguished masculine from feminine roles, that of warfare, was conspicuously absent from the monastic life: monks like women were *inermes*. Conversely, within the monastery, a woman could transcend the 'weakness' of her sex and become, not perhaps 'virilised',[10] but desexualised. Thus the same literary and spiritual culture was offered in monasteries to both girls and boys; and in this same asexual milieu, a woman as abbess of a double monastery[11] could exercise the political authority which in the secular world, at all levels including the

[6] *MGH SSRM* 4, cap 5, p 342. See Riché, 'Note d'hagiographie mérovingienne: la *Vita S. Rusticulae*', *AB* 72 (1954) pp 369–77, showing this to be a seventh-century text.

[7] *MGH SSRM* 5, caps 8 and 12, pp 54, 56. For the site, a *villa* in the *pagus* of Langres, see Krusch's comments *ibid* pp 43, 56 n 2. Could paternal *saltus* be classed as *eremus*?

[8] J. Guerout, 'Les Origines et le premier siècle de l'Abbaye', Y. Chaussy *L'Abbaye royale Notre-Dame de Jouarre,* ed Y. Chaussy (Paris 1961) pp 1–67.

[9] *Vita Geretrudis,* cap 6, *MGH SSRM* 2, p 460. For *Sippenkloster* ('kin-group monasteries') as aristocratic cult-centres, see Prinz, *Mönchtum,* pp 489–503.

[10] So, Riché, *Education,* p 457, with, however, valuable comments on the place of women in monastic culture.

[11] See Guerout, 'Origines', esp pp 34 *seq*; also J. Godfrey, 'The Double Monastery in early English history', *AJ* 79 (1974) pp 19–32.

monarchic,[11a] was formally monopolised by men. The point to stress is the absence of any principle of matriarchy.[12] Aristocratic women propose and dispose *ex officio* in a context where their sex is irrelevant. If through the contingencies of mortality or inheritance they temporarily wield power in secular society, they do so primarily in virtue of, and by means of, biologically-ascribed status which marital status will normally match and reinforce.[13]

To all of this, the position of a Merovingian queen, at any rate from the later sixth century, stands in something of a contrast. For it *could* be (not necessarily, but usually—and the mere possibility is what matters here) achieved and constituted exclusively through her husband. This happened when it became royal practice, first in Burgundy, then in Austrasia and Neustria, to choose as consort a low-born woman or even a slave.[14] From this same period we have evidence that the birth or status (whether queen or concubine) of a king's bed-fellow could not affect the status or succession-rights of her sons,[15] and it may be that

[11a] Ganshof, 'Statut', p 54, stresses the inability of women, despite their *Rechtsfähigkeit* in private law, to receive or transmit royal power in their own right: Kingship was an *hereditas aviatica.* (For one small caveat, see below p 7). Ganshof's point must modify the notion that the Merovingians treated their realm simply as personal property, in view of the changes made in inheritance law by Chilperic I (561–84), on which see Ganshof, pp 34–5.

[12] This is certainly not to deny the importance of ties with and through maternal kin. See K. Leyser, 'The German aristocracy from the ninth to the early twelfth century', *PP* 41 (1968) pp 25–53, and 'Maternal kin in early medieval Germany: a reply', *PP* 49 (1970) pp 126–34, though Leyser deals with periods later than the Merovingian.

[13] This seems true of the seventh-century marriages on which details are given in hagiographic sources. I have found only one clear case of an asymmetrical marriage in Gregory of Tours' *L*[*ibri*] *H*[*istoriarum*] (the so-called *History of the Franks*) and here the mother's status is higher than the father's: see *LH* x, 8, ed B. Krusch and W. Levison, *MGH SSRM* 1 (2 ed Berlin 1937–51) p 489 (the parents of Tetradia - *nobilis ex matre, patre inferiore.*) For an alleged attempted exception to this conjugal matching by a Frankish aristocrat see below p 17.

[14] For details see [E.] Ewig, 'Studien [zur merowingingischen Dynastie]', *Frühmittelalterliche Studien* 8 (1974) pp 15–59 at 39 *seq. LH* iv, 25 and 26, pp 156–7, provides confirmation that low-born queens were not usual in the mid-sixth century.

[15] *LH* v, 20, p 228. See [Ian] Wood, 'Kings, [Kingdoms and Consent]', *Early Medieval Kingship*, ed P. H. Sawyer and I. N. Wood (University of Leeds 1977) pp 6–29 at p 14. On the distinction between queen (*regina*) and concubine (*concubina*) in Gregory and Fredegar, see Ewig, 'Studien', pp 38–9, 42–4. There is only once certain case of a concubine's son succeeding to the kingship in the later sixth century and through the whole later Merovingian period: Theudebert II. See below p 15. But Sigibert III is another probable case. Pauline Stafford rightly points out to me that the queen-concubine distinction is too simple, betraying an ecclesiastical perspective: matters were often more complicated. But in the light of the very scarce Merovingian evidence it seems impossible to say how much more so in the cases that have concerned me here.

the principle enunciated by Gregory of Tours reflected a new situation. Certainly, from the time of Guntramn and Chilperic, the typical Merovingian king expressed the uniqueness of his monarchic status, his freedom from the norms that constrained his aristocratic subjects, by marrying a woman who, far from bringing him potent affines or rich dowry, owed everything to her relationship with him. Even if the royal bride was, as occasionally in the sixth century, a foreign princess,[16] her situation in practice might be little different from the ex-serving maid's. Her dependence on her husband's generosity and favour, when her own kin were far away and her people reckoned, perhaps, the enemies of the Franks, might be similarly complete. A Visigothic princess (Spain being one source of foreign brides for Merovingians) might keep in touch with her fatherland, but dynastic discontinuity there might in the fairly short run cut her personal link with the reigning house.[17] The fate of the Spanish princess Galswinth at Chilperic's hands[18] was no different from that of the ex-slave Bilichild at Theudebert II's.[19] And Galswinth did not find her avenger in any Spanish king.

The wife of a Merovingian, then, enjoyed a position both dependent and precarious, resting as it did on her personal, sexual association with a husband whose interests or fancy could all too easily attach him to her supplanter. A Merovingian ex-wife often cuts a pathetic figure, especially if she was sonless, or if her sons quarrelled with, or pre-deceased, their father.[20] Radegund, opting for ascetic virtuosity,[21] is an exception that also proves the rule. A Merovingian wife might have the title of queen, but there is no evidence that she underwent any special inauguration ritual (apart, presumably, from the marriage-ritual itself) that would have paralleled her husband's to his kingship.

[16] Ewig, 'Studien', p 39.

[17] See below p 9.

[18] *LH* iv, 28, pp 160–1.

[19] [*The Fourth Book of the Chronicle of*] *Fred*[*egar*], ed J. M. Wallace-Hadrill (London 1960) cap 37, p 30.

[20] *LH* iii, 27 (Deuteria—though she did have a son, Theudebald); iv, 25 (Marcatrude —childless); iv, 26 (Ingoberg —sonless); v, 39 (Audovera—see below p 8 n 29). Nantechild, ex-wife of Dagobert, retained her queenly status and re-emerged to prominence at her husband's death because she had an infant son (Clovis II) for whom she became regent, whereas the two queens who superseded her in Dagobert's favours both seem to have been childless: *Fred* caps 60, 79, pp 50, 67.

[21] *LH* iii, 7, p 105. It is probably significant that Radegund was childless. On her spirituality see E. Delaruelle, 'Sainte Radegonde, son type de sainteté et la chrétienté de son temps', *Études Merovingiennes,* Actes des Journées de Poitiers, 1952 (Paris 1953) pp 65–74.

Yet the very limitations on the extent to which the queen was enmeshed in political and familial structures could also give her, under certain conditions, a paradoxical freedom. We can look at this under two aspects: the economic and the sexual-genetic. Whereas a female aristocrat usually inherited some wealth in land or retained a stake in family estates, a queen of low or servile birth acquired wealth exclusively from or through her husband; and because a fair proportion of such acquired wealth tended to be in movables,[22] there was probably rather less contrast in practice between the resources of a Bilichild and a Galswinth than the difference in original status might seem to suggest. The association of queens with treasure is a recurrent theme of Merovingian history, and the uses of treasure were manifold. First as goldbringer or gold-receiver, then as guardian of the royal hoard in a primitive 'capital' during the king's absences at war, a queen could personally control sufficient treasure to support political activities on her own account. Fredegund was generous enough in deploying hers to taunt the Franks for their niggardliness;[23] plotters against Clothar II solicited his queen's alliance, asking her to send them secretly 'all the treasure she could[24]. Given the indispensability of treasure to political success in the Merovingian world, in the seventh and the eighth centuries no less than in the sixth,[25] the queen's access to such resources could put her in a strong position, despite her relative weakness in terms of the direct control of land. Politically as personally, a queen's

[22] This seems to have been true of the bride-price (*dos*—to be distinguished from dowry) in barbarian laws: see Ganshof, 'Statut', p 28 with nn 66–8. It is not clear from *LH* ix, 20, p 437 what proportion of the five *civitates* given to Galswinth by Chilperic constituted the *dos* and what was morning-gift. But it is clear that kings gave land as well as moveables to their wives: see *LH* vi, 45, p 318 (Fredegund). For Balthild's estates, see below, p 40 n 204.

[23] *LH* vi, 45, p 318. Compare *LH* iv, 26, p 159 (Theudechild), and vii, 4, p 328 (Fredegund again).

[24] *Fred* cap 44, pp 36–7. The bishop of Sion asks Bertetrude 'ut thinsauris quantum potebat secretissime ad Sidonis suam civitatem transferrit, eo quod esset locum tutissimum'. Perhaps episcopal treasuries had something of the function of banks. On the Burgundian background to this episode see Ewig, '[*Die fränkische*] *Teilreiche* [*im 7. Jahrhundert* (613–714)]', *Trierer Zeitschrift* 22 (Trier 1953) pp 85–144 at p 106.

[25] *Fred* cap 45, p 38; cap 67, p 56; cap 75, p 63; cap 84, p 71. The Continuator of Fredegar, *ibid* cap 9, p 88 shows the importance of treasure for Plectrude, widow of Pippin II, in 714–5. Hincmar, *De Ordine Palatii*, cap 22, *MGH Cap* 2, p 525, shows the continuing intimate connexion of the queen with treasure in the ninth century. See below n 234. For the continuance of taxation and tolls throughout this period, see F. Lot *L'Impot foncier et la capitation personnelle sous le Bas-Empire et a l'époque franque* (Paris 1928), and Ganshof, 'A propos du tonlieu sous les mérovingiens', *Studi in honore di Amintore Fanfani* (Milan 1962) 1, pp 291–315.

'rootlessness' might mean the advantage of greater freedom of manoeuvre.

The queen's initial offer to her husband of sexual services could obviously serve as a power-base as long as she retained his affections. Fredegund's is probably the best-documented case of a king's passion giving his consort long-term political ascendance.[26] Aside from such personal predilections, however, the strength of the conjugal bond—a point on which Germanic and ecclesiastical attitudes converged, though from different premises[27]—meant that a monarch's status rubbed off on his bed-fellow so that, while no queen could reign in her own right, a queen as widow could become a repository of royal powers for the time being apparently quiescent, a vehicle on which claims to the royal succession could be carried to a second husband. Admittedly, in every such case known to me, the queen was not low-born but herself of noble or royal family.[28] Still, her capacity to transmit a claim to rule seems to have arisen from her association with a reigning king; and in the interregnum created by his death, given an indeterminate succession system (whether dynastic or elective), the queen would function as an inhibitor of conflict if her second husband could make his claim stick.

[26] *LH* iv, 28, p 161; v, 18, p 240 (Fredegund had 200 pounds of silver to offer as a bribe); v, 34, p 220; etc. For a caution about Gregory's bias, see below p 10. Fredegund is vividly evoked in the novel of M. Brion, *Frédégonde et Brunehaut* (Paris 1935).

[27] Ganshof, 'Statut', pp 15 *seq*, cites evidence not only from the laws but from legal acts (wills; land-grants) showing the rights of wives and widows in conjugal property. Roman law here influenced barbarian laws. Of course divorce was allowed in barbarian as in Roman codes. But McNamara and Wemple, 'Divorce', pp 98 *seq*, seem to overstress both the disadvantaged position of wives as compared with that of husbands, and the importance of the divergence between barbarian and ecclesiastical law on this point. Divorce and inheritance need to be treated together, as do law and practice, in both areas. I am not convinced by those who argue that the cases of Clothar I (*LH* iv, 3) or Dagobert (*Fred* cap 60, p 50) show the practice of royal polygamy, though these two kings offer the most conspicuous examples of serial monogamy.

[28] For the Lombards, see *Fred* caps 51, 70, pp 42, 59; and the comments of [*K. A.*] Eckhardt *Studia* [*Merovingica*], *Bibliotheca Rerum Historicarum* 11 (Aalen 1975) p 141. For the Anglo-Saxons, the evidence is conveniently assembled by W. A. Chaney, *The Cult of Kingship in Anglo-Saxon England* (Manchester 1970) pp 25–8, though the inferences there drawn concerning matrilineal royal succession are quite unwarranted. For the Merovingians, see *LH* iii, 6, iv 9; and perhaps *Fred* cap 44, p 37; also below p 10. The men concerned in all these cases where information is available already had a claim to the kingship, which suggests that marriage with the late king's widow strengthened, but did not constitute, such a claim. See also [R.] Schneider, *Königswahl* [*und Königserhebung im Frühmittelalter*] (Stuttgart 1972) pp 246–8, where however the notion of *Einheirat* ('endogamy') seems of doubtful relevance.

In Gaul, however, unlike Lombard Italy or Visigothic Spain, filial succession remained normal. Thus the only way a queen could secure her position, both in her husband's lifetime and especially after his death, was to produce a son who survived.[29] Because of the frequent succession of minors, regents might govern for relatively long periods (even though the age of majority was fifteen)[30] and a queen-mother clearly had a strong claim to the regency. Hers was not the only claim: the role of *nutritor*, literally 'male nurse', which in fact contained that of a regent, thereby illustrating once again the political significance of personal closeness to the king even when he was a child,[31] was appropriated by mayors of the palace on several occasions in the sixth and seventh centuries.[32]. But a dowager queen could normally hope to act as regent for her own son. If a dowager queen were childless or had only daughters, then her husband's death would obviously mean her exclusion from power. But even if she had a young son, she might have difficulty in maintaining that physical proximity to him on which a regent's power depended. An infant prince might be reared on a country estate;[33] he would probably be in the care of a nurse. The moment of his father's death might find his mother far away. In any event, what determined a boy-prince's success in claiming the royal succession also directed his mother's future: namely, the attitude of the aristocracy, or, immediately, of a few well-placed aristocrats. A widowed queen was thrown back on the personal ties she had formed during her husband's lifetime, and on her own political skill: for on these depended how much treasure and influence (the two were not unconnected) she might be able to salvage.

[29] For the position of a widowed queen with only daughters, see *LH* iv, 20 (Ultrogotha). For the risks of sonlessness during the husband's lifetime see *LH* iv, 26 (Ingoberg) and possibly iii, 7 (Radegund). See also below p 18, and for another probable seventh-century example (Gomatrude), see *Fred* cap 58, p 49. There were the additional risks of very high infant mortality (Fredegund lost four sons in infancy) and of sons growing up to quarrel with their father and being killed on his orders (Audovera lost two of her three sons this way, and the third also predeceased his father).

[30] Ewig, 'Studien', pp 22–4.

[31] For the potential importance of the nurse's position, see *LH* ix, 38, pp 458–9, where a royal nurse and her male assistant conspire with powerful aristocrats.

[32] Venantius Fortunatus, *Carmina* vii, 16, *MGH AA* 4, pp 170–1 (Condan, preceptor of Theudebald and *de facto* mayor of the Austrasian palace); *LH* v, 46, p 256 (Gogo—see below p 41); *Fred* caps 86, 88, pp 72, 75 (Otto; Grimoald). On Otto see [H.] Ebling, *Prosopographie* [*der Amtsträger des Merovingerreiches* (*613–741*)] (Munich 1974) pp 66–7.

[33] *LH* vi, 41, p 314.

Throughout Merovingian history, the fates of widowed queens in interregna highlighted the persisting power of bishops and *leudes*.[34]

So far I have laid stress on the precariousness and contingency of queens' positions rather than any inherent advantages accruing from their associations with monarchy, and on the relatively small extent to which the queen's powers were integrated into ongoing political or social structures: beyond personalities, episcopacy, aristocracy, kingship can be said to have existed as institutions, but it is much harder to identify anything that could be called 'queenship'. I want now to consider in more detail two queenly careers, not simply to illustrate but to amplify, and perhaps qualify, the above generalisations, and by exploring more fully the mechanisms of queenly activity to get at what seem to me some of the main forces and fundamental continuities in Merovingian politics. I begin with some basic biographical information on each.

First: Brunhild.[35] A Visigothic princess who maintained links with Spain till her last years, Brunhild's kinship link with the ruling dynasty there was severed when Liuva II was murdered in 603. Sisebut (612–21) whose *Vita* of Desiderius of Vienne[36] is the earliest surviving source for Brunhild's regency and is also violently hostile, was therefore no relative of hers. Nor was Witteric (murderer of Liuva II) whose daughter Ermenberga was sought as a bride for Brunhild's grandson Theuderic in 607.[37] These facts, I shall argue, are relevant to the unfolding of Brunhild's Spanish connexion.

Born *c*545–50, Brunhild was sought in marriage by Sigibert (apparently continuing an Austrasian tradition of foreign dynastic marriages)[38] in 566. Her Arianism was no obstacle, and she swiftly abandoned it. Gregory of Tours, our chief source for Brunhild's life up to 591, has no unfavourable comment to make on her: he introduces her on her arrival at Sigibert's court as good-looking and shrewd with a

[34] *LH* v, 1, p 194; vii, 7, p 330. See Wood, 'Kings', pp 6–7, 10–11; also below pp 12, 19.

[35] The best scholarly study remains [G.] Kurth, '[La reine] Brunehaut', in *Études Franques*, 2 vols (Paris, Brussels 1919) 1, pp 265–356, with full references to the nineteenth-century literature. (Kurth's paper first appeared in 1891). See also Ewig, '[Die fränkischen] Teilungen [und Teilreiche (511–613)]', *AAWL*, Geistes- und Sozialwissenschaftlichen Klasse, 9 (Wiesbaden 1952) pp 689 *seq*. For the chronology of Brunhild's life, I have relied on Ewig, 'Studien'.

[36] *MGH SSRM* 3, pp 620–7. See below pp 27-8.

[37] *Fred* cap 30, p 20.

[38] Ewig, 'Studien', p 40.

large dowry of treasures.[39] But Gregory's view of Brunhild must be set in a literary as well as an historical context: Chilperic figures in Gregory's drama as 'the Nero and Herod of our time',[40] Fredegund is his female counterpart in villainy, and Brunhild for whose sister Galswinth's death the evil pair are responsible[41] is therefore an avenger on the side of the angels. Twenty years after Galswinth's murder, the mutual hatred between Brunhild and Fredegund was as strong as ever.[42] Clearly the pursuit of this vendetta is one main theme in Brunhild's whole life.[43]

But another, equally significant, is Brunhild's identification with the family into which she had married. Of the various aspects of her collaboration with her husband and, later, her son praised in the courtly verse of Venantius Fortunatus, none is more revealing than her patronage of the cult of St Martin, the Merovingians' *Reichsheiliger*.[44] It was said after Sigibert's death that she had 'held the realm under her husband.'[45] She had joined him on his last campaign against Chilperic, bringing treasure to him at Paris. She was there, with treasure and children, when the news of his assassination arrived.[46] But though deprived of this treasure and of the custody of her children and exiled to Rouen, she retained an impressive quantity of personal treasure[47] as well as the special association with kingship adhering even to the widow of a Merovingian king. Very soon, Merovech, son of Chilperic and stepson of Fredegund, came to Rouen and married her.[48] *Aima-t-elle réelement Merovée?*[49] Kurth's delightful question must remain unanswered. But it is not fanciful to guess that Merovech's motive was

[39] *LH* iv, 27, p 160: '. . puella elegans opere, venusta aspectu, honesta moribus atque decora, prudens consilio et blanda colloquio . . . cum magnis thesauris. .' For Gregory's own personal relations with Brunhild, see below p 13 n 59, and p 24. He is hardly, therefore, a dispassionate witness.

[40] *LH* vi, 46, p 319.

[41] *LH* iv, 28, p 161.

[42] *LH* ix, 20, p 439: '. . . odium, quod inter illas olim statutum est, adhuc pullulat, non arescit.'

[43] This is rightly stressed by [J. M.]Wallace-Hadrill, [*The*] *Long-Haired Kings* (London 1962) pp 134–5, 205.

[44] Venantius Fortunatus, *Carmina* x, 7, pp 239–41. See Prinz, *Mönchtum*, pp 32–3.

[45] *LH* vi, 4, p 268.

[46] *LH* v, 1, p 194.

[47] *LH* v, 18, p 221: Brunhild had left five bundles with the bishop of Rouen for safekeeping, of which two were alleged to be stuffed with 'species et diversis ornamentis . . . quae praeciebantur amplius quam tria milia solidorum; sed et saccolum cum nummismati auri pondere, tenentem duo milia'.

[48] *LH* v, 2, p 195.

[49] Kurth, 'Brunehaut', p 280.

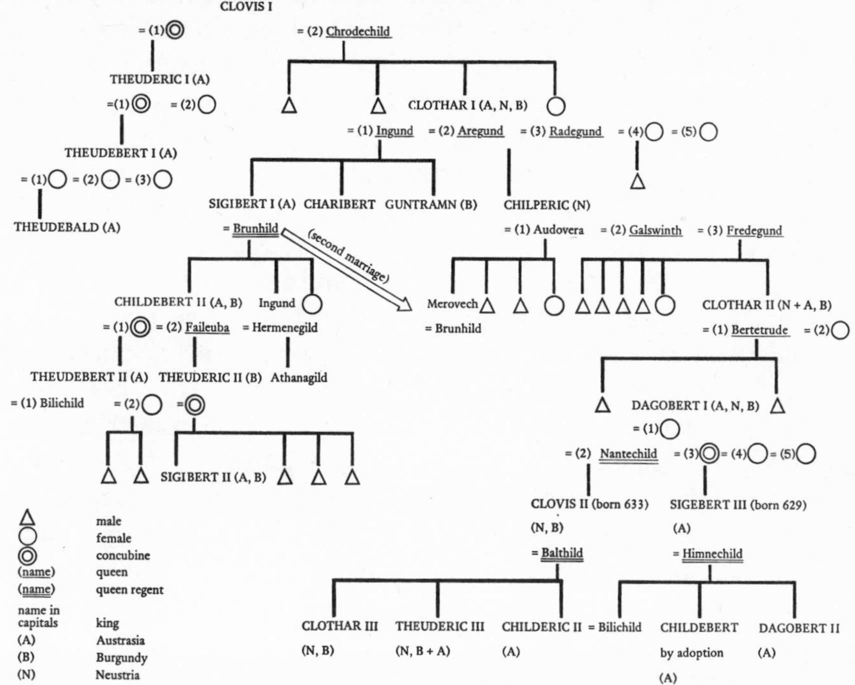

TABLE SHOWING THE MEROVINGIANS, THEIR QUEENS AND CONCUBINES

the staking of a claim to Sigibert's kingdom.[50] As it turned out, Sigibert's young son Childebert proved more acceptable to a majority of the Austrasian magnates. Brunhild herself commanded enough personal loyalty from some of those magnates for them to request and get her liberation from Chilperic.[51] And Merovech's rejection by 'the Austrasians' when he attempted to rejoin Brunhild (577) may not, as Kurth surmised, have meant her humiliation but the carrying out of her wishes. For as long as her son was king, she could hope to retrieve her position. Kurth portrays the period 576–84, that is, until Childebert attained his majority, as 'eight years of humiliation' for Brunhild at the hands of the Austrasian aristocracy.[52] But there is no evidence that Childebert's *nutricius* Gogo was hostile to her: he may, indeed have been her appointee both in this capacity and in the royal chancery.[53] Brunhild could conduct her own relations with Spain, using the bishop of Châlons as an envoy.[54] Even the driving into exile of her 'faithful supporter' duke Lupus of Champagne was the work of a faction, not an 'anti-royal'aristocracy as a whole. Brunhild had been strong enough to prevent faction-fighting from erupting into open warfare in a threatened attack on Lupus when, in Gregory's fine phrase, 'girding herself manfully, she burst into the midst of the opposing ranks', and her *industria* prevailed. Against these facts, Ursio's taunt that Childebert's realm 'is being kept safe by our protection, not yours' should not be understood as implying Brunhild's eclipse.[55]

When Childebert reached his majority in 585[56] however, Brunhild's position became a commanding one. Dispensing with a 'tutor', she now took over her son's guidance herself,[57] and pope Gregory the

[50] Ewig, 'Studien', p 33.

[51] *LHF* cap 33 p 299. See Kurth, 'Brunehaut', pp 281–2.

[52] Kurth, 'Brunehaut', p 28.

[53] For the letter written for Childebert to the Lombard king Grasulf by Gogo, see *MGH Epp* 3, no 48, p 152. Riché, *Education,* p 222, suggests that Brunhild 'brought Gogo into the royal chancellery'. For Gogo as *nutricius,* see *LH* v, 46, p 256. According to the *Chronicle of Fredegar,* iii, cap 59, *MGH SSRM* 2, p 109, Gogo was one of the envoys sent to Spain to fetch Brunhild.

[54] *LH* v, 40, p 247. The date is 580.

[55] *LH* vi, 4, p 268: '. . ."Recede a nobis, o mulier. Sufficiat tibi sub viro tenuisse regnum; nunc autem filius tuus regnat, regnumque eius non tua, sed nostra tuitione salvatur . . . "Haec et alia cum diutissime inter se protulissent, obtenuit reginae industria, ne pugnarent.'

[56] Ewig, 'Studien', p 22.

[57] *LH* viii, 22, p 389: '. . . regina mater curam vellit propriam habere de filio'. As Ewig points out this did not, of course, involve a formal legal position, but rather a personal relationship.

Great would soon afterwards treat 'both the government of the realm and the education of your son' as evidence of Brunhild's qualities.[58] A family compact between the Austrasian and Burgundian branches of the dynasty was achieved at Andelot (586) where her continuing hostility to Fredegund is transparent.[59] Fredegar makes her responsible for Chilperic's assassination and names the man she hired for the job:[60] against this, the argument from Gregory's silence, given his bias, may not be as telling as Kurth supposed—which is only to say that Brunhild carried out her family duties according to her Germanic lights. Family duty marched with political interest within Austrasia: those Austrasian magnates who had opposed Brunhild not surprisingly found support in Neustria.[61] But now able to back her aristocratic supporters with the full weight of royal resources, the queen mother crushed her opponents within Austrasia, demonstrating then and later her capacity to exercise the eminently royal virtues of rewarding loyalty, avenging wrongs done to those under her protection, and revenging herself on personal enemies.[62] Her famous 'foreign relations' with Spain and with Constantinople were in fact extensions of family relations, on the one hand forging further links with the royal dynasty in Spain and, after her daughter Ingund's marriage to Hermenegild and his unsuccessful revolt against his father Leuvigild,[63] trying to recover her little grandson Athanagild from the Byzantine imperial protectors to whom he had fled;[64] on the other hand identifying with a new Frankish assertiveness expressed as clearly in Baudonivia's *Vita* of Radegund[65] as

[58] Gregory the Great, Ep vi, 5, in *MGH Epp* 1, p 383: 'Excellentiae vestrae praedicandam ac Deo placitam bonitatem et gubernacula regni testantur et educatio filii manifestat'. The date is 595.

[59] *LH* ix, 20, pp 434–9, for the text. For the date, see [W. A.] Eckhardt, '[Die] *Decretio Childeberti* [und ihre Uberlieferung]', *ZRG GAbt* 84 (1967) pp 1–71 at 66 *seq*. In the subsequent diplomatic exchanges between Guntramn and Childebert and Brunhild, Gregory of Tours himself served as the latter's envoy. This closeness to the Austrasian court is noteworthy.

[60] *Fred* iii, 93 in *MGH SSRM* 2, p 118: '. . . ab homine nomen Falcone'.

[61] *LH* ix, 9, p 421.

[62] *LH* ix, 9–12, pp 421–7. Brunhild's relations with Lupus, Ursio and Berthefried, illustrating the varieties of just deserts, should be compared with the earlier episode recounted in *LH* vi, 4, pp 267–8. Brunhild's concern for someone under her protection is shown in the story of Sichar, *LH* ix, 19, pp 433–4.

[63] See J. N. Hillgarth, 'Coins and chronicles: propaganda in sixth-century Spain and the Byzantine background', *Historia* 15 (Wiesbaden 1966) pp 483–508; and E. A. Thompson, *The Goths in Spain* (Oxford 1969) pp 64–73.

[64] The evidence is contained in the *Epistolae Austrasicae*, nos 25–48, *MGH Epp* 3, pp 138–53.

[65] *MGH SSRM* 2, pp 358–95, II cap 16 at p 388: in acquiring a piece of the true cross,

in the diplomatic exchanges of earlier Austrasian kings,[66] and now epitomised in Brunhild's appeal to the empress Anastasia (wife of Maurice) to join with her in bringing the benefits of peace 'between the two peoples'![66a]; Beneath the Roman verbiage of *pax* and *caritas* is a thoroughly gentile consciousness of Frankish-Roman parity.

Childebert, who had inherited Burgundy on Guntramn's death in 593, himself died aged only twenty-six in 596, leaving Austrasia to the ten-year-old Theudebert, Burgundy to nine-year-old Theuderic.[67] Brunhild as de facto regent for both young kings now entered the last and most active phase of her career. She and her son had had their Austrasian supporters. Now she needed, and found, support from members of a more southerly aristocracy, of mixed 'Roman' and barbarian origins, long used to collaboration with kings. Asclepiodotus, former head of Guntramn's chancery, had carried his expertise to Childebert, whose great *Decretum* of 596 he probably drafted, and he remained influential during Brunhild's regency.[68] I shall examine presently other bases of the old queen's continuing power, but here briefly consider her position in the royal family. She had vetoed Childebert's marriage to the Agilolfing Theodelinda (the pair had been betrothed before 589) presumably to counter the hostile influence of that princess's Austrasian and Lombard connexions.[69] But she seems to have approved Childebert's eventual marriage with his ex-mistress Faileuba, who may possibly have been a woman of low birth.[70] If this was so, and Childebert was following Guntramn in raising a low-born concubine to queenship, we might speculate that Brunhild assented the more readily because Faileuba, lacking powerful aristocratic connexions

---

Radegund tells King Sigibert she will act 'pro totius patriae salute et eius regn: stabilitate'. 'Sicut beata Helena . . . quod fecit illa in orientali patria, hoc fecit beata Radegundis in Gallia', comments Baudonivia. Radegund commends her foundation, *ibid* p 389, 'praecellentissimis dominis regibus et serenissimae dominae Bronichildi'.

66 *MGH Epp* 3, nos 18, 19, 20, pp 131–3, esp no 20, p 133, where Theudebert I lists 'quae gentes nostrae sint, Deo adiutore, dicione subiectae', and asks Justinian 'ut . . . in communi utilitate iungamur'.

66a *MGH Epp* 3, no 29, p 140: ' . . . dum inter utramque gentem pacis causa conectitur, coniuncta gratia principum subiectarum generent beneficia regionum', and no 44, p 150, another appeal to the empress to return Brunhild's little grandson Athanagild 'et inter utramque gentem per hoc, proptitiante Christo, caritas multiplicetur et pacis terminus extendatur'. These letters date from 584 and 585.

67 *Fred* cap 16, p 11, Paulus Diaconus, *Historia Langobardorum* iv cap 11, *MGH SSRL* p 120: 'Brunichildis tunc regina cum nepotibus adhoc puerulis . . . regebat Gallias'.

68 Eckhardt, '*Decretio Childeberti*', pp 70–1.

69 *Fred* cap 34, p 22. I accept the interpretation of Ewig, 'Studien', p 40, n 145.

70 Ewig, 'Studien', p 42.

of her own, posed less of a threat to Brunhild's ascendance than a noblewoman might have done. Over the marriage of her elder grandson Theudebert II, a concubine's son,[71] Brunhild had no control. His coming-of-age in 600 saw, hardly coincidentally, her expulsion from Austrasia,[72] presumably because magnates hostile to her found the young king ready to assert himself. Soon after, he married Bilichild, a former slave of Brunhild herself with no kind feelings for her former mistress.[73] Once queen, Bilichild's position could not be affected by Brunhild's taunts about her base origin—so long as the Austrasian magnates approved of her. Had withdrawal of that approval, and perhaps also her lack of a son, anything to do with her murder in 611?[74] The case of Bilichild could show that a queen who was an ex-slave was just a bit more vulnerable to changing currents of aristocratic support than was a princess like Brunhild: certainly her fate was unusually harsh. Theuderic II (Faileuba's son)[75] provides a marked contrast to his half-brother. Having given a welcome to his grandmother when she sought his court in 600,[76] Theuderic remained close to her for the rest of his life. That he never married was due to Brunhild's influence (I see no reason to reject the evidence of the *Vita Columbani* on this point):[77] the raising of a concubine to queenly status would have created a new power in the *aula regis* and so weakened Brunhild's position in general and her freedom to choose Theuderic's heir(s) in particular. This freedom played a crucial part in the network of personal loyalties which upheld the old queen for loyalty required long-term prospects dependent, in turn, on predictions of who would control the royal succession. I shall return to this point below. Only one other action of Brunhild needs mentioning here: her renunciation in 613 of the allegedly 'traditional' practice of dividing a Merovingian's realm

71 *L[iber] H[istoriae] F[rancorum]*, cap 37 *MGH SSRM* 2, p 306.

72 *Fred* cap 19, p 12. The attempt of Kurth, 'Brunehaut', p 310, to gloss over this is unconvincing.

73 *Fred* cap 35, pp 22–3. On the probable date of this marriage (601–2), see Ewig, 'Studien', p 26.

74 *Fred* cap 37, p 30: 'Belechildis a Teudeberto interfecitur'.

75 *LHF* cap 37, p 306. Both Theudebert and Theuderic were sons of Childebert according to *LH* viii, 37 and ix, 4. But there seems no reason to doubt that Brunhild goaded Theuderic to attack Theudebert by alleging that the latter was a gardener's son and thus no kin at all to Theuderic: *Fred* cap 27, p 18. If Theuderic believed this, his subsequent treatment of Theudebert and his sons is even less surprising: *Fred* cap 38, p 32, and *LHF* cap 38 pp 307–9.

76 *Fred* cap 19, p 13.

77 *V[ita] C[olumbani]* I, cap 18, *MGH SSRM* 4, p 86. This chapter and much of the next two are borrowed almost verbatim by *Fred,* cap 36, pp 23–9.

between his sons. Theuderic in 612 had defeated Theudebert and gained control of Austrasia. His sudden death just as he was marching against Clothar II of Neustria (Fredegund's son) created an interregnum of the usual dangerous kind. How did Brunhild respond? 'Her endeavour was to make Sigibert [Theuderic's eldest son, then aged eleven] his father's successor',[78] in other words, to maintain, at least for the time being, the union of Austrasia and Burgundy. By this date there was no question, I think, of dividing Theuderic's inheritance among his *four* sons. But why was the two-fold division of 596 (already foreshadowed in 589) not followed in 613? Should not Brunhild have bought off the Austrasian 'separatists' and so forestalled their alliance with Clothar? The answer, in my view, lies not in the old queen's alleged 'centralising' ambitions nor in her adherence to *Romanentum* against *Germanentum*,[79] but in a short-term bid to rally her old and new supporters among the Burgundian and Austrasian aristocracy in a final thrust against Clothar II. There is nothing to suggest that, had she won, she would have resisted the inevitable pressures—since young princes were available—to redivide the *regnum* by allocating kings to the Neustrians and Austrasians. Her supporters among them would surely have expected such a pay-off. Brunhild's mistake in 613 was, as Ian Wood has recently pointed out,[80] to overestimate the support she commanded among the aristocracy, especially and fatally the very Burgundian office-holders she had believed loyal. The politics were as ever those not of *raison d'état*[81] but of family interests, of self-preservation, of manoeuvring among shifting aristocratic loyalties. Brunhild's game was the old one, only now she made her first bad miscalculation and lost all.

Before looking more closely at some key aspects of Brunhild's

[78] *Fred* cap 40, p 32: 'Brunechildis . . . Sigybertum in regnum patris instituere nitens . . .

[79] So, Ewig, 'Teilungen', pp 705–8, 715. For a similar view, see H. Löwe, 'Austrien im Zeitalter Brunichilds. Kampf zwischen Königtum und Adel', H. Grundmann, *Handbuch der deutschen Geschichte* (9 ed, rev B. Gebhardt Stuttgart 1970) pp 124–7. This view seems standard in German historiography. The alleged evidence (the *chaussées Brunehaut*) for Brunhild as a 'Roman' road-builder or maintainer was demolished by Kurth, *Histoire poétique des Mérovingiens* (Paris 1893) pp 424 *seq.*

[80] Wood, 'Kings', p 13.

[81] So, Kurth, 'Brunehaut', p 306 and 350–1: 'elle prétendit soumettre à l'autorité d'une femme des gens qui ne reconnaissaient pas même celle d'un homme'. Kurth's contrast between the would-be despot Brunhild, an inevitable failure, and the *monarchie temperée* of the Carolingians seems to have had a strong influence on francophone historiography: see H. Pirenne, *Mohammed and Charlemagne*, trans B. Miall (London 1939) pp 265 *seq*, and F. Lot, in F. Lot, C. Pfister and F. L. Ganshof, *Les Destinées de l'Empire en Occident de 395 a 888* (2 ed Paris 1940–1) pp 265–6; 297–8; 314–15.

success, I turn now to Balthild,[82] and a sketch of her career which, much shorter than Brunhild's, is also less variously documented, the main source being the *Vita Balthildis* written soon after her death (in 680 or soon after).[83] Born in England probably in the early 630s, Balthild was brought as a slave-girl to Gaul and bought (in 641 or after) by Erchinoald, mayor of the palace of Neustria.[84] Her hagiographer's stress on her low birth (she was one of those 'poor' whom God 'raises from the dust and causes to sit with the princes of his people', and a 'precious pearl sold at a low price')[85] must be taken seriously, in view of the usual contemporary hagiographical delight in noble ancestry.[86] She was good-looking, (had doubtless caught Erchinoald's eye) and she was also canny—*prudens et cauta*.[87] Erchinoald himself is said to have wished to marry her after his wife's death, but this seems implausible, given all the other evidence of aristocratic marriage patterns.[88] The hagiographer introduced this detail, I suggest, in order to deploy the chastity motif obligatory in the *Vitae* of female saints[89] and otherwise unusable in the special case of Balthild. Divine providence caused the girl to spurn the king's minister so as to be saved for the king himself—Clovis II, son of Dagobert. Clovis probably married Balthild as soon

[82] The only usable biography remains [M. J.] Couturier, *Sainte Balthilde,* [*reine des Francs*] (Paris 1909) which, despite its devout and rather rambling style, should not be dismissed as by [L.] Dupraz, [*Le*] *Royaume* [*des Francs et l'ascension politique des maires du palais au déclin du VIIe siècle (656–680)*] (Fribourg en Suisse 1948) p 223 n 3. For useful preliminary remarks on Balthild, see [W.] Levison, *England* [*and the Continent in the Eighth Century*] (Oxford 1946) pp 9–10 with a full bibliography of the source materials at p 9, n 4.

[83] *MGH SSRM* 2, pp 475–508, version 'A', with the ninth-century reworking, 'B', in parallel columns. For the dates of both versions, see Krusch's introduction, *ibid* pp 478–9. The 'A' *Vita* was evidently written by a nun at Chelles, and commissioned by some monks—perhaps those of Corbie?

[84] *MGH SSRM* 2, cap 2, p 483.

[85] *Ibid.* These are standard topoi in references to low-born holy people: the references are to 1 Kings 2, 8 and Ps 112, 7, as is observed by [F.] Graus, [*Volk, Herrscher und*] *Heiliger* [*im Reich der Merowinger. Studien zur Hagiographie der Merowingerzeit*] (Prague 1965) pp 411–12. For another example, Gerbert writing of himself, see *Lettres de Gerbert, 983–887,* ed J. Havet (Paris 1889) no 217, p 229.

[86] See Prinz, 'Heiligenkult [und Adelsherrschaft im Spiegel merowingischer Hagiographie]', *HZ* 204 (1967) pp 529–44. Low birth was perceived as hard to reconcile with holiness. Version 'B' of the *Vita* makes Balthild into a noble lady: *claro sanguine*; and she was later depicted as belonging to an Anglo-Saxon royal family! See Couturier, *Sainte Balthilde,* p 2, n 2.

[87] *MGH SSRM* 2, cap 2, p 483; cap 3, p 485: 'prudens et astuta virgo'.

[88] *Ibid* cap 3, p 484. Ian Wood suggests to me, however, that Erchinoald, a kinsman of Dagobert on his mother's side, may have been deliberately imitating royal practice.

[89] Graus, *Heiliger,* pp 410 *seq.* The authoress of this *Vita* clearly had before her Venantius' *Vita Radegundis.*

as he came of age in 648.[90] 'Astute' as ever, Balthild had no illusions about her position. Pregnant in 649, she confided her anxieties to Eligius, most influential of Dagobert's courtiers and a holy man still evidently at the heart of royal affairs: what would happen to the realm (did she mean, to herself?) if she carried only a girl-child? Eligius reassured her that she would give birth to a son, and put his money where his mouth was: 'he had a piece of metalwork made which was suitable for a boy-baby and ordered it to be kept for his use until he was born'.[91] Balthild duly had her son—the future Clothar III, followed by Theuderic (III) and Childeric (II).[92] Already during her husband's lifetime, her great influence was evident: she seems to have organised the care of the king's entourage of young aristocrats at the court—that cradle of royal servants; and she controlled, with the help of her almoner Genesius, quantities of treasure for disbursement to the poor and other pious causes.[93] The hagiographer paints the picture of a *palatium* in which all revolves around the queen. Other sources stress the role of Erchinoald in maintaining peace throughout Clovis II's reign.[94] Balthild and her former master probably coexisted by each concentrating on different areas of activity, and the Neustrian aristocracy, whether dazzled still by Dagobert's glories or gratified by the restitution of his unjust exactions after his death during the conciliatory regency of Nantechild (died 641/2),[95] were satisfied. But the best argument from silence for Bathchild's strong position during Clovis II's lifetime might be that despite his womanising, he did not

[90] *LHF* cap 43, p 315. On the date, see Ewig, 'Studien', p 26.

[91] *Vita Eligii*, ii, 32, *MGH SSRM* 4, p 717. Riché, *Education*, p 231 with n 354, seems slightly to misinterpret this passage: I cannot see that Eligius's present for the baby can possibly have been 'a teething-ring' which would have been equally suitable for a boy or a girl.

[92] For the birth-order of the three boys, I follow that implied by the near-contemporary *Passio Leudegarii* I, cap 5, *MGH SSRM* 5, p 287, in preference to that given by *LHF* cap 44, p 317. See [L.] Levillain, '[Encore sur la] Succession [d'Austrasie au VIIe siècle]', *BEC* 105 (1945,6) pp 29–30 at p 305, n 1. The *filiola* who lived with Balthild at Chelles and died just before she did must, as the 'B' *Vita* and Krusch agree, have been a god-daughter. (After all, Clovis II had died in 657!) Although Clovis II is said to have had other women (*LHF* cap 44, p 316) he is not known to have had any children except by Balthild.

[93] *MGH SSRM* 2, pp 485–7. 'Auri vel argenti largissima munera' are disbursed. On the role of Genesius, see Ewig, '[Das Privileg des Bischofs Berthefrid von Amiens für Corbie von 664 und die] Klosterpolitik [der Königin Balthild]', *Francia* 1 (1973) pp 63–114 at pp 107–8 with n 86: '. . . eine Art Grand Aumônier'.

[94] *Fred* cap 84, p 71. Compare the aggressive and tightfisted Erchinoald depicted in the *Vita Eligii*, i, caps 20, 27, *MGH SSRM* 4, pp 711, 714.

[95] *Ibid* cap 80, p 68.

endanger her position (as Dagobert had done Nantechild's) by raising another woman to the status of queen.[96] Both the moral and the political backing of Balthild's ecclesiastical connexions must have helped her here.

Balthild's situation changed with the deaths of Clovis and, soon after, Erchinoald (657, 658/9).[96a] She now became regent for her son Clothar III, who significantly, succeeded to an undivided realm, excluding at least for the moment his two little brothers. The *Vita Balthildis* and the *Liber Historiae Francorum*[97] both stress the decisive roles of the Neustrian aristocracy. No doubt the many personal bonds forged during Balthild's years as 'nurse to the young men' in the *palatium* now stood her in good stead. The Neustrians' choice of Ebroin, a former *miles palatinus,* to succeed Erchinoald as mayor must have had Balthild's consent.[98] It has been alleged that Balthild and Ebroin between them pursued a systematic policy of reunifying the Merovingian *regnum,* first by imposing the Neustrian prince Childeric II on the Austrasians, then by abolishing the Burgundian mayoralty of the palace thus uniting Neustria and Burgundy.[99] On an alternative hypothesis, the unification-policy was 'only neustro-burgundian, not pan-frankish'.[100] Neither view offers an entirely convincing interpretation of the *Vita's* account of Balthild's actions. The complications surrounding the export of Childeric II boil down to Merovingian family politics with two dowager queens playing typical roles. It is possible that the coup of Grimoald and his son Childebert III was even part of the same family politics, in a broad sense, if indeed they too had Merovingian blood in them.[101] The most plausible reconstruction of

[96] *Ibid* cap 84, p 71.

[96a] Clovis II died between 11 September and 16 November 657: see Levison, 'Das Nekrologium von dom Racine', in *NA* 35 (1910) p 45. For the date of Erchinoald's death, see Dupraz, *Royaume,* p 245 with n 1.

[97] *Vita* cap 5, *MGH SSRM* 2, p 487; *LHF* cap 44, p 317.

[98] *LHF* cap 45, p 317; *Fred* (Continuator) cap 2, p 80, *Vita Balthildis,* cap 5, p 487. See [J.] Fischer, [*Der Hausmeier*] *Ebroin* (Bonn 1954) pp 82 *seq,* whose case for Ebroin's low birth seems, however, unproven and his explanation of Ebroin's rise therefore unconvincing. (His picture of the regent and 'her' mayor as two *Willensmenschen* risen from nothing through their own energies yet fated to clash because of the very strength of their wills, has a splendidly Wagnerian quality, at once romantic, epic and sexist: 'Früher oder später musste es zwischen ihnen zur entscheidenden Auseinandersetzung kommen, und der weniger Starke musste dem Stärkeren weichen'!)

[99] Dupraz, *Royaume,* pp 239 *seq,* 351 *seq.*

[100] Fischer, *Ebroin,* p 87. See also Ewig, 'Teilreiche', pp 121 *seq.*

[101] On the evidence for Grimoald's coup, Levillain, 'Succession', remains fundamental, and for a cogent restatement of his views in the light of subsequent research, see Ewig, 'Noch einmal zum "Staatsstreich" Grimoalds', *Speculum Historiale, Festschrift*

the events of 662, in my view, is that Childebert's childless death left Grimoald in a dangerously exposed position rather like that of a dowager queen. He had exiled Dagobert, son of Sigibert III, in 656[102] and to recall him would have been, at best, difficult and time-consuming for Grimoald. With Austrasian enemies to cope with, Grimoald had little time to afford. But he did have custody of Dagobert's sister Bilichild and perhaps also of her mother, Sigibert's widow Himnichild. To play this 'trump-card', Grimoald needed to find a Merovingian husband for Bilichild. There was no alternative but to seek him in Neustria. Thus the initiative in 662 was an Austrasian one,[103] and the outcome was a Merovingian family compact: the seven-year-old Childeric II was sent (perhaps it was Balthild's decision to choose her third in preference to her second son) to be betrothed to his first cousin Bilichild—a unique case of Merovingian in-marriage—while her mother assumed the regency,[104] all with the backing of a powerful section of the Austrasian aristocracy.[105] At this point, Grimoald became expendable and thus the sole victim of these arrangements. In him

---

J. Spörl (Munich 1965) pp 454–7. But in what follows I have accepted some revisions suggested by H. Thomas, 'Die Namenliste des Diptychon Barberini und der Sturz des Hausmeiers Grimoald', *DA* 25 (1969) pp 17–63, and further modified by Eckhardt, *Studia*, pp 152 *seq*, who also argues that Grimoald was descended in the maternal line from the Austrasian king Theudebald. But even if Levillain and Ewig are right, and Grimoald was killed in 657 rather than 662 (see following note) my view of Balthild's actions in the latter year would be unaffected.

[102] *LHF* cap 43, p 316: 'Decedente vero tempore, defuncto Sighiberto rege, Grimoaldus filium eius parvolum nomine Dagobertum totundit Didonemque Pectavensem urbis episcopum in Scocia peregrinandum eum direxit, filium suum in regno constituens. Franci itaque hoc valde indignantes Grimoaldo insidias preparant, eumque exementes ad condempnandum rege Francorum Chlodoveo deferunt. In Parisius civitate in carcere mancipatus, vinculorum cruciatu constrictus, ut erat morte dignus, quod in domino suo exercuit, ipsius mors valido cruciatu finivit'. Levillain argues that the *LHF* account must be accepted entirely: thus, Grimoald's death must precede Clovis (II)'s, in autumn 657. Those who argue that Grimoald's death must be dated to 662, on the grounds that his son Childebert III could not otherwise have been sustained as king in Austrasia until that date, must emend the *LHF*'s 'Chlod*oveo*' to 'Chlod*ochario*' or 'Chlo*thario*', that is, Clothar III. This emendation is not merely 'arbitrary' as Levillain alleges: for evidence of just this confusion of names in seventh- and eighth-century *diplomata*, see Dupraz, *Royaume*, pp 382–4.

[103] *Vita Balthildis* cap 5, p 487: '. . . Austrasii pacifico ordine, ordinante domna Balthilde, per consilium quidem seniorum receperunt Childericum, filium eius, in regem Austri'. Only by mistranslating 'ordinante' could Dupraz, *Royaume*, p 355, infer that Balthild 'gave orders' and 'imposed' her own solution. See further, Schneider, *Königswahl*, pp 163–4.

[104] Himnechild continued to subscribe Childeric II's *diplomata* until he came of age: see Ewig, 'Studien', p 23. For the assassination of Childeric and Bilichild in 675, see *LHF* cap 45, p 318.

[105] For the role of Wulfoald, see Ewig, 'Teilreiche', p 123.

Merovingian blood, if any, was much diluted. Perhaps the narrower family of Dagobert I's descendants closed ranks against more distant kin, the *indignatio* of the Neustrians against Grimoald was genuine, and his execution in Paris a kind of vengeance for the exile of Dagobert's grandson.[106] In all this, it is impossible to see Balthild as imposing her son—still less Neustrian control—on the Austrasians. She acts within limits defined by the Austrasians themselves, and her response restores harmony within both family and *regnum*. The *Vita's* depiction of her as a peace-bringer is not mere hagiographical convention.

As for her 'neustro-burgundian policy', it is possible to interpret Clothar III's succession in both Neustria and Burgundy as evidence of aristocratic interests in *both* regions, rather than only of royal design. The gradual cessation of the practice of dividing the realm in the course of the seventh century was not the result of kings' (or queens') decisions alone.[107] The *Burgundofarones* had something to gain from access to the *palatium* of a king who was theirs and the Neustrians' alike.[108] Nor can I see much evidence for a formal extinction of the Burgundian mayoralty by Balthild. It is arguable, anyway, that their laws and customs mattered more to the Burgundians than a mayoralty.[109] Scholarly discussion of the whole issue has turned on the interpretation of a phrase in the *Vita Balthildis:* 'The Burgundians and the Franks were made as one'.[110] What seems to have been unnoticed hitherto is that not merely this sentence but the whole final section of chapter 5 of the *Vita* echoes a remarkable passage in the Book of Ezechiel. The context (Ezechiel chapter 36) is a divine promise to the prophet that the *gentes* shall be put to shame and Israel renewed and exalted. In the following chapter, God sets Ezechiel down in the valley of the bones and brings them to life. He then tells the prophet to take two sticks, one to signify Israel and the other Judah:

> And join them one to another into one stick; and they shall become one in thine hand . . .

[106] Above n 102.

[107] This is a basic assumption in Dupraz's book. See also Ewig, 'Teilreiche', pp 110 *seq.*

[108] *Fred* cap 44, p 37; cap 55, p 46. For later Burgundian resistance to Ebroin because he denied them direct access to the *palatium*, see *Passio Leudegarii* I, cap 4, *MGH SSRM* 5, p 287.

[109] *Fred* cap 54, p 46: the Burgundians decide to do without a mayor of the palace after the death of Warnacher (626), preferring *cum rege transagere. Passio Leudegarii* I, cap 7, p 289, shows the Burgundians' concern to preserve their *lex vel consuetudo*. The Burgundian mayoralty seems not to have been revived after the death of Flaochad, a Frankish appointee of Nantechild, in 642. See also Ewig, 'Teilreiche', pp 106–7, 120.

[110] *Vita*, cap 5, pp 487–8: 'Burgundiones vero et Franci facti sunt uniti'.

> And when the children of thy people shall speak unto thee saying, Wilt thou not shew us what thou meanest by these?
>
> Say unto them, Thus saith the Lord God . . . Behold, I will take the children of Israel from among the heathen . . .
>
> And I will make them one nation . . . and one king shall be king to them all: and they shall be no more two nations, neither shall they be divided into two nations any more at all . . .
>
> Moreover I will make a covenant of peace with them; it shall be an everlasting covenant with them: and I will place them, and multiply them, and will set my sanctuary in the midst of them for evermore.[111]

The hagiographer's purpose throughout his fifth chapter is to show Balthild as the instrument of divinely-ordained concord between the once-warring kingdoms. The queen is presented, not as the author of specific new constitutional arrangements, but—in almost apocalyptic terms—as the inaugurator of a new era of peace. There is a significant contrast, as well as a similarity, here with the note caught by Ewig in the early eighth-century *Continuator* of Fredegar's identification of the Franks with Israel and of their war-leader Charles Martel with Joshua:[112] clearly the insistence on the Frank's providential role is a common theme, but a female ruler cannot be the lieutenant of a God of Battles. Here, in a warlike age, the obstacles to an ideology of 'queenship' are as evident as the hagiographer's ingenuity.

One final point to make here concerns Balthild's loss of power, which, as with Brunhild in Austrasia, coincided with her son's coming of age. Like Brunhild, Balthild found regency imposed its own time-limit and tenure was non-renewable. Balthild's retirement to her foundation of Chelles in late 664 or 665 was no voluntary move. Though her hagiographer glosses over it,[113] the threat of force is strongly suggested by the *Vita Eligii*.[114] Whether or not Ebroin was

111 Ezechiel 37; 17–18, 20–2, 26 (Authorised Version). The vulgate reading of verse 17 is: 'Et adjunge illa unum ad alterum tibi in lignum unum; et erunt in unionem in manu tua'.

112 Ewig, 'Zum christlichen Königsgedanken im Frühmittelalter', *Das Königtum*, ed T. Mayer *Vorträge und Forschungen* 3 (Konstanz 1956) pp 7–73 at 51 *seq*.

113 *Vita Balthildis* cap 10, p 495: 'Erat enim eius sancta devotio, ut in monasterio [Chelles] . . . conversare deberet. Nam et Franci pro eius amore hoc maxime dilatabant nec fieri permittebant . . . Et exinde . . . permiserunt eam subito pergere ad ipsum monasterium. Et fortasse dubium non est, quod ipsi principes tunc illud non bono animo permississent . . .'

114 *Vita Eligii* ii, 32, p 717: '. . . iure regio exempta'. The last of Clothar III's *diplomata* subscribed by Balthild is dated 6 September 664: *MGH DD* 1, no 40, p 38.

directly involved,[115] those responsible were clearly a powerful section of the Neustrian aristocracy. The very violence of these *principes*' reaction implies the reality of Balthild's power: as her *Vita* puts it, they had acted against her will and feared her vengeance.[116] But their success also showed how precarious was a queen-mother's position if those 'whom she had tenderly nurtured' should turn against her. Her elimination could be more decorously handled, but, like Grimoald, she had become expendable. The dowager's phoney vocation, the mayor's judicial murder, could be arranged without the political upheavals of an interregnum.

So far, I have portrayed two queens acting in a thoroughly secular context of kingly courts and counsels, treasure, armed force and aristocratic politics. But other, equally important, non-secular types of power in the Merovingian world must now be considered if we are fully to appreciate these queens' activities, or their posthumous reputations. The saints—the holy dead—were believed to incorporate supernatural power which could seem random, inexplicable in its operations.[117] Those who could claim to mediate such power, to render it intelligible, to enable 'human strategy [to be set] at work on the holy'[118] were the bishops, the holy men and the monks in the towns and countryside of Gaul. Both the power and the exponents thereof predated the Merovingians: Clovis and his successors had to come to terms with them. We must now examine how, first, Brunhild and then Balthild did so.

If the Frankish kings from the fifth century onwards wielded a territorial authority from city bases, the collaboration of bishops was

[115] Judgements on this point have been very subjective. See Fischer, *Ebroin*, pp 98–104.

[116] *Vita* cap 10, p 495: '. . . nec fieri permittebant, nisi commotio illa fuisset per miserum Sigobrandum episcopum, cuius superbia inter Francos meruit mortis ruinam. Et exinde orta intentione, dum ipsum *contra eius voluntatem* interfecerunt, metuentes *ne hoc ipsa domna contra eos graviter ferret ac vindicare ipsam causam vellet*, permiserunt eam subito . . .' etc (above n 113.) A few lines further on, p 496, the *Vita* gives a further revealing glimpse of Balthild's position: 'Habuit enim tunc non modicam querelam contra eos, quos ipsa dulciter enutriverat, pro qua re falso ipsi eam habuissent suspectam, vel etiam pro bonis mala ei repensarent. Sed et hoc conferens cum sacerdotibus citius, eis clementer cuncta indulsit . . .' For the Sigobrand episode, see below p 41.

[117] For a fine account, full of fresh insights, see now [P.] Brown, 'Relics [and Social Status in the Age of Gregory of Tours]', The Stenton Lecture for 1976 (University of Reading 1977), with references to previous work. Also indispensable is Graus, *Heiliger*, Brown's paper must be supplemented for the seventh century by Prinz, 'Heiligenkult', and *Mönchtum*; and Ewig, 'Milo [et eiusmodi similes]', *Bonifatius-Gedenkgabe* (Fulda 1954) pp 412–40, at 430 *seq*.

[118] Brown, 'Relics', p 14.

indispensable. Appointments of, and relations with bishops remained key aspects of royal action through the sixth and most of the seventh centuries:[119] and rulers had scope for action precisely because, though episcopacy was part of the 'Establishment', bishops, especially prospective ones, needed outside support to secure their local positions. Had 'senatorial blood, episcopal office and sanctity' *really* 'presented a formidable united front,'[120] Merovingian kings—and queens too—could never have been as formidable as they sometimes were. Brunhild is a case in point. As a consort, she, like other sixth-century queens had probably used her influence in episcopal elections, notably, according to Venantius, that of Gregory of Tours himself.[121] Better documented is her intervention at Rodez in 584, where her influence was invoked by one of the participants, count Innocentius, in a power-struggle in the nearby city of Javols. When the count transferred his interests to the see of Rodez, Brunhild's support secured him the bishopric in an election which scandalised even Gregory by the fierceness of the competition.[122] Brunhild's own interest here might have been connected, I suggest, with her continuing efforts to secure the restitution of her sister Galswinth's morning-gift which included the city of Cahors.[123] The dioceses of Rodez and Cahors were contiguous, and bishop Innocentius's harrassment of the neighbouring see[124] may have exerted some of the pressure which achieved the transfer of Cahors into Brunhild's possession in 586. Her continuing interest in this region, in which Frankish and Visigothic powers competed, and the key position of

[119] D. Claude, '[Die] Bestellung der Bischöfe [im merowingischen Reiche]', *ZRG KAb t* 49 (1963) pp 1–77. For some general aspects of episcopal collaboration, see Wood, 'Kings'. It is tempting to correlate the absence of queenly regencies in England in the seventh century (the year-long reign of Seaxburh, widow of Cenwalh of Wessex, apparently in her own right, in 672–3 is quite exceptional) or later, with the relative weakness of episcopal power there as well as with the ubiquity of warfare: there was no substitute therefore for an adult warrior king. An obvious further correlation would be with the persistance of dynastic discontinuity in the English kingdoms into the ninth century. See below p 46.

[120] So, P. Brown, *Religion and Society in the Age of Saint Augustine* (London 1972) p 131, quoted and renounced, with admirable open-mindedness, by Brown himself: 'Relics', p 17. See also his reservations, 'Relics', pp 19–20, about Prinz, '[Die bischöfliche] Stadtherrschaft [im Frankenreich]', *HZ* 217 (1974) pp 1–35, which, however, remains an important article.

[121] Venantius Fortunatus, *Carmina* v, 3, lines 11–15, p 106: 'Huic Sigibercthus ovans favat et Brunechildis honori'.

[122] *LH* vi, 38, p 309. For the previous context at Rodez see *LH* v, 46.

[123] *LH* ix, 20, see above n 22.

[124] *LH* vi, 38, p 309.

Rodez are still evident twenty years later.[125] The other vital area for the queen's control of episcopal appointments after 600 was Burgundy proper. She must surely have been behind the elections of Aridius to Lyons and of Domnolus to Vienne in 603. She appointed Desiderius to Auxerre in 605.[126] Gregory the Great complained in 595 that no-one obtained a bishopric in the *regnum Francorum* without paying for it.[127] Assuming twelve to fifteen vacancies per annum, Claude has made the interesting calculation that the royal profits from simony over the *regnum* as a whole could have reached ten thousand solidi in the later sixth century.[128] Despite later accusations, I do not think that Brunhild's practice here was unusual, nor that she was responsible for a peculiarly bad attack of this 'contagion' in the late sixth century.[129] Of course the money was useful to her, as to the other strong rulers who profited from this source. But it was not the chief consideration. Whether or not they proved their devotion in hard cash, Brunhild needed episcopal allies and servants. They if anyone could control the cities, their very simony being proof of one vital attribute of power;[130] they could influence their aristocratic lay kinsfolk; and they could serve as counsellors and envoys, deploying their useful network of

[125] The evidence lies in three letters, two of them apparently addressed to the bishop of Rodez, by Bulgar, count of Septimania during the reign of the Visigothic king Gunthimar (610–2): *MGH Epp* 3, *Epp Wisigothicae* nos 11, 12 and 13, pp 677–81. The letters to the bishop of Rodez are violently hostile to Brunhild and Theuderic, accusing them of making an alliance with the pagan Avars, and making it clear that Gunthimar was sending money to Theudebert. The Auvergne region was, of course, an Austrasian enclave. Bulgar's third letter, evidently addressed to a Burgundian bishop (here Brunhild and Theuderic are *gloriosissimi reges*), reveals that Brunhild was negotiating with Gunthimar for two towns in Septimania which had been granted to her personally by her cousin king Reccared but taken back by the Visigoths, presumably after Reccared's death in 601 or his son's in 603. Brunhild was meanwhile holding two Visigothic envoys captive as a bargaining counter. For anti-Brunhild propaganda in this festering Visigothic-Frankish conflict, see below p 27. The treatment of Bulgar's letters by Kurth, 'Brunehaut', pp 313–4, is rather confused.

[126] *Fred* cap 24, p 15; cap 19, p 13 with Wallace-Hadrill's n 1. The case of Desiderius of Auxerre, and the inaccuracy of Fredegar's 'legendary' account, are discussed by Kurth, 'Brunehaut', pp 308–10.

[127] Ep v, 58, *MGH Epp* 1, p 369. Compare *Ep* ix, 213, *MGH Epp* 2, p 198.

[128] Claude, 'Bestellung der Bischöfe', p 59 n 290.

[129] *Vita Eligii* II, 1, p 694: 'Maxime de temporibus Brunehildis infelicissimae reginae . . . violabat hoc contagium catholicam fidem'. A similarly harsh view of Brunhild ('le mauvais génie de la maison de Sigebert . . .'!) is taken by E. Vacandard, 'Les elections episcopales', in *Études de Critique et d'Histoire* (Paris 1905) pp 159 *seq.*

[130] For a nice example from the 660s, of wealth as a qualification for episcopal office, see the contemporary *Passio Praejecti*, cap 12, *SSRM* 5, p 232: when Praejectus solicits the bishopric of Clermont, the *plebs* ask him 'si se sciebat tantam pecuniam auri argentique metalli habere, unde hoc opus queat subire'.

personal connexions. The bishops, for their part, could achieve no concerted action, could undertake no moral reform, without royal sponsorship. This pope Gregory understood very well when he directed his appeals to Brunhild.[131] The collaboration of queen, bishop and pope is apparent in Brunhild's foundations at Autun: a nuns' house dedicated to the Virgin, a *Xenodochium* associated with a male convent whose abbot was to be royally appointed, and a church dedicated to St Martin served by secular clergy and destined to provide the queen's tomb.[132] Brunhild's interest in Autun is significant. Continuing the eastward reorientation of the 'Burgundian' kingdom implicit in Guntramn's choice of Chalon for his *sedes regia*,[133] Brunhild, while cultivating links with the Rhone cities especially Lyons, also entrenched royal influence firmly in a major centre of sixth-century cult and culture, a point of articulation between the two broad zones of Martinian and Rhone-based monasticism, a citadel, finally, of Gallo-Roman aristocratic power which was close to the frontier with 'barbarian' Gaul.[134]

Brunhild's association with Syagrius of Autun is only the most striking instance of what must be seen as a characteristic and inevitable mode of royal government in the Merovingian *regnum*. Bishops were there in the *civitates*, and kings, from Clovis onwards, who wanted to govern in and from cities therefore had to work with bishops. This rather than any common commitment to *Romanentum* and Roman governmental principles, or any adherence to a '*parti romain*',[135] or any absolutist ambitions on the part of a cultured Visigoth grown into a 'Burgundian "lady-centralist" ',[136] accounts for Brunhild's relations with the bishops of the realms she ruled and, beyond them, with the pope. In Burgundy, naturally, the bishops were *Romani*, but it was not

[131] *Epp* viii, 4; ix, 213; xi, 46, *MGH Epp* 2, pp 5–8; 198–200; 318–9.

[132] *Epp* xiii, 11–13, *MGH Epp* 2, pp 376–81, where also the editor, L. M. Hartmann, convincingly defends the authenticity of these privileges, and suggests that Gregory based his wording on that of Brunhild in her original request. For Brunhild's tomb, see Kurth, 'Brunehaut', pp 347, 352–6.

[133] Ewig, 'Résidence [et capitale pendant le haut Moyen Age]', *RH* 230 (1963) pp 25–72, at p 48.

[134] See Gregory the Great, Epp ix, 214, 218 and 222 *MGH Epp* 2, pp 200, 205–10, 213–14 (contacts with Syagrius of Autun) and Epp ix, 208 and 230, pp 195–227 (contacts with Spain via Autun). Riché, *Education*, pp 179 *seq*, 268–70, with maps on pp 170 and 269; Prinz, *Mönchtum*, pp 60–1, 136, 140 with maps 5, 6 and 9; and Stroheker, *Adel*, pp 121–2, 163–4 (for the Syagrii and Desiderii).

[135] So, Delaruelle, 'L'Église romaine et ses relations avec l' Église franque jusqu'en 800', in *SS Spoleto* 7, i (1960) pp 143–84, at p 160.

[136] So, Prinz, *Mönchtum*, p 542.

their Romanity which determined Brunhild's favour, any more than ethnic affinity governed her choice of lay officials: her alleged partiality to 'Romans' is belied by the number of Frankish and Burgundian appointments mentioned by Fredegar.[137]

The exception to the record of harmony between Brunhild and her bishops is the case of Desiderius of Vienne, first exiled, later stoned to death, according to Fredegar on 'the wicked advice of Aridius of Lyons and of . . . Brunhild'.[138] If all we had was Fredegar's threadbare account of this apparently arbitrary action, it might be tempting to explain Desiderius' fate in terms of factionalism in the Burgundian episcopate and the traditional rivalry between Lyons and Vienne. But the remarkable *Vita Desiderii* written by the Visigothic king Sisebut (612–21), and a second *Vita* written in the eighth century by a cleric of Vienne throw more light on the affair.[139] Sisebut is violently hostile to Brunhild, not I think because he held her responsible for the dismissal of Theuderic II's Visigothic bride (who after all was no relation of Sisebut's)[140] nor through any genuine concern for the sanctity of Desiderius, but because he is writing propaganda for Septimanian consumption. His *Vita* is, as Fontaine has brilliantly shown, 'a hagiographic pamphlet' designed to show how a Toledan king could respect a Gallo-Roman aristocrat and to incite opposition to Frankish rule.[141] And here, significantly, as in the letters of count Bulgar of Septimania (written about 610)[142] Brunhild the 'nurse of discords' is completely identified with the Merovingians. Sisebut stresses the role of Brunhild's protégé, the mayor of the palace Protadius in bringing about Desiderius's exile and suggests that the terror of Brunhild and Theuderic at Protadius's death made them avenge themselves on

[137] *Fred* caps 24, 28, 29, pp 16, 19, mentions Protadius, Claudius and Ricomer as 'Romans by birth'; but he also mentions the promotions of the Franks Quolen (cap 18, p 12), and Bertoald (cap 24, p 15), while the constable Eborin and the chamberlain Berthar (caps 30, 38, pp 20, 31–2) were also presumably Franks. Duke Rocco, probably a Burgundian, served as Brunhild and Theuderic's envoy to Spain in 607 and only turned against her in 613. (caps 30, 42, pp 20, 34). Among bishops, the Austrasian Frank Leudegasius of Mainz was an ally of Theuderic in 612 (cap 38, p 31) while Lupus of Sens, deposed after 614 for his previous loyalty to Brunhild, came from a Frankish family in Orleans: *Vita Lupi, MGH SSRM* 4, caps 1, 11, p 179, 182.

[138] *Fred* cap 32, p 21.

[139] Both *Vitae* are edited by Krusch in *MGH SSRM* 3, pp 630–45.

[140] cap 30, p 20: Ermenburga was the daughter of Witteric, murderer of his predecessor and himself murdered by Gunthimar in 610.

[141] J. Fontaine, *Isidore de Séville et la culture classique dans l'Espagne wisigothique* (Paris 1959) p 841 nn 1 and 2.

[142] *MGH Epp* 3, pp 677–81, at 677: 'iurgiorum auctrix'.

Desiderius. The eighth-century *Vita* hints at popular opposition to Desiderius in Vienne. But both *Vitae* agree that the basic reason for Desiderius' loss of royal favour and eventual death was his sharp criticism of royal *mores*—specifically of Theuderic's concubines.[143] How credible is it that Brunhild would have let such an issue embroil her in an uncharacteristic conflict with a leading bishop? Why did she not ensure that her grandson took a wife and became respectable in the eyes of an ecclesiastical moralist? Such a marriage, argued Kurth, could not have endangered Brunhild any more than concubines already did: 'will anyone seriously maintain', he asked, 'that a sensual king submits more willingly to the influence of his wife than that of his mistress?'[144]

To understand Brunhild's motives, we must look at one more episode: her relations with St Columbanus. She must have met him long since, when he first arrived in the *regnum Francorum* c591 and found patronage from her son Childebert.[145] From the outset Columbanus' *peregrinatio* had a strong inner-worldly objective, namely the restoration (or application) of *religio* to *fides*,[146] which could only be achieved with political support. It was a matter of building up a network of personal relations and loyalties, of education: and this took time. The history of Luxeuil is obscure until quite late in Theuderic's reign but it is clear that some Austrasian and Burgundian aristocrats had been patronising the monastery in the 590s.[147] and there is no sign of any royal hostility. The first mention in the *Vita Columbani* of Theuderic's attitude to the saint stresses his veneration: 'he had often come to [Columbanus] at Luxeuil and with all humility begged the help of his prayers'.[148] Brunhild too recognised his support as worth having. Columbanus seems to have been in the habit of coming to visit Brunhild and the royal family. In 609 she sought the holy man's blessing for her great-grandsons, the eldest of them born in 602.[149] We should note the lateness of the evidence for conflict between the queen and the saint. If for years he had been complaining about Theuderic's failure to marry, it was only in 609 that the political consequences of

143 *MGH SSRM* 3, pp 635, 640–1.

144 Kurth, 'Brunehaut', p 322.

145 Jonas, *VC* cap 6, *MGH SSRM* 4, p 72 with Krusch's n 3. See [G. S. M.] Walker, [*Sancti Columbani Opera*], *Scriptores Latini Hiberniae*, 2 (Dublin 1957) introd, pp x–xi, xxi *seq*.

146 *VC* cap 5, p 71. Compare Columbanus's ep 2, Walker, pp 12–23.

147 *VC*, I, caps 10, 14 and 15, pp 76, 79 and 81. For another possible case (Agilus) see Prinz, *Mönchtum*, pp 126, 217, 356–7.

148 *VC*, I, cap 18, p 86; *Fred* cap 36, p 23.

149 *VC*, I cap 19, p 87. *Fred* cap 21, p14 gives the date of Sigebert's birth.

his objections became explicit when he denied the claim of Theuderic's sons to succeed to the kingship. Now and only now Brunhild appears as 'a second Jezebel',[150] her sin the primal one of pride: but it is pride of a specific kind, which fears to lose long-held status, power and wealth, and it has a specific manifestation of hostility to the *vir Dei* whose moralising threatens that position. Theuderic had nothing to lose by compliance and indeed, Brunhild 'could see that he was yielding to the man of God'. But for her, what might be at stake was control of the *aula regis,* the court, and thus the real power and influence which made a queen's position worth having. Columbanus's hagiographer Jonas, for all his bias, had hit the nail squarely on the head: being the king's bedfellow, even being the mother of his sons, was not at all the same thing as being queen. Brunhild knew this. She must have known it when in Childebert's reign she had had a queen as daughter-in-law. But in such situations, personalities counted for much, and Faileuba did not strike contemporaries as considerable. And in any case that was all long ago when perhaps Brunhild herself had had little choice. In the early 600s she was old, had long grown used to power and did not want to retire: there was no contemporary sentiment against gerontocracy. Her aim now was to secure the future for her line; thus to get Theuderic's sons accepted as his prospective heirs. And there was a final element in her motivation, perhaps still an essential one: Fredegund's son lived and ruled in Neustria. Could Theuderic be counted on, without Brunhild at his side, to pursue the vendetta to its necessary end? Desiderius had already been eliminated probably by means of an intended exile that went wrong.[151] Columbanus too must now be exiled—for Brunhild rightly judged that the abrasive old Irishman would never be pressurised into silence when he saw principle at stake. The initiative was hers. The allegedly 'fundamental' hostility of the bishops, or, alternatively, of 'the monasticism of the Rhone region', have in my view been exaggerated. Despite Columbanus's rudeness, despite the awkward dispute over the dating of easter,[152] the bishops of Brunhild's realm had left the Irish to their eccentricities; as for

[150] *VC,* I, cap 18, p 86: '. . . mentem Brunechildis . . . secundae ut erat Zezebelis, antiquus anguis adiit eamque contra virum Dei stimulatam superbiae aculeo excitat quia cerneret viro Dei Theudericum oboedire'. It is worth noting that Sisebut, despite his violent antipathy to Brunhild, does not label her a 'Jezebel'. But his *Vita* is stylistically very different from Jonas's work.

[151] Kurth, 'Brunehaut', p 329, argues this on the basis of the second *Vita Desiderii, MGH SSRM* 3, cap 9 p 641.

[152] Columbanus, epp 1–3, Walker, pp 12–25, with Walker's comments, pp xxv–vi.

'monasticism', the delay in the appearance of Luxeuil's influence in southern Gaul (neatly demonstrated in Prinz's maps) had more to do with pre-existing deep-rooted traditions and patterns of aristocratic patronage and monastic practice than with positive or principled 'opposition'.[153] Jonas should still be believed, I think, when he says that it was Brunhild herself who 'worked upon the bishops' and on the lay magnates and *auligae* as well as the king, to co-ordinate an anti-Columbanan front. It was natural for Jonas to see a parallel with the biblical archetype of the wicked queen who sought to destroy God's mouthpiece, the holy man. Knowing as he did the details of Brunhild's life and death, Jonas must have relished other reminiscences of Jezebel: like her, Brunhild was a foreigner and a king's daughter; like her, Brunhild attacked a personal enemy (Naboth=Desiderius) by bringing false charges against him and then had him stoned to death; like her, Brunhild met a dreadful fate—*et equorum ungulae conculcaverunt eam.*[154] Jonas's audience, likewise connoisseurs of the Books of Kings, could readily supply these motifs, once given the identification of Brunhild with Jezebel; and readers of the *Vita Columbani* who wrote about Brunhild subsequently gained access to useful new 'material'. In the *Liber Historiae Francorum*, the aged Brunhild titivates herself in a pathetic attempt to seduce her conqueror Clothar II, just like Jezebel who, hearing of king Jehu's arrvail, *depinxit oculos suos stibio et ornavit caput suum;*[155] while in the eighth-century *Vita* of Desiderius, Brunhild becomes Jezebel in this second context, *alone* responsible for the bishop's death in which the motif of stoning is emphasised.[156] So influential, indeed, was Jonas's work, so definitive his portrayal of Brunhild that in Frankish hagiography she came to rank with Ebroin as a stereotype of villainy.[157] If in one tenth-century *Vita* she appears in a less awful light when, struck by the saint's power she becomes his patron, this simply proves that a hagiographer could best show the greatness of *his* holy man by pitting him successfully against the wickedest of Wicked Queens.[158]

[153] Prinz, *Mönchtum,* p 148 and n 137, stresses this 'opposition'. Reservations similar to mine, though based on other evidence, are voiced by Ian Wood, 'A prelude to Columbanus: the monastic achievement in the Burgundian territories' (in the press). I am very grateful to him for letting me see this paper in advance of publication.

[154] 3 Kings 16: 31; 19: 1–2; 5–16, 23; 4 Kings 9: 30–37. For Jonas' use of typology in the *Vita Columbani,* see J. Leclercq, 'L'univers religieux de St Columban', *Aspects du Monachisme hier et Aujourd'hui* (Paris 1974) pp 193–212 at 201 *seq.*

[155] *LHF* cap 40, p 310, influenced by 4 Kings 9: 30–33.

[156] *MGH SSRM* 3, cap 9, p 641.

[157] Graus, *Heiliger,* pp 373–4.

[158] *Vita Menelei, MGH SSRM* 5, caps 3–11, pp 150–4.

Brunhild, then, had not been born bad, but nor had she exactly had badness thrust upon her: in the hagiographer's terms, she deserved her reputation and had indeed challenged the authority of a saint and opposed heavenly by earthly power. That this action was untypical of her, that it was forced on her in a particular time and situation by the need to survive politically, could not concern the monks who reviled her memory. That she was very unlucky to have crossed the path of the one great charismatic of her age and that her posthumous fate was in a sense accidental: none of this could concern the generations of monks in whose collective memory this Jezebel lived on. But it must concern modern historians and cause us to rethink some of the sweeping generalisations and value-judgements out of which our predecessors, two or three generations ago, fashioned their own improbable images of Brunhild as benevolent despot or great soul.

Balthild's image is, of course, timeless: she was and is a saint.[159] But she was also, for some contemporaries, a Jezebel. The paradox, and the apparent contrast with Brunhild, invite our attention. Balthild's *Vita* makes it clear that she had grasped the uses of piety, both as a means to secure personal status and as a political instrument. There is a touch of Uriah Heep about her oft-praised 'humility' but this may be the hagiographer's fault, not hers. What is new and remarkable here is the depiction of a specifically royal sanctity.[160] This is apparent first in her activities as Clovis II's consort. In the intimate atmosphere of the court, Balthild structures her personal relationships 'correctly' in terms both of the hagiographer's values and of her own interests: 'to the great men she showed herself like a mother, to the bishops like a daughter, to the young men and boys like the best sort of nurse.' In a rather wider context too, she has the right priorities, loving 'bishops as fathers, monks as brothers and the poor as their pious nurse'; she does not infringe the magnates' sense of status but accepts their counsels when appropriate, she encourages the young men to monastic studies, and uses her influence with the king 'humbly but persistently' on behalf of churches and the poor.[161] Clovis assigns her the chief of his palace

[159] *LThK* 2, col 50 (Ewig) *sv* 'Balthildis'. Her feast-day is 30 January. If we may trust Ewig, 'Klosterpolitik', p 62, she is still capable of making a nocturnal visit to reprove a detractor!

[160] This is most evident in her remission of the capitation-tax and her prohibition of the slave-trade in Christian captives: 'datasque praeceptiones per singulas regiones, ut nullus in regno Francorum captivum hominem christianum penitus transmitteret', *Vita* caps 6 and 9, pp 488, 494.

[161] *Vita* cap 4, pp 485–6.

clerks, his *fidelis famulus* Genesius, to administer her charitable works: as the *Vita's* term *assiduus* implies, he was a force to be reckoned with in the Neustrian palace at this time. Further promotion was assured: he would become bishop of Lyons, 'on Christ's orders' (and doubtless Balthild's) in 660.[162]

Already during Clovis's lifetime, Balthild had had close ties with Eligius, bishop of Noyon from 641, and probably also Audoenus (Dado), bishop of Rouen from 641.[163] These men were at the centre of a friendship-network which spanned the entire *regnum Francorum* and had a remarkable capacity to persist and to reproduce itself over generations—from the 620s through to the 660s and probably later.[164] In so far as it transcended the boundaries of the *Teilreiche,* it could be troublesome for a king: Sigibert III forbade Desiderius of Cahors to attend a council at Bourges because that was in his brother's realm, and Desiderius could invite only his Austrasian friends to celebrate the foundation of the monastery of St Amantius at Cahors.[165] But Clothar II and Dagobert had made the network work for them, using its members first as lay officials and close advisers, later as bishops in major *civitates.* A hefty attack on simony made by the bishops themselves was directed against local aristocratic, rather than royal malpractice.[166] Control of episcopal appointments, simoniac or otherwise, remained essential for rulers. It seems likely, for instance, that Chrodobert became bishop of Paris late in Clovis's reign because of his already close connexions with Audoenus and with Balthild.[167]

When Clovis died late in 657, Balthild as queen mother naturally had a good claim to the regency, but her established friendships, especially

[162] *Ibid* pp 486–7.

[163] *Vita Eligii,* ii, 32, p 727. See also Vacandard, [*Vie de*] *Saint Ouen,* [*evêque de Rouen*] (Paris 1902) pp 249–55.

[164] The main evidence lies in the letter-collection of Desiderius of Cahors (died 650) *MGH Epp* 3, pp 191–214. Audoenus survived until 684. For the friendship-circle, see Levison's introduction to the *Vita Audoini, MGH SSRM* 5, pp 536–7; Sprandel, *Adel,* pp 16–7, 33; Riché, *Education,* pp 236 *seq.* Wallace-Hadrill, *Long-Haired Kings,* pp 222–3.

[165] Desiderii, *Ep* ii, 17, p 212; *Ep* i, 11, p 199.

[166] Council of Chalon-sur-Saône (647–53) cap 16, *Concilia Galliae 511–695,* ed C. de Clercq, *CCSL* 148A (Turnhout 1963) p 306.

[167] He seems to have belonged to Audoenus' circle, if the 'bishop Chrodobert' to whom Audoenus sent a copy of his *Vita Eligii* can be identified with the then bishop of Paris: see Krusch's comments in *MGH SSRM* 4, pp 650–1 and Vacandard, *Saint Ouen,* pp 236–7. But Vacandard's apparent identification of the bishop with a Rodebert, mayor of the palace in 655, is mistaken for the latter was still addressed as mayor in 663: see Ebling, *Prosopographie,* pp 112–13. The mayor and the bishop could well be relatives however.

with Genesius, allowed her to make the claim effective. There is no evidence of any demand at this point for a division of the Neustro-Burgundian realm, which, while suggesting the absence of any strong Burgundian secessionist movement, could also indicate the smoothness of the transmission of royal power. Audoenus and Chrodobert are named in the *Vita Balthildis* as the key supporters of the regency,[168] and Ebroin's appointment as mayor some months afterwards must have been made on their, as well as the queen's, 'advice'. In 657-8, then, the *regnum Francorum* remained at peace—no mean tribute to the degree of governmental stability and continuity which episcopal underwriting helped ensure.

But the maintenance of royal power was not just a simple matter of keeping inherited episcopal allies. The trouble was, there were bishops and bishops: the 'good' ones, as the *Vita* engagingly terms them (they certainly included Eligius and Audoenus) urged the queen on to prohibit simony specifically in episcopal appointments,[169] where the 'bad' ones, by implication, preferred to work the familiar systems. Whatever financial profits this meant foregoing Balthild continued to exercise her power to appoint. Politics based on personalities, families and factions were the reverse of static: to remain in any sort of control, a ruler had to be able to place his/her supporters in key positions. Earlier Merovingians had been able to exercise considerable freedom in appointing patricians, dukes and counts. The development of hereditary offices, restricting the scope of royal action,[170] heightened the need to secure the right bishops. Against this background, the scanty evidence for Balthild's episcopal appointments becomes significant. Three cases are known. In the first is recorded only the bare fact that through her influence Erembert, who came originally from the Chartres region, became bishop of Toulouse.[171] Aquitaine was clearly not yet outwith the scope of royal intervention. The second and third cases relate to Burgundy which contained, in my view, not a separatist movement, but aristocratic factions operating in cities as well as countryside. As in Brunhild's time, Autun and Lyons were two key cities in the region.

[168] *Vita* cap 5, p 487: '. . . suscepit ilico . . . Chlotharius quondam Francorum regnum, tunc etenim precellentibus principibus Chrodobertho episcopo Parisiaco et domno Audoeno seu et Ebroino maiore domus . . .'

[169] *Vita* cap 6, p 488: '. . . exortantibus bonis sacerdotibus . . .'

[170] A. R. Lewis, 'The Dukes in the *Regnum Francorum*, A. D. 550–751', *Speculum* 51 (1976) pp 381–410 at 398–9; Sprandel, 'Struktur und Geschichte', pp 43–7, 60–1.

[171] *Vita Eremberti*, *MGH SSRM* 5, p 654. This *Vita* was composed *c*800, but its accuracy on this point is accepted by Ewig, 'Teilreiche', p 127.

In Autun, faction-fighting kept the see vacant for two years (probably 660–2)[172] until Balthild took the initiative. She had already provided herself with the man for the job when she summoned to the court a learned, experienced and above all *strenuus* man from Poitiers—Leudegarius. It is tempting to suggest that Balthild needed a replacement for Genesius in the royal chapel and, probably on Audoenus' advice, sought an 'outstanding teacher of clerics'. His subsequent move from chapel to bishopric replicated that of Genesius. In the short run he proved the wisdom of Balthild's choice by restoring Autun to peace and good government.[173]

Balthild's interventions in Toulouse and Autun evoked little contemporary comment. But the third case involved more complications: Genesius's appointment to Lyons followed a violent episode in which his predecessor was killed. According to *Acta* which seem to have a genuinely seventh-century base,[174] bishop Aunemundus and his brother, the prefect of Lyons, were sons of a previous prefect and the family had built up a virtual monopoly of local power through using their influence at the courts of Dagobert and Clovis II. There Aunemundus had had a typically successful career as a lay office-holder before being appointed to Lyons, surely with royal support, about 650 (he baptised the infant Clothar III who was born in that year). But the *Acta* stress envy in what sounds like a local context as the cause of Aunemundus' downfall.[175] The bishop and his brother were accused of treason *(infidelitas)* and summoned to appear before the boy-king Clothar and the regent Balthild at an assembly at Mareuil, a royal *villa* near Orleans. The brother appeared, was found guilty and executed.

172 *Passio Leudegarii* I, cap 2, p 284.

173 *Ibid* I, caps 2, 3, pp 284–6. See also Riché, *Education,* pp 363–4.

174 *Acta sancti Aunemundi, AASS* Sept vii (Brussels 1760) pp 744–6. See A. Coville, *Recherches* [*sur l'histoire de Lyon du Vme au IXme siècle*] (Paris 1928) pp 366 *seq.*

175 *Acta* p 744: '... nullusque de aliqua re ad suum profectum quidquam valebat impetrare, nisi sua suggestione (that is, Aunemundus's) Clotario tertio principi deportaret ... Ideo dum sublimitatis suae gloriam ac brachium vindicaret extentum, nec non et a fratribus celsior videretur in coetu, cunctis incidit in odium. Qui tractare eum seditiose coeperunt sub clandestina accusatione dicentes, quasi regnum ejusdem Clotarii ... evertere moliretur occulte ...' Dupraz, *Royaume,* p 343 n 1, and Fischer, *Ebroin,* p 92, both state, citing the *Acta,* that the bishop's accusers were *maiores natu ducesque.* But what the *Acta* in fact say is that these magnates appeared at the assembly at Mareuil, as one would expect. The *Acta* imply, rather, the identity of accusers and *fratres*—presumably the 'brethren' of the church of Lyons. A few lines later, the *Acta* tell how Aunemundus asked forgiveness from the *fratres* at Lyons for any injuries he had done them, including unfair seizure of their goods. For further evidence of Aunemundus' local power, see below n 181.

When Aunemundus himself failed to appear, pleading illness, the regent sent *duces* with instructions to bring him to the royal court and to kill him only if he resisted. On their way there, near Chalon, Aunemundus was murdered one night by two armed men whose action was deeply regretted by the *duces* themselves.[176] Now the local tradition about these events had got fairly confused by the time the surviving (late-medieval) texts were written.[177] But the crucial points so far as Balthild is concerned are, first, that these *Acta* ascribe to her neither the initiative in Aunemundus' accusation nor the responsibility for his death, and second that the identity or gentile origin of Aunemundus's accusers is not stated. To erect on this basis a theory of a 'Burgundian autonomist party' who had 'conspired against the Neustrian *palatium*' in sharp reaction against Balthild's 'programme of compulsory "union" '[178] is to pile figment on fantasy. We simply know too little about the alleged treason of Aunemundus and his brother and have no indication that any others but these two were involved. It is more likely, I think, that the episode belongs in a context of family or factional rivalries in and around Lyons, and that the accusers of Aunemundus and his brother were other local aristocrats, not Neustrian centralists. The whole affair is reminiscent of a situation recorded in the *Passio Praejecti,* where a dispute over land in the Auvergne between the bishop of Clermont and a local magnate is brought to the king's court and settled, but the royal decision is soon followed by violence on the spot when the bishop is murdered by other local enemies.[179] The interplay, rather than conflict, between royal and aristocratic interests, the circulation of power from court to provinces and back, seem to me as characteristic of Merovingian politics in the 660s and 670s as in the days of Gregory of Tours. In our Lyons case, anyway, the death of Aunemundus left the way open for Balthild to appoint Genesius, who not only survived but established a strong base for intervention in the politics of the *regnum* over the next twenty years.[180]

Unmentioned in any contemporary Frankish source, apparently without repercussions in the history of the *regnum Francorum,* the

[176] *Acta* p 745. The *duces* had promised the abbot of Luxeuil that Aunemundus would be safe.

[177] Coville, *Recherches,* pp 372 *seq.*

[178] So, Dupraz, *Royaume,* pp 342–4, 352–4; Fischer, *Ebroin,* pp 90–8.

[179] *MGH SSRM* 5, caps 23, 24, pp 239–40.

[180] Genesius died in 679. For his career, see Coville, *Recherches,* pp 416–21.

Aunemundus affair might seem irrelevant to Balthild's reputation. But because the young Wilfrid happened to have established close relations with Aunemundus and to have stayed for three years in Lyons, whence he subsequently acquired some information about the bishop's death, the story was translated in a new 'Wilfridian' version to an Anglo-Saxon literary milieu.[181] Thus, strangely, Balthild who had begun life in England returned there in posthumous tradition, not as a saint—but as a 'malevolent queen . . . just like the most impious queen Jezebel'.[182] Eddius may have borrowed the motif from the *Vita Columbani*, but he could equally well have used it independently, for his *Vita Wilfridi* is rich in biblical typology. Jezebel was the obvious type for a queen who persecuted a holy man, and Eddius actually used the same motif again later in his work in reference to the 'wicked' queen Iurminburg, second wife of Ecgfrith of Northumbria and Wilfrid's violent enemy until her later *conversio*.[183] Eddius wrote over half a century after Aunemundus's death, and based his account of it upon Wilfrid's reminiscences. He asserts that the 'evil-wishing queen Balthild' persecuted the church of God; that she had nine bishops put to death ('not counting priests and deacons'!) and one of these was 'bishop Dalfinus' (=Aunemundus)[184] whom certain dukes had most malignly ordered to come before them; and that Wilfrid not only was present at the bishop's 'martyrdom' but offered himself to the same fate, only to be spared by the dukes when they learnt that he was 'from overseas, of the English race from Britain'. So, concludes Eddius, Wilfrid, though denied a martyr's palm, was already a confessor—'just like John the apostle and evangelist who sat unharmed in a cauldron

[181] Eddius, *Vita Wilfridi*, ed Levison, *MGH SSRM* 6, cap 6, p 199; ed [B.] Colgrave, p 14. Bede *H*[*istoria*] *E*[*cclesiastica gentis Anglorum*], ed [C.] Plummer (Oxford 1896) v, 19, p 325. Plummer, vol 2, pp 316–20, established the chronology of Wilfrid's life. During Wilfrid's first visit to Lyons on his way to Rome in 653, the bishop of that city offered him his niece in marriage together with 'a good part of Gaul' (*bona pars Galliarum*); *Vita* cap 4, ed Levison, p 197.

[182] *Vita Wilfridi* cap 6, p 199 (Levison). One of the two manuscripts of Eddius gives the reading 'Brunhild' instead of 'Balthild', as do some manuscripts of Bede, *HE*: see Levison's comment here p 199 n 3, and Colgrave's, p 154. Colgrave's suggestion that this may be a reminiscence of the Brunhild of the Volsung saga is surely incorrect.

[183] *Vita Wilfridi*, cap 24, p 218 (Levison), p 48 (Colgrave). I am grateful to Joan Nicholson for reminding me of Eddius's other Jezebel.

[184] The name 'Dalfinus' is not, as often alleged, evidence of Eddius's inaccuracy. Coville, *Recherches*, pp 381–5, shows that Aunemundus's brother is not named at all in any early Lyons source, that Aunemundus, typically in this period, had two names, and that his second name (Dalfinus) was simply 'borrowed' for his brother by late medieval reworkers of the story.

of boiling oil . . .'[185] Eddius's aim here is not factual reporting,[186] but the establishment of Wilfrid's saintly credentials at an early point in his *Vita*.

Now if we date Aunemundus's death to 660 with Levison and Ewig,[187] there is clearly a chronological problem involved in accepting Eddius's story, for Wilfrid left Lyons, at the latest, in 658.[188] Further the details of place, time and circumstances recorded in the *Acta* (where of course Wilfrid is not mentioned at all) actually contradict those of Eddius's account. Levison observed these discrepancies but left the matter unresolved; while Coville claimed the discrepancies were insignificant and on Eddius's 'authority' dated Aunemundus' death to 658.[189] I suggest another conclusion, namely, that Wilfrid was not in fact present at Aunemundus's death, and that Eddius's account therefore derives from information which Wilfrid acquired on one of his subsequent visits to Gaul (or perhaps from some other *peregrinus*) on which either Eddius or Wilfrid himself superimposed the tale of Wilfrid's youthful heroism—satisfying to upholders of Germanic and monastic values alike.[190] The motivation behind this tale need not concern us further, though Wilfrid's later connexion with Dagobert II and Eddius' very hostile attitude to Ebroin[190a] are no doubt relevant. Here the point is simply that the *Vita Wilfridi*, and Bede who depends on it, while they explain Balthild's otherwise surprising 'bad name in her native country',[191] need not seriously affect our assessment

[185] *Vita Wilfridi* cap 6, pp 199–200 with n 2 (Levison); p 14 (Colgrave, who gives a possible source of the St John anecdote in the note on p 155.)

[186] For pertinent views on Eddius's method, see R. L. Poole, 'St Wilfrid and the see of Ripon', *EHR* 34 (1919) pp 1–22, and H. Mayr-Harting, *The Coming of Christianity to Anglo-Saxon England* (London 1972) pp 139 *seq*.

[187] Levison, *Vita Wilfridi*, pp 163–4; Ewig, 'Teilreiche', p 95.

[188] *Vita*, ed Colgrave, pp 14–5; Plummer at p 317 of Bede, *HE*, vol 2.

[189] Coville, *Recherches*, p 389; also Fischer, *Ebroin*, pp 95–6. But there is a further difficulty in accepting that Wilfrid, if he had really experienced Balthild's malevolence at first hand, could have been consecrated bishop in 664 at the Neustrian royal villa of Compiègne, by courtesy of Clothar III and presumably also Balthild: Bede, *HE* iii, 28, p 194, with Plummer's notes, vol 2, pp 198, 317.

[190] R. Woolf, 'The ideal of men dying with their lord in the *Germania* and in The Battle of Maldon', *Anglo-Saxon England* 5 (1976) pp 63–81; Graus, *Heiliger*, pp 63–4, 101.

[190a] *Vita*, caps 25, 27, 33, pp 219–20, 228 (Levison); 50, 52, 68 (Colgrave). Poole, 'St Wilfrid', pp 4 *seq*, notes some inaccuracies in Eddius' information on Frankish affairs.

[191] Levison, *England*, p 10. Balthild might have been expected to have had a glowing reputation in England, given the close links of Chelles and Jouarre with various English houses: see A. Lohaus, *Die Merowinger und England, Münchner Beiträge zur Mediavistik und Renaissance-Forschung* (Munich) 1974 pp 53 *seq*, and P. Sims-Williams, 'Continental influence at Bath monastery in the seventh century', *Anglo-Saxon England* 4 (1975) pp 1–10.

of Balthild's regency and, more particularly, of her interventions in local politics and her relations with bishops. Ewig has seen 'the conflict between Aunemundus and Balthild' as signifying a new development in the Neustro-Burgundian realm: the diocese was changing from an 'area associated with an office' to 'the area of a lordship' and Balthild, so Ewig implies, was thus engaged in a new struggle against episcopal 'territorial politics'.[192] I have argued, however, that the fate of Aunemundus was the result rather of a local conflict than of one between centre and province; that Eddius should not be invoked to suggest, as Ewig does, that Aunemundus's case is typical of many others during Balthild's regency; and that the relationship between ruler and *civitas*-politics evident in this case is not a new but a rather traditional one. Evidence of a 'structural change' in the seventh century must be sought elsewhere.

One last aspect of Balthild's dealings with the holy, its custodians and interpreters, remains to be considered: her *Klosterpolitik*.[193] Since the evidence for it begins in 655 and continues throughout the regency, we can fairly assume that she was at least partly responsible for it already as Clovis II's queen. The extant text of the privilege of bishop Landericus for St Denis has been tampered with by later forgers, but its genuine parts can be supplemented by Clovis II's confirmation of it which has survived in the original dated 22 June 655.[194] Clearly the bishop gave up certain rights he had formerly exercised in respect of the monastery: he could no longer exact payment for certain liturgical functions, nor interfere in the disposition of the monastic revenues nor dip into the monastic treasury. What prompted such substantial concessions of wealth and power? Landericus is explicit enough: he grants his privilege 'because the request of the king is for us like a command which it is extremely difficult to resist'.[195] During Balthild's regency this episcopal privilege was complemented by a grant of royal immunity, whereby the king took the monastery under his protection

[192] Ewig, 'Milo', pp 430–3. (His terms are *Amtsgebiet, Herrschaftsgebiet* and *Territorialpolitik.*)

[193] On what follows, Ewig, 'Klosterpolitik', is fundamental, as also is his 'Beobachtungen zu den Klosterprivilegien des 7. und frühen 8. Jhdts', *Adel und Kirche. Festschrift G. Tellenbach* (Freiburg 1968) pp 52–65.

[194] Landericus' privilege: [J. M.] Pardessus, [*Diplomata, Chartae . . . et instrumenta aetatis Merovingicae*], 2 vols (Paris 1843,9) 2, no 320, pp 95–7. Clovis II's confirmation: *MGH DD* 1, no 19, pp 19–21; facsimile in P. Lauer and C. Samaran, *Les Diplomes originaux des Merovingiens* (Paris 1908) no 6.

[195] Pardessus, p 96: '. . . quia supradicti domni Clodovei regis petitio quasi nobis iussio est, cui difficillimum est resisti'.

and put himself under the saint's protection, in return for releasing the monastery from fiscal obligations and other public services, making it 'immune' to the entrance of public officials in the performance of fiscal or judicial functions.[196] What was taking place was a redistribution of resources between three parties, bishop, monastery and king. The bishop's loss was the monastery's gain: so much the privilege made clear. But when at the same time the monastery became an immunist, the king while reallocating the burdens of royal administration could also hope to gain in terms of close, permanent, mutually-beneficial relations with the monastery and more effective control through, for example, royal intervention in abbatial appointments.[197] Finally, and also of vital importance from the king's standpoint, the establishment of the *laus perennis* at St Denis, which Dagobert seems unsuccessfully to have attempted,[198] was achieved in 655 by the introduction there of the *sanctus regularis ordo,* that is, the mixed Benedictine-Columbanan Rule of Luxeuil.[199] The monks' prayers were the instrument by which their royal protector on earth sought the benefits of heavenly protectors: Ewig is surely right to stress the importance 'for the court, [of] the cultic-liturgical business of monasticism'.[200]

The new arrangements at St Denis not only foreshadowed but provided the model for a whole series of similar ones precisely during Balthild's regency. On the one hand, there were two new foundations: Corbie, founded by Balthild and Clothar III between 657 and 661 and granted a privilege by the bishop of Amiens in 664 at Balthild's 'pious request',[201] and Chelles, effectively refounded on a royal *villa* where Chrodechild (Clovis's queen) had long ago established a little convent of nuns and a church dedicated to St George.[202] For Corbie, Balthild had monks and abbot imported from Luxeuil, for Chelles, nuns and abbess

[196] For the significance of privilege and immunity, see Levillain, 'Études [sur l'abbaye de Saint-Denis a l'époque mérovingienne]', *BEC* 87 (1926) pp 21–73. Clothar III's concession of immunity during Balthild's regency is not extant.

[197] Explicitly stated in the privilege of the bishop of Amiens for Corbie, ed Krusch in *NA* 31 (1906) pp 367–72 at p 369: '. . . quem unanimiter congregatio ipsius monasterii . . . dignum elegerint, data auctoritate a praefato principe vel eius successoribus. . .'

[198] *Fred* cap 79, p 68.

[199] See Prinz, *Mönchtum,* pp 105–6, 167–9, and Ian Wood's forthcoming paper, 'A prelude to Columbanus'.

[200] Ewig, 'Klosterpolitik', pp 112–13.

[201] *NA* 31 (1906) p 367. *Vita Balthildis* cap 7, pp 490–1.

[202] *Vita Balthildis* cap 7, pp 489–90, cap 18, pp 505–6, *Vita Bertilae, MGH SSRM* 6, cap 4, p 104. Chelles' function of prayer for king, queen and *proceres* is stressed by the dying Balthild herself: *Vita,* cap 12, p 498, urging the abbess to maintain this

from Jouarre. On the other hand there was the reorganisation of the communal life of old basilicas by the introduction therein of the *sanctus regularis ordo*. The *Vita Balthildis*, remarkably detailed and explicit on this topic, lists the main basilicas and makes it clear that Balthild's actions were coherent and well-planned—in Ewig's word, a 'policy':

> throughout the senior basilicas of the saints, lord Dionisius [St Denis near Paris], lord Germanus [St Germain at Auxerre], and lord Medardus [St Medard at Soissons], and also St Peter [St Pierre-le-Vif at Sens] and lord Anianus [St Aignan at Orleans] and also St Martin [at Tours], and everywhere else that her attention affected, she commanded the bishops and abbots, persuading them for the sake of zeal for God, and directed letters to them to this end, that the brethren settled in these places should live under the holy regular discipline. And in order that they [that is, the brethren] might willingly acquiesce, she ordered that a privilege should be granted them, and at the same time she granted them immunities, so that it might please them the better to pray for the mercy of Christ the highest king of all on behalf of the king and for peace.[203]

If we accept Ewig's plausible suggestion that 'everywhere else' probably included St Marcel at Chalon-sur-Saône, St Symphorien at Autun, St Bénigne at Dijon, St Hilary at Poitiers, St Lupus at Troyes and St Sulpicius at Bourges,[204] then with the *Vita's* six we have a list of nearly all the major cult-sites of seventh-century Gaul. Brunhild had cultivated St Martin's patronage and Dagobert St Denis's. But Balthild was mobilising a whole regiment of saints, enlisting the forces of the holy in every *civitas*. Perhaps still more confidence-inspiring was the placing of such forces right within the *palatium* itself: Clovis II (at Balthild's instigation?) had appropriated the arm of St Denis for the palace-oratory, outraging the monks thus deprived;[205] and it may well have been Balthild herself who acquired St Martin's *cappa* for the royal relic-collection[206] (it is first documented there in 679)[207] though in

'consuetudo, ut ipsa domus Dei bonam famam, quam coeperat, non amitteret, sed amplius semper in affectu caritatis cum omnibus amicis . . . permaneret in dilectione . . .'

203 *Vita* cap 9, pp 493–4.

204 'Klosterpolitik', p 111. with n 43. Balthild's generosity to a group of Norman monasteries in the diocese of Rouen, to Luxeuil and 'the other monasteries of Burgundy', to Jouarre and Faremoutiers, and to the monasteries of Paris itself is stressed in *Vita* cap 8, pp 493–4, listing forests, *villae* and *pecunia innumerabilis.*

205 *LHF* cap 44, p 316.

206 So, Ewig, 'Klosterpolitik', p 112.

207 *MGH DD* no 49, p 45.

this case no opposition is recorded. Thus in the burial-places of the royal dead[208] and in the home-base of the living king, direct contacts were made between the Merovingian family and the sources of supernatural power—contacts which superimposed new centripetal forces on a previously localised field.

Playing for such high stakes, Balthild knew the risks she ran. Not every bishop was enthused by the new monasticism; and even if a bishop happily granted privileges to his own new foundation in the countryside, it would be naive to assume that he granted the same privileges equally gladly to the ancient basilica on his own doorstep in or by the city.[209] I am struck by the documents' emphasis on the bishop's economic loss, especially the renunciation by bishop Landericus of what was evidently an existing practice of carrying off from the monastery and into the city gold and silver bullion and cash which had been placed in the monastery.[210] The bishop of Amiens expressly renounced the same practice in the Corbie privilege,[211] but in his case the profit or loss was hypothetical. The bishops of Paris, Auxerre, Soissons and the rest must have faced a real loss of resources. The *Vita Balthildis* gives no hint of any compensation. For the brethren who served the basilicas, on the other hand, the new obligations Balthild laid on them were offset by new 'freedoms' which included financial incentives.[212] Balthild's policy then, might have been expected to arouse opposition, if anywhere, from bishops, which would make royal control of episcopal appointments all the more essential. Perhaps it is in this context that Balthild's 'fall' should be understood. Sigobrand, presumably her appointee to the see of Paris, alienated some powerful aristocrats by his *superbia*:[213] was he trying to recoup some of the losses his see had suffered because of his predecessor Landericus's enforced concessions to St Denis? Did the 'commotion' which caused

[208] Their significance is indicated by Ewig, 'Résidence', pp 48–52.

[209] Ewig, 'Klosterpolitik', p 109, rightly stresses that bishops might perceive Balthild's demands as 'an unheard-of imposition'.

[210] *MGH DD* 1, no 19, p 20.

[211] *NA* 31 (1906) p 369. The broader economic context which these references hint at cannot be discussed here. But for some archaeological and artistic evidence that might suggest continuing Neustrian prosperity, see Maillé, *Jouarre*, pp 112–14, p 206 *seq.* and for other evidence, F. Vercauteren, 'La vie urbaine entre Meuse et Loire du VIe au IXe siècle', in *SS Spoleto* 6, ii (1959) pp 453–84 at 478–9.

[212] *Vita Balthildis* cap 9, pp 493–4, (quoted above) suggests that the inducements to the *fratres* were well-planned: '. . . ut hoc libenter adquiescerent, privilegium eis firmare iussit [!], vel etiam emunitates concessit, ut melius eis delectaret pro rege . . . exorare'.

[213] Above p 23, and n 116.

Sigobrand's death signify the limits set by aristocratic interests to Balthild's policy in a situation of fierce competition for scarce resources (especially around Paris)? Balthild's wealth was clearly vast, both in treasure and in land; but had she enough to sustain lavish generosity to monasteries all over Neustria and Burgundy and at the same time to maintain bishops in their powerful yet dependent positions as lynchpins of royal government? In the event, the precariousness of her position as mere regent was exposed, and those whom she had 'sweetly nurtured' in the palace—including, probably, Ebroin—decided to dispense with her. Personal bonds held only so long as they were reinforced by real or prospective benefits. Balthild's regime had not been anti-aristocratic, nor, if she had gained prestige, had she done so at the aristocracy's expense; but their benefits were not apparent. With deadly accurate irony, the 'princes', according to Balthild's hagiographer, now 'suddenly permitted her'[214] to retire to Chelles which she had so richly endowed. There she died, perhaps in 680, after fifteen years of exemplary humility in the convent;[215] there she soon found her hagiographer and there her memory was kept green and her cult defended against the sceptical.[216]

Balthild had attempted, as Ewig observes, 'a structural change in the Merovingian church'.[217] But this could not fail to have consequences also for non-ecclesiastical politics. To be sure of this, we need only recall the implications of the Carolingians' *Reichskirche* for their whole political position, especially in the ninth century when royal exploitation of the church's resources replaced, to a significant extent, an eroded secular power-base.[218] Ewig thinks that Balthild's fall made her attempted 'structural change' quite abortive.[219] I am not so sure. True, we lack the evidence which might show whether or not a Childeric II

[214] Above *ibid*, and p 22 n 113. The role of the *sacerdotes* at this point is interesting: they intervene, not to save Balthild but to re-establish peace between her and the *seniores* and thus to nip in the bud her *non modica querela* (feud ?) against them. The implication is that she might have pursued the quarrel even in 'retirement'.

[215] For the date, see Krusch's introduction to the *Vita*, p 476. In describing Balthild's convent years, her hagiographer lavishly deploys the motifs of female asceticism: the influence of Venantius' *Vita Radegundis* is clear, and we are assured no less than thrice that Balthild was an *exemplum humilitatis* (caps 11, 12, 16, pp 496, 498, 502).

[216] Their existence must be inferred from the reference in the *Vita* cap 1, p 482 to *detractores*. In caps 18–9, pp 505–7, the hagiographer tries to establish Balthild's saintly credentials by setting her in a line of holy queens: Chrodechild, Ultrogotha and Radegund.

[217] 'Klosterpolitik', p 113.

[218] See C. -R. Brühl, *Fodrum, Gistum, Servitium Regis* (Cologne 1968) pp 50 *seq*.

[219] 'Klosterpolitik', p 113.

or even a Theuderic III landed himself and his court more often than his predecessors had done on the hospitality of monastic communities, or used monastic lands to reward trusty warriors, or dipped into monastic treasuries when need arose. We do know, however, that towards the end of the seventh century, there were 'organisational connexions' between Corbie and the royal chancery[220] and that there were similarly close and continuous links between the ruling dynasty and both St Denis[221] and Chelles.[222] After Balthild, there were still powerful Merovingians—the more powerful, I suggest, because of what she had done. The real threat to such rulers was not bad blood but assassination. Against that the only remedy in the early middle ages, so the Carolingians' experience implies, was the dynastic prestige that came of contact with supernatural power. Precisely that contact was what Balthild had effected so forcefully. But it took time and a more thorough Christianisation of Frankish society for sentiments of legitimacy to grow, and so the Carolingians reaped what Balthild had sown. It was apt enough, therefore, that in the time of Louis the Pious, the abbess of Chelles, who was also the emperor's mother-in-law, staged in the imperial presence a splendid *translatio* of Balthild's remains into a fine new church dedicated to the arch-protectress, the Virgin.[223] Ewig's claim that 'not constitutional or political but religious aspects primarily determined [Balthild's] actions'[224] seems to me in one sense a truism, in another misleading. For those 'religious' aspects were at one and the same time political: to appropriate relics, to commandeer prayers, to pressurise bishops, to make dependents and allies of urban as well as rural monastic communities—all this was to gain power at once this-worldly and other-worldly. Balthild's tenure of that power was brief, partly, at least, because of the inherent weakness of her position as a mere regent, a married-in woman. But in terms of what she attempted, she must be judged a rarely gifted and creative early medieval politician.

In sketching the careers of Brunhild and Balthild, I have tried to grasp both the fortuitous and the significant in their reputations as 'Jezebels'. I have therefore had to consider some aspects of royal power

[220] See Prinz, *Mönchtum,* p 174 and works cited there, n 114.

[221] Ewig, 'Résidence' p 52; Levillain, 'Études', *BEC* 87 (1926) pp 21–73 and 91 (1930) pp 1–65.

[222] B. Bischoff, 'Die Kölner Nonnenhandschriften und das Skriptorium von Chelles', *MStn,* 2 vols (1966) 1, pp 16 *seq* at 26–7.

[223] *Translatio Balthildis, MGH SS* 15, pp 284–5.

[224] 'Klosterpolitik', p 113.

and of its interrelations with what in the sixth and seventh centuries was believed to be the power of the holy. Though we in the twentieth century tend to place these two types of power in separate compartments, it is precisely their interrelations which make for some fundamental continuities in the Merovingian period. If it is hard to make 'a clear distinction between religion and politics'[225] in establishing the motivations of Brunhild, Balthild and their contemporaries, perhaps, without discarding useful categories, rather than seeking lines of division, we should look for points of intersection and ask how far we can understand the religious *as* political, and vice versa, in the Merovingian world. It is in the changing location of such points of intersection that we can find evolution, and a kind of dialectic. In the sixth century, there are important cult-sites mainly in *civitates,* in which royal and episcopal power mutually reinforce each other, in the early seventh century, land-based aristocratic power creates new religious centres in the countryside; and in the mid-seventh century royal power is redefined and extended (in intent, at least) in relation to rural as well as urban centres. Thus from the activities of Brunhild and Balthild, which serve so conveniently to identify two of these three phases, we can make some useful inferences about the modes of Merovingian royal power and its adaptation, by means of new religious forms, to economic and social changes.

Can we also make any useful inferences about women, or about royal women, in the sixth and seventh centuries? There is no simple answer. In comparing her position with that of a female aristocrat, we observed the queen's special character. And while her position had its disadvantages these are hard to attribute specifically to her femininity. The weakness of ineligibility for kingship she shared with all non-Merovingian men; that of the non-institutionalisation of her power, with even very powerful male contemporaries, including mayors of the palace. A queen who possessed the right personal qualities could command the loyalty of warriors, and if, as a woman, she could not wield armed force herself, she could direct armies in a strategic sense. Wallace-Hadrill once asked how women could have prosecuted a

[225] *Ibid,* where Ewig himself recognises the problem.

feud except by using hired assassins;[226] but I have suggested that her grandson's campaign against Clothar II may have been instigated by Brunhild precisely to prosecute her feud against the son of Fredegund. Balthild, on the other hand, used her power most effectively without recourse to armed force. All this prompts the question of whether the exercise in person of command on battlefields was always so indispensable a function of successful early medieval rulership as is usually assumed. Perhaps even a seventh-century Merovingian queen, like a Byzantine emperor (or, in the eighth-century, an empress)[227] or most modern rulers, could either like Brunhild have her battles fought for her, or like Balthild use political as an alternative to military action.

Our discussion of these two queens' careers has indicated, less the alleged drawbacks of a woman's position than a kind of strength inherent precisely in its domestic location. A king might win or confirm his power on the battlefield, but he exercised it in the hall, and this we have seen to be the prime area of the queen's activity. Here in the royal *familia* the distribution of food, clothing, charity, the nurturing of the *iuvenes*, the maintenance of friendly relations between the *principes,* the respectful reception of bishops and foreign visitors: all fell to the queen's responsibility. Thus the organisation of the household, the woman's sphere, became a political function in the case of the *aula regis.* The centrality of *Hausherrschaft* to early medieval kingship has long been recognised.[228] But its implications for the queen's position, perhaps less clearly appreciated hitherto, have emerged in strikingly similar ways in both Brunhild's and Balthild's careers: Brunhild braves even Columbanus's wrath to preserve all the *dignitates* and *honor* that only control of the *aula regis* has given her, while Balthild makes the *palatium* her power-house as long as she controls the network of friendships and clientage that radiates from it. In so far as later Merovingians remained powerful, it was their activity in the palace that made them so. Wallace-Hadrill lists the judgements, the confirmations, the arbitrations, the confiscations and the exemptions which had been, and in the late Merovingian period remained, the peacetime functions of kingship.[229] In all these queens could be active too:

[226] *Long-Haired Kings,* p 135. Men, including kings, used assassins sometimes: Gregory and Fredegar give several examples.

[227] See Sir Steven Runciman's paper in *Medieval Women*, ed. D. Baker (Oxford 1978).

[228] W. Schlesinger, *Beiträge zur deutschen Verfassungsgeschichte des Mittelalters* (Göttingen 1963) 1, pp 9 *seq,* partly translated in F. L. Cheyette, *Lordship and Community in Medieval Europe* (New York 1968) pp 64 *seq.*

[229] *Long-Haired Kings,* pp 237–8.

Brunhild ransomed captives.[230] Balthild remitted taxes,[231] and behind the dry *diplomata* how often can a queen's influence be suspected? Praejectus owed to Himnechild the favourable outcome of his land-dispute.[232] Indeed episcopal *Stadtherrschaft,* and the whole complex of relations between bishops and rulers, need to be linked to the *Hausherrschaft* of kings and queens. When Chilperic sought the support of one bishop against another 'traitorous' one, the whole exercise was conducted through face-to-face contact in the palace; and though the king's first move was a threat to sabotage the bishop's local power-base in his own *civitas,* his second was a conciliatory offer of an alfresco snack of specially-cooked chicken and pea soup.[233] If banquets still play an important role in modern diplomacy, how much the more useful instruments were food-prestations and commensality to an early medieval king. The distinction between public and private action becomes redundant in the context of the royal hall. All this explains why in the case of a queen, domestic power could mean political power.[234] Their realisation and effective exploitation of this possibility go far to explain the achievements of Brunhild and Balthild.

But in the end, it is not just as female but as royal figures that the pair have commanded our attention. That both were able to function as regents at all is significant. In no other early medieval kingdom did queen regents recurrently rule as they did in the late sixth- and seventh-century *regnum Francorum.*[235] It could be argued that such regencies are symptomatic of aristocratic power. For whereas elective monarchy tends to produce a sequence of mature kings who may consolidate royal power at the expense of their magnates (and even of

[230] Paulus Diaconus, *Historia Langobardorum* iv, 1, *MGH SSRL,* p 116.

[231] *Vita* cap 6, p 488: the capitation-tax had apparently been causing parents to prefer infanticide to rearing offspring, so Balthild by removing the *impia consuetudo* also removed the inducement to an impious crime. Her financial loss would of course be compensated by a *copiosa merces* of a heavenly kind.

[232] *Passio Praejecti* cap 24, *MGH SSRM* 5, p 239–40.

[233] *LH* v, 18, pp 219–20.

[234] This equation, and its relevance to the queen's position, was made explicitly by Hincmar in reference to ninth-century *palatium* organisation, in his *De Ordine Palatii* cap 22, *MGH Capit* 2, p 525: 'De honestate vero palatii seu specialiter ornamento regali necnon et *de donis annuis militum* . . . ad reginam praecipue et sub ipsa ad camerarium pertinebat'. Thus the king could be freed 'ab omni sollicitudine *domestica vel palatina*' to turn his mind to the *status regni*! Here again, Carolingian arrangements show continuity with Merovingian.

[235] The contrast with seventh-century England was noted by Wallace-Hadrill, *Early Germanic Kingship in England and on the Continent* (Oxford 1971) p 92.

many magnates' lives)[236], hereditary monarchy, with son(s) succeeding father, though it may exclude princes who had hitherto been eligible, in practice ensures that there will be minorities during which those princes and other magnates can collaborate with the queen-mother in ruling the kingdom. On this view the regimes of Brunhild and Balthild would represent the product of aristocratic interests. But the very fact that those interests are centred still on the royal *palatium* suggests that our queens' regencies are also symptomatic of dynastic strength. The long-term Merovingian monopoly of Frankish kingship should be explained primarily in terms of concentrations of monarchic power from Clovis to Sigibert and Chilperic, and during the reigns of Clothar II and Dagobert, and only secondarily in terms of aristocratic reactions to that power. If magnates exploited minorities, they did not create the conditions for them: filial succession became normal as a consequence of the activity and the will of kings.

The careers of Brunhild and Balthild, therefore, highlight the Merovingians' monopoly of kingship, as well as some of the modes and potential resources of royal government in the Frankish realm which made that monopoly possible and conditioned its operation in practice. The extent of these queens' political success thus helps confirm what the work of Ewig and others have shown of the fundamental structures of Merovingian politics in *palatium* and *civitas*. At the same time, Brunhild and Balthild focus our attention on the ebb and flow of power through those structures, on the dynamic relationships and the personalities that shaped the course of Merovingian history. Both queens, acting in areas of life dominated by men, were depicted as having masculine traits: Brunhild defied a posse of armed enemies *viriliter*[237]—'like a man'—while to Balthild was attributed that most manly of virtues—*strenuitas*.[238] Each ruled like a Merovingian, with a Merovingian's authority. Each earned the ill-name of 'Jezebel' in certain quarters not because female rulership was seen as a monstrous incongruity but because these particular rulers in the exercise of their

[236] For the spectacular bloodbath following the accession of the Visigothic king Chindaswinth in 641, see *Fred* cap 82, pp 69–70. On the differing consequences of indeterminate and hereditary father-son succession, see Goody, *Succession*, pp 29 *seq*; compare also the remarks of Pauline Stafford, below pp 79–100. I am grateful to John Gillingham for discussion of this point.

[237] *LH* vi, 4, p 268.

[238] *LHF* cap 43, p 315: '. . . pulchram omnique ingenio *strenuam*'. Compare *Vita Bertilae* cap 4, *MGH SSRM* 6, p 104: '[Baltechildis] . . . *viriliter* gubernabat palatium'.

power offended particular influential men. If we want to redress the gross unfairness of their posthumous reputations, we shall do them less than justice to consider them *only* as women. Like their contemporary female saints[239]—or like any climber of the Matterhorn—they are distinguished as *homines:* as human beings.

[239] See the evidence assembled by Kurth, *Études Franques,* I, pp 161–7, for women *homines* in Merovingian texts.

2

ON THE LIMITS OF THE CAROLINGIAN RENAISSANCE[1]

EINHARD tells us that Charlemagne had a special liking for 'those books of St Augustine called *The City of God*'.[2] If only he had told us why. Did Charlemagne demand readings from book 5 on the happy Christian emperors?[3] Or was he, as Ladner suggests, particularly attracted by 'the idea of a society embracing earth and heaven, a society which a man could join through personal renewal'? If Ladner is right, then, he tells us, we should talk not of a Carolingian renaissance—'secondary classicising features notwithstanding'—but of a Carolingian reform 'as just one phase in the unfolding history of the realisation of the Reform idea in Christian history' and specifically 'an attempt to recreate the religious culture of the fourth and fifth centuries'.[4] But *is* Ladner right about Charlemagne? I have my doubts: perhaps what he really enjoyed most was book 22's meaty chapter on the resurrection of the flesh or its rattling good miracle-story.

Of course, it is possible to insist on the primary quality of those 'classicising features', yet still deny that there was a Carolingian renaissance. Le Goff has done so precisely because of the lack of creativity in Carolingian culture: 'peut-il y avoir une renaissance avare?'[5] Schramm rejected the biological metaphor of birth and growth as, quite simply, inappropriate to what was happening in Charlemagne's time,[6] apparently discounting the metaphor's Caro-

[1] The wording of my title is a deliberate echo of [H.] Liebeschütz, 'Wesen und Grenzen [des karolingischen Rationalismus]', in *A*[*rchiv*] [*für*] *K*[*ultur*]*g*[*eschichte*], 33 (Berlin 1950) pp 17 *seq*, and [H.] Löwe, 'Von den Grenzen [des Kaisergedankens in der Karolingerzeit]', in *DA*, 14 (1958) pp 345 *seq*.

[2] *V*[*ita*] *K*[*aroli Magni*], ed O. Holder-Egger, *MGH SRG* (1911) cap 24, p 29.

[3] As implied by [J. M.] Wallace-Hadrill, [*Early Germanic*] *Kingship* [*in England and on the Continent*] (Oxford 1971) p 104. Compare H. X. Arquillière, *L'augustinisme politique* (2 ed Paris 1955) cap iv, esp pp 164, 196.

[4] [G.] Ladner, 'Die mittelalterliche Reform-Idee und ihr Verhältnis zur Renaissance', in *MIÖG* 60 (Vienna 1952) p 54 with n 109.

[5] [J.] Le Goff, *Les Intellectuels au Moyen Age* (Paris 1969) p 14.

[6] [P. E.] Schramm, *K*[*aiser,*] *K*[*önige und*] *P*[*äpste*] (Stuttgart 1968) 1, pp 27 *seq* and esp 336 *seq*. E. Patzelt, *Die karolingische Renaissance* (Berlin 1923, repr Graz 1965) also rejected the notion of a renaissance under Charlemagne but on other grounds. Schramm dismisses this book too glibly: though many of her arguments must be abandoned

lingian currency and ignoring too the fact that concepts of rebirth and renewal were then, as often in Christian history, intimately linked and even interchangeable[7] (for metaphor after all need follow neither logical nor biological rules). It is not difficult to resist Schramm's appeal that we abandon this renaissance in favour of a bloodless *correctio.*[8] Far more seductive is Riché's suggestion, on the very last page of *Education et Culture* after pages of proliferating renaissances in the seventh and eighth centuries, that there were two Carolingian renaissances—one in Charlemagne's time and another 'true' one in the ninth century[9]. But we should resist any temptation thus to split up a single continuous historical process, intelligible only as such. Let us for the moment accept at least Lehmann's minimal definition of the Carolingian renaissance as 'a rebirth of studies—especially the Latin language and the writings of classical Rome'.[10] In this sense, the deliberate historiographical evocation of the fourteenth-sixteenth century renaissance seems perfectly acceptable. But the question of whether or not the Carolingian renaissance, like the later one, had broader dimensions than this cannot be evaded:[11] it is indeed implicit in the quest for limits.

Three characteristics of early medieval Christian mentality conditioned Carolingian concepts of rebirth in such a way that this renaissance amounted to more than simply 'a rebirth of studies' yet at the

---

in the light of subsequent research, Patzelt was in my view correct in emphasising continuities between the Merovingian and Carolingian periods. But she gave no consideration to law.

[7] See J. Trier, 'Zur Vorgeschichte des Renaissance-Begriffes', in *AKG*, 33 (1950) pp 45 *seq*, and 'Wiederwuchs', *AKG* 43 (1961) pp 177 *seq*. For further references and a fine analysis of the concepts involved here, see the indispensable work of Ladner, *The Idea of Reform* (rev ed New York 1967) and the same author's very useful summary in *RAC* 6 (1966) cols 240 *seq* under 'Erneuerung'. In 'Gregory the Great and Gregory VII: a comparison of their concepts of renewal', in *Viator*, 4 (Berkeley 1973) pp 1 *seq* at pp 24–5, Ladner has some interesting comments on the Carolingian renaissance, expanding the few scattered remarks in *The Idea of Reform*, and promising a full treatment of this subject in a forthcoming book, now eagerly awaited.

[8] Schramm's main reason for preferring this term was that it expressed the *actio* of Charlemagne himself. The false assumption here is that the 'biological' birth-process in the case of human beings excludes any positive exercise of the will. Could Schramm not have cast Charlemagne in the metaphorical role, if not of mother, then of midwife?

[9] [P.] Riché, *Education* [*et culture dans l'Occident barbare*] (3 ed Paris 1973) p 552.

[10] P. Lehmann, 'Das Problem der karolingischen Renaissance', in *SS* Spoleto 1 (1954) pp 309 *seq*.

[11] I omit any consideration of the political aspects of Carolingian imperial *renovatio*, on which see Schramm, *Kaiser, Rom und Renovatio* (Leipzig 1929) and *KKP*, 1 pp 215 *seq*, and Löwe, 'Von den Grenzen'.

same time was relatively restricted both in intention and in effect. First, the Carolingian scholars who operated with these concepts did so within the framework of clerical culture: *eruditio* was to be reborn in order to serve and promote the ends of Christian *sapientia* as determined by a tiny elite of clergy and monks.[12] Lay involvement was inevitably passive and at second hand. Second, the habit of thinking of these same scholars—as, it seems, of their illiterate contemporaries—was typological. Just as the old testament was fulfilled in the new, so antiquity was reborn or renewed in christendom: *nova antiquitas et antiqua novitas.*[13] Like Marx's *Aufhebung*, Carolingian ideas of rebirth transcended any crude polarisation of 'conservative' and 'revolutionary'. Carolingian scholars perceived their present as fully continuous with the Roman, and especially the Christian-Roman, past. This sense of continuity through renewal presents, I think, a noteworthy contrast to the renaissance ideologies of the fifteenth/sixteenth and, in some degree, even the twelfth centuries. Historians prone to emphasising the alleged novelties of the Carolingian age should at least consider the implications of re-viewing it in Carolingian perspective. Third, and perhaps especially in this period of Christian expansion, the rebirth metaphor could have reference to baptism, the *sacramentum regenerationis* through which a person is reborn into the church.[14] In this case, the rebirth, being a personal matter, could be interpreted more directly in terms of prevailing notions of community. I shall return to this point below.

The distinct yet related ideas of individual and social or institutional rebirth[15] have not been neglected by Ullmann, whose great merit in *The Carolingian Renaissance and the Idea of Kingship* has been to seek to locate the rebirth of scholarship in the context of Carolingian society.

[12] Compare W. Edelstein, *Eruditio und Sapientia. Weltbild und Erziehung in der Karolingerzeit* (Freiburg i. Breisgau 1965) *passim*, esp pp 22 and 85 n 35, some penetrating criticisms of J. Fleckenstein, *Die Bildungsreform Karls des Grossen als Verwirklichung der 'norma rectitudinis'* (Bigge-Ruhr 1953).

[13] This phrase from the *Libri Carolini* forms the title of a remarkable book by [E.] Dahlhaus-Berg, *Kölner Historische Abh*, 23 (Cologne 1975) with pp 35 *seq* esp relevant in the present context.

[14] For the immediate liturgical situation, see Dahlhaus-Berg, *Nova Antiquitas*, pp 94 *seq* and for the wider background, [W.] Ullmann, [*The*] *C*[*arolingian*] *R*[*enaissance and the Idea of Kingship*] (London 1969) pp 6 *seq* with additional references on p 191, to which should be added the baptismal liturgy itself, as in, for example, J. Deshusses, *Le sacramentaire gregorien, SpicFr* 16 (1971) no 1086, p 379: 'Deus . . . qui te regeneravit . . .' Still valuable is [K.] Burdach, *Reformation,* [*Renaissance, Humanismus*] (Berlin 1918) esp pp 37 *seq*.

[15] The distinction was drawn by Ladner, 'Erneuerung', col 262.

'What I fail to understand', he writes, '. . . is how there could be a literary and cultural movement . . . floating in a vacuum, and having no links with the society surrounding it'.[16] What Ullmann argues, if I read him correctly, is that in the 'totalitarian' world of this medieval Christian society, personal renewal implies institutional renewal: those same Christian norms which applied to the baptised individual were, he suggests, applied quite naturally to society as a whole. 'The effect which this Carolingian renaissance in the social sense was to produce in the public field was a "baptism" on the largest conceivable scale'. To the question of how this was achieved, Ullmann answers: by the absorption of 'ecclesiology . . . into the governmental system itself'. For, 'just as the individual, through the juristic effects of baptism was incorporated in, or absorbed by, the Church, in the same way the component groups of Frankish society were absorbed within the corporative union of the Church'. Ullmann goes on to argue that the major instrument of his social and governmental renaissance was 'the law applicable to the whole of Frankish society'; and in subsequent parts of the book, he attempts to show how Carolingian legislation aimed at the suppression of 'Frankish or Germanic or any other naturally grown habits and usages' by 'the laws of God'. Ullmann's novel approach seems to me to focus upon a vital question, and his concern with law points to a fruitful source of answers. In what follows, however, viewing the problem from a different stand-point and Carolingian law in a different perspective, I reach some different conclusions.

I begin, I confess, with a nagging doubt as to whether in the Carolingian period individual Christian renewal was so significant an ideological theme as to imply social renewal either in theory or practice. Ullmann rightly asks: 'are cultural phenomena not at all times intimately and indissolubly linked with society?'[17] Yes indeed, but the links may be complex and indirect, as, for instance, when a cultural renaissance occurs in a time of social and political disintegration: scholars have sometimes been known to inhabit ivory towers. Moreover, the institutionalisation of governmental ideas may be more or less complete, or scarcely realised at all. In any given case, we need to know what institutions are available[18] and how far these are functionally

[16] *CR*, p 5. My further quotations are from pp 8, 9, 11 and 22 of the same work.

[17] *CR* p 5.

[18] Their importance in relation to law is stressed by E. Forsthoff, 'Zur Problematik der Rechtserneuerung', in *Naturrecht oder Rechtspositivismus?*, ed W. Maihofer (Darmstadt 1966) pp 83 *seq*.

autonomous with respect to other social phenomena. In the present case, we have to ask whether Charlemagne and his church (including both clerical and monastic orders) were really in a position to seek, let alone effect, 'the transformation of contemporary society in accordance with the doctrinal and dogmatic notions of Christianity, as it was seen in patristic lore'.[19] I am enough of a traditionalist to claim that the renaissance-idea of the Carolingian period had rather severe limits. I shall now try to delineate some of them, limiting myself first to the area of law.[20]

If rebirth and renewal ideas were used fairly often by Carolingian writers in reference to learning and religious culture, they were scarcely ever applied to law.[21] What did occasionally appear were notions of emending or correcting the law.[22] Now these terms are certainly found in the vocabulary of Christian renewal ideology. But it was not from thence that they were brought to bear on Carolingian law. Rather, we have here to deal with two other sources, both legal and both of directly political relevance. First, the idea that a monarch's function was to codify and correct the law of his people stems from late Roman practice as transmitted through the sub-Roman successor-kingdoms.[23] The creation of Charlemagne's empire, in gaining direct access to the lively Roman-legal traditions of Lombard Italy and Visigothic Spain to some extent revived this influence.[24] Thus when Charlemagne stated his desire to remedy defects in the law, he followed in the footsteps of Rothari and Recceswinth.[25] Church

[19] Ullmann, *CR*, p 7.

[20] In arguing that law was an integral part of this renaissance, Ullmann, *CR*, though on somewhat different premises, takes the same view as [F.] Heer, 'Die "Renaissance"-Ideologie [im früheren Mittelalter]', in *MIÖG*, 57 (1949) pp 48–9.

[21] Heer, 'Die "Renaissance"-Ideologie', p 49, nn 67 and 69, cites two poetic examples. I am aware of two other references to *leges renovare*: Cathwulf, *MGH Epp* 4, p 50, and the mid-ninth century *Vita Lebuini Antiqua*, *MGH SS* 30, p 793, referring to the assemblies of the eighth-century Saxons: 'renovabant leges et praecipuas causas adiudicabant'. For the late classical background to this idea, see Ladner, 'Erneuerung', col 263.

[22] For example Einhard, *VK* cap 29, p 33; *MGH Cap* 1, no 33, p 92. But such expressions remained uncommon: see [G.] Köbler, [*Das*] *Recht* [*im frühen Mittelalter*] *Forschungen zur deutschen Rechtsgeschichte* 7 (Cologne 1971) p 225.

[23] [E.] Ewig, '[Zum christlichen] Königsgedanken [im Frühmittelalter]', in *Das Königtum. Vorträge und Forschungen* 3 (Konstanz 1956) pp 32 *seq*; Wallace-Hadrill, [*The*] *Long-haired Kings* (London 1962) pp 37 *seq*, and *Kingship*, pp 32 *seq*.

[24] For Italy, see below pp 55-6 with n 33; for Visigothic law in the Carolingian realms, see Ullmann, *CR*, p 81 with n 2.

[25] *Edictum Rothari*, ed F. Beyerle, *Die Gesetze der Langobarden* (Weimar 1947) prologue, p 16; Leovigild: Isidore, *Historia Gothorum*, cap 5, *MGH CM* 2, p 288;

councils of the sixth and seventh centuries had also adopted the emendation terminology of Roman law,[26] but such ecclesiastical models were, I think, of only secondary importance to a Carolingian practice representing continuity with the earlier gentile *regna*, and not something peculiar to the Carolingian renaissance.

Second, Charlemagne also inherited a specifically Frankish tradition of hegemonial imperialism enshrined in the laws issued by successive Merovingian kings for the *gentes* over whom they held sway.[27] Charlemagne was too shrewd to neglect so politically-useful a legacy: his mental sustenance included, after all, alongside Augustine's books, tales of the deeds of his predecessors.[28] Einhard seems to imply a causal link between Charlemagne's reception of the *imperiale nomen* and his concern with gentile legislation.[29] But why assume merely Roman imperial influence here?[30] Charlemagne may have been at least as strongly imbued with a *non*-Roman imperial idea. He attempted no more than had those Merovingians who 'added to the laws what had to be added . . . modified them in accordance with the *lex christianorum* . . . and gave a written law to each *gens*'. The words are those, not of any representative of the Carolingian

Recceswinth: *Lex Visigothorum Recc.* I, 1, 9, *MGH Leg* 1, 1, p 40, and Erwig, *ibid* 2, 1, 1, p 45. Compare Clothar II's *Edictum*, *MGH Cap* 1, no 9, p 20. The ultimate model was the preface to Justinian's Nov vii, referring to one law 'quae priores omnes et renovet et emendet et quod deest adiciat et quod superfluum est abscidiat'.

[26] Köbler, *Recht*, pp 215 *seq*.

[27] For interpretations along these lines, compare Wallace-Hadrill, *Long-haired Kings*, pp 213–14, and 'A background to St Boniface's mission', in *Early Medieval History* (Oxford 1975) p 139; and H. Wolfram, 'The shaping of the early medieval principality', in *Viator*, 2 (1971) p 45. On the 'Rome-free imperial idea', C. Erdmann, *Forschungen zur politischen Ideenwelt des Frühmittelalters* (Berlin 1951) esp pp 22 *seq* remains fundamental. See now also E. E. Stengel, *Abhandlungen und Untersuchungen zur Geschichte des Kaisergedankens im Mittelalter* (Cologne 1965) pp 260 *seq*, 289 *seq*, and Schramm, *KKP*, 1, pp 250 *seq*, both of whom, however, underestimate the significance of pre-Carolingian gentile-imperial ideas. Löwe, 'Von Theoderich dem Grossen zu Karl dem Grossen', in *DA*, 9 (1952) pp 367, n 54 and 383 *seq* provides a valuable corrective, though he has relatively little to say on Merovingian sources. I hope to deal elsewhere with the evidence, legal, liturgical and otherwise, for a Merovingian concept of gentile, hegemonial, imperial kingship.

[28] Einhard, *VK* cap 29, p 33.

[29] *Ibid*: 'Post susceptum imperiale nomen cum adverteret multa legibus populi sui deesse . . . cogitavit quae deerant addere . . .'

[30] So, [F.] Ganshof, *Recherches* [*sur les Capitulaires*] (Paris 1958) pp 98 *seq*, and 'Charlemagne's programme of imperial government', in *The Carolingians and the Frankish Monarchy* (London 1971) pp 55 *seq*.

renaissance, but of the prologue to the *Lex Baiuvariorum.*[31] Charlemagne's abortive efforts at further codification of gentile laws marked no new departure, but the end of a road.

The fact that most Carolingian capitularies cannot be classed as legislation at all may be linked with the feebleness of Roman-legal traditions in this period. Previous barbarian legislation, from the fifth through to the eighth century, had been far more open than the Carolingians' to Roman-legal influence,[32] whether through the persistence within the regna of *romani*, that is, men living under, and in some cases learned in, Roman law in its late-imperial form, or through access, direct or indirect, to the surviving practice of Roman law in Italy.[33] By comparison, Carolingian Gaul was poverty-stricken: the study of Roman law was never included in Charlemagne's programme of *correctio* nor in ninth-century curricula.[34] Certainly Roman-legal texts were copied in Carolingian monasteries (though often simply by way of scholarly exercises) and sometimes used by churchmen to defend ecclesiastical privileges. But all this hardly adds up to a 'renouveau des études juridiques'.[35] And if we leave the cloister to consider the secular legal practice of the Carolingian period, we are confronted not with renewal but with a process of change continuous from the sixth and much accelerated from the early eighth century, whereby new economic and social conditions imposed legal usages very different from those envisaged even in the most 'vulgar' Roman law.[36] In those regions of the empire inhabited by *romani*, despite the

[31] Ed E. Schwind, *MGH Leg* 1, 1, pt 2, p 202. (The edition of K. Beyerle has unfortunately been inaccessible). For the date—probably seventh-century—see F. Beyerle, 'Die süddeutschen *Leges* [und die merowingische Gesetzgebung]', in *ZRG GAbt* 49 (1929) pp 373 *seq*, and 'Die beiden süddeutschen Stammesrechte', in *ZRG GAbt* 73 (1956) p 124.

[32] See Riché, *Education*, pp 489 *seq* (Alamannia and Bavaria), 387 *seq* and 455 *seq* (Lombard kingdom). The more 'Romanising' laws of the Burgundian and Gothic kingdoms are contrasted with those of the Franks, Lombards and Anglo-Saxons by [G.] Astuti, 'Note critiche [sul sistema delle fonti giuridiche nei regni romano-barbari dell'occidente]', in *Atti della Accademia Nazionale dei Lincei*, 377, 8 ser 25 (Rome 1970) pp 319 *seq*, at 325 *seq*. For a similar contrast on general grounds, see L. Musset, *The Germanic Invasions, 400–600* (London 1975) pp 67 *seq* and 211.

[33] See Riché, 'Enseignement [du droit en Gaule du VIe au XIe siècle', in *Ius Romanum Medii Aevi* 5b, bb (Brussels 1965), p 15, and the interesting suggestions of [D. A.] Bullough, '*Europae Pater*: Charlemagne and his achievement in the light of recent research', in *EHR*, 85 (1970), pp 92 *seq*.

[34] Riché, 'Enseignement', pp 16 *seq*.

[35] *Ibid* p 16.

[36] [J.] Gaudemet, 'Survivances [romaines dans le droit de la monarchie franque du Ve au Xe siècle]', in *Tijdschrift voor Rechtsgeschiedenis*, 23 (Harlem 1955) pp 149 *seq*,

persistence of Roman-legal formulae in many documents, basic transactions of property and marriage increasingly came to be regulated —as elsewhere—by the custom of an evolving feudal society. This trend pre-dated and underlay changes in the procedures of public courts generalised under Charlemagne and his successors.

Ganshof has recently shown that not a single Roman-law text was used in its entirety in Charlemagne's capitularies, and that even in the ninth century there is very little sign of Roman law influencing the secular legislation of Louis the Pious or Charles the Bald.[37] These facts are intelligible in the light of Carolingian legislative methods: legal problems would be brought up by provincial administrators and judges to be discussed at the great assemblies and dealt with according to whatever legal expertise was available.[38] If *romani* were among those consulted, bits of Roman legal procedures and even substance might be adopted and given general currency. But this was a product of practical need and eclectic political power, and it was realised by practising law-men. There is nothing to suggest any conscious or systematic Romanising policy planned and executed by ecclesiastics for whom law, to be valid, had to be Roman and Christian. In canon law where deliberate effort towards standardisation *was* made, we now know that great diversity persisted throughout the ninth century and beyond.[39] How much more so in the realm of secular law, where legislative and administrative decisions were actually shaped very often by laymen. In 802 when Charlemagne thought to revise the gentile laws, 'he called together the dukes and counts with the rest of the

---

esp p 205: 'Si la renaissance carolingienne se traduit par des références plus fréquent plus nombreuses et plus variées . . . aud droit romain *dans les oeuvres de doctrine et dans les collections canoniques*, cette période semble au contraire correspondre à une regression due rôle effectif du droit romain *dans la pratique*'. (My stresses.)

[37] 'Droit romain [dans les capitulaires]', in *Ius Romanum Medii Aevi*, pt i, 2b, cc α–β (1969), pp 14 *seq*.

[38] The evidence is given, though not fully appraised, by Ganshof, 'Droit romain', and *Recherches*, esp pp 22 *seq*, 47 *seq*. The similarly ad hoc ways by which capitulary-texts were transmitted are indicated in W. A. Eckhardt, *Die Kapitulariensammlung Bischof Ghaerbalds von Luttich* (Göttingen 1955); reviewing this book, Wallace-Hadrill, *Tijdschrift voor Rechtsgeschiedenis*, 24 (1956) p 472, notes that texts had to be translated from the vernacular into Latin, and then back again. On the nature of the capitularies, and on other matters, I am grateful to Rosamond McKitterick (née Pierce) for valuable criticisms of an earlier version of this paper.

[39] See R. Kottje, 'Einheit und Vielfalt des kirchlichen Lebens in der Karolingerzeit', in *ZKG*, 76 (1965) pp 323 *seq*, and now H. Mordek, *Kirchenrecht und Reform im Frankenreich* (Berlin 1975) esp pp 151 *seq*.

Christian people [that is, the magnates] along with the legislators'[40]—and these *legislatores* (the term itself seems significant) were none other than the laymen learned and practised in the secular laws.[41] Such men were often, no doubt, imbued with notions of Christian ethics presented to them by priests.[42] But the church's teachings were at once too specific and too vague to have much direct relevance to the legal life of every day. Riché has observed a widespread anxiety on the part of conscientious laymen—just those, one could add, who were involved in jurisdiction—as to how far 'carnal men' could follow what looked like clerics' rules.[43] It is hard to believe that such anxieties were dispelled by the often banal prescriptions of an Alcuin or a Jonas. Lay society continued to operate with its own values. The fundamental ethic of *fidelitas* pre-existed the church's concern with it, and remained despite ecclesiastical glossing a largely secular affair.[44] Carolingian theology was in some degree laicised as it absorbed and reproduced the features and vocabulary of the *comitatus*.[45] On the other hand, with the obvious exception of legislation specifically concerned with the clergy and the monks, Carolingian capitularies show a Christian influence that, far from being attributable to the Carolingian renaissance, is a longstanding feature of gentile law: the

[40] *Annales Laureshamenses*, *sa* 802, ed G. Pertz (Hanover 1826), *MGH SS* 1, p 38.

[41] The term *legislatores* here exactly reflects the character of early medieval law and law-making: see below p 62. These men seem to be identical with those termed *iudices* in other texts: see Ganshof, *Recherches*, p 22 and *Carolingians*, p 69 and p 156 n 45 for *iudices* (in southern Gaul) as '*scabini* under another name'. Compare *Lex Baiuv*, prol, p 201: 'viri sapientes qui in regno . . . legibus antiquis eruditi erant', presumably identical with the *judices*, *ibid* XVII, 5; and *Edict. Rothari*, cap 386, p 93: 'iudices et antiqui homines' have helped to compile the code. Law-men of this type seem to me meant by the phrase *legis doctores* in a judgement of Pippin III shortly before 751, ed J. Tardif, *Monuments historiques* (Paris 1866) no 54, p 45. Riché, 'Enseignement', p 14, and 'Le renouveau culturel à la cour de Pépin III', *Francia*, 2 (Munich 1975), p 64, implies that the reference here may be to Roman law. But the passage as a whole reads: '. . . sicut proceres nostri seu comitis palacii nostri vel *reliqui* legis doctores judicaverunt', (my stress) which suggests a *lex*, that is *Lex Salica*, with which laymen normally associated with Frankish judgement-finding would be familiar.

[42] On Carolingian 'Laienspiegel', with rich bibliographical data, see H. H. Anton *Fürstenspiegel und Herrscherethos in der Karolingerzeit*, *Bonner Historische Forschungen* 32 (Bonn 1968) pp 83 *seq* and 213.

[43] [*La*] *Vie Quotidienne* [*dans l'Empire Carolingien*] (Paris 1973) pp 99 *seq*.

[44] See [W.] Schlesinger, *Beiträge* [*zur deutschen Verfassungsgeschichte des Mittelalters*] (Göttingen 1963) 1, pp 33 *seq*, 316 *seq*.

[45] D. H. Green, *The Carolingian Lord* (Cambridge 1965), esp pp 115 *seq*, 288 *seq*, shows that this process long antedates the Carolingian period, but in caps 10 and 11 argues for major developments precisely then. See now also Wallace-Hadrill, 'War and Peace in the early Middle Ages', in *Early Medieval History*, esp pp 31 *seq*.

historian impressed by the Augustinian overtones of Carolingian *pax* and *iustitia*[46] should be no less appreciative of these same ideas on the part of a Gundobad or a Clothar II.[47]

Did the Carolingian renaissance then have no effect on secular legal practice or—which is something different—on ideas about secular law? Its direct effect was significant in practical terms in only one sense: Carolingian scholars copied and preserved the texts of the laws, and ecclesiastical institutions in using these texts (as, for instance, St Gall in a whole series of land cases appealed to the *Lex Alamannorum*)[48] contributed to their continuing vitality. The formal characteristics of later Carolingian capitularies owed much to the improved latinity achieved through the renaissance of scholarship. On the other hand, a tendency to rely on the written word in legal procedures, though it probably increased simply through the readier availability of scribes, was already common in the vulgar private law of the fifth century and had shown continuous if patchy development in the practice of the barbarian kingdoms.[49]

Turning now to ideas about law, I briefly consider three important areas in which there seems little evidence of change occurring as a consequence of the Carolingian renaissance. Firstly: both lay and clerical ideas about the making of secular law continue to display that same creative ambiguity which is embodied in the barbarian *leges* themselves: the law is the people's but the king gives it authority. *Volksrecht oder Königsrecht*[50] is a non-issue, since where the king is a *Volkskönig*, law is at once gentile and royal. For Charlemagne, a

[46] So, Ewig, 'Königsgedanken', pp 63 *seq*, and 'La monocratie dans l'Europe occidentale', in *Receuils Jean Bodin* 21 (Brussels 1969), p 89. That some new conception of *pax* led Charlemagne into a frontal attack on feud is rightly questioned by Wallace-Hadrill, *Long-haired Kings*, pp 145 *seq*, and *Kingship*, pp 107 *seq* (where his own immediately following remarks imply the inaccuracy of the designation of the *Admonitio Generalis* (789) as 'legislation against feud').

[47] *Lex Burgundionum*, ed de Salis, *MGH Leg* 1, 2, 1, pp 30–1; *Edictum Clotharii*, in *MGH Cap* 1, no 9, pp 22–3.

[48] Köbler, *Recht*, p 99.

[49] L. Stouff, 'La formation des contrats par l'écriture dans le droit des formules du Ve au XIIe siècle', in *Nouvelle Revue Historique du Droit Français et Etranger*, 11 (Paris 1887), esp pp 259, 274 *seq*; Gaudemet, 'Survivances', pp 185 *seq*, 199 *seq*.

[50] See, with further references, [R.] Buchner, [*Die*] *Rechtsquellen* (Weimar 1953) [*Beiheft* to W. Wattenbach and W. Levison, *Deutschlands Geschichtsquellen im Mittelalter. Vorzeit und Karolinger*], pp 4 *seq*, suggesting *Stammesrecht* as preferable to either of these terms. F. Beyerle, 'Die süddeutschen *Leges*', pp 388 *seq*, asserts a sharp distinction between *Weistum* and *Satzung*, but shows that this cannot be simply aligned with the *Volksrecht/Königsrecht* division. Compare also his 'Über Normtypen und Erweiterungen der *Lex Salica*', in *ZRG GAbt* 44 (1924) pp 216 *seq*, where this same

public criminal was *infidelis noster et francorum*.[51] Where Ullmann classes the capitularies of 'the Carolingian age' all together as 'royal instruments'[52] indicative of a 'descending theme of government', Ganshof traces a shift from the 'absolute' royal legislative power of Charlemagne and (until 830) Louis the Pious to the 'conditional' power of Charles the Bald who promulgated laws with the *consensus populi*.[53] Both these views seem to me over-schematic: is not the truth of the matter that the *consensus* element in legislation was there, if in a subordinate role, all along? The shift occurred not in the realm of public law but in that of politics. Under Charlemagne, and still more clearly under Charles the Bald, the *verbum regis* was spoken only after consultation with those who were to hear and obey it. And it had to be *heard*: this was a face-to-face society organised by rules whose legitimacy depended on (amongst other things) their public oral pronouncement.[54] If Charlemagne, on one occasion at least, denied this, he was up against the conviction of his far-away Italian subjects that *capitula legibus addenda* were validly-made only when the emperor in person issued them in a formal *adnuntiatio* to the Italians themselves.[55] The sense of participation on the part of the *populus* is understandable. Were the learned cleric's views essentially different? Even Hincmar, more interested in the relation of kingship to law than any other Carolingian thinker, and himself well enough versed in canon and Roman law, had relatively little to say to kings about *leges condere* compared with his intense concern that they should *leges servare*.[56] Hincmar might have had a hand in drafting the very capitulary which mentions aristocratic *consensus* alongside royal *constitutio*;[57] and he it was, so Devisse plausibly suggests, who brought

---

non-alignment is clear. Schlesinger, *Beiträge*, p 30, observes that 'Königliche Herrschaft und adlige Herrschaft waren ursprunglich ebensowenig unterschieden wie Königsrecht und Volksrecht'. I am suggesting that the distinction remained blurred *in practice* in the Carolingian period.

51 *MGH Cap* 1, no 67, p 156. 52 *CR* pp 30 and 10.

53 *Recherches* pp 29 *seq*.

54 A. Dumas, 'La parole et l'écriture dans les capitulaires carolingiens' in *Mélanges Halphen* (Paris 1951) pp 209 *seq*.

55 *MGH Cap* 1, no 103, p 212. The episode is discussed by Ganshof, *Recherches*, p 21.

56 J. Devisse, *Hincmar et la Loi* (Dakar 1961). On Hincmar's legal and political thought see below, chapter 7, pp. 133-71.

57 Edict of Pîtres (864), in *MGH Cap* 2, no 273, p 313: '. . . lex consensu populi et constitutione regis fit . . .' Compare Hincmar, *De Ordine Palatii*, cap 8, ed V. Krause, *MGH Cap* 2, p 520: 'reges capitula . . . generali consensu fidelium suorum . . . promulgaverunt'. For Hincmar's presence in 864, see H. Schrörs, *Hinkmar, Erzbischof von Reims* (Freiburg-i.-Breisgau 1884) pp 232, 573.

into the vocabulary of west Frankish public law the pregnant phrase *consilium et auxilium*, already replete with feudal-governmental meaning.[58] But then Hincmar was well attuned to the sentiments of his lay fellow-*fideles*: a stickler for canon law when a Lotharingian royal divorce threatened the west Frankish realm, he practised a quite Nelsonian collusion when it came to accommodating aristocratic interests in another royal divorce affair.[59]

Secondly: the personality principle continued throughout the ninth century fundamental in secular law.[60] The laity's attachment to it can be inferred from their insistence on repeated royal assurances that the *lex unicuique competens* would be preserved.[61] Few scholar-clerics have left any record of their views, which could suggest that they simply accepted current aristocratic assumptions.[62] Such acquiescence is implicit in the fact that Hincmar assumes the personality of laws, and actually extends the principle to the canons as 'the tribal law of the priesthood',[63] even when he reminds that such laws will not apply at the final divine tribunal or insists that excessively cruel *lex saeculi* should be suppressed

[58] Devisse, 'Essai sur l'histoire d'une expression qui a fait fortune: Consilium et auxilium au IXe siècle', in *Moyen Age*, 23 (Paris 1968) pp 179 *seq*.

[59] See the subtle and plausible argument of C.-R. Brühl, 'Hinkmariana II. Hinkmar im Widerstreit von kanonischem Recht und Politik in Ehefragen', in *DA*, 20 (1964) pp 48 *seq*.

[60] Buchner, *Rechtsquellen* pp 4 *seq*; Astuti, 'Note critiche', pp 325 *seq*, with rich bibliography of recent literature at p 333, n 18. Gaudemet, 'Survivances', p 158, n 23, observes that in the edict of Pîtres of 864 (see above n 57) the concept of gentile law appears to have a territorial rather than a personal sense. Compare the development from gentile to regional (and pseudo-gentile) solidarities sketched by Ewig, 'Volkstum und Volksbewusstsein im Frankenreich des 7 Jhdts', in *SS Spoleto* 5 (1958) pp 587 *seq*. Such a gradual evolution of territoriality out of the personality of laws seems more plausible than the sharp break alleged by Schlesinger, *Beiträge*, p 44. But I can see no evidence of any Carolingian attempt to unify the law over the whole realm such as Devisse, 'Essai', p 181, n 11, suggests might be ascribed to Charles the Bald. This is not to deny the influence of Visigothic legislation in other respects on ninth-century clerics: see Ullmann, *CR*, p 81 with n 2.

[61] Thus, the *Pactum* of Coulaines (843), *MGH Cap* 2, no 254, p 253 *seq*. Compare also *ibid* pp 281, 296, 330, 339, and very similar expressions of the same principle in the Ostrogothic and Merovingian realms: Cassiodorus, *Variae* VII, 3, in *MGH AA* 12, p 203, and *Passio Leodegarii*, in *MGH SRM* 5, p 289 (here the *lex vel consuetudo* has become linked with the *patria*).

[62] For some evidence of this, which also suggests a 'territorialisation' of the personality principle–that is, the gentile law is attached to an estate, and only secondarily to the people who work on it—see W. Goffart, *The Le Mans Forgeries* (Cambridge, Mass., 1966) pp 144, 236; and H. Krause, 'Königtum und Rechtsordnung in der Zeit der sächsischen und salischen Herrscher', in *ZRG GAbt* 82 (1965) p 8.

[63] See [K. F.] Morrison, [*The*] *Two Kingdoms* (Princeton 1964) pp 35, 90 *seq*.

so that God's justice may prevail.[64] If Hincmar's tolerance here could be held typical of Carolingian scholars, Agobard is a well-publicised alleged exception. Others shared his concern for imperial unity, but he alone proceeded to ask if diversity of laws was not an obstacle to the unity of that *divina operatio*, the *corpus christi*.[65] Like so much else in Agobard's writings—his objections to the ordeal; his 'rational' scorn of sorcery—this is impressively modern-sounding. But its underlying assumptions prove to be far from modern, for it depends on an eschatology, probably derived from Tychonius as well as Augustine which opposed the *corpus* of God's empire to the *corpus diaboli*.[66] Agobard does not seriously challenge the personality of laws in principle: he attacks the *lex Gundobada* in particular, both because, as a southwesterner and a *romanus*, he had an outsider's aversion to the Burgundians and their interminable feuding, and because having access to the historical records of Lyons, he knew Gundobad to have been an Arian, and could not countenance the survival of a heretic's laws within a Christian empire. For various reasons, Agobard's views are *sui generis*. In general, the Carolingian renaissance made no dent in the principle of the personality of laws[67]—indeed may even have fostered it, in so far as Carolingian scribes copied and multiplied the texts in which that principle was enshrined.

Thirdly: the essential characteristic of early medieval law, so a number of German scholars have recently argued, was its lack of 'any assumption of a legal order resting either on statute or on customary law'.[68] A man could impose legal obligations on himself

[64] *De raptu viduarum*, in *PL* 125 (1852) col 1026; *De Ordine Palatii* pp 524 *seq*.

[65] See his letter to Louis the Pious *Adversus legem Gundobadi*, ed E. Dümmler, *MGH Epp* 5, pp 158 *seq*.

[66] E. Boshof, *Erzbischof Agobard von Lyon* (Cologne 1969) pp 41 *seq*; compare also Liebeschutz, 'Wesen und Grenzen', pp 33 *seq*. I am grateful to Ian Wood for his helpful suggestions here.

[67] The further erosion of the principle during the ninth century (the process had begun much earlier) was due, not to the Carolingian renaissance but to the growing regionalisation and feudalisation of social and political relationships. Compare n 60, above. It is worth noting the still gentile imperialism of Agobard's proposed solution to the Burgundian problem, when he requests the emperor 'ut eos [Burgundiones] transferret ad *legem Francorum*; et ipsi *nobiliores* efficerentur ...' (My stress).

[68] [K.] Kroeschell, 'Rechtsfindung', in *Festschrift fur H. Heimpel* (Göttingen 1972) 3, pp 498 *seq* at p 512. See also his '[Recht und] Rechtsbegriff', im 12 Jht', in *Vorträge und Forschungen*, 12 (1968), pp 309 *seq*; W. Ebel, *Die Willkur* (Göttingen 1953) esp pp 37 *seq*; H. Hagemann, '*Fides facta* und *wadiatio*. Vom Wesen des altdeutschen Formalvertrages', in *ZRG GAbt* 83 (1966) pp 1 *seq*, esp 28 *seq*; Köbler, *Recht*, esp pp 211 *seq*.

by the giving of a pledge (*fides facta*), and he was subject to the decision of a court. Studies of legal vocabulary suggest that the law (*lex*) did not condition, but was contained in, the judgement. Kroeschell has concluded that 'there prevailed a purely formal concept of law'.[69] In other words, secular law in the early middle ages was what experienced men declared to be and used as the law, whether this was written or unwritten. Kern's ritualistic and unchanging medieval law, the famous 'good old law' that could only be found, not made, is a myth. On the contrary, since law was never identified simply with what was just, it could undergo a constant process of alteration.[70] There is a Comte-ian ring about all this—sounded rather too strongly by Kroeschell. Early medieval men were no positivists: *ius* never lost its association with *iustitia*.[71] Yet the contrast stands between early medieval law on the one hand, and, on the other, classical Roman, later medieval and modern law:[72] between a law lodged in the practice of courts, palpably manmade, without system, not needing to be written, and bounded by the need to regard men's 'subjective' statuses—and a written, systematised law representing a permanent 'objective' statement of abstract justice, a law which judges merely applied and executed, a law bounded by the requirements of continuity, predictability, and conformity with explicit norms. What is significant in the present context is the fact that the Carolingian period belongs so unequivocally on the early medieval side of the line: for the *Rechtshistoriker* familiar with the jurisprudence of the gentile *Leges*, that of the Carolingian sources evidently presents no aberrant features, and any new trends discernible from the ninth

[69] 'Rechtsfindung', p. 513.

[70] Kern's thesis was set out in 'Recht und Verfassung im Mittelalter', in *HZ* 120 (1919), trans S. B. Chrimes in *Kingship and Law in the Middle Ages* (Oxford 1968) part 2, pp 149 *seq*. For penetrating revisions of Kern, see H. Krause, 'Dauer und Vergänglichkeit im mittelalterlichen Recht', *ZRB GAbt* 75 (1958) pp 206 *seq*, whose title epitomises 'einen anscheinend unauflöslichen Gegensatz' in medieval law (p 217): 'Ein konstituierender Faktor des Rechts ist die Länge der Zeit, das Element der Dauer—ein konstituierender Faktor des Rechts ist die Macht des gegenwärtigen Herrschers, das Element der Vergänglichkeit'. For further observations and recent literature, see also Ullmann, *Law and Politics in the Middle Ages* (London 1975) pp 30 with n 1, 48 with n 2.

[71] As noted, against Kroeschell, by Köbler, *Recht*, p 226. Kroeschell's recent reply, 'Rechtsfindung', p 510, n 66, is unconvincing. I hope to return elsewhere to this problem.

[72] I follow here Kroeschell, 'Rechtsbegriff', esp pp 325 *seq*. Kroeschell's book *Haus und Hausherrschaft im frühen deutschen Recht* (Göttingen 1958) has unfortunately been inaccessible.

century onwards are less remarkable than the continuities.[73] I would stress the continuing absence of precisely those social and economic changes, especially urbanisation and the development of business practices, which help to explain the appearance in certain areas in the twelfth and thirteenth centuries of 'a new, objective law'.[74] This is by no means to deny that later developments were in some ways foreshadowed in the Carolingian period: the notions of equality before the law and of tutorial rulership can be found in ninth-century documents, as Ullmann has recently shown.[75] Yet foreshadowings these remained, and though of great interest as such, they appeared in the ninth century very rarely and were then much less significant, quantitatively and qualitatively, than the areas of continuity with a pre-Carolingian past.

Earlier in this paper, I mentioned the distinction between personal and institutional rebirth, and Ullmann's thesis of baptismal rebirth as the paradigm of a whole social-ecclesiological renaissance. Now, inverting that model, instead of viewing a hypostatised 'Christian rebirth idea' as the autonomous source of a legal-governmental programme, I suggest we see the interpretation of baptismal rebirth by Christians of the Carolingian age as itself heavily conditioned by prevailing legal conceptions. A man knew what it meant to be born into membership of the Frankish, or Bavarian or Burgundian *gens*; and this coloured his notion of baptism as admission to the Christian society. A Salian Frank, for instance, established his public legal identity as against the men of other *gentes* by the way he behaved in certain situations—dealt with his property, transacted a marriage, responded to an accusation. He was also a Christian, and this too

[73] Despite the innovations in Germanic legal terminology from the ninth century onwards observed by Köbler, 'Richten—Richter—Gericht', in *ZRG GAbt* 87 (1970) pp 57 *seq*, esp 108 *seq*, and assigned by him to clerical influence, Kroeschell, 'Rechtsfindung', p 513 sees no change in the assumptions inherent in persisting traditional procedures.

[74] Kroeschell, 'Rechtsbegriff', p 333, though the causal factors are here barely hinted at. Despite the qualifications of Kroeschell, p 320, and 'Rechtsfindung', pp 508 *seq*, I share the reservations of Köbler, *Recht*, p 226, as to the aptness in this context of the modern categories of 'objective' and 'subjective' law. On his own admission, Kroeschell's major contrast is in fact between two types of 'objective' law, which suggests the need for a new classification.

[75] *CR*, pp 116, 122.

was a matter of external behaviour: he did not eat meat in lent, he buried his dead in the church's cemetery, he did not go to public gatherings on Sundays.[76] Baptism had little to do with doctrinal conviction or ethical transformation, even in the case of adults:[77] private penance and remission at once compensated for and confirmed this fact.[78] When pagans were mass-baptised by force, Alcuin's was a rare voice of protest; and even Alcuin expounded baptism not in terms of rebirth but as the incurring of liability to receive and obey certain instructions, his only concession being the proposal that the new laws be imposed gradually—prohibitions first and positive commands later.[79] In practice he knew that the main effect of baptism for a Saxon or Avar was liability to pay tithes, and not even Alcuin could work a rebirth metaphor into that!

Carolingian lay piety, so far as we can reconstruct it, was dominated at aristocratic level by a barely Christianised warrior ethic[80] and at a popular level by the effort to project within each individual relations of command and subordination (between soul and body) which mirrored those of feudal society,[81] and by the need to propitiate Israel's vengeful God of Battles by certain prescribed acts. Small wonder that Mosaic law was held the model of all gentile law.[82] In the Carolingian period, sorcery flourished, external acts and

[76] For these and other similar requirements, see the *Capitulatio de partibus Saxoniae* (785), *MGH Cap* 1, no 26, pp 68–70.

[77] The normal practice of child-baptism had long since transformed the catechnmenate from 'einer Belehrungs- und Erziehungsinstitution zu einer Folge von Zeremonien rein liturgischen Charakters': so, Dahlhaus-Berg, *Nova Antiquitas*, pp 94 *seq* with further references. The candidates for adult-baptism were conquered Saxons and Avars.

[78] Compare B. S. Turner, 'Origins and traditions in Islam and Christianity', in *Religion*, 6 (1976), pp 13 *seq* at 25–6.

[79] *MGH Epp* 4, no 111, pp 159–62. The date is 796 following the victory over the Avars: Alcuin hoped to avoid a repetition of the forced conversion of the Saxons. Compare the comments of Wallace-Hadrill, *Kingship*, p 102.

[80] This aspect is stressed by A. Waas, 'Karls des Grossen Frommigkeit', in *HZ*, 203 (1966), pp 265 *seq*. See also J. Chélini, 'Les laïcs dans la société ecclésiastique carolingienne', in *I laici nella societa cristiana dei secoli XIo-XIIo, Acta della terza Settimana internazionale di studio Mendola, 1965* (Milan 1968), pp 23 *seq*; [J.] Leclercq, *The Spirituality of the Middle Ages* (London 1968) pp 68 *seq*; Riché, 'Les bibliothèques de trois aristocrates laïcs carolingiens', *Moyen Age*, 69 (1963) pp 87 *seq*, *Vie Quotidienne*, pp 215 *seq*, and Introduction to Dhuoda's *Manuel pour mon fils*, *SCP* (1975), esp pp 24 *seq*. For further references, see above nn 43 and 46.

[81] This is especially clear in the short sermon, probably by Paulinus of Aquileia, ed by Leclercq in *RB*, 59 (1949) pp 159–60, esp lines 42 *seq*, where the preacher develops a series of striking oppositions: *imperium—servitium*; *erigitur—humiliatur*; *inebriatur et pascitur—fame torquetur*; *pretiosi vestes—veteres panni* . . . etc.

[82] Köbler, *Recht*, p 88.

material objects being used alike to placate a jealous deity and to manipulate other supernatural powers.[83] The gentile churches resisted such an extreme manifestation, but had long since come to terms with a religiosity of the physical. This process of acculturation[84] was now carried a significant stage further when clerics liturgified the ordeal, elaborated the symbolism of oil rituals, restructured without restraining the practice of private penance, and promoted, while not always successfully controlling, a great upsurge in the cult and social deployment of relics.[85] We should not forget that all this went on, relatively unpublicised, alongside and beneath the Romanising trend of the 'official' renaissance of the Carolingian church. I am certainly not denying that at least some Carolingian clerics sought a religious renewal that would penetrate lay society, at peasant as well as aristocratic level: sermons and *specula* directed at laymen, still more than the relevant capitularies, offer eloquent testimony to this attempted *Volksaufklärung*.[86] The case of Louis the Pious shows, perhaps, that the effort was not wholly unsuccessful. But were more than a handful of laymen—and the direct evidence is confined to rulers and aristocrats—ever really affected by it? The piety of Charles the Bald, who aspired to a divinely-blessed warrior-kingship and had clerical anointing applied to his queen as a 'fertility charm',[87] hardly seems more 'spiritualised', more 'ethically-transformed' than that of Charlemagne. Dhuoda recommended her son to read the works of the fathers, yet she herself 'n'a sans doute pas retenu de ses lectures tout ce qu'on aurait souhaité. Elle a été particulièrement séduite par la symbolique des

[83] Riché, 'La Magie Carolingienne', in *Comptes Rendus de l'Académie des Inscriptions et Belles-Lettres* (Paris 1973) pp 127 *seq*.

[84] Le Goff, 'Culture cléricale et traditions folkloriques dans la civilisation mérovingienne', in *Annales* 22 (1967), pp 780 *seq*.

[85] For these developments see Gaudemet, 'Les Ordalies au Moyen Age', in *Recueils Jean Bodin*, 17 (1965), pp 99 *seq*, and the evidence in *MGH Leg* 5, *Formulae* ed K. Zeumer (1886), pp 604 *seq*; my paper, 'Symbols in context: rulers' inauguration rituals in Byzantium and the west in the early Middle Ages', below, pp. 259 *seq.*; C. Vogel, *Le pécheur et la pénitence au Moyen Age* (Paris 1969) pp 43 *seq*, and R. Pierce, 'The "Frankish" penitentials', *SCH* 11 (1975) pp 31 *seq*; H. Fichtenau, 'Zum Reliquienwesen im früheren Mittelalter', *MIÖG*, 60 (1952), pp 60 *seq*, and Riché, *Vie Quotidienne*, pp 320 *seq*.

[86] So, Ullmann, *CR*, p 36, with a full appraisal of the sermon literature; compare also Bullough, *The Age of Charlemagne* (2 ed London 1973) pp 115 *seq*.

[87] So, E. H. Kantorowicz, 'The Carolingian King in the Bible of San Paolo fuori le Mura', in *Late Classical and Medieval Studies in Honour of A. M. Friend* (Princeton 1955) p 293. See also Wallace-Hadrill, *Kingship*, pp 124 *seq*, esp 135 (where, however, the reference of the capitulary of Pîtres is to confirmation-anointing, not royal consecration).

nombres . . .'[88] Without sharing Riché's value-judgement, we can agree that the significant point concerns not so much what texts Dhuoda read as how she read them, and we may well doubt whether, had Herchenfreda, mother of Desiderius of Cahors, written to her son not just letters but a whole book of exhortation, it would have been so very different from Dhuoda's.[89] I am suggesting that here again the Carolingian world can be understood only in the perspective of the Merovingian centuries and that its lay piety, if not the transmission of its learning, was fully continuous with that of the earlier *regna.*

The less frequented route seems to have led to a familiar destination. For my conclusion is that the limits of the Carolingian renaissance hardly exceeded, even in the ninth century, the dimensions of a religious culture that was largely confined to the clerical and monastic orders—what contemporaries in fact so often meant by the term *ecclesia.* At the same time, in lay society, pre-Carolingian legal and religious ideas and practices—and, I suspect, (though this has been beyond the scope of this paper) political ones too—persisted and evolved with a momentum of their own, affected but not determined by ecclesiastical *novitas.*

A cultural renaissance obviously depends on economic and political factors for its patronage and on social factors too for its personnel; but its base in society may be narrow and its unfolding relatively autonomous. This situation, which prevailed for instance in late Byzantium, was essentially that of the Carolingian renaissance, not least because the Carolingian church was, and could see itself as, in some sense *altera respublica.*[90] Within the priestly and monastic orders with their structural coherence and growing sense of identity expressed in the bid for full legal autonomy, ideas of rebirth and renewal could transcend the personal and be, at least to some degree, institutionalised, especially in the sphere of law. The third, lay, order, by contrast, with its relatively undifferentiated forms of social and legal organisation,

[88] Riché, Introduction to Dhuoda's *Manuel,* p 31. Riché continues: 'Mais sommes-nous ici dans le domaine de la spiritualité ou plutôt dans celui de la culture intellectuelle? Il est vrai que pour Dhuoda il n'y avait pas de frontières'. Here Riché raises, without resolving, a major problem in the methodology of historians of 'culture'.

[89] Herchenfreda's letters are preserved in the *Vita Desiderii,* ed Krusch, *MGH SRM* 4, pp 569–70. For some details of their contents, see Riché, *De l'éducation antique à l'éducation chevaleresque* (Paris 1968) pp 42–3. Riché himself suggests the comparison with Dhuoda.

[90] Paschasius Radbertus, *Epitaphium Arsenii,* ed E. Dummler, *ADAW* (1900) p 63. See also Morrison, *Two Kingdoms,* pp 36 *seq* and *passim,* where, however, the theme of 'dualism' is overstated.

its legal and religious conceptions alike embedded in the mentalities of kin-group and *comitatus*, could neither generate nor genuinely accommodate the idea of rebirth. It was not until the twelfth century, tentatively, and the fifteenth and sixteenth centuries confidently, that laymen—often lawyers—used ideas of rebirth and renewal which originated in the church or drew inspiration from Christian reform traditions to shape ideologies for radical transformations of law and politics in lay society.[91] The paradox was that these transformations depended on rapidly-accelerated processes of social differentiation: only in an increasingly secularised society could Christian laymen try to institutionalise a renaissance for themselves.

[91] For the twelfth century, see Ullmann, *Law and Politics*, pp 83 *seq*, and Kroeschell, 'Rechtsbegriff', esp 326 *seq*; for the fifteenth and sixteenth centuries, see J. H. Franklin, *Jean Bodin and the Sixteenth-century Revolution in the Methodology of Law and History* (New York 1963), D. R. Kelley, *Foundations of Modern Historical Scholarship. Language Law and History in the French Renaissance* (New York 1970), and *The Francogallia of François Hotman*, ed R. Giesey and J. H. M. Salmon (Cambridge 1972). Burdach, *Reformation*, p 55, writes that although the idea of rebirth and reform existed throughout the middle ages, before the twelfth century 'es war verblasst und erstarrt zu einer dogmatischen Formel der Sakramentenlehre', but in the later middle ages 'verwandelt jenes Bild sich in den Ausdruck eines . . . Gefühls und Verlangens *rein menschlicher Art*' (my stress) as expressed in the ideal of the *nova vita*. Again, p 96, Burdach refers to 'die langsame Säkularisierung des Gedankens der Wiedergeburt' from the fourteenth century onwards.

3

ROYAL SAINTS AND EARLY MEDIEVAL KINGSHIP

THE problem I want briefly to focus on concerns the significance of the saint-king in early medieval cosmology: what is his relationship to the sacral king of so many pre-industrial societies?[1] A commonly-accepted view has been that the sacral king was, quite simply, the immediate ancestor of the saint-king. To quote the recent but in some respects old-fashioned work of W. A. Chaney on Anglo-Saxon kingship: 'The sacral nature of kingship. . . . would lead the folk to expect God to honour the *stirps regia*. The recognised form of this in the new religion was sainthood.'[2] Christianity, so Chaney implies, simply makes a saint out of the sacral king: in essentials, nothing is changed.

This view has been rightly challenged. But we need, if possible to go further, and to substitute an alternative general interpretation of the phenomenon of the saint-king. The task has been made easier by recent research. Two contributions seem particularly important. First I would like to consider a paper by the Polish scholar K. Gorski on 'The birth of states and the saint-king', published in 1968 but originally delivered in 1965.[3] In this short but penetrating study, Gorski suggested that the appearance of saint-kings in certain kingdoms of Scandinavia and eastern Europe could be used analytically as an index of progress towards state-formation. Royal cults reflect 'the potential of the power of early

[1] Amid a vast literature the following works are especially helpful, and provide further bibliographical references: R. Folz, 'Zur Frage der heiligen Könige', in *Deutsches Archiv* 14 (Weimar 1958) pp 317 ff; O. Nachtigall, 'Das sakrale Königtum bei Naturvolkern', in *Zeitschrift für Ethnologie* 83 (Berlin 1958) pp 34 ff; *The Sacral Kingship. Contributions to the VIIIth International Congress of the History of Religions* (Leiden 1959); [H.] Wolfram, ['Methodische Fragen zur Kritik am "Sakralen" Königtum'], in *Festschrift O. Höfler* (Vienna 1968) pp 473 ff; L. Makarius, 'Du roi magique au roi divin', in *Annales* 25 (1970) pp 668 ff.

[2] *The Cult of Kingship in Anglo-Saxon England* (Manchester 1970) p 81. Compare the review by R. Brentano in *Speculum* 47 (1972) pp 754 f.

[3] 'La naissance des états et le "roi-saint" ', in *L'Europe au IXe au XIe Siècles*, edd T. Manteuffel and A. Gieysztor (Warsaw 1968) pp 425 ff. I have translated the passages quoted from the original French.

medieval state organisations – a potential which the Church might or might not reinforce'. Gorski offered as an explanation of the differential incidence of saint-kings in the various nascent states, the relative strength of political power already attained and the correspondingly variable attitude of the church: in brief, where political power was weak, the church sought to strengthen it by promoting the cults of royal saints. The one country where no saint-king appeared – Poland – was characterised by a uniquely strong kingship at a rather early date, so that 'the Church, considering monarchical power as not only consolidated but even excessive and disposed to tyranny, was not inclined to venerate a saint-king upon its altars'.

The great merit of Gorski's approach is its concentration on the relationship of religious authority to political power. Thus, following the time-honoured gelasian principle, we recognise that there are two equally necessary parties to this case. But the flaw in the argument also seems clear: its misinterpretation of the functional relationship of the 'feudal Church' to secular power. To Gorski, the whole question presents itself as 'a problem of feudal ideology'. But whatever its relevance to eastern Europe between the ninth and eleventh centuries, this way of viewing the problem is less helpful for the early medieval west – where, after all, saint-kings first appear. We can only hope to explain their incidence (why, for example, in seventh-century, rather than eighth-century Northumbria? and why not in late ninth-century Francia?) by exploring their significance to those who cultivated them.

Gorski lamented the absence of any structural study of early medieval sanctity. But even as he spoke, the gap was being largely filled by the Czech, F. Graus, whose important work, *Volk, Herrscher und Heiliger* was published also in 1965. Here are exposed the essential characteristics of the early medieval concept of sanctity, as revealed in merovingian hagiography. In brief, sainthood was defined by reference to monastic-ascetic values and it was virtually monopolised by representatives of the monastic and clerical orders of society. Graus went on to examine the specific case of the saint-king, taking into account evidence from western Europe as a whole. Saint-kings, he concluded, fell into two main categories: those who abandoned their kingdoms to become monks; and those who died as 'martyrs', innocent and often unresisting victims, either in battle or at the hands of traitors. They were not saints in virtue of their royalty, but in spite of it.[4] They qualified for sainthood

4 [F.] Graus. [*Volk, Herrscher und Heiliger im Reich der Merowinger*] (Prague 1965) pp 390 ff.

either through the act of renouncing the world, most spectacular in their case because they had most to lose, or through self-subjection to defeat and death, in a conspicuous reversal of normal values showing themselves lacking in *felicitas* or in that martial valour which fights to the death.

In the hierarchy of early medieval values, sanctity was therefore not only superior to all other statuses including that of kingship, but it was available only to those who had withdrawn from the *ordo secularis*. Sanctity and secularity were, in effect, mutually exclusive. To bring about a rapprochement between them was one of the main conceptual tasks facing the early medieval church. By the tenth century, the saint-queen[5] and the saint-nobleman[6] were achieving recognition as acceptable models of *this*-worldly sanctity displayed in 'everyday life'. But the saint-king presented considerably more difficulties. Even in the eleventh century, he was still presented by clerical biographers as a 'crowned monk'.[7] How are we to account for this delay in bringing him, so to speak, down to earth?

Graus rejected the notion that sacral kingship had any widespread existence at all in pre-christian western Europe.[8] But it seems to me that it is precisely the recognition of sacral traits in early medieval kingship which can help answer our question. Gorski had already made the significant observation that there was never any 'saint-emperor' in Byzantium. The point has been taken up by a byzantinist scholar, who objects that there was a peristently 'sacral' element in byzantine imperial power.[9] But there is an obvious misunderstanding here, arising at least in part from confused terminology: English seems to be the only language which not only distinguishes *sacral* from *sacred*,[10] but (unlike Greek, Latin, French or German) also has two separate words for the

[5] For the *Vita* of queen Matilda, wife of Henry the Fowler and mother of Otto I, see Graus pp 410 ff. I am also indebted to suggestions made in conversation by Mr Karl Leyser.

[6] For the *Vita* of Gerald of Aurillac, see D. Baker, 'Vir Dei: secular sanctity in the early tenth century', in *SCH* 8 (1972) pp 41 ff.

[7] J. T. Rosenthal, 'Edward the Confessor and Robert the Pious: 11th Century kingship and biography', in *Medieval Studies* 33 (Toronto 1971) pp 7 ff, at p 11. See also [F.] Barlow, [*Edward the Confessor*] (London 1970) pp 256 ff.

[8] For this debate, and the views of Höfler, Baetke and others, see Wolfram; also K. Hauck, *Goldbrakteaten aus Sievern* (Munich 1970) and now the perceptive comments of [J. M.] Wallace-Hadrill, [*Early Germanic Kingship in England and on the Continent*] (Oxford 1971) cap I.

[9] See the short notice of Gorski's paper in *BZ* 61 (1968) p 184.

[10] The German *sakral* is a very recent borrowing from English, where the term 'sacral' was coined by the pioneer anthropologists of the later nineteenth century.

substantive 'saint' and the adjective 'holy' (or 'sacred'). Sacrality involves the transmission of otherworldly powers into this world, crosscutting the line between nature and supernature. Sacral rulership therefore transcends the distinction between clerical and secular (in societies where such a distinction is made at all). It constitutes an ascribed not an achieved status, for its bearer possesses magical powers by definition. Nothing has to be proved or approved: sacrality goes with the job, is carried in the blood. There was nothing here to attract, and much to repel, the christian churchman attempting to construct a model of royal sanctity. The riskiness of the enterprise was clear when there were always 'some people', as William of Malmesbury anxiously noted, who would claim that Edward the Confessor's healing powers flowed *non ex sanctitate sed ex regalis prosapiae hereditate*.[11]

In the end, the church was able to come to terms with a saint-king who was the exponent of specifically royal virtues in the world of men, yet posed no threat to the clergy's working monopoly of sacral powers.[12] In the first place, the church developed its own objective and differentiated idea of useful rulership, whose type was the *rex iustus*. Wallace-Hadrill has recently suggested that Bede's kings, notably the *sanctissimus* Oswald, were already sketches for the church's eventual full-scale portrait of christian kingship.[13] With the eighth- and ninth-century development of the practice of royal anointing, along with its accompanying ideology, clerical theorists could present kingship as an office within the *ecclesia*, clerically-conferred (*per officium nostrae benedictionis*) and clerically-conditioned in content and exercise.[14] In principle, the suitable candidate required the approval of both clergy and people, and he could achieve his kingly status only through the

[11] *Historia Regum* ed W. Stubbs, *RS* 90 (1887) II, i, p 273. See M. Bloch, *Les Rois Thaumaturges* (Strasbourg 1924).

[12] We must take into account that strain in christian tradition which always regarded earthly power with misgivings. Compare Graus, p 432: 'Der heilige König ist in der Hagiographie nicht Garant des Wohlergehens, sondern zu seiner Schilderung wird ... nur der Topos vom goldenen Zeitalter verwendet. Diese "gehemmte" Entwicklung hat ihren letzen Grund wohl in der Erkenntnis kirchlicher Kreise, dass selbst ein "guter König" nur bedingt den "christlichen Idealen" entsprechen konnte.' Even in the eleventh century, Gregory VII repeated (*Reg* VIII, 21) the idea that royal dominion was the work of the devil – by that date, not such a common view. The origins of this specifically western line of christian political thought were clearly traced by W. H. C. Frend, *Martyrdom and Persecution in the Early Church* (London 1965).

[13] Wallace-Hadrill, cap IV. Compare Graus, pp 416 ff, where too little account is taken of the positive and 'useful' aspect of Bede's image of kingship.

[14] See W. Ullmann, *The Carolingian Renaissance and the Idea of Kingship* (London 1969). The quotation is from the crowning-prayer of Hincmar's *Ordo* for Louis the Stammerer, 877 (*MGH Capit*, II, 461) which reappeared in many subsequent *Ordines*.

sacral ministrations of the clergy. The anointing rite was the means whereby the *electus* was made, not replete with magical powers, but capable, through grace, of fulfilling his this-worldly royal function.[15] Once 'useful' qualifications were clear, the notion of 'useless' kingship too could acquire juristic definition;[16] and the so-called coronation-oath could become a constitutional check.[17] Thus the consecrated king was the church's model of desacralised rulership.

In the second place, the concept of sanctity itself[18] could be not only sharply differentiated from sacrality but turned against it. For what distinguishes a saint from a sacral or holy person is the very obvious, but crucial, fact that a saint is dead: it is his bones (real or believed) which are the object of a cult. The living determine the criteria of sanctity and establish the qualifications of the prospective saint. His life and/or death must be adjudged worthy, and his relics must be believed to work wonders. As the subject of a critical assessment, therefore, the saint must achieve and be assigned his status. However positively kingship may be valued, if sanctity has to be earned and recognised there can be no sanctification of royalty *per se*. I cannot see the church's *auctoritas*, operated increasingly from the eleventh century as a papal monopoly,[19] functioning here as a simple adjunct of 'feudal' political institutions. Even if the initiative in promoting a saint's cult was usually clerical, popular acceptance was essential to its success. Cowdrey has shown in relation to the peace movement of the eleventh century how saints were summoned into cooperative action by clergy and people.[20] The general point is no less valid for royal saints in particular. It is significant that all but a few of these cults remained obscure and localised, while some, for example that of Edgar at Glastonbury, never got off the ground. Family interest and clerical support were not enough to guarantee long-term or widespread recognition:[21] a more public utility had to be demonstrated.

For royal saints, manipulated by the living, provided not just a model

15 Compare my paper, 'National synods, kingship as office, and royal anointing', ch. 10 below, pp. 239 ff.

16 See E. Peters, *The Shadow King* (New Haven 1970).

17 See W. Ullmann, *Principles of Government and Politics in the Middle Ages* (London 1961) pp 143 ff, 186 ff.

18 On the origins of the christian idea of the saint, see Graus, part III; A.-J. Festugière, *La Sainteté* (Paris 1949); and the penetrating remarks of P. Brown, *Religion and Society in the Age of St Augustine* (London 1972) p 142.

19 See E. W. Kemp, *Canonisation and Authority in the Western Church* (Oxford 1948).

20 'The Peace and Truce of God in the Eleventh Century', in *PP* 46 (1970) pp 42 ff.

21 Graus pp 390 ff; Wallace-Hadrill pp 81 ff.

but a yardstick of kingly conduct and performance in office. Such a tool was useful to other workmen than clerics and princes. Thus St Edward the Confessor was a potent figure in twelfth-century England less for propagandisers of beneficent royalty than for those who, in order to put limits on royalty's operations, were already making what Jolliffe so aptly termed the advance 'from law to politics'.[22] Even from the arch-example of a dynastic saint-king, Joinville points the following moral: Louis IX's canonisation 'has brought great honour to those of the good king's line who are like him in doing well, and equally dishonour to those descendants of his who will not follow him in good works. Great dishonour, I repeat [Joinville's emphasis is significant] to those of his line who choose to do evil. For men will point a finger at them and say that the saintly king from whom they have sprung would have shrunk from doing such wrong.'[23] The prediction was accurate: in 1314, Philip IV was forced by his subjects to confirm the liberties his saint-grandfather had allowed, just as in England a century earlier, Edward the Confessor's sanctity which 'was known to include the remission of taxes'[24] was held up against the tyrannous king John. There is more than coincidence here: it was because the saint-king's past was *not* that of sacral kingship that he had at least a potential future as a symbol of constitutional monarchy.

22 J. E. A. Jolliffe, *Angevin Kingship* (London 1963). On St Edward, see [J. C.] Holt, [*Magna Carta*] (Cambridge 1965). J. C. Russell, 'The Canonization of opposition to the king in Angevin England', in *C. H. Haskins Anniversary Essays* (Boston 1929) pp 279 ff, comments interestingly on the implications for English royalty of the popular 'sanctification' of anti-royal leaders, without, however, noting that a saint-king could play a similar role.

23 *Chronicle of the Crusade of St Louis*, trans M. R. B. Shaw (London 1963).

24 Holt p 96. Compare Barlow pp 265 ff.

4

CHARLES THE BALD AND THE CHURCH IN TOWN AND COUNTRYSIDE

'THE CHURCH in town and countryside' is a fruitful theme. But for early medievalists it is an especially challenging one. We first have to establish our right to participate at all. There is a classic tradition of interpreting western history, and the history of western Christianity too, in terms of an opposition between town and countryside:[1] but according to exponents of this tradition, from Marx and Engels through Weber and Troeltsch to some contemporary historians, the early middle ages present a dull, townless void between antiquity and the eleventh or twelfth century. We have to begin then, by affirming that there were towns in the early middle ages. To justify this, we must do more than point out continuity in the terminology used by late classical and early medieval writers. We need to show that places existed which functioned as towns. Biddle[2] has given a useful archaeologist's list of functional criteria: defences, a planned street-system, a market, a mint, legal autonomy, a role as a central place, a relatively large and dense population, a diversified economic base, plots and houses of 'urban' type, social differentiation, complex religious organisation, a judicial centre.

Biddle suggests that if a place fulfils three or four at least of these criteria, it merits serious consideration as a town. At this point, the early medieval ecclesiastical historian can rub his or her hands: not only are we qualified to join actively in discussion, but we have a particularly good qualification to do so—simply because in the early middle ages it was churches, episcopal and monastic, which provided the major, if not quite the only, *foci* for town life on the criteria

[1] See for example K. Marx, *Pre-capitalist Economic Formations*, ed E. Hobsbawm (London 1964) pp 35–6, 77–8, 127 *seq*; F. Engels, *The Peasant War in Germany*, ed L. Krieger (Chicago/London 1967) pp 33 *seq*; [M.] Weber, *Economy* [*and Society*], ed G. Roth and C. Wittich, 3 vols (New York 1968) 3, cap 16, pp 1212–62; E. Troeltsch, *The Social Teaching of the Christian Churches*, 2 vols (London 1931) 1, pp 254 *seq*; C. Haase, 'Die mittelalterliche Stadt als Festung', *Die Stadt des Mittelalters*, ed C. Haase, 3 vols (Darmstadt 1969) 1, pp 377–408, and other essays in the same collection.

[2] 'Towns', *The Archaeology of Anglo-Saxon England*, ed D. M. Wilson (London 1976) pp 99–150 at p 100.

specified above.[3] If 'a role as a central place' and 'complex religious organisation' go without saying, the defensive, economic, and governmental functions of ecclesiastical centres seem to me equally characteristic and peculiar—certainly for ninth-century west Francia on which I propose to concentrate.

But by way of preliminary, I want to make two points, one specific, one general. The first concerns the economic features of our ecclesiastical towns: they are centres not primarily of production but of consumption and, to a lesser but increasingly significant extent, of exchange. As consumers of rural products, the town-dwellers—religious specialists and those who service them—clearly exist in intimate dependence on the countryside. But those who produce for or supply the urban élite are also its dependants. There is no merchant class, no bourgeoisie: only agents and servitors of churchmen. This explains why there is no qualitative distinction between the religiosity of town and countryside such as Weber and Troeltsch posited for later medieval Christendom and Gellner for north African Islam.[4] My second, general, introductory point is this: that compared with any other society I can think of since urban civilisation began at all, the differentiation of town and countryside in the early medieval west had quite peculiar implications. Elsewhere towns were the locations of political power. And if political and religious institutions were structurally differentiated, it was the religious ones, if any, which shifted to the countryside.[5] The growth of the Christian church within the Roman empire, and especially during 'the birth of the Middle Ages', had consequences specific to the early medieval west: institutional continuity of the church in old urban centres; the transformation of those old centres and the growth of new ones under ecclesiastical direction or at least strong influence; the disappearance or attenuation of certain urban functions in these centres as barbarian lay political power was established in the countryside; and a spatial

[3] [J.] Hubert, 'Évolution [de la topographie et de l'aspect des villes de Gaule du Ve au Xe siècle]', *SS Spoleto* 6 (1959) pp 529–58 at 540 *seq*; [R.] Latouche, [*The*] *Birth* [*of Western Economy*] (London 1967) pp 97 *seq*; E. Ennen, *Die europäische Stadt des Mittlelalters* (Göttingen 1972) caps 1, 2; [G.] Duby, [*The*] *Early Growth* [*of the European Economy*] (London 1974) pp 97 *seq*, esp p 106.

[4] [E.] Gellner, '[A pendulum swing theory of] Islam', *Annales Sociologiques* (Paris 1968) pp 5–14.

[5] For pioneering attempts at a comparative approach, see Weber, *Economy* 3, pp 1226 *seq*, 1236 *seq*, 1260–2, and Gellner, 'Islam'. But the uniqueness of developments in the early medieval west remains to be explored.

dislocation between lay and ecclesiastical power which meant that kings, though based in the countryside, had to find some mode of access to the towns through relations with the church. Balthild's interference with urban and sub-urban cult-sites throughout her Neustro-Burgundian realm shows the interaction of all these themes[6]. In the ninth century, that interaction took other forms—arising from the terms on which the early Carolingians had set about the reconstruction of ecclesiastical culture and institutions after the disintegration of the late seventh and early eighth centuries.[7] Reform depended, as in the eleventh century, on maximising material resources: no scriptoria without sheep and cows! Carolingian royal and aristocratic piety ensured that the reformed church had its riches. Herlihy[8] has calculated that church lands over western Christendom as a whole tripled in area between 751 and 825, rising from ten to over thirty per cent of the total of land cultivated. No contemporary power-holder could neglect such a trend, and kings especially were bound to claim some benefits from it. I start from the assumption that this royal exploitation could be, not wanton plundering, but a highly discriminating exercise the pattern of which may be clearer if we apply the distinction between town and countryside. And since Charles the Bald has the reputation of an arch-exploiter, his activities seem worth closer examination.

First then, what was the interest of the church in the countryside to Charles the Bald? Following an ancestral tradition which may well predate the Carolingians,[9] Charles used church lands to reward, and secure the loyalty of, his vassals and his counts. In his father's reign, clerical protests against this practice had become noisy; but though Louis the Pious probably tried to stop making new appropriations, he did not revoke those of his ancestors.[10] During the wars of 840–3, further spoliations, royal and otherwise, had been made. Charles the Bald therefore began his effective reign under intensified pressure to restore ecclesiastical property. He did so, as twenty-four surviving

[6] See my 'Queens as Jezebels: the careers of Brunhild and Balthild in Merovingian History', above, chapter 1, pp. 1-48.

[7] E. Ewig gives a fine survey in *Handbook of Church History*, ed H. Jedin and J. Dolan 3 (London 1969) sections 1, 3 and 4.

[8] 'Church property on the European Continent, 701–1200', *Speculum* 36 (1961) pp 81–105.

[9] [É.] Lesne, [*Histoire de la*] *Propriété* [*ecclésiastique en France*], 6 vols (Lille 1910–43) 1, pp 446–50; 2, pp 1–9.

[10] Lesne, *Propriété*, 2, ii (1922) pp 148 *seq.*

charters testify.[11] But did this mean that he was having to 'despoil his own domains to buy off revolt'?[12] Can we infer from such acts of restitution increased royal weakness, measured in terms of loss of control of lands? Let us look at a case where we know what actually happened next. In 845, with Hincmar at his elbow, Charles restored substantial properties to the church of Rheims.[13] But his vassals were not thrown off their estates. They now became, instead, vassals of the archbishop[14] and were told by the king to pay their due rents (*nonae et decimae*)[15] to the church. In practice, though, what mattered was that Charles's men retained their benefices and through them their personal link with the royal benefactor; so that, when one such vassal wished to pass on his benefice to his son, he applied not to Hincmar but to Charles.[16] Where is the alleged loss of royal political control?

It is true that ninth-century churchmen had successfully vindicated their exclusive rights—in principle—to the disposition of church property.[17] A vassal holding such property no longer held it from the king (*verbo regis*) but from an ecclesiastical *rector*.[18] Churchmen recognised, nevertheless, that in practice royal needs had still to be met in the interests of the realm as a whole. Paschasius Radbertus, writing in 852, attributed a shrewd assessment of the situation to Wala of Corbie a generation before: 'If the state (*respublica*) cannot survive without the help of church property, a procedure and a system (*modus et ordo*) must be sought' so that laymen could receive such property without damage to the church.[19] New rules were found. But as Southern said in another context:[20] '. . . though the system had its . . . philosophers, it was also, as practical men knew, capable of being

[11] [G.] Tessier, [*Receuil des Actes de Charles II le Chauve*], 3 vols (Paris 1943–55) 3, pp 213–15.

[12] [J. M.] Wallace-Hadrill, [*Early Germanic*] *Kingship* [*in England and on the Continent*] (Oxford 1971) p 127.

[13] Tessier, 1, no 75, pp 210–13.

[14] Tessier, 1, no 99, pp 262–5.

[15] G. Constable, 'Nona et decima', *Speculum* 35 (1960) pp 224–50.

[16] Hincmar of Rheims, *De villa Noviliaco, PL* 125 (1879) col 112.

[17] [W.] Goffart, [*The Le Mans*] *Forgeries* (Cambridge, Mass. 1966).

[18] Lesne, *Propriété*, 2, i, pp 164 *seq.*

[19] *MGH SS* 2, ed G. H. Pertz (Hanover 1829) p 549. On this passage, see W. Wehlen, *Geschichtsschreibung und Staatsauffassung im Zeitalter Ludwigs des Frommen, Historische Studien* 418 (Lübeck/Hamburg 1970) p 114, and for the meaning of *respublica* (in some ninth-century contexts equivalent to *Staatsgut*) pp 33 *seq*, 53–4. It is worth stressing that Paschasius was writing this in the context of the reign of Charles the Bald, not Louis the Pious.

[20] *The Making of the Middle Ages* (London 1959) p 140.

manipulated to give much the same results as had been obtained in a . . . cruder age. The whole secret lay in knowing the ropes, and in sensing how far one could go.' Charles the Bald knew the ropes. On the lands of the church of Laon he confided so many vassals to the bishop that the lands of the see were hardly adequate to support them and additional royal grants had to be promised.[21] Given the loyalty and the effective generalship of the bishop in question, Charles had nothing to lose by having his vassals become the bishop's: service to church and realm were then perfectly congruent. Moreover, those vassals persisted in regarding the king as the real source of their benefices, appealing to him against the bishop when the latter tried to evict them. But in that case it was not the king or his men but the bishop himself who could be depicted as despoiling church property, and at the same time betraying his king.[22]

Continuing effective royal disposition of the lands of churches (whatever theory might say) could in fact work to the benefit of those churches as corporate institutions. Individual bishops or abbots sometimes presided over the despoiling of their own churches' lands.[23] In such circumstances royal protection could mean what it said. It was to protect the abbey's lands against abbots who might 'make grants to laymen more inordinately than was fitting' that the monks of Fleury sought the king's help.[24] Charles dispatched four *missi* to establish the true extent of the abbey lands, and in a diploma recording the findings of the inquiry he commanded '. . . that no future abbot . . . should presume to subtract to any degree from the named manors, but from them should both strenuously perform our [military] service . . . and take care to provide adequately for the monks', whom Charles naturally expected to pray for himself, his family and the stability of the realm.[25] Charles' candour is refreshing: in his view the

[21] Hincmar of Laon, *PL* 124 (1879) col 1029.

[22] *PL* 126 (1879) cols 495, 583, Mansi 16, cols 649–50. See Lesne, *Propriété*, 2, i, pp 278 *seq*; [J.] Devisse, *Hincmar*, [*Archevêque de Reims 845–882*], 3 vols (Geneva 1975–6) 2, pp 738–85, esp p 775, n 402, where it becomes clear that the central issue is not legal but political.

[23] Lesne, *L'Origine des Menses dans le temporel des églises et des monastères de France au IXe siecle* (Lille 1910) pp 63 *seq*; but the comments on pp 59–60 need modifying in the light of [F.] Felten, 'Laienäbte [in der Karolingerzeit'], *Mönchtum, Episkopat und Adel zur Gründungszeit des Klosters Reichenau*, ed A. Borst (Sigmaringen 1974) pp 397–431.

[24] Tessier, 1, no 177, pp 465–9 at 467: '. . . propter rerum diminutionem quas praeteriti praelati ejusdem monasterii inordinatius quam decuit saecularibus attribuerunt. . . .'

[25] *Ibid* p 468: '. . . ut nullus abbas futurus de eodem momasterio eligendus secundum nostram indulgentiam et sanctorum episcoporum privilegium de nominatis villis vel locis aliquid diminuere praesumat, sed de ipsis et nostrum servitium strenue peragat,

interests of *servitium nostrum* and of the monastic community went hand in hand, and both had to be defended against the arbitrary action of self-interested abbots. Interestingly, the passage referring to secularisations of Fleury lands by abbots (*praelati*) caused two respectable nineteenth-century editors[26] to treat this diploma as 'suspicious': abbots, they declared, did not do that sort of thing.

Charles the Bald exercised a special control over the lands of royal abbeys, especially in Neustria. Like his immediate predecessors, he could grant abbacies, with their appurtenant vast estates, to able clerics who made their careers in the royal service.[27] More often than those predecessors, Charles sometimes granted abbacies to laymen.[28] The disposition of St. Martin's at Tours, for instance, successively to well-connected clerics and powerful laymen, played a key part in the king's policy in western Neustria.[29] Lay abbacies tended to lead to dismemberment of monastic holdings, they were uncanonical and aroused episcopal protest;[30] but they continued to provide Charles with a useful fund of lands for distribution. Alternatively, he could keep royal abbeys for himself or for members of his own family, in which case royal agents ran the monastic estates directly. Abbey lands became, in other words, an extension of the royal domain. Thus in 864 Charles commanded his counts 'that the manors of our royal domain and also the manors of the monasteries which we hold conceded and granted to our wife and our sons and daughters, and which are under the royal immunity, shall maintain their existence within the counties and be preserved intact with due respect paid [to their

---

adjunctis vassallorum annuis donis et aedificiis monasterii et munitione, consueto adjutorio, et ipsis servis Dei in eodem loco habitantibus congrua stipendia ministrare studeat' and a few lines above: '. . . quatenus et praesentes et secuturi ejusdem loci monachi absque ulla penuria stipendiorum valerent Domnino libere militare, et delectaret eos pro nobis et stabilitate regni nostri uxorisque ac prolis Dominum exorare'. The military service owed from monastic lands and by abbots in person is discussed by [F.] Prinz, *Klerus und Krieg* (Stuttgart 1971) pp 105 *seq*, 120–2.

26 M. Prou and A. Vidier, cited by Tessier, 1, p 466.

27 [K.] Voigt, [*Die Karolingische*] *Klosterpolitik* [*und der Niedergang des westfränkischen Königtums*] (Stuttgart 1917); Lesne, *Propriété*, 2, ii, bks 1 and 2; Ewig, 'Descriptio Franciae', *Karl der Grosse*, ed W. Braunfels, 4 vols (Düsseldorf 1965–8) 1, pp 160 *seq*.

28 This development and its significance have been ably demonstrated by Felten, 'Laienäbte', esp 408 *seq*, 421 *seq*.

29 J. Boussard, 'Les destinées de la Neustrie du IXe au XIe siècle', *Cahiers de Civilisation Medievale* 11 (Poitiers 1968) pp 15 *seq*.

30 See Hincmar's comments in *Ann* [*ales*] *Bert* [*iniani*], *sa* 866, ed F. Grat, J. Vielliard and S. Clemencet (Paris 1964) pp 126; 131; 132 (here the culprit is Charles himself).

special status].'[31] In 867 Charles himself assumed the abbacy of St. Denis, consigning its economic management to provost, dean and treasurer, and the organisation of its military service (*cura militiae*) to a *maior domus*.[32] The monks themselves seem to have collaborated willingly in these arrangements:[33] after all they stood to benefit from the king's attention. This was a case of mutual advantage. Hence the lack of any clerical criticism of Charles' action.

Of further significance was the use to which Charles put his *Klosterpolitik* in providing for two of his four sons who reached maturity.[34] It may seem only a short step from setting up your daughters as abbesses, as Charles' predecessors had done, to making oblates and in due course abbots of your legitimate sons. But this latter, Charles's innovation,[35] had large political implications. It enabled Charles to break with the Frankish royal tradition, so assiduously followed by Charlemagne and Louis the Pious and continued also by east Frankish kings down to the 880s, of partitioning the realm between all of a king's legitimate sons. No doubt the spur was shortage of sub-kingdoms: Charles only had two.[36] But the availability of royal monasteries provided an alternative to dismembering the fisc, or more dangerously, disinheriting his younger sons. Like appanages, rich abbeys might with luck keep princes happy, and unlike appanages, they did not carry the risk of heritability, for Charles's sons were properly professed monks. From the king's standpoint, it was also potentially very useful to have such important

[31] *MGH Cap* 2, ed A. Boretius and V. Krause (Hanover 1897) no 272 (edict of Pîtres) cap 5, p 313: 'Volumus et expresse comitibus nostris mandamus, ut villae nostrae indominicatae, sed et villae de monasteriis, quae et coniugi nostrae et filiis ac filiabus nostris concessa atque donata habemus, quaeque sub immunitate consistunt, cum salvamento et debita reverentia in comitatibus illorum consistant'.

[32] *Ann Bert sa*, pp 134–5. See further Voigt, *Klosterpolitik*, pp 87 *seq*.

[33] Tessier, 2, no 379, pp 347–50 (an original), where, p 350, Charles calls himself abbot *fratrum electione*. On royal abbacies, see Lesne, *Propriété*, 2, ii, pp 172–84.

[34] For the abbacies held by Lothar (St Germain at Auxerre and perhaps St Jean at Réome) and Carloman (St Amand, St Riquier, Lobbes, St Médard at Soissons and St Arnulf at Metz) see Voigt, *Klosterpolitik*, pp 38 *seq*. Two younger boys may also have been destined for the church: sent for education to St Amand, they died there in 865 or 866. See *MGH Poet* 3, ed L. Traube (Berlin 1896) pp 677–8. For this and other dealings of Charles the Bald with St Amand, see now the important article of Rosamond McKitterick, 'Charles the Bald and his library', *EHR* 95 (1980), pp. 28-47. I am very grateful to her for letting me see this in advance of publication.

[35] I had thought this point hitherto neglected until I found that Lesne, as usual, had already seen it: *Propriété*, 2, ii, pp 167–8.

[36] See Boussard, 'Neustrie'; and W. Kienast, *Studien über die französischen Volksstämme des Frühmittelalters* (Stuttgart 1968).

abbeys as those of St. Medard (Soissons), St. Amand, St. Riquier, and St. Germain (Auxerre) firmly in filial hands. The system worked well until 870 when the abbot of St. Medard, having seen one of his two elder brothers die and his father then acquire part of Lotharingia, made a desperate bid for a realm of his own and was ruthlessly suppressed.[37] But Charles had set a precedent: later monarchs from the Ottonians onwards would dispose of surplus princes by dedicating them to the service of God—a strategy which of course presupposed effective (if indirect) control of churches and their lands.

I turn now to Charles's dealings with the church in the towns: what specifically urban services could the church offer? Despite its rural bases, Frankish royal power had always had important links with *civitates*.[38] But relations that had been quite informal and personalised under the Merovingians became rather less so under the Carolingians. Not that churchmen now occupied permanent posts in royal government, though they did act very frequently on special commissions, for example as *missi dominici* sitting alongside counts in public courts held in *civitates*.[39] But in general terms, it was because permanent, thus urban, central places came to play a more conspicuous part in ninth-century administration that more, and more varied, governmental activity was required of churchmen, especially bishops.[40] On the supply side, the workings of the Carolingian renaissance produced more experts capable of drafting complex legislative documents or compiling estate surveys. On the demand side, growing defence problems created new needs. As an initial response individual churchmen, like the bishops of Orleans and Chartres, led local resistance to the Vikings from their *civitates*.[41] When Charles implemented something like a defence policy for the realm (at any rate those regions worst affected) he looked to the church not merely to contribute but to bear the main burden. Fortification was largely an urban task, in that whole cities or monasteries were enclosed in walls.[42] Danegeld, the alternative method

[37] *Ann Bert sa* 870, 871, 873, pp 178–9, 194.

[38] F. Prinz, 'Die bischöfliche Stadtherrschaft im Frankenreich vom 5. bis zum 7. Jht', *HZ* 217 (1974) pp 1–35; see further my comments in chapter 1, above.

[39] For example *MGH Cap* 2, no 261, p 278.

[40] F. Ganshof, *The Carolingians and the Frankish Monarchy* (London 1971) pp 206–7; W. Ullmann, 'Public welfare and social legislation in the early medieval councils', *SCH* 7 (1971) pp 1–39.

[41] *Ann Bert sa* 854, p 69. See also Prinz, *Klerus und Krieg*, pp 124 *seq.*

[42] F. Vercauteren, 'Comment s'est-on défendu, au IXe siècle, dans l'empire franc, contre les invasions normandes?', *Annales du XXXe Congres de la Fédération archéologique et*

of defence, meant urban and episcopal organisation.[43] Bishops had to contribute from their own treasuries; they also had to collect the sums due from other ecclesiastical contributors throughout their dioceses. Like the Merovingians' tax-system, that of Charles the Bald was run in and from *civitates*—which explains why the famous Danegeld edict of 877, after specifying the central role of bishops, ended by requiring contributions also from 'traders and people living in *civitates* . . . in proportion to their resources'.[44]

Since Lot showed that the church was effectively the sole bearer of this financial burden, we have learnt more about the sources of the church's wealth in the ninth century.[45] It is not just a matter of dethesaurisation. When bishops like those of Rheims and Orleans, or the monks of St. Riquier and St. Bertin, could undertake large and often long-term building programmes, when successive bishops of Auxerre could disburse quantities of silver and cash for the adornment of every parish church in the diocese,[46] it looks as if urban ecclesiastical centres, episcopal and monastic, were able to dispose of increasing cash incomes deriving not only from increased revenues from vast, well-managed estates, but also from the growth of the markets they controlled. It is in this context of ninth-century economic growth—not universal, by any means, but concentrated precisely in those centres with which I am now concerned—that we can look at Charles the Bald's new exploitation of what was for him surely the most important of the church's urban services: hospitality. Charles's itinerary, compared with those of his predecessors, shows a striking increase in the frequency of stays at *civitates*.[47] Only rarely was an ancient royal palace available: Charles restored the one

---

historique de Belgique (Brussels 1936) pp 117–32; Hubert, 'Évolution', pp 550–7, with figs 15, 16.

43 F. Lot, 'Les tributs aux Normands et l'Église de France au IXe siècle', *BEC* 85 (1924) pp 58–78.

44 *MGH Capit* 2, no 280, p 354.

45 The fundamental work is Lesne, *Propriété*, esp vols 2 (1936) and 6 (1943). See further, works cited above p 76 n 3; and Duby, *Rural Economy and Country Life in the Medieval West*, trans C. Postan (London 1968).

46 Rheims: *MGH SS* 13, ed G. Waitz (Hanover 1881) pp 478–9; Orleans: *MGH SS* 15, ed W. Wattenbach, 2 parts (Hanover 1887/8) p 497; St Riquier: Hariulf, *Chronicon Centulense*, ed F. Lot (Paris 1894) pp 53–4; St Bertin: *Cartulaire de l'abbaye de St Bertin*, ed B. Guerard (Paris 1841) p 109, and *MGH SS* 15, pp 513–44; Auxerre: *MGH SS* 13, pp 396–7. See also Lesne, *Propriété*, 3, pp. 91 *seq;* 6, pp 425 *seq.*

47 [C.-R.] Brühl, *Fodrum*, [*Gistum, Servitium Regis*] (Cologne 1968) pp 39 *seq.* It would be misleading to neglect the continuing preponderance of Charles's stays on royal manors, though even here the overwhelming preference for two of them, Quiersy

at Senlis *c*860.[48] Early in his reign, he had got into the habit of visiting himself and his court on the bishop's own residence, the *episcopium*. Later Charles more often chose to say in the palaces built within royal or episcopal monasteries and what needs stressing here is the urban, or more precisely sub-urban, character of these monasteries: St. Denis near Paris, St. Medard at Soissons, St. Martin at Tours, St. Sernin at Toulouse, St. Germain at Auxerre, St. Remi at Rheims, St. Mesmin at Orleans.[49] How is this new royal practice to be explained? Brühl who first drew attention to it explained it mainly in terms of dwindling royal land resources[50]—in particular of the famous 'squandering of the fisc' for which every scholar who has read his Dhondt (and every student his Barraclough) knows Charles the Bald was responsible.[51] Given political pressures which forced him to travel rapidly and continuously about his realm moving far more frequently than any previous or later Carolingian (he seldom spent more than a few weeks, or even days, in one place), Charles found his remaining fisc lands inadequate to sustain his court. Instead the burden had to be imposed on a reluctant church. Of course, all this is partly true, though I think the alleged squandering of the fisc by Charles has been much exaggerated.[52] But I would suggest a positive as well as a negative reason for his changed choice of residence. Why could he not have solved his accommodation problem by staying frequently on rural episcopal or monastic manors (something he in fact did, but rarely)?[53] One obvious reason for choosing urban ecclesiastical sites was veneration for the saints who rested there. But Charles's motivation for visiting a place, as expressed in his own charters, was

---

and Compiègne, is strikingly suggestive of new possibilities for the concentration of supplies. But what concerns me here is the nonetheless notable increase in the urban component in Charles's itinerary.

[48] Brühl, 'Königspfalz [und Bischofsstadt]', *Rheinische Vierteljahrsblätter* 23 (Bonn 1958) pp 206–7.

[49] On all these monasteries, the last two controlled respectively by the bishops of Rheims and Orleans, see Brühl, 'Königspfalz'. There is little additional information, for present purposes, to be found in Brühl's recent work, *Palatium und Civitas* 1 (Cologne 1975).

[50] 'Königspfalz', pp 269–74; *Fodrum*, pp 50–2.

[51] J. Dhondt, *Études sur la naissance des principautés territoriales en France IXe–Xe siècle* (Bruges 1948), pp 264–6, 272–4; G. Barraclough, *The Crucible of Europe* (London 1976) pp 88–9.

[52] I hope to defend this view at length elsewhere.

[53] For example *Ann Bert sa* 846, p 52, Épernay, a manor of the church of Rheims restored in 845, Tessier, 1, no 75; Hincmar, *MGH Epp* 8, i, ed E. Perels (Berlin 1939) p 72, Neauphles, a manor of the church of Rouen.

surprisingly pragmatic: he might come 'for the sake of prayer (*orationis causa*)' but he might equally well come 'to make arrangements for other affairs of our realm'.[54] Another likely reason for staying in *civitates* was the partial survival of the Roman road system that linked them.[55] But the main reason surely was that the *civitates* and monastic urban centres were becoming wealthier, and the churches which could tap that wealth by controlling markets were therefore in a good position to sustain the new royal demands—sustain, and perhaps also to benefit from them. The bishops at the synod of Meaux-Paris in 845 registered a famous complaint which is conventionally cited to show their rooted opposition to Charles's new impositions. This is what the bishops said:

> It should be suggested to [the king] that . . . he should enter the episopal residence . . . in a respectful manner whenever he may stay in a *civitas* to claim his due hospitality, and should not allow women in . . . Also the immunities granted by previous emperors and kings prohibit excessively long visits from kings, their magnates and their secular followings . . . [From now on] when your journeying brings you to *civitates*, let your majesty give orders that the houses within a *civitas* be free from the exactions of plunderers; because [what is happening now is that] all who used to bring their goods to the *civitates*, both to keep them in safe storage and to sell them more peacefully there, are refraining from doing so, existing immunities are being infringed, and the citizens are being . . . not just oppressed but plundered by the visitors [that is, the king's entourage] and prevented from selling their goods . . .[56]

[54] Tessier, 1, no 18, p 44 (for Corbie); 2, no 240, pp 43, 44 (St Martin, Tours). References to *orationis causa* belong only to the early part of the reign. See Brühl, *Fodrum*, pp 45–6, 104.

[55] Brühl, *Fodrum*, pp 62 *seq*. For the realm of Charles the Bald, this topic is in need of further study.

[56] *MGH Capit* 2, caps 26, 27, p 405: 'Suggerendum est . . . regiae dignitati, ut episcopium . . . reverenter introeat, et . . . quando orationis et debitae susceptionis gratia in transitu convenienti civitatem ingressus fuerit, habitaculis episcopalibus reverenter inhabitet, et non diversoria feminarum magnificentia sua et religio venerabilis ibidem fieri permittat. . . . Sed et inmunitates praecedentium imperatorum ac regum ab huiusmodi longiori et diuturna conversatione et commoratione regum et quorumcumque potentium ac secularium personarum in episcopio prohibent. . . . Vestra studebit magnitudo obnixius observare, ut, quando transitus vester iuxta civitates acciderit, inmunes et liberas vestra dominatio iubeat a depraedationum exactionibus fieri mansiones intra civitatem, quia omnes, qui sua ad civitates deferebant, ut et salva quaeque ibi haberent et illa plus pacifice venderent, iam et hoc refugiunt et pristinae inmunitates et confir-

This protest is interesting because it is equivocal. The complaint is not about royal visits as such: had the 'citizens' and the suppliers of the urban market been able to rent out lodgings and sell their wares, instead of having them appropriated, would not everyone have been happy? We know that Charles subsequently imposed many times upon ecclesiastical hospitality; but there is a notable absence of subsequent complaints.[57] Rheims was visited more often than any other *civitas*, but there is no sign at all that it was ruined[58]—rather its flourishing scriptoria and new buildings indicate the contrary. When Charles visited Auxerre in September 861, his court occupied all the available accommodation in and around the *civitas*.[59] But no clerical complaint is recorded: perhaps women were kept out of the churchmen's way. Is it possible that Charles's urban subjects, both ecclesiastical governors and the citizens for whom they were responsible, had begun to appreciate the benefits of increased consumer demand? Charles himself, after all, was highly sensitive to commercial considerations. He husbanded his revenues from tolls;[60] and in the enormous capitulary of 864 he provided for a sophisticated coinage reform, including a *renovatio monetae*, and for a firm royal control of mints (all but one of them in *civitates*).[61] Charles granted land to churches surprisingly rarely (surprisingly, that is, if you think of him an inveterate fisc-squanderer) but he did have other valuable things to give: to Corbie, a bridge and rights to tolls thereon;[62] to the bishop of Paris, the Grand Pont with its mills, and later, the right to dispose of some newly-built houses;[63] to the monks of St. Denis control of a weekly market at

---

mationes infringuntur, dum et cives ab hospitibus opprimuntur et ab his, a quibus non solum opprimuntur, verum et diripiuntur, sua non solum vendere prohibentur, sed et propter direptionem post eos cum gemitu clamare coguntur'.

57 The ravaging of the countryside by the king's troops was occasionally complained of, but is hardly relevant in the present context.

58 Hincmar's only complaints about royal demands for hospitality occur in a thoroughly disingenuous letter to pope Hadrian II, *PL* 126, col 183, in which Hincmar affects to exculpate himself from complicity in Charles's invasion of Lotharingia! Even M. Devisse, *Hincmar*, 1, p 458, n 596, is moved to observe: 'la sincérité de l'argumentation, cette fois, n'est pas éclatante'. In the very same letter, Hincmar affirms the king's rights to hospitality at bishops' expense.

59 Lupus of Ferrières, *ep* 115, *Correspondance*, ed L. Levillain, 2 vols (Paris 1935) 2, p 162.

60 Ganshof, 'A propos de tonlieu à l'époque carolingienne', in *SS Spol* 6, ii (1959) pp 485–508 at 496–7.

61 *MGH Capit* 2, no 273, pp 310–32, at 314–20 (caps 8–24). See M. van Rey, 'Die Münzprägung Karls des Kahlen', *Die Stadt in der europäischen Geschichte. Festschrift E. Ennen*, ed W. Besch and others (Bonn 1972) pp 153–84.

62 Tessier, 1, no 18, pp 42–4.

63 Tessier, 1, no 186, pp 491–2; 2, no 391, pp 374–5.

Cormeilles;[64] to the bishop of Châlons-sur-Marne a mint and (carefully specified) the profits thereof.[65] It seems that from about 860 onwards, Charles was trying to establish regalian rights over the foundation of markets as well as over the profits of trade.[66] Certainly he knew how to invest in, as well as to exploit, the urban wealth of churches.

So far I have surveyed in a general way Charles the Bald's use of ecclesiastical resources first in the countryside, then in towns. Now I want briefly to bring these strands together by looking at royal policy in action at a particular place and time: Auxerre and Burgundy in 858–9. This was the great crisis-point of Charles's reign, when his realm was invaded by his half-brother Louis the German and most of the aristocracy deserted him. So did the archbisop of Sens, whose treachery represented a major military loss for Charles. But fortunately for him, the rest of the episcopate stayed loyal and explained why, in terms both of principle and of self-interest, in the famous Quiersy letter addressed to Louis the German. That the church 'saved Charles's kingdom' in this sense is well-known.[67] Less well-known is the church's contribution to Charles's political come-back. In late September 858, hearing of Louis' long-threatened invasion, Charles made for Burgundy.[68] To the monk Heiric writing a generation later, it was clear that Charles came to Auxerre 'having lost all hope of earthly help' to commit his cause to God and St. Germain.[69] No doubt. But Auxerre had other attractions too. Charles had two powerful friends there: the bishop, Abbo, who had close connexions with the court and whose brother and uncle had been bishops of Auxerre before him, and the abbot of St. Germain's, Charles's cousin Hugh who already held this office in 853.[70] The church in Auxerre was wealthy, whether we measure that by the silver it could distribute, the marble it could buy or the school it could support.[71] Charles's political influence

[64] Tessier, 2, no 323, pp 210–12.

[65] Tessier, 2, no 277, pp 120–1.

[66] T. Endemann, *Markturkunden und Markt in Frankreich und Burgund vom 9. bis 11 Jhdt.* (Constance 1964) pp 27–34; 40–8; 98 *seq;* 210–11.

[67] On all this see [J.] Calmette, [*La*] *Diplomatie* [*carolingienne*] (Paris 1901, repr 1977) pp 34 *seq*, 51 *seq*.

[68] *Ann Bert sa* 858, pp 78–9.

[69] *MGH SS* 13, pp 403–4.

[70] Abbo: *MGH SS* 13, p 398, and Lupus, *Correspondance,* 2, nos 95, 96, pp 108–115; Hugh: Calmette, *Diplomatie,* pp 42, 60.

[71] *MGH SS* 13, pp 396–8, 403–4; E. Jeauneau, 'Les écoles de Laon et d'Auxerre au IXe siècle', *SS Spol* 19 (1972) pp 495–522.

there, attested by episcopal and abbatial appointments before 858, was further shown when his cousin Conrad became count in that year.[72] It was from Auxerre, after staying in the palace he himself had probably had built in the precincts of St. Germain's,[73] that Charles set out soon after 9 January 859, to mobilise resistance to the invaders in Burgundy. With the recently-appointed young bishop of Laon at his side, Charles rallied his vassals from church lands in the region, and by the end of January had marshalled enough troops to cause the invader's support to wane and Louis himself to withdraw.[74] There are frustrating gaps in our information but the outlines of the picture are clear. When Charles to survive had to use every instrument at his disposal, from family connexions to saintly intercession, what really tipped the scales was his ability to exploit the carefully-husbanded resources of the church in town and countryside. A last point worth noting is that Burgundy was a conspicuous area of economic activity in the ninth century and later, activity of which Charles himself was among the early sponsors.[75]

My conclusion is two-fold. First, I am sure Émile Lesne was right to focus on ecclesiastical property as a crucial determinant of the relations between the king and the church in ninth-century Francia. Lesne's approach was criticised fairly recently on the grounds that it was 'too narrowly material' and took insufficient account of 'changes in the law' during the early Carolingian period.[76] I cannot share such reservations; and if I must plead guilty to narrowness, I can only find solace in the company of a materialist monseigneur. Of course Wallace-Hadrill is right to stress how much books (produced in

[72] L. Auzias, *L'Aquitaine carolingienne* (Paris 1937) p 295, n 58 (where, however, the grant of the abbacy of St Germain to Hugh is misdated). See also Calmette, *Diplomatie*, pp 42, 58 (but the reference to Heiric, *MGH SS* 13, pp 401–2, seems misplaced: Heiric praises the generosity to St Germain of Conrad senior, father of the man made count in 858 – which only goes to show the longstanding Welf connexion with Auxerre).

[73] Brühl, 'Königspfalz', pp 171–2.

[74] *MGH Epp* 8, no 126 p 52; *Ann Bert sa* 859, p 80, See Calmette, *Diplomatie*, pp 58–9.

[75] The map at the end of Endemann, *Markturkunden*, is suggestive. For evidence of Charles's interest in the region, see Tessier 2, no 326, pp 218–23; no 354, pp 287–8; no 365, pp 315–17; no 378, pp 342–7. See also Latouche, *Birth*, p 221, and Duby, *Early Growth*, pp 104–5. No doubt an influx of refugees had an effect on economic growth in Burgundy. But it would be premature to claim a direct connexion between that growth and relative freedom from Viking raids. Notwithstanding the arguments of Wallace-Hadrill, 'The Vikings in Francia', Stenton Lecture for 1974 (University of Reading 1975) pp 13–18, the question of the Vikings' impact on economic developments in western and, especially, northern Francia seems to me still open.

[76] Goffart, *Forgeries*, p 6.

ecclesiastical centres) meant to Charles the Bald;[77] but I think that land and money, bed and breakfast meant even more.[78] It is probably true that Charles had little alternative to exploiting the church. But that does not mean that such exploitation was bad policy. When Wallace-Hadrill points out that for the monks of St. Calais in dispute with the bishop of Le Mans, 'the only escape' from episcopal domination was 'into the arms of the king',[79] he has put his finger on the vulnerability of the church. The need of churches for royal protection (*tuitio*) was greater, in the end, than the king's for ecclesiastical support (*suffragium*)—which makes me unable to follow Wallace-Hadrill when he claims that Charles's 'unprecedented and unwelcome reliance on bishops and abbots for hospitality and the upkeep of his court was bound in the long run to play into their hands'.[80]

This brings me to my second conclusion: that it is false to see Charles's exploitation of the church as, in Brühl's word, *rücksichtslos*[81] —wanton, ill-considered—and ultimately self-defeating, a view which seems currently to be widely shared. It was not Charles, after all, who created the vulnerability of the church. Ecclesiastical property-holding was always, and inevitably, at the mercy of lay politics. I have tried to show that Charles, far from ruining the churches' material base, generally sought to strengthen it when he could; and was able to do so, and exploit it at the same time, because he worked within an economy which, however tentatively and patchily, was showing the first signs of expansion. The analogy I would like to evoke is not that of a cake which, though its slices may vary, has fixed limits of total size, but that of a healthy cow which you can not only milk without killing, but whose production you can greatly increase if you improve its feed. Charles the Bald was no cynic: he seriously meant to protect the church, and on the whole contemporaries believed that he did so.

[77] Wallace-Hadrill, 'A Carolingian Renaissance Prince: the Emperor Charles the Bald', *Proceedings of the British Academy* 64 (1978), pp 155-84. There is much valuable information on books written for Charles the Bald in the article (cited in n 34 above) by McKitterick.

[78] Compare the presentation of the Ottonians by J. Gillingham, *The Kingdom of Germany in the High Middle Ages*, Historical Association (London 1973). Brühl, 'Königspfalz', p 274, n 703, contrasts Charles's 'system' with that of the Ottonians, whereas I am more impressed by the similarities.

[79] Wallace-Hadrill, *Kingship*, p 126: by implication, royal arms are preferable to aristocratic ones.

[80] *Ibid* p 127.

[81] Brühl, *Fodrum*, p 52.

Hincmar and others held up hard standards for the king to meet. They obeyed him because Charles, despite his many problems, did not fall so far short of the model *minister Dei*. In the end, I hope that my view of the relation of political practice to clerical ideology is not incompatible with the views of Wallace-Hadrill and Ullmann; for if, as Wood recently wrote,[82] they move in the same world, it is surely one roomy enough to contain political, social and economic historians too.

[82] *Early Medieval Kingship* (University of Leeds 1978). If there is currently something of a 'Carolingian Renaissance' amongst younger British medievalists, this is largely due to the influence, direct and indirect, of these two scholars.

5

LEGISLATION AND CONSENSUS IN THE REIGN OF CHARLES THE BALD

In a recent comment on some Carolingian historical writing, Professor J. M. Wallace-Hadrill spoke of 'a nice mixture of ruthlessness and fantasy'.[1] It is a rare achievement to have coped as he has with this and other early medieval mixtures: he has seemed as much at home at Brebières or Clichy as at St Denis; he has conveyed vividly the excitement of both 'matters of the mind' and 'their startling physical background'; he has explained equally convincingly the bloodfeud's function in Merovingian society, and the interest of Carolingian scholars in *Lex Salica*, and he has discerned in Frankish legal sources 'the public reason of the Franks'.[2] The following notes on the capitularies of Charles the Bald are offered in gratitude for many insights and a generous supply of counsel and aid.

Since F.-L. Ganshof published his fine work on Carolingian capitularies,[3] his views have been developed in two main ways. First, increasing attention has been given to the survival of capitularies in private collections rather than in remnants of an official archive; and while new editions are still urgently needed, much progress has been made in understanding the ways in which

[1] Wallace-Hadrill, *Early Medieval History* (Oxford, 1975), p. 17.

[2] Review of W. A. Eckhardt, *Die Kapitulariensammlung Bischof Ghaerbalds von Lüttich* (Göttingen, 1955), in *Tijdschrift voor Rechtsgeschiedenis*, XXIV (1956), pp. 471–2.

[3] F. L. Ganshof, *Recherches sur les Capitulaires* (Paris, 1958), with references to earlier literature.

Charlemagne's capitularies, at least, were produced and preserved.[4] Second, Ganshof's contrast between Charlemagne's capitularies, given binding force 'by the ruler's ban alone', and those of Charles the Bald, where the consent of the aristocracy has become a condition of validity, has been refined by the argument that the written text in the case of Charles the Bald's capitularies, unlike his predecessors', had come to possess a 'dispositive character' and was no longer merely an *aide-mémoire* to orally-promulgated legislation.[5] On the whole, however, recent research has tended to focus, as Ganshof did, on Charlemagne's reign at the expense of his successors, and to reaffirm Ganshof's belief that the references to 'consent' in Charles the Bald's capitularies signify the progressive weakening of the Carolingian monarchy from *c*.830 onwards.[6] But these later capitularies, though quarried for historical data, have never been systematically explored; nor have they been looked at in the context of political practice, as collective 'public reason'. Even a brief and preliminary survey seems timely.

Over fifty capitularies have survived from the reign of Charles the Bald, including fourteen which are records of meetings between

[4] A start was made by S. Stein, '*Lex* und *Capitula*: eine kritische Studie', *MIÖG*, XLI (1926), pp. 289–301, and 'Étude critique des capitulaires francs', *Le Moyen Age*, LI (1941), pp. 1–75. Although he reached the wrong conclusions, he directed attention to the MSS. See also W. A. Eckhardt, 'Die *Capitularia Missorum Specialia* von 802,' *DA*, XII (1956), pp. 498–516; R. Schneider, 'Zur rechtlichen Bedeutung der Kapitularientexte', *DA*, XXIII (1967), pp. 273–94; D. Hägermann, 'Zur Entstehung der Kapitularien', in *Festschrift P. Acht* (Kallmütz, 1976), pp. 12–27; G. Schmitz, 'Wucher in Laon. Eine neue Quelle zu Karl der Kahlen und Hinkmar von Reims', *DA*, XXXVII (1981), pp. 520–58; the best discussion in English is R. McKitterick, *The Frankish Church and the Carolingian Reforms* (London, 1977), pp. 18 ff.; also W. Ullmann, *Law and Politics in the Middle Ages* (London, 1961), pp. 203 ff. and *The Carolingian Renaissance and the Idea of Kingship* (London, 1969), pp. 30–5; for capitularies in the broad context of early medieval legislation and kingship, P. Wormald, '*Lex Scripta* and *Verbum Regis*', in P. H. Sawyer and I. N. Wood (eds), *Early Medieval Kingship* (Leeds, 1977), pp. 105–38.

[5] Schneider, 'Rechtliche Bedeutung'.

[6] Hägermann, 'Entstehung', makes important qualifications to this argument, but concludes (p. 27) that instead of 'a fundamental constitutional change', there was 'a significant shift of accent'. E. Magnou-Nortier, *Foi et fidelité* (Toulouse, 1976), pp. 98 ff., offers a more radical reassessment with a remarkable analysis of the ideological content of four of Charles the Bald's capitularies. But I am not convinced by her interpretation of the term *convenientia* (which does not recur in Charles' later capitularies and seems unlikely to be an import from Roman law via the Midi), or by her general account of a 'restructuring of the French monarchy' in this reign.

Charles and (one or more) other Carolingian rulers.[7] Though a number of these texts have not been transmitted in the form of *capitula*, i.e. are not divided into numbered sections or 'chapters', nearly all of them fall within Ganshof's broad substantial definition of capitularies as 'prescribing rules of law and ordering their implementation, and/or prescribing measures in particular cases'.[8] What proportion has survived of the total number that may have been produced? We can only begin to answer that question by looking at how our texts have been preserved. Early in Charles' reign, at the Council of Ver in 844, it looks as if no agreed 'official' text was produced there and then.[9] Some months later, Lupus of Ferrières in a letter to Hincmar of Rheims regretted that the king 'had not agreed in the first place to the recommendations which he sought and got at Ver', and recalled: 'I sent you [Hincmar] these same canons, or, as you call them, *capitula*, which I then marshalled with my pen. Posterity will, I think, judge them fair, and God will not be unmindful of my devotion.'[10] Hincmar, present at Ver, had evidently had to wait for Lupus to produce the capitulary text. From the early 850s, efforts were made to have a given capitulary text available at the palace from the time of issue, for copying by 'the archbishops and their counts'(!)[11] This rule does not suggest that many copies were envisaged, and the copying itself was evidently left to scribes attached to the archbishops and counts – hardly a surprising arrangement, given the very small number of chancery

[7] See R. Schneider, *Brüdergemeine und Schwurfreundschaft* (Lübeck-Hamburg, 1964).

[8] Ganshof, *Recherches*, p. 12. Appendix 1 lists these texts. All were edited by A. Boretius and V. Krause, *MGH, Capit.* II, except for no. 58, which falls within Ganshof's classification of 'capitulary-like texts' (*Recherches*, pp. 11–12), and has been edited by Schmitz, 'Wucher in Laon', pp. 556–8. That *ordines* of royal consecration should also be thus classified has been well argued by Ullmann, *Law and Politics*, pp. 207–8.

[9] No doubt the council had worked from a written agenda and some record of proceedings was kept. cf. McKitterick, *Frankish Church*, pp. 23–5, on ecclesiastical councils.

[10] Lupus, *Ep.* 43, in *Correspondance*, ed. L. Levillain (2 vols. Paris, 1927–35), I, p. 182.

[11] As originally prescribed by Louis the Pious in 825, *MGH, Capit.* I, no. 150, c.26, which reappears in the collection of Ansegis, ed. A. Boretius in *MGH, Capit.* I, Bk II, c.24, p. 419, and was cited from there in the capitularies of Servais (853) and Pîtres (864), *MGH, Capit.* II, no. 260, c.11 and no. 273, c.36 (appendix 1, nos. 17, 39).

notaries operating at any one time.[12] We have no way of knowing how regularly the repeated directives about the keeping of a palace text were carried out. No example of such a text survives.[13] An episode in 862 where 'counsellors' tried to suppress a capitulary text suggests that, at this date anyway, the drawing-up of capitularies was in the hands of a very small group of close royal advisers who, especially if a capitulary was not promulgated, could have taken texts away with them to 'private' archives.[14]

I would like to pursue further the question of capitularies' survival by considering three manuscripts:

1. Hague 10 D 2, written at Rheims in the third quarter of the ninth century, contains a series of West Frankish capitularies dating from between 843 and 856, and including virtually every capitulary known from these years.[15] The last piece in the collection contains references to ten of the earlier items. I have suggested elsewhere that Hincmar may have been responsible both for this last capitulary, and for the collection of which Hague 10 D 2 is an early copy.[16] If so, ought we to ask whether he was acting in a 'public capacity', 'entrusted' with the construction of a state archive, or in a private capacity as one interested in collecting, preserving and even composing capitularies (among other legal texts)? The question is, I think, *mal posé*: it presupposes a hard and fast dividing line which was constantly transgressed in ninth-century practice. I shall return to this point.

2. Most of Yale Beinecke 413[17] is in the hand of a scribe,

[12] cf. Ganshof, *Recherches*, p. 64. On the chancery of Charles the Bald, see G. Tessier, *Receuil des Actes de Charles le Chauve* (3 vols, Paris, 1944–55), III, pp. 46 ff.

[13] And see below, p. 95, for reservations about the alleged link between a copy of Ansegis and Charles the Bald. If there was a copy of Ansegis in Charles' palace archive late in the reign, was anyone there to use it as a legislative data-bank? The mandate tentatively dated by Schmitz to 868 (1, no. 58) tells Hincmar to prepare a dossier of Ansegis-citations on a particular issue (usury).

[14] *Annales de Saint-Bertin*, ed. F. Grat, J. Vielliard and S. Clemencet (Paris, 1964), (hereafter cited as *Annales*), pp. 94–5.

[15] See appendix 1. This MS was cited by the *MGH* editors as Haagensis 1. For details (and dating by B. Bischoff) see P. Classen, 'Die Verträge von Verdun und Coulaines, 843, als politische Grundlagen des west-fränkischen Reiches', *HZ* CXCVI (1963), pp. 28 *et seq*.

[16] 'Kingship, law and liturgy in the political thought of Hincmar of Rheims', below, chapter 7, pp. 148-9.

[17] See appendix 1. This MS, formerly Chester Beatty 11, and before that Phillipps 10190, was listed by the *MGH* editors as Cheltenhamensis 10190 and cited as

Ingobert, who also copied out a bible apparently presented to Charles the Bald by Hincmar *c.*870.[18] The manuscript consists of a fine copy of the capitulary collection of Ansegis, followed by six capitularies of Charles the Bald. Ingobert wrote in the last of the additional capitularies at a later date than the rest, which probably means that the manuscript remained in its original Rheims *scriptorium* from *c.*864 to *c.*873. The rationale behind this particular series of six seems to be that all these capitularies cite from Ansegis' collection, the first of them being the earliest of Charles the Bald's capitularies to do so.[19] This Ansegis connection is important, for no fewer than four Ansegis-manuscripts can be attributed to Hincmar's Rheims *scriptorium*.[20]

3. A manuscript still extant at Beauvais in the early seventeenth century, and used by Sirmond in his remarkable edition of Charles the Bald's capitularies,[21] has since been lost, but two copies of it survive in the Vatican library, both made in the early modern

---

Middlehill. It has been very thoroughly described by E. G. Miller, *The Library of A. Chester Beatty* (2 vols, Oxford, 1927), I, pp. 50–2, II, plates xxviii–xxx; and in less detail in Sotheby's catalogue, 24 June 1969, pp. 20–3. I am grateful to Yale University Library for lending me a microfilm of the MS.

[18] See Sotheby's catalogue, 24 June 1969, p. 21, for the identification by Bischoff of Ingobert's hand. On the San Paolo Bible, see R. McKitterick, 'Charles the Bald and his library', *EHR*, XCV (1980), pp. 41–2. As against the strong paleographical links with Rheims, the arguments that have been adduced for a Soissons origin for this manuscript seem to me weak. There may be another pointer towards Rheims in the list of addressees of the Quiersy capitulary in 857 (appendix 1, no. 26) in this manuscript: Bishop Hunfrid (of Thérouanne), and Counts Ingiscalc and Berengar. Clearly the original of this text was destined for the Ternois *missaticum* (cf. the list of *missi* here in the Servais capitulary of 853, appendix 1, no. 17: Bishop Folcoin (succeeded by Hunfrid in 856), Ingiscalc and Berengar): a likely explanation is that Hincmar's *scriptorium* was responsible for multiplying and distributing capitulary texts throughout the Rheims province, and an exemplar that happened to contain the Ternois names had remained in the Rheims archive to be copied by Ingobert in the 860s.

[19] See appendix, no. 14, *MGH, Capit.* II, no. 259, c.4. On the proceedings at this assembly, see J. Devisse, *Hincmar, archevêque de Reims, 845–882* (3 vols, Geneva, 1975–6), I, p. 91.

[20] See Devisse, *Hincmar*, III, p. 1078, and *idem*, *Hincmar et la Loi* (Dakar, 1962), pp. 64–9; and Schmitz, 'Wucher in Laon', pp. 540–1. Interestingly, Hincmar cites from Ansegis quite often in *De Ecclesiis et Capellis*, written in 857 or 858 (ed. W. Gundlach, 'Zwei Schriften des Erzbischofs Hinkmars von Reims', *Zeitschrift für Kirchengeschichte*, X (1889), pp. 92–145.

[21] J. Sirmond, *Capitula Caroli Calvi et successorum* (Paris, 1623); Ganshof, *Recherches*, pp. 7 ff., thinks this work unworthy of mention.

period: Vaticanus reginae Christinae 291 and Vaticanus 4982.[22] The coverage of capitularies in the lost manuscript overlaps to a small extent with, but largely continues, that of Hague 10 D 2: taken together, these manuscripts could suggest an attempt at the systematic preservation of Charles the Bald's capitularies. I am tempted to make this juxtaposition, first because the lost manuscript contained a number of capitularies in whose composition Hincmar seems to have been involved;[23] second because none of the capitularies preserved in the lost manuscript is of later date than 876,[24] in other words, all fall within the period when Hincmar can plausibly be assigned a major role in the composition of capitulary texts; and third because several other manuscripts containing capitularies of Charles the Bald have been traced to a Rheims origin or exemplar.[25]

In appendix 1, I list Charles the Bald's capitularies chronologically, as do the manuscripts, rather than using the categories of the *Monumenta* editors (though for convenience I also give *Monumenta* numbers).[26] The appendix shows in which of the four manuscripts

[22] See Boretius' conspectus in *MGH, Capit.* II, p. xxviii (where, however, the Servais capitulary of 853 (appendix 1, no. 17) has been accidentally omitted from the contents of Vat. 4982). The contents of these two MSS are very similar indeed, but Vat. 4982 is probably closer to the exemplar as it includes the capitularies of Epernay (appendix 1, no. 10) and Meersen 847 and 851 (appendix 1, nos. 11 and 12) where Vat. Reg. 291 omits these. Further, Vat. Reg. 291 contains two additional capitularies which suggest the use of other sources in an attempt at more complete coverage: the *Decretio Childeberti* (596) and the *Conventio* of Furon (878). These other sources could well be of Rheims origin: the *Decretio* occurs (twice) in the Rheims MS Paris BN Lat. 10758, while the Furon text is given by Hincmar in the *Annales*, pp. 230–4.

[23] Especially the Quiersy oaths and the Quiersy letter of 858 (appendix 1, nos. 29, 30) and the Pact of Tusey (appendix 1, no. 40). Hincmar's hand in no. 29 is likely: see J. Devisse, 'Essai sur l'histoire d'une expression qui a fait fortune: *consilium et auxilium* au IXe siècle', *Le Moyen Age*, LXXIV (1968), pp. 187–8; and in no. 30, is certain: Hincmar *Ep*. 126, *MGH, Ep*. VIII, p. 64. For no. 40, cf. *Annales, s.a.* 865, p. 116, and see Devisse, *Hincmar*, I, pp. 449 ff., (where, however, as elsewhere in Devisse's work, Tusey near Toul is confused with Douzy, near Sedan.)

[24] This is true on the assumption that Vat. 4982 is nearer the original collection: see above, n. 22.

[25] Paris BN Lat. 4638; 4761; 9654; and cf. 10758 (with capitularies of Charlemagne and Louis the Pious, and Ansegis' collection). The Rheims connection was already noted by E. Bourgeois, *Le Capitulaire de Quierzy-sur-Oise (877)* (Paris, 1885), pp. 23, 25: still a valuable study; and by Stein, 'Étude critique', pp. 51–2. (Stein's implied inference that Hincmar forged the capitularies of Charles the Bald's predecessors is absurd, yet Stein had a feel for the grain of the evidence).

[26] Like the *MGH* editors, I have taken 'capitulary' in a broad sense, to include 'capitulary-like texts': see above, n. 8. Such a classification clearly corresponds to the view of ninth-century compilers.

just discussed each capitulary was preserved. Out of 58 capitularies, only 12 are not found in one (or more) of these four manuscripts, and of those 12 texts, 6 can be associated with Hincmar as author or preserver.[27] Of the 46 capitularies in one or more of our four manuscripts, Hincmar's authorship has been suggested, in whole or in part, for 19,[28] and I would think it likely for at least a further 5.[29] In other words, Hincmar's hand can perhaps be seen in the writing-up of 30 out of the 58 surviving capitularies, and, if a Hincmar-connection for the four manuscripts is accepted, in the preservation of a further 23. Now it is clear that Hincmar was not the only author or preserver of capitularies in Charles the Bald's reign. But what seems beyond doubt is the major role of Hincmar in the maintenance and indeed the climaxing (whether judged on formal or substantial criteria) of the Carolingian capitulary tradition. Other Carolingian contemporaries of Charles the Bald 'prescribed and ordered the application of rules of law' and took 'measures for particular cases':[30] it was no difference in political practice but a highly differential degree of interest in written law on the part of the clerical elite, and specifically of Hincmar, as compared with prelates in other kingdoms, which accounted for the distinctiveness of the West Frankish capitularies between *c*.840 and *c*.880.

[27] The twelve texts not in any of the four manuscripts (numbers refer to appendix 1): 4, 27, 33, 43, 51, 55–7, 58, 22, 42 and 46. The six that can be linked with Hincmar: 22, 42 and 46 (on these royal consecration *ordines*, see C. A. Bouman, *Sacring and Crowning* (Groningen, 1957), pp. 8–9, 112 ff.); 33 (on the *Libellus contra Wenilonem*, see 'Kingship, law and liturgy', below, ch. 7, p. 142 and n. 3); 43 (on the Pacts made at Metz either in 867 or 868, see Devisse, *Hincmar*, I, p. 453, and P. McKeon, *Hincmar of Laon and Carolingian Politics*, Urbana, 1978, pp. 210–1); and 58 (on the preservation of this text, see Schmitz, 'Wucher in Laon', esp. p. 552).

[28] See Devisse, '*Consilium et auxilium*', for appendix 1, nos. 2, 12, 18, 20, 28, 29, 31, 32, 33, 34, 38, 40, 43; and the *MGH* editors for nos. 22, 26, 30, 42, 45, and 46.

[29] Appendix 1, nos. 36, 37, 39, 44 and 50; also possibly 13, 14, 15, 16 and 17. Detailed discussion of Hincmar's role awaits further study.

[30] See n. 8; on capitularies in the Italian kingdom, see C. Wickham, *Early Medieval Italy* (London, 1981), pp. 60–2. The possibility that capitularies were issued by Louis the German, but have been lost, was suggested by H. Conrad, *Deutsche Rechtsgeschichte* (Karlsruhe, 1954), I, p. 187. The kind of occasion on which capitularies might well have been promulgated is noted frequently by Hincmar in the *Annales*: e.g., *s.a.* 872, p. 186; 873, pp. 190, 193; 875, p. 197 (East Francia); and *s.a.* 864, p. 105, 866, pp. 132–3 (Middle Kingdom). As Ganshof stressed (*Recherches*, p. 102), the positive evidence for the persistence of the capitulary tradition after 840 really comes only from the reign of Charles the Bald; but that fact has of course specific significance for the way in which the relevant texts were preserved.

This is not the place for anything more than a brief indication of the scope and formal sophistication of these texts. The Capitulary of Servais (November 853: see appendix 1, no. 17) has been held to signify 'a remarkable restoring to order of the kingdom'.[31] Here was affirmed the principle of the collective liability of free Franks to denounce and pursue criminals in their locality; practical means to enforce this were the oaths required of free men and the hundredman's role in linking local and central measures to suppress disorder.[32] A total of forty-three *missi* were named in a dozen *missatica* in Francia and Burgundy.[33] The Edict of Pîtres (June 864: see appendix 1, no. 39) was conceived on a grand scale in thirty-seven *capitula* (which run to seventeen pages of *Monumenta* text).[34] The single largest topic was coinage reform (cc.8–24):[35] the siting of mints, the duties of moneyers, penalties for rejecting new coin (including careful specification of type of flogging to avoid permanent health damage), were all spelled out in detail. As for the formal characteristics of this capitulary, the frequent reference to Ansegis is very striking, and allowed the author(s) to place the measures taken at Pîtres solidly within the framework of recent Frankish legislation.[36] Yet there is no sense here of merely formulaic repetition: the older provisions were often modified or supplemented, and as in the capitularies of Charlemagne and Louis the Pious we find a wealth of data about quite specific governmental problems: for instance the need to secure the supply of horses both for military and communications purposes; the difficulties posed for royal estate-managers by the growth of a peasant land-market and the consequent dismemberment of tenurial units that were also fiscal

[31] Devisse, *Hincmar*, I, p. 290 with n. 26.

[32] *MGH, Capit*, II, p. 274. cf. *Capit. de missis instruendis* (829), *ibid.*, p. 8.

[33] *ibid.*, pp. 275–6. The first *missaticum* here covers the Rheims area, and Hincmar is the first *missus* named.

[34] *ibid.*, pp. 310–28. cf. *Annales* p. 113: 'Generale placitum habet in quo annua dona . . . recipit . . . Capitula etiam ad triginta et septem consilio fidelium more praedecessorum ac progenitorum suorum regum constituit et ut legalia per omnem regnum suum observari praecepit'.

[35] See P. Grierson, 'The *Gratia Dei Rex* coinage of Charles the Bald', in M. Gibson and J. Nelson (eds), *Charles the Bald: Court and Kingdom*, (BAR International Series, CI, 1981), pp. 41–2; D. M. Metcalf 'A sketch of the currency in the time of Charles the Bald', *ibid.*, pp. 73–4.

[36] There are 24 references to, or citations from, Ansegis, plus 1 reference to the collection of Benedict the Levite, and 5 to Roman law, as well as several others to previous capitularies of Charles the Bald (notably appendix 1, nos. 17 and 26).

units; conflicts of interest between lords and peasants over labour services and the earnings of migrant workers.[37]

As always with medieval legal sources, we are left with the question of how far rules reflect social reality: how widespread or long-term were the problems dealt with at Pîtres in June 864? In this and other capitularies, we can sometimes suspect that remedies are being prescribed for quite local and/or short-term problems. For instance, peasant migration, here said to be 'recent' and the result of 'the persecution of the Northmen', may have been affecting only the lower Seine valley, and perhaps even there only certain estates, and we have no way of telling whether it was more widespread than that here referred to (via Ansegis) as having occurred in the time of Charlemagne and Louis the Pious[38] (when, presumably, it was due to factors other than the Vikings). Again, peasant resistance to lords' new demands for the cartage of marl may have been quite widespread, or may have been merely a local phenomenon. We have two near-contemporary cases where charters show that groups of peasants have appealed to the king and lost, and in the earlier of these it is polyptych evidence that clinches the lord's case.[39] Could it be that the 864 capitulary is another kind of reflection of the outcome of a single similar case, an apparent generalizing of the particular?[40] It looks very much as if such an interpretation might work for the famous denunciation of lay abbots by the Council of Ver:[41] in this case, we know the author, Lupus, and his particular grievance against the lay-abbot Odulf at the time of this council – and indeed, he himself makes the connection explicit in his letter to Hincmar, cited above.[42] It is obvious, too, that a specific factional conflict, centring on the court, lies behind the references in the Capitulary of Coulaines (843) to persons pursuing private interests and influencing the king improperly.[43] Again, external,

[37] cc.26, 30; 29 and 31: *MGH, Capit.* II, pp. 321, 323–4.
[38] c.31, with reference to Ansegis III, 18.
[39] Pippin I of Aquitaine, charter no. XII, in L. Levillain (ed.), *Receuil des Actes de Pépin I et de Pépin II* (Paris, 1926), pp. 44–7 (original dated 828); Charles the Bald, charter no. 228, in Tessier, *Receuil*, ed. Tessier, II, pp. 7–9 (original dated 861).
[40] P. Wormald, '*Lex Scripta*', pp. 112–13; cf. some early modern Scottish parliamentary legislation and the illuminating comments of J. Wormald, *Court, Kirk and Community* (London, 1981), p. 27.
[41] Appendix 1, no. 6, c.12, *MGH, Capit.* II, pp. 385–6.
[42] Lupus, *Ep.* 43, in *Correspondance*, ed. Levillain.
[43] Appendix 1, no. 2, and cf. also no. 1: *MGH, Capit.* II, pp. 254–5, 402.

this time charter, evidence points fairly clearly to at least one of the individuals concerned: the chamberlain Vivian.[44]

To see why any particular topic was the subject of a capitulary, we have to understand the text as the residue – all that survives – of the proceedings of an assembly. The agenda would be the product of initiatives not only from the king and his close advisers but also from individuals and groups among the aristocracy. Collective deliberations and decision-making could translate private concerns and grievances into public law: thus, in the Edict of Pîtres, statements on peasant labour services and migrants' earnings appear alongside the decrees on coinage reform and the defence of the realm. Politics is the common denominator, in as much as dealings involving king and aristocracy lie behind all these affairs, and the assembly is the forum in which power is negotiated. A lively impression of the assembly's central role in the earlier part of the reign is conveyed in some of Lupus' letters: the operation of networks of patronage and the activity of favoured magnates as brokers between the king and other nobles supplement but are no substitute for personal participation at assemblies. Lupus regards these occasions with a keen anticipation that sometimes carries more than a hint of anxiety. Attendance is at once a burden and an opportunity: a summons is a demand for service, specifically military service, and for gifts, but also a personalized signal of the king's attention. Refusal of such a summons, on whatever excuse, is dangerous.[45]

How large was the attendance at the summer assembly which still in Charles the Bald's reign was a gathering of the Frankish host for campaign? Enough information even to hazard a guess is very rare. In late summer 843, most of the bishops and abbots of Francia proper, Neustria, northern Aquitaine and Burgundy seem to have been present, and we can name five lay magnates probably with the king through the autumn and present at Coulaines in November. In this case, we can piece together evidence from the list of subscribers to a monastic privilege plus several charters.[46] Occasionally,

[44] Tessier, *Receuil*, I, nos. 24, 28, 30, 31. See also F. Lot and L. Halphen, *Le Règne de Charles le Chauve* (Paris, 1909), pp. 86, 88, 153 n. 2.

[45] Lupus, *Epp*. 15, 16, 17, 28, 36, 41, 45, 47, 58, 60, 67, Levillain, *Correspondance*, I, 72, 74, 111, 112, 123, Levillain, *Correspondance*, II.

[46] Synodal privilege for St Lomer: Mansi XIV, cc.795–6: see Lot and Halphen, *Règne*, p. 85, n. 4, 86, n. 1. For the charters see n. 44 above: evidence for Harduin, Vivian and (in conjunction with Lupus *Ep*. 32) Adalard (who also appears in the St

charters can be linked with assemblies;[47] but even in the early years of the reign when charters are relatively plentiful, the absence of lists of subscriptions severely limits the usefulness of charters as indicators of attendance at assemblies.[48] Royal judgements, though very rare, do carry lists of subscribers and this makes the three such texts we have from Charles the Bald's reign particularly significant. Two dated within a week of each other can be read as showing 18 counts as well as 25 archbishops and bishops and 6 abbots with the king at the palace of Verberie in late October/early November 863.[49] The third shows the king attended by nine counts at Rouy (near Laon) in April 868.[50] Unfortunately neither occasion can be linked with a capitulary nor indeed identified with an assembly; but both hint at the numbers of magnates that could be present when important business was being discussed. In two cases, the scale of an assembly is indicated in the capitulary emanating from it: it is clear that most of the forty-three *missi* named in the capitulary of Servais were present there.[51] They represent a majority of the bishops and perhaps also of the counts in the Frankish and Burgundian parts of the kingdom. In the capitulary of Quiersy (June 877; see appendix 1, no. 56), 10 bishops, 4 abbots[52] and 16 counts are named, all but three of whom were at the assembly,[53] and the list certainly includes only a proportion of those present.[54]

Lomer text). The Capitulary of Coulaines, *MGH, Capit.* II, pp. 253–4: evidence for Warin and Richwin.

[47] The one striking case relates to attendance at St Sernin's, Toulouse, in May/June 844: cf. Tessier, *Receuil*, nos. 36–56. But one or two charters can be linked with a number of other assemblies: e.g. Tessier, no. 157 with the Synod of Verberie (appendix 1, no. 15); Tessier, nos. 191–193bis with the Assembly of Quiersy in 857 (appendix 1, no. 26); see also appendix 2.

[48] Contrast the Anglo-Saxon charter evidence discussed by S. Keynes, *The Diplomas of King Aethelred 'the Unready' 978–1016* (Cambridge, 1980).

[49] Tessier, *Receuil*, II, nos. 258, 259.

[50] *ibid.*, no. 314.

[51] Appendix 1, no. 17, *MGH, Capit.* II, p. 271: the prologue addressed to the *missi* specifies that if anyone has had to be absent from the assemblies of Valenciennes (appendix 1, no. 16) or Servais where this capitulary was agreed, still he is to carry out its instructions.

[52] For their importance, see K.-F. Werner, 'Gauzlin von Saint-Denis', *DA*, XXXV (1979), pp. 395–462.

[53] *MGH, Capit.* II, cc.12, 15, p. 359. Hincmar's letter to Louis the Stammerer, *PL* CXXV, c.987.

[54] Only those magnates staying in Francia with Louis the Stammerer are mentioned; but some, at least, of those present at Quiersy would be going with Charles to Italy.

Nearly all Charles the Bald's assemblies, especially in the latter half of the reign, were held in Francia proper, usually at one of the palaces on the Oise or the Seine.[55] Enemies of the king might be captured in the provinces but were brought back to Francia to be sentenced at an assembly by the judgement of the Franks.[56] Disputes between magnates might be settled in the assembly-forum, as at Pîtres in 862 when Charles 'at the request of his faithful men' forestalled an outbreak of violence by reconciling two such opponents.[57] Similar rivalries and reconciliations are attested at another great summer assembly at Pîtres in 864.[58] Here too, the royal changes in, or confirmations of, comital personnel that were the outcomes of such manoeuvring, were publicly announced.[59] While aristocratic politics remained centripetal with the court still the natural forum for competition between nobles and for peaceful resolution of conflicts by king and faithful men acting in concert, equally, the king could use the assembly as a convenient locale for orchestrating support. It is clear that political arrangements of this kind continued in practice throughout the reign of Charles the Bald.

The fragmentary evidence makes it hard to draw up a full list of the assemblies during the reign. We no longer, as in the reigns of Charlemagne and Louis the Pious, have the Royal Frankish Annals with their consistent interest in the where and when of assemblies. The Annals of St Bertin, which cover Charles's reign and are in some sense a continuation of the Royal Frankish Annals, are essen-

[55] See appendices 1 and 2. See also C.-R. Brühl, *Fodrum, Gistum, Servitium Regis* (Cologne, 1968), p. 40 with nn. 145-7, and cf. the evidence for Anglo-Saxon assemblies discussed by P. Sawyer, 'The Royal *Tun* in Pre-Conquest England', in P. Wormald ed., *Ideal and Reality. Studies in Frankish and Anglo-Saxon Society* (Oxford, 1983), pp. 277, 286-99.

[56] This was prescribed at Quiersy, 857 (appendix 1, no. 26), *MGH, Capit.* II, cc.4, 6, p. 287. For actual cases, see *Annales, s.a.* 849, p. 58. (Charles of Aquitaine); 852, p. 64 (Pippin II of Aquitaine); 866, p. 130 (William, son of Odo); 870, p. 171, and 871, p. 184 (Carloman). Probably another case is Gauzbert in 853 (Regino of Prüm, *Chronica, s.a.* 860, *MGH, SRG*, p. 78). Bernard of Septimania was condemned by judgement of the Franks, but Prudentius thinks it worth noting that he was executed in Aquitaine, not Francia: *Annales, s.a.* 844, p. 45.

[57] *ibid.*, pp. 92–3.

[58] *ibid.*, pp. 113-14. In one case, conciliation was unsuccessful: hostility between Bernard, son of Bernard, and Robert flared immediately afterwards. Perhaps there is an allusion to this episode in Hincmar's *De Ordine Palatii*, c.31, ed. T. Gross and R. Schieffer, *Fontes Iuris Germanici Antiqui* (Hanover, 1980), pp. 88-9. But the reconciliation of Egfrid proved more lasting.

[59] *Annales, s.a.* 864, p. 114; 865, p. 124; 867, p. 137; 868, p. 151; 872, pp. 185-6; 877, pp. 212-13. Cf. the role of the Merovingian court noted by I.N. Wood, 'The ecclesiastical politics of Merovingian Clermont', in Wormald ed., *Ideal and Reality*, pp. 42-6.

tially a private work.[60] Under Prudentius' authorship, up to 861, they contain only a few random mentions of assemblies: for instance, neither Coulaines, 843, nor Servais, 853, appears. Several summer assemblies are known only from a chance reference in a letter of Lupus', or from the Chronicle of St Wandrille with its curious attempt at 'official' coverage from 847–51.[61] But from 861 until the end of Charles' reign, a fairly complete list (see appendix 2) of twice-yearly assemblies can be constructed from the Annals of St Bertin – for we are now back with Hincmar (when can we ever be far from him in Charles the Bald's reign?), this time as contemporary historian, consciously reverting to the pattern of the Royal Frankish Annals.[62] Information on assemblies becomes more detailed and systematic than ever in the annals from 868–77. In 868, for instance, the king is said to have received the annual gifts at Pîtres in mid-August, and to have 'summoned certain leading men of his kingdom, both some of the bishops, and others' to meet him at Quiersy at the beginning of December. The term 'counsellors' is used increasingly frequently for the clearly small group of leading men who advises on major decisions. Under 874, Hincmar records: 'Charles held a meeting with his counsellors on the feast of the Purification of Holy Mary [2 February] at the monastery of St. Quentin . . . He held the general assembly at the manor of Douzy on 13 June and received the annual gifts.'[63]

Another piece of evidence can now be brought into the picture: Hincmar's description in the last few chapters of the *De Ordine Palatii* of how 'the healthy condition of the whole realm was

[60] Below, chapter 8, pp. 173-94. By 'private work', I mean that the annals were not written at court, had no 'official' status, and were never intended for circulation.
[61] Lupus, *Epp*. 28, 67; *Chronicle of St. Wandrille*, ed. J. Laporte, (Rouen-Paris, 1951), pp. 78–85.
[62] Below, chapter 8, p. 185. The work and the author have recently been reconsidered with characteristic insight by J. M. Wallace-Hadrill, 'History in the mind of Archbishop Hincmar', in R. H. C. Davis and J. M. Wallace-Hadrill (eds), *The Writing of History in the Middle Ages. Essays presented to R. W. Southern* (Oxford, 1981), pp. 43-70.
[63] See appendix 2 for these and other references to the *Annales*. The role of the counsellors was stressed particularly by Hincmar in his later years: see H. Löwe, 'Hinkmar von Reims und der Apocrisiar. Beiträge zur Interpretation von *De Ordine palatii*', in *Festchrift für H. Heimpel* (Göttingen, 1972), pp. 197–225, esp. 221 ff., and cf. the comments on the term *primores regni* in the *Annales*, *idem*, 'Geschichtsschreibung der ausgehenden Karolingerzeit', *DA*, XXIII (1967), p. 10 with n. 39.

maintained' by the holding of twice-yearly assemblies whose business was dealt with by means of 'lists of separately-headed chapters' (*denominata et ordinata capitula*).[64] At the general assembly, 'the whole aristocracy' (*universitas maiorum*), lay and clerical, attended, 'the more influential to frame counsel, the less important men to hear that counsel and sometimes similarly to deliberate on it, and to confirm it, not because they were forced to do so, but from their own understanding and freely-expressed opinion.'[65] Such assemblies were also the occasions for the aristocracy to hand over their gifts to the king. The other assembly was attended only by the more influential men, the leading counsellors. It was held in winter, to take stock of what would have to be done in the coming year. Its transactions were confidential: the same matters would be brought up again at the general summer assembly, where, 'as if nothing had been previously worked out concerning them, they were now subject to the new counsel and consent of the people, policies were found, and, under God's leadership, arrangements made along with the magnates, for putting good order into effect.'[66] The next chapter (c.31) details the qualities required in counsellors: loyalty, wisdom, the ability to withstand pressures of political friends and relatives, and a commitment to confidentiality. Recruitment should be by merit, from among the pool of the king's palace servants (*ministeriales palatini*). After explaining how the palace officers should conduct less important affairs, Hincmar describes in detail (c.34) how the counsellors dealt with assembly business:

[64] The new edition of T. Gross and R. Schieffer has a German translation and notes by Schieffer. The passages I refer to are in cc.29-36, pp. 82-93. See H. Anton, *Fürstenspiegel und Herrscherethos in der Karolingerzeit* (Bonn, 1968), pp. 288 ff.; Löwe, 'Apocrisiar'. The text is translated in D. Herlihy, *History of Feudalism* (New York, 1970), pp. 208-27. But I use my own translation to bring out the ambiguities of the original.

[65] *De Ordine*, c.29, pp. 84–5. 'Counsel' translates Hincmar's *consilium*, which Herlihy renders misleadingly as 'decisions', and Schieffer as 'Beschlüsse' (conclusions, decrees), though further down the same page he translates as 'Rat' (counsel, advice). (Schieffer complains, p. 83, n. 195 of Hincmar's 'schwankende Terminologie'!)

[66] *ibid.*, c.30, pp. 86–7. The implication here that legislation was promulgated only at summer assemblies, though obviously an oversimplification, holds true in general: see appendix 1.

So that it should not look as if [the counsellors] had been summoned without good reason, at the outset, both those matters which the king (through God's inspiration) had found to be in need of attention, and those which, since the counsellors' departure from the last assembly, had been brought to the king's notice from far and wide as especially important, were laid before them by the king's authority to be discussed and carefully pondered. The documents consisted of lists of chapters each with a separate heading. When the counsellors had received these chapters, they considered each sometimes for a day, sometimes for two days, or even three or more, as the gravity of the matter required. Messengers chosen from the palace servants went back and forth between them and the king supplying them with answers on whatever queries they thought had to be asked. All this time, no outsider came near them. Finally each matter on which a conclusion was reached was explained orally to the glorious prince in his presence, and whatever his divinely-bestowed wisdom might choose, all would follow. The same process was gone through once, twice or as many times as the number of chapters demanded, until, by God's mercy, all the problems that had had to be dealt with on that occasion were smoothed out.[67]

The difficulty of translating certain words and phrases in this and other passages reflects what may appear to us as the ambiguous, even contradictory, nature of Carolingian political action: who is making the decisions here, and who is taking initiatives? The king 'finds' the agenda, the counsellors 'find counsel', the people 'find what is required, by their counsel and consent'. The counsellors 'reach conclusions'; the king 'chooses'; all 'follow'. It seems to me artificial to claim that there is a special insistence here on the king's authority, to contrast this with Hincmar's 'accent on the collaboration of the counsellors' in another near-contemporary work, and to infer that c.34 of the *De Ordine Palatii* reflects conditions in the reign of Charlemagne rather than that of Charles the Bald.[68] I am not convinced, either, by the argument that c.29 describes the assem-

[67] *ibid.*, pp. 90–3.

[68] So Schieffer, p. 93, n. 219, following Löwe, 'Apocrisiar', p. 223, where the *De Ordine* is compared with the *Acta* of the Synod of St Macra-de-Fismes, *PL* CXXV, cc, 1069–86, esp. 1085. On these *Acta* as 'the end-product of the development of Hincmar's thought', see Anton, *Fürstenspiegel*, pp. 236 ff. cf. below, 'Kingship, law and liturgy', pp. 139-40, n. 5. But for the political context of Fismes, see now Schmitz, 'Hinkmar von Reims, die Synode von Fismes 881 und der Streit um das Bistum Beauvais', *DA*, XXXV (1979) pp. 463–86. For a perceptive comment on *De Ordine*, c.34, see F. Kern, *Gottesgnadentum und Widerstandsrecht* (rev. edn Darmstadt, 1954), pp. 266–7.

blies of Louis the Pious, rather than those of Charles the Bald.[69] Such claims have, of course. been lent colour by the well-known fact that some, at least, of the *De Ordine Palatii* was, as Hincmar asserted, not his own work but that of Adalard of Corbie (d.826). But it is equally clear that much of it was Hincmar's own composition.[70] I believe the chapters on assemblies and capitularies are more likely to fall into that latter category, and that Hincmar had in mind the practice of the 860s and 870s.

As far as assemblies are concerned, the twice-yearly pattern and the specific forms of attendance and deliberation, at winter and summer meetings respectively, can be seen from appendix 2 to correspond rather well with what the Annals of St Bertin record, especially for the last decade of Charles the Bald's reign. And since Hincmar, as author of these Annals, was concerned that this information should be recorded, it seems reasonable to expect a similar interest to be reflected in his reworking of, or additions to, the *De Ordine Palatii*. Equally noteworthy is the correspondence between c.34's very detailed interest in the nature and function of *capitula* in assembly business, the references to *capitula* in the Annals of St Bertin, and Hincmar's role in the composing and keeping of capitulary texts (we recall Lupus' 'canons, or as you, [Hincmar], call them, *capitula*').[71] But most significant of all is the complex way in which the action, and interaction, of assembly participants is described. I do not hear in c.34 just one 'accent' on the king's role: on the contrary, the counsellors' 'collaboration' sounds an equally strong note, while the 'understanding' of the people provides a ground-bass with which king and counsellors harmonize. Lines of communication, and of influence, run between all these participants. Initiatives might come from one or several different points. There is no doubting the king's central role: the assemblies physically centred, after all, on the king's palace. But the king operated through a generalized 'authority' and a series of informal pressures

[69] Löwe, 'Apocrisiar', pp. 221–2. J. T. Rosenthal, 'The public assembly in the time of Louis the Pious', *Traditio* XX (1964), pp. 25–40, is a useful discussion, but his distinction between military and other assemblies seems to me artificial.

[70] Admirably demonstrated by Löwe, 'Apocrisiar', with reference to recent literature.

[71] Above, p. 93. cf. also Charles the Bald's order to Hincmar (appendix 1, no. 58) to prepare his dossier of canonical and Carolingian legislation on usury *capitulatim*. Was the king teasing Hincmar for this penchant? I think Schmitz, 'Wucher in Laon', p. 543, is right to detect 'a malicious undertone' in Charles' telling Hincmar that where canons and capitularies are concerned, 'you know better'.

on individuals. 'Counsel' engaged a select group of magnates, then a wider range of greater and lesser nobles, in collective deliberation:[72] hence, whatever the origin of a given item on the agenda, each participant could feel himself involved in decision-making. This is not to suggest that the system was 'democratic': rather, that assemblies were natural forums for the exertion of magnate influence and of the demands of the 'less important' for protection and support;[73] for the interplay of interest between patrons and clients, and of competition between patrons and between clients; and, last but not least, for royal contact with and influence on individuals and groups among both greater and lesser aristocracy. The formation of 'opinion' was the product of these complex and multiplex interactions of people in a locale where the king's peace prevailed: in a society where so many transactions directly involved coercion, meetings of the assembly seem to have stood out in Hincmar's mind as occasions when men, even *minores*, did not act 'because they were forced to do so'. The picture may have been idealized, but it did, I think, accurately represent a contemporary reality: assembly politics were consensus politics, and that consensus – achieved through political processes of persuasion and brokerage, of authority as well as power, of what Balandier has called, in another context, 'the dialectic of contestation and conformity'[74] – is what is represented, quite literally, in the

[72] Clearly evidenced in the surviving form of the Capitulary of Quiersy (877) (appendix 1, no. 56): 'Haec capitula constituta sunt a domno Karolo . . . cum consensu fidelium . . . de quibus ipse definivit et de quibusdam a suis fidelibus responderi iussit.' These responses have been preserved along with the *capitula*: as the *MGH* editors observe, p. 355, the capitulary can hardly have been promulgated in this form. The exchange recorded in c.4, pp. 356–7, seems especially revealing of the direct style of assembly proceedings: *Charles* 'How can we be sure that when we get back (from Italy) our kingdom will not have been disturbed by anyone?' *Fideles* 'As far as that is concerned . . . our answer is that there are the oaths we made to you, and the profession that all of us, clerics and laymen, gave to you at Quiersy . . . we have kept these up till now, and we intend to go on keeping them. So you certainly can believe us [Unde pro certo nos veraciter credere potestis].' In this same c.4, when Charles asks how he can feel confident about his son (Louis the Stammerer), he is told: 'None of us can or should do more than you can to keep him safe . . . so it is up to you to make the right arrangements.' There seems no reason to see anything new in these frank and familiar dealings. On assembly proceedings and the formulation of capitularies through discussion, see Ganshof, *Recherches*, pp. 22–9, and for the political background to Quiersy, Werner, 'Gauzlin', pp. 410 ff.

[73] A nice example: Tessier, *Receuil*, no. 228, cf. n. 39 above.

[74] G. Ballandier, *Political Anthropology* (London, 1972), p. 66.

terminology of 'consent', 'consultation', 'counsel and aid' in the capitularies of Charles the Bald. It was not just that changes in the procedures and penalties of Frankish law required the formal expression of the people's consent as well as royal promulgation.[75] An apparently classic statement of this principle does indeed occur in the 864 capitulary: 'law comes into being by the consent of the people and by the establishment of the king.'[76] (Less often remarked is the context – a change in the procedures for delivering summonses – and the mention of consensus in five other procedural contexts elsewhere in the same capitulary.)[77] But more significant, and to the capitulary's redactor(s) evidently quite compatible with this technical application of consent to legal change, is the invocation of the 'consent of the faithful men' in the prologue of the 864 text, and in several other capitularies of this period, with reference to political decision-making in general. It is important to stress that there was nothing new in such usage: a number of examples can be found in the capitularies of Charlemagne and Louis the Pious.[78] Therefore if it appears – and no more frequently – in Charles the Bald's capitularies, it need not, surely, be understood in terms of a 'shift of legislative initiative from the kingship to the aristocracy':[79] rather, in the context I have described, it at once expresses and appeals to a sense of 'common utility'[80] on the part of all, or most,

[75] For important qualifications to previous hypotheses about the distinction between *Volksrecht* and *Königsrecht*, see E. Kaufman, *Aequitatis Iudicium. Königsrecht und Billigkeit in der Rechtsordnung des frühen Mittelalters* (Frankfurt, 1959), pp. 60–92; also Ganshof, *Recherches*, pp. 30 ff.; Wormald, '*Lex Scripta*', pp. 109–10.

[76] c.6, *MGH, Capit.* II, p. 313.

[77] cc.15, p. 316 (differentials in punishments for refusing coin), 25, p. 321 (capital penalty for those selling to Vikings), 33, p. 325 (standardizing calculation of lifting of bann for returning warriors), 34, p. 326 (rules about redemption or release of slaves), 34, p. 327 (penalty for selling Christians into slavery).

[78] The texts are assembled and ably discussed by Hägermann, 'Entstehung', pp. 19–22.

[79] So Hägermann, 'Enstehung', p. 27. There are certainly more references to *consensus*, in this general sense, in Louis the Pious's capitularies than in Charles the Bald's. Kern, *Gottesgnadentum*, pp. 142–3 with n. 305, rightly stresses that the meaning of 'consensus' varies with political circumstances.

[80] This phrase, which occurs in *De Ordine*, c.31, had appeared in Charlemagne's capitularies: *MGH, Capit.* I, pp. 162, 208. In such contexts, 'usefulness' assumed a genuinely political, and not only moral, content in the later eighth and ninth centuries: see E. Peters, *The Shadow King* (Yale, 1970), pp. 47–72. cf. such terms as *utilitas populi, utilitas publica*. Of course these expressions, like the concept of the state (*res publica*), derive from Roman law and political theory, but they were resurrected in the ninth century, I think, less because of their potential for hierocratic theorists, than precisely because they reflected contemporary political realities as perceived by lay as well as ecclesiastical participants. This point scarcely

members of a political community which really did remain a going concern throughout Charles the Bald's reign.

In c.35 of the *De Ordine Palatii*, Hincmar gives a vignette of the king's role during the general assembly. Interestingly, it is at this point that we are told that 'if the weather was set fair, the assembly would be held outdoors . . .' If requested, the king would join the counsellors in their closed session, and in an atmosphere of good-fellowship (*familiaritas*) would listen to their debates. Otherwise,

> he would be occupied with the rest of the assembled people, receiving gifts, greeting important men, swapping stories with people he didn't see often, expressing sympathy with the old, sharing their pleasures with the young, and so forth, involving himself in spiritual as well as secular affairs.[81]

This could, of course, be any Carolingian king about his business: perhaps it is an idealized Charlemagne, or even a composite royal image. But Hincmar could also be drawing on his memories of Charles the Bald's assemblies, and of Charles' speeches on those occasions. For instance, in his *adnuntiatio* at Pîtres in 864, Charles thanked his faithful men for their attendance 'fully and in peace', adding wryly: 'even if not all of you, as we wanted, have been keeping the peace since our last assembly, still most of you have'.[82]

---

emerges from the otherwise admirable discussion of L. Wehlen, *Geschichtsschreibung und Staatsauffassung im Zeitalter Ludwigs des Frommen* (Lübeck-Hamburg, 1970), pp. 8–11; 91–104.

[81] Hincmar, *De Ordine*, c.35, pp. 92–3. The meaning of *familiaritas* has to be inferred not only from this passage but from its two other appearances in the *De Ordine*, cc.27 and 32, pp. 80, 88. (cf. also *familiarius* in c.18, p. 66, and *familiariter* in c.31, p. 86.) In the *De Ordine*, Hincmar consistently uses 'familiarity' in something like its colloquial sense in modern English, i.e. 'intimate acquaintanceship'. This sense of the word is not taken account of in J.-F. Niermeyer, *Mediae Latinitatis Lexicon Minus* (Leiden, 1976), *s.v.* 'familiaris', 'familiaritas'.

[82] *MGH, Capit.* II, p. 311. For another possible instance of Charles' irony, see above, n. 71. cf. Hincmar's letter to Charles, *PL* CCXXVI, c.97, where Devisse, *Hincmar*, II, p. 727, n. 6, sees a veiled allusion to a royal taunt: 'some people', says Hincmar, 'accuse us bishops of wanting to spend all day parabling through written communications' (*per scripturas parabolare* – the pun is lost in translation). The best example of Charles' black humour is his treatment of Archbishop George of Ravenna after the battle of Fontenoy, recorded, I think from eye-witness sources (perhaps George himself), by Agnellus, *Liber Pontificalis Ecclesiae Ravennatis*, c.174, *MGH, SRL*, p. 390. For the young Charles' close and informal relationship with his faithful men, see Nithard, *Histoire des fils de Louis le Pieux* II.4, ed. P. Lauer (Paris, 1926), p. 46. There is no real evidence that Charles' political style changed in later life, despite the hostile remarks about his 'Greek' imperial costume in the Annals of Fulda, *s.a.* 876, *MGH, SRG*, p. 86.

In context, Charles' repeated assurances that he will 'preserve to each man his law and justice'[83] should be interpreted not as symptoms of weakness (of monarchy 'descended from its throne' in Halphen's sense),[84] nor as statements of new constitutional principle (of 'the birth of contractual monarchy' in Magnou-Nortier's sense),[85] but as affirmations of a thoroughly traditional ideal relationship of mutual trust and collaboration between king and aristocracy: the 'familiar face' (in both senses) of Frankish politics. This image, this ideology, has been preserved for us – thanks, not least, to Hincmar's efforts – in the capitularies of Charles the Bald. It was in his reign, and probably at Rheims, that a scribe headed Ansegis' collection: 'capitula episcoporum, regum et maxime omnium nobilium francorum'.[86] For each of the noble Franks, his 'law' in the subjective sense[87] was his status, his social standing, his fair treatment according to 'the law(s)' in the objective sense of customary norms and procedures including the judgement of his peers. Hence Charles the Bald's care in having political enemies condemned 'by the judgement of the Franks'. Hence the evident requirement that any change in those customary procedures as practised in public courts should be made, should 'come into being', 'with the consent of the Franks', as well as 'by the establishment of the king'. Capitularies, duly consented to and established, themselves became laws, part of that law (in the general sense), composed of both statute and codified 'gentile' custom, which was the collective possession of the king's faithful men.[88] The law of all constituted the framework that guaranteed and preserved the law of each. Bishops, and still more kings with authority, had a crucial function in law-making that maintained 'the stability of the king-

[83] For such promises at Coulaines (843), Quiersy (858) and several other occasions through the reign, see Nelson, 'Kingship, law and liturgy', below, pp. 147 ff.

[84] In Lot and Halphen, *Règne*, p. 96.

[85] *Foi et fidelité*, pp. 98 ff.

[86] Beinecke 413, fol. 2b. For other MSS with this *incipit*, see *MGH, Capit*. I, p. 394, n.(a).

[87] For the sense of 'lex unicuique competens', see above, n. 83. cf. the closely related meaning of 'iustitia' in, for instance, the capitularies of Servais, c.2, *MGH, Capit*, II, p. 271, and Quiersy (858), *ibid*., p. 296.

[88] For examples of these various meanings of law (*lex, leges*), see the Edict of Pîtres, c.2, *MGH, Capit*. II, p. 312 (divine and human law in general); c.3, p. 312 (the due law of each); c.6, p. 313 (customary procedures of Frankish law); c.33, p. 325 (law-makers: *conditores legum*).

dom';[89] but it was not surprising if for one well-informed contemporary – perhaps Hincmar himself? – the capitularies belonged in a special way – *maxime* – to 'all the noble Franks'.

[89] *Stabilitas regni*, a traditional phrase in Merovingian and Carolingian charters, gained a new lease of life in ninth-century capitularies.

APPENDIX 1

Capitularies of Charles the Bald

No.	*Date*	MGH *no.*	MGH *title*	*MS transmission* Hague 10 D 2	Vat. reg 291/ Vat. 4982	Beinecke 413
1	Oct 843	[293]	Capitula in synodo acta quae habita est apud Lauriacum	x		
2	Nov 843	254	Conventus in villa Colonia	x		
3	Jun 844	255	Capitulare Septimanicum apud Tolosam datum	x		
4	Jun 844	256	Praeceptum pro Hispanis			
5	Oct 844	227 [293]	Synodus ad Theodonis villam habita	x		
6	Dec 844	291	Concilium Vernense	x		
7	Apr 845	292	Synodus Bellovacensis	x		
8	Jun 845 }	293	Concilium Meldense-Parisiense	x (in part)		
9	Feb 846 }					
10	Jun 846	257	Notitia de conciliarum canonibus in villa Sparnaco a Karolo rege confirmatis	x	x	
11	Feb 847	204	Conventus apud Marsnam primus	x	x	
12	summer 851	205	Conventus apud Marsnam secundus	x	x	
13	Apr 853	258	Conventus Suessionensis	x		
14	Apr 853	259	Capitulare missorum Suessionense	x	x	x
15	Aug 853	294	Synodus Vermeriensis	x		
16	Nov 853	206	Conventus apud Valentianas	x	x	
17	Nov 853	260	Capitulare missorum Silvacense	x	x	x

18	Feb 854	207	Conventus apud Leodii habitus	x (in part)	x	
19	Jun 854	261	Capitulare missorum Attiniacense	x	x	
20	Jul 856	262	Capitula ad Francos et Aquitanos missa de Carisiaco	x	x	
21	Aug 856	295	Concilium optimatum Karolo II datum	x	x	
22	Oct 856	296	Coronatio Iudithae Karoli II filiae			
23	Jul/Sept 856	263	Primum missaticum ad Francos et Aquitanos directum		x	
24	Sept 856	264	Secundum missaticum ad Francos et Aquitanos		x	
25	Sept/Oct 856	265	Tertium missaticum ad Francos et Aquitanos		x	
26	Feb 857	266	Capitulare Carisiacense		x	x
27	post-Feb 857	267	Allocutio missi cuiusdam Divionensis			
28	Mar 857	268	Conventus apud Sanctum Quintinum		x	
29	Mar 858	269	Sacramenta Carisiaci praestita		x	
30	Nov 858	297	Epistola synodi Carisiacensis ad Hludowicum regem Germaniae directa		x	
31	May/June 859	298	Synodus Mettensis		x	
32	Jun 859	299	Synodus apud Saponarias habita		x	
33	Jun 859	300	Libellus proclamationis adversus Wenilonem			
34	Jun 860	242	Conventus apud Confluentes		x	
35	post-Jun 860	270	Capitula post conventum Confluentinum missis tradita		x	
36	Jun 861	271	Constitutio Carisiacensis de moneta		x	
37	Jun 862	272	Capitula Pistensia		x (in part)	x
38	Nov 862	243	Conventus apud Saponarias		x	

No.	*Date*	MGH *no.*	MGH *title*	*MS transmission* *Hague 10 D 2*	*Vat. reg 291/ Vat. 4982*	*Beinecke 413*
39	Jun 864	273	Edictum Pistense		x	x
40	Feb 865	244	Pactum Tusiacense		x	
41	Feb 865	274	Capitulare Tusiacense in Burgundiam directum		x	
42	Aug 866	301	Coronatio Hermintrudis reginae			
43	867 or 868	245	Pactiones Mettenses			
44	Jul 869	275	Capitula Pistensia		x	
45	Sept 869	276	Electionis Karoli capitula in regno Hlotharii factae		x	
46	Sept 869	302	Ordo coronationis Karoli			
47	Mar 870	250	Pactiones Aquenses		x	
48	Aug 870	251	Divisio regni Hlotharii II		x	
49	Sep 872	277	Sacramenta apud Gundulfi-villam facta		x	
50	Jan 873	278	Capitulare Carisiacense		x	x
51	Jun/Jul 874	303	Synodus Attiniacensis			
52	Feb 876	220	Karoli II imperatoris electio		x	
55	Feb 876	221	Karoli II capitulare Papiense		x	
54	Jun/Jul 876	279	Synodus Pontigonensis		x	
55	May 877	280	Edictum Compendiense de tributo Nordmannico			
56	Jun 877	281	Capitulare Carisiacense			
57	Jun 877	282	Capitula excerpta in conventu Carisiacensi coram populo lecta			
58	853–75 (?868)		Mandate to Archbishop Hincmar			

APPENDIX 2

Assemblies of Charles the Bald, 860–77

	Date and place	*Capitulary(ies) issued (see appendix 1)*	*Annals of St Bertin ref. (see n. 14 for Grat edn)*	*Charters issued (see n. 12 for Tessier edn)*
860	Jun: Coblenz	34, 35	83	
	?Nov: Ponthion			221, 222
861	Jul: Quiersy	36		229, 230
862	?Jan: Senlis		88: regni primores consulens.	237
862	Jun: Pîtres	37	91: omnes primores . . . convenire fecit.	
	Nov: Savonnières	38	94	
863	? : Soissons		98	
	?Nov: Auxerre		104: consilio fidelium suorum.	261
864	Jun: Pîtres	39	113–4: generale placitum habet in quo annua dona . . . recipit.	269
865	Feb: Douzy	40, 41	116: cum fidelibus consideratis . . .	
865	?Jul: Attigny		118	
	?Dec: Rouy		124	
866	?Jun: Pîtres		127: hostiliter ad locum . . . pergit.	
867	(Aug: Chartres)		136: placitum suum . . . condixit.	
	Aug: Compiègne		137: populus . . . hostiliter veniat.	
868	Aug: Pîtres		150–1: anna dona . . . accepit . . . placitum.	
	Dec: Quiersy		151: quosdam primores . . . sibi accersivit.	
869	Jul: Pîtres	44	153: placitum.	326
	Nov: Gondreville		167: denuntians se . . . venturum . . . ut . . . ad se venturos suscipiat.	330

	Date and place	Capitulary(ies) issued (see appendix 1)	Annals of St Bertin ref. (see n. 14 for Grat edn)	Charters issued (see n. 12 for Tessier edn)
870	Jul: Meersen	48	171–5: colloquium.	
	Nov: Rheims		177: plurimos fidelium . . . convenire faciens.	
871	Aug: Douzy		181–2: synodum.	349
	Dec: Senlis		184: placitum cum suis consiliariis habuit.	
872	?Jun: Senlis		185	
	Sept: Gondreville	49	188: placitum.	365
873	Jan:Quiersy	50	189: cum consilio fidelium suorum . . . leges . . . promulgavit.	
	? ? (Neustria)		192: hostem denuntiat versus Brittaniam.	
874	Feb: St Quentin		195–6: cum suis consiliariis placitum . . . tenuit.	369, 370, 371, 372
	Jun: Douzy		196: generale . . . placitum . . . tenuit, ubi et annua dona sua accepit.	
	?Dec: Herstal		197: placitum . . . conlocutio.	
875	Aug: Ponthion		198: quoscumque potuit de vicinis suis consiliariis obviam sibi venire praecepit . . . et suppetias in itinere suo accepit.	402, 403
876	Jan: Pavia	52, 53	200: placitum suum.	
	Jun: Ponthion	54	201–16: synodum . . . indixit.	409, 410, 411
	Nov: Samoussy		210: placitum suum . . . condixit.	
877	Jun: Quiersy	55, 56, 57	212–14: placitum suum generale habuit, ubi per capitula . . . ordinavit . . .	428

6

THE CHURCH'S MILITARY SERVICE IN THE NINTH CENTURY: A CONTEMPORARY COMPARATIVE VIEW?

COMPARISONS are odorous'. Modern historians, far from sharing Dogberry's repugnance, have found the scent of the comparative method irresistible. 'Perhaps even the future of our discipline' depended on its pursuit, wrote Marc Bloch in 1928.[1] Since then, comparison has become fashionable enough, and hardly remarkable in our contemporaries' work. Remarkable it certainly is, however, in the ninth century. I would like to begin by quoting a passage written in 857 or 858 by Archbishop Hincmar of Rheims:

> In the regions [of the English] the bishoprics and monasteries are not so endowed with ecclesiastical property as they are in these Gallic regions; and for this reason, military services are not rendered from the bishoprics of those [English] regions, but [instead] the costs of rewarding those who fight (*stipendia militiae*) are allocated from public resources (*ex roga publica*). Here, on the other hand, in our regions, our clergy, instead of being given a fourth part of the bishopric's income from renders and offerings, have an appropriate share (*pars congrua*) assigned them; then another share is assigned for lighting of churches, and another share goes to the hospices for the poor; but then a share goes to the fighting-men who are listed under the name of 'housed ones' (*casati*); and finally a share goes to the bishop and those who are under his direct command. Thus, at the dictate of necessity and the urging of reason, the rulers of provinces and churches have established

[1] 'A contribution towards a comparative history of European societies', in *Land and Work in Medieval Europe* (London 1967) pp 44–81. This paper originally appeared in the *Revue de Synthèse Historique* in 1928.

> customary arrangements appropriate to the respective qualities of provinces and quantities of church property.[2]

This passage, with its explicit cross-Channel comparison and modern-sounding relativist note, has received little comment from modern historians—partly, perhaps, because it occurs in one of the less well-known of Hincmar's works.[3] In fact that work, the *De Ecclesiis et Capellis*, is one of Hincmar's most interesting. As for the passage I have just quoted, I believe it is worth some attention in the context of the theme of 'the Church and war'.

I want to ask three questions of this ninth-century comparison. the first is: how far can we believe what Hincmar has to say of 'the regions of the English'? Hincmar alleges that warriors in ninth-century England were 'paid' at 'public expense'; that English bishoprics and monasteries did not owe any specific military service; and that the reason for this was the 'English' Church's relatively poor endowment with landed wealth. On the face of it, the first point hardly fits with recent accounts of Anglo-Saxon military institutions: that is, of a recruitment system in which service was owed by the 'whole people' and calculated on the basis

[2] *De Ecclesiis et Capellis*, ed W. Gundlach in *Zeitschrift für Kirchengeschichte* 10 (1889) pp 92–145 at p 135. (I cite this hereafter as *dEC*.) A new edition is being prepared by the MGH. Hincmar's covering letter sending the work to Charles the Bald is printed in *MGH* Epp 8 pp 52–5. The division of episcopal revenues into four (?equal) parts (for bishop, clergy, the poor, and church buildings) was laid down by Gelasius I: *Decretum Gelasii* in the Dionysio-Hadriana, Decreta Gelasii c 27, in *PL* 67, col 310. On the application of these arrangements in Gaul, see M. Rouche, 'La matricule des pauvres, évolution d'une institution de charité du Bas-Empire jusqu'à la fin du Haut Moyen Age', in M. Mollat ed, *Etudes sur l'Histoire de la Pauvreté.* 2 vols (Paris 1974) pp 83-110, esp 86-7, also J. Devisse, '"Pauperes" et "paupertas" dans le monde carolingien: ce qu'en dit Hincmar de Reims', in *Revue du Nord* 48 (1966) pp 273–87, esp 277 with n 15. Hincmar contrasts the Gelasian four-way division with the contemporary practice of a five-way division 'in these Gallic regions'.

[3] Until Gundlach's edition from Leyden Universitätsbibliothek MS 141, the work was known of only from Flodoard's mention, *Historia Remensis ecclesiae* III, 18 in *MGH SS* 13 p 508. It is therefore not printed with the bulk of Hincmar's works in *PL* 125 and 126. The work's interest was appreciated by P. Imbart de la Tour, *Les origines religieuses de la France: les paroisses rurales du IXe au XIe siècle* (Paris 1900), and by [E.] Lesne, *Histoire* [*de la propriété ecclésiastique en France*, 6 vols (Lille 1905–43)] 2 part ii (1926) who discussed part of the passage quoted above at pp 272–3 without, however, distinguishing between land and income from land. That Hincmar had both in mind is clear from his re-examination of the subject ten years later in the *Pro Ecclesiae Libertatum Defensione*, *PL* 125, cols 1050–1. See also the fine commentary on the *dEC* in [J.] Devisse, *Hincmar* [*Archevêque de Reims, 845–882*, 3 vols (Geneva 1975-6) 2 pp 829-45, noting the interest of the comparative passage (pp 839–40) but without any discussion of its relevance to the military service of the ninth-century church.

of one warrior for so many hides of inherited land.[4] In such a system the question of payment by the state did not arise: men came to the muster bringing their own provisions and, like the West Saxon levies of 893, 'having completed their period of service and come to the end of their food-supplies',[5] they expected to go home. Further, it is clear that church lands too were assessed for such contributions of warriors in the ninth century.[6] Hincmar then seems not to have been talking about the *fyrd*. Perhaps he had in mind the specialist warriors of the king's and ealdormen's retinues—men who certainly did expect a 'stipend', in the short run money and in the longer term land.[7] Asser in his *Life* of Alfred is explicit about the king's generosity with money to his fighting-men.[8] True, he mentions royal gifts of estates only in the context of Alfred's rewarding of his ecclesiastical helpers (including Asser himself),[9] but Alfred surely gave some lands to his *faselli*, and presumably his father King Æthelwulf had done so too.[10] Hincmar may be thought to imply that he believed that in England all such grants were made from the fisc and that the English kings who were his contemporaries did not try to exploit church lands or

[4] See [N.] Brooks, ['The] development [of military obligations in eighth- and ninth-century England', in P. Clemoes and K. Hughes edd, *England before the Conquest: Studies . . . presented to Dorothy Whitelock* (Cambridge 1971)] pp 69–84: a fine study that does justice to previous scholarship on this subject. Equally indispensable is E. John, *Orbis Britanniae* (Leicester 1966) pp 128–53, esp 139–42, placing military organisation firmly in social context.

[5] *Anglo-Saxon Chronicle* edd J. Earle and C. Plummer, *Two of the Saxon Chronicles Parallel* (Oxford 1892) s.a. 894 for 893 pp 85–6.

[6] Brooks, 'Development' p 70 and *passim*.

[7] See John, *Orbis Britanniae* pp 118–22. There is no direct evidence before the late tenth century, however, that the *fyrd* was organised on the lines of ealdormanic followings writ large.

[8] Asser, *Life* [*of King Alfred* ed W. Stevenson (Oxford 1904 repr 1959)] c 100, p 88.

[9] Asser, *Life* cc 77, 81, pp 62, 67–8. The monasteries given to Asser by Alfred were evidently royal proprietary churches.

[10] Asser, *Life* cc 53, 55, pp 41, 44, mentions Alfred's *fasselli*. In c 76, p 60, listing the many peoples (including *pagani* – Danes!) from whom Alfred's following was recruited, Asser says the king 'endowed them all with money and estates'. (For the likely meaning of *potestas* here: 'power over lands', see D. Whitelock, *EHD* vol 1 (2nd edn London 1979) p 293, n 1.) Alfred's few surviving charters include two that perhaps represent grants to members of his following: *CS* 2 nos 581, 568. (For their likely genuineness see D. Whitelock, 'Some charters in the name of King Alfred', in [M.H.] King and [W.M.] Stevens edd *Saints, Scholars and Heroes,* [*Studies in Honor of C.W. Jones* (Collegeville Minnesota 1978)] pp 77–98.) The argument of H.P.R. Finberg, *West Country Historical Studies* (Newton Abbot 1969) pp 11–28 (even allowing for the reservations noted by Whitelock, *EHD* p 522) suggests that some of the lands which Æthelwulf booked to himself in *CS* no 451 may have been intended for distribution to his following.

revenues, on the Carolingian model, to reward members of their *militia terrestris*. But given the pressing need of these kings, with Viking attacks increasingly serious from c850 onwards, to secure the service of their aristocracy, and given also the degree of control they exercised over the disposition of bishoprics and at least some rich minsters, it is difficult to believe that they never used episcopal or minster lands to make the equivalent of precarial grants. Mercian and Northumbrian kings had almost certainly done so a generation and more earlier.[11] It looks as if Egbert of Wessex did so too in the 820s and 830s.[12] I know of no evidence on the point from Æthelwulf's reign; but from Alfred's there is a hint in a letter of Pope John VIII to the archbishop of Canterbury that 'the king and others' have been 'wronging the house of the Lord' in a way the archbishop is urged to 'resist strenuously, making your service honourable'.[13] Vikings were not the only beneficiaries of Canterbury's material losses in the ninth century.

Hincmar says that military services were not rendered from English bishoprics as such. But was it just a coincidence that in 825, King Egbert 'sent Bishop Ealhstan and Ealdorman Wulfheard to Kent with a great force and they drove King Baldred over the Thames'; or that in 848 'Ealdorman Eanwulf with the men of Somerset and Bishop Ealhstan . . . fought against a Danish host . . . and made great slaughter . . . and won the victory'; or that in 871 Ealhstan's successor Heahmund was slain at the battle of Meretun?[14] As for the landed resources of the English church, charter evidence shows, *pace* Hincmar, that bishoprics and a very large number of minsters had been generously endowed with ecclesiastical property before the mid-ninth century.[15]

But if I hesitate to accept Hincmar's statements about ninth-century practice in England, that is not only because it jars with

[11] The evidence is ably discussed by P. Wormald in 'Bede, the *Bretwaldas* and the Origins of the *Gens Anglorum*', in Wormald ed., *Ideal and Reality* (Oxford, 1983).

[12] This is implied in *CS* no 421. For very interesting comments on the political context of this charter, see Wormald in J. Campbell ed *The Anglo-Saxons* (London 1982) p 140.

[13] I quote from Whitelock's translation of this letter in *EHD* p 882.

[14] *Anglo-Saxon Chronicle* s.a. 823 for 825, 845 for 848, 871, pp 60, 64, 72.

[15] For example, for the Canterbury evidence, see Brooks, *The Early History of the Church of Canterbury* (Leicester, 1984); for Winchester, see Finberg, *The Early Charters of Wessex* (Leicester 1964) pp 218–20; for Worcester, see Wormald in Campbell ed, *The Anglo-Saxons* pp 122–3 and the map *ibid* p 71 showing the large number of minster endowments up to c850.

what Anglo-Saxon evidence we have: it is also because, despite appearances to the contrary, Hincmar himself cannot be read as a contemporary witness here. What we might assume, given the intensification of contacts between Wessex and Francia precisely in the 850s,[16] to be hard data gained from a well-placed West Saxon informant, in fact comes from an authoritative text written over two and a half centuries before: Hincmar's source, as might have been guessed from the reference to the regions of 'the English', where a ninth-century insular informant would probably have distinguished between Mercians and West Saxons, is Gregory the Great's letter to Augustine, the famous 'Responses' recorded by Bede in the *Ecclesiastical History*.[17] Note that Hincmar cites what is to be 'found' there in the present tense: the churches '*are* not so endowed . . .'. The answer to my first question then is that the credibility of Hincmar's 'ninth-century' data for England must be rated low: which does not, however, make his comparison valueless from a historical standpoint, as we shall see in a moment.

The second question which I think worth asking is whether Hincmar in this passage throws any special light on the military service of the Frankish Church. For in this Hincmar was himself deeply implicated. True, we know a good deal about this from other sources.[18] On some aspects, capitularies are perfectly frank. Here is an example from Charlemagne's reign:

[16] See P. Stafford, 'Charles the Bald, Judith and England', in M. Gibson and J. Nelson edd, *Charles the Bald:* [*Court and Kingdom*, B.A.R. International Series 101 (Oxford 1981)] pp 137–51. Hincmar was closely involved personally in these contacts: he performed Judith's consecration in 856 for which he remodelled an English *ordo* (see Nelson, 'The earliest surviving royal *Ordo*', in B. Tierney and P. Linehan edd, *Authority and Power: Studies presented to Walter Ullmann*; below, ch. 15, pp 341-60)and he had a hand in the Capitulary of 864 in which Charles the Bald's imposition of a new obligation to build fortifications was almost certainly influenced by recent West Saxon developments (see Brooks, 'Development' p 81; and for the capitulary see 'Legislation and consensus in the reign of Charles the Bald', above, chapter 5, pp 98-9.

[17] *Historia Ecclesiastica Gentis Anglorum* ed Plummer (Oxford 1896 repr 1975) 1, 27, p 48. The best discussion of this letter in its historical context is H. Mayr-Harting, *The Coming of Christianity to Anglo-Saxon England* (London 1972) pp 60–4, 269–71. Gregory's position and missionary concerns gave him in some ways a genuinely relativist outlook. Whether Hincmar cited Gregory's letter from Bede is uncertain: Devisse, *Hincmar* 2 p 822, n 696 shows there is no evidence for Hincmar's having a text of the *Ecclesiastical History* before the 870s. Hincmar could have cited from Pseudo-Isidore though again his use of this is late, and sparing, or from the Register of Gregory's letters (Devisse, *Hincmar* 3 p 1434, n 2): though Hincmar's own references to a *Regestum* are only from 870 onwards (*ibid*, p 1495, n 4), this seems his likeliest source in this passage in the *dEC* where he also refers to two other letters of Gregory.

[18] Lesne, *Histoire*, 2(ii) pp 456 *seq* remains indispensable. See also [F.] Prinz, *Klerus und Krieg*

> No bishop or abbot or abbess...is to presume to give or sell a mail-shirt or a sword to an outsider (*extraneus*) without our permission, but only to their own vassals. If it should happen that a rector has in a church or holy place more mail-shirts than there are fighting-men of that church, he is to ask the king what should be done with them.[19]

Each rector then was responsible for the service owed by his—or her—own church: for equipping, and in the case of a bishop or an abbot personally leading, that church's warriors on campaign. This obligation was as far as I know never questioned by any Carolingian churchman: so firm was the *Einstaatung* of the Frankish Church.[20] The reforming Council of Ver in 844, for instance, was concerned that 'military affairs should suffer no disadvantage from the absence of bishops' who might be prevented by physical weakness or excused by royal indulgence from personal service with the army. The solution offered was that the bishops should place 'their men coming forward for the state (*res publica*)' under the command of a layman whom they considered suitably 'useful'.[21] We can guess both from ninth-century casualty-lists and from such private sources as letters that ecclesiastical contingents formed a very important component in Carolingian armies.[22] Charles the Bald's main complaint against Archbishop Wenilo of Sens in 859 was that he had not only failed to deliver to his king his due 'solace' (the euphemism is an old one but it is interesting to

[*im früheren Mittelalter* (Stuttgart 1971)] and *idem*, 'King, clergy and war at the time of the Carolingians', in King and Stevens edd, *Saints, Scholars and Heroes*, pp 301–329, though both the book and the article are patchy in their treatment of the ninth century.

19 *MGH* Capit 1, no 74, c 10, p 167. The obligation of abbesses is rightly insisted on for the tenth century by L. Auer, 'Der Kriegsdienst des Klerus [unter den sächsischen Kaisern', in] *MIOG* 79 (1971) pp 316–407; 80 (1972) pp 48–70 at 63–4.

20 The term is Prinz's, *Klerus und Krieg* pp 65, 91. See also Nelson, above, chapter 4, pp 75-90.

21 *MGH* Capit 2, no 291, c 8, p 385. In the same year, the Council of Thionville, *ibid* no 227, c 3, p 114, complained about lay-abbots, but acknowledged that monasteries served not only '*divina religio*' but also '*utilitas rei publicae*'.

22 See e.g. *Annales Regni Francorum*, ed F. Kurze *MGH SSRG* (Hannover 1895) s.a. 753, p 11; *Annales Laureshamenses*, s.a.791, *MGH SS* 1 pp 34–5; *Annals of St Bertin*, ed F. Grat et al (Paris 1964) s.a. 833, 834, 844, 876 pp 9 (with note g.), 13, 46–7, 209; Archbishop Hetti of Trier to Bishop Frothar of Toul, *MGH Epp* 5 pp 277–8; Lupus [of Ferrieres,] *Correspondance.* [ed L. Levillain, 2 vols (Paris 1927-35)] 1. Epp 15, 17, 34, 35, 45, and 2. Epp 72, 83; Hincmar, *MGH Epp* 8 p 206, and a vivid passage in *dEC,* p 132, on the need for an efficient commissariat.

find it recurring in this Hincmarian text),[23] but had offered it instead to Charles' enemy. Charles was able to recover his position thanks not least to the loyalty of bishops whose 'solaces' evidently were forthcoming.[24] In 865 Charles issued particularly explicit orders about the service he demanded from the church in the Burgundian part of his realm:

> If men unfaithful to us join in rebellion, all our faithful men in each missaticum, bishops and abbots and counts and the abbesses' men, and the counts and our vassals and the other faithful men, are all to make arrangements to assemble. Our missi . . . are to be responsible for ensuring that each bishop, abbot and abbess should send his or her men there on time with the whole quota required, each contingent along with its banner-man (*guntfanonarius*) who, together with our missi, is responsible for his comrades.[25].

Nor was West Francia exceptional: in every Carolingian kingdom, the *militia ecclesiae* was vital to the king's successful prosecution of war—service regularly demanded and apparently for the most part assiduously performed.[26]

How did the system actually work? It is often argued that its basis was the precarial grant, which allowed royal vassals to be installed on church lands for what was effectively a rent (ninths and tenths).[27] But it looks as if such men, militarily important as they certainly were, remained in practice the king's men,[28] and

23 *MGH* Capit 2, no 300, cc 6–7, 14 pp 452–3. The euphemism appears already in the reign of Childebert II: *MGH* Capit 1, no 7, p 16.

24 See above, chapter 4, pp. 87-8.

25 *MGH* Capit 2, no 274, c 13, p 331. The mention of banners in relation to *ecclesiastical* contingents is noteworthy (and overlooked by C. Erdmann, *Die Entstehung des Kreuzzugsgedankens* (Stuttgart 1935) in his important chapter on holy banners). This seems to be the earliest recorded instance of the word *guntfanonarius*.

26 East Francia: e.g. *Annals of Fulda*, ed Kurze, *MGH SSRG* (Hannover 1891) s.a. 872, 883, pp 76, 100; Notker, *Gesta Karoli*, ed H. Haefele, *MGH SSRG* (Berlin 1959) bk 2, c 17, p 83: a description, perhaps drawn from his own experience rather than from historical evidence, of Charlemagne's bishops, abbots and chaplains '*cum comitibus suis*' at the siege of Pavia in 774. (It is clear from the context that the reference is to military followings rather than 'attendants' as translated by L. Thorpe, *Two Lives of Charlemagne* (Harmondsworth 1969) p 163.) Italy: e.g. *MGH* Capit 2, no 221, c 13, p 103 ('*episcopi . . . in suis domibus cum suis vassallis*'); no 218, c 4, p 96: '*. . . abbates vel abbatissae si plenissime homines suos non direxerint, ipse suos honores perdant (!) et eorum bassalli et proprium et beneficium amittant*'.

27 G. Constable, 'Nona et decima' *Speculum* 35 (1960) pp 224–50.

28 Above, 'Charles the Bald and the Church', pp 78, 88, with further references. The exceptionally-rich evidence for the see of Laon is discussed by P. McKeon, *Hincmar of*

being perhaps of high status (counts, for example) and already powerful in their own right were more likely to answer a direct royal summons to the host than to form part of a church contingent. Who then were the *homines ecclesiae*? Part of the answer is that they were vassals picked by the bishop (or abbot or abbess), many of them probably his own kinsmen[29] and beneficed on episcopal lands. The rest of the answer is suggested by Hincmar in the passage I began by quoting: they were the *casati*, 'the housed ones', and those under the bishop's direct command.[30] For such warriors, whether endowed with a homestead (and thus enabled to marry) and a parcel of land, or resident still in their lord's establishment, a sizeable benefice might be a future hope: in the meantime they depended on distributions of moveable wealth, including money, and equipment to keep them 'prepared' for war. They formed the bishop's military household, and (assuming that Hincmar's 'shares' (*partes*) were equal) two-fifths of the bishop's income was spent largely on their support (though some non-military personnel will have been included among 'those under his direct command'). There is no doubting the importance of episcopal vassals in general, or of contingents of free tenants mobilised on occasion by ecclesiastical lords. But it may be suggested that perhaps the key element in the ninth-century system was composed of bodies of virtually full-time soldiers, maintained out of churches' moveable resources and available for service alongside the king's and his counts' and magnates' own household troops. In terms of sheer military experience, such men could make a unique contribution to the host. These were the professionals. Under able and committed leaders, they would fight fiercely and effectively against whatever enemy might threaten, not excluding the Vikings. Such a group, I think, were the men of the abbey of Corbie who acquitted themselves valiantly against a Viking attack in 859, and were led in person by their young abbot,

Laon and Carolingian Politics (Urbana-Chicago-London 1978) esp pp 179–85; but there is no reason to think the arrangements here unusual.

29 As in the case of Hincmar of Laon: *PL* 124, col 981. Cp below p 129, n. 47.

30 The distinction between the bishop's military *familia* in this narrower sense, and the larger body of vassals whom he led to war is impossible to document directly from ninth-century sources. But Hincmar seems to refer to the former in *dEC* p 135; and there may be another reference in Lupus, *Correspondance*, 1, Ep 16, p 96: '*Homines nostri . . . censu rei familiaris in . . . servitio effuso, onere paupertatis gravantur*' (though Levillain translates: '. . . revenu de leur patrimoine').

Odo. Lupus of Ferrières wrote to him in mingled congratulation and distress:

> I'm particularly anxious . . . when I recall your way of pitching yourself unarmed right into the thick of battles. Your youthful energy gets drawn into them by your greediness for winning! I advise you, out of well-wishing affection, be content with only putting your troops in position—for that's as much as is suitable to your [monastic] vow—and leave it to the fighting-men (*armati*) to carry out their 'profession' with instruments of war.[31]

Lupus' reservations are about Odo's personal engagement in warfare, and the risks he runs, not about his church's military service against those whom the classically-inspired Lupus calls not 'pagans', but 'barbarians' or 'pirates'.

Hincmar's evidence is important, therefore, in helping to qualify the notion that the institutionalised military service of the Carolingian Church changed from a precarial base producing 'noble fief-holders' in the ninth century, to a ministerial base producing episcopal (or abbatial) retinues of warrior-dependants in the tenth century.[32] For Hincmar implies that the episcopal military household already in the 850s played an important role in the service of the Carolingian state, and indeed it probably had done so for the past century. Hincmar thought fifty a fair upper limit for a bishop's retinue when he toured his diocese.[33] In 870 the bishop of Laon came to an assembly contrary to royal orders 'with the whole company of his men' in 'an armed band' (*armata manu*). The bishop was told by royal officers that 'ten or twelve *casati homines*' plus clergy and servants would be considered an adequate entourage for this synodal appearance. The rest of his men should be 'prepared for the defence of the fatherland against the Vikings'.[34] Clearly the bishop's total following contained well upwards of a dozen men. This implies a scale of episcopal military

[31] Lupus, *Correspondance* vol 2, Ep 106 p 138. I have tried in my translation to bring out the play on words and ideas between Odo's monastic profession (*propositum*) and the profession of the *armati* ('*quod instrumentis bellicis profitentur*').

[32] Prinz, *Klerus und Krieg* p 166.

[33] *dEC* p 127, quoting VII Toledo, c 4 presumably via the Hispana, *PL* 84 col 407–8. (For the versions current in the ninth century, see Devisse, *Hincmar* vol 3 p 1409). But Hincmar asserted (*dEC* p 136) that his fellow bishops regularly violated this limit, travelling around their dioceses '*cum hoste collecta*'!

[34] Mansi 16, col 663.

retinue comparable with those documented for the East Frankish realm in the tenth century;[35] and I can see no reason for thinking the bishop of Laon unique, or even unusual, in the ninth, except in the sense of being unusually well-documented.

One or two further implications of general interest for the ninth century can be noted here. First, the ability of bishops and abbots to maintain followings on this scale indicates (if it does not presuppose) the growth of a money economy to facilitate the payment of renders and offerings, and the accumulation of episcopal incomes, in cash; for while some transfers to warriors were made in kind (weapons, for instance), it seems likely that the 'annual gifts' they received were in coin.[36] If this was already so in the ninth century, as it remained quite largely in the twelfth, then any monochrome picture of 'the feudal system' as one in which land was virtually the sole reward for military service, beneficed vassals the major and crucial component in armies summoned by kings, and liability neatly calculated on a standard ratio of land to men, is plainly in need of some retouching, as Prestwich and Gillingham have recently shown for England.[37] In Carolingian kingdoms too, the quotas of warriors due from churches in particular were apparently arranged bilaterally between king and bishop (or abbot or abbess): thus in 865, missus and banner-man together were to check that such an agreement had been carried out. In a given quota, the bishop's military household would form a key element. A useful periodisation of medieval military systems taking full account of the Church's part therein would therefore stress continuities through the early and central Middle Ages, say, from the seventh to the twelfth centuries, and contrast the later

[35] Lesne, *Histoire*, 2, ii, pp 481–2. Cp K. F. Werner, 'Heeres-organisation und Kriegführung im deutschen Königreich des 10 und 11 Jhdts.', in *SS Spoleto* 15 (1968) pp 791–843, esp pp 820–30 (repr in Werner, *Structures politiques du monde franc* (London 1979)), Auer, 'Kriegsdienst des Klerus' in *MIOG* 79 (1971) pp 376–7, and 80 (1972) p 68, nn 31–3. These figures will include members of episcopal *familiae* along with beneficial vassals.

[36] The implication of Hincmar's *De Ordine Palatii*, c 22 is that the West Frankish king's military following were paid annual gifts in cash. Asser c 100 explicitly mentions annual cash payments by Alfred to his bellatores, and Alfred in his will (Whitelock, p 536) left 200lb, to 'those who follow (*folgiađ*) me'. For the abbot of Fleury's annual gifts to his *vassalli*, see G. Tessier, *Receuil des Actes de Charles II le Chauve*, 3 vols (Paris 1943–55) 1, no 177, p 468. See also below, p 127 n. 39.

[37] J. O. Prestwich, 'The Military Household of the Norman Kings', in *EHR* 96 (1981) pp 1–35; J. B. Gillingham, 'The introduction of knight service into England', in R. A. Brown ed, *Proceedings of the Battle Conference* 4 (1982) pp 53–64.

Middle Ages when qualitative economic change permitted armies to be supported on tax revenue raised from ecclesiastical sources among others: a development which eased at least some of the most practical and embarrassing problems of the Church's involvement in war and in general made kings and princes less dependent on the Church's military service. A second aspect of the way in which the ninth-century Frankish Church organised its service may be significant. Through their recruitment of fighting-men, bishops and abbots and abbesses could provide a channel of social mobility to their *casati homines*, not differing in kind from the advancement of vassals by lay aristocrats[38] but perhaps operating on a larger scale and more continuously, in so far as money oiled the system (churchmen are conspicuous as lenders, and borrowers, in the ninth century).[39]

So much for what Hincmar's account of the allocation of episcopal revenues in West Francia has to tell us about the Frankish Church's *militia*, its 'solace' to the Carolingians. It is time to pose my third and last question: why did Hincmar affect the use of the comparative method? For in fact the difference he purported to explain did not exist. The English churches, I have argued, owed military service to their kings just as Frankish churches did; and so too did the Italian churches which Hincmar again alleged were unfamiliar with 'the heavy custom of our regions'.[40] The

[38] Cp Werner, 'Untersuchungen zur Frühzeit des französischen Fürstentums (8.–10. Jdts)', in *Die Welt als Geschichte* 18 (1958) pp 256–89; 19 (1959) pp 146–93; and the important contribution of C. B. Bouchard, 'The Origins of the French Nobility: a Reassessment', in *American Historical Review* 86 (1981) pp 501–32.

[39] Condemnations of the practice of usury by ecclesiastics are frequent in the ninth century. (There is a good example in *dEC* p 121). The taking of cash-payments by clergy of all ranks but especially bishops is also condemned. (Again, the *dEC* offers several examples: pp 107, 113, 123–4, 127). Both the bishops attacked by Hincmar (Rothad of Soissons, and Hincmar of Laon) were accused of simony, and one of pawning church plate. For the scale of the church's cash-contribution to successive Danegelds in Hincmar's time, see F. Lot, 'Les tributs aux Normands et l'Eglise de France au IXe siècle' in *BEC* 85 (1924) pp 58–78. All this should be set in the context of the relatively extensive monetisation of the economy of Charles the Bald's kingdom demonstrated by D. M. Metcalf, 'A sketch of the currency in the time of Charles the Bald' in Gibson and Nelson edd, *Charles the Bald* pp 53–84, and of the increasing tendency for the renders of peasants on ecclesiastical estates to be paid in cash.

[40] *MGH Epp* 8, no 198, p 206. In *dEC* p 135, Hincmar cites two letters of Gregory I to Italian bishops alongside the letter to Augustine: conditions in England and Italy are alleged to be the same and contrasted with the military service owed by the church in 'these Gallic regions'. But for the real situation in Italy, see above 123, n 26, and C. Wickham, *Early Medieval Italy* (London 1981) pp 137, 140–2.

truth is that Hincmar—'incorrigible Hincmar', as M. Devisse was once moved to exclaim[41]—was not really concerned with the practice of contemporary English or Italian churches. He was no true forerunner of the Annales School. And yet his 'comparative method' was neither entirely bogus nor redundant. For Hincmar was trying to come to terms with a genuine contrast, not in space but in time: the contrast between the Church of the Apostles and the Fathers, not so richly endowed with worldly wealth and in which a bishop and his clergy might realistically hold their goods in common, and the Frankish Church of his own day with its vast estates and revenues, its bishops wielding power that had an unmistakeably economic and political, as well as legal and spiritual, basis.[42] It was Hincmar who imagined Frankish lay magnates jeering at him and his episcopal colleagues: 'those villains, those non-noble men . . . *Their* ancestors did not help [previous kings] to rule their kingdoms'. And instead of insisting as he easily could have done that Frankish bishops were noble to a man, Hincmar offered this hypothetical riposte:

> When God came in flesh . . . and disposed the government of His kingdom, he did not choose for this purpose rich men and noble men, but poor men and fishermen. And as it is written, 'He hath chosen the base things of the world and things which are despised to confound the things that are mighty'.[43]

Of course the debate is imaginary, the context polemical and the assertion unique in Hincmar's work (and indeed in early medieval writing, I think). But the very fact that Hincmar wrote this, even once, suggests that at least at this stage of his career he was conscious of the paradox that an 'established' Church, beneficiary over centuries of the gifts of the faithful, would be rich and its pastors aristocratic, where Christ and his followers had been poor and lowly. The apostles had had resources that were the mere

[41] Devisse, *Hincmar* 2 p 603.

[42] Hincmar shows his awareness of the contrast in a torrent of appeals to St. Paul and the age of the Apostles: *dEC* pp 125–36. He also attempts to rationalise the transition from apostolic arrangements to the acquisition of landed wealth by the Church: *ibid* pp 135–6. For similar concerns in Pseudo-Isidore and their specific ninth-century context, see the penetrating comments of W. Goffart, *The Le Mans Forgeries* (Cambridge, Mass. 1966) ch 1 esp p 20.

[43] *MGH* Capit 2, no 297, pp 440–1.

minimum required to enable them to preach the Gospel.[44] The situation of their ninth-century 'successors' was very different: they were accused of greed for worldly goods, not only by laymen but by their own parish clergy (prime victims of that cupidity) and by Hincmar himself.[45] The *De Ecclesiis et Capellis* is amongst other things a passionate appeal to the higher clergy to be content with modest personal consumption. But it is more than that. In it Hincmar offers one solution to the dilemma of the institutionalised Church. How could a church that was already so rich insist, as ninth-century churchmen so often did, on not just retaining lands but on gaining, or re-gaining, yet more? Because, answered Hincmar, their income was required to enable the Church to perform its military service to the kingdom that defended it. Hincmar was not justifying a system based on precarial grants that were, after all, still regarded in principle as mere temporary expedients.[46] He envisaged a more permanent solution in warriors maintained by and closely attached to ecclesiastical lords. Not the Church's warfare but the Church's wealth was the real problem. And the war, long since justified, would now justify the wealth.

For Hincmar this was a viable solution, first and foremost because the Church's military service could be conceived in ninth-century West Francia as a public service.[47] Hincmar saw in his own time as in the early Church a state which provided the benefits of peace and order to its subjects. He began the *De Ecclesiis et Capellis* by quoting St. Augustine: '"Honour the king." Don't say, "What does the king mean to me?" What then do possessions mean to you? Possessions are possessed through the laws of kings.'[48] For Hincmar as for Augustine, the ruler's *raison d'être* was his function in making and preserving law. To apply law within, to protect a law-ordered society from external attack, force would sometimes be necessary: the Church's offering of military 'solace'

[44] *dEC* pp 129–32.

[45] Such complaints were not new in the ninth century; nor was Hincmar then the only one to make them. But the depth of his concern in the *dEC* is very striking.

[46] Constable, 'Nona et decima'.

[47] Cp above 122-3, nn 21, 26: and Hincmar of Laon's self-justification in *PL* 124, col 981, admitting that he had granted benefices on episcopal lands to his own kinsmen, but insisting that this benefitted both church and state.

[48] *dEC*, prefatory letter, *MGH Epp* 6, no 108, pp 53–4. For this theme in Hincmar's political thought, see Nelson, 'Kingship, law and liturgy [in the political thought of Hincmar of Rheims', below, chapter 7, pp 133-71.

to the ruler thus had automatic justification. Hincmar's view of the Carolingian state may have been rosy but it had a basis in political reality. Ninth-century churchmen did not only preach peace as the end of war but joined king and lay magnates in practical efforts to achieve it, as when the assembly of Soissons in 853 agreed that no public courts should be held in Lent except to deal with 'concord and making peace between disputants'—a curious foreshadowing of the Truce of God.[49]

Secondly, Hincmar could readily justify in patristic terms the Church's participation in warfare that was defensive, as it was increasingly often in the ninth century, and could also be presented as Christian (the Bretons though not pagans could be branded 'false Christians').[50] A saint seen by a monk in a vision defending his earthly *familia* and its property wore helmet and mail-shirt, and he felled his Viking enemy with blows none the less lethal for being invisible.[51] For centuries the Church had invoked God's power to 'destroy the enemies of your people'.[52] Now the Frankish bishops assured their king that he had been anointed (another symptom of the close entente between Church and state) like the victorious warrior-kings of the Old Testament, his role 'to defend from the wicked by royal strength the holy Church, that is, the Christian people committed to you by God'.[53] Because churchmen had to join in that defence, war had become a fact of ecclesiastical life. Pope Nicholas I in a moment of irritation at Frankish kings who used their bishops' military duties as an excuse for inaction on

[49] *MGH* Capit 2, no 259, c 8, p 269. The foreshadowing was noticed by Devisse, *Hincmar* 1 p 499 n 166. See also J. M. Wallace-Hadrill, 'War and Peace in the Early Middle Ages', in his collected essays, *Early Medieval History* (Oxford 1975) pp 19–38, esp 31–5, for a fairly optimistic assessment of the Carolingian Church's success in preaching peace (though I cannot share his view that 'Frankish bellicosity' had come to be in need of reactivating in the ninth century: there is too much evidence not only for inter-Frankish violence, but also – and contrary to a currently-fashionable view—for local and spontaneous resistance to the Vikings! Cp Lupus' letter, above p23).

[50] *PL* 125, col 966. For the Vikings as *pagani*, see Wallace-Hadrill, 'The Vikings in Francia', in *Early Medieval History* pp 222–7 (though in my view exaggerating the 'positive force' of Viking paganism in reality).

[51] *Translatio Sancti Germani Parisiensis*, cc 29, 30, ed C. de Smedt, *Analecta Bollandiana* 2 (1883) pp 90–1, 92.

[52] So, one of the prayers in time of war in the Gelasian Sacramentary ed L. C. Mohlberg, *Liber Sacramentorum Romanae Aeclesiae Ordinis Anni Circuli* (Rome 1960) p 215.

[53] Prayer at the handing over of the sceptre, *Ordo* of Louis the Stammerer (877), *MGH* Capit 2, no 304, p 461. For Hincmar's authorship, see Nelson, 'Kingship, law and liturgy', below, chapter 7, pp. 138, 152.

other important business, might denounce such 'secular service' as reprehensible, quoting 2 Timothy 2:4: *Nemo militans Deo implicat se negotiis saecularibus*.[54] But how *un*typical a protest this was (both of Nicholas and his contemporaries) can be gauged from Hincmar's thinking this very same excuse appropriate in a carefully-worded letter to Nicholas written only months later.[55]

We know more of Hincmar's thoughts than those of other ninth-century churchmen. But in finding a new application of Augustine's compromise with a violent world, he probably spoke for them all. The institutionalised warfare of the Church was not just permissible but necessary: in practical terms because it sustained the Carolingian state, in ideological terms because it transcended the opposition between apostolicity and landed wealth. The solution was *zeitbedingt* in both senses of that useful word: it was needed by churchmen at a particular time and it required the conditions of that time. In the tenth century, changed conditions—the collapse of the Carolingian state in West Francia and in Italy—left a mere warrior-clergy, so it is often claimed, without institutional support, at the mercy of the feudal laity. Yet even in those kingdoms (and the East Frankish case needs no further labouring since the solid demonstrations of Werner and Auer) something of the ninth-century system survived—and more perhaps than Erdmann allowed for—into the age of the Crusades. The liturgy of knighthood has ninth-century West Frankish roots (I am thinking of the benediction *super militantes* in the Leofric Missal),[56] and the earliest dubbing rituals should be linked with the warrior-households of particular bishops, that is, with the *familiae* of particular saints.[57] Can we believe that any wide gulf separates these *milites* from, on the one hand, those warriors of Carolingian bishops and abbots and abbesses who went to war behind their banners and kept their mail-shirts in holy places, and on the other, the *militia sancti Petri* and the soldiers of Christ?[58] At least, to end

[54] *MGH Epp* 6, no 38, pp 309–10.

[55] *MGH Epp* 8, no 198, p 206.

[56] Ed F. Warren (Oxford 1883) p 232. See below, 'Earliest surviving royal *Ordo*', esp 348, n 37, and 350, n 41.

[57] G. Duby, *Les Trois Ordres* (Paris 1978) p 358. This point is missed by J. Flori, 'Chevalerie et liturgie' in *Le Moyen Age* 84 (1978) pp 245–78, 434–8.

[58] I. S. Robinson, 'Gregory VII and the Soldiers of Christ', in *History* 58 (1973) pp 169–92 esp 179.

where I began, there are comparisons that may repay some further sniffing out.

7

KINGSHIP, LAW AND LITURGY IN THE POLITICAL THOUGHT OF HINCMAR OF RHEIMS

OVER the past three decades, Hincmar of Rheims has attracted increasing scholarly attention from various points of view: K. Weinzierl, J. Devisse and M. David have discussed his use of civil and canon law; J. M. Wallace-Hadrill, C.-R. Brühl, H. Fuhrmann and H. Löwe have shown the interrelation of law and politics in his thought and action; M. Andrieu and C. A. Bouman have revealed his large contribution to the development of royal and episcopal consecration rites; K. F. Morrison and Y. M.-J. Congar have thrown fresh light on his ecclesiology; H. H. Anton has given detailed consideration to his work in the genre of the 'mirror of princes'; and W. Ullmann has offered some thought-provoking comments on his political ideas.[1] All of these studies are relevant to Hincmar's view of kingship, but the conclusions towards which they tend, implicitly or explicitly, are far from unanimous, especially in relation to Hincmar's treatment of law. Was he, as Weinzierl maintains, a consistent and high-minded defender of the ancient law of the church, or should we follow Brühl and Fuhrmann in seeing him as a more eclectic figure who could manipulate law to suit political interests? Did his emphasis on law serve in the main

1. K. Weinzierl, 'Erzbischof Hinkmar von Reims als Verfechter des geltenden Rechts', in *Episcopus. Studien über das Bischofsamt ... Kardinal von Faulhaber ... dargebracht* (Regensburg, 1949), pp. 136–63; J. Devisse, *Hincmar et la Loi* (Dakar, 1962), and *idem*, 'Essai sur l'histoire d'une expression qui a fait fortune: "*Consilium et auxilium*" au IXe siècle', *Le Moyen Age*, (1968), 179–205; M. David, 'Le serment du sacre du IXe au XVe siècle', *Revue du Moyen Age Latin*, vi (1950), parts 1, 2 and 3, *passim*; J. M. Wallace-Hadrill, 'Archbishop Hincmar and the authorship of Lex Salica', *Tijdschrift voor Rechtsgeschiednis*, xxi (1953), 1–29, reprinted in *The Long-haired Kings* (London, 1962), and *idem.*, 'The Via Regia of the Carolingian age', in B. Smalley, ed., *Trends in Medieval Political Thought* (Oxford, 1965); C. R. Brühl, 'Hinkmariana II. Hinkmar im Widerstreit von kanonischem Recht und Politik in Ehefragen', *Deutsches Archiv*, xx (1964), 48–77; H. Fuhrmann, *Einfluss und Verbreitung der pseudoisidorischen Fälschungen* (Stuttgart, 1972–4); H. Löwe, 'Hinkmar von Reims und der Apokrisiar', in *Festschrift für H. Heimpel* (Göttingen, 1972), iii, 197–225; M. Andrieu, 'Le sacre épiscopal d'après Hincmar de Reims', *Revue d'Histoire Écclésiastique*, xlviii (1953), 22–73; C. A. Bouman, *Sacring and Crowning* (Groningen, 1957); K. F. Morrison, *The Two Kingdoms* (Princeton, 1964); Y. M.-J. Congar, *L'Écclésiologie du haut moyen-âge* (Paris, 1968); H. H. Anton, *Fürstenspiegel und Herrscherethos in der Karolingerzeit* (Bonn, 1968); W. Ullmann, *The Carolingian Renaissance and the Idea of Kingship* (London, 1971).

to enhance royal power, as Morrison implies, or, as Devisse has argued, to limit it? Did he hold the king answerable to God alone, as David would contend, or did he press the hierocratic claim attributed to him by Ullmann, and assert a right of episcopal surveillance over the king? By re-examining these questions, I hope to show that Hincmar's theory of restraints on Christian kingship had a firmer and more extensive juristic basis than has been generally realized.

It is clear that Hincmar placed special emphasis on the legal aspects of the royal function itself.[1] Augustine had long since distinguished the person from the office of the king in the following terms:

Aliter enim servit, quia homo est, aliter, quia etiam rex est; quia homo est enim, servit vivendo fideliter, quia vero etiam rex est, servit leges justa praecipientes et contraria prohibentes convenienti vigore sanciendo.[2]

For Hincmar as for Augustine, an essential component of the royal office was the making and preservation of law, new royal laws being created to conserve the public rights and interests enshrined in existing laws. Herein lay the king's claim on his subjects' obedience.[3] While Hincmar also echoed the patristic notion that an evil king was established by God as a punishment for sinners, and therefore should not be resisted,[4] his originality lay

1. See Devisse, *op. cit.* pp. 74 ff., and the very pertinent brief remarks of Wallace-Hadrill, 'The Via Regia', pp. 35 ff. Anton, *op. cit.* pp. 307 ff., seems rather to underestimate the importance of law.

2. Ep. 185, *Corpus Scriptorum Ecclesiasticorum Latinorum*, lvii. 17 f.

3. In *De Regis Persona et Regio Ministerio*, c. 16, *Patrologia Latina* (hereafter PL) 125, col. 845, Hincmar quoted the passage from Augustine cited above, and *ibid.*, c. 27, quoted from Pseudo-Cyprian, *De XII Abusivis Saeculi*, c. 12: 'Populus sine lege'. (Ed. S. Hellmann, Texte und Untersuchungen, pp. 58 ff.) Anton, *op. cit.* pp. 78 and 105, notes that the royal function *leges renovare*, *leges statuere*, etc., was already present in earlier Carolingian writings. For Hincmar's views, see *De Divortio*, PL 125, col. 754; *Schedula*, PL 126, col. 627; letter to Louis III, PL 126, col. 119, declaring that the king had been elected 'ad regimen regni *sub conditione debitas leges servandi*'. Devisse, *op. cit.* p. 79, rightly infers that for Hincmar, the king who transgressed the *leges* was *ipso facto* deprived of office. The objection of Morrison, *op. cit.*, p. xii, is unconvincing. See *infra*, pp. 270 ff. M. Jacquin, 'Hincmar et Saint Augustin', *Mélanges C. Moeller* (Louvain, 1914), pp. 328 ff., mainly criticizes Hincmar's theological methods. For Augustine's influence on his idea of kingship, see Anton, *op. cit.* pp. 286, with n. 719, and 300 f. For Hincmar's own MSS. of Augustine, see F. M. Carey, 'The Scriptorium of Reims during the Archbishopric of Hincmar', in *Classical and Medieval Studies in Honor of E. K. Rand* (New York, 1938), esp. pp. 51 ff.

4. *De Regis Persona*, c. 1, PL 125, col. 834: 'Quod bonos reges Deus facit, malos permittit'. *Cf.* Ep. 15, PL 126, col. 98, quoting Rom. xiii. But, in this same letter, Hincmar distinguishes between *potestas* as an institution, ordained by God, and the behaviour of individual power-holders: 'Sicque [fideles] non resistunt ordinationi Dei. . . . Resistunt autem *iniquis iniquorum operibus et mandatis*'. Ep. 15 goes on to provide a resolution for the tension in Hincmar's thought: ' "Regem honorificate et obedite regi quasi praecellenti" (I Pet. ii. 17, 13): videlicet qui regis regum obedit mandatis, et eius custodit judicia. *Alioquin* ut sanctus Petrus dicit: "Obedire oportet Deo magis quam hominibus" ' (Act. v. 29). A *rex*, therefore, is to be obeyed, whereas an *iniquus*, as a mere man, is not. Morrison, *op. cit.* p. 229 with n. 41, seems to miss the

in his insistence on a much more positive evaluation. The king as legislator and as executor of justice through conformity with his own and his predecessors' laws was truly acting on God's behalf.[1] It was the high value he set on this royal service which made Hincmar so concerned that the king should be bound to the observance of laws, once made. Too much was at stake for the option of merely tolerating an unworthy king to carry great conviction. Hincmar's anxiety for the maintenance of the law caused him not only to revalue the royal office but to confront, more resolutely than any previous Christian thinker, the problem of controlling its exercise.

In one sense, of course, the priesthood already controlled the Christian king when penitential discipline was imposed on him as an individual sinner.[2] But although in the case of a ruler, the priest's jurisdictional power affected his tenure of office as well as his person, the Frankish bishops who, in the first half of the ninth century, wished to pronounce upon the way in which rulership was exercised, faced the difficulty that the ruler's power had origins quite outside their control. The events of 833 demonstrate the point. The deposition of the emperor Louis the Pious was then declared by the divine judgment of battle, which the bishops only confirmed.[3] God's agents were Louis's rebellious subjects. The bishops accordingly did not claim themselves to have deposed the emperor, for they had, after all, played no part in his making[4]; and they were

---

point. Anton, *op. cit.* p. 297 with nn. 760 and 761, gives an excellent commentary on this passage, but without noting that Hincmar's definition of a *rex* here centres on the making and keeping of law: 'Et de legibus quibus ecclesia moderatur et christianitas regitur, Christi Domini sapientia dicit: "Ego sapientia habito in consilio: per me reges regnant, et legum conditores justa decernunt" (Prov. viii. 12, 15). Conditores quippe legum non nudo verbo, sed scripto leges condiderunt et condunt.... Quas non illi reges custodiunt de quibus Deus ... dicit: "Ipsi regnaverunt, et non ex me: principes exstiterunt, et non cognovi" (Hos. viii. 4). Sed illi reges eas [leges] condunt *atque conservant*, de quibus item Dominus ... dicit: "Per me reges regnant" '. See *infra*, pp. 260 ff.

1. *De Regis persona*, c. 16, PL 125, col. 844: 'Reges regi regum serviant Domino ... *et leges dando pro ipso*'.

2. See O. D. Watkins, *A History of Penance* (London, 1920), ii, 665 ff.; B. Poschmann, *Penance and the Anointing of the Sick* (trans. F. Courtney, London, 1964), pp. 135 ff.

3. I follow L. Halphen, *Charlemagne et l'Empire Carolingien* (Paris, 1947), pp. 291 ff. See also T. Schieffer, 'Die Krise des Karolingischen Imperiums', in *Festschrift G. Kallen* (Bonn, 1957), pp. 12 ff., and E. Boshof, *Erzbischof Agobard von Lyon* (Cologne, 1969), pp. 245 ff. The biographer of Wala of Corbie saw the desertion of Louis's troops as the manifestation of a *iustum Dei iudicium*: Monumenta Germaniae Historica (hereafter MGH), Scriptores II, p. 565. The bishops in their *Relatio* of 833 declared that Louis had been deprived of imperial power by a *iudicium divinum*: MGH Capitularia Regum Francorum (hereafter Capit.) II, p. 53. For Hincmar's interpretation of these events, see *infra*, p. 136, n. 2.

4. Louis had been crowned and anointed king by the pope in 781; crowned emperor by his father in 813; crowned and anointed emperor by the pope in 816: for details, see Brühl, 'Fränkischer Krönungsbrauch', *Historische Zeitschrift*, cxciv (1962), 322. Whatever *caracter* was supposed to have been conferred through the anointing evidently gave no more immunity from deposition than did a bishop's consecration. But it may well have been regarded as indelible: just as a deposed bishop could be reinstated without requiring any re-consecration (*cf.* the case of Ebbo of Rheims in 840, Capit.

also chary of drawing any such inference from their subsequent imposition of penance. They grounded their action on the *cura animarum*, and Louis's disqualification from bearing arms, which in practice rendered him incapable of ruling, was so to speak a side-effect of the penance imposed on him.[1]

The development of penitential theory during the Carolingian period enabled the bishops in 833 to use public penance as the penalty for misgovernment construed as a public sin; but they could construct no juristic claim to depose a ruler who was directly answerable only to God – hence the significance of the *iudicium dei* – nor could they claim jurisdiction over his office itself, however abused. The confession and penance of Louis, unlike his prior deposition derived, legally speaking, from an act of self-limitation. On this basis, there could be no sound episcopal case for the trial and judgment of the emperor.[2] In the changed conditions of the reign of Charles the Bald, the West Frankish bishops strove to increase the prestige of the royal office and to operate through it.[3] Yet the king's power, though seriously weakened, was still

---

II, pp. 111 f.), so Louis at his restoration in 834 was not re-anointed, though he was re-crowned both then (Sunday, 1 Mar.), and the following year (Sunday, 28 Feb. 835). These *Befestigungskrönungen* are discussed by Brühl, *ubi supra*, pp. 278 f.

1. In their *Relatio* of 833, the bishops stressed how great had to be their 'sollicitudo . . . circa salutem cunctorum' (Capit. II, p. 51). Their concern for Louis was 'ne animam suam perderet' (*ibid.* p. 53). *Cf.* Capit. II, p. 447, the declaration of the synod of Savonnières (859): 'Episcopi namque secundum illorum ministerium ac sacram auctoritatem uniti sunt ut mutuo consilio atque auxilio reges regnorumque primores atque populum sibi commissum in Domino regant et corrigant'. Devisse, art. cit. (*supra*, p. 133, n. 1), p. 192, suggests Hincmar's authorship here. For ecclesiastical penalties imposed on kings, see F. Kern, *Gottesgnadentum und Widerstandsrecht im früheren Mittelalter* (2nd rev. ed., R. Buchner, Münster, 1954), pp. 338 ff. For disqualification from bearing arms, see *Relatio*, Capit. II, p. 55; *Annales Fuldenses* s.a. 834, ed. F. Kurze, p. 27; Penitential of Halitgar (c. 840) III, c. 7, in PL 105, col. 678. Ullmann, *op. cit.* pp. 66 f., notes the peculiar relevance of this penalty in the case of kings, whose raison d'être in contemporary eyes lay mainly in their military function.

2. *Cf.* M. David, *La Souveraineté et les Limites juridiques du Pouvoir monarchique du IXe au XVe siècle* (Paris, 1954), p. 119: 'A quoi bon un procès quand la peine précède le jugement?' Hincmar, ignoring this drawback, later revalued the bishops' role in 833. In *De Divortio*, quaestio vi, PL 125, cols. 757 f., Hincmar insisted that Heb. xiii, 17 ('Obedite praepositis vestris . . .' etc.), applied to *et reges*; then quoted Gelasius on *pontificalis auctoritas*; mentioned Ambrose's excommunication of Theodosius ('ab ecclesia separavit, et per poenitentiam revocavit'); and went on: 'nostra aetate pium Augustum Ludovicum a regno dejectum, *post satisfactionem* episcopalis unanimitas . . . et ecclesiae *et regno* restituit'. A few lines later, Hincmar developed the idea that a true king was not subject to law in the sense that he was just by definition, and 'lex non est posita justo sed injustis. . . . Adulter, homicida, *injustus*, raptor, et aliorum vitiorum obnoxius quilibet, vel secrete, vel publice *judicabitur a sacerdotibus*, qui sunt throni Dei, in quibus Deus sedet et per quos sua decernet judicia'. Here without exploiting the argument based on the consecration of kings by bishops (see pp. 139 ff. *infra*), Hincmar wrung the last ideological ounce from the bishops' spiritual jurisdiction. *Cf.* also his argument of 868, *infra*, pp. 163 f.

3. For the background here, see J. Reviron, *Les idées politico-religieuses d'un evêque du IXe siècle: Jonas d'Orléans et son De institutione regia* (Paris, 1930), pp. 94 ff. and 113 ff.; E. Delaruelle, 'En relisant le *De Institutione Regia*', in *Mélanges Halphen* (Paris, 1951), pp. 185 ff.; and Ullmann, *The Growth of Papal Government* (3rd edn., London, 1970), pp. 125 ff.

strong enough to threaten ecclesiastical interests as the demands on royal resources grew more pressing.[1] Hincmar therefore, for all his confidence in Christian rulership, still faced as archbishop the problem of defining and controlling its function. Augustine's *rex-homo* distinction might have enabled him to reconcile the divine ordination of the royal *office* with the episcopal control of the king's *person*.[2] But the events of 833 had effectively shown that an episcopal claim to the disposition of the ruler's office (and this would be equally true of an emperor or a king) could find no basis in spiritual jurisdiction over his person. That claim could be lodged successfully only with the episcopal mediation of the office itself.

For almost a century before 848, the papacy had virtually monopolized the inauguration-anointings of Frankish kings and emperors.[3] But in 848, the performance of the royal rite was appropriated by West Frankish bishops, probably at the instance of Hincmar himself.[4] Thereafter Hincmar's strong personal interest in

---

On the synods of the early part of Charles the Bald's reign, see F. Lot and L. Halphen, *Le règne de Charles le Chauve (part 1: 840–853)* (Paris, 1909), pp. 74 ff. (no further volumes appeared); H. Barion, *Das fränkisch-deutsche Synodalrecht des Frühmittelalters* (Bonn, 1931, repr. Amsterdam, 1963), pp. 290 ff.; C. de Clercq, 'La législation religieuse franque depuis l'avènement de Louis le Pieux jusqu'aux Fausses Décrétales', *Revue de Droit Canonique*, v (1955), 280 ff. and 390 ff.

1. This emerged clearly in the case of Hincmar of Laon. See H. Schrörs, *Hinkmar, Erzbischof von Reims* (Freiburg i. B., 1884), pp. 295 f.; E. Lesne, *Histoire de la Propriété ecclésiastique en France* (Lille–Paris, 1926), II, ii, 382 ff.; and *infra*, pp. 160 f. For Charles the Bald's growing political weakness and consequent dependence on the church, see Brühl, *Fodrum, Gistum, Servitium Regis* (Cologne, 1968), pp. 50 ff.; F. Prinz, *Klerus und Krieg* (Stuttgart, 1971), pp. 73 ff., 123; Wallace-Hadrill, *Early Germanic Kingship* (Oxford, 1971), pp. 125 ff. Hincmar's protests in 868 against royal interference in the affairs of the church of Laon reveal the still extensive scope of royal authority, at any rate in this northern see: *Pro ecclesiae libertatum defensione quaterniones*, in PL 125, cols. 1035–70, esp. 1051 ff., and *cf.* similar ideas in a late work (881), *De officiis episcoporum*, PL 125, cols. 1087–94. For Rheims' recovery of lost land and rights, see G. Tessier, *Receuil des Actes de Charles II le Chauve* (Paris, 1943), i, 210 ff. and 262 ff. For Hincmar's views on the deployment of these resources by the *successores apostolorum*, see Capit. II, p. 432. *Cf.* on the general social problem, K. Bosl, 'Potens–Pauper', in *Frühformen der Gesellschaft in mittelalterlichen Europa* (Munich, 1964), pp. 114–15, and Devisse, '*Pauperes* et *paupertas* dans le monde carolingien. Ce qu'en dit Hincmar de Reims', *Revue du Nord*, xlviii (1966), 273 ff.

2. W. Mohr, *Die Karolingische Reichsidee* (Münster, 1962), p. 145 n. 583, complaining, somewhat unfairly, that L. Knabe, *Die gelasianische Zweigewaltentheorie* (Berlin, 1936), pp. 77 f., and David, *op. cit.* pp. 121 f., had 'overlooked' the fact that Hincmar distinguished between the power of kingship and the king's personal conduct.

3. For the possibility of papal influence on Pippin's anointing in 751, and the role of Boniface as *servus et legatus apostolicae sedis*, see W. Levison, *England and the Continent in the Eighth Century* (Oxford, 1946), pp. 88 ff. and 119 ff.; and the comments of F. L. Ganshof in *Settimana Spoleto* VII (1960), ii. 396 f. Frankish bishops may have anointed Frankish kings in 768 and 771, though P. E. Schramm, *Kaiser, Könige und Päpste* (Stuttgart, 1968), I, 197 ff. with nn. 10 and 20, plausibly suggests that *consecratio* in these contexts may mean no more than a blessing. From then on, certainly, until 848, every anointing of a Frankish king or sub-king (or emperor) was performed by a pope: for details, see Brühl, 'Krönungsbrauch', *passim*.

4. *Annales Bertiniani*, s.a. 848, ed. F. Grat (Paris, 1964), p. 55. L. Levillain, 'Le sacre de Charles le Chauve à Orléans', *Bibliotheque de l'École des Chartes*, lxiv (1903), 31 ff., regarded the anointing as a royal makeshift. Lot and Halphen, *op. cit.* p. 194 with n. 2,

royal anointing and its liturgical elaboration is attested by the four *Ordines* which he composed, and by many allusions in his writings.[1] He recognized that rulers achieved power, historically and in his own times, by various means, some, like heredity and election, admissible by ecclesiastical norms, and others inadmissible, like force or intrigue.[2] The former were direct expressions of God's will, while the latter were merely permitted, rather than willed, by God.[3] In the ninth century, the West Frankish bishops in anointing their kings appeared, like Samuel and Nathan in the Old Testament, as visible mediators of the divine will.[4] According

rightly criticize Levillain's interpretation, as does P. Zumthor, *Charles le Chauve* (Paris, 1957), p. 116. *Cf.* Schramm, *König von Frankreich* (2nd edn. Weimar, 1960), i. 17. Earlier views assume royal initiative; but see now Ullmann, *Carolingian Renaissance*, pp. 79 ff. Technically, this was an anointing only to the kingship of the Aquitainians, but it was evidently regarded by Hincmar and by Charles himself, at least when convenient to do so, as an anointing to the whole West Frankish realm: see the letter of the synod of Quierzy (858), Capit. II, p. 439 (for Hincmar's authorship, *cf.* his own admission in *De coercendis rapinis*, PL 125, col. 955), and the *Libellus adversus Wenilonem* (859), Capit. II, p. 451. These references strongly support the argument from silence that Charles had received no other anointing as West Frankish king, *e.g.* at his designation or accession. Since the Orleans anointing was an Aquitainian affair, Hincmar's absence is explicable: *cf.* E. Dümmler, *Geschichte des ostfränkischen Reichs* (2nd edn. Leipzig, 1887), i. 337, n. 3. Wenilo of Sens officiated because Orleans was in his province. Hincmar was a stickler for metropolitan rights, and had himself been consecrated by Wenilo: J. D. Mansi, *Conciliorum Collectio* (Florence–Venice, 1759–78), xv, col. 794. But even if not present, Hincmar's already great political influence and his liturgical interests make him the likeliest source for the idea of the anointing. Between Easter (25 Mar.) when he was recognized by the Aquitainians at Limoges, and May when he was consecrated there, Charles visited north-eastern France: see G. Tessier, *Recueil*, i. 284–6, no. 107 issued in April at Quierzy, and 286–8, no. 108 issued in May at Compiègne. He could well have contacted Hincmar during this period.

1. Hincmar's *Ordines*, preserved in a now lost Liège MS., were edited by J. Sirmond, *Hincmari . . . opera* (Paris, 1645), i. 741 ff., and are conveniently reprinted in Capit. II, pp. 425 ff., 453 ff., 456 f., and 461 f. On Hincmar's liturgical work and technical mastery, see the valuable study of Bouman, *op. cit.* (*supra* p. 133, n. 1), esp. pp. 103 and 112 ff., and in relation to the episcopal consecration-rite, Andrieu, 'Le sacre épiscopal', *passim*. See also A. Sprengler, 'Die Gebete der Krönungsordines Hinkmars von Reims', *Zeitschrift für Kirchengeschichte*, lxiii (1950/51), 245 ff.

2. *De Divortio*, quaestio vi, PL 125, cols. 756 ff. In hereditary or elective succession, God acts *ministerio angelorum et hominum*. Previous commentaries on this passage have been superseded by that of Anton, *op. cit.* pp. 295 ff.

3. *Cf.* p. 134, n. 4 *supra*.

4. See Hincmar's references to the bishops as *locum tenentes* for Samuel in the synodal letter of 858, Capit. II, p. 439; *De Divortio*, PL 125, col. 632; *De fide Carolo regi servanda* (875), PL 125, col. 979; and, for the related assumption of identity between episcopal and divine action, synod of Meaux (845), c. lxxi, Capit. II, p. 415, and synod of Quierzy (858), *ibid.* p. 428. A major component in the typology of the prophet was the correction of erring rulers: see *De Divortio*, PL 125, col. 756, for the precedents of Nathan and David, Samuel and Saul, Ahias and Jeroboam. For some implications of royal anointing in this context, see p. 142 *infra*. See also Anton, *op. cit.* p. 347, but surprisingly neglecting the Old Testament models in Hincmar's *Ordines*: in the anointing-prayer of 877, there are references to the victories of Abraham, Moses and Joshua, to the humility of David and the wisdom and peace of Solomon. Hincmar was influenced here by St Paul's similar list of *exempla* in Heb. xi, whence also (v. 33) he borrowed the wording for the central passage in the anointing-prayers of 869 and 877. By placing this after a quotation from the *Benedictio chrismatis*, Hincmar produced an explicit linkage of anointing with the successes of the Old Testament heroes 'qui per fidem vicerunt

to Hincmar, Charles the Bald was 'crowned and consecrated to the Lord in the possession of the kingdom [of Lotharingia] by the agency of the bishops'.[1] Earlier Frankish tradition was permanently breached when a king could no longer be made without the bishops' explicit intervention.

Hincmar reaffirmed Isidore's statement that secular princes had to render account to God for the *ecclesia* committed to them for protection by Christ.[2] But he did not forget Gelasius's observation that the *sacerdotes* had to render account *pro ipsis regibus hominum.*[3] These two notions of responsibility could now be fused, for the consecration which carried the king into the ranks of the governors of the *ecclesia* also represented in concrete terms the mediation of a specific *ministerium* by the bishops of a given kingdom. Useful and necessary as kingship was, it was an office in which a suitable candidate could be installed only by the hands of those directly accountable to God.[4] Thus Hincmar linked the bishops' responsibility at the Last Judgment with the earthly manifestation of their authority:

> . . . tanto gravius pondus est sacerdotum, quanto etiam pro ipsis regibus hominum in divino reddituri sunt examine rationem; et tanto est dignitas pontificum maior quam regum quia reges in culmen regium sacrantur a pontificibus, pontifices autem a regibus consecrari non possunt.[5]

---

regna et operati sunt iustitiam atque adepti sunt promissiones'. See Capit. II, pp. 457 and 461. Rich evidence for the influence of Old Testament models is to be found in eighth- and ninth-century prayer-texts, including regal benedictions. The topic awaits detailed study. The fine work of R. Kottje, *Studien zum Einfluss des A.T. auf Recht und Liturgie des frühen Mittelalters, 6.–8. Jht.* (Bonn, 1964), deals with other matters.

1. Hincmar's *Adnuntiatio* immediately preceding the consecration of 869, Capit. II, pp. 340 f.: 'non incongruum videtur istis venerabilibus episcopis, si vestrae unanimitati placet, ut *in obtentu regni*, unde vos ad illum sponte convenistis et vos ei commendastis, *sacerdotali ministerio* ante altare hoc *coronetur et sacra unctione Domino consecretur*'. Morrison, *op. cit.* (*supra* p. 133, n. 1), pp. 187 f., argues that the consecration of the king's person to the Lord, and his receiving his royal title through episcopal benediction, are mutually exclusive. But the above passage, read in full, shows the inappropriateness of Morrison's sharp distinction.

2. *Sent.* iii. 51, no. 6, in PL 83, col. 723 f. E. Ewig, 'Zum christlichen Königsgedanken im Frühmittelalter', in *Vorträge und Forschungen*, (ed. T. Mayer, Constance, 1956), iii, 31 f., contrasts this with Gelasian theory. *Cf.* similar notions of responsibility in Pseudo-Cyprian, c. 9, ed. cit. p. 53; Cathwulf, MGH Epp. IV, p. 503; Jonas, *De Instit. Reg.*, ed. cit. pp. 145 f.; and the episcopal statements of 829 and 836, MGH Concilia II pp. 652 and 716. Anton, *op. cit.* pp. 317 f., nn. 887–93, cites further references in Hincmar's writings, but neglects his liturgical work where the same idea underlies the blessing, 'Clerum ac populum' in the *Ordo* of 869 and the sceptre formula of 877.

3. Ep. 12, c. 2, ed. A. Thiel, *Epistolae pontificum Romanorum genuinae* (Braunsberg, 1868), pp. 350 f. On the doctrine of responsibility here, see my note in *Journal of Theological Studies*, xviii (1967), 154 ff., and the important revisions of M. H. Hoeflich, 'Gelasius I and the Roman Law: one further word', *ibid.* xxvi (1975), 114 ff. The passage is quoted in the synodal letter of 858, Capit. II, p. 440.

4. *Cf.* the *adnuntiationes* of Adventius and Hincmar in 869, Capit. II, pp. 338 ff., and p. 138, n. 4, *supra.*

5. PL 125, col. 1071, in the *acta* of the synod of Fîmes, Apr. 881. *Cf.* also *ibid.* cols. 1087 f.; the contemporary letter to Louis III, PL 126, col. 119 (with the correction of Anton, *op. cit.* p. 344, n. 1038); and the so-called *Ad episcopos*, Hincmar's last extant

If the bishops' obligation to render account was at once a privilege and a burden, their indispensable role as consecrators gave them *maior dignitas* – a term which implied not only superior sacramental powers but also superior governmental position.[1] In Hincmar's view, he and his colleagues, uniquely qualified as they were to consecrate their king to his office, acquired thereby a jurisdiction over him. Hincmar modelled his conception of this jurisdiction on the analogy of the metropolitan's position with regard to his suffragans[2] and here he invoked the principle:

ab his potes *iudicari* a quibus potuisti *ordinari*.[3]

---

work, PL 125, cols. 1007 ff. Probably influential here was Heb. vii. 7: 'Quod minus est a meliore benedicitur'. For further comments on Hincmar's use of the Gelasian theme, see Knabe, *op. cit.* pp. 88 f. and Mohr, *op. cit.* pp. 144 f. In the *De Ordine Palatii* in Capit. II, p. 519, written also in 881, Hincmar quoted Gelasius on two *ordinationum officia*, without adding that one was superior to the other or mentioning the consecration of kings. On the work, and the circumstantial reasons for this omission, see Anton, *op. cit.* pp. 288 ff. and 346 with n. 1044. *Cf.* also Löwe, art. cit. pp. 219 ff. But even here, when writing for the court, Hincmar insisted on the significance of the king's anointing in the view of its ministrants: 'In sacra regum historia legimus, quia principes sacerdotum, quando sacra unctione *reges in regnum sacrabant . . . legem in manum eius dabant* ut scirent, qualiter se ipsos regere et pravos corrigere et bonos in viam rectam deberent dirigere'. *Cf.* similar statements at Fîmes, PL 125, col. 1071; in the *De Divortio*, PL 125, col. 757; and in the sceptre formula of 877, Capit. II, p. 461. On the sources of these ideas, Anton, *op. cit.* pp. 57, n. 58, and 309, n. 834.

1. The dual meaning has attracted little attention in this context. See s.v. 'Dignitas' in H. G. Heumann, rev. E. Seckel, *Handlexikon zu den Quellen des römischen Rechts* (9th edn. Jena, 1907), for both the general sense of prestige and the technical sense, in late imperial law, of an official post in the civil government. Morrison, *op. cit.* p. 117, n. 1, notes the official sense of the term, but does not consider Hincmar's use of it. Although his usual word for 'office' was *officium*, less often *ministerium*, Hincmar did sometimes use *dignitas* in this sense of a specific post or function: *e.g.* in PL 125, cols. 1040, 1041; PL 125, col. 700; PL 125, col. 1007 and elsewhere, quoting Gelasius, Tract. IV, c. 11, ed. Thiel, p. 568 ('dignitatibus distinctis officia potestatis utriusque [Christus] discrevit').

2. See E. Perels, 'Eine Denkschrift Hinkmars im Prozess Rothads von Soissons', *Neues Archiv*, lxiv (1922), 43 ff.; *Opusculum LV Capitulorum* in PL 126, cols. 290–494 (hereafter *LV Capit.*); *Epistola de iure metropolitanorum* in PL 126, cols. 189 ff. Among many citations from canon law, references to canons of the African church are particularly frequent: I have counted over fifty instances (including repetitions) in *LV Capit. Cf.* also the critical apparatus in Perels, *ubi supra*. Schrörs, *op. cit.* pp. 392 f., and Anton, *op. cit.* p. 334, n. 985, indicate a few of Hincmar's citations of African canons without stressing the significance of this source. Metropolitan jurisdiction, a major theme of African councils, was something of special concern to Hincmar: see *Dictionnaire de Droit Canonique*, art. 'Afrique' (G. Bardy), i. 296 ff.; P. Monceaux, *Histoire Littéraire de l'Afrique chrétienne* (Paris, 1905), iii. 80 ff. and 211; and for Hincmar's views, E. Lesne, *La hierarchie épiscopale en Gaule et en Germanie, 742–882* (Lille, 1905), pp. 122 f. and 171 f.; F. X. Arnold, *Das Diozesanrecht nach den Schriften Hinkmars von Reims* (Vienna, 1935), pp. 53 ff.; H. G. J. Beck, 'Canonical Election to suffragan bishoprics according to Hincmar of Rheims', *Catholic Historical Review*, xliii (1957), 137 ff.; Fuhrmann, *op. cit.* (*supra* p. 133, n. 1), i. 219 ff., ii. 255.

3. *LV Capit.*, PL 126, col. 378. *Cf.* a lengthier statement of the same point in a letter to the bishop of Laon, PL 126, col. 559: 'Si potui propter ministerium mihi collatum exorare deum et tu per impositionem manuum mearum fieres ordinatus episcopus, possum et debeo *eodem ministerio* te obtestari per auctoritatem ut facias quod facere debet episcopus'. Here, col. 559, and in another letter, *ibid.* col. 276, Hincmar writes of the bond of quasi-filial obligation which binds a new bishop to his consecrator(s).

Hincmar drew his inspiration from texts that were available in the contemporary Pseudo-Isidorian collections. In c. xv of the Capitula Angilramni, for instance, which dealt with the restriction of a bishop's jurisdiction to the clergy of his own diocese, Hincmar could find the statement:

Nam qui eum *ordinare* non potuit, nec *iudicare* ullatenus poterit.[1]

Similarly a false decretal of Pseudo-Calixtus, cc. xiii and xiv, dealt with the impermissibility of a metropolitan's interfering with his suffragan's powers over the priests in their dioceses:

Quia sicut *ordinatio*, ita eius et *iudicatio* . . . Nam qui *ordinare* non poterit, qualiter *iudicabit*?[2]

The context of these pronouncements would hardly have commended them to Hincmar.[3] But in c. xxiv of the Capitula Angilramni, he could find a similar text in a more congenial setting:

Quandocumque aliquis episcoporum criminatur congregatis omnibus eiusdem provinciae episcopis causa eius audiatur, ut non occulte iudicetur vel dampnetur, quia ab aliis *iudicari* prius non potest, nisi ab his quibus *ordinari* potuit.[4]

This canon is partly based on Antioch, c. xv,[5] but the explicit linking of *ordinari* and *iudicari* has no ancient precedent. Here, as in the other cases cited above, the link seems to have been forged by ninth-century Frankish clerics, and it suggests a significant new emphasis on the crucial role in consecration rites of the bishops as mediators of office conceived as the emanation of divine grace. Hincmar's use of the *ordinari-iudicari* principle involved an original twist: as archbishop, he virtually monopolized it so as to amplify,

1. *Decretales Pseudo-Isidorianae*, ed. P. Hinschius (Berlin, 1863), p. 761. On the Capitula Angilramni, see G. May, 'Zu den Anklagebeschränkungen in den Capitula Angilramni', *Zeitschrift für Kirchengeschichte* (1961), lxxii. pp. 106 ff., and Fuhrmann, *op. cit.* i. 161 ff. and 217 with n. 85 for their use by Hincmar. Because of their transmission along with the work of Pseudo-Isidore and their origin in the same circles, Fuhrmann includes them under the heading 'Pseudo-Isidorian'. The wording of Capit. Angil. c. xv finds close parallels in two false decretals, Ps.-Julian, c. xii, ed. cit. p. 468, and Ps.-Sixtus, c. vi, ed. cit. p. 192.

2. Ed. cit. p. 139. *Cf.* the reappearance of this text in eleventh-century collections: *Anselmi episcopi Lucensis collectio canonum*, VI, c. 114, ed. F. Thaner (Berlin, 1906–15), p. 324, and c. 194 of the Collection of Seventy-four Titles, *ibid.*

3. A basic issue in the case of Rothad of Soissons (see pp. 157 f. *infra*) was that of a bishop's jurisdiction over a priest in his own diocese, when Hincmar as metropolitan claimed power to intervene. See Schrörs, *op. cit.* pp. 239 ff., and Fuhrmann, *op. cit.* ii. 254 ff.

4. Ed. cit. p. 768.

5. *Ecclesiae Occidentalis Monumenta Iuris*, ed. C. H. Turner (Oxford, 1913), II, ii. 280 f. *Cf.* Pseudo-Isidore, ed. cit. p. 271. A form of this canon was transmitted in the Dionysio-Hadriana, c. xciii, PL 67, col. 162. On this collection, see p. 159, n. 1 *infra*. The basic principle here is implicit in other early canons, but none explicitly links *ordinari* and *iudicari*.

rather than (as the Pseudo-Calixtine decretal had implied) to limit, metropolitan powers. The archbishop's canonically-based right to consecrate suffragans to their offices could now be presented as the basis of his jurisdiction over every aspect of their official conduct.[1]

Hincmar's real masterstroke was to grasp the relevance of the episcopal case to the royal case. Obviously existing canon law did not yet cater for the consecrated king; but once he, like the bishop, was anointed into his office – and Hincmar was in no doubt about the constitutive nature of this rite[2] – the two cases could be treated as analogous, and canonical rules transferred from one to the other. Just as the bishop, through his consecration, joined the ranks of the governors of the *ecclesia* and became thereby subject to the rules of that body, so now the king, being, in his official capacity, *consecratus domino*, and receiving his office through the mediation of those same governors, entered the realm of the rules that bound them. Charles the Bald expressed Hincmar's ideas when he referred to his own anointing,

> a qua consecratione . . . proici a nullo debueram, saltem sine audientia et *iudicio episcoporum*, quorum ministerio in regem sum consecratus.[3]

Through his consecration, then, the king, like the bishop, became answerable to the judgment of his episcopal consecrators, and Hincmar, logically enough, made this the ground of their *maior dignitas*. The form and the substance of this jurisdiction now invite further exploration.

1. On Hincmar's methods in relation to canon law, see Fuhrmann, *op. cit.* i. 113 ff., and 121 f.: 'Wo Hinkmar die Falschen Dekretalen im Wege standen, verstand er es, sie auch für sich passend zu machen'. *Cf. ibid.* 205 with n. 35, for another comparable Hincmarian 'Verfälschung'.

2. See the preliminaries to the consecration of 869, Capit. II, pp. 338 ff., quoted in part, *supra* p. 139, n. 1; the anointing-prayer of the 869 *Ordo*: 'Ungat te in regni regimine . . .'; the *Ordo* of 877, *ibid.* 461: '. . . in regni regimine sublimiter colloca.'; the *Pro Ecc. Lib. Def.*, PL 125, col. 1040, where Hincmar told Charles: '. . . *episcopali et sacerdotali unctione* et benedictione *regiam dignitatem* potius quam terrena potestate *consecuti estis*'. Morrison, *op. cit.* p. 187, mistranslates this passage and disregards the *Ordines*. For the constitutive nature of the royal anointing, see also the *Benedictio regis in regno*, in the second ('B') of the *Benedictionals of Freising*, ed. R. Amiet (Henry Bradshaw Society vol. 88 for the years 1951 and 1952, publ. 1974) 100–1.

3. *Libellus contra Wenilonem*, c. 3, Capit. II, p. 451. The passage continues: '. . . et qui throni Dei sunt dicti, in quibus Deus sedet et per quos sua decernit iudicia; quorum paternis correptionibus et *castigatoriis iudiciis* me subdere fui paratus et in praesenti sum subditus'. For the basic meaning of *consecratio* in Christian usage as dedication to a particular function, see art. 'Consecratio' (L. Koep) in *Reallexikon für Antike und Christentum*, iii. 281 ff. See, for the background to the *Libellus*, Halphen, *Charlemagne et l'Empire Carolingien*, pp. 359 ff., and for Hincmar's probable authorship, Lot and Halpen, *op. cit.* p. 193 with n. 1. For a similar statement, see Charles's letter to Pope Hadrian II, PL 126, col. 881, complaining that the pope had misjudged him since he had been 'nullo crimine publico *in audientia episcopali legaliter et regulariter accusatum, minime autem convictum*'. *Cf.* also *ibid.* cols. 876 and 883, and the synodal letter of 858, Capit. II, p. 439. Hincmar's lack of consistency in expressing such views is understandable: as Anton, *op. cit.* p. 342, observes, Hincmar's statements were 'weitgehend tagespolitisch beeinflusst'.

In the first place, it became desirable to establish firm criteria on which an episcopal judgment could rest. This could most suitably be done at the time of the king's inauguration. Although from the mid-ninth century, the Frankish magnates often intervened decisively in the choosing of kings, and Hincmar readily acknowledged their role here,[1] the formal procedures of election came under clerical influence, in striking contrast with earlier Frankish custom. Not surprisingly, the procedures adopted showed similarities with the corresponding phase of episcopal ordination. From the fifth-century onwards, the episcopal ordinand had had to satisfy his consecrators of his doctrinal orthodoxy and personal suitability, and these assurances became the formal preliminaries to the consecration itself.[2] In the ninth century, Frankish bishops, certainly in the province of Rheims, had to give oral and written professions of faith and obedience as a precondition of their consecrations.[3]

The giving of written professions by bishops elect may well have been in West Frankia, as in contemporary England, a fairly recent innovation.[4] Although monks and nuns gave *professiones* 'of a rather different kind' from an early date, clerics do not seem to have done so before the seventh century,[5] and then, only from Visigothic Spain is there clear evidence for the demand of written professions

1. *Cf.* the preliminaries to the consecration of 869, Capit. II, p. 339, and Hincmar's account of the events leading up to that of 877, Ann. Bertin., ed. cit., p. 219. See also Hincmar's careful statement to Louis III, PL 126, col. 119: 'Non vos me elegistis in praelatione ecclesiae sed ego cum collegis meis et ceteris Dei *ac progenitorum vestrorum fidelibus* vos elegi ad regimen regni'. See the fine discussion of W. Schlesinger, 'Karlingische Königswahlen', in *Beiträge zur deutschen Verfassungsgeschichte* (Göttingen, 1963), i. 88 ff., esp. 135 ff.

2. *Statuta Ecclesiae Antiqua*, ed. Andrieu, *Les Ordines Romani du haut moyen âge* (Spicilegium Sacrum Lovaniense xxiv, Louvain, 1951), iii. 616 f. See also *idem.*, 'Le sacre épiscopal', pp. 31 ff.

3. The evidence was first published by Sirmond, *Concilia Antiqua Galliae* (Paris, 1615), ii. 651 ff., reprinted by E. Baluze, *Capitularia Regum Francorum* (Paris, 1677), ii. 614 ff., and thence conveniently in PL 87, cols. 915 ff. From the province of Rheims survive the profession of Adalbert of Thérouanne (871(?)–87) and the examination of Willebert of Châlons (868–78). For the profession of Hincmar of Laon, see *infra*, p. 161, n. 1. See T. Gottlob, *Der kirchliche Amtseid der Bischöfe* (Bonn, 1936, repr. 1963), pp. 150 ff.; Andrieu, 'Le sacre épiscopal', pp. 31 ff.; Beck, 'Canonical election', pp. 158 ff. Hincmar of Rheims' archiepiscopal profession, promising due subjection and obedience to the pope, and aid for his own suffragans, is printed, and its authenticity defended, in MGH Epp. VIII, Karolini Aevi VI, fasc. i, no. 1. *Cf.* Gottlob, *op. cit.* p. 31 and n. 136.

4. So Gottlob, *op. cit.* p. 150, seems to infer. On the English professions from the late eighth century onwards, see now the indispensable work of M. Richter, *Canterbury Professions* (Canterbury and York Society, vol. lxvii, Torquay, 1973). Richter suggests, p. xxxvii, that 'the purpose of their introduction into England may well have been to reassert the authority of the archbishop of Canterbury after the short-lived metropolitan ambitions of the bishopric of Lichfield under Hygebeorht at the end of the eighth century'. In some ways, this English context is unlike those of seventh-century Spain or ninth-century West Frankia: see p. 144 *infra*.

5. L. Hertling, 'Die Professio der Kleriker und die Entstehung der drei Gelübde', *Zeitschrift für Katholische Theologie*, lvi (1932), pp. 148 ff.

from ordinands of every grade as a prerequisite to consecration.[1] Behind this 'Spanish symptom' were specific circumstances to which Dr Michael Richter has recently drawn attention: social and political tensions which evoked a strong central government, its power manifested in the series of great Toledan councils to which 'members of the ruling class' both lay and ecclesiastical 'were called together at regular intervals'; and a similarly centralized church, headed in the later seventh century by an archbishop of Toledo intent upon establishing for the metropolitan see an effective primacy strengthened by the regular practice of episcopal profession. Richter has concluded that 'the profession of obedience . . . sanctions a pronounced hierarchical structure of the Church'.[2]

At least as far as the national church was concerned, many of these conditions were reproduced in the West Frankish kingdom in the mid-ninth century. In a time of political crisis, the episcopate became increasingly conscious of its own unity and responsibility – a consciousness at once the cause and the effect of frequent synodal activity[3] – and the archbishop of Rheims was using all his resources of political influence and canonical expertise to bring his suffragans under firmer metropolitan control.[4] It is against this background that the extant episcopal professions should be considered. Compared with contemporary English examples, they are surprisingly long and detailed, and their association with the formal examination immediately preceding the consecration-rite is clear. The archbishop himself posed the whole series of searching questions concerning moral and educational qualifications, and it was he who finally received the ordinand's written profession of doctrinal orthodoxy and obedience 'to the privileges of the church of Rheims'. Orthodoxy was defined by reference to the canons of previous councils, the *placita*, which were read out to, and acknowledged by, the ordinand and a copy of which he formally 'received' from his consecrators

1. See Richter, *op. cit.* pp. xii ff. It was clearly the episcopal practice of giving a written profession of obedience to the *ordinatores* which influenced Hincmar's shaping of the king's commitment: see pp.153 f. *infra*. Priestly, monastic and other professions are thus of no direct relevance here. David, *La Souveraineté*, pp. 90 ff., obscures this point.

2. *Op. cit.* pp. xv f.

3. See the works cited *supra*, p.136, n. 3, and my paper, 'National synods, kingship as office, and royal anointing: an early medieval syndrome', *SCH*, vii (1972), below, ch. 10, 239 ff. Some neglected aspects of Charles the Bald's government, suggesting continuing efforts at central control, have rightly been stressed by J. Campbell, 'Observations on English government from the tenth to the twelfth century', *Trans. R. Hist. Soc.*, xxv (1975), esp. pp. 44 ff.

4. See Schrörs, *op. cit.* pp. 318 ff.; Perels, *art. cit.* pp. 44 ff.; Beck, 'The selection of bishops suffragan to Hincmar of Rheims', *Catholic Historical Review*, xlv (1959), 273 ff. Lesne, *La hierarchie épiscopale*, pp. 57 ff. and 259 f., discusses metropolitan privileges at Rheims, Sens and elsewhere. On Rheims–Sens rivalry later in the ninth century and its impact on royal consecrations, see Schramm, *König von Frankreich*, pp. 112 ff.

and electors after his consecration.[1] Through his profession, therefore, he personally subscribed to the laws of the church – quite literally underwrote them. If obedience was a crucial part of any suffragan's profession, so also (and this has been less often stressed) was his 'confirmation' of the canonical *regulae*: in Hincmar's view, this aspect of episcopal incorporation in the church's government seems to have complemented the role of synodal *assensus* in the creation of the church's law.

Given his concern with discipline, with subordinating the bishop's office to metropolitan jurisdiction and with clarifying the rules governing its conferment, Hincmar's interest was naturally in episcopal, rather than monastic or priestly, profession: in a written and legally-enforceable obligation, rather than a vocational commitment. His emphasis on the written documents involved in the election and examination of a bishop was part of a more general insistence on conformity with written law – whether the *regulae* of the church or the *leges et statuta* of Christian princes.[2] Since both

1. The profession of Adalbert, PL 87, col. 916: '. . . sed et observationes ac regularia mandata, sacrorumque conciliorum *placita*, quae post ordinationem episcopalem in libellis canonicis secundum morem ecclesiasticam *propriis subscriptionibus roboratis collecta*, et mihi tradenda coram omnibus praedixistis, me servaturum profiteor, et omnibus supra scriptis cum cordis et oris professione subscribo.' *Cf.* the *examinatio* of Willebert, PL 87, col. 915: following the ordinand's satisfying the doctrinal requirements laid down in the *Statuta Ecclesiae Antiqua*, 'Tunc relecta sunt ei *placita* quae episcopus iam ordinatus ab ordinatoribus et electoribus suis suscipere debet'. Hincmar's use of the term *placita* to mean conciliar decrees was certainly influenced by ancient canons, esp. c. xxi of the Carthaginian canons of 419: 'Ut ordinandis episcopis vel clericis prius ab ordinatoribus suis *placita conciliorum auribus eorum inculcentur* ne se aliquid contra statuta concilii fecisse poeniteant'. The reading *ordinandis* is correctly given by Hincmar in the preface to the *LV Capit.*, PL 126, cols. 292 f., following the Dacheriana, III, c. cxxxv, ed. J.-L. D'Achéry, *Spicilegium sive collectio veterum aliquot scriptorum* (2nd edn., Paris, 1723), i. 561, where the Dionysio-Hadriana gives *ordinatis*, in at least one version, PL 67, col. 189. Hincmar continues, *loc. cit.*: 'Quae [placita] a me tibi ordinando inculcata sunt . . . Quando librum sacrorum canonum et regulam pastoralem beati Gregorii . . . in manum misi, . . . ipsos libros . . . te ita observaturum consensione tua confirmastis'. He concludes by quoting c. xiii of the council of 419 (see p. 158, *infra*), Ep. 84 of Leo I, 'de sua erga leges consensione si contra illam fecerit', and finally, I Carthage, c. xiv: 'Quae vel facta vel dicta superius comprehensa sunt, vel ab aliis conciliis conscripta, quae secundum legem inveniuntur, custodire nos oportet. Si quis vero statuta supergressus corruperit, vel pro nihilo habenda putaverit, si laicus est communione, si clericus est honore privetur.' *Cf.* Hincmar's argument in *De Ordine Palatii*, c. 15, ed. cit. p. 523: 'Neque iuxta decreta ex sacris canonibus promulgata beati Gregorii praetoria . . . debent [episcopi] inutiliter observare, ne incurrant iudicium ut contra *placita canonum sibi in ordinatione sua tradita* facientes ipsi sibi honore privent ecclesiastico'. On *privatio honoris*, see p. 157, *infra*. On the significance of the synodal *assensus* for Hincmar's ecclesiology, see Morrison, *op. cit.* pp. 19 and 91 ff., and the brilliant sketch of Congar, *L'Ecclésiologie*, pp. 169 ff., noting, p. 174, of the mid-ninth century: 'Nous sommes donc à un moment ou . . . les structures canoniques entrent dans la conception *dogmatique* de l'Église' (his stress). Professor Ullmann kindly points out to me that the result was precisely 'une conception *juridique*'.

2. *Cf.* the reference to laws made 'non nudo verbo sed scripto', in the letter to Charles the Bald, *supra* p. 242, n. 4, and also the text quoted *infra*, p. 163, n. 3. For Hincmar's appreciation of written law, see Devisse, *Hincmar et la Loi*, pp. 88 ff., and Morrison, *op. cit.* pp. 88 ff. For the wider background, see F. Ganshof, 'The use of the written word in Charlemagne's administration', in *The Carolingians and the Frankish*

king and bishop performed similarly ministerial functions, since both were similarly consecrated, Hincmar when designing formal preliminaries to a king-making rite logically drew on the existing well-developed model of the episcopal examination and profession, with their peculiarly apt stress of office defined by reference to laws. Interestingly enough, in the earlier Spanish case also, there are obvious parallels between the undertakings which kings had to give on oath before they could be inaugurated, and the *adnotatio placiti* demanded of every cleric before he could receive his *honor*.[1] The introduction of the profession changed nothing in the content of the office, nor in men's expectations of the office-holder. What was new was the personal, public and written commitment to specific laws and rules. For from this it followed that quite precise conditions could be set on the assumption of office, and that these conditions thereafter stood as the terms on which the office was held. If the conditions were to operate effectively, their breach would have to entail the application of equally precise juristic sanctions. Here Hincmar was able to provide a neater and more theoretically-convincing solution than those adumbrated in seventh-century Spain.[2]

Part of the explanation for Hincmar's achievement lies in his own legal knowledge and liturgical creativity. Another no less important part lies in the political creativity of the West Frankish

---

Monarchy (London, 1971), esp. p. 126 with n. 6. The stress on written documents in Charles the Bald's capitularies is no less remarkable: see Devisse, art. cit. (*supra*, p. 133, n. 1), p. 182, and Campbell, art. cit., p. 48. Underlying these Carolingian efforts at governmental consistency and continuity was, I suggest, in practice if not in legal theory, a trend in public law analogous to that traced in private law by L. Stouff, 'La formation des contrats par l'écriture dans le droit des formules du V au XII siècle', *Nouvelle Revue Historique du Droit Francais et Etranger*, xi (1887), 249 ff., esp. 259 and 274 f.: both in the later empire and in the barbarian kingdoms, the written document was regarded in common practice, though not in theory, as 'le principe de la force même du contrat'.

1. *Cf.* the wording of XI Toledo, c. 10, PL 84, col. 475: '. . . ut unusquisque qui ad ecclesiasticos gradus est ascensurus, non ante honoris consecrationem accipiat, quam *placiti sui adnotatione* promittat, ut fidem catholicam . . .' etc., with IV Tol., c. 3, PL 84, col. 396: '. . . non ante conscendat [rex] regiam sedem, quam . . . pollicitus fuerit . . .', etc., and Lex Visig. II. i. 6, MGH Leges I, p. 51: '. . . non ante quispiam solium regale conscendat quam iuramenti foedere . . . promittat', etc., the royal oath occurring here in precisely the context of succession to the *res regni*, *i.e.* the official, not personal resources of the king. For comparable notions in episcopal and royal contexts, see Ullmann, 'A note on inalienability', *Studi Gregoriani*, ix (1972), esp. 123 f. with n. 30. On Visigothic royal oaths, see David, 'Le Serment,' pp. 39 ff. Hincmar may have been familiar with the Toledan councils through the Hispana: see p. 156, n. 3 *infra*. Ullmann, *Carolingian Renaissance*, p. 81 with n. 2, suggests that he may also have been familiar with the Visigothic laws. The question of direct Spanish influence needs further investigation.

2. The limitations of seventh-century Visigothic theory are well brought out by P. D. King, *Law and Society in the Visigothic Kingdom* (Cambridge, 1972), pp. 44 ff. The removal of Wamba (683) shows parallels with the case of Louis the Pious in the exploitation of penitential discipline. Though Wamba had been anointed king by the archbishop of Toledo, the latter's successor Julian did not claim an episcopal jurisdiction over the king arising from that fact.

fideles, laymen and clerics alike, who from the early 840s helped to create a new polity: the West Frankish realm. Active participants already at Strasburg (842) and Verdun (843), these men joined with Charles the Bald in making the *pactum* of Coulaines in November 843.[1] They promised to uphold the *honor regis*, while Charles in turn 'granted' (the term is *perdono*, but the context here imposes on it a promissory sense) certain guarantees for the *honor ecclesiae* and, significantly, the *honor fidelium*:

Legem vero unicuique competentem sicut antecessores sui tempore meorum praedecessorum habuerunt, in omni dignitate et ordine, favente deo, *me observaturum perdono*.[2]

The pact signalized not confrontation but a hoped-for working partnership between king, clergy and *populus*. The *lex* acknowledged by the ancestors of king and subject alike set limits on the arbitrary exercise of the king's will and, at the same time, imposed obligations on the *fidelis*. Thus at the outset of Charles's de facto rule, the law appeared as the guarantee of the social and political relations which underpinned the realm: subjectively, it enshrined what were perceived as the 'fair dues' of the *fidelis*, while objectively, as the king's law, laid down, for example, in the pact of 843 itself, it preserved the structure of the state as a whole. The drafter(s) at Coulaines succeeded in expressing and in giving shape to contemporary political realities; and the pact, written down and preserved, became the source of subsequent definitions of the terms on which royal power was exercised. At Beauvais (845) and at Quierzy (858), Charles gave to the bishops renewed commitments to uphold ecclesiastical privileges, while for their part the bishops

1. Capit. II, pp. 253 ff. The fundamental study is by P. Classen, 'Die Verträge von Verdun und Coulaines, 843, als politische Grundlagen des westfränkischen Reiches', *Hist. Zeitschrift*, cxcvi (1963), 1 ff. See also Schlesinger, 'Die Auflösung des Karlsreiches', in *Karl der Grosse*, ed. H. Beumann (Düsseldorf, 1965), i. 792 ff., esp. 838 ff. Devisse, art. cit., throws valuable light on the interrelation of political theory and practice in Charles the Bald's reign, though apparently without reference to Classen's work. For the role of the *fideles* in 842 and 843, see Nithard, *Historiarum libri IV*, iii. 5 and iv. 4 (ed. P. Lauer, Paris, 1926), pp. 100 ff. and 130; and Capit. II, pp. 171 ff.

2. Capit. II, p. 25. Devisse, art. cit., p. 181 with n. 11, interprets *lex competens* in terms of a 'gentile' personality of laws, and suggests interestingly that a demand for the affirmation of this principle could have arisen at this time in response to rumours that Charles, under clerical influence, was considering the substitution of the territoriality principle as exemplified in Visigothic law. Again, the possibility of Spanish influence deserves attention. But *lex competens* in association here with a man's *dignitas* and *ordo* has as much to do with feudal as 'gentile' politics. For the history of these and similar notions in Frankish public law, see Kern, *Gottesgnadentum*, pp. 294 ff., and p. 149, n. 1 *infra*. Devisse insists, similarly, *ubi supra*, that *perdonare* here retains its original sense of concession. I prefer to follow Lot and Halphen, *op. cit.* p. 93 and David, 'Le serment', p. 53, n. 26, whose interpretation takes into account the total context. Classen, 'Die Verträge', p. 30, points out that as early as 845/6, the synodists of Meaux–Paris altered the wording of 843: '. . . nostram magnificentiam observaturam *promittimus*'. This was bringing *nomen* into line with *res*: a royal concession not concealed by the assumed magnificence of the royal 'we'!

in their *Consilium* of 856, and Hincmar himself in 868, reminded Charles of what had been settled at Coulaines.[1] At Meersen (851), Charles declared that he and his *fideles* would act together to ensure that 'et vobis lex et iustitia conservetur, et vos nobis sicut antecessores vestri nostris antecessoribus fecerunt, debitum honorem et auxilium exhibeatis', and again, in 858, he undertook, *sicut fidelis rex*, to keep every one of his subjects *honoratum ac salvatum*.[2] Church and lay *fideles* were to thrive together.

Whoever may have composed the text of the pact of 843, there can be little doubt as to who plagiarized and publicized, built on and elaborated its terms in the decades that followed: everything points to the key role played by Hincmar both in the continuing quest for consensus and in the persistent emphasizing of specific royal commitments. He is surely the likeliest candidate for the role of collector of a series of West Frankish public documents covering the years 843 to 856 and beginning with the *pactum* of Coulaines.[3] Ten of the pieces in this collection are referred to in the *Consilium* addressed to Charles the Bald by the bishops assembled at Bonneuil in 856. Although direct evidence is lacking, Hincmar's prominence at this time and his masterminding of so many synods in the 840s and 850s make his presence at Bonneuil very likely. The *Consilium* itself bears some hallmarks of his hortatory style in addressing kings: a string of previous royal commitments is cited, stress is laid on the king's subscription of laws *manu propria*, and Charles is finally enjoined, '[haec capitula] diligenter et frequenter ad memoriam reducatis ac relegatis'.[4] If Hincmar's authorship is

1. Capit. II, pp. 387 f. (Beauvais), 296 (Quierzy), and 424 (*Consilium* of 856). For Hincmar's appeal to earlier promises in the *Pro Ecc. Lib. Def.*, PL 125, col. 1066, see *infra*, pp. 163-4. See also Schramm, *König von Frankreich*, pp. 68 f., and C. Odegaard, 'Carolingian Oaths of Fidelity', *Speculum*, xvi (1941), 282.

2. Capit. II, pp. 74 (Charles's *Adlocutio* at Meersen) and 296 (promise of 858). For other borrowings from the text of Coulaines, see Capit. II, pp. 398 f. (Meaux–Paris, 845–6), 303 (Pîtres, 862), 333 f. (Pîtres, 869), 339 (Metz, 869), 355 f. (Quierzy, 877). *Cf.* also Hincmar's *Instructio* to Louis the Stammerer, Nov. 877, in PL 125, cols. 987 f.

3. Classen, 'Die Verträge', pp. 28 ff., analyses the content of this collection and notes the possibility that Hincmar was responsible: see esp. his comments, p. 28, n. 1 and 29, n. 2, on the Hague MS. 10 D 2 (cited in Capit. II as 'Hague MS. 1'). Devisse, art. cit., seemingly independently, lends support to this view on internal stylistic evidence, though he does not discuss the collection as such.

4. Capit. II, pp. 424 f. *Cf.* Hincmar's advice to Louis III, PL 126, col. 292: 'diligenter relegi eam [professionem] facite coram vobis'; also *Pro Ecc. Lib. Def.*, PL 125, col. 1040: 'illa quae ... subscripsistis ... ante oculos et mentis et corporis revocare debetis'. For comparable evidence of Hincmar's references to previous royal commitments, see p. 148, n. 1 *supra*. For the collection of materials in the cathedral archive of Rheims, see Lesne, *Histore de la Propriété Ecclésiastique*, iv. 812 f., and Fuhrmann, *op. cit.* iii. 672, n. 141 and 726, n. 318. Devisse, art. cit., says nothing about the *Consilium*, which admittedly lacks the particular 'Hincmarian' verbal traits with which Devisse is concerned. The lack of direct evidence of Hincmar's presence at Bonnueil need not be significant: only a chance reference in Flodoard has preserved the fact of his presence at Quierzy in 857 (Schrörs, *op. cit.* pp. 77, 274 with n. 23), yet V. Krause, 'Hincmar von Reims der Verfasser der sog. *Collectio de raptoribus* im Capitular von Quierzy, 857', *Neues Archiv*, xviii (1893), 303 ff., argues convincingly that Hincmar wrote the

accepted for the *Consilium*, then, given their almost identical list of *capitularia*, the collection of public documents can probably also be assigned to him.

The incorporation of a royal commitment into the clerically-conducted procedures of later Carolingian king-making was certainly Hincmar's work.[1] There is no sign of any formal promise before the consecration of Charles in 848, nor of his son in 855, neither rite being conducted by Hincmar.[2] In 869, however, Hincmar was responsible both for the rite whereby Charles was consecrated to the kingdom of Lotharingia and for the formalities which preceded it.[3] Though not built into the rite itself, these

---

Admonitio which accompanied Charles's legislation. A further sign of Hincmar's influence might be seen in the citation here, Capit. II, pp. 285 ff., of relevant capitularies of Charlemagne and Louis the Pious: for other examples of Hincmar's drawing on such sources, see p. 163, n. 3 and p. 170, n. 3 *infra*.

1. See David, 'Le serment', pp. 127 ff., and Bouman, *op cit*., p. 141. Earlier instances of rulers' promises, in many cases unrelated to accession, are given by Kern, *Gottesgnadentum*, pp. 294 ff. For some Visigothic evidence, see p. 254, n. 1 *supra*. For the Franks, see the sixth-century case of Charibert, Gregory of Tours, *Historiae Francorum*, ix. 30, ed. B. Krusch and W. Levison, 1951, MGH SS. rer. Merov., i. pp. 448 f.: '. . . rege populus hic sacramentum dedit; similiter etiam et *ille cum iuramento promisit*, ut leges consuetudinesque novas populo non infligeret . . .'. These mutual commitments show a certain similarity to those of Coulaines. I know of no other example from the intervening period, though, for a promise by a new Burgundian mayor of the palace 'per epistolas etiam et sacramentis' to preserve to each his 'gradum honoris et dignetatem seo amiciciam', *cf*. Fredegar, *Chronicle*, iv. c. 89, ed. Wallace-Hadrill, pp. 75 f. In 813 when Charlemagne crowned Louis co-emperor, the latter had to promise obedience to a series of paternal admonitions including an injunction that 'nullum ab honore suo sine causa discretionis eiecisset': Thegan, *Vita Ludovici*, ed. W. Pertz, MGH SS. II, pp. 591 f. But Louis's undertaking was given to his father, not to his subjects. *Cf*. the comments of Schlesinger, 'Karlingische Königswahlen', p. 93, on the 'Machtvollkommenheit' of Pippin and Charlemagne. Kern, *op. cit*. pp. 300 and 304 f. neglects the important distinction, since observed by Schramm, *Kaiser, Könige und Päpste*, ii. 180, between royal commitment (*Verpflichtung*) and royal instructions issued to the people (*Vorschriften*). *Vorschriften* may well have been issued by the early Carolingians, but *Verpflichtungen* are a ninth-century development. Yet, though formally so different, their similarity of content to earlier *capitula* and *precepta* should be noted: *cf*. my comments on the comparable Anglo-Saxon material in *SCH*, xi; below, chapter 14, pp. 335-6. The early Carolingians' promises to the popes, discussed by Schramm, *op. cit*. i. pp. 149 f., are not relevant here. (The reference of Morrison, *op. cit*. p. 201 and n. 68, is very misleading.)

2. But the evidence on both events is meagre: on 848, see p. 137, n. 4 *supra*; on 855, the sole source is Ann. Bertin., ed. cit., p. 71, and except under Hincmar's authorship, as these annals were from 861 to 882, such a source could not be expected to give details of royal inaugurations. For the different nature of the evidence for 869 and 877, see *infra*.

3. Capit. II, pp. 337 ff.: the preliminaries, and 456 f.: the rite, in the form of a protocol, *i.e.* instead of rubrics, having short statements in the perfect tense indicating how the *Ordo* was actually performed. Such explicit details are rare in contemporary liturgical books: Andrieu, 'Le sacre épiscopal', pp. 40 ff. The significance of the protocol form was noted by Schramm, 'Ordines-Studien II: die Krönung un Frankreich', *Archiv für Urkundenforschung*, xv. 1 (1938), 12, and by Bouman, *op. cit*. pp. 8 f., who however wrongly used the term to designate all four of Hincmar's *Ordines*. On the single MS., now lost, see p.138, n. 1 *supra*; the preliminaries too were in this and another lost MS., but Hincmar also gave them in full in the Ann. Bertin. Schramm, *König von Frankreich*, pp. 27 f., noting the formal similarities with procedure at synods, observes: 'Wie von selbst müsste sich da das Verfahren, durch das die Kirche seit alters Beschlüsse einer Versammlung herbeiführte, zur Nachahmung anbieten'.

formalities were conducted by the officiating clergy inside the church, and were presented by them as necessary preliminaries to the royal anointing. Adventius of Metz informed the congregation on the bishops' behalf:

... Videtur nobis, si vobis placet, ut, sicut *post illius verba* vobis manifestabimus, signo certissimo demonstrabimus, quia illum a deo *electum* et nobis datum *principem* credimus ...

Et si illi placet, dignum ipsi et *necessarium nobis* esse videtur, ut ex eius ore audiamus, quod a christianissimo rege fideli et unanimi in servitio illius populo, unicuique in suo ordine convenit audire ...

The bishops sought not only a unilateral undertaking from the *princeps electus*[1] but a reaffirmation of the mutual understandings between him and his leading subjects. Charles's *Responsio*, appropriately addressed to the people 'faithful and unanimous in his service', was not quite the *Herrschereid* that Schramm has claimed. It was, almost verbatim, a repetition of the terms of Coulaines, here given a new significance by their setting. For Charles's *Responsio* of 869 was represented as the precondition of his being made king of Lotharingia. In form it was neither a promise nor an oath, but an announcement: 'Know ye that I preserve . . .' etc.[2] Its true analogues were the *adnuntiationes*, the formal public statements made by Charlemagne and his successors which thus became binding law.[3] From the time of Charlemagne onwards, the *adnuntiatio*, like the oath, tended to get written down,[4] an understandable development

1. Calling Charles *rex noster*, Capit. II, p. 340, Hincmar seems to have referred only to the kingship of the West Franks. Adventius of Metz spoke for the Lotharingians in calling Charles *princeps noster*, and again, 'a deo electus et nobis datus *princeps*'. For Adventius's role, see O. G. Oexle, 'Die Karolinger und die Stadt des hl. Arnulf', *Frühmittelalterliche Studien*, i (1967), 351 ff. For the constitutive character of anointing see p. 142, n. 2 *supra*. *Cf.* the 'Frühdeutsch' *Ordo*, where the ruler is termed *princeps* until the anointing and only thereafter, *rex*: C. Erdmann, *Forschungen zur politischen Ideenwelt des Frühmittelalters* (Berlin, 1951), pp. 83 ff. See also Ullmann, 'Der Souveränitätsgedanke in den Krönungsordines', *Festschrift P. E. Schramm* (Wiesbaden, 1964), i. 77, n. 24. H. Wolfram, *Intitulatio* (Graz–Cologne, 1967), pp. 145 ff., shows the use of *princeps* in eighth-century titles to designate one who exercised royal *potestas* without the royal *nomen*.

2. Capit. II, p. 339: 'Sciatis me honorem et cultum Dei . . . conservare et unumquemque vestrum . . . honorare . . . et unicuique in suo ordine *secundum sibi competentes leges* tam ecclesiasticas quam mundanas *legem et iustitiam* conservare; in hoc, ut honor regius et potestas ac debita obedientia atque adiutorium . . . ab unoquoque vestrum . . . mihi exhibeatur'. The reciprocal nature of the obligations is here explicit. *Cf.* similar wording and involvement of the *populus* in Charles's *Adlocutio* at Meersen, 851, quoted *supra*, p. 148. This text also appears in the collection of documents discussed *supra*, p. 148.

3. For examples, see Nithard, iii. 5, ed. cit. pp. 100 ff.; Capit. II, pp. 68 ff., 72 ff., 153. At these meetings of Carolingian brother-kings and their *fideles*, as Classen, 'Die Verträge', p. 31 observes, it is Charles whose *adnuntiationes* particularly stress 'die Rechte der Fideles als Mitträger des Staates'. On the *adnuntiatio* and the verbal promulgation of law, especially under Charlemagne, see A. Dumas, 'La parole et l'écriture dans les capitulaires carolingiens', *Mélanges Halphen* (Paris, 1951), pp. 209 ff.

4. Classen, 'Die Verträge', p. 15. Note the parallel, unmentioned by Classen, of Adventius' *adnuntiatio* in 869 which in most MSS. seems to have been headed: '. . . haec quae sequuntur capitula Adventius episcopus . . . publice populo et *scripto* et verbis

in view of the increasingly vital role played by clerics in the promulgation and the preservation of public law and their increasing awareness of the need, not least in their own interests, for governmental consistency and continuity. In the political context of the West Frankish kingdom, a royal *adnuntiatio*, once given permanent and tangible form as a written text, and kept for reference in a cathedral archive, assumed a new and particular importance. On the one hand, the *fideles* had a strong interest in holding Charles the Bald to the terms of public statements they heard from his own lips, yet increasingly the *fideles* in contact with the king comprised only the great magnate families, operating in practice as factional groups, while legally, it has been argued, they remained the recipients of royal commands.[1] On the other hand, Hincmar and his colleagues could now become the custodians of the law not only in fact, as scribes and keepers of the texts in which laws were fixed and preserved, but also in juristic theory, as king-makers and definers of the royal function *leges servandi*. The king's *adnuntiatio*, which the *fideles* received as a command, was therefore at the same time, from the episcopal standpoint, a royal undertaking in so far as the king was bound to obey his own just laws. Juxtaposed to the king-making rite, the 'announcement' of the *electus* was now endowed with a conditional sense, and became indistinguishable in function from a public promise given to the king-makers. This explains why Hincmar could invoke Charles's *Responsio* of 869 as a '*promissio* ... quam verbo *et scripto*, antequam rex consecraretur, *episcopis* fecerat'.[2]

denuntiavit'. For the sources, see the comments of Boretius, Capit. II, pp. 337 f. The same MSS. give Charles's *responsio* the heading: 'Post haec Karolus rex haec quae sequuntur ... cunctis qui affuerunt *denunciavit*'. Schramm, *Kaiser, Könige und Päpste*, ii. 149, suggests that a written document could have been involved here also: for confirmation, see *infra*. For the transition from spoken to written word, see Charles's statement at Coblenz, Capit. II, p. 153: '... capitula a communibus fidelibus nostris *dictata* et nobis *relecta* nos observaturos promisimus'. Compare the verbal forms of 842 with Ann. Fuld., s.a. 876, ed. cit. p. 89: '... cuius sacramenti textus *theutonica lingua conscriptus in nonnullis locis habetur*'. For the written oath, see H. Mitteis, *Lehnsrecht und Staatsgewalt* (Weimar, 1933), p. 61 with Classen, *ubi supra*, p. 15, n. 3. *Cf.* also p. 145, n. 2 *supra*.

1. For the legal position of the *fideles*, see Ullmann, *Carolingian Renaissance*, pp. 115 f., and *idem.*, 'Schranken der Königsgewalt im Mittelalter', in *Hist. Jahrbuch*, xci (1971), 13. *Cf.* also Wallace-Hadrill, 'Via Regia', p. 39, noting, however, practical resistance 'of an untidy sort' on the part of the *populus*. Classen, art. cit., shows the significance of Coulaines in the developing reciprocal relations between *rex* and *fideles*. It was the disunity of the latter which came to pose the most acute political problem: *cf.* the acute comments of Löwe art. cit. (*supra* p. 133, n. 1) 222 ff. I cannot follow Ullmann, *Carolingian Renaissance*, p. 112, in stressing only the divergence between the aims and interests of 'the hierarchy and the king on the one side and the magnates on the other'.

2. Flodoard, *Historia Remensis Ecclesiae*, iii. c. 18, MGH Scriptores XIII, p. 508 = Hincmar's Register no. 356 in Schrörs, *op. cit.* p. 544: 'Karoli regi de XII abusivis colligens dicta patrum et *constitutiones regum*, sed et de promissione sua eum admonens, quam verbo ...' etc. Schrörs dates this '870–5' and observes, p. 583, n. 135, that 869 must have been the occasion referred to. Though the text of this letter is lost, the fact that it existed deserves more attention.

At the next West Frankish king-making, in 877, Hincmar brought form and function more closely into line. Now built into the *Ordo* proper was a *Petitio episcoporum*, requesting a guarantee of ecclesiastical rights and privileges, to which the king replied with a *Promissio*: 'I promise and grant . . .'[1] The term 'grant' (*perdonare*), a throwback to the wording of Coulaines from which the promise itself was ultimately derived, was now hardly consistent with the obligatory nature of the king's commitment. Here, the distinction between *promittere* and *perdonare* was blurred, only the former's sense remaining.[2] The promise concerned ecclesiastical interests alone. But the new king had also given, a week before his consecration, a more general commitment. After promising to uphold the *regulae* of the church, Louis the Stammerer had continued:

Polliceor etiam me servaturum *leges et statuta* populo qui mihi ad regendum misericordia dei committitur, pro communi consilio fidelium nostrorum, secundum quod praedecessores mei, imperatores et reges, gestis inseruerunt, et omnino inviolabiliter tenenda et observanda decreverunt.[3]

The reference to *leges et statuta* was no mere conventional phrase. The insistence on the maintenance of (written) laws as the essence of divinely sanctioned rulership reflected Hincmar's views on government in general. *Leges et statuta* had their counterpart in the *regulae ecclesiasticae*: just as the bishops' subscriptions appended to synodal decrees affirmed and confirmed their binding force, so did the royal subscription in the making or reissuing of secular laws, and just as a bishop's profession at his ordination committed him to maintain the canonical *regulae*, so the king's profession appropriately bound him to observe *inviolabiliter* the laws which his predecessors had made or which he himself might make in the future.

The royal undertaking of 877 followed nearly two months of negotiations between the young Louis the Stammerer and the great men of the realm as to the disposition of various *honores*. Louis's preparedness for concessions made possible the fulfilment of Charles's deathbed command designating Louis as his heir and directing the dowager Richildis to hand over to her stepson the regalia: sword, clothing, crown and sceptre. The *honores* were duly

1. Capit. II, pp. 364 f.: 'Promitto et perdono . . .'. *Cf.* a further reference to 'hanc spontaneam promissionem meam'.

2. *Cf. supra*, p. 147, n. 2.

3. Capit. II, pp. 364 f.; and Ann. Bertin., ed. cit., p. 221, where the editor assumes that Hincmar misplaced events and that the *professio* actually followed the anointing. But the view of A. Boretius, Capit. II, p. 364, is certainly preferable: the Ann. Bertin. account should be received as it stands. There were two episcopal petitions, the first associated with the distribution of *honores* (*infra*, p. 153), the second, demanding confirmation of ecclesiastical privileges, built into the *Ordo* itself. Both the *professio* of 30 Nov. and the royal *promissio* of 8 Dec. were responses to episcopal requests. For further details, see Boretius, *ubi supra*.

assigned to those who demanded them: *pactis honoribus singulis quos petierunt*.[1] The formal agreement here implied was presumably the occasion on which Louis gave his promise to preserve the laws and statutes for his people. In his subscription, he used for the only time the title:

misericordia domini dei nostri et electione populi rex constitutus.[2]

The *fideles'* acceptance of Louis, sealed by the agreement on the disposition of *honores*, was the reality behind this notion of an *electio populi*. There is no evidence of any other secular formality. The swearing of *fidelitas* by the magnates was coming to be seen in theory as in fact as the expression of their choice of king. But that choice was depicted by ecclesiastical writers, and perceived no doubt by the *fideles* themselves, as a manifestation of the divine will. God acted through the agency of the *populus*.[3] Hence the *electio* of Louis's title, as in canon law usage, bore the connotation of divine approval and was therefore both apt for the occasion and quite compatible with the invocation of the *misericordia dei*.

It was Hincmar himself who gave Louis's first promise the label *professio*, while the bishops' petition was answered with a *promissio* in the *Ordo* proper. Schramm observed that Hincmar was clearly very conscious of an analogy with the bishops' commitment: 'the forms of the church set the pattern for those of the state in those areas where they were already further developed'.[4] But he did not go on to link the profession specifically with consecration to office, which for Hincmar was the essential common factor in the royal and episcopal *Ordines*. M. David has stressed the parallel between royal professions on the one hand, and monastic and clerical professions in general on the other, concluding that the clergy had in some way incorporated the king into their ranks and made him

1. Ann. Bertin., ed. cit., p. 221. For these events, see Schramm, *König von Frankreich*, pp. 54 ff. (though, p. 56, wrongly terming Richildis Louis's 'mother'). Brühl, 'Hinkmariana', p. 72, presents an ingenious and plausible explanation of the rift at this time between lay *primores* (counts and lay abbots) and bishops: the former insisted, as a condition of their accepting Louis, that he repudiate his first wife and marry a lady of their rank and choosing. Episcopal objections were set aside.

2. Ann. Bertin., *loc. cit. Cf.* the comment of Schramm, *König von Frankreich*, pp. 55 f.: 'Das ist um so auffällender, als gar keine Wahlversammlung stattgefunden hätte'. But the swearing of *fidelitas* by the *primores* now took the place of any formal election: see Schlesinger, 'Karlingische Königswahlen', pp. 135 ff. This is also suggested by Adventius's words in 869, Capit. II, pp. 340 f.: 'Non incongruum videtur . . . ut in obtentu regni, unde vos ad illum *sponte convenistis et vos ei commendastis* . . . Domino consecretur', and by Charles's response to the *populus*: 'vos acclamastis me Dei electione ad . . . gubernationem hic advenisse'.

3. *Cf.* though in reference to the Anglo-Saxons, my comments in *SCH*, xi (1975); below, ch. 14, pp. 335ff. For a different view of Louis's title, see Ullmann, *Carolingian Renaissance*, p. 96: *misericordia Dei* and *electio populi* are 'two irreconcilables'.

4. *König von Frankreich*, p. 55.

into 'a kind of cleric'.[1] But the *rex et sacerdos* conception cannot legitimately be invoked in such vague terms here. Schramm was surely right to discern a precise and exclusive analogy with episcopal profession. What is relevant is Hincmar's idea of the king as a *minister*, that is, one holding an office of government over the *populus christianus* and responsible for the welfare of the *ecclesia*. Hincmar himself, as a bishop, had refused to make the apparently unconditional personal commitment (*in omnibus*) involved in the oath of the lay subject to the king, insisting instead on the qualified commitment of a profession *secundum ministerium suum*. His fierce protest to Charles the Bald over this issue is well-known.[2] It is worth noting the appearance of the distinction between profession and oath in close conjunction with Hincmar's account of Louis's profession of 877: as part of the agreement between the king and his *fideles*, the bishops commended themselves and their churches, making a profession (*profitentes juxta suum ministerium*), whereas the abbots[3] and other lay magnates commended themselves, promising fidelity with oaths (*sacramentis*). It can be no coincidence, therefore, that Louis is described only a few lines later as giving a profession – a type of promise made by an office-holder rather than an individual, and by which the interests of the *ecclesia* were always reserved.[4]

In Hincmar's account, two other features of Louis's profession are also significant. Not only was it made to the bishops, but it was written down, and the document, signed by the king, was likewise handed over to the bishops:

> Ad suprascriptam vero episcoporum petitionem haec quae sequuntur rex Hludowicus professus est *episcopis*, et istam ipsam donationis scripturam manu sua *eis dedit*. . . .[5]

Thus, like the promise within the *Ordo*, the profession remained in the archiepiscopal archive, to be brought out and held up to the king whenever the bishops might consider timely a reminder of its contents.[6] Hincmar's stress on the profession as a written document

1. *La Souveraineté*, p. 104; and p. 128, n. 31: 'le monarque, par le sacre, cesse d'être un simple laic'. But David cites evidence from a later period, whose relevance to the ninth century cannot be assumed. On theocratic kingship, see the sensible remarks of H. Fichtenau, *Das karolingische Imperium* (Zurich, 1949), p. 66, n. 58, and, from a different standpoint, W. Dürig, 'Der theologische Ausgangspunkt der mittelalterlichen liturgischen Auffassung vom Herrscher als Vicarius Dei', *Hist. Jahrbuch*, lxxvii (1958), 176 ff. *Cf.* also Anton, *op. cit.* pp. 110 f.

2. On the letter of 876, PL 125, cols. 1125 f., see R. Boutruche, *Seigneurie et Féodalité* (Paris, 1959), pp. 185 f., 200, and now the exhaustive discussion of Anton, *op. cit.* pp. 321 ff.

3. Clearly lay abbots: *cf. supra* p. 153, n. 1.

4. See Schlesinger, 'Karlingische Königswahlen', p. 120; Anton, *op. cit.* p. 327.

5. Ann. Bertin., ed. cit. p. 221.

6. *Cf. supra* p. 148, n. 4 and p. 151, n. 2. See also Hincmar's admonition to Louis III, PL 125, col. 112: 'Recordamini, quaeso, *professionis vestrae* quam in die consecrationis vestrae promisistis'. The reference here is to the *promissio* given in response to the bishops' petition in the *Ordo* itself, as in Capit. ii, p. 370. In terming this a profession, Hincmar suggests the functional similarity of the two commitments.

bearing the royal signature, quite distinct from the simply verbal undertakings still prevalent in lay society, illustrates his extension of canonical practice to cover the royal case, through a specific analogy with episcopal profession.

The profession of 877 included a guarantee not only for the ecclesiastical *regulae* but for secular *leges* too. Hincmar was implicitly claiming that the bishops were responsible for the surveillance of all the king's official actions, including, that is, the protection of the *honor fidelium*, the interests of the *populus* enshrined in the laws,[1] as well as of the institutional church.[2] The bishops' reception of the profession from the king presupposed their qualification to judge whether or not the king was performing his function of preserving rather than destroying the laws, and maintaining rather than undermining the subject's *iustitia*. Though the notion of the king as *tutor regni*[3] remains only implicit in the profession, the limitation placed on his freedom of action in the ongoing interests of the ruled is as noteworthy here as the infusion of further content into the *maior dignitas pontificum*.

But did the analogy between royal and episcopal professions have still more concrete significance in terms of episcopal jurisdiction? M. David has argued that Hincmar, in demanding from the king a profession rather than an oath, also had another purpose in mind. While on the one hand he wanted to impose conditions upon the king, on the other, he was anxious to preserve the kingship from an excessive and dangerous limitation of powers. He therefore preferred the profession, whose breach entailed only excommunication, to the oath, whose breach meant deposition from office.[4] Hincmar, in other words, had no intention of claiming for the episcopate the right to depose an unjust king. Now it is true that the distinction between penalties on which David based his argument can be found in twelfth-century canon law.[5] What is more questionable is its relevance to the ninth-century situation, and in particular to the thought and practice of Hincmar.

1. See the text of the profession, *supra* p. 152. Though given to the bishops, Louis's commitment was equally to preserve the laws 'for the *populus*' and 'in accordance with the collective counsel of our *fideles*'.

2. For the king's protective function in regard to church lands, see *Pro Ecc. Lib. Def.*, PL 125, col. 1051; and further references in Anton, *op. cit.* pp. 330 ff.

3. See Ullmann, *Carolingian Renaissance*, pp. 122 f., 177 ff., and *idem.*, *Law and Politics in the Middle Ages* (London, 1975), pp. 205 f. The notion appeared, but was hardly worked out, in the ninth century.

4. David, 'Le Serment', pp. 60 ff., 104, n. 92, and *idem.*, *La Souveraineté*, pp. 96 ff. and 128. Schramm, *Kaiser, Könige und Päpste*, i. 181, calls David's interpretation 'plausible'.

5. David, *La Souveraineté*, pp. 90 ff., cites evidence from Gratian on various types of profession from various periods. But, as he himself shows, pp. 100 ff., the distinction between lying and perjury was not entirely clearcut even in the twelfth century, and the penalty for the latter offence could vary. *Cf. idem.*, 'Parjure et mensonge dans le Décret de Gratien', *Studia Gratiana*, iii (1955), 119 ff., esp. 130 f.

David recognized one difficulty for his own interpretation: in the *Pro ecclesiae libertatum defensione*, Hincmar asserted that the penalty for a broken profession was deposition: *privatio honoris.*[1] David tried to minimize the significance of this statement, however, by claiming first, that it was made 'incidentally', and second, that it was not in conformity with the theory or practice of ninth-century canon law. Since Hincmar could have had no 'serious intention' of rejecting the contemporary norm, the *privatio honoris* passage, David assured us, should be dismissed.[2] But the problem here is more complicated than David's cursory account implied. Three objections to his view can be made. The first concerns the interpretation of the law itself. In David's presentation, the single authoritative text appears as II Carthage, c. xiii:

Qui contra suam professionem vel subscriptionem venerit, ipse se *ab hoc coetu separavit.*[3]

David himself had little doubt that excommunication was the penalty here prescribed. But the meaning of this single sentence should be appraised in the context of the whole canon from which it is taken. Canon xiii, the last issued by the synod of 390,[4] deals

1. PL 125, col. 1040. *Cf. supra* p. 163, n. 1.

2. David, *La Souveraineté*, p. 128, n. 30: 'Nous ne pensons pas qu'Hincmar ait sérieusement l'intention par là de s'inscrire en faux contre la réglementation canonique en vigueur de son temps, et qui ne préconise pas un deposition'.

3. Mansi III, col. 697. *Cf.* David, *La Souveraineté*, p. 92 with nn. 17 and 19. The canons of this council were not included in the collection of Dionysius but were transmitted through the Hispana: see F. L. Cross, 'History and fiction in the African canons', *Journal of Theological Studies*, n.s. xii (1961), 247 n. 1. On the still unresolved problems connected with the Hispana's reception in Gaul from the eighth century onwards, see Fuhrmann, *op. cit.* pp. 151 ff. and 665 f. (The work of G. Martinez Diez has unfortunately been inaccessible.) In the *LV Capit.* c. xxxiv, PL 126, col. 420, Hincmar advised: 'Lege Breviarium Africae provinciae canonum sedi apostolicae missum, et ab eadem sede corroboratum'. This *Breviarium*, containing I Carthage 'in fronte', seems to have consisted of a collection of African canons like that of the Hispana. For the existence of such a collection, on which the Hispana itself drew, in sixth-century Gaul, see F. Maassen, *Geschichte der Quellen und der Literatur des canonischen Rechts im Abendlande* (Graz, 1870), pp. 772 ff. For II Carthage, c. xiii in the Hispana, see PL 84, col. 188. From here it entered the work of Pseudo-Isidore, ed. cit., p. 296. *Cf.* also the version in Benedictus Levita II. 304 and III. 158, in PL 97, cols. 782, 818: 'Qui contra professionem vel subscriptionem suam venerit, *in concilio deponatur*'. Capit. Angilramni c. iv, ed. cit., p. 767, gives: 'Si quis contra . . ., si clericus fuerit *deponatur*, si laicus anathematizetur'. There is presumably a borrowing here of a distinction found *ibid.* c. xliv, ed. cit., p. 765, derived from I Carthage, c. xiv, quoted *supra* p. 145, n. 1. It was the Capit. Angilramni form which reappeared in the eleventh-century collections of Anselm and the Seventy-four Titles: see ed. cit., p. 166. This may help to explain why no use seems to have been made in the eleventh-century or later of an argument from breach of profession to justify the deposition of a king or emperor by the pope. On the formal characteristics of canons of the 'Si quis contra . . .' type, see J. Studtmann, 'Die Pönformel der mittelalterlichen Urkunden', *Archiv für Urkundenforschung*, xii (1932), 251 ff.

4. On this council *sub Genethlio*, see Monceaux, *Histoire Littéraire*, iii. 225 ff., and on its canons, Maassen, *op. cit.* pp. 151 f.

with the formal ratification of the preceding decrees. The presiding bishop asked his colleagues for their assent:

Omnia ergo quae *a coetu gloriosissimo statuta* sunt, placet ab omnibus custodiri? Ab universis episcopis dictum est: Placet, placet, custodiantur ab omnibus. Geneclius episcopus dixit: Si, quod non opinamur, ab aliquo fuerit violata, quid statuitis? Ab universis episcopis dictum est: Qui contra . . . (etc).[1]

Here, separation from the episcopal legislative body could only signify deposition[2] – removal from the *coetus gloriosissimus*, whose subscriptions confirmed the synodal decrees. And in fact the canon bears the title, unmentioned by David 'Ut episcopus qui contra professionem suam in concilio habitam venerit, *deponatur*'.[3] Closely comparable is the final canon of I Carthage, also concerned with the future observance of decrees just made, and specifying, for clerics, the penalty of *privatio honoris*.[4] Thus, even if it could be shown that Hincmar relied on II Carthage, c. xiii in punishing episcopal breach of profession, it would remain likely that deposition was inferred to be the prescribed penalty.

The second objection to David's view relates to his absolute distinction between excommunication and deposition as penalties. The case of Rothad of Soissons is relevant here. This was one of only two cases of episcopal deposition in which Hincmar as metropolitan was directly involved.[5] The issue turned on the obedience owed by a suffragan to his archbishop, and the latter's claim to jurisdiction. Two stages are discernible in this case: first, in 861, what amounted to a suspension from office, and second, in 862, a definitive sentence of deposition which was in principle irreversible. The *acta* of the synods which pronounced these judgments are

1. Mansi III. col. 697. *Professio* is used here for the formal acknowledgment of the binding authority of canons, especially those establishing basic doctrine. A bishop expressed this in putting his *subscriptio* to synodal decrees. Thus regular synodal attendances evoked a series of professions. For the more specific sense of profession at ordination, see p. 145, n. 1 *supra*. Documentary form was common to both types. Although Richter, *op. cit.* p. xxi, states that 'a profession . . . could be given either orally or in writing', Hincmar's emphasis is on the written document, which of course could be read out aloud.

2. Monceaux, *op. cit.* iii, 227, interprets the canon thus.

3. Hispana, PL 84, col. 188, and Pseudo-Isidore, ed. cit., p. 296. Note also the unequivocal formulations of Benedictus Levita and Capit. Angilramni, cited p. 156, n. 3 *supra*.

4. I Carthage, c. xiv, Mansi III, col. 158, quoted p. 145, n. 1, *supra*, in Hincmar's citation. For his source, see p. 156, n. 3 *supra*.

5. The other case was that of Hincmar of Laon: see *infra*, pp. 160f. For the Rothad case, see Hincmar of Rheims's letter to Nicholas I, MGH Epp. VIII. i. pp. 144 ff.; Perels, art. cit., *passim*; the comments of Schrörs, *op. cit.* pp. 238 ff. and Register, nos. 85, 86 and 89; and Fuhrmann, *op. cit.* ii. 254 ff. In such cases, deposition was a last resort. The preferred method was abdication, if necessary under heavy pressure as in the case of Ebo of Rheims, MGH Concilia II, p. 702. Hincmar tried to persuade both Rothad and Hincmar of Laon to subscribe their own condemnations: Fuhrmann, iii. 629 ff.

unfortunately lost. Hincmar himself, however, reports the 861 sentence thus:

Hincmarus ... synodo conprovinciali ... Rothadum ... *episcopali privat communione* secundum decreta canonum, donec obediat.[1]

Rothad's removal from *episcopal* communion was clearly something more than straightforward excommunication. Simply because a bishop was involved, it must in fact have meant provisional suspension from office – removal from the *coetus episcopalis*.[2] Perhaps a time-limit was specified for Rothad's return to obedience, for the following year, again in Hincmar's words, '... quoniam corrigi noluit ... *deponitur*'.[3] Although Hincmar seems to be distinguishing between suspension and final deposition, the former nevertheless implied the possibility of the latter. It is reasonable to infer that in Rothad's case, *privatio episcopalis communionis* constituted an imminent threat of deposition, unless amends were forthcoming. Thus, far from being mutually exclusive categories of penalty, excommunication and deposition could be sequentially related in the case of an office-holder within the *ecclesia*: the provisional suspension from office which excommunication necessarily involved could, if the guilty man proved obdurate, be finalized as deposition.

The third objection is yet more damaging to David's case. The fact is that Hincmar, though he certainly had access to it, seems nowhere to have cited II Carthage, c. xiii. What he did cite – and there was a critical difference between these two related texts – was the thirteenth of 138 canons collected and formally approved by the council of Carthage of 419. Often termed the *Codex Ecclesiae Africanae*,[4] this collection was incorporated in full into the second redaction of the *Codex Canonum* of Dionysius Exiguus,[5] and thence

1. Ann. Bertin., ed. cit., p. 86.

2. F. Kober, *Die Suspension der Kirchendiener nach den Grundsätzen des canonischen Rechts dargestellt* (Tübingen, 1862), pp. 33 f., 102. On the legal aspects of the comparable case of the excommunication/suspension of Henry IV by Gregory VII, see Ullmann, *Growth of Papal Government*, pp. 299 ff., and Morrison, 'Canossa: a revision', *Traditio*, xviii (1962), 141.

3. Ann. Bertin., ed. cit., p. 92. Nicholas I overrode this judgment: see Fuhrmann, *op. cit.* ii. 257 ff.

4. The name was given by the seventeenth-century historian C. Justel. See Maassen, *op. cit.* pp. 173, n. 2 and 173 ff. on the canons, which were based on the legislation of previous councils including that of 390.

5. On the formation and structure of the collection of African canons in the first and second recensions of Dionysius's work, see Cross, 'History and fiction', pp. 233 ff. and 240 with n. 3 on the MSS. of other early texts including the African canons. Cross's exposition partly supersedes Maassen, *op. cit.* pp. 422 ff. and 771 ff., and P. Fournier and G. Le Bras, *Histoire des Collections Canoniques en Occident* (Paris, 1931), pp. 18, n. 2 and 24 ff. Dionysius's second recension is printed in PL 67, cols. 39 ff. with the African canons at cols. 181 ff. Some of the canons of 419 were also printed from another early sixth-century collection, MS. Vat. Lat. 1342, following Justel's edition, in PL 56, cols. 863 ff. Some canons are numbered differently, and show small variants, in the different collections: see *e.g. infra*, p. 159, n. 3.

into the Dionysio-Hadriana, which became 'the most significant *Liber canonum*'[1] of the ninth-century Carolingian church. It was the Dionysio-Hadriana, both as it stood and in combination with other material, which shaped Hincmar's canonistic thought.[2] Less often remarked, the African canons in particular seem to have been a major influence, probably because they were largely concerned with the problems of provincial organization and discipline which so much exercised Hincmar himself. The thirteenth canon of 419 is a case in point. As transmitted in the Dionysian version, it reads:

> Ut non liceat episcopum nisi a plurimis ordinari; sed si necessitas fuerit, vel a tribus ordinetur episcopis.
>
> Aurelius episcopus dixit: Qui ad haec dicit sanctitas vestra? Ab universis episcopis dictum est: A nobis veterum statuta debere servari, sicut et inconsulto primate cuiuslibet provinciae tam facile non praesumant multi congregati episcopi episcopum ordinare: nisi necessitas fuerit, tres episcopi, in quocumque loco sint, eius praecepto ordinare debebunt episcopum. Et si quis contra suam professionem vel subscriptionem venerit in aliquo, *ipse se honore privabit.*[3]

Here the penalty of deposition is explicitly prescribed for breach of profession. Hincmar cited this canon, 'Si quis . . . se honore

1. So, H. Mordek, 'Dionysio-Hadriana und Vetus Gallica – historisch geordnetes und systematisches Kirchenrecht am Hofe Karls des Grossen', *Zeitschrift für Rechtsgeschichte*, Kan. Abt. xliv (1969), 58. Fournier and Le Bras, *op. cit.* pp. 94 f., inclined to regard the Dionysio-Hadriana, given to Charlemagne by Pope Hadrian in 774, as a kind of 'official code' for the Carolingian church. Any impression of uniformity in ninth-century practice must now be qualified in the light of Kottje, 'Einheit und Vielfalt des kirchlichen Lebens in der Karolingerzeit', *Zeitschrift für Kirchengeschichte*, lxxvi (1965), 323 ff., showing the variety of materials which continued to be copied, though the Dionysio-Hadriana was particularly widespread in north-eastern France and the Rhineland. See also Mordek, *ubi supra*, and *idem*, 'Die Rechtssammlungen der Handschrift von Bonneval', *Deutsches Archiv*, xxiv (1968), 339 ff. See now *idem*, *Kirchenrecht und Reform im Frankenreich* (Berlin, 1975).

2. See Schrörs, *op. cit.* pp. 389 ff., and Weinzierl, art. cit. (*supra*, p. 241, n. 1), pp. 148 f. Kottje, 'Einheit und Vielfalt', p. 337, n. 60, lists two Rheims MSS. of saec. IX med. containing the Dionysio-Hadriana, and also, p. 340, n. 70, two Rheims MSS. of the Dacheriana dating from Hincmar's period.

3. PL 67, col. 188. The Dacheriana, ii. c. lxiii, ed. cit., p. 539, gives: 'Ut episcopus qui contra suam possessionem (!) in concilio habitam venerit, deponatur. Si quis contra suam possessionem et subscriptionem venerit in aliquo ipse se honore privabit. Geneclius episcopus dixit: Omnia ergo . . .' etc. A comparison with II Carthage, c. xiii, quoted *supra*, p.156, shows that the compiler of the Dacheriana (or of his model) rearranged the sentence-order, and inserted the canon 'Si quis contra . . .' in its Dionysio-Hadriana form. MS. Vat. Lat. 1342 (*supra*, p. 158, n. 5), PL 56, col. 867, gives as 'c. xii' of the 419 council a version of this canon which conflates its two forms thus: 'Si quis . . . ab hoc coetu separabitur'. Modern editions of these collections are urgently needed. Meanwhile, David, *La Souveraineté*, p. 92, n. 19 justifiably remarks: 'Il subsiste une incertitude sur le contenu original de ce canon'. All that is relevant in the present context, however, is what form or forms were available in the ninth century. David overlooks both the variety of canonical sources, and the presence of the text specifying *privatio honoris* in the Dionysio-Hadriana itself. The association of the profession with consecration in this text is noteworthy, in view of Hincmar's concerns.

privabit', not just once and 'incidentally' as David has alleged, but at least eight times[1]: often enough and consistently enough, therefore, to show that this if anything represented his canonical norm. Yet he had available in the Hispana and in Pseudo-Isidore an alternative text prescribing, not the unequivocal *privatio honoris* but *separatio coetus*, whose initial meaning at least was excommunication. It would be false to argue that Hincmar necessarily preferred the Dionysio-Hadriana to other possible sources: whatever reservations he had about some Pseudo-Isidorian texts, he was prepared to exploit others when it suited him, and even to tinker with them on his own account.[2] If he chose to cite the thirteenth canon of 419, this was less for its source, the Dionysio-Hadriana, than for its content. This can be demonstrated by a closer examination of the contexts and purposes of the various citations.

Four of them occur in connection with the one case of episcopal deposition in which Hincmar was intimately involved and on which fairly full information has survived: the case of Hincmar of Laon.[3] The elder Hincmar summoned all his resources of canonistic learning to justify the sentence imposed on his nephew. These were public arguments, designed to convince other experts, including the papacy. One of the main charges brought against the bishop of Laon was precisely breach of his professions, the one given at the time of his consecration to his uncle the metropolitan of Rheims, the other at the synod of Attigny (870) when he reaffirmed his promise of obedience 'to the privilege of Hincmar, metropolitan

1. For details, see *infra*, and for a clear allusion in the *De Ordine Palatii*, *supra*, p. 145, n. 1. No significance seems attached in ninth-century usage to a distinction between deposition as a penalty imposed by an ecclesiastical authority, and self-deposition as apparently prescribed in c. xiii of 419. In any case, a sentence obviously had to be declared and enforced by an ecclesiastical authority; the varying syntax used *e.g.*, in 1 Carthage, c. xiv (*honore privetur*) and c. xiii of 419 (*se honore privabit*) would make no difference to the practical outcome. The active voice only emphasizes that the wrongdoer deserves his own punishment. The implication of all the African disciplinary canons is that jurisdiction and enforcement are the responsibility of the appropriate authority – in the present case, a provincial council. See art. 'Déposition et Dégradation des clercs' (E. Vacandard) in *Dict. de Théologie Catholique*, iv. 451 ff., esp. 498 f.

2. See p. 142 with n. 1 *supra*. Some earlier commentators tended to exaggerate the conflict between 'old law', as represented by the Dionysio-Hadriana, and the 'new law' of Pseudo-Isidore, and thus to see Hincmar as simply committed to the former: see Schrörs, *op. cit.* pp. 389 ff., and esp. Weinzierl, art. cit. (*supra*, p. 133, n. 1). But *cf.* now Fuhrmann, *op. cit.* iii. 664 ff., arguing that Hincmar believed both these collections to be the work of Isidore of Seville. Despite the important characteristic tendencies of Pseudo-Isidore, both in ninth-century episcopalist and in eleventh-century papalist aspects, elements of continuity with older law also need emphasis.

3. *LV Capit.*, preface and c. xxxii, PL 126, cols. 292 and 414; *Schedula sive Libellus* presented to the council of Douzy (871), cc. xvii and xxxiv, PL 126, cols. 589 and 627. *Cf.* also Hincmar's parody of the same canon, *infra*, 161. At the first of these citations, Sirmond, *Hincmari . . . Opera*, ii. 389 misleadingly referred to 'II Carthage, c. xiii', reproduced by Migne, *loc. cit.* Morrison, *op. cit.* p. 108, n. 29 gives: 'Council of Carthage I (!) c. 13'. On the conflict between the two Hincmars, see Fuhrmann, *op. cit.* iii. 651 ff., with full bibliographical details.

of the province of the church of Rheims'.[1] When the archbishop claimed, and his colleagues accepted, on the basis of the thirteenth canon of 419, that the recalcitrant bishop must be deposed, and when, moreover, the sentence itself was swiftly carried out, there can be little doubt that this canon, far from being cited 'incidentally', was held authoritative, and far from being mere theory, determined Hincmar of Rheims' actual conduct of the case against his nephew. So much was it a familiar part of Hincmar's canonistic equipment that he could paraphrase it ironically: his nephew might more aptly be said by his own recent actions to have declared his own condemnation in the words: '*Ego Hincmarus contra meam professionem vel subscriptionem veniens, sponte me honore privavi*'.[2] Clearly, in the view of the elder Hincmar, this Carthaginian canon provided firm grounds for punishing a breach of episcopal profession by deposition from office.

Hincmar cited this same canon again in a letter (June 881) to Louis III, protesting about the young king's intervention in the election to the bishopric of Beauvais.[3] The king had expressed the hope that Hincmar would prove *in omni utilitati regni proficuus et devotus*, to him as to his predecessors. Hincmar answered that Louis should preserve what they had preserved, rather than try to force him in his old age to abandon the *sacrae regulae* which he had faithfully observed for thirty-six years in episcopal office. If I were to do so, Hincmar continued, '*a gradu episcopali ... merito decidam*'. For according to sacred canons decreed by the holy spirit: 'Si quis contra suam professionem vel subscriptionem venerit in aliquo, *ipse se honore privabit*'. The king could therefore reap little profit from compelling the archbishop to an action which would ipso facto render the latter liable to deposition.

The canon appears, finally, in a short work written in July 882, following the settlement of the Beauvais dispute: *Quae exsequi debeat episcopus, et qua cura tueri res et facultates ecclesiasticas*.[4] Hincmar's theme was the inviolability of the church's temporal possessions and the consequently strict limits on a bishop's freedom of action, since not only secular powers but bishops themselves were bound by the earlier legislation of councils and kings. Again Hincmar suggested that it was futile either for a king to command, or for a bishop to take, any action which meant breach of the latter's profession, for the canons had decreed: 'Si quis contra suam

1. *LV Capit.*, preface, PL 126, col. 292; *Schedula*, cc. ix, xiii, xxxiii, PL 126, cols. 575, 583, 624; the promise of Attigny, PL 124, col. 999, on the political context of which see P. McKeon, 'Le concile d'Attigny (870)', *Le Moyen Age*, lxxvi (1970), 414 ff.

2. *Schedula*, c. xvii, PL 126, col. 589.

3. PL 126, col. 115. On the Beauvais affair, see Schrörs, *op. cit.* pp. 436 ff., and Beck, 'The selection of bishops', pp. 303 ff.

4. PL 125, cols. 1087 ff. Schrörs, *op. cit.* p. 439, n. 101 justifies the date, though p. 556, at Register no. 507, he wrongly gives 'July, 881'.

professionem vel suam scripturam venerit in aliquo, *ipse se honore privabit*'.[1]

Hincmar twice cited this same canon in relation to the office of a king. In the *De Divortio*, addressed to the Lotharingian bishops in 860 and protesting against their support for Lothar II's divorce, Hincmar argued that the king must keep the laws to which he had himself subscribed. Canon xiii of 419 was then quoted in justification, though with the word *professio* omitted. Kings could not claim, Hincmar continued, that this canon applied only to bishops, for all Christians acquired both royal and priestly dignity through their baptismal anointing. A king, therefore, who acted against the *conscriptio* of his own hand in contravening the *leges* was deprived of both the title and the office of king *in oculis dei*.[2] M. Devisse has admired the sophistication of Hincmar's argument, discerning here 'the germs of a real contract theory'.[3] But perhaps more noteworthy are the limitations imposed on Hincmar by the facts of the Lotharingian situation in 860: king Lothar never had made a royal profession, which left only the appeal to the more general notion of

1. The whole passage, PL 125, col. 1094, reads: 'Episcopo etiam nuper ordinato agere talia vel talibus consentire non praecipiat [rex], unde se ipsum perdat et coram Deo ecclesiasticam gratiam amittat. Cum coram omnibus et electoribus et ordinatoribus suis districtissime professus ante ordinationem suam fuerit, et *propria manu subscripserit* sacras regulas sanctorum conciliorum, quantum scierit et potuerit, servaturum. Qui sacri canones spiritu Dei conditi, et totius mundi reverentia consecrati ita decernunt: 'Si quis contra suam professionem . . . (etc.)'. Qui autem res et facultates ecclesiasticas Belvacensis ecclesiae ipsius consensu vel favore pessumdare praesumpserint, qui auctoritatem eas illis dare vel consentire non habuit, sollicitissime caveant, ne suprascriptas sacrorum canonum sententias, ab omnibus nobis episcopis, ad quorum notitiam ipsorum sacrilegia pervenerint, intentatas, suscipiant, et ab omni christianorum societate modis omnibus separentur'. The reading *scriptura* instead of *subscriptio* seems to have been present in the manuscript used by Sirmond, *Hincmari . . . Opera*, ii. 768, and may well represent a copyist's error, esp. since the word *scriptura* (though in another sense) appears a few lines earlier in the same text.

2. PL 125, col. 700: '[Imperatores et reges] ita praedecessorum suorum bene statuta debent in omnibus conservare, sicuti sua constituta a suis successoribus cupiunt conservari. Et non leve regibus vel quibuscunque aliis videtur infringere *quod suis student manibus roborare*, quia ex divina doctrina, et apostolica traditione, tam maxima res semper ab ipsis primis saeculis manus confirmatio fuit, ut de ipsis apostolorum vicariis, illi ipsi apostolorum vicarii supercoelesti auctoritate decreverint, 'Ut qui contra suam subscriptionem in aliquo venerit, ipse se privet honore'. Et non dicant reges hoc de episcopis et non est de regibus constitutum: sed attendentes quia si sub uno rege ac sacerdote Christo, a cujus nominis derivatione christi domini appellantur, in populi regimine sublimati et honorati esse desiderant, . . . cum sint homines sicut et ceteri, et partem cum his in regno coelorum habere volunt qui sacro peruncti sunt chrismate, quod a Christi nomine nomen accepit, qui exinde unxit sacerdotes, prophetas, reges et martyres, ille unctus oleo laetitiae prae consortibus suis, quique fecit eos in baptismate reges et sacerdotes Deo nostro, et genus regium ac regale sacerdotium, secundum apostolos Joannem et Petrum (Apoc. ii. 26; 1 Pet. ii. 9): intellegant et credant se in oculis Dei privari regii nominis et officii dignitate, quando si illud placitum Deo fuit quod manu firmaverunt, faciunt contra manus suae conscriptionem, licet illud nomen usurpent ante oculos hominum terrena et instabili potestate'. In the citation of the African canon, 'Ut qui' has been substituted for 'Si quis' to produce a subordinate clause flowing on from 'decreverint'. Significantly, the canon is cited in the context of legislation, a point neglected by Anton, *op. cit.* p. 294, n. 753.

3. *Hincmar et la Loi*, p. 75, n. 4.

the royal promulgation of laws, and though he had been anointed king, Lothar's consecrators had been those very bishops who now connived at what Hincmar insisted was a breach of the laws. For these reasons, whatever appeal his own theory might have had for contemporary clerics in general, Hincmar when he addressed the Lotharingian bishops in this particular case could argue for the application of canon xiii to Lothar only because of the initiation-anointing which the king shared with all other Christians – *sicut et ceteri.*[1] Yet it was impossible to construct on this basis juristic sanctions specifically on the royal office; and absence of any control on earth meant leaving any royal breach of the laws to divine judgment, so that in practice a king's *privatio dignitatis* could be said to have occurred only *in oculis dei.*[2]

In 868, Hincmar addressed a strongly-worded protest to Charles the Bald against infringements of the *libertates ecclesiae*. Again an appeal was made to canon xiii of 419 to establish that the king was subject to the laws, but this time the canon could be cited in full, for Charles as king had given explicit written undertakings which could readily be identified as professions.[3] At Beauvais in 845, Charles

1. For Lothar II's anointing, see Brühl, 'Fränkischer Krönungsbrauch', p. 295 and n. 3, and Ann. Bertin., ed. cit. p. 72 with the editor's comments, p. lxii. In *De Divortio*, PL 125, cols. 756 ff., Hincmar portrays the Lotharingian bishops as 'Hofabsolutisten', in whose view '[rex] nullorum legibus vel judiciis subjacet, nisi solius Dei, qui eum in regno ... regem constituit'. See Anton, *op. cit.* pp. 307 f., 317, and, for earlier stigmatizations of these bishops as 'pliable', 'subservient', etc., Dümmler, *Gesch. des ostfränk. Reichs*, pp. 3 ff., 19; Halphen, *Charlemagne*, p. 376; Fichtenau, *Karolingische Imperium*, pp. 235 ff. But *cf.* J. Haller, *Nikolaus I und Pseudoisidor* (Stuttgart, 1936), pp. 5 ff., for a more realistic interpretation of the bishops' interests. When the existence of Lothar's realm itself was not threatened, these men could be far from subservient: see Capit. II, pp. 441 ff. and 463 ff.; Mansi, xv, col. 614: Lothar II's *Contestatio* (862), presumably written by Archbishop Gunther of Cologne, which contains an interesting and hitherto little noticed application of Gelasian doctrine. No sharp contrast should be drawn between West Frankish and Lotharingian political ideas at this period: Devisse, 'Consilium et auxilium', p. 190, and n. 51, shows the probable influence of Hincmar himself on Lothar II's *Adlocutio* (857), Capit. II. p. 295. But in the circumstances of 860, the Lotharingian bishops naturally rallied uncompromisingly to their king, so that Hincmar could not then expect their co-operation in asserting the king's subordination to 'laws and judgments'. In any case, Hincmar's theory of juristic restraints remained his own, even if many of his assumptions were shared. The practice of royal anointing was a necessary, but by no means sufficient, cause of that theory's development.

2. But the implications of this *privatio* might be greater than Morrison, *op. cit.* p. 229, allows: see p. 134, n. 4 *supra*. Hincmar was aware that *christus* meant 'anointed', but the association was developed here only in relation to baptismal anointing. The two quotations from the *Benedictio chrismatis* were later used by Hincmar to much greater effect in the *Ordines* of 869 and 877; but in 860, their specific relevance to the consecrated king had to be ignored: *cf.* preceding note.

3. *Pro Ecc. Lib. Def.*, PL 125, col. 1040. After quoting the legislation of Theodosius and Louis the Pious, Hincmar continues: 'Unde non solum ea quae a decessoribus et praedecessoribus vestris bene statuta sunt servando, vos firmitatem eis dare oportet, verum et illa quae ipsi gessistis, et *manu propria subscripsistis*, et cum maxima obtestatione vos servaturos perpetuo promittentes, *in manibus sacerdotum ad vicem Dei tradidistis*, ante oculos et mentis et corporis revocare debetis. Et non modica necessitas vobis incumbit, ut *si contra ea in aliquo* egistis, hoc quantocius emendare, et de caetero ne

had given a promise *cum maxima contestatione* to maintain ecclesiastical interests, and Hincmar in rehearsing its terms was careful to stress its permanently binding quality. Its recipients, Hincmar insisted, were not only the bishops present in 845 or even their absent colleagues throughout the whole realm, but all their successors too.[1] The episcopate, like the laws themselves, transcended time. Charles's promise had been drawn up in a formal document, signed by the king and placed in the bishops' hands; and in 868 Hincmar could refer back to it, and to the promise of Quierzy (858),[2] as well as to Charles's subscriptions of his own and his predecessors' laws. Precisely in this legal context, therefore, Hincmar could now relate Charles's *professiones*, and thus the relevance of canon xiii itself, to the royal anointing: because Charles had acquired his royal *dignitas* through an anointing and benediction performed by bishops, he could be considered bound by the same rules as applied to the bishops themselves as consecrated holders of office, and because after his baptismal anointing Charles had received another and specifically royal anointing, the application of canon xiii now no longer depended on the position which the king as a Christian individual shared with *ceteri fideles*, but on his tenure of public office under conditions clearly defined in terms of written law.

At this point, surely, Hincmar was on the threshold of asserting the king's liability to deposition for any breach of his profession and, as a corollary, the authority to depose of the recipients and custodians of that profession: the *praepositi ecclesiae*. But Hincmar did not proceed to this logical conclusion. Instead, leaving canon xiii hanging in the air, and in effect retreating to the familiar position of 833,[3] he shifted his argument to the penitential jurisdiction of the church. He admitted now to Charles, as he had to Lothar's bishops, that in practice a bad ruler, deposed in the eyes of God,

contra illa faciatis, cavere summopere procuretis. Quia enim post illam unctionem qua cum caeteris fidelibus meruistis hoc consequi, quod beatus Petrus apostolus dicit: 'Vos genus electum, regale sacerdotium' (1 Pet. ii. 9), episcopali et spirituali unctione ac benedictione regiam dignitatem potius quam terrena potestate consecuti estis: attendere subtili intellectu debetis, quoniam ad diffinitionem sancti spiritus, quam synodali auctoritate protulit, excepti non estis: 'Si quis, inquit, contra suam professionem vel subscriptionem venerit, ipse se honore privabit'. Here again Hincmar cites this canon in the context of written law. *Cf.* Anton, *op. cit.* p. 331 with n. 966, for the fine catena of legal authorities appealed to by Hincmar in this passage.

1. PL 125, col. 1041: 'Haec . . . cunctis diebus vitae vestrae vos servaturos promisistis, eisdem episcopis, qui praesentes aderant, et caeteris regni vestri episcopis, qui corpore praesentes non aderant, *et omnibus eorum successoribus*, et omnibus episcopis in regno vestro consistentibus, et *in manibus eorumdem episcoporum* ad eorum petitionem dedistis'. *Cf.* the reference later in the same work, col. 1066, to the oath by which Charles swore the *capitulum* of Beauvais: 'coram Deo et angelis eius, in fide et dextera vestra, per spatam vestram *iurantes*'. Clearly both promise and oath were involved in 845. Hincmar and his colleagues had to take account of Germanic tradition as well as canonical practice: both streams converged in Carolingian kingship. For the oath on the sword, see Schramm, *Kaiser, Könige und Päpste*, i. 180.

2. PL 125, col. 1042. See p. 148, n. 1 *supra*.

3. See pp. 135 f. *supra*.

could 'often' retain power in the eyes of men.[1] But he did not consider the alternative possibility: that a bad ruler might by due legal process enforced by ecclesiastical authorities be deposed on earth. He cited from the Old Testament the case of David, made king through the agency of Samuel, and later held accountable by Samuel's successor Nathan for the breach of his profession in becoming proud when he had promised humility:

> ... superbiendo David ... faciens *contra professionem suam* ... dignitatem regiam, quam peccando perdidit, confessus coram Nathan poenitendo recuperavit.[2]

Then in the New Testament there was Peter, who broke his profession in denying Christ:

> ... faciens *contra suam professionem* ... confessus ... coram omnibus apostolis ... apostolatum quem negando perdiderat, confitendo et flendo recepit.

Thus, Hincmar concluded, anyone who confessed, repented and corrected whatever he had done in breach of his profession 'ad honorem redire, et in honore praevalet, Domino miserante, manere'. To deny this would be to challenge the authority of Matthew xvi, 19, where Christ had conferred these powers of jurisdiction on the *praepositi eiusdem ecclesiae*.[3] Only shortage of space and time, said Hincmar, prevented him from explaining how the exercise of these powers conformed to the *sacrae regulae*. These limitations did not prevent him from rehearsing now verbatim the promises of Beauvais and Quierzy given by Charles to the contemporary *praepositi ecclesiae*. The consequence of failure to fulfil these promises was clear: loss of *regia dignitas*. But the mechanics of earthly deposition remained unspecified. Hincmar drew back from the assertion that bishops had power to depose the consecrated king who broke his profession, although his own treatment of liturgy and law had seemed to prepare the way for precisely that. It is not hard to understand why Hincmar hesitated to put forward a revolutionary claim, for which neither biblical history nor ecclesiastical tradition afforded any precedent, and whose political implications in this time of waning royal authority have been seen by M. David[4] as too dangerous for Hincmar to risk exposing. And yet it is worth recalling that in 859 Charles himself, at Hincmar's prompting and in the crisis of foreign invasion, had stated the possibility of his being 'thrown

1. PL 125, col. 1040: 'Quod licet non fiat, sicut saepe solet accidere, in oculis hominum, fit tamen semper in oculis Dei'.
2. *Ibid.* The reference is to II Reg., xii.
3. PL 125, col. 1041. Here Hincmar quotes, without attribution, from Augustine, Ep. 185: see p. 134 *supra*. He was probably quoting from memory, since his text of Matt. xvi, 19 diverges slightly from Augustine's and is closer to the Vulgate.
4. 'Le serment', pp. 60 ff., and *La Souveraineté*, pp. 96 ff.

out from his [royal] consecration (*proici a consecratione*) by the trial and judgment of the bishops (*audientia et iudicium episcoporum*)'.[1] Nothing that Hincmar wrote subsequently involved an abandonment of this position. M. David seems to ignore the possibilities inherent in Hincmar's argument of 868 when he treats the two *exempla* here as confirming his own belief that Hincmar contemplated only the excommunication, never the deposition, of a king who violated the laws: 'Hincmar fait état de cette privation d'*honor* seulement pour signaler qu'à condition de faire penitence, le coupable peut recuperer son poste'.[2] But in the case of a bishop, as the events of 861/2 had shown, suspension from office could be the prelude to total deposition if penitence were not forthcoming. Addressing Charles the Bald in 868, Hincmar for reasons of tact and tactics chose to cite *exempla* where such penitence was offered, and where, therefore, loss of *honor* proved temporary. His immediate object was to urge the king to mend his ways, not to provoke confrontation *à l'outrance*. But his argument left open the possibility, in theory at least, that the penalty of deposition might be exacted later if the voice of the *praepositi* went unheeded; and the juristic basis for such a claim was explicitly stated in the thirteenth canon of 419, that *diffinitio sancti spiritus*, made manifest by synodal authority, from which the king himself was not exempt.

Although Hincmar never cited this canon explicitly to Louis III, he did, in two letters of June 881, implicitly extend its application to the king. In the first letter, when he quoted the canon in relation to his own office, he had appealed also to the king's profession, and could therefore conclude:

Si vobis consensero, ut contra divinas et humanas leges, et contra vestram et meam, coram pluribus in synodo episcopis cohibentibus, professionem faciatis, me perdam, et vos non salvabo.[3]

1. See p.142, n. 3 *supra*.

2. *La Souveraineté*, p. 128, n. 30. The source of the two *exempla*, unnoticed by M. David, is Augustine's Ep. 185, CSEL lvii, pp. 39 f. Hincmar quoted this same passage verbatim in *LV Capit.*, c. xx, PL 126, col. 357, arguing that no man-made law is immutable, and that changing circumstances may mean that laws have to be changed. Relating this principle to the question of whether penitent *lapsi* should retain their offices, he quoted Augustine to this effect: the norm was that such men should be deprived of office permanently, for the sake of *rigor disciplinae*, not through *desperatio indulgentiae*, yet discretion must be used, and if the penitent showed true humility, especially if he held high office so that whole peoples, as well as himself, were affected, then severity might be relaxed. In arguing that the church uses discretion in exercising its authority, Hincmar stresses the scope of ecclesiastical jurisdiction. Fuhrmann, *op. cit.* i. 204 ff., notes that Hincmar was not always willing to allow that penitent *lapsi* might be restored, even *post dignam satisfactionem*, and shows, p. 205 with n. 34, that the passage from Augustine's Ep. 185, and also a false decretal (Ps.-Calixtus, cc. xix–xx) which borrows from it, both relate to deposition from office, not excommunication, in the case of clerics. Hincmar's use of Augustine's *exempla* will therefore hardly bear M. David's interpretation.

3. PL 126, col. 115. *Cf. supra* p. 161.

Given the conclusion he drew in his own case, Hincmar's close linking of 'your and my profession' implied that the king was liable to the same penalty as the bishop, namely deposition.

In the second letter, having stressed the condition – *debitas leges servandi* – under which the king had acceded, Hincmar pointed out the illegality of Louis's action in the Beauvais election,

> . . . contra regulas ecclesiasticas, contraque antiquorum et christianorum regum leges, contraque praedecessorum ac progenitorum vestrorum promulgationes sed et contra illorum consuetudinem.

This was immediately followed up by a much firmer warning:

> . . . vos videte ne pro hoc illicito facto canonicas sustineatis sententias, vel in hoc saeculo, vel in futuro.[1]

The last three words left the threat of deposition oblique, but there could be no doubt as to the content of the 'canonical sentences'. The king who acted *contra regulas contraque leges* deprived himself of kingship. The execution of the sentence *in hoc saeculo* might remain in suspense, but the king's liability to deposition was clear.

There is one further piece of evidence which suggests that not only Hincmar but many of his clerical contemporaries may have been able to contemplate the deposition of kings. In the West Frankish realm, from the mid-ninth century, there seems to have been a fairly widespread knowledge and use of three privileges granted by Gregory the Great at the request of Queen Brunhilda and her son to a foundation at Autun, all three containing the same remarkable penalty formula:

> Si quis vero *regum*, sacerdotum et judicum atque *saecularium personarum*, hanc constitutionis paginam cognoscens, contra eam venire tentaverit, potestatis *honorisque sui dignitate careat*.[2]

It is hardly likely, given the absence of any supporting evidence, that the pope was here foreshadowing another Gregory in independently threatening kings with deposition[3]: perhaps he was

1. PL 126, cols. 119 f.

2. Register XIII, 11–13, MGH Epp. II, pp. 376–81.

3. Despite the suggestion of Ullmann, *Law and Politics in the Middle Ages* (London, 1975), p. 124, Gregory I did not, in my view, intend any claim to papal jurisdiction over kings, still less any right to depose them. For Gregory VII's exploitation of his predecessor's penalty-clause in just this sense, see his letter to Hermann of Metz, Register IV, 2 and VIII, 21, MGH Epp. Sel. II, ed. E. Caspar, i. 294 and ii. 550. See Caspar's comments at ii. 550, n. 2, with other instances of Gregory VII's use of this text; also Caspar, 'Gregor VII in seinen Briefen', *Hist. Zeitschrift*, CXXX (1924), 15 f. The pronouncement of judgment on kings was a key issue in the polemics of the later eleventh century. Apologists of Henry IV, who never doubted the genuineness of Gregory I's penalty-clause, challenged Gregory VII's interpretation of it: judgment, they held, remained in God's hands. See *De unitate ecclesiae conservanda*, ii. 15, MGH Libelli de Lite II. p. 227, and for an indictment of Gregory VII's misuse of his source, *Contra epistolam Hildebrandi*, iii. 9, *ibid.* pp. 391 f.

simply basing his words on those of Brunhilda in her original request.[1] In the present context, the relevant point is the familiarity of this passage to Hincmar and his contemporaries. Flodoard's notice of a letter of Hincmar's to the widow of Charles the Bald shows that Bishop Pardulus of Laon had borrowed Gregory's penalty-formula in a privilege which he drew up at Charles's request, sometime between 842 and 869, for the convent of Orrigny.[2] In quoting this passage to a dowager queen, Hincmar naturally made no attempt to apply the threat of deposition, although he was protesting vigorously at her violation of the Orrigny privilege. But the emphasis he placed on the authority of the penalty-formula – the words were not those of Pardulus but of 'the blessed pope Gregory' – imply his awareness of their implications. Again, precisely this penalty-formula of Gregory's was used in a privilege for the church of Beauvais, confirmed with the consent of Charles the Bald by 'the bishops of four provinces'. Hincmar quoted this part of the Beauvais privilege both in a public letter of 881 and in the *Quae exsequi debeat episcopus*.[3] His audience, both at the royal court

1. So L. M. Hartmann in MGH Epp. II, p. 378, n. 6, mentioning similar penalty-formulae in decrees of Merovingian councils and in the *Liber Diurnus*, and, likewise stressing parallels in the *Liber Diurnus*, Anton, *Studien zu den Klosterprivilegien der Päpste im frühen Mittelalter* (Berlin, 1975), pp. 54 f. with nn. 47, 48. (I am grateful to Ian Wood for this reference.) But in these other cases, the penalty is always excommunication, not deposition, and kings are never specified. Although the binding of successors 'forever' appears in Merovingian diplomas and in Marculf's formulae, these texts offer no true parallels for Gregory's penalty-clause. Hartmann's suggestion has been widely accepted: see F. Homes Dudden, *Gregory the Great* (London, 1905), ii. 84 f., and Anton, *Studien*, p. 55, n. 48, with further references. Studtmann, 'Die Pönformel', pp. 268 f., skates over the problem. Still worth consulting, though apparently ignored by Anton, is J. Mabillon, *De re diplomatica* (Paris, 1681), ii. c. 9, pp. 104 ff., citing two Roman synodal penalty-formulae of 680 and 704 in which kings are specified, though only excommunication is prescribed. (See now MGH Scriptores rer. Merov. VI, pp. 227 and 247.) *Cf.* similar features in the formulae discussed by P. Sims-Williams, 'Continental influence at Bath monastery in the seventh century', *Anglo-Saxon England*, iv (1975), 5 f. But the closest parallel to Gregory's formula, hitherto apparently unnoticed, appears in XVI Toledo, c. x, PL 84, col. 544: 'Si quis sane regum succedentium cunctas huius constitutionis nostrae definitiones custodire aut adimplere distulerit ... ex divino iudicio rebus omnibus et honore praesenti in seculo careat ...' (I omit the lengthy spiritual penalties here). The possibility of a direct influence should be noted. It remains doubtful whether the Visigothic bishops drew any more practical inferences from the formula than did Gregory I. The genuineness of Gregory's privileges for Autun in their entirety was convincingly shown by Hartmann, *loc. cit.*; see also Anton, *Studien*, p. 55, n. 47. The untenable view that the penalty-formula is an eleventh-century forgery is unfortunately repeated in the revised edition of Kern, *Gottesgnadentum*, pp. 186, n. 397, and 395.

2. Flodoard, *Historia Remensis ecclesiae*, iii. c. 27, MGH SS. XIII, p. 549. Schrörs, *op. cit.*, Register no. 557, does not give the full text. Hincmar's letter can be dated 877–82. For the privilege itself, see Tessier, *Receuil*, ii. 520, no. 197 bis.

3. PL 126, cols. 250 f.; PL 125, col. 1091. The suggestion of E. Loening, *Das Kirchenrecht im Reiche der Merowinger* (Strassburg, 1878), ii. 392, n. 2, that Hincmar himself forged Gregory's privileges for Autun, is unacceptable. Equally so is the view of Lesne, 'Nicholas Ier et les libertés des monastères des Gaules', *Le Moyen Age*, xxiv (1911), 301 ff., that the privileges were forged in ninth-century Frankia. For the manuscript evidence against this, see Hartmann, *loc. cit.* The hypotheses of Loening and Lesne cannot accommodate the use of Gregory's privileges by popes Nicholas I

and at synodal gatherings was being familiarized with the idea that specified illegal acts entailed the deposition of office-holders whether royal or episcopal.

While recent scholarship has highlighted the importance of law in Hincmar's political ideas, there has remained a tendency to regard the restraints he placed upon kingship as essentially moral, not juristic.[1] Hincmar, on this reading, was concerned to stress the king's spiritual duties, to urge his conformity to Scriptural models, and to keep before him the threat of divine judgment. From the evidence considered above, however, Hincmar can be seen, as by some earlier scholars,[2] to have claimed not only sacramental *auctoritas* but a specific jurisdiction over the consecrated king. It seems clear that he both designed and used restraints of a concrete legal type, finding in liturgy and law the requisite juristic models and instruments. In the painful struggle towards a positive response to contemporary political change, Hincmar was forced to modify western ideological tradition as evolved before, and especially during, the reign of Charlemagne, in order to cope with the new realities of the reign of Charles the Bald.[3] For Hincmar's interests as a statesman were basically practical: law and liturgy served him as means to political ends.[4] Though he subjected more than one

---

and John VIII: for details, see Caspar, 'Gregor VII', p. 15, n. 1, observing that Nicholas reproduced the penalty-formula 'ohne das anstössige *regum*' while John included it. Caspar's denial of any significance in this ninth-century papal usage may perhaps be questioned. (I have been unable to follow up his reference to the unpublished Berlin dissertation (1922) of E. Hufe.) Dependence on the same Gregorian source can be demonstrated in the privilege of Nicholas I for St Calais (Jaffé-Ewald 2735 – unmentioned by Caspar): see Lesne, *ubi supra*, p. 301 with n. 3, noting several signs of this dependence, but failing to draw attention to the St Calais penalty-formula, ed. Perels, MGH Epp. Kar. Aevi IV, p. 683: 'Haec autem constituta volumus omnibus omnino modis inviolabilia ... permanere, et a nemine vel *regum* vel episcoporum vel alicuius ordinis violari ... unde constituimus ut primus quisque hoc [*i.e.* violation of the privilege] molitus fuerit, *sui honoris dignitate privetur, sive sit saecularis*, sive sit ecclesiastica persona: deinde ab ecclesiasticae communionis societate fiat alienus'. Perels, *ibid.* p. 680, n. 2 and Lesne, *ubi supra*, pp. 301 ff., treat the St Calais privilege as spurious. But W. Goffart, 'The privilege of Nicholas I for St Calais: a new theory', *Revue Benedictine*, lxxi (1961), 287 ff., has argued strongly that it is genuine. If so, its penalty-clause deserves closer attention than it has received. So also does Hincmar's publicization of Gregory's formula.

1. See Morrison, *op. cit.* pp. 227 ff.; Anton, *op. cit.* p. 329 with n. 953.

2. See, though without any analysis of the juristic evidence, H. Lilienfein, *Die Anschauungen von Staat und Kirche im Reich der Karolinger* (Heidelberger Abhandlungen, Hft. 1, 1902), pp. 100 ff.; G. Ehrenforth, 'Hinkmar von Reims und Ludwig III von Westfranken. Eine kirchenrechtliche Untersuchung', *Zeitschrift für Kirchengeschichte*, xliv (1925), p. 97.

3. See Wallace-Hadrill, 'The Via Regia', pp. 36 ff., and esp. 38, on ideas of resistance to unjust kings: 'Sooner or later, someone would want to limit kingship itself: Hincmar very nearly did'. I would go just one step further than this.

4. *Cf.* the pertinent remarks of Brühl, 'Hinkmariana', pp. 76 f.: for Hincmar, as for the Lotharingian bishops during the controversy over Lothar II's divorce, 'stand das fränkische Staatswohl letzten Endes hoher als das kanonische Recht ... [Aber] es wäre ganz ungerecht, Hinkmar daraus einen Vorwurf machen zu wollen'.

king to harsh criticism, to penance and even to excommunication,[1] Hincmar could hardly have seen any episcopal claim to depose kings as either desirable or practical politics. It was not that his thought, as has been suggested,[2] lacked originality or coherence: rather, his objective was a new kind of consensus, a new structure of political relations, by means of which the realm could achieve *soliditas*. This theme provides the unity in Hincmar's public life, linking the 'programme' of Coulaines with that of Fîmes (881).[3] It can be no coincidence that such terms as *communis* and *communiter* appear with a new frequency in a political sense in the public documents of Charles the Bald's reign.[4] Then, as often in medieval political thought, ecclesiology influenced the concept of the state[5]: king, clergy and *populus*, recognizing their collective stake in the *communis salus*, were now to act together in the interests of their *communis utilitas*.[6] All, and not only the king, had to accept the limits implied here.

In the working out of some of these implications, Hincmar's thought is impressive not only for its originality and coherence

1. For Hincmar's excommunication of Lothar I, see MGH Epp. v, p. 605, and Flodoard's notice of an absolution, *Hist. Rem. Ecc.*, iii. c. 10, ed. cit. p. 483 (Schrörs, Register no. 76). For threats to excommunicate Charles the Bald, see *Pro Ecc. Lib. Def.*, PL 125, col. 1058, and a letter of 868, PL 126, col. 97. For the penance imposed on Louis III, see PL 126, col. 250. *Cf.* also Hincmar's very explicit citations of the *exemplum* of King Ozias (II Paral. xxvi, 16 ff.) in *Pro Ecc. Lib. Def.*, PL 125, cols. 1049, 1057 ff., and the decrees of Fîmes, PL 125, col. 1071: 'Ozias ... de templo a sacerdotibus *ejectus* ...' For the Ozias theme in other ninth-century sources, as a warning to kings not to go 'extra ministerium verstrum', see Anton, *op. cit.* pp. 410, n. 225 and 435.

2. M. David, 'Le serment', p. 121.

3. For *soliditas regni* as an objective at Coulaines, see the preface, Capit. II, p. 253. The decrees of Fîmes are in PL 125, cols. 1069 ff.: in the preface, col. 1071, Hincmar and his colleagues declare themselves 'non nova condentes sed quae a maioribus nostris secundum tramitem sanctarum scripturarum *statuta*, et a christianis imperatoribus ac regibus *promulgata*, et usque ad haec periculosa nostrae infelicitatis tempora fuere *servata*, quasi lumina in malignorum operum tenebras ... devocamus'. The synodal decrees treated as a whole the affairs of church and state, and were meant to be observed by all in the realm. C. vi: *Admonitio ad regem et ministros reipublicae*, included twenty-one passages from capitularies, the last of them from that of Meersen (851), with its guarantees for the *lex et iustitia* of every *fidelis*: see p. 148 *supra*. C. viii contained a sketch of Charlemagne's government as a deliberately-idealized model: 'et ad capitium lecti sui tabulas cum graphio habebat, et quae sive in die sive in nocte de *utilitate sancti ecclesiae* et de *profectu et soliditate regni* meditabatur, in eisdem tabulis adnotabat ... et quando ad placitum suum veniebat, omnia subtiliter tractata plenitudine consiliarorum suorum monstrabat et *communi consilio* illa ad effectum perducere procurabat'. If legislation remains in the king's hands, its implementation is seen to rest on consensus: *cf.* Capit. II, p. 307 (Pîtres, 862): 'illa capitula quae consensu fidelium nostrorum fieri iussimus'; *ibid.* p. 313 (Pîtres, 864): 'consensus populi'. Hincmar depicts Charlemagne in terms made familiar by Charles the Bald. See the fine comments of Löwe, 'Hinkmar', pp. 222 ff., on this and comparable passages in Hincmar's late works: '... was aussieht wie ein Lob der Vergangenheit, was in Wirklichkeit die freilich nicht sehr erfolgreiche Mahnung an die Gegenwart, sich vom Nutzen des Königs, des Reiches und der Kirche durch keine egoistischen Interessen abbringen zu lassen'.

4. See Capit. II, Index Verb., s.v. 'Communis'.

5. See S. Wolin, *Politics and Vision* (Boston, 1960), pp. 127 ff.

6. For these and similar linked concepts, see Capit. II, pp. 73, 253, 328, etc.

but also for its realism and firm basis in Frankish political traditions. He applied to kingship, on the one hand, that order and functional definition which he found, in principle at least, in the church's own internal organization, so that the king's office acquired the same clear juristic delimitation as the bishop's.[1] He appealed to law, on the other hand, less in abstract terms than as a surviving and still evolving common denominator of rights and interests, a publicly-acknowledged regulator of relations between the main competitors for power in the West Frankish realm.[2] Hence the shrewdly utilitarian nature of his attempts at a long series of great public gatherings to commit king, clergy and *populus* together to the preservation of both the *regulae* and the *leges et statuta*. At this constitutional level, affirming the identity of the laws with the public interest, Hincmar could transcend any antithesis between the juristic and the moral. His own lifetime (805/6–882) spanned the Carolingian Empire from its heyday to its dissolution: his political thought forms a bridge between the ideologies of theocratic and feudal kingship.[3]

1. For Hincmar's parallel role in producing similarly-constructed royal and episcopal consecration-rites, see Bouman, *Sacring and Crowning*, pp. 112 ff.

2. *Cf. supra* pp. 146 f.

3. I am very grateful to Mr John Gillingham, Professor J. M. Wallace-Hadrill and Professor Walter Ullmann, who kindly offered constructive criticisms of an earlier draft of this paper. If errors of fact or of judgment remain, they are my responsibility alone.

8

THE ANNALS OF ST. BERTIN

I

Though the keeping of annals or chronicles had never entirely ceased in Western Europe since the fall of the Roman Empire, the eighth and ninth centuries brought changes that were qualitative as well as quantitative.[1] Before Charlemagne's reign, annalists had been at work in several monasteries in the British Isles and then on the Continent; and one branch of Charlemagne's family had sponsored the keeping of something rather like annals of the Frankish realm.[2] Still, it was not until Charlemagne's time, specifically with the organising of a royal chapel

ABBREVIATIONS

AB	*Annales de St. Bertin*, ed. F. Grat et al. (Paris, 1964)
AM	*Annales du Midi*
ARF	*Annales Regni Francorum*, ed. F. Kurze, MGH SSRG (1895)
Astron	*Anonymi Vita Hludovici Pii*, ed. G. Pertz, MGH SS II, pp.607–48
Calmette	J. Calmette, *La Diplomatie Carolingienne* (Paris, 1901)
DA	*Deutsches Archiv*
Devisse	J. Devisse, *Hincmar archevêque de Reims, 845–882*, 3 vols. (Geneva, 1975, 1976)
EHR	*English Historical Review*
Ermold	Ermold le Noir, *Poème sur Louis le Pieux et Épitres au Roi Pépin*, ed. E. Faral (Paris, 1932)
FMS	*Frühmittelalterliche Studien*
LMA	*Le Moyen Age*
Lot and Halphen	F. Lot, L. Halphen *Le Règne de Charles le Chauve, 840–851* (Paris, 1909)
Lupus	Loup de Ferrières, *Correspondance*, ed. L. Levillain (Paris 1927–35)
MGH	*Monumenta Germaniae Historica*
MGH Cap.	MGH *Capitularia Regum Francorum*
MGH Epp. KA	MGH *Epistolae Karolini Aevi*
MGH SS	MGH *Scriptores in Folio*
MGH SSRG	MGH *Scriptores Rerum Germanicarum*
Nithard	Nithard, *Histoire des Fils de Louis le Pieux*, ed. P. Lauer (Paris 1926)
PL	J.-P. Migne, *Patrologia Latina*, 221 vols. (Paris, 1841–64)
RB	*Revue Bénédictine*
Tessier	G. Tessier, *Receuil des Actes de Charles II le Chauve*, 3 vols. (Paris, 1943, 1952, 1955)

[1] Wattenbach-Levison 1953, pp.245ff.; Hoffmann 1958.*
[2] Wattenbach-Levison 1953, pp.161ff, 180ff.; Wallace-Hadrill 1960.

* For full references to notes in this chapter, *see* pp. 193-4 below.

and a 'chancery' (the two cannot be rigidly distinguished) at his court, and the basing of that court at Aachen for at least part of each year from 794 onwards, that the *Royal Frankish Annals* became a court product, kept up by royal chaplains or notaries.[3] Charlemagne himself is usually said to have inspired this development, but palace clerks had their own reasons for writing contemporary history: 'no learned man doubts, I think', wrote one learned man of the period, 'that it is the most ancient practice, habitual for kings up to now, to have whatever things are done or happen written down in annals for posterity to learn about'.[4] The stress here seems to be on the historical consciousness of the learned rather than any use-value to the king. Given the character of the palace personnel and a culture common to the scholars in monasteries and palace alike, the transfer of monastic annal-writing to the court was a natural move. Once the annals were there, it is possible that the king, or at any rate his counsellors, occasionally consulted them and felt glad to know that 'the most ancient practice' was revived. But there is no evidence that Charlemagne tried to publicise or circulate them, still less use them for propaganda – a point I shall return to later.

Palace clerks writing up contemporary 'doings and events' worked under severe difficulties in ninth-century Francia. Court scholars were expected when necessary to double as warriors, and not all kings would have responded as good humouredly as Pippin of Aquitaine did to cack-handed Ermold: 'Lay your weapons aside brother, and better stick to your books!'[5] The extent to which the court remained itinerant, even when courtiers were not actually campaigning, made documents hard to collect and store. The ninth-century royal archive was termed the *armarium*[6] – the cupboard – which is probably just what it was. Written material, then, was not very plentiful for the court annalist: in the main he noted, rather, what he had witnessed, or what oral informants had witnessed. The court was a centre to which such information flowed. But rumour was rife: it was no cliché when a ninth-century annalist wrote that the king learned some piece of news 'for certain' or 'by a not uncertain messenger'.[7] Sheer problems of communication were enormous, and sometimes added to deliberately by Carolingian rulers.[8]

I have glanced first at the production of the *ARF*, in the time of Charlemagne and Louis the Pious, because the *Annals of St Bertin* began life as a continuation thereof. Perhaps I should have said, '*so-called* Annals

[3] Fleckenstein 1959, pp.40ff., 74ff., Malbos 1966. In what follows, the *Royal Frankish Annals* are referred to as the *ARF*.

[4] Smaragdus, *Vita S. Benedicti Anianensis*, *MGH*, *SS XV* i, p.201.

[5] Ermold, *In Honorem Hludowici*, line 2019, p.154, Cp. Lupus, Ep. 72, ii, p.12.

[6] Ganshof 1958, pp.65ff.

[7] E.g. *AB* s. a. 875, pp.196, 198; 862, p.87; 869, p.156. Cp. 871, pp.182–3.

[8] *AB* s. a. 837, p.22; 864, pp.105, 112. Cp. Lupus, Epp. 35, 45, 101, i, pp.154, 186; ii, p.124; Hincmar Ep. 169, MGH Epp. *KA* VI, i, pp.158–9.

of St Bertin' (though I think it's too late to propose an alternative label) for despite their monastic ring, these annals have no other connection with St Bertin's than the accident that the earliest manuscript was probably copied out there.[9] In the manuscripts (and there are not many), the *AB* immediately follow the *ARF*. There is no new heading, no break at all: the *AB* annalist simply takes up the story in 830 where the *ARF* left off in 829. Yet there must have been some kind of break in production at this point, because most manuscripts of the *ARF* do *not* continue with the *AB*.[10] It seems that the break coincides with a change in authorship in circumstances which also contributed to a dispersal of copies of the *ARF*: the arch-chaplain Hilduin, who had exercised some kind of supervision over the annals' production up to 830, in that year joined the revolt of Louis the Pious' sons and fell into disgrace. Hilduin's successor as arch-chaplain, Fulco, evidently included the continuance of the annals-tradition amongst his responsibilities, until he in turn was moved to a new job away from the court in 835.[11] The first five years of the *AB* thus predictably show continuity of themes and general style with the earlier *ARF*, especially perhaps with those covering the 820s. The picture is somewhat skewed by the fact that Fulco's annals cover years of political upheavals – Louis the Pious' removal from power in 833, his temporary replacement by his eldest son Lothar, followed by Louis' recovery early in 834 – which must have made the keeping of court annals peculiarly hard. It looks as if, though information was being collected throughout, the annals for the early 830s were not written up in their present form until 834. Louis the Pious is consistently depicted as a wronged father, with all the stress laid on his virtues of magnanimity, paternal feeling, patience in adversity – 'as is his custom', comments the annalist[12] – and finally, clemency. His enemies, especially Ebbo, archbishop of Rheims, who stage-managed Louis' enforced penance (and hence de facto deposition) at Soissons, are equally consistently depicted in hostile terms: their traits, the very opposite of Louis', are disobedience, disloyalty, filial impiety, cruelty. The annalist tried to maintain the *ARF* tradition in recording the ruler's itinerary, especially where he spent Easter and Christmas each year, when and where assemblies were held and at which one the annual gifts were handed over. But inevitably the entries for 832–3 became a chronicle of the conflict between Louis and his sons, with other events neglected. In 834, the annalist's horizon could widen again: he recorded a Danish attack on Frisia, and had more detailed information on affairs in Italy and in Neustria.[13]

[9] Levillain 1964, pp.v, xviff. In what follows, the *Annals of St Bertin* are referred to as the *AB*.

[10] Compare Kurze 1895, preface, with Levillain 1964, pp.xxiiff.

[11] Grierson 1940a, pp.277ff.; Levillain 1964, pp.viiiff.; Malbos 1966.

[12] *AB* s. a. 832, p.7.

[13] *AB* s. a. 834, pp.14–5.

It is worth asking what court chaplains and clerks, in particular Fulco himself, actually did when Louis was imprisoned and Lothar with his own entourage temporarily took up quarters at Aachen. No doubt those of Louis' clerks who stayed loyal to him thought fit to lie low for a while: as the *AB* say under 833, 'some of those against whom the rebels' wrath raged most fiercely slipped away and took themselves off to the lands of their friends and faithful men'.[14] Palace clerks had personal links with monasteries – Fulco himself was abbot of St Wandrille as well as of St Hilaire at Poitiers – and would seek refuge there. The resumption of annal-writing at Louis' court must have had to wait till the spring or summer of 835. This same year brought another change of arch-chaplain with Louis' appointment of his half-brother and stand-by, Bishop Drogo of Metz,[15] while Fulco went to administer the archdiocese of Rheims following Ebbo's removal from office, formalised in February 835. Unlike his two predecessors as arch-chaplain, Drogo had episcopal responsibilities, which he took seriously. Because he had to spend much time away from the court, Drogo assigned the task of keeping up the annals to one of the palace chaplains. A single surviving manuscript reveals the existence of a copy of the annals from 830 onwards which may have been made late in 837, for it contains part of the annal for that year but breaks off before the *AB* account of the winter assembly at Aachen.[16] This copy of the *AB* annals for 830 to 837 was preserved at Metz in the twelfth century: presumably it had been made for Drogo, who as arch-chaplain, though not based at court, continued to take an interest in the annals if not actively to supervise them.

II

One of Louis the Pious' palace clerks, then, took over the *AB* in 835. Given that he had been trained in the chapel and continued to work there, residing at the court with access to information, written and oral, coming in there, his annals, like Fulco's, show predictable continuity of style and content with the preceding *ARF*. This continuity in the annals as long as they were being kept up at the court transcends any changes of authorship as between one clerk, or group of clerks, and another. It seems wiser, therefore, not to split the *AB* in the conventional way, like Gaul, into three parts, according to authors, but rather to split it into two: the part written at the court, and the part written elsewhere. The appearance of a new annalist in 835 is, then, relatively insignificant in terms of the character of the *AB*. Still, it is time to identify our clerk as

14 *AB* s. a. 833, p.9.
15 Oexle 1967, pp.347ff.
16 Levillain, pp.xxxixff. This is Grat's MS 'M'.

Prudentius.[17] He was a Spaniard by origin, probably from a refugee family who sought their fortune north of the Pyrenees early in Louis the Pious' reign[18] and were doing well enough in Gascony by about 820 to send one of their boys to Louis' court, eventually to take up service in the chapel. Prudentius' family connexions may have had some effect on his access to information about the Spanish March, Gascony and even Spain itself, but the *AB* yield disappointingly little evidence and virtually none of Prudentius' correspondence survives[19] to help our understanding of him. More important than his biological connexions, anyway, seem to have been the new social ones of common outlook, experience, culture and personal interest which he made at Louis' court. Two men in particular were there in the 830s who had a major influence on his subsequent career: Lupus, abbot of Ferrières from 840, and Wenilo, archbishop of Sens from 836 or 837.[20] Both these men had powerful connexions within the Frankish realm: henceforth the Spaniard could hope through them, as well as through Carolingian patronage, for power there too. In the ninth century, an able palace clerk could reasonably expect to end up a bishop.

Prudentius kept writing the *AB* from 835 to 861, when he died on the job. But because his situation changed radically during this period, so too did the nature of the *AB*. Until 840, the annals continued to centre on the movements and doings of Louis the Pious – his campaigns, his whereabouts on the major feasts, his assemblies, his relations with his sons. Where else than at court could Prudentius have got the information that on 26 December 838, a terrible flood happened in Frisia after which 'the number of people drowned was very carefully counted: 2,437 deaths were reported'?[21] Who but a palace clerk would have been so shattered by the conversion to Judaism ('rumour spread the news') of the palace clerk Bodo who had, so to speak, defected while on a visit to Rome?[22] Only at court could Prudentius have used the text of a letter sent by the West Saxon King Æthelwulf to Louis in 839 reporting an English priest's vision of supernatural warning: 'if Christian people do not quickly do penance for their various vices and crimes . . . then all of a sudden pagan men will lay waste their land with fire and sword'.[23] The interest in Viking activities, and in the Anglo-Saxons' response to them, would recur in Prudentius' annals in later years.[24] But while he remained at Louis'

17 Wattenbach-Levison 1957, pp.348f.

18 Cp., though with no mention of Galindo-Prudentius, Higounet 1949.

19 MGH, Epp. KA III, pp.323–4, 631–3.

20 Levillain 1927; Werner 1959, pp.164ff.

21 *AB* s. a. 839, p.28. The event is recorded between references to Lent and Easter (6 April) 839 presumably because details were not available at the court until March.

22 *AB* s. a. 839, pp.27–8.

23 *AB* s. a. 839, pp.29–30.

24 See Pauline Stafford's paper in M. Gibson and J. Nelson edd., *Charles the Bald: Court and Kingdom*, BAR International Series 101 (Oxford, 1981), pp. 137-51.

court, the image of imperial success was kept as bright as possible. According to Nithard's later and plausible account, there was a conspiracy against Louis in 838, but the *AB* say nothing of it. Prudentius, knowing the emperor might see his work, gave the impression that Louis' arrangements for the royal inheritance of his youngest son Charles were quite secure; but Nithard, writing in very different circumstances, would reveal the opposition Louis' plans aroused.[25]

Where was Prudentius when, on 20th June 840, the old emperor died? Levillain[26] has suggested that already during the winter of 839–40 Prudentius was attached to the court of the young Charles at Poitiers in Aquitaine and remained with him, or with the Empress Judith, thereafter. This would mean that Prudentius' career shifted fairly smoothly from one court to another, in which case his annals should reflect simply a transfer of personal adherence from the old emperor to Charles. But perhaps things were more complicated. It may well be that Bishop Ebroin of Poitiers had already taken up the office of arch-chaplain to Charles in 839,[27] but to claim that Prudentius was on his staff from this time onwards, one would look for evidence either in Lupus' correspondence, perhaps, of a personal connexion between the two men, or in the *AB* for Prudentius' closeness to Charles in 840. The former line is a dead-end; the latter leads in another direction, for the 840 annal, after recording Louis' death on an island in the Rhine 'within sight of the palace of Ingelheim',[28] has practically no more to say, and nothing at all about Charles' doings. I think that Prudentius, along with Drogo of Metz, the archbishops of Mainz and Trier and many others, was at Louis' deathbed[29] and so, like Drogo and the rest, faced an agonising choice: to which of Louis' sons to offer his allegiance and his service?[30] A comparison of the *AB* for 840 and 841, taken together with Nithard's very full account of these years, shows that Prudentius had no detailed knowledge of Charles' movements until the autumn of 841. I suggest, therefore, that like Drogo and others he did not join Charles until news of Lothar's defeat at Fontenoy (25 June) had made that the obvious option. Prudentius duly recorded where Charles spent Christmas in 841 (Châlons) and both Easter and Christmas in 842 (Herstal and St Quentin);[31] and that was the last time he noted Charles' whereabouts at a major feast. Like the early 830s, the years 840–3 were exceptional: continuing political crisis, frequent changes of personnel, moves and campaigns must have made a court chaplain's life hard, a court annalist's

[25] Nithard, i, c. 6, p.26.
[26] 1964, p.xiii.
[27] Grierson 1934, pp.241ff.; Oexle 1969, pp.166f.
[28] *AB* s. a. 840, p.36.
[29] Astron, c. 63, p.647.
[30] Cp. Grierson 1934, pp.244f.
[31] *AB* s. a. 841, p.40; 842, pp.41, 43.

harder still. Under such conditions, the annal for 842 was something of an achievement, including as it does not only details of the activities of all three Frankish kings and a careful record of Charles' marriage, but also information on Vikings in the Channel and Saracens in the Mediterranean.

The next development in Prudentius' career, and one with a decisive effect on the *AB*, was his appointment to the bishopric of Troyes, usually dated sometime between 843 and 846.[32] This can probably be pinned down more closely. Lupus reveals that he and Prudentius, almost certainly a bishop by then, were engaged on an official mission in the autumn of 844, and he addresses Prudentius as a bishop in April 845.[33] Then there is the evidence of the *AB* themselves which imply some kind of break late in 843: no more information is given after August under that year (which means that Charles' Breton campaign, the assemblies of Germigny and Coulaines, and Charles' wintering at Tours[34] are all unmentioned) while, on the other hand, the 844 annal seems to be settled in a pattern followed by Prudentius thereafter, that is, under each year there is usually some information on events in Italy, especially concerning the papacy, on Viking activities, and on Louis the German, with sometimes a scrap on the British Isles or Spain. Where these scraps can be checked, incidentally, the information seems accurate, as in the notices of Viking attacks on Ireland under the year 847 and of a great Irish victory under 848: the Annals of Ulster bear this out and the movements of Irish scholars on the Continent suggest likely lines of communication.[35]

But Prudentius' *AB* from 844 onwards are different in a more fundamental way from the *AB* of the 830s and from the *ARF*. They are not only less full but also much more scrappy, because the ruler's deeds and diplomacy no longer provide a linking theme. The sentences jerk along from one lump of information to the next, not because Prudentius' Latinity is weak, but because there is nothing resembling a continuous narrative. Prudentius' problems may have arisen partly from trying to keep too many balls in the air at once, in so far as he was interested in the doings not just of one Carolingian ruler but of several; but they arose, too, from the spasmodic, patchy way in which news reached him. The annals for 844 and 849, for instance, with their confused and fragmentary accounts of events in far-off Aquitaine, show how hard it was for Prudentius to arrange his material in a coherent time-sequence. The explanation for the changed character of Prudentius' annals from 844 to

[32] Duchesne 1910, ii. p.456; Wattenbach-Levison 1957, p.349.

[33] Lupus, Epp. 40, 41, i, pp.170, 172–4.

[34] Lot and Halphen, pp.74ff.

[35] *AB* s. a. 847, p.54; 848, pp.55–6. Cp. Chadwick 1958, pp.101ff. I am grateful to Glenn McKee for discussion of this point.

861 lies, I think, in his absence, most of the time, from Charles' court, and his living, again most of the time, at Troyes which during this whole period hardly figured at all in Charles' itinerary.[36] Chronic illness may have been another reason why Prudentius visited the court and attended assemblies less often than some other bishops.[37]

Some historians have found it hard to account for Prudentius' silences on what in the view of those same historians were quite important events. Lot and Halphen, for instance, wondering why Prudentius failed to mention the Synod of Ver (844) or the so-called First Colloquy of Meersen (847), were moved to suggest that this was because neither meeting produced successful results. Frankly it is hard to see why the Second Colloquy of Meersen (851) should be thought any more 'important' in terms of results, though this was the criterion, so Lot and Halphen allege, on which Prudentius not merely mentioned it, but included verbatim the text that emanated from it, in the *AB*.[38] Yet if this really was the criterion on which Prudentius inserted, or omitted, material, why do the *AB* say nothing of the Synod of November 849 at Paris when theological matters which Prudentius certainly thought important were settled in a manner which he thought successful?[39] Two reasons of a quite different kind may be advanced for Prudentius' placing of the Meersen *capitula* in the 851 annal: first, this was a very lean year in terms of other information, and since 850 had been still worse (it is by far Prudentius' shortest annal) he may simply have been grateful for more, and ready-made, material, especially at a time when he was much preoccupied with writing a bulky theological treatise;[40] second – and the point is not quite so obvious as it looks – Prudentius was able to get hold of the Meersen text, for whether or not he was himself present at Meersen,[41] he was certainly in contact at this time, unusually, with the king and with his own metropolitan Wenilo of Sens,[42] both of whom were. Anyway, the 851 annal is the exception that proves the rule: normally Prudentius was in no position to have such an 'official document' at his disposal.

This raises a wider problem: Prudentius' annals have generally been seen as, still, an 'official' work, and the obligations of a 'courtier' ('d'un

36 A charter issued at the monastery of Moutier-la-Celle, Troyes, on 10 January 859, Tessier 1, no. 201, pp.512–4, seems to give the only evidence for Charles' presence at Troyes during Prudentius' episcopate. For the circumstances of January 859, see above p. 88.

37 *AB* s. a. 861, p.85; MGH Epp. KA III, p.633.

38 Lot and Halphen, pp.129 n. 2, 179 n. 1, 227 n. 2.

39 Lot and Halphen, pp.208, 213 n. 3. This synod, unmentioned by Devisse 1975, vol. 1, pp.127ff., might throw a different light on reactions to Gottschalk in 849 from that offered by Devisse.

40 PL. 115, cols 1011–1352.

41 Lot and Halphen, p.228 n. 1.

42 Devisse 1975, vol. 1, pp.146, 152f.

courtisan, ou tout au moins partisan') have been invoked to explain both what Prudentius said or did not say, and how he said it.[43] Everything was presented, according to Levillain, in a way that favoured 'his master' (Charles) which produced 'faults so obvious that historians . . . are unable to let themselves be led into error' (!) Well, whatever Prudentius' 'faults', they are surely not those Levillain alleges. For Prudentius *did* give information discreditable to Charles, and indeed explicitly criticised him in more than one place;[44] while what he did not do in any annal after than for 841[45] was to put in any phrase or even epithet that might have flattered the king. Odd if this was the best a 'courtier' could do . . .

Löwe, evidently recognising the inadequacy of such a view as Levillain's, has offered his own explanation of those *AB* passages in which Prudentius criticised Charles: 'his (critical) position corresponds to the rise of the West Frankish episcopate to a position which it could claim to control and direct the West Frankish king, and, seen from this perspective, . . . it was quite understandable that after Prudentius' death, his work was carried on by Hincmar of Rheims'.[46] But on this analysis, it becomes strange that an episcopal spokesman should have neglected even to mention the alleged 'episcopalist' triumphs of Ver and Meaux-Paris (844, 845),[47] and depicted the events of autumn in 858 in such very un-'episcopalist' colours. Those events, and Prudentius' treatment of them, have a good deal to tell us about ninth-century political realities, not least as they affected bishops. Louis the German's invasion of the realm of his half-brother Charles did not come out of the blue:[48] a sizable faction of the aristocracy of Charles' realm had promised Louis their support, and were as good as their word. Among these were Wenilo Archbishop of Sens and Odo Count of Troyes.[49] And what then was Prudentius' position, with his metropolitan and his local count gone to welcome the invader? We can only guess at the degree of Prudentius' complicity when Louis came to Troyes in November and made it briefly his base in West Francia.[50] By the

[43] Levilain 1964, pp.xiiif.

[44] *AB* s. a. 846, p.52; 853 p.68; 855, p.70. Under 846, the forthright criticism of Charles' attitude to 'episcopal warning' at the Assembly of Epernay looks to me like a Hincmarian interpolation (I hope to defend this view elsewhere), as do the comments on Gottschalk and the Synod of Quierzy under 849, pp.56–7. For a different view, see Schrörs 1884, p.101 n. 55, and Devisse 1975, vol. 1, p.128. On the other hand the much less forthright criticisms of Charles' intrigues with the Slavs (853) and his weak line on heresy (855) seem to me Prudentius' own. For their context, see below, p. 182.

[45] *AB* s. a. 841, p.37.

[46] Wattenbach-Levison 1957, p.349. Cp. Löwe 1967, p.7 and n. 23.

[47] Lot and Halphen, pp.126ff., 145ff.; Ullmann 1972, pp.98f.

[48] Calmette 1901, pp.34ff.

[49] *Libellus proclamationis domni Caroli regis adversus Wenilonem* cc. 7–14, MGH, Cap II, pp.452f.; *Annals of Fulda* s. a. 858, ed. Kurze, MGH, SSRG, pp.49ff.

[50] *AB* s. a. 858, p.79.

following spring, Charles had recovered his position and Louis had withdrawn eastwards. How did Prudentius write up all this? Neglecting even to mention Wenilo or Odo, he recounted the moves of Louis and Charles without comment or explanation – so baldly, in fact, that a later West Frankish copyist of the *AB* was moved to insert a sentence at the beginning of the 858 annal summarising the year's events in a way sympathetic to Charles.[51] Yet if Prudentius wrote no criticism of Louis into his annals, Hincmar of Rheims, his suffragans and his colleague of the province of Rouen had rallied in practical, military support of Charles and dispatched a beautifully 'episcopalist' letter of protest to the invader.[52] Prudentius' failure to conform at this point to any ideological stereotype should make us look for another interpretation of his conduct: he seems to have been on the fringe, at least, of a group of nobles with whom Wenilo and Odo were involved and some of whose members had been in incipient revolt since 853[53] – which might be linked, in turn, with the criticisms of Charles in the *AB* under the years 853 and 855. Even if the composition of this group remains obscure, and its consistency of policy questionable, there can be little doubt that the way in which Prudentius wrote his annals was determined less by any abstract principles than by his personal political loyalties and connexions.

This brings us to the last problem of Prudentius' section of the *AB*, the curious passage at the end of the entry for 859: 'Pope Nicholas faithfully confirmed and catholicly decreed concerning the grace of God and Free Will, the truth of Double Predestination and about the blood of Christ, how it was shed for all believers?[54] Now without going into theological details, it's enough to note here that this alleged papal pronouncement belongs in a saga of doctrinal controversy over the teachings of Gottschalk.[55] Hincmar and many of the Frankish bishops had condemned these teachings, but Prudentius and others had sympathised with them; and in the 859 annal a similar sympathy was attributed to the pope himself. Some have said that Prudentius invented this 'decree' of Pope Nicholas;[56] others have suggested he recorded a

51 *AB* s. a. 858, p.78 n. as., from MS 'O'. Cp. Werner 1959, p.165 n. 79.

52 MGH, Cap. 2. pp.432ff. Cp. Hincmar's comment in Ep. 126, MGH, Epp. KA VI, i, p.64. See Halphen 1947, pp.313ff.

53 Werner 1959, pp.163ff.; Oexle 1969, pp.191ff.

54 *AB* s. a. 859, p.82.

55 Vielhaber 1956; Devisse 1975, vol. 1, pp.118ff. See also the paper of David Ganz in Gibson and Nelson edd., *Charles the Bald*, pp. 353-73.

56 The now lost fragment of the *AB* transcribed by Bolland in the seventeenth century had a marginal note against this passage of the 859 annal: 'Hic Prudentius eps de Nicolao scripsit quod ut fieret voluit; sed quia factum fuerit, verum non dixit'. For the likelihood that this note, and the MS itself, were Hincmar's own, see Ganshof 1949, and Levillain 1965, pp.xviiif. This is Grat's MS 'C'.

current rumour.[57] But Prudentius makes the statement sound perfectly authentic. Is what he says in fact incredible? I think not. Thanks to recent work, it is fairly clear that Gottschalk's teachings remained in circulation as long as they did because he had found powerful friends and patrons throughout his career. Then, of course, his 'heresy' became a peg on which to hang other, political, interests. Thus Gottschalk's friends came to include some of Hincmar's opponents.[58]

In the light of all this, we can now look at a letter written by Hincmar in 866 – for him an especially difficult year. Charles had insisted on appointing to the vacant see of Bourges (a place vital to ruling Aquitaine) his tried and trusted clerk Wulfad. But there was a snag: Wulfad had originally been consecrated in holy orders by Hincmar's predecessor Ebbo who, though deposed from office, as we saw, in 835, had been briefly reinstated at Rheims by Lothar in 840 and during the few months before he was expelled again in 841 had consecrated a number of clerks, including Wulfad. The issue raised in 866 was that of the finality of Ebbo's deposition, which it was of course vital for Hincmar to maintain. Charles, to be fair, did not wish to challenge this, but was determined to put in his man at Bourges. Both he and Hincmar set about enlisting the support of the pope.[59] And amidst all this, to Hincmar's alarm, the friends of Gottschalk were, predictably, again rearing their heads. 'It's said he has many supporters', wrote Hincmar[60] in September to Eigil, Archbishop of Sens, just then leaving on a mission to Rome. One of these supporters, Hincmar continued, had been Prudentius, 'as his writings show' – referring to his work on Predestination. 'He also', added Hincmar, 'in the *Annals of the Deeds of our Kings* which he put together (i.e. our *AB*) inserted the following in the events of the year 859 to confirm his own opinion . . .' and Hincmar then quoted the offending passage about Nicholas' 'decree'. 'We have never heard this from anyone else', Hincmar went on, 'nor read it anywhere else. Therefore since those *Deeds* (again, the *AB*) in which these things are written have just now come in to the hands of a number of people, it is necessary that you (Eigil) have a word with the pope about the matter, lest scandal come from it into the Church.' After hastily adding that no mention should be made of his own name ('for his mind is said to be moved against me, and many people are writing to him against me'), Hincmar wanted to make clear to Eigil exactly which annalistic text he meant: evidently it was not all that familiar to

57 McKeon 1974, p.105.

58 Ganz 1979.

59 See Charles's letter to Nicholas I, PL. 124, cols. 867–9, 870–5. Hincmar Ep. 185, MGH Epp. KA VI, i, pp.187ff. Cp. Devisse 1976, vol. 2, pp.600ff.; McKeon 1978, pp.62ff.

60 Ep. 187, MGH Epp. KA VI, i, pp.194f.

the Archbishop of Sens. 'That set of *Annals* I am talking about, the king has: it is that very same book which he lent to me in your presence, and which I returned to him in your presence in the church where he commended you to us.' The reference must be to the year 865 when Eigil was consecrated to Sens. Then, at any rate, the king was in possession of Prudentius' section of the *AB*. But Hincmar's words need not imply that he had had it for long before that. On the contrary, Hincmar says that it is only recently (*iam*) that Prudentius' annals have come into the hands of 'a number of people'. His words also suggest that this text was special, even unique:[61] Hincmar had had to take his copy from the king's manuscript, and the researches of Grat and others have shown that there is no evidence for the existence of any other manuscripts in the ninth century besides these two. Amazingly, this letter of Hincmar has been cited as indicating that not only Charles the Bald but, by extension, Charlemagne too kept a text of the royal annals close by him 'in the chancery' for handy reference, and allowed open access to it: 'there was no thought of keeping the royal annals as an official secret' (!).[62] But surely Hincmar's letter implies that Charles had never had a copy of Prudentius' annals during Prudentius' lifetime, but, when Hincmar wrote in 866, had only recently acquired the unique manuscript. We don't know what happened to Prudentius' papers and library when he died, but we do know that Charles appointed as his successor one of the palace notaries Fulcric.[63] I suggest that Prudentius' annals only then got into the hands of the king, and in due course, of others, perhaps because Charles wanted to draw their attention to the 859 annals with its evidence of Nicholas' soft line on predestinationist heresy.

To summarise my view of Prudentius' annals: written, on Hincmar's evidence, as 'Deeds of our Kings', they were, from 844 onwards, produced neither at nor for the court, and not especially preoccupied with only the West Frankish realm. Given Prudentius' connexions with a group which was in touch with Louis the German at various points in the 850s, the fairly consistent interest shown in Louis' deeds in this part of the *AB*, and specifically the treatment of the events of 858, find an explanation. If, as Levillain apparently believed, Prudentius' annals were intended for Charles' eyes, then the question would have to be faced: how could he have written into them criticisms of Charles? The thing to remember is the simple fact of Prudentius' situation: geographically, politically, personally, he was removed from the court.

[61] But Hincmar does seem to have had, or seen, a copy of Fulco's section of the *AB* already in 859 or 860. He termed this text: 'Annales domni Ludovici imperatoris', and referred to the passage in the 835 annal covering Ebbo's deposition, PL. 125, col. 391, Cp. Levillain 1965, pp.xvif.

[62] Wattenbach-Levison 1953, p.248.

[63] Tessier 3, p.73.

In other words, the association of annal-production with the Carolingian royal chapel was broken after 843. Charles the Bald seems to have made no attempt to re-establish it, and indeed allowed the office of arch-chaplain to lapse after 860. Löwe has argued that this helps to explain the end of the court-annalistic tradition.[64] But any relationship here seems to be the other way round: one reason an arch-chaplain was no longer needed was that by 860 the production of annals had long since ceased to be part of his responsibilities. I shall return presently to the wider question of how this came to be so.

III

It's time now to consider the last and best-known section of the *AB* – Hincmar's section, covering the years 861 to 882 when Hincmar died. Levillain was perhaps a little carried away when he likened Hincmar's annals to the *Mémoires* of Saint-Simon,[65] but it's true that, compared with Prudentius' section, they are often entertaining and occasionally, even, quite gripping. If we begin by asking why Hincmar took up the annalist's pen at all,[66] the first thing to notice is that he reverts, in some respects, to the old style of the *ARF*. He records the royal itinerary in some detail, with special note taken of where the king spends Easter and Christmas. Assemblies and synods are fairly thoroughly recorded, and there is much detailed information about diplomatic exchanges. Hincmar, himself a Frank and kinsman of at least two counts, is also interested in the actions and appointments of leading aristocrats.[67] He attempts fuller coverage overall: his annals average at 5+ pages per annum as against 1½ for Prudentius' section and 2½+ for the *ARF* in the 820s.[68] We recall that Hincmar had the *ARF* and Fulco's annals before him in Prudentius' manuscript, and that he had begun his career as a palace clerk, a protégé of Hilduin who was probably responsible for the annals' production in the 820s.[69] A certain nostalgia for those good old days, a somewhat aggrieved determination to reaffirm their sound practices in the teeth of modern decline, were later to be leitmotifs in Hincmar's *De Ordine Palatii*,[70] and may well have inspired him when in

[64] Löwe 1967, p.3.

[65] Levillain 1965, p.xiv.

[66] The near-total neglect of the *AB* in Devisse 1975–6, is surprising. Büchting 1887, does not consider the general question of Hincmar's motivation.

[67] Löwe 1967, p.10 n. 39, points out that Hincmar sometimes depicts them as acting as a group: *the primores*.

[68] To make this rough and ready comparison, I used Waitz's edition of the *AB*, MGH, SSRG.

[69] Malbos 1966.

[70] MGH, Cap. II, pp.517ff. Cp. Löwe 1972.

861 he set about continuing the *AB* where Prudentius had left off. Also relevant, perhaps, may have been Hincmar's youthful acquaintance with historical writing in the form of the *Gesta Dagoberti*: this again was an interest to which he returned later in life with the *Vita Remigii*.[71] A further biographical point is surely important: in 861, Hincmar had recently completed two very large works, the first of them involving, as Devisse has shown,[72] a major programme of re-education – the *Third Treatise on Predestination*, and the *De Divortio*. With these off his desk, this indefatigable pen-pusher may well have been in search of a new theme.

But in one vital respect, Hincmar was indeed continuing Prudentius' work rather than resuming the *ARF* tradition: he was not writing annals at the court, annals which the king should or might see, but writing at Rheims, we may guess for his own *familia* of clerks, for posterity too perhaps, but above all for himself. Hincmar's need to judge the conduct of others and to justify his own is one of the most striking traits in his personality, and its prominence in his annals differs only in degree, not in kind, from what we find in his works designed for publication. It largely accounts for the much greater fulness of his section of the *AB* compared with Prudentius', for when Hincmar's style looks at his most 'official', it is in fact very subjective. When he quotes from 'official documents', which he does relatively often and at tedious length, they are being used as pièces justificatives for Hincmar's own position or actions in a given case. For instance, the proceedings before Charles' consecration as king of Lotharingia at Metz in 869 are given in full,[73] partly because Hincmar designed and stage-managed the ritual on this occasion (as on others: like present-day Heralds, he clearly found these matter fascinating and important) and partly because he wished to reproduce his own speech justifying his officiating in someone else's archdiocese (reason enough to pull, triumphantly, out of the mitre the myth of Clovis' heaven-sent oil 'of which we (at Rheims) still have some'!). Again, when he gives the text of a letter sent by two Lotharingian archbishops to their colleagues, we find that he has doctored it.[74] Apparently his motive here, since the two Lotharingians were fiercely critical of the pope, was to dissociate himself from an extreme position with which they had tried to identify the entire Frankish episcopate. (Hincmar could, on occasion, himself criticise the pope very freely in the *AB*, but only when his personal position was threatened.)[75] It was not that Hincmar lacked a conception

71 Wallace-Hadrill 1953; Devisse 1976, vol 2, pp.1092; 1004ff.

72 Devisse 1975, vol. 1, pp.244ff., 386ff.; 1976, vol. 3, pp.1351ff.

73 *AB* s. a. 869, pp.158–64. Cp. MGH, Cap. II, pp.337ff.

74 *AB* s. a. 864, pp.107–10, where also the variants from the text as given in the *Annals of Fulda* are given in the apparatus. See also the comments of Levillain, p.108, n. 1.

75 *AB* s. a. 865, pp.118–9.

of textual authenticity; rather that, in the *AB* as in other works, he manipulated documentary evidence as a means to what he saw as higher, polemic, ends.[76] The mémoires-analogy is certainly more useful to an understanding of Hincmar's purposes in the *AB* than the charge that he often 'forgot his duty as an historian'.[77]

Criticism of others is, I've said, a notable feature of Hincmar's annals. He loosed his shafts over a wide range of people, from the men of Toulouse, 'with their usual perfidy', to Hagano, 'a crafty and very greedy Italian bishop', to Charles' uncle, Count Conrad, 'with his arrogant yet superficial knowledge of the world which brought little benefit to himself, still less to others',[78] to – finally – Prudentius whose unfinished annal for 861 he continued as follows:[79]

> 'Prudentius Bishop of Troyes, originally named Galindo, a Spaniard by birth, was at first a very learned man . . . But later, excited by bitter feelings, he became a very keen defender of (Gottschalk's) heresy against certain bishops . . . Then he died, still scribbling away at many things that are mutually contradictory and contrary to Faith. Thus, though he had been worn down by illness for a long time, he put an end at once both to living and to writing.'

As we've already seen, Hincmar had personal reasons for hostility to Prudentius and a more than theological stake in the Predestination controversy. But when we turn to Hincmar's criticisms of Charles the Bald, the situation may seem a very different one. For Löwe[80] has argued that these reflect 'not just personal rancour but a political will', a consistent policy – a kind of episcopalist policy – which involved setting up certain standards for royal behaviour. Löwe's account of Hincmar's views might be translated (without, I hope, too much misrepresentation) into the following list of concrete prohibitions:

1. the king should not negotiate with Vikings: he should fight them.
2. the king should stop giving churches and church lands to laymen.
3. the king should stop claiming control of top ecclesiastical appointments.
4. the king should not get involved in Italy when he should be at home fighting Vikings.
5. the king should never flout the rules of canon law as expounded by me, Hincmar.

[76] Devisse 1975, vol. 1, p.96; 1976 vol. 2, pp.657ff., 798f. For a broader perspective on early medieval attitudes, see Fuhrmann 1972, vol. 1, pp.65ff.

[77] Büchting 1887, p.22.

[78] *AB* s. a. 863, pp.97, 98; 862, p.95. Cp. the comment on the deaths of Robert and Ramnulf, s. a. 866, p.131, and the jibes at Rothad s. a. 862, pp.91f.

[79] *AB* s. a. 861, pp.84–5.

[80] 1967, p.9.

We can test Löwe's argument first, by looking at all the instances of negotiations with Vikings, and so on, recorded in the *AB* to see whether Hincmar reacts *consistently* to royal breaches of his 'rules'; and second, by invoking the help of other sources, to see if Hincmar in the *AB* has not sometimes shelved a problem of his own by omitting certain awkard facts. Let's then, look briefly at the points on our list in turn.

1. *How to deal with Vikings*. True, under the years 865 to 866, Hincmar does criticise, more or less explicitly, lack of resistance to the Vikings, and, implicitly, the making of treaties with them.[81] On the other hand, he records details of Danegeld payments without comment,[82] and under 873, in what reads like an eye-witness account, he approves Charles' skill in negotiations with the Vikings at Angers when according to other contemporary information with a different bias, he could actually have crushed these Vikings by force.[83]

2. *Giving churches to Laymen*. Yes, Hincmar does lodge bitter complaints on this score under 866.[84] On the other hand, under 867 he records without adverse comment that Charles himself assumed the abbacy of Hincmar's old house, St Denis.[85]

3. *Ecclesiastical appointments and royal control*. Yes, there are sharp protests under 866 about royal interference in the case of Wulfad, and under 876 in that of Ansegis of Sens.[86] On the other hand, there are no complaints about other episcopal and abbatial appointments made by the king, and Hincmar is quite sympathetic to Charles in his presentation of the case of Hincmar of Laon under 868–871.[87]

4. *Involvement in Italy*. In fact there is no explicit criticism on this score in the *AB*, and the two instances of irony Löwe[88] finds under 877 are not directed against the Italian involvement itself. Hincmar did complain in another work in 875,[89] but his view may have become more favourable by 877.[90]

[81] *AB* s. a. 865, p.124; 866, p.125; Löwe 1967, p.7 n. 24.

[82] *AB* s. a. 861, p.86; 877, p.213.

[83] *AB* s. a. 873, pp.194–5. Cp. Regino *Chronicon* s. a. 873, ed. Kurze, MGH, SSRG, pp.105ff. See Werner 1959b, pp.99ff.

[84] Above, n. 78.

[85] *AB* s. a. 867, p.135, Cp the grants of St Aubin's, Angers, to Salomon, St Hilaire, Poitiers, to Acfrid, St. Maurice, Agaune, to Boso, etc.: *AB* s. a. 863, p.96; 867, p.140; 869, p.167.

[86] *AB* s. a. 866, p.129; 876, p.202.

[87] *AB* s. a. 868, pp.151–2; 869, p.152; 871, p.181. See McKeon 1978.

[88] 1967, p.8 n. 32.

[89] *De fide Carolo regi servanda c.* 12, PL. 152, col. 967.

[90] A possible inference from the *AB* s. a., and from the role assigned to Hincmar at Quierzy in June: MGH, Cap. II, *c.* 12.

Before dealing with the last point on our list, we can already register some doubts about Löwe's presentation of the *AB* evidence. Hincmar's criticisms of Charles come in very specific contexts, and two short periods – 865–6, and 876 – stand out as years of complaint. The first of these was, as we've seen, the time of Wulfad's appointment to Bourges and of Hincmar's reawakened anxiety over the heresy of Gottschalk and his suspected patrons in high places. It was also a period of temporary enstrangement from the king. The 876 situation shows striking similarities: Charles had tried to railroad the appointment of Ansegis of Sens as Primate of Gaul and Ansegis had superseded Hincmar in the royal counsels. By contrast, during periods when Hincmar and the king were close, or at any rate not in conflict, even debateable royal actions evoked no overt criticism in the *AB*. When Charles attacked Provence in 861, for instance, Hincmar expressed his disapproval in a letter to a Provencal magnate whose help he wanted to protect the property of the church of Rheims in that region, but as annalist he simply recorded Charles' moves, reserving his critical comments for the conduct of the king's troops.[91] When Charles made a similar swoop on Lotharingia in 869, Hincmar had his own reasons (based no doubt on his church's interests) for approving, and confided his view somewhat coyly in the *AB*.[92] In 873 again, the *AB* show Hincmar firmly aligned with Charles over his dealings with the Loire Vikings and also his treatment of his son Carloman (whose revolt had evidently occasioned a good deal of damage to the property of Hincmar's church).[93] I think we have to conclude that the distinction between 'personal rancour' and 'political will' is rather misleading in the terms Löwe has proposed, and that there is no consistent ideological position to be found in Hincmar's section of the *AB* any more than in Prudentius'. Different responses to similar pieces of royal behaviour reflect, not mere 'personal rancour', but changes in Hincmar's political situation.

Finally, we should glance at Hincmar's alleged consistency in the application of canon law. Christian marriage will serve as a good example, for Hincmar in the *AB* and elsewhere has much to say in the 860s about the famous divorce case of Lothar II. In this, and in other similar cases, Hincmar is usually claimed to have upheld, unequivocally, the law of the Church.[94] By applying the rules, Hincmar could pronounce Lothar's marriage indissoluble, childless though it might be. The fact was that if Lothar died without heirs who were indisputably legitimate, then his uncle Charles the Bald could

[91] Ep. 142, MGH Epp. KA VI, i, p.115; *AB* s. a. 861, p.87.
[92] *AB* s. a. 869, p. 157.
[93] *AB* s. a. 873, p. 190.
[94] Weinzierl 1949; Devisse 1975, vol. 1, pp.383ff., 459ff.

hope to inherit all or part of his kingdom – which of course is what happened in 869. Most historians have been rightly suspicious of Charles' motives in preaching adherence to the canon law on marriage, yet those same historians have believed in Hincmar's complete integrity.[95] Only quite recently has it been noticed that there was another strictly comparable case of royal divorce on which Hincmar took a different line.[96] In his annal for 878, Hincmar wrote that when the pope came to West Francia, Louis the Stammerer (son and heir of Charles) asked for his wife (whom Hincmar did not name) to be consecrated queen, 'but he could not get his way'.[97] The reader is left with the impression that the lady is the same one mentioned in the record of young Louis' marriage under the year 862.[98] Why, then, was the pope so uncooperative? It turns out that although the 862 wife was still living, the 878 wife was a different lady. Evidently at the insistence of Charles near the end of his reign, and for clear political motives, Louis had been made to repudiate his first wife and make another alliance, and the whole affair was arranged *with Hincmar's connivance*! I should add that some very clever detective work was needed to expose this Hincmargate. Fortunately, on this subject Hincmar the letter-writer[99] proved to have been less discreet than the author of the *AB*. The interesting historiographical point is that Hincmar was found out, so to speak, only when the possibility of his guilt on such a score could be conceived of. Perhaps it's not surprising that the process of revision has been long and painful. For the realities of the ninth-century politics are often obscured from us in the clerically-produced texts of the period, and not least in the *AB*, by the writer's use of a code in which political conflicts are expressed as theological or canonistic ones. To reconstruct the context and purposes of Hincmar's work without anachronism is a delicate business.

In the end, to summarise, Hincmar's annals have to be read, not as bad history, not merely as mémoires, certainly not as the reflection of an episcopal programme, but as a series of subjective and more or less instantaneous perceptions of and reactions to contemporary political events in which Hincmar was himself more or less directly involved. There is no evidence that Hincmar ever revised his section of the *AB*. When he died, he left, it seems, a single manuscript, from which all extant manuscripts or fragments of the *AB* in other works (with a single exception)[99a] are derived. This time, no successor continued with

[95] Calmette, pp.80ff.; Devisse 1975, vol. 1, pp.439ff.
[96] Brühl 1964, pp.60ff.; Werner 1967, pp.437ff.
[97] *AB* s.a. 878. p.227.
[98] *AB* s. a. 862, p. 91.
[99] Schrörs Reg. nos. 404, 480,. from Flodoard in MGH SS XIII, pp.513, 510.
[99a] See above, n. 16.

a further instalment of the 'Deeds of our Kings'.

But if such categories as 'history' or 'mémoires' are clearly unapt, the *AB* also raise doubts about the usefulness of conventional distinctions betweeen 'public' and 'private', 'official' and 'unofficial' historiography. We are forced to consider what was the function of annals or chronicles of the realm in the early Middle Ages. If they were used by or potentially useful to kings, why did not only Charles the Bald but other ninth-century Carolingians too allow the Carolingian tradition of court annals to lapse? But a prior question must be: why were court annals ever written under any Carolingian? As I suggested at the beginning of this paper, annal-keeping had always been the product of clerical, not royal enthusiasm, specifically of the interest of a small number of palace clerks assembled in the first place by Charlemagne to cherish the reborn Latin learning. It was the very growth of this royal protegé which led in due course to the emptying of the nursery. Despite Heiric's fulsome eulogy of Charles the Bald's palace as a home of learning,[100] there is very little evidence for a court school in his reign.[100a] In place of the tight-knit court circle of Charlemagne and even of Louis the Pious, there came in the next two generations a dispersal of scholarship into a number of regional bases, loosely but effectively linked, as the Predestination debates, for instance, showed, by ties of personal affection and alliance and shared political as well as scholarly concerns. Yet while poetry or theology or music thrived in monasteries and episcopal cities, this dispersal brought an end to court annal-keeping. What had been a spin-off of the first, constricted, phase of the Carolingian Renaissance was outmoded in the more expansive, diverse and decentralised ecclesiastical culture of mid-ninth-century Francia.

The question of why Charles the Bald was not concerned to maintain the court-annals tradition in turn becomes less pressing if we jettison the false notion of Carolingian royal annals as in any sense propaganda. It was because the youthful Charles, fresh from Walahfrid's tutorship, was indeed concerned with the representation of his cause to posterity that in 840 he asked Nithard to write, not annals, but a history of royal family conflicts. Disillusioned perhaps with the outcome of that commission (if he ever even saw Nithard's increasingly dyspeptic Third and Fourth Books) Charles apparently did not repeat that attempt. As for propaganda, of course like any pre-modern ruler, Charles was concerned to influence and cajole contemporary aristocratic opinion. Great assemblies, consultations, oath-takings, public addresses, ritual displays were instruments all of which Charles exploited vigorously. But court

[100] *Vita Sancti Germani*, verse preface in MGH Poet III, p.756; prose preface in PL. 124, col. 1131ff. Cp. McKitterick 1980, and her paper in Gibson and Nelson edd, *Charles the Bald*, pp. 385-400.

[100a] I am grateful to Peter Godman for discussion of this point. See his comments in Gibson and Nelson edd., *Charles the Bald*, p. 302.

annals, in Latin, hardly came into this category. Their political irrelevance becomes clear, finally, if they are contrasted with the contemporary *Anglo-Saxon Chronicle*. It seems that Alfred did what no Carolingian ever thought of doing with the *ARF* or the *AB*: arranged for the copying and circulation of a revised text of the *Chronicle*[101] which, since it was in the vernacular, men could hear, if not read.[102] The medium could affect the message. Modern ideas of propaganda are, of course, as Professor Whitelock reminds us,[103] anachronistic for ninth-century England; but certainly the potential audience of the *Anglo-Saxon Chronicle* was no mere clerical coterie. Contrary to a recent tendency to see Continental influence in Alfredian historiography,[104] I would now stress the differences between English and Frankish annal-keeping in the ninth century, and suggest that the Alfredian *Chronicle* hailed from a distinctively insular tradition.[105] If Grimbald, whether at St. Bertin's or during his stay at Rheims,[106] ever saw Hincmar's manuscript of the *AB*, there is not to my mind the slightest trace of this to be found in subsequent *Chronicle*-production across the Channel. In the case of the *AB*, indispensability to historians is in inverse proportion to contemporary impact; and in that respect, a better modern analogue, for all its limitations, than Saint-Simon's *Mémoires* might be the *Diary* of Samuel Pepys.

101 Cp. Sisam 1953, pp. 140ff.
102 Wormald 1977.
103 Whitelock 1977.
104 Wallace-Hadrill 1950; John 1966, p.39; Nelson 1967; Parkes 1976, pp.165ff.
105 Cp. Harrison 1976; Bately 1979.
106 Grierson 1940b.

REFERENCES

BATELY, J., 1979: 'Bede and the Anglo-Saxon Chronicle', in *Saints, Scholars and Heroes, Studies in Medieval Culture, in honour of C. W. Jones*. eds. M. H. King, and W. M. Stevens, Minnesota 1979.

BRÜHL, C. R., 1964: 'Hinkmariana. II: Hinkmar im Widerstreit von kanonischem Recht und Politik in Ehefragen', in *DA* 20, 1964, pp.55–77.

BÜCHTING, E., 1887: *Glaubwürdigkeit Hincmars von Reims im dritten Teile der sogenannten Annalen von St. Bertin*, Halle 1887.

CHADWICK, N., 1958: *Studies in the Early British Church*, Cambridge 1958.

DAVIS, R. H. C., 1971: 'Alfred the Great: Propaganda and Truth', in *History* 56, 1971, pp.169–82.

DUCHESNE, L., 1910: *Fastes Episcopaux de l'ancienne Gaule* (3 vols.), vol. 2, Paris 1910.

FLECKENSTEIN, J., 1959: *Die Hofkapelle der deutschen Könige* vol. 1 MGH Schriften 16/1, Stuttgart 1959.

FUHRMANN, H., 1972: *Einfluss und Verbreitung der pseudoisidorischen Fälschungen* (3 vols.) vol. 1, Stuttgart 1972.

GANSHOF, F., 1949: 'Notes critiques sur les *Annales Bertiniani*' in *Mélanges F. Grat* (2 vols.), vol. 2, Paris 1949, pp.159–74.

GANSHOF, F., 1958: *Recherches sur les Capitulaires*, Paris 1958.

GANZ, D., 1979: review of Devisse, *Hincmar*, in *Revue Belge de Philologie et d'Histoire* LVII, 1979, pp.711–18.

GRIERSON, P., 1934: 'Hugues de St. Bertin: était-il archichapellain de Charles le Chauve?' in *LMA* 44, 1934, pp.241–51.

GRIERSON, P., 1940a: 'Abbot Fulco and the date of the *Gesta abbatum Fontanellensium*', in *EHR* 55, 1940, pp.275–84.

GRIERSON, P., 1940b: 'Grimbald of St. Bertin's', in *EHR* 55, 1940, pp. 529–61.

HALPHEN, L., 1947: *Charlemagne et l'Empire Carolingien*, Paris 1947.

HARRISON, K., 1976: *The Framework of Anglo-Saxon History*, Cambridge 1976.

HIGOUNET, C., 1949: 'Les Aznar', in *AM* 61, 1949, pp.5–14.

HODGKIN, R. H., 1924: 'The Beginning of the Year in the English Chronicle', in *EHR* 39, 1924, pp.497–510.

HOFFMANN, H., 1958: *Untersuchungen zur karolingischen Annalistik*, Bonn 1958.

JOHN, E., 1966. *Orbis Britanniae*, Leicester 1966.

KURZE, F., 1895: Introduction to *Annales Regni Francorum, SS rer Germ*, Hannover 1895.

LEVILLAIN, L., 1927: Introduction to *Loup de Ferrières, Correspondance*, Paris 1927.

LEVILLAIN, L., 1964. Introduction to *Annales de Saint-Bertin*, edd. F. Grat *et al.*, Paris 1964.

LEVISON, W., see Wattenbach, W.

LÖWE, H., 1957: see Wattenbach, W.

LÖWE, H., 1967: 'Geschichtsschreibung der ausgehenden Karolingerzeit', in *DA* 23, 1967, pp.1—30.

LÖWE, H., 1972: 'Hinkmar von Reims und der Apokrisiar', in *Festschrift für H. Heimpel* (3 vols.) Göttingen 1972, vol. 3, pp.197–225.

MALBOS, L., 1966: 'L'annaliste royal sous Louis le Pieux', *LMA* 72, 1966, pp.225–33.

McKEON, P. R., 1974: 'The Carolingian Councils of Savonnières (859) and Tusey (860) and their Background', in *RB* 84, 1974, pp.75–110.

McKEON, P. R., 1978: *Hincmar of Laon and Carolingian Politics*, Urbana-Chicago-London, 1978.

McKITTERICK, R., 1980: 'Charles the Bald (823–877) and his library: the patronage of learning', in *EHR* 95, 1980, pp.28–47.

NELSON, J. L., 1967: 'The Problem of King Alfred's Royal Anointing', in *Journal of Ecclesiastical History* 18, 1967, pp.145–63 ; see below, chapter 13, pp. 309-27.

OEXLE, O. G., 1967: 'Die Karolinger und die Stadt des heiligen Arnulf', in *FMS* 1, 1967, pp.250–364.

OEXLE, O. G., 1969: 'Bischof Ebroin von Poitiers und seine Verwandten', in *FMS* 3, 1969, pp.138–210.

PARKES, M., 1976: 'The paleography of the Parker manuscript of the *Chronicle*, laws and Sedulius, and historiography at Winchester in the late ninth and tenth centuries', in *Anglo-Saxon England* 5, 1976, pp.149–171.

SCHRÖRS, H., 1884: *Hinkmar, Erzbischof von Reims*, Freiburg i.B., 1884.

SISAM, K., 1953: *Studies in the History of Old English Literature*, Oxford 1953.

ULLMANN, W., 1972: *A Short History of the Papacy*, London 1972.

VIELHABER, K., 1956: *Gottschalk der Sachse*, Bonn 1956.

WALLACE-HADRILL, 1950: 'The Franks and the English in the Ninth Century: Some Common Historical Interests', in *History* 35, 1950, pp.202–18, repr. in *Early Medieval History*, Oxford 1975.

WALLACE-HADRILL, 1953: 'Archbishop Hincmar and the authorship of Lex Salica', in *Tijdschrift voor Rechtsgeschiednis* 21, 1953, pp.1–29, repr. in *The Long-haired Kings*, London 1962.

WALLACE-HADRILL, 1960: *The Fourth Book of the Chronicle of Fredegar*. Oxford 1960.

WATTENBACH W., and LEVISON, W., 1953, 1957: *Deutschlands Geschichtsquellen im Mittelalter*, revised ed. by H. Löwe, Heft 2, Heft 3, Weimar 1953, 1957.

WEINZIERL, K., 1949. 'Erzbischof Hincmar von Reims als Verfechter des geltenden Rechts', in *Episcopus. Studien über das Bischofsamt . . . Kardinal von Faulhaber . . . dargebracht*, Regensburg 1949, pp.136–63.

WERNER, K. F., 1959a: 'Untersuchungen zur Frühzeit des französischen Fürstentums (9.-10.Jht.); IV', in *Die Welt als Geschichte* 19, 1959, pp.146–93.

WERNER, K. F., 1959b: 'Zur Arbeitsweise des Regino von Prüm', in *Die Welt als Geschichte* 19, 1959, pp.96–116.

WERNER, K. F., 1967: 'Die Nachkommen Karls des Grossen bis um das Jahr 1000 (1.-8. Generation)', in W. Braunfels ed., *Karl der Grosse, Lebenswerk und Nachleben*, vol. 4: Das Nachleben, Düsseldorf 1967, pp.403–79.

WHITELOCK, D., 1977: *The Importance of the Battle of Edington*, Westbury 1977.

WORMALD, C. P., 1977: 'The Uses of Literacy in Anglo-Saxon England and its Neighbours', in *Transactions of the Royal Historical Society* 27, 1977, pp.95–114.

9

PUBLIC *HISTORIES* AND PRIVATE HISTORY IN THE WORK OF NITHARD

There is no historians' consensus about the ninth century. Opinions have been both highly judgmental and bewilderingly disparate. The most common diagnosis has been of disintegration and decline: the terminal illness of the Carolingian state. But some more sanguine observers have claimed to find here transformation and a political creativity decisive for the future of western Europe. On any reckoning, the ninth century was an important period. Yet it remains as true as when Walter Schlesinger made the observation twenty years ago that a history of the ninth century in and for itself has still to be written.[1] When it is, an interpretation of the events between 840 and 843 will surely be given a central place. For it was during those years that Carolingian Europe underwent most obviously those changes which historians have held characteristic and seminal in the century as a whole. At the beginning of 840 the Carolingian Empire persisted as a political entity; in 843 it no longer did so. The quest for an understanding of what happened during these critical years must start from a thorough reexamination of the relevant sources, and a number of recent studies show that this task is already well under way.[2] But one text, though not wholly neglected by modern scholarship, still stands in need of closer attention and reappraisal: the *Histories* of Nithard.[3]

My thanks are due to Stuart Airlie, Paul Fouracre, David Ganz, Rosamond McKitterick, Thomas Noble, and Michael Wallace-Hadrill for invaluable criticisms and to my colleague John Gillingham and the members of the "Charles the Bald" Special Subject classes of 1977–84 in the University of London for many thought-provoking questions and comments on Nithard. This paper, originally read to the Cambridge Medieval Group, is dedicated to the memory of my teacher and friend Kathleen Hughes.

[1] Walter Schlesinger, "Die Auflösung des Karlsreiches," in *Karl der Grosse, Lebenswerk und Nachleben,* ed. Wolfgang Braunfels and Helmut Beumann, 5 vols. (Düsseldorf, 1965–68), 1:795, n. 6. Schlesinger gives some examples of historians' varied judgments on the ninth century. See also Bernd Schneidmüller, *Karolingische Tradition und frühes französisches Königtum* (Wiesbaden, 1979), pp. 5–13.

[2] Two outstanding examples are Peter Classen, "Die Verträge von Verdun und von Coulaines als politische Grundlage des westfränkischen Reiches," *Historische Zeitschrift* 196 (1963), 1–35, and Wolfgang Wehlen, *Geschichtsschreibung und Staatsauffassung im Zeitalter Ludwigs des Frommen* (Lübeck and Hamburg, 1970).

[3] Ed. with French translation as *Histoire des fils de Louis le Pieux* by Philippe Lauer (Paris, 1926).

The special value of Nithard's evidence has long been recognized. He was not only a strictly contemporary witness of the events he described but closely involved in them, and for the years 840–42 in particular no other informant offers anything approaching the scope or detail of Nithard's work. Thus Ferdinand Lot and Louis Halphen, for instance, in the first part of their study of the early years of Charles the Bald's reign relied on Nithard more than on any other source and lamented his death as "an irreparable loss to History."[4] Historians have of course been aware that such dependence on Nithard presents a problem insofar as this author was prejudiced in favor of the patron who commissioned his work, Charles the Bald. But the problem has generally been disposed of without difficulty. The nature of Nithard's bias has been thought obvious and straightforward: he presented a uniformly hostile picture of Charles's eldest brother, Lothar, his rival and chief enemy in 840–42, while Charles himself was allegedly the "hero" of Nithard's work. It has therefore seemed relatively easy to allow for Nithard's bias and to claim at the same time that this does not affect the basic reliability of his account of events.[5] This assessment has recently been restated with

---

All references below are to this edition. That of Ernst Müller, MGH SSrG (Hannover, 1907, repr. 1965) has been reproduced with German translation by Reinhold Rauer, *Quellen zur karolingischen Reichsgeschichte,* 1 (Darmstadt, 1955). The English translation by Bernard S. Scholz, *Carolingian Chronicles* (Ann Arbor, 1970), is marred by some serious errors (see below nn. 98, 102, 113). All translations from Nithard in this paper are my own. The sole early manuscript of the work, Paris B.N. lat. 9768, dates from the late tenth century (Lauer, p. xiv, "fin de IXe siècle," is evidently a misprint as the manuscript also contains the *Annales* of Flodoard up to the year 948, in the same hand as Nithard's *Histories*). In the manuscript the work is divided into four books, but its title and chapter divisions have been supplied by modern editors. The one detailed appreciation of Nithard's work remains Gerold Meyer von Knonau, *Ueber Nithards vier Bücher Geschichten: Der Bruderkrieg der Söhne Ludwigs des Frommen und sein Geschichtsschreiber* (Leipzig, 1866). More recent but briefer are the important studies of Wehlen, *Geschichtsschreibung,* pp. 57–105, and Hans Patze, "*Iustitia* bei Nithard," in *Festschrift für Hermann Heimpel zum 70. Geburtstag am 19. September 1971,* 3 vols. (Göttingen, 1972), 3:147–65, both mainly concerned with examining Nithard's political ideas through his vocabulary. The article of Klaus Sprigade, "Zur Beurteilung Nithards als Historiker," *Heidelberger Jahrbücher* 16 (1972), 94–105, has unfortunately been inaccessible. A useful short account of Nithard's work (in Flemish, with French summary) is François-Louis Ganshof, "Een historicus uit de IXe eeuw: Nithard," *Mededelingen van de Koninklijke Vlaamse Academie voor Wetenschappen, Letteren en Schone Kunsten van Belgie,* Klasse der Letteren, jaarg. 33, no. 3 (Brussels, 1971). For the extensive bibliography on Nithard's texts of the Strasbourg oaths (see below, pp. 210-11), see Heinz Löwe's revised edition of Wilhelm Wattenbach and Wilhelm Levison, *Deutschlands Geschichtsquellen im Mittelalter,* 3 (Weimar, 1957), pp. 353–57, esp. n. 204; and Roger Wright, *Late Latin and Early Romance in Spain and Carolingian France* (Liverpool, 1982), pp. 122–26.

[4] Ferdinand Lot and Louis Halphen, *Le règne de Charles le Chauve,* 1: (*840–851*) (Paris, 1909), p. 115, and pp. 13–61 passim. Nithard's work is also the basis of the narrative of Ernst Dümmler, *Geschichte des ostfränkischen Reiches,* 3 vols., 2nd ed. (Leipzig, 1888), 1:139–88.

[5] So, Meyer von Knonau, *Ueber Nithards vier Bücher,* pp. 81–82. See also Max Manitius, *Geschichte der lateinischen Literatur des Mittelalters,* 3 vols. (Munich, 1911–31), 1:658–59; Joseph Calmette, *L'effondrement d'un empire et la naissance d'une Europe* (Paris, 1941), p. 264; Löwe in *Deutschlands Geschichtsquellen,* 3:353–55.

admirable candor by Franz Brunhölzl: Nithard, he says, makes a refreshing change from the medievalist's usual fare of "learned monks and ingenuous armchair scholars" for Nithard was a man of action who wrote in a simple "unaffected" style.[6] The assumption, it seems, is that directness of style goes with uncomplicated content, and that Nithard, the bluff soldier, tells it straight.

That assumption, as military historians can assure us, is false.[7] I shall try to show that Nithard's work is more complicated than most previous commentators have acknowledged, that it is in fact a work of art shaped and composed to convey a series of interpretative judgments, and that Nithard for all that he was a man of action possessed a true historian's artifice in the selection and presentation of what he wanted to tell. I shall argue that Nithard's work encodes a private history and that the public *Histories* reassessed in its light may have more to say than has usually been realized about the complex realities of Carolingian politics and the often contradictory values motivating ninth-century participants.

Most historians who have stopped to consider the purpose of Nithard's work have been content to note that he wrote on Charles's orders and thus implicitly to assume that a bias in Charles's favor characterizes the whole of the work. The usual corollary has been a further assumption that Nithard would have gone on writing had not death cut him short: in other words, the work as we have it is incomplete.[8] Some commentators, however, have noticed a change of tone in the last part of the *Histories*. Thus its most recent editor, Philippe Lauer, observed that Nithard when he was writing this part, in the winter of 842–43, seemed to have been "envahi par la misanthropie."[9] But Lauer suggested no explanation of the reason or timing of Nithard's affliction, nor did he link it to the hypothesis that Nithard deliberately gave up writing his work at this point.[10] B. S. Scholz, on the other hand, having

[6] *Geschichte der lateinischen Literatur des Mittelalters* (Munich, 1975), 1:399–400. For a similar view see Ganshof, "Een historicus," pp. 18–20.

[7] See, for instance, the assessment of the memoirs of military men by Sir Basil S. Liddell Hart, *The Other Side of the Hill*, rev. ed. (London, 1951), p. 10: they are "usually more concerned with their own interests and the service of their own reputations than with the service of history. Nothing can be more misleading than the carefully-framed account of their own actions that statesmen and generals, of any country, provide when they compile their accounts in their own time and way. There is a better chance of reaching the truth by a searching process of questioning them. . . ." Interestingly, Ganshof, "Een historicus," p. 20, compares Nithard's soldierly virtues of soberness, clarity, and matter-of-factness with those of another soldier-historian, Ammianus Marcellinus. But Ronald Syme, *Ammianus and the Historia Augusta* (Oxford, 1968), pp. 94–95, 142–53, shows that though Ammianus's efforts to be truthful are on the whole successful, still "passion and prejudice claim their rights."

[8] See, in addition to the works cited in nn. 4 and 5 above, J. M. Wallace-Hadrill, "A Carolingian Renaissance Prince: The Emperor Charles the Bald," *Proceedings of the British Academy* 64 (1978), 155–84, at p. 159.

[9] Lauer, *Histoire*, p. xi. Compare Ganshof, "Een historicus," p. 17 ("vervuld van droefheid").

[10] That Nithard's work is complete as we have it was argued by Müller, *Nithardi historiarum libri IV*, p. vi.

noticed the gloomy tone of the last part of the *Histories,* explained this in terms of Nithard's understandable response to a worsening political situation — to the "rising anarchy" he saw about him in the winter of 842–43.[11] Hans Patze has distinguished carefully between the first part of Nithard's work, which was royally commissioned, and the latter part, which was not; but he has argued at the same time that the search for *iustitia* remained Nithard's theme and "the service of Truth" his aim throughout the *Histories,* which he completed in the spring of 843.[12]

What has been noticed, then, are changes of tone and of addressee in the course of Nithard's work. But the implications of these changes have not been thoroughly explored, nor has an adequate explanation been given for them. Were political conditions in late 842 or early 843 really much worse than in 840 or 841? Had public morals really declined? And was anarchy really "rising"? In terms of any objective assessment and indeed of the hopes Nithard himself expressed, the situation in the winter of 842–43 was surely better than it had been at any time since he began writing. Charles, allegedly the hero of Nithard's work, was strengthening his position in West Francia and in Aquitaine; now Lothar was at last negotiating in earnest for a settlement with his younger brothers; and most important of all, the leading members of the Frankish aristocracy themselves were eager for peace.[13] Again, if Nithard wrote the first part of his work for a king (and royal readership was a common enough inspiration for medieval authors), why did he continue writing not only without any royal instruction but clearly, in the end, without any intention of pleasing a royal reader? (Even modern authors seldom write solely for "the service of Truth"!) And why, finally, did Nithard end his work as and when he did? If he did not simply abandon it, in what sense could he have considered it complete?

It is worth tracing in some detail the ways in which Nithard's work changed over the period of twenty months or so during which he wrote, before we attempt any explanation in terms of altered motives. A useful

[11] Scholz, *Carolingian Chronicles,* p. 30. Ganshof, "Een historicus," p. 17, suggested that Nithard felt "revulsion" at prevailing conditions in the *regnum Francorum.*

[12] Patze, "*Iustitia,*" pp. 161, 163.

[13] Nithard, *Histoire* 4.6, p. 140. Hincmar, writing more than thirty years later, saw both aristocracy and kings impelled to make peace because of the sufferings caused by war: PL 125:986. Nithard, *Histoire* 4.4, p. 132, shows Charles's improved position in Aquitaine. Compare the *Annales Bertiniani* (hereafter AB), ed. Félix Grat, Jeanne Vielliard, and Suzanne Clémencet (Paris, 1964), s.a. 842, 843, pp. 42, 44 — brief and neutral mentions of Charles's moves through Aquitaine but implying his freedom of maneuver. See also below, n. 115. Support for Charles in the Spanish March may be indicated by two grants to faithful men in that region: *Recueil des actes de Charles II le Chauve,* ed. Georges Tessier, 3 vols. (Paris, 1943–55), 1, nos. 15 (dated 24 December 842) and 17 (23 January 843). Charles spent Christmas 842 at the major palace of Quierzy where his marriage was celebrated: AB, p. 43. For the subsequent role of Quierzy in Charles's itinerary throughout his reign, see Carlrichard Brühl, *Fodrum, Gistum, Servitium Regis* (Cologne, 1968), pp. 40–41.

approach is to look in turn at the four books of which the *Histories* is composed and especially at the preface to each of them. The first is addressed explicitly to Charles the Bald, Nithard's lord (*dominus*):

> You ordered me, before we entered the city of Châlons, to commit to memory by the office of my pen the deeds done in your time.[14]

Thus Nithard clearly dates the conception of his work to May 841 when Charles, evidently with Nithard in his following, entered Châlons-sur-Marne only a month or so before the battle of Fontenoy. The preface continues with a request to Charles to pardon the work's shortcomings and an explanation of the need to cover in book 1 the deeds of "your pious father" in order to expose the truth about the events of 840–41. The preface to the second book follows as part of a narrative planned to the end of book 2 with its description of Fontenoy:

> Having explained as well as I could . . . the origins of your dissensions, so that any reader wanting to know why, after your father's death, Lothar decided to persecute you and your brother can make out . . . whether or not he acted justly, now I shall show with what forcefulness and effort Lothar set about pursuing his ends.[15]

Again Charles is requested to forgive the work's omissions and to make allowances for the difficult conditions under which it was written. At the end of book 2 Nithard says that he was "writing these things," that is, his account of Fontenoy, on Tuesday 18 October when there was a solar eclipse.[16] Nithard, then, wrote books 1 and 2 as parts of a whole: together they constituted a fulfillment of Charles's request at Châlons and presented events in the perspective of Charles's God-given victory at Fontenoy. Yet that victory had been no foregone conclusion at the time when the work was commissioned. Though a military confrontation with Lothar then seemed inescapable, Charles's conduct was plainly going to require a good deal of justification. If he won, he would have defeated his eldest brother, who was also his godfather, and would therefore have flouted religious obligations as well as the norm of fraternal concord that was so insistently preached in Frankish aristocratic society.[17] If he lost, it might be all the more necessary that an

[14] Nithard, *Histoire,* preface to book 1, p. 2.

[15] Ibid., preface to book 2, p. 36. The references to Lothar's "forcefulness and effort" (*virtus, industria*) are surely ironic. That books 1 and 2 were planned as a whole has rightly been stressed by Patze, "*Iustitia,*" p. 158.

[16] Nithard, *Histoire* 2.10, p. 76.

[17] Ibid. 2.1, 2, pp. 38, 40, for Lothar's godparentship of Charles. See also Astronomer, *Vita Hludovici Pii* 60, ed. Georg Pertz, MGH SS 2:644. Nithard, *Histoire* 2.4, p. 48, records an appeal to Lothar for fraternal behavior. For this theme in the Strasbourg oaths, see below, p. 210. For fraternal love invoked in Carolingian agreements, see Reinhard Schneider, *Brüdergemeine und Schwurfreundschaft: Der Auflösungsprozess des Karlingerreiches im Spiegel der Caritas-Terminologie in den Verträgen der karlingischen Teilkönige des 9. Jahrhunderts* (Lübeck and Hamburg, 1964). The

apologia for his cause should already have been committed to parchment, and any defense of Charles's actions in terms of principle could also cover the actions of his supporters — including Nithard.

Now it is certainly possible to argue that Nithard, and his patron, never conceived of any audience but posterity for such an apologia. Nithard himself, after all, writes of contemporary Frankish nobles who preferred even death to "leaving an unworthy memory to their descendants."[18] Yet in the prefaces to books 1 and 2 Nithard does not claim to be addressing posterity but writes directly to Charles. Further, in the second preface he seems to envisage a wider audience than the king alone: he writes for "anyone" trying to judge Lothar's motives and assess his conduct against standards of justice which, whatever Augustinian accretions they had acquired, were firmly rooted in Frankish political practice.[19] It would be unrealistic to suggest that Charles ever intended Nithard's work to be widely "published" or circulated: Charles lacked resources and time for any such project; but above all he had no need of it. The contemporary audience he wanted to reach, I think, was small and localized: it consisted of the leading men in his own camp, together with their vassal followings and perhaps contingents of free men.[20] These *primores,* who before Fontenoy may have numbered no more than a dozen or so, and those they led were typical actors in Carolingian politics.[21] They formed Charles's

---

noblewoman Dhuoda in her handbook of moral instruction for her elder son William, *Manuel pour mon fils,* ed. Pierre Riché (Paris, 1975), 1.7, p. 116, and 10.4, p. 352, reminds the youth of his obligations towards his little brother. This work has been perceptively discussed by Jürgen Hannig, *Consensus fidelium* (Stuttgart, 1982), pp. 201–5, and by Peter Dronke, *Women Writers of the Middle Ages* (Cambridge, Eng., 1984), pp. 36–54.

[18] Nithard, *Histoire* 2.10, p. 70.

[19] Patze, "*Iustitia,*" pp. 151–54. For the broader context of Frankish royal succession and inheritance practice, see Peter Classen, "Karl der Grosse und die Thronfolge im Frankenreich," *Festschrift für Hermann Heimpel,* 3:109–34. Classen's argument that on the fundamental issue of the nondivision of Francia the project of 806 was the forerunner of 817 does not seem to have been overturned by Dieter Hägermann, "Reichseinheit und Reichsteilung," *Historisches Jahrbuch* 95 (1975), 278–307. Classen's concluding remarks, pp. 132–34, suggest the toughness of the tradition of dividing the realm. The preface to the so-called *Ordinatio* of 817, MGH Capit 1, no. 136, pp. 270–71, with its mention of deliberations "according to the custom of our ancestors," shows the traditional role of the aristocracy in the making of such divisions. Contemporary notions about eligibility for royal succession are discussed by Silvia Konecny, *Die Frauen des karolingischen Königshauses* (Vienna, 1976), pp. 33–44.

[20] On the composition of ninth-century armies, see my comments in "The Church's Military Service in the Ninth Century: A Contemporary Comparative View?" *Studies in Church History* 20 (1983), 15–30 ; see above, chapter 6, pp. 117–32.

[21] See Karl Ferdinand Werner, "Untersuchungen zur Frühzeit des französischen Fürstentums (9.–10. Jht.)," 1–3, *Die Welt als Geschichte* 18 (1958), 256–89, and 4, ibid., 19 (1959), 146–93; idem, "Bedeutende Adelsfamilien im Reich Karls des Grossen," *Karl der Grosse,* ed. Braunfels and Beumann, 1:83–142, English translation in *The Medieval Nobility,* ed. Timothy Reuter (Amsterdam, 1979); and Karl Brunner, *Oppositionelle Gruppen im Karolingerreich,* Veröffentlichungen des Instituts für Österreichische Geschichtsforschung, 25 (Vienna, 1979). Nithard implies that Charles's faithful men in 840–41 were a relatively small group. For its

"constituency," his "public," without whose military and political support his cause whatever its justice in theory would have been lost in practice. Before Fontenoy the most conspicuous member of this group was probably Adalard.[22] In the autumn of 841 Charles's uncle Hugh of St. Quentin was a notable adherent.[23]

Why should Charles have believed such men to be susceptible to an apologia written in Latin, to *Histories* in the classical style?[24] He might have relied (like Henry V before Agincourt) on chats beside the campfires to maintain his men's morale. But Charles knew that his followers had been subjected like himself, if perhaps less intensively, to the teaching program of the Carolingian Renaissance.[25] Some, at least, of the laymen among them probably knew enough Latin to be able to follow a straightforward narrative. We know of several of their aristocratic contemporaries who were certainly capable of doing so.[26] They could also have had access through Latin, as

---

composition see below, Appendix 1, pp. 234-5. For the size of Charles's entourage later in the reign, see Nelson, "Legislation and Consensus in the Reign of Charles the Bald," in *Ideal and Reality in Frankish and Anglo-Saxon Society,* ed. Patrick Wormald (Oxford, 1983), pp. 202–27 at 211–12 ; see above, chapter 5, pp. 100-1.

[22] As implied by Charles's marriage to a woman identified both by Nithard and by Prudentius in the AB, p. 43, as "Adalard's niece." For Adalard's career, see Ferdinand Lot, "Note sur le sénéchal Alard," *Le moyen âge* 21 (1908), 185–201, reprinted in *Recueil des travaux historiques de Ferdinand Lot,* 3 vols. (Geneva, 1968–73), 2:591–607; and, for some revisions, Werner, "Untersuchungen," 2, pp. 274–76, and 4, pp. 155–56. The careers of Adalard and his brother Gerard diverged in the autumn of 840 when Gerard "defected" to Lothar: Nithard, *Histoire* 2.3, p. 44. René Louis, *Girart, comte de Vienne,* 3 vols. (Auxerre, 1945), 1:44 and n. 2, suggested that the two brothers looked after each other's interests after 843 in the kingdoms of Charles and Lothar respectively. This is plausible, but in 840–42, and specifically at the battle of Fontenoy, the hedging of bets had surely given place to real fraternal conflict.

[23] Hugh was a son of Charlemagne by his concubine Regina: Karl Ferdinand Werner, "Die Nachkommen Karls des Grossen bis um das Jahr 1000," in *Karl der Grosse,* ed. Braunfels and Beumann, 4:403–79 at 445. See also Philip Grierson, "Hugues de Saint-Bertin: Etait-il archichapellain de Charles le Chauve?" *Le moyen âge* 44 (1934), 241–51; and Löwe in *Deutschlands Geschichtsquellen,* 5:545.

[24] Manitius, *Geschichte,* p. 659, lists the classical authors Nithard seems to have read, but claims that, apart from reminiscences, these had no effect on Nithard's style. Lauer, *Histoire,* p. xiii, also takes this view. But David Ganz kindly points out to me that the influence of Sallust, and perhaps Vergil, was probably greater than Manitius allowed. The question is important, but cannot be pursued here.

[25] For Charles's own education and its background, see Rosamond McKitterick, "Charles the Bald (823–877) and His Library: The Patronage of Learning," *English Historical Review* 95 (1980), 28–47, especially 29–31; and, in addition to the works there cited, Reto Radwolf Bezzola, *Les origines et la formation de la littérature courtoise en occident,* 2 vols. (Paris, 1958–60), 1:195–213.

[26] Lay book-ownership is suggestive: see Pierre Riché, "Les bibliothèques de trois aristocrates laïques," *Le moyen âge* 69 (1963), 87–104, and Rosamond McKitterick, "Some Carolingian Law-Books and Their Function," in *Studies on Medieval Law and Government Presented to Walter Ullmann on His Seventieth Birthday,* ed. Brian Tierney and Peter Linehan (London and New York, 1980), pp. 13–28. For aristocratic recipients of works of moral instruction, see Hans

Charles himself did, to some knowledge of Roman and Jewish history and of the history of their own Frankish people.[27] Nithard, as we know from his work, had a well-developed idea of the state and of "public utility."[28] There is no reason (making due allowance for the scarcity of our source material) to suppose that Nithard, layman as he was, was unique in this respect. Nor should we confine ourselves to literary tradition transmitted through classical texts in seeking sources for such ideas. Would not an important part have been played, too, by political experience? I have in mind the habit of participating in collective discussion and decision making at assemblies, notably those general *placita* summoned each year by Charlemagne and Louis the Pious.[29] The capitularies that are residues of assembly proceedings have survived in ecclesiastical archives, but they reveal, surely, patterns of thought and practice that were not only clerical. The laymen in Charles's following in 840–41 would have attended assemblies in previous years, and therefore for them the language of public utility, the common interest, and so forth, current in capitularies long before Nithard used it, expressed not only an ideal but the reality of political effort in which they had been personally

---

Hubert Anton, *Fürstenspiegel und Herrscherethos in der Karolingerzeit* (Bonn, 1968), pp. 83–86, and Pierre Toubert, "La théorie du mariage chez les moralistes carolingiens," in *Il matrimonio nella società altomedievale,* Settimane di Studio del Centro Italiano di Studi sull'Alto Medioevo, 24 (Spoleto, 1977), 1:233–85. Lay aristocrats who received correspondence in Latin may have had it translated by clerics in their households but, equally, may have understood *spoken* Latin. Hincmar of Rheims addressed letters to thirteen laymen (excluding kings), most of them counts and in the West Frankish kingdom: MGH Epp 8, ed. Ernst Perels, nos. 49, 68, 70, 103 (and 142), 105 (and 173), 136, 155, 174, 175, and Flodoard, *Historia Remensis ecclesiae* 3.23, 26, ed. Johann Heller and Georg Waitz, MGH SS 13:530, 543–44. The ability to understand spoken Latin was general among free men in the Rheims area in the 850s: Jean Devisse, *Hincmar, archevêque de Reims,* 3 vols. (Geneva, 1975–76), 1:335. This situation is likely to have characterized the West Frankish as distinct from the Middle or East Frankish kingdom: see Michael Richter, "Die Sprachenpolitik Karls des Grossen," in *Sprachwissenschaft* 7 (1982), 412–37. Wright, *Late Latin,* chap. 3, presents an interesting argument for the identity of late Latin and Romance as languages, but with different pronunciations, without however considering the implications for aristocratic lay literacy (e.g., p. 117: "Nithard . . . was exceptional").

[27] The world chronicle of Freculf of Lisieux, PL 106:919–1258, begins with the Creation and ends with the death of Gregory the Great, the time when "Roman governors were expelled from Italy and Gaul and the Franks and the Lombards succeeded to those realms" (col. 1258). Writing in the 820s, Freculf dedicated the second of the work's two books to the empress Judith to help in educating Charles the Bald. The work and its readership deserve further study. For lay aristocrats' history books, including the *Histories* of Gregory of Tours, see Riché, "Les bibliothèques," pp. 99, 103; and for Dhuoda's reading of Old Testament history, see Hannig, *Consensus fidelium,* pp. 203–4.

[28] Wehlen, *Geschichtsschreibung,* pp. 33–56, 61–66, 96–105. Despite the thought-provoking comments of Johannes Fried, "Der karolingische Herrschaftsverband im 9. Jh.," *Historische Zeitschrift* 235 (1982), 1–43, especially 11–14, and his justified insistence on the personal character of Carolingian political obligation, ideas of public authority, the state, and office did exist in the ninth century: see my contribution to *The Cambridge History of Medieval Political Thought* (forthcoming).

[29] See above, chapter 5, pp. 91-116.

involved. It is no coincidence that when, a generation after Nithard, Hincmar of Rheims offered the West Frankish magnates, as well as the king and the bishops, a blueprint for reform, he focused on assemblies along with the running of the king's household as the key to preserving the "well-being of the realm." Hincmar stressed that the "wise men" on whose counsels that well-being depended were drawn from the laity as well as the clergy.[30] Of course the two groups had interests that were in some ways distinct, as when, for instance, count opposed bishop in a particular locality. But I think it is misleading to suggest that they had radically divergent, still less incompatible, sets of political ideas when they were united in so much political practice.[31] A Frankish noble sent as a youth to the king's court where spiritual and secular "militias" rubbed shoulders, with a Latin education that had familiarized him with moral standards of behavior in public office (via Isidore and Alcuin) and with a profoundly Christian view of history (via the Bible, Gregory of Tours, or Freculf of Lisieux), and after years of attending assemblies where he heard, and later read, decisions on public business formulated in legislation (via capitularies): such a man had learned to be responsive to other messages than the "most ancient songs" alone.[32] At such a man Alcuin and Jonas of Orléans directed works of moral guidance and collections of private prayers. Such a man, so Hincmar believed, could be appealed to through the *De ordine palatii* — which is not to say that he could not also have enjoyed the heroic verse of the *Ludwigslied.*[33] If William, son of

[30] *De ordine palatii,* ed. Thomas Gross and Rudolf Schieffer, MGH Fontes Iuris Germanici Antiqui (Hannover, 1980), pp. 84–88. See also Heinz Löwe, "Hinkmar von Reims und der Apocrisiar," in *Festschrift für Hermann Heimpel,* 3:197–225 at 200, 221–25.

[31] Dhuoda, *Manuel* 3.8, 10, 11, pp. 166, 174, 192–96, urges her son among the *commilitones* in the "royal and imperial hall" to imitate the "great ones" there and to attach himself to worthy priests, to eat meals with them as often as possible and seek their intercession, and not to criticize "as many do" clergy who though great *in saeculo* fail to live up to their office. Towards the end of Charles's reign Heiric of Auxerre described the palace as a *schola* where scholarly no less than military disciplines were practiced daily: MGH Poet 3:429. See also Pierre Riché, "Charles le Chauve et la culture de son temps," in *Jean Scot Erigène et l'histoire de la philosophie,* Colloques internationaux du CNRS, 561 (Paris, 1977), pp. 37–46, reprinted in Riché, *Instruction et vie religieuse dans le haut moyen âge* (London, 1981), and Rosamond McKitterick, "The Palace School of Charles the Bald," in *Charles the Bald: Court and Kingdom,* ed. Margaret Gibson and Janet L. Nelson, BAR International Series, 101 (Oxford, 1981), pp. 385–400.

[32] Charlemagne's catholic tastes are well known: Einhard, *Vita Karoli* 29, ed. Oswald Holder-Egger, MGH SSrG (Hannover, 1911), p. 33. Thegan, *Vita Hludovici Imperatoris* 19, ed. Georg Pertz, MGH SS 2:594, says that Louis the Pious "despised the pagan songs he had learned in his youth." Given the date and polemic nature of Thegan's work, too much should not be made of this apparent contrast between Louis's court and his father's. Charles the Bald may have shared his grandfather's tastes: the anonymous poet of the *Carmen de exordio gentis Francorum,* MGH Poet 2:141–45, offered Charles the models of his ancestor St. Arnulf of Metz and Charlemagne as well as Louis the Pious, hence perhaps a latinized and Christianized version of the theme of the "ancient songs."

[33] The *Ludwigslied* was written by a monk or cleric and preserved in a monastic library, yet its author thought the vernacular appropriate to celebrate the victory of a Frankish king in 881.

Bernard of Septimania, could use the *Manual* of social and spiritual instruction his mother, Dhuoda, wrote for him when he joined Charles's following in 841, could he not also "use" some political advice? Nithard's *Histories,* I suggest, was aimed at William and his like, as well as at the king himself.

If Charles's followers did indeed constitute Nithard's "public," then certain features of his work can be seen to have had a specific rationale. His "uncluttered" style would pose few problems for anyone who had wrestled with Gregory of Tours's Latin (or for that matter with Dhuoda's); it may even have been designed for oral delivery. Nithard's neglect of biographical details for important actors in his story has left puzzles for "posterity" (in the shape of modern historians) but makes good enough sense if he was writing for contemporaries who knew those actors well.[34] Again, some of Nithard's omissions become understandable if we picture him writing book 2 in the weeks following Fontenoy for an audience consisting in part of men recently recruited into Charles's camp as a result of that battle. For instance, Nithard does not mention the important fact that late in 840 Pippin II of Aquitaine managed to install his candidate Rodulf as archbishop of Bourges.[35] But in the post-Fontenoy situation, when Charles was strengthening his hand in Aquitaine and perhaps already bidding for Rodulf's support, Nithard might have thought it wiser to keep silent on Pippin's earlier success.[36] He is similarly silent on Pippin's role at Fontenoy and indeed neglects the Aquitanian dimension of a battle which in fact settled the long-term future of Aquitaine.[37] Another of Nithard's silences may be explicable in the context

---

See J. M. Wallace-Hadrill, *The Frankish Church* (Oxford, 1983), pp. 387–88: "It is possible that the poem was recited at court." Compare the brilliant evocation of a single barbarian, Christian culture among the Anglo-Saxon aristocracy by Patrick Wormald, "Bede, *Beowulf* and the Conversion of the Anglo-Saxon Aristocracy," in *Bede and Anglo-Saxon England,* ed. Robert T. Farrell, BAR, British Series, 46 (Oxford, 1978), pp. 32–95 especially 49–58.

[34] See Appendix 1, below, pp. 234-5, for suggested identifications of Hugh, Gerard, and Theutbald. I would further identify Guntbold (*Histoire* 2.6, p. 54, and 3.2, p. 86) as archbishop of Rouen and Joseph (ibid. 1.7, p. 30, and 4.3, p. 124) as bishop of Ivrea.

[35] See Léon Levillain, *Recueil des actes de Pépin I et Pépin II, rois d'Aquitaine (814–848)* (Paris, 1926), p. clxxvii and n. 6.

[36] Levillain's statement, ibid., that Rodulf stayed loyal to Pippin II "until 848 at least" needs qualifying if Tessier, *Recueil,* no. 42 is accepted as genuine: see Tessier's comments at p. 116. It seems likely that Charles would have already been trying to win over Rodulf's support during the negotiations leading up to the Treaty of Verdun in 843, when Charles was successful in having Pippin II excluded from a share in the Carolingian *regnum.*

[37] Nithard, *Histoire* 2.10, pp. 68, 74, says that Lothar tried successfully to defer the coming battle until Pippin should have arrived. See also AB, p. 38. The importance of Pippin's role during the battle is stated by Agnellus, *Liber pontificalis ecclesiae Ravennatis,* ed. Oswald Holder-Egger, MGH SSrerLangob 174, p. 390, an account which seems to rest on an eyewitness report either from Archbishop George of Ravenna himself (compare AB, p. 38) or from a member of his household. That Aquitanian contingents fought especially fiercely on both sides is implied by Andreas of Bergamo, *Historia,* ed. Georg Waitz, MGH SSrerLangob 7, p. 226, again apparently well informed (unusually for him) about affairs north of the Alps and perhaps dependent on a Ravenna source. See also the *Miracula Sancti Genulfi,* ed. Oswald Holder-Egger, MGH SS

of the situation after Fontenoy: his omission of what was probably an immediate consequence of the battle's outcome — the flight of Lothar's supporter Archbishop Ebbo of Rheims "fearing the rule, and the wrath, of Charles."[38] This was a major success for Charles since Ebbo had also carried his suffragans and provincial clergy with him (however unwillingly) in supporting Lothar in 840.[39] By the autumn of 841 two such men (and there may well have been others) were in Charles's camp, both of them influential adherents to Charles's cause: Bishop Immo of Noyon and Abbot Hugh of St. Quentin, Charles's uncle.[40] With such men in his potential audience, Nithard could well have chosen to draw a veil over Ebbo's departure.

Similar considerations could apply to the positive aspects of book 2, that is, to events Nithard chose to deal with at particular length. Two instances are worth looking at. The first is the story of the arrival of envoys from Aquitaine at Charles's camp at Troyes in April 841. Its context in Nithard's narrative is important: shortly before this passage he has presented Charles's position as desperate and then, after noting the beginnings of an upturn in his fortunes, Nithard stresses Charles's isolation and the energy of Lothar's countermoves. He goes on:

> A truly wonderful and most notable thing happened to Charles that Easter Saturday. For neither he nor anyone in his following had anything at all apart from the clothes they stood up in and their weapons and horses. Charles was just getting out of his bath and was about to put on again the same clothes he had taken off beforehand when suddenly, there at the door were envoys from Aquitaine carrying a crown and all his royal gear! Who can fail to be amazed that so few men, quite obscure men, too, were able to carry so many talents of gold and so huge a quantity of jewels over so great a distance without coming to any harm, while all kinds of violence were threatening on every side? Even more amazing is how they managed to arrive at just the right place and exactly the day and hour required, when not even Charles himself knew where he and his men would be. It seemed that this could only have happened by God's grace and with his approval. And through this [Charles] inspired wonder in all who fought along with him and encouraged them all to a confident hope that things would go well for them. And Charles and the whole cheerful band busied themselves with celebrating Easter.[41]

Now according to Nithard himself a few pages earlier, Charles had sent instructions from western Francia about two weeks before to the Aquitanians

---

15:1208: though this is a tenth-century work, its information on the ninth century was thought reliable by Léon Levillain, "Les Nibelungen historiques et leurs alliances de famille," *Annales du Midi* 49 (1937), 337–407 at 406. According to Nithard, *Histoire* 2.9, pp. 64–66, Charles himself was swayed by those who advised him to join up with his mother and "the Aquitanians" before advancing against Lothar, but Nithard gives the impression that he himself opposed this advice.

[38] Letter of the clergy of Rheims, ed. Albert Werminghoff, MGH Conc 2:812.

[39] Devisse, *Hincmar,* 1:86–87.

[40] Nithard, *Histoire* 3.3, pp. 90–92.

[41] Ibid. 2.8, pp. 60–62.

to meet him at Attigny and, given the geography involved, it was something less than miraculous that Aquitanian envoys should have met up with him at Troyes.[42] Nithard makes no comment on the efficiency of Charles's communications.[43] What he does say in the very next sentence is that envoys from Lothar now arrived at Troyes and were entertained at Charles's table. It was fortunate that Charles's baggage had arrived.

What was Nithard trying to convey to his audience in this story? He himself was one of the loyal band left with "nothing except the clothes they stood up in," yet filled with new hope by the Aquitanians' arrival. There is no reason to doubt Nithard's sincerity in presenting the event as, in effect, a miracle — the result of divine intervention. But Nithard's account does suggest that Charles exploited it (may even have stage-managed it) to boost his men's morale. This, Nithard says, was precisely its effect on Easter Saturday 841. And the dramatic little story was, I think, intended in its turn to have a similar effect on Nithard's audience in the autumn of that same year when, despite Fontenoy, Lothar continued to resist and Charles had to make further demands on his supporters' loyalty.

A second and parallel instance of Nithard's artifice is his account of Fontenoy. This, as Patze has rightly insisted, was the very heart of Nithard's apologia for Charles: the justice of his cause was manifest in this judgment of God.[44] Nithard, in fact, spends far longer on the preliminaries to the battle than on the battle itself. His intention is clearly to show that all the approved resources of negotiation, of diplomatic pressure, of ritualized maneuver had been exhausted, that Charles and his ally Louis the German had done all they could to resolve the dispute at a political level, and that it was Lothar himself who had forced a military solution upon them by rejecting every alternative. Patze has observed that the quest for justice is a leitmotiv in Nithard's very detailed narrative here. But a second theme, to my mind as significant, is the role of Charles's and Louis's followers during what is in effect (if in unusual circumstances) a prolonged assembly. The two kings are counseled and supported at every step by their men, and in what is

[42] Ibid. 2.6, p. 54.

[43] Nithard's story has been taken to show the difficulty of travel in the ninth century by Marc Bloch, *Feudal Society* (London, 1961), pp. 61–62, and by Pierre Riché, *La vie quotidienne dans l'empire carolingien* (Paris, 1973), p. 28.

[44] Patze, "*Iustitia*," pp. 156–59. Compare the view of Kurt Georg Cram, *Iudicium belli: Zum Rechtscharakter des Krieges im deutschen Mittelalter* (Münster and Cologne, 1955), pp. 20–47, that the battle of Fontenoy itself, and the events immediately preceding and following it, represented a customary legal procedure for ascertaining the judgment of God. Patze, p. 156, n. 13, rightly criticizes Cram for taking too little account of the specific historical context of Fontenoy. But Patze's own stress on the "programmatic" aspect of Charles's actions, that is, his presentation of himself as a seeker after "justice," is quite compatible with Cram's understanding of the preliminaries to the battle as procedural devices which were, all the same, very far from playacting. The efforts to avoid battle and the bloodiness of the conflict when it ensued were equally real.

almost their last attempt to come to terms with Lothar, they and their men decide "unanimously with common consent" to select from among their number "noble, wise, and well-intentioned men including some bishops and some laymen" to present their just cause.[45] Now it is possible that Nithard rehearsed all this for Charles's benefit. But did the king need quite such lengthy reassurances about a justice that coincided so neatly with his own interests? What is harder to believe is that Nithard went into these details with posterity in mind: to later generations would not the to-and-fro of envoys, the exchange of claim and counterclaim, seem tedious, even irrelevant, by comparison with the divinely awarded victory that in itself provided all the justification Charles needed? Again, it seems more likely that Nithard wrote book 2's final chapters for a contemporary audience: the men in Charles's camp in the autumn of 841.

But why did Charles's men still need so much reassurance after what should have been the decisive confirmation that they were both morally and politically on the right side? Frank Pietzcker has suggested a possible answer: Nithard had to gloss over an unpleasant truth, namely, that Fontenoy was not a battle fairly fought according to what the Franks accepted as the rules of war, but a treacherous surprise attack launched by Charles and Louis on Lothar's still-sleeping camp at dawn in flagrant violation of a truce arranged to last until 8 a.m.[46] Thus when Nithard said that Charles and Louis, having "struck camp" at dawn, waited until 8 a.m. to join battle "as their men had sworn they would," he was actually telling a downright lie.[47] Nithard's motive, according to Pietzcker, was to preserve the reputation of his hero, Charles. It might further be argued, pursuing Pietzcker's line of thought, that Nithard intended at the same time to conceal the guilt of all those concerned, that is, all of Charles's and Louis's followers, and that his work was offered to this audience as a salve to raw consciences. Such speculations would have some point if one of the sources favorable to Lothar laid a charge of treachery against Charles and Louis. But none seems to do so.[48] If Nithard's account not only of the battle but of the lengthy negotiations preceding it is an elaborate fiction, it is hard to place "in the literary-propagandistic arena,"[49] assuming an audience of Nithard's own contemporaries.

[45] Nithard, *Histoire* 2.9, p. 68.

[46] "Die Schlacht bei Fontenoy," *Zeitschrift der Savigny-Stiftung für Rechtsgeschichte,* Germanistische Abteilung 81 (1964), 318–42. The argument is based on an analysis of Nithard, *Histoire* 2.9–10.

[47] Nithard, *Histoire* 2.10, p. 76.

[48] Neither Agnellus nor Andreas implies it: see above, n. 37. Nor does the *Annals* of Xanten, ed. Bernhard von Simson, MGH SSrG (Hannover, 1909), p. 11. The *Versus de bella* (sic) *que fuit acta Fontaneto,* ed. Ernst Müller, MGH SSrG (Hannover, 1907), pp. 52–53, hints that some important person(s) on Lothar's side defected at the last minute to Charles and Louis. The poem's author, Angilbert, had fought on Lothar's side. If he was a layman, we have another example of a lay writer in the early 840s to set alongside Nithard and Dhuoda.

[49] So, Pietzcker, "Schlacht," p. 332.

Glossing over or distortion is not the same thing as lying outright. Propaganda in a situation that is still wide open can be effective only when it is credible.[50]

The needs of Nithard's audience were at once simpler and more complex than Pietzcker's hypothesis would imply. There was no question of any "cover-up." When all due allowance is made for the difficulty of distinguishing between factual reporting and propaganda, Nithard's record may be judged truthful. But for Charles's followers, including Nithard, the real problems arose from genuine conflicts of values: "justice," as so often, was equivocal. If a case in law and in Christian morality could be made for Charles, another equally substantial case could be made for Lothar. There were no absolutes governing the succession to the Frankish realm: here not even a judgment of God could be recognized as decisive, or even recognized at all.[51] Norms of fraternal solidarity existed, but it was sometimes justifiable to breach them. Among the Frankish aristocracy fidelity owed to a lord was a fundamental obligation, yet even this might have to compete with other claims which could override it in a particular case. So much would depend on circumstances. And for this reason, I suggest, the wealth of circumstantial detail in Nithard's first two books, especially in the last two chapters of book 2, makes sense as a justification — constructed with all the care and sympathy of an insider — of the precise series of choices made by the men who followed Charles. If I am right, then Nithard's work as originally conceived and executed up to the end of book 2 could legitimately be called "public *Histories*" in a triple sense: first, as dealing with public, political events; secondly, as intended not only to be read by posterity, but to be heard and read by a contemporary public, that is, by a section of society considered as consumers; thirdly, as directed at *the* public (of the West Frankish realm) in the specific sense used by some political scientists, that is, a clearly defined group of political actors operating in the given society as "a central agency for the regulation of public affairs."[52]

The argument that Nithard wrote for this contemporary audience may be strengthened if we go on to consider book 3. As Patze has pointed out, its

[50] Propaganda can of course take the form of outright lying in a closed situation, that is, when a regime is in firm enough control to blatantly misrepresent the immediate past: see Janet L. Nelson, "The Rites of the Conqueror," *Proceedings of the Battle Conference on Anglo-Norman Studies*, 4/1981 (Woodbridge, Eng., and Totowa, N.J., 1982), pp. 117–32 with notes 210–21 at pp. 218–19, below, pp. 397-8, n. 97, for two likely examples from later in the Middle Ages.

[51] Hrabanus Maurus, *Liber ad Otgarium* 15, PL 112:1411, condemned Charles's and Louis's depiction of Fontenoy as a judgment of God. Compare the situation in 833 when Lothar's supporters claimed the Field of Lies as a judgment of God, but Louis the Pious's supporters (including Hrabanus) thought otherwise.

[52] Michael G. Smith, *Corporations and Society* (Londón, 1974), pp. 82, 84–86, and especially 93–94 and 98. For some of the difficulties in defining "public" historiography in the ninth century, see above, chapter 8, pp. 191-2.

preface makes it clear that Nithard had originally planned to end his story with Fontenoy and that he went on writing only with some reluctance.[53] Perhaps it was Charles's pressure that made him continue, but Nithard does not state explicitly that this was so, nor does he address Charles directly in this third preface (in contrast to the previous two). Patze sidesteps the problem of motivation here: for him, since *iustitia,* Nithard's central theme, had been revealed at Fontenoy, the battle's aftermath is inevitably an anticlimax. Yet if Charles apparently no longer felt a pressing need for a continued apologia, then it is hard to see why Nithard should have thought his lord's conduct after Fontenoy needed further justification to posterity. According to Patze, Nithard's purpose in writing book 3 was "now only to serve the Truth in the usual way"(!).[54] But the continuity with book 2 is not complete. The third preface, unlike the first and second, offers no explicit condemnation of Lothar's conduct, and Nithard is in no hurry to criticize Lothar for failure to accept the "divine judgment" manifested at Fontenoy.[55] As in books 1 and 2, both Charles's leadership and the crucial role of his following emerge strongly. But there are new stresses, too, on reconciliation among the Franks, on the need for continuing devotion to "the public interest," on Charles's winning of new adherents after Fontenoy, and on the close entente between Charles and Louis the German and between their followers.[56] Again, precisely these emphases are intelligible in terms of an appeal to a contemporary audience. Nithard continued to address his fellow supporters of Charles, but his immediate concerns had shifted somewhat since Fontenoy. Now he needed to win support for a new effort at a negotiated settlement in which the claims of all three brothers, including Lothar, could be accommodated. This in Nithard's view required the maintenance of the close alliance between Charles and Louis, for it could only be as a result of their combined pressure that Lothar would be brought to terms.[57] Hence in book 3 Nithard presented Louis, and the alliance itself, in such a favorable light as to enlist the continued commitment of Charles's men. Given that the composition of his audience had altered to some extent, Nithard was careful to recognize the importance of those recently recruited to Charles's camp. Lothar's continued resistance was a problem to be faced together: the narrative of book 3 showed how the problem could be overcome by preserving a united front.

[53] Nithard, *Histoire,* preface to book 3, pp. 78–80; Patze, "*Iustitia,*" p. 158.

[54] "*Iustitia,*" p. 161.

[55] But Lothar's rejection by God is implicit in a "miraculous" rising in the waters of the Seine "under a clear sky," which prevented him from crossing the river: Nithard, *Histoire* 3.3, p. 94. Soon afterwards, Lothar's planned "deception" of his brothers was thwarted by Charles's firm adherence to his alliance with Louis, while Lothar's own ally, Pippin II, regretted his choice: ibid. 3.4, p. 100.

[56] Ibid. 3.1, pp. 80–82; 3.2, p. 84; 3.3, pp. 90–92, 94; 3.5, pp. 100–112.

[57] Ibid. 3.3, pp. 94–96; 3.5, pp. 102–8; 3.7, pp. 112–14.

This overriding concern helps to account for the attention (on any reckoning extraordinary) that Nithard pays to the Strasbourg oaths of February 842.[58] He first presents in Latin the declarations which he tells us Charles and Louis made, in the *lingua Teudisca* and the *lingua Romana* respectively, to each other's followers. That is, Charles addressed Louis's men in Frankish (or Old High German) and Louis addressed Charles's men in Romance (or French). Whether or not Nithard himself had a hand in drafting these texts,[59] his specification of the vernaculars emphasizes the importance of total intelligibility on this occasion, for the kings' audience consisted not just of magnates but of the whole *plebs,* that is, the lesser aristocracy as well. The kings asserted the traditional values of *fraternitas* and *Christianitas* and their objectives of *pax, iustitia,* and the welfare of the *populus Christianus.* Then (and Nithard has not weakened this theme by previous overuse) they recalled the "divine judgment" of Fontenoy and condemned Lothar for willfully ignoring it. Then each king absolved his own men from their obligations of loyalty to him should he renege on his commitment to his brother. These undertakings were summarized in short oaths whose texts Nithard gives in the vernaculars. First Louis in Romance, then Charles in German swore to help the other "as any man ought in right to preserve his brother, so long as he in turn does the same for me," and never to enter into separate negotiations with Lothar against the other brother's interests.[60] Then the *populus* of each king swore, each in its own language — and again Nithard gives vernacular texts — to give no aid to its royal lord should he attempt to act against his brother. Each man evidently swore the oath individually. But by the use of the collective noun *populus* Nithard highlights the collective nature of these commitments. It was the aristocracy who as a group underwrote the kings' agreement, and it was their power to withdraw their loyalty on which all relied as the sanction binding the kings to their oaths.[61] Nithard's pursuit of

[58] Ibid. 3.5, pp. 102–8.

[59] As suggested by Wright, *Late Latin,* p. 123.

[60] Louis's oath, in Romance, is given by Nithard, 3.5, p. 104, as follows: "Pro Deo amur et pro christian poblo et nostro commun salvament, d'ist di in avant, in quant Deus savir et podir me dunat, si salvarai eo cist meon fradre Karlo et in aiudha et in cadhuna cosa, si cum om per dreit son fradra salvar dift, in o quid il mi altresi fazet et ab Ludher nul plaid nunquam prindrai, qui, meon vol, cist meon fradre Karle in damno sit." Ruth Schmidt-Wiegand, "Eid und Gelöbnis im mittelalterlichen Recht," in *Recht und Schrift im Mittelalter,* ed. Peter Classen (Sigmaringen, 1977), pp. 55–90 at 62–68, observes that written, Latin models lay behind some of the phraseology of the kings' oaths, but that their being spoken was what made them legally binding.

[61] The oath of Charles's *populus* (termed *fideles* in AB, p. 40) is given by Nithard, *Histoire* 3.5, pp. 106–8: "Si Lodhuuigs sagrament que son fradre Karlo jurat conser at et Karlus, meos sendra, de suo part non l'ostanit, si io returnar non l'int pois, ne io ne neuls cui eo returnar int pois, in nulla aiudha contra Lodhuuig nun li iu er." Schmidt-Wiegand, "Eid und Gelöbnis," p. 68, finds the oaths of the faithful men more influenced than the kings' by spoken language. Wright, *Late Latin,* p. 125, finds some difficulty in accounting for the production of a vernacular text for the West Frankish *populus* "not many [of whom] could have been likely to be able to read at all, let alone from a baffling orthography. . . ." I am not sure that assuming rather more

peace and the common good was based on a thoroughly realistic grasp of the means to the end. His treatment of the Strasbourg oaths ensured that no reader or hearer of book 3 would miss his message.

The third preface offers one further pointer towards the conclusion that Nithard continued writing for an immediate "propagandistic" reason. He was anxious

> in case someone, tricked by some means or other, should dare to give an account of recent events otherwise than as they really happened.[62]

Nithard's anxiety might be attributed to a disinterested concern for truth and the correct informing of posterity. More probably it had an immediate and pragmatic cause: fear that Charles's men might be subjected to an alternative view of events emanating from Lothar's camp. For Charles need not have been alone in appreciating the utility of an apologist who could address noble Franks in terms they understood. Lothar, in Nithard's view, was quite capable of "trickery"[63] and was an expert practitioner of those "solicitings" of rivals' supporters that were the stuff of Carolingian politics.[64] Nithard himself tells us that Lothar's "partisans," so far from accepting Fontenoy as a divine judgment in Charles's and Louis's favor, spread a rumor that Charles had been killed in the battle and Louis put to flight.[65] Here indeed was an alternative view of events! Nithard was surely realistic to fear that such "disinformation" might be given literary form. Under the circumstances, and despite the tension inherent in pursuing reconciliation through the recording of conflict, it was not surprising that Nithard in his own words "settled for adding a third book."[66]

The preface to the fourth and last book contains an echo of the first preface, but it is set in so different a context as to carry a very different meaning. Nithard tells of his personal anxieties, his mind moved by "many grievances," he himself driven by the "blasts of fortune."

> But meanwhile if I find any free time, what objection can there be if, as it was commanded, I take pains to commit to memory by the office of my pen the deeds

---

widespread literacy will resolve Wright's problem, given his basic hypothesis (see above, n. 26), but the idea of "Nithard, or whoever it was" producing the second vernacular oath because "they felt they were sufficiently pleased" with the first is rather engaging!

[62] Nithard, *Histoire,* preface to book 3, p. 80.

[63] Ibid. 2.4, p. 46: Lothar looks for a trick (*astus*) by which to deceive Charles. Compare 2.2, p. 42; 2.7, p. 58; 2.9, p. 68; 4.3, p. 128.

[64] Ibid. 2.8, p. 62. Compare 2.2, p. 40, and similar tactics in 2.3, p. 44, and 2.4, p. 48. The inducements involved are explicit in 2.1, p. 38, where Lothar promises "unicuique honores a patre concessos se concedere et eosdem augere velle." For examples of such tactics after 843, see the Second Colloquy of Meersen (851), ed. Alfred Boretius, MGH Capit 205.2, p. 72, and the *Libellus contra Wenilonem,* ibid. 300.7, p. 452.

[65] Nithard, *Histoire* 3.2, p. 86.

[66] Ibid., preface to book 3, p. 80: "tertium libellum ut adderem acquievi."

> of our princes and our magnates? I shall therefore apply myself to this fourth book, and if I am unable to be of any use in other public affairs in future, at least by my own effort I can clean up the blot of error for posterity.[67]

The echo of the first preface here has an ironic ring. Nithard's tone is no longer positive and optimistic but resigned. His reference to fortune is perhaps more than a Sallustian flourish; it implies a sense of the vanity of human endeavor, even a loss of confidence in his ability to discern the workings of divine providence in the affairs of men.[68] Nithard no longer hoped, as he had once done, to influence his contemporaries: book 4 would be appreciated by posterity alone. Whereas in the first preface Nithard had told Charles that he would record "the deeds done in your time," deeds in which Charles by implication would appear a central figure, in the fourth preface the reference is to "deeds of our princes and our magnates" in general. The royal "command" mentioned in the fourth preface is simply the original one of May 841: the fourth book itself is not addressed to Charles and lacks the first three books' occasional admiring or sympathetic reference to Charles and to the justice of his cause.[69] The deeds of Charles and his men no longer provide any kind of theme and when Nithard does mention Charles's marriage to "Adalard's niece," he follows this up with a little diatribe on Adalard's political vices — hardly a fit passage for the man who had just become Adalard's nephew-in-law.[70] Still less fit for Charles's consumption is the final passage of book 4 (and of the *Histories*) where Nithard bitterly evokes "the times of the great Charles of happy memory" to make a stark contrast with his own times:

> Then this people walked on one and the same straight highroad of the Lord and there was peace and concord everywhere. But now — what a difference! — everywhere dissensions and feuds. Then there was everywhere plenteousness and gladness; now everywhere penury and sadness. . . . Then the very elements were favorable; now everywhere they are hostile. . . .[71]

If the changed tone of book 4 as compared with the earlier books can hardly be attributed to Nithard's objective observation of worsening political conditions or declining moral standards on the part of the Frankish nobility, then it is time to look for an alternative explanation.

[67] Ibid., preface to book 4, p. 116.

[68] Compare the comments of Heinz Löwe, "Geschichtsschreibung der ausgehenden Karolingerzeit," *Deutsches Archiv* 23 (1967), 1–30 at 29–30, à propos Regino of Prüm.

[69] It is Louis the German, rather than Charles, who attracts special praise from Nithard now — notably in 4.4, p. 132. See below, n. 118.

[70] Ibid. 4.6, p. 142. Compare Lupus of Ferrières, *Correspondance,* ed. Léon Levillain, 2 vols. (Paris, 1927–35), ep. 31, 1:144: "ne metuatis potentes . . . ," followed by a citation of Psalm 144.3. This may be a criticism of Adalard but it is discreetly veiled.

[71] Nithard, *Histoire* 4.7, p. 144.

Our attention can be redirected now from society in general to Nithard's own career — to the private history which runs through the public *Histories*. Unfortunately there is no direct evidence for it before 840.[72] But Nithard's receiving of *honores* from Louis the Pious implies a position of some influence at Louis's court,[73] while parts of book 1, for instance, the accounts of Guntbald's role in 830, of the casualties in the Neustrian battle of 834, and of Charles's investiture in 838, suggest firsthand, if not necessarily continuous, familiarity with the court during Louis's reign.[74] A recipient of *honores* may be assumed to have attended some of the assemblies, and probably to have fought in some of the campaigns, of the 820s and 830s. For his description of the lands granted to Charles in the winter of 837–38 Nithard used a document which may well have been produced at the Aachen assembly where the grant was made.[75] Furthermore Nithard, as he himself tells us, was a grandson of Charlemagne through his mother, Bertha,[76] and thus belonged to the "royal family" in the wider sense understood by contemporaries. The position of such a man in the Carolingian period was problematical because of the political and social significance attached to royal blood.[77] Biological closeness to the ruler could carry dangers as well as

[72] According to the family tree attached to Werner, "Nachkommen," Nithard was born "before 800." For justification of this date, see Konecny, *Frauen*, p. 76.

[73] Nithard, *Histoire* 2.2, p. 42.

[74] Ibid. 1.3, p. 12; 1.5, p. 20; 1.6, p. 27.

[75] Ibid. 1.6, pp. 24–26, with Lauer's comments at n. 3. Compare AB, pp. 22–23. Nithard presumably got access to this document in 841 as a result of Charles's commission.

[76] Nithard, *Histoire* 4.5, p. 138.

[77] So, for instance, Dhuoda, *Manuel* 3.8, pp. 166–70, devotes a chapter to the special respect due to the "inclitos atque praeclaros seniori tuo regiae potestatis eximios parentes atque propinquos," before going on to speak of *optimates* in general. Paschasius Radbertus lays striking emphasis on membership of the royal kindred in his *Vita Adalhardi* 7 and 50, PL 120:1511, 1534 (this Adalard was a first cousin of Charlemagne). Thegan, *Vita Hludovici* 36, MGH SS 2:597, says that Bernard, count of Barcelona, belonged to the *stirps regia* (his father, William of Gellone, was apparently related through his great-grandmother to Charlemagne's mother: see the family tree in Eduard Hlawitschka, "Die Vorfahren Karls des Grossen," in *Karl der Grosse,* ed. Braunfels and Beumann, 1, following p. 72). Hincmar of Rheims, noting the death of Charles the Bald's brother-in-law William (AB, s.a. 886, p. 130), specifies not his affinal but his blood relationship to the king. (Levillain, "Nibelungen historiques, II," *Annales du Midi* 50 [1938], 34–43, argues ingeniously that William was Charles's *sobrinus* because his grandfather was the brother of Charles's grandmother Hildegard, mother of Louis the Pious.) Despite some attempts in this period to narrow the circle of those eligible for royal succession, a relatively large range of claims remained possible, including some through women: see Werner, "Nachkommen," p. 410, n. 14, and Konecny, *Frauen,* pp. 33–44, 126–33. Nithard was not the only son of one of Charlemagne's daughters to achieve some prominence: for Louis see below, Appendix 1, p. 235, and for Richbod, below, p. 224. Both men are noted as grandsons of Charlemagne *ex filia* in the AB: Louis in Hincmar's section, s.a. 867, p. 134, and Richbod in Prudentius's section, s.a. 844, pp. 46–47. The broader context of such relationships is discussed by Donald Bullough, "Early Medieval Social Groupings: The Terminology of Kinship," *Past and Present* 45 (1969), 3–18. See also Karl Schmid, "Zur Problematik von Familie, Sippe und

advantages. Nithard is the sole supplier of our information on some interesting cases in point. He tells us, for instance, of Charles the Bald's half sister Hildegard, who apparently tried to hold Laon for Lothar in the aftermath of Fontenoy and was swiftly dealt with by Charles:

> He promised her in the nicest possible way all the kindness a brother owes a sister, provided that she would agree to show favor to him, and he gave her permission to depart for whatever destination she wished.[78]

If Hildegard's behavior to Charles had seemed unsisterly, she had done right by her full brother Lothar. Fraternal discord inevitably posed problems for sisters. As for Charles, brotherly he might wish to be, but in the political circumstances of summer 841, he had no alternative to the expulsion of his sister from a key stronghold. Again, it is Nithard who records what happened to Charlemagne's three youngest sons, Drogo, Hugh, and Theoderic, after their father's death: at first they were favored by their half brother Louis the Pious and made his table companions, but after the revolt of Louis's nephew Bernard, king of Italy, in 817, they were tonsured and put in monasteries for fear that they might "solicit the people," in other words, seek aristocratic support, "and follow Bernard's example."[79] Later Nithard reports the alignments of Drogo and Hugh in the great family conflict of 840–41.[80] Now, too, he mentions Bernard's son Pippin and makes it clear that this great-grandson of Charlemagne had been given lands, presumably by Louis the Pious, somewhere between the rivers Meuse and Seine.[81] Probably identifiable as another close kinsman is the "Arnulf" whom Nithard

---

Geschlecht, Haus und Dynastie beim mittelalterlichen Adel," *Zeitschrift für die Geschichte des Oberrheins* 105 (1957), 1–62, which, however, deals mainly with East Frankish material. The situation in ninth-century West Francia may have been somewhat different: see below n. 157.

[78] Nithard, *Histoire* 3.4, p. 98. Konecny, *Frauen,* p. 96, speculates on the possible identity of Hildegard's husband. But see below, Appendix 1, p. 290, for the suggestion that two daughters assigned to Louis the Pious by Werner, "Nachkommen," pp. 447, 450, should in fact be regarded as daughters of Pippin I of Aquitaine. Hildegard was probably abbess of Notre Dame, Laon, but since there is no evidence that she was married, there seems no reason to dub her a "lay abbess." The fact that Nithard accords her no ecclesiastical rank is irrelevant here: compare the identifications suggested above, n. 34.

[79] Nithard, *Histoire* 1.2, pp. 6–8. Drogo, Hugh, and Theoderic were sons of Charlemagne's old age by concubines. Illegitimacy did not, of course, automatically debar a man from royal succession: see Konecny, *Frauen,* pp. 41–44, and, for the broader context, Konrad Bund, *Thronsturz und Herrscherabsetzung im Frühmittelalter* (Bonn, 1979). For Bernard's revolt see Thomas F. X. Noble, "The Revolt of King Bernard of Italy in 817: Causes and Consequences," *Studi medievali* 15 (1974), 315–26, and Konecny, *Frauen,* pp. 38, 88, 160–63, noting the bias of the sources on 817 and the evidence of later ninth-century practice.

[80] Nithard, *Histoire* 2.10, p. 74; 3.2, 3, p. 90.

[81] Ibid. 2.3, p. 44. Werner, "Untersuchungen," 5, *Die Welt als Geschichte* 20 (1960), 92–93, argues that Pippin had probably been given the countship of Beauvais, and assumes that he was confirmed in it by Charles in 842 or 843, held it continuously thereafter, and transmitted it to his son sometime before 877. If so, the fact that Pippin's life from 841 is undocumented may indicate that he never played an important role at Charles's court.

mentions in a context that implies he had been given a countship in this same region.[82] That both Pippin and Arnulf opted for Lothar's side in 840 or 841 evidently caused problems for Charles in an area where it was crucial for him to hold supporters. Nithard, again our only informant, shows that these surplus royal kinsmen, like other great nobles, had to decide which of the rival Carolingian claimants to a share in Louis the Pious's inheritance they should support. Nithard implies, further, that the decisions of these men were additionally important because they influenced others. Charles, Louis the German, and Lothar all sometimes chose envoys from among their Carolingian kin.[83] But if the family conflict of 840–41, like previous similar conflicts in the reigns of Charlemagne and his son, gave such royal kinsmen political importance and new prospects of serviceability, hence of advancement and reward, it presented them at the same time with some hard choices. For the very object of the conflict, Francia, was the region where their own honors lay.

The dilemma is nicely illustrated by the example of Pippin, son of Bernard of Italy. Nithard records that when in the autumn of 840 Lothar pushed westwards across the Meuse towards the Seine,

> Pippin and the others chose to despise their oaths, to break their faith in the way that serfs do, rather than to lose their lands for a short while.[84]

Pippin's lands must thus have lain squarely within the area assigned to Charles by his father in 839, an arrangement to which Lothar had agreed and the Frankish magnates had sworn.[85] But Nithard does more than condemn the conduct of Pippin and the others who went over to Lothar: he contrasts it implicitly with an alternative model he has just given us:

> [Charles] chose Nithard and Adalgar as his envoys to Lothar. . . . Because these envoys refused to turn to Lothar and abandon their good faith, Lothar deprived them of the honors which his father had given them.[86]

This "Nithard" is none other than the author himself,[87] and from the context of this passage it looks as if the honors he lost in the autumn of 840 lay in the Meuse valley where Lothar was then active. And if Nithard lost these lands, then Lothar no doubt assigned them to someone else, perhaps to one of the "defectors" whom Nithard lists a few lines further on, a group of nobles from "beyond the Charbonnière," that is, from the area between

[82] Nithard, *Histoire* 2.6, pp. 54–56. See Werner, "Nachkommen," p. 446.
[83] Nithard, *Histoire* 2.2, 10, pp. 40, 74; 3.3, p. 90.
[84] Ibid. 2.3, p. 44: ". . . more servorum fidem omittere, iuramenta contempnere."
[85] Ibid. 1.6, p. 26.
[86] Ibid. 2.2, pp. 40–42.
[87] Though Nithard elsewhere refers to himself in the first person (*Histoire* 2.10; 4.1, 5), this identification seems certain given the character of book 2 and the circumstances of the work's commissioning by Charles.

this ancient forest boundary (running approximately between modern Louvain and Charleroi) and the Meuse.[88] Though not all Charles's supporters left him, Nithard stresses what a small band they were in the winter of 840–41, when Charles's fortunes were at their lowest ebb. Charles and his men were very close; he discussed his plans with them and when he asked their advice,

> it was easy to make up their minds what to do. Since they had nothing left besides their lives and bodies, [Charles's men] chose to die nobly rather than to betray and abandon their king.[89]

This nobleness forms a striking contrast with the "serflike" conduct of Pippin and the rest. Lothar himself, according to Nithard, recognized the mettle of Charles's men, knowing that they would resist him "strenuously" however much he might try to bribe or threaten them.[90] After describing Louis the German's joining up with Charles, Nithard praises Louis's men in similar terms:

> They feared that if brother should fail to help brother [that is, should Louis fail to help Charles] then they [Louis's men] would leave an unworthy memory to their descendants. They preferred penury, even death, to losing their unconquered name.[91]

Louis's men were actually engaged in a campaign directed against Louis's brother Lothar, yet their good reputation depended on their lord's acting in a brotherly way. The conflict of values was a real one: a son could justly claim a share in the paternal inheritance, yet this set him in competition with the brother he should love. It was not only in the case of kings that fraternal rights or acceptable ambitions clashed with fraternal obligations: all the stress in a Frankish noble's education might be on solidarity between brothers, yet brothers' careers could diverge, even compete,[92] and fraternal

[88] Nithard was writing from a point west and south of the Charbonnière. For the location of this frontier in the Middle Ages, see H. Vander Linden, "La forêt Charbonnière," *Revue belge de philologie et d'histoire* 2 (1923), 203–14, and F. L. Ganshof, "Carbonaria Silva," in *Handworterbuch zur deutschen Rechtsgeschichte,* ed. Adalbert Erler and Ekkehard Kaufmann, 3 (Berlin, 1966), cols. 589–90. For its significance in Merovingian and Carolingian times, see Eugen Ewig, "Descriptio Franciae," in *Karl der Grosse,* ed. Braunfels and Beumann, 1:157–58; Classen, "Verträge" (cited above, n. 2), p. 6 with nn. 1 and 2; and below, n. 107.

[89] Nithard, *Histoire* 2.4, p. 46.

[90] Ibid.

[91] Ibid. 2.10, pp. 68–70.

[92] The sons and grandsons of Count Welf, father of the empress Judith, offer several instances: see the evidence presented by Gerd Tellenbach, "Exkurs über die ältesten Welfen im West- und Ostfrankenreich," in *Studien und Vorarbeiten zur Geschichte des grossfränkischen und frühdeutschen Adels,* ed. Tellenbach (Freiburg, 1957), pp. 335–40 (though Tellenbach himself did not draw the same inference as I have done). Adalard and Gerard offer another case: though modern historians agree on the fraternal relationship between these two, no ninth-century text

disputes over the division of family property may have been common in the ninth century.[93] For a noble individual such dissonance between norm and experience would often be painful. Therefore though nobles sometimes exploited the fraternal conflicts of kings, the concern described by Nithard in the passage just quoted should not be dismissed as mere cynical playacting. Furthermore, as Nithard shows in the case of Bernard of Septimania awaiting on the sidelines the outcome of Fontenoy, a noble's optimal self-interest could not be easily calculated.[94] Several ninth-century casualty lists suggest that the often idealized duty of a faithful man to his lord could involve all too real sacrifice.[95]

For many of Nithard's Frankish contemporaries, including, I believe, many of those who read and heard his work, such dilemmas will have been recent and vivid realities. Thus both Nithard's very detailed presentation of the preliminaries to Fontenoy and the brevity of his account of the actual battle can be seen as accommodating the sensibilities of his audience. Nithard had to explain Fontenoy. He did not, as Pietzcker argued, have to explain it away. But he could not have thought of glamorizing it. Far more attention is also given to the elaborate rituals of legitimation and reconciliation that followed Fontenoy than to the battle itself.[96] Nithard's values did not differ from those of Carolingian churchmen; he did believe that bishops had special access to the will of God. He and his patrons were therefore perfectly genuine in invoking episcopal pronouncements. Like Villehardouin appealing to ecclesiastical approval for the Latins' attack on Constantinople in 1204,[97] Nithard and his fellow Franks needed to believe in the church's authority.

Thus far Nithard may be seen to have reflected the concerns of his fellow participants. But there is one point in his narrative where he calls attention in an unusually explicit way to his own part in events. In his account of Fontenoy he names only two of the combatants, apart from the warring

---

specifies it or links their careers. They apparently fought on opposite sides at Fontenoy: above, n. 22.

[93] Describing one such attempted division, Odo of Glanfeuil says that a quarrel broke out "as often happens in such a business" (*ut in tali adsolet negotio*) and one brother slew the other: *Miracula Sancti Mauri*, ed. Oswald Holder-Egger, MGH SS 15:470. Odo's account of the refoundation of Glanfeuil suggests tension and finally a compromise between close kinsmen over control of a family monastery: ibid., pp. 467–68. See Otto G. Oexle, "Bischof Ebroin von Poitiers und seine Verwandten," *Frühmittelalterliche Studien* 3 (1969), 138–210 at 149–60.

[94] Nithard, *Histoire* 3.2, pp. 82–84. For perceptive comments on twelfth-century nobles in a comparable situation, see Edmund King, "King Stephen and the Anglo-Norman Magnates," *History* 59 (1974), 180–94.

[95] Nithard, *Histoire* 1.5, p. 20; AB, pp. 13, 46–47, 131, 209.

[96] The battle is dealt with in fourteen lines of Lauer's edition (*Histoire* 2.10, pp. 76–78) whereas three times as many lines are devoted to the aftermath (ibid. 3.1, pp. 80–82).

[97] Villehardouin, *The Conquest of Constantinople,* trans. M. R. B. Shaw (Harmondsworth, 1963), chap. 11, pp. 84–85.

kings, and these are Adalard and himself. After saying that Louis and Charles were victorious in their sectors of the battle, Nithard goes on:

> But the part [of Lothar's forces] that fought at Solmet against Adalard and the others, to whom I gave no small assistance, struggled bravely . . . but in the end they fled.[98]

Nithard implies that this part of the battle was the hardest-fought one, and he claims that his own role was significant here. What matters is not so much the trustworthiness of the claim (for we have no means of checking that) but the reason that Nithard makes it at all — and with a rare use of the first person singular. It looks as if when he was writing the final chapter of book 2 in October 841 he wished to bring his own services to the attention of Charles and also of his followers and at the same time to associate himself with Adalard, then nearing the height of his influence in Charles's camp. Adalard is named three times in book 3 and his role in winning support for Charles in Francia is implicitly approved by Nithard.[99] It looks as if Nithard hoped to gain personally from his connection with Adalard,[100] expecting that the man he felt he had helped so signally at Fontenoy would feel in return some sense of obligation and would use his influence with the king to promote Nithard's own interests. For Nithard surely believed that anyone familiar with books 2 and 3 would regard this expectation as reasonable. By publicizing his connection with Adalard he hoped to enlist widespread sympathy for his own concerns.

Those concerns centered, I think, on the recovery of his lost lands in Francia. In the autumn of 841 Nithard may well have felt confident of getting them back. Even when Lothar, unbowed by Fontenoy, had reaffirmed his extensive territorial demands, Charles had replied that

> it seemed to him utterly unfitting that he [Charles] should yield up the realm between the Meuse and the Seine which his father had given him, especially because so many nobles (*tanta nobilitas*) from there had chosen to follow him and it would be quite wrong for them to be deceived in their loyalty to him.[101]

Charles went on to ask that further negotiations be deferred "since winter was coming on," but that in the meantime "each should have the honors which [Louis the Pious] had given him." Nithard would have been a conspicuous beneficiary by such terms, but Lothar predictably spurned them. By the spring of 842, however, it seemed that Lothar was no longer in a position to call the tune. Charles and Louis the German could draft at Aachen a division of the *regnum Francorum* which apparently excluded Lothar al-

[98] Nithard, *Histoire* 2.10, pp. 76–78. Scholz's translation, *Carolingian Chronicles,* p. 154, has Adalard fighting on Lothar's side.

[99] Nithard, *Histoire* 3.2, 3, pp. 84, 86, 90.

[100] For the possibility of a further kin tie between the two men, see below, p. 232.

[101] Nithard, *Histoire* 3.3, pp. 94–96.

together, confining him to Italy.[102] Such a division could never have been expected to stick; as the sequel made clear, it was a means of exerting pressure on Lothar to come to the conference table. But their successes over the previous months had made Charles and Louis more than ever determined to hold on to the regions which they considered politically vital and which Lothar had tried correspondingly hard to withhold from them. In Louis's case, the region in question consisted of an enclave on the west bank of the Rhine around Ingelheim and including Mainz, Worms, and Speyer.[103] In Charles's case the vital area, according to Nithard, lay north and east of the Charbonnière between the rivers Scheldt and Meuse. After Lothar had been forced to flee from Francia (Nithard simply calls it "the realm") in March 842, Charles and Louis could agree to a division which, while purporting to partition the whole of Francia between them in order to give them a strong bargaining position in future negotiations with Lothar, was really intended to secure for each his area of special interest in addition to the kingdom he already effectively held.

Nithard clearly thought this agreement important and he spelled out the criteria used in drawing the detailed boundaries:

> not so much the fertility or equal territorial extent of each share, as the family connections, interests, and commitments of everyone involved.[104]

Nithard's depiction of the basis for the 842 division in what we might call explicitly sociological rather than geographical or constitutional terms is perhaps our single most important piece of evidence for the central political role of the Carolingian aristocracy. This settlement, like its more famous sequel ratified at Verdun in 843, was a product of Frankish consensus politics. So familiar was this context of ninth-century practice that Nithard felt no need to labor the point: indeed his touch was so light that most modern historians had failed to register it at all until the late Peter Classen sharpened our perceptions. In Nithard's account of the 842 agreement

[102] Ibid. 4.1. pp. 116–20. Nithard says: "Evenitque Lodhuvico omnis Frisia. . . ." Scholz, *Carolingian Chronicles,* p. 166, renders: "Louis received all of Francia . . ." — a rather different proposition!

[103] Dümmler, *Geschichte,* 1:205–6, notes the strategic and ecclesiastical significance of this area. Louis the Pious stayed quite often in his palaces at Ingelheim, Worms, and Mainz: see Brühl, *Fodrum, Gistum,* p. 21. For fisc lands here, see Wolfgang Metz, *Das karolingische Reichsgut* (Berlin, 1960), pp. 113, 118, 123, 130.

[104] Nithard, *Histoire* 4.1, p. 120: "non tantum fertilitas aut equa portio regni quantum affinitas et congruentia cujusque aptata est." My translation is based on the interpretation of Classen, "Verträge," pp. 10–12, which seems to me preferable to earlier views. F. L. Ganshof, "Zur Entstehungsgeschichte und Bedeutung des Verträges von Verdun," *Deutsches Archiv* 12 (1956), 313–30 (English translation in Ganshof, *The Carolingians and the Frankish Monarchy* [London, 1971], pp. 289–302), is an illuminating study which identifies the nature of royal resources but because the focus remains on the kings rather than on the aristocracy misses the significance of *affinitas* and *congruentia.*

"everyone involved" included not just the two kings[105] but their boundary commissioners, twelve chosen by Charles and twelve by Louis from among their leading supporters, and these men in turn took account of the connections and interests of their peers, their friends and clients, and their noble comrades of the past months' campaigning. Nithard himself was one of these commissioners[106] and he leaves us in little doubt about his approval of their work. Charles, he goes on, left Aachen and "crossed the Meuse to put his kingdom in order." The *Annals* of St. Bertin confirms this, adding that Charles spent Easter at Herstal, one of the most ancient Carolingian holdings.[107] When within a few weeks Lothar took the hoped-for initiative in reopening negotiations with his brothers, there was, according to Nithard, a sense of relief on the part of Charles and Louis and "all their people."

What happened next evoked from Nithard an unmistakable cry of protest, even of pain. The three envoys sent by Charles and Louis found Lothar unwilling to accept the terms they brought. Lothar put his own position plainly:

> He would not have, he said, in the part [that is, the share of the divided *regnum*] they offered him the wherewithal to make good to his own supporters that which they had lost.

Nithard goes on — with another of his rare uses of the first person:

> For this reason — and I do not know by what trickery they were deceived — the envoys increased Lothar's share of the *regnum* so that it extended as far as the Charbonnière.[108]

The additional concession, so Nithard implies, made all the difference: Lothar accepted the revised terms. This was a crucial stage, therefore, in the negotiations that led to Verdun where in 843 a division of the *regnum Francorum* was settled for that generation. Charles can have had no illusions about the price to be paid. It was an offer he had once made before in a last urgent attempt to avert battle at Fontenoy.[109] Then Lothar had rejected it.

[105] If that had been Nithard's meaning, would he not have written *utriusque* instead of *cujusque,* picking up his *uterque* (referring to Charles and Louis) earlier in the same sentence?

[106] Nithard, *Histoire* 4.1, p. 120: ". . . quorum unus extiti."

[107] AB, s.a. 842, p. 41. On the history of Carolingian (Pippinid) holdings in the Haspengau (Hesbaye), see Matthias Werner, *Der Lütticher Raum in frühkarolingischer Zeit* (Göttingen, 1980), pp. 347–54, 441–51. According to the *Annales Mettenses priores,* s.a. 688, ed. Bernhard von Simson, MGH SSrG (Hannover, 1905), p. 2, Pippin, the first mayor of the palace, in the early seventh century "populum inter Carbonariam silvam et Mosam fluvium . . . gubernabat." But Werner stresses, p. 347, that this text was written c. 800 and may well reflect a contemporary rather than earlier regional identity.

[108] Nithard, *Histoire* 4.3, pp. 124–26.

[109] Ibid. 2.10, p. 72. Significantly, Louis the German, too, had then offered a correspondingly large concession, foregoing his enclave west of the Rhine. Pietzcker, "Schlacht," p. 129, suggests

But his acceptance of it now, a year later when the alternative of a military victory no longer seemed available, proved its significance in terms of political gain. The lands between the Charbonnière and the Meuse did, it seems, provide Lothar with the "wherewithal" he needed to supplement his territories further east. For here around Herstal were estates that had been Pippinid before they became Carolingian. Being ancient they may well have been intensively exploited, and being fairly near Aachen they had probably received careful attention from royal estate managers over at least the past two generations. As well as the fisc lands proper, such abbeys as Nivelles and Lobbes and the see of Cambrai were major royal assets in the vicinity.[110] This was the area, together with the region laden with similar assets between the Scheldt and the Seine, which was said by a well-informed East Frankish contemporary to constitute "the best part of the *regnum Francorum*."[111] Such assets provided the means whereby kings "made good their supporters' losses." Benefices, land grants "in propriety," *honores* were the expected compensations and rewards of faithful service, and an adequate supply of them was an essential condition of a king's credibility.[112] Thus the loss of the region between the Charbonnière and the Meuse was a heavy price for Charles to be willing to pay in 842 even if it bought peace. Nithard evidently thought it unacceptably heavy.

But what for Nithard was the truth of the situation may not have been the whole truth. Nithard implies that Charles himself had not authorized his negotiators to make such a concession but that the envoys were "deceived" into doing so on their own initiative. Yet Charles did not renege on the offer, and on Nithard's own showing, it was an offer Charles had made before, in June 841. Moreover Nithard says of Charles's negotiators while working on the details of the division of the *regnum* a few months later that "they dared not agree to anything without their lord's authority."[113] All

---

that the offers were not intended seriously and may even be inventions of Nithard's. But Pietzcker underestimates the difficulties of Charles's and Louis's position at that point and gives no reason for Nithard's alleged invention.

[110] Compare the list of royal assets in the 870 division of what had been Lothar II's kingdom: MGH Capit 2.251, pp. 193–95.

[111] *Annals* of Fulda, ed. Friedrich Kurze, MGH SSrG (Hannover, 1891), s.a. 838, p. 28. This is not to deny that the major concentrations of Carolingian fisc lands lay further east and southeast. But Carolingian lands west of the Meuse and old Merovingian fisc lands west and southwest of the Scheldt were clearly very important assets for ninth-century rulers and perhaps were preferred sources of endowment for royal kinsfolk.

[112] Exactly this point had been made a century before Nithard wrote, by Bede in his letter to Archbishop Egbert of York, *Venerabilis Baedae opera historica,* ed. Charles Plummer (Oxford, 1896), p. 415 (English translation by Dorothy Whitelock, *English Historical Documents,* 1, 2nd ed. [London, 1979], no. 170, p. 805).

[113] Nithard, *Histoire* 4.3, p. 138. (The translation of this chapter in Scholz, *Carolingian Chronicles,* p. 171, is in part incomprehensible.) On the role of the negotiators, see Gerd Tellenbach, "Die geistigen und politischen Grundlagen der karolingischen Thronfolge," *Frühmittelalterliche Studien* 13 (1979), 184–302 at 205–6, 255.

things considered, it seems likely enough that Charles had authorized his envoys to offer the crucial concession in the summer of 842 should that seem necessary because of Lothar's intransigence. It might also have seemed in Charles's best interests. For Lothar had commanded a good deal of support between the Meuse and the Scheldt in 840.[114] Perhaps Charles had found during the weeks following Easter 842 that putting that region "in order" was more difficult than he had hoped, in other words, that too many of Lothar's supporters there could be neither dislodged nor won over by "solicitings" from Charles's side. If so, it might well have seemed to Charles and his advisers more prudent to yield an unpromising claim and to make a show of concession in this area in order to consolidate substantial power elsewhere. The defeat of Pippin II at Fontenoy had reopened brighter prospects for Charles in Aquitaine, where he did in fact concentrate a good deal of effort later in 842.[115] It may therefore have been a shrewd calculation of potential advantage as well as the urgent need for peace which induced Charles to replace on the negotiating table the lands between the Meuse and the Scheldt.

Why then Nithard's talk of "deception"? Why the bitterness of his reaction to the terms brought back to Charles's camp by his chief envoy, Adalard? Neither the envoys nor the king, I think, had really been deceived: rather it was Nithard himself who felt cheated and saw Charles's abandonment of the Meuse line as a sad turning point in the negotiations and a consequence of "trickery." For it was in this disputed region between the Meuse and the Scheldt, surely, that Nithard's own lost honors lay: lands which (among others) Lothar maintained were indispensable to "rewarding his faithful followers." One of Lothar's men had no doubt already been rewarded with the lands confiscated from Nithard two years before; now Lothar had no intention of seeing his supporter "dis-honored."[116] In the spring of 842

[114] Nithard, *Histoire* 2.3, p. 44. A number of Carolingian estates in the Haspengau may have helped to supply the palace at Aachen, which was to be by far the most frequent residence of Lothar I after 843 and later of Lothar II: see Brühl, *Fodrum, Gistum,* pp. 31–32. Lothar II granted renders from several estates in this region to the chapel at Aachen: MGH DD GermKarol, 3, ed. Theodor Schieffer, Lothar II, no. 43, p. 454.

[115] Nithard, *Histoire* 4.4, p. 132. Compare AB, p. 42. Charles's presence at Agen and then Castillon-sur-Dordogne in late August 842 is attested by two charters: Tessier, *Recueil,* nos. 10, 11. The assertion of Lot and Halphen, *Règne de Charles le Chauve,* p. 84, n. 3, that Pippin II remained master of Aquitaine in 843 rests on the misdating of an alleged grant: see Levillain, *Actes de Pépin I et de Pépin II* 55, pp. 217–21.

[116] The terms *exhonorare* and *inhonoratio,* signifying deprivation of *honores* in the sense of offices and lands, are used by Paschasius Radbertus: *Vita Adalhardi* 36 and 45, PL 120:1528, 1533, and *Epitaphium Arsenii,* ed. Ernst Dümmler, *Abhandlungen der königlichen preussischen Akademie zu Berlin,* Phil.-Hist. Klasse (1900), pp. 75, 76. Nithard uses the phrase *honoribus privare: Histoire* 2.2, p. 42, and 4.4, p. 132. From the second of these cases it is clear that Lothar in the late summer or autumn of 842 dis-honored some men who had supported him until the spring of that year and only abandoned him "compelled by necessity" when he had left Francia

when Charles had been able to move from Aachen into the area west of the Meuse, Nithard's hopes of recovering his lands had probably been high. Did he perhaps even see his lands again at this time? In any event he seems in the early summer to have felt still confident of permanent restitution, for he welcomed Lothar's reopening of talks with Charles and Louis.[117] But then Lothar wrested the concession that took his western frontier up to the Charbonnière.

Where did this leave Nithard? He can have seen little advantage in transferring his allegiance now to Lothar (if he even considered this course), for Lothar had his own faithful men to reward, to maintain or reinstate. Nithard's forfeited lands could hardly have been on offer in that quarter. He had pinned his hopes elsewhere. He had supported Charles consistently since 840 at considerable personal cost.[118] He had written two books of the *Histories* not from an armchair but under the difficult circumstances of camp and campaign because his chosen lord had requested it. He surely expected that fidelity would receive its due, and he went on writing after Fontenoy in the confidence that even if the king should prove slow to deliver the reward, then Adalard, who had incurred a special debt of his own to Nithard at Fontenoy, would jog the king's memory. In the first three books of his work Nithard thus presented for men au fait with recent events his own, as well as Charles's, case. According to the rules of Carolingian politics, both Charles and Adalard owed Nithard much; hence Nithard had every reason to expect that his own sacrifice would prove to have been only "for a short while."[119] Instead, because of the "trickery" of 842, Nithard's services did not get their

---

(Nithard again calls it the *regnum*) for the Rhone valley. My hypothetical Lothar supporter who had received Nithard's *honores* in 840 may have been one of those whom Lothar thus deprived in 842. But if so, this clearly did nothing to help Nithard. Noble concern to acquire, or retain, honors granted by kings is evident in *Histoire* 2.1, p. 38, 3.2, p. 84, and 3.3, p. 96. In 3.2 the term *honores* has the general sense of lands rather than a specific connection with office: see the comments on this passage of Joachim Wollasch, "Eine adlige Familie des frühen Mittelalters," *Archiv für Kulturgeschichte* 39 (1957), 151–88 at 187–88. The term probably has this general sense elsewhere in Nithard (the *honores* of 2.2, p. 42, seem to be identical with the *facultates* of 2.3, p. 44) and in many other sources from the mid-ninth century onwards. The change in the word's meaning seems to have occurred during Nithard's lifetime: compare the still-restricted sense of *honores* in the *Annales regni Francorum,* ed. Friedrich Kurze, MGH SSrG (Hannover, 1895), s.a. 828, p. 174, with the broad connotation implicit in AB, s.a. 839, p. 31: Louis the Pious endowed some of Lothar's men "non solum proprietatibus verum etiam beneficiariis honoribus." The semantic history of the term would repay further study.

117 Nithard, *Histoire* 4.3, p. 126.

118 The distinctly favorable attitude shown by Nithard towards Louis the German in book 4 (especially 4.4, p. 132, where Louis is said to have crushed the Stellinga revolt *nobiliter*) could suggest that Nithard in late 842/early 843 contemplated seeking Louis as an alternative patron to Charles. But this is more probably a literary device, contrasting with the favorable treatment of Louis and Charles *together* in book 3, to point up what Nithard saw as a divergence between the brothers' conduct from mid-842 onwards. In any event Nithard remained in Charles's kingdom: see below, p. 225.

119 Nithard, *Histoire* 2.3, p. 44.

due acknowledgment: his Carolingian maternal kin colluded in his "disinheritance" thereby making his sacrifice a permanent one. What was left to him was the lay abbacy of his father's monastery of St. Riquier and custodianship of the paternal tomb.[120] No longer, it seems, a favored or prominent member of Charles's entourage, Nithard withdrew to St. Riquier during the winter of 842–43. One of the last events mentioned in his work is the translation at St. Riquier of his father's body "incorrupt even though not embalmed": a clear sign of sanctity.[121] It was this side of his ancestry as well as his descent from Charlemagne that Nithard now wished to stress. For it was this that distinguished him from his kinsman Abbot Richbod, another of Charlemagne's grandsons.[122] Richbod had received the regular abbacy probably from Lothar in 840,[123] and Nithard's sharing of the lordship of St. Riquier constitutes one of the earliest instances of a double abbacy of this kind.[124] The arrangement in Nithard's case is unlikely to have been very harmonious. It may be significant that Nithard omits even to mention Richbod's presence at the translation of Angilbert's body though a contemporary source from St. Riquier has recorded that Richbod presided on that occasion.[125] In such circumstances Nithard can hardly have regarded a mere

[120] According to his epitaph, composed by a St. Riquier monk probably in 853, Nithard "for a short time (*modico*) held the title of *rector,*" that is, of lay abbot: ed. Ludwig Traube, MGH Poet 3:310–11, with the editor's comments at p. 268. For the career of Angilbert, Nithard's father, see Löwe, *Deutschlands Geschichtsquellen,* 2:236–40.

[121] Nithard, *Histoire* 4.5, p. 138. The date was 5 November.

[122] Werner, "Nachkommen," p. 448, argues rightly that there are no grounds for assuming that Bertha was Richbod's mother: "Die Inhaberschaft von S.-Riquier, das Angilbert unterstand, [ist] keine genügende Grundlage für die Annahme, Bertha habe auch noch von einem anderen Manne Kinder gehabt als von Angilbert!" I would add that Nithard's failure to mention Richbod would be surprising had the two men been half brothers. The likelihood is that their mothers were half sisters.

[123] The date at which Richbod became abbot is nowhere stated, though it was certainly before October 842: see below, and n. 125. Werner, "Nachkommen," gives 840 on the family tree but without explaining why in the accompanying notes. Assuming that Richbod's predecessor as abbot sided (like Nithard) with Charles the Bald, Lothar would have wanted to install his own man at St. Riquier in late summer 840, when he was bidding for control of the area between the Charbonnière and the Seine. Compare his giving of St. Josse to Rhuoding: Lupus, *Correspondance,* ep. 19, 1:104, and of St. Wandrille to Joseph of Ivrea: *Annales Fontanellenses priores,* ed. Jean Laporte, Société de l'histoire de Normandie, 15th ser. (Rouen and Paris, 1951), p. 75. Conversely, when Charles gained a measure of control in the Paris-Sens area in late 840, he was able to oust the abbots of St. Denis and Ferrières, who had accepted Lothar, and instead place his own supporters in these key posts: the archchancellor Louis in the one, Lupus in the other.

[124] I accept here a suggestion of Lauer, *Histoire,* p. v. See below, Appendix 2.

[125] The epitaph of Angilbert, MGH Poet 3:314–15. A renewal by Charles of privileges for the monks of St. Riquier (Tessier, *Recueil,* no. 22, pp. 53–55) oddly fails to mention an abbot. Tessier points out the difficulty in dating this grant: it is preserved only in Hariulf's *Chronicle,* written in the eleventh century, where it is dated 844, but that is certainly wrong and is probably the result of willful alteration by Hariulf. Tessier suggests instead 21 May 843, but 842 seems equally likely: either way, Charles has to be given an otherwise unattested stay at Compiègne.

share in what was after all his own patrimonial abbey (and not Richbod's) as a satisfactory compensation for the lands he had lost in 840. But there is no evidence of his receiving any other compensation. Charles's resources were limited and in 842–43 he had other, younger claimants to satisfy.[126] In them Nithard showed no interest, any more than he showed sympathy for Charles's activities in Aquitaine or appreciation for the political adroitness of Charles's marriage to Adalard's niece.

Nithard's world had narrowed. He wrote no longer for the public to whom books 1, 2, and 3 had been addressed. Book 4's savage criticism of Adalard could never have been intended for a court audience in 842–43, nor could the implicit indictment of Charles in book 4's final comparison of the wretched present with the golden past of the "great Charles" ever have been thought fit for the eyes of Nithard's former patron and confidant. Nithard went on writing book 4 out of an understandable sense of grievance, venting his bitterness perhaps to a circle of faithful intimates at St. Riquier, men whose interest in their saint-patron Angilbert Nithard might hope to exploit against his rival Richbod.[127] And with book 4 Nithard completed his *Histories,* allowing himself a writer's ironic satisfaction in ending with a flourish of literary symmetry belied by the cruel disjuncture within his work and his life.[128] He had done with writing. Little more than a year later on 14 June 844 he was killed in Aquitaine in the battle of the Angoumois, fighting again for Charles in another round of Carolingian family conflict.[129] His

---

For Charles's itinerary in the relevant periods, see Lot and Halphen, *Règne de Charles le Chauve,* pp. 54, 62. I suggest the absence of reference to an abbot in this grant may have arisen from Charles's reservations about Richbod's position or perhaps from awkwardness on the monks' part over the anomalous situation of the double abbacy. But presumably this was just the sort of compromise Charles and Lothar had to accept as part of the settlement at Verdun. See below, Appendix 2.

[126] For instance, Odo, future count of Châteaudun, Robert, future count of Angers, and Richwin, future holder of a countship in the Rheims area, perhaps Rheims itself: for their careers, see Werner, "Untersuchungen," 4, pp. 152–69. Charles distributed lands of the church of Rheims to these men and others. Hincmar, *Vita Sancti Remigii,* ed. Bruno Krusch, MGH SSrerMerov 3:324, says this happened "when Lothar, Louis, and Charles, after their father's death, divided the *regnum* between themselves." Werner, "Untersuchungen," 4, p. 157, infers that the distribution of Rheims lands must therefore be dated after Verdun (August 843), but Hincmar's reference could be to some time during the months of negotiations preceding Verdun. (Hincmar was writing the *Vita Remigii* nearly forty years after that.) Another claimant on Charles's favor at this time was Vivian, first attested as Charles's chamberlain in Tessier, *Recueil,* no. 19, p. 46, dated 18 February 843. My impression is that Odo, Robert, Richwin, and Vivian all belonged to Charles's generation, rather than to Nithard's.

[127] The tone of these final chapters seems to me to support the view that Nithard's monastic retirement was the result of something other than a genuinely religious *conversio,* such as Einhard may have experienced.

[128] Patze, "*Iustitia,*" p. 163, nicely observed that *Histoire* 4.7 balances 1.1 in harking back to the days of Charlemagne.

[129] I defend this view below in Appendix 2.

work, left at St. Riquier, remained almost totally obscure until its discovery in the sixteenth century.[130]

I have suggested that a "private history" runs through Nithard's work, revealing and in part explaining changes in his reactions to public events. It is in book 4 that the private history comes most obviously to the surface of the narrative and here, too, with the change in Nithard's audience, that his work ceases to be public in the sense of no longer being addressed to a relatively wide group of political actors. Yet it would be false to infer a contrast between "the objective account" of books 1–3 and "the subjective view" of book 4, as if the Nithard who served "truth" or "history" in the first three books descended to a baser aim in the fourth. An apologia designed for a contemporary public may be as subjective as a more private and explicitly personal writing up of experience: neither is fiction yet both blend fact with interpretation. From the historian's standpoint this means, on the one hand, that nothing in Nithard's work can be taken simply at face value or out of its specific context in ninth-century politics.[131] On the other hand, once our witness is allowed to speak in that context and asked the right questions, what matters is not only his factual reliability (insofar as that can be checked) but also his plausibility as a guide to contemporary values, motives, and expectations. Nithard's *Histories* should be listened to not just for what happened in 840–43 but for something of why it happened and what it meant to those involved. As the late Kathleen Hughes said of early Celtic historians: "From a sympathetic and sensitive questioning of what they were attempting, history emerges."[132]

In conclusion I want to focus briefly on two aspects of the Carolingian period where Nithard's work is particularly illuminating. First, if Nithard wrote for a contemporary public of the kind I have suggested, then the *Histories* points towards the possibility that a genre of political polemic existed in the ninth century. The near-total loss of such writings is hardly surprising, for the survival of a work like Nithard's is a matter of pure luck.

[130] For the manuscript in question, see above, n. 3. It was at St. Médard, Soissons, in the eleventh and twelfth centuries and at Paris in the fifteenth century. There is no clear evidence that other manuscripts existed. Müller in the preface to his edition of Nithard, p. ix, notes one possible citation of the *Histories* by a medieval author: Hucbald of St. Amand (writing in the early tenth century). But the passage is so brief and so specific (it concerns the three classes of Saxon society) that it is tempting to surmise a now lost source for both Nithard and Hucbald at this point. Lauer, *Histoire,* p. xvii, neglecting Hucbald, claims as the sole citation of Nithard by any medieval author a "mention" in an anonymous thirteenth-century *Historia regum Francorum,* but I have been unable to trace this work beyond the reference in André Duchesne, *Historiae Francorum scriptores coaetanei,* 2 (Paris, 1639), p. 357. For the postmedieval history of Nithard's work, see Lauer, *Histoire,* pp. xv–xviii.

[131] An example of what seems to me a decontextualized reading is given above, n. 43.

[132] "The Early Celtic Idea of History and the Modern Historian," Inaugural Lecture in the Readership in Celtic Studies founded by Nora Chadwick (Cambridge, Eng., 1977), p. 24.

Like a number of other ninth-century *pièces d'occasion* — Paschasius's *Epitaphium Arsenii,* Ermold's *Poem on Louis the Pious,* Hincmar's *De ordine palatii,* the *Ludwigslied,* several politically inspired visions of the next world, or (to go further afield) Asser's *Life of Alfred* — Nithard's *Histories* survived in a single early manuscript.[133] But it is not hard to see why such ephemera, partly unintelligible outside their immediate historical context and often by "unknown" authors, were not thought by learned monks of later generations to have educational value and were therefore rarely copied or preserved. Though not all the works just listed were written for quite the kind of audience Nithard addressed, it can be argued that some were[134] and that others were aimed at groups which if more restricted than Nithard's public nevertheless had a stake in political affairs.[135] Again, though most of these authors had an eye to a royal reader, in practice the court — in the sense of the king's entourage — regularly expanded to include many or most of the king's leading men: Compiègne (or Chippenham) at assembly time probably contained virtually all those involved in "the regulation of public affairs" of the kingdom.[136]

To speak of a genre may sound less like exaggeration if we note other works relating to particular occasions or issues. Agobard's polemic of 833 is an obvious example.[137] For the crisis year of 858 the *Annals* of Fulda preserves what sound like extracts from the manifesto of a group of West Frankish nobles inviting Louis the German to take over Charles's kingdom.[138] The famous Quierzy letter masterminded by Hincmar is a demarche similarly intended for a far wider audience than Louis the German alone.[139] Other ninth-century crises could have evoked comparable literature, notably such bouts of Carolingian family conflict as the disputed successions to Lotharingia in 869–72 (I include Carloman's revolt)[140] and to Italy after 875. Nor need we exclude laymen from the audience of polemic produced in

[133] For Nithard's work, see above, nn. 3 and 130. For the works of Paschasius, Ermold, Hincmar, and Asser referred to here, the relevant standard editions give details on unique early manuscripts. Examples of visions surviving in unique manuscripts are given by Devisse, *Hincmar,* 2:821, n. 688, and 823, n. 697. The interest of the *Ludwigslied* for historians (as distinct from linguists) has only recently been stressed by Karl Ferdinand Werner, "Gauzlin von Saint-Denis," *Deutsches Archiv* 35 (1979), 395–462 at 433–37, and 434, noting the unique manuscript of the poem.

[134] The *De ordine palatii*; the *Ludwigslied*; perhaps Asser's *Life of Alfred.*

[135] For instance, the Corbie monks or the Rheims clergy at whom the *Epitaphium* and the *Visio Bernoldi* respectively were addressed.

[136] See my comments above, chapter 5, pp. 100-8.

[137] *Libri duo pro filiis et contra Judith uxorem Ludowici Pii,* ed. Georg Waitz, MGH SS 15:274–79.

[138] *Annals* of Fulda, pp. 49–50. On an alternative view, this could be propaganda produced by Louis the German's entourage.

[139] MGH Capit 297, 2:427–41. Hincmar himself said that "illa capitula" were intended for Charles the Bald too: MGH Epp 8:64.

[140] See Peter R. McKeon, *Hincmar of Laon and Carolingian Politics* (Urbana, Ill., 1978), pp. 120–31.

what we tend to think of as exclusively ecclesiastical causes célèbres: the indictment of Archbishop Wenilo of Sens,[141] the arguments for and against the promotion of Wulfad to the see of Bourges,[142] the debates over Lothar II's divorce[143] were all essentially political issues that were discussed not only in terms of canon law.

If polemic was produced in the ninth century for all those — kings, higher clergy, and lay aristocrats — involved in affairs of state, it follows that we should be chary of any assumption that laymen as such had any distinctive outlook on politics, still less "secular" political ideas that could be seen as in any sense opposed to the much better evidenced clerical ideology of this period. On the one hand, the views and values of lay political actors had been and continued to be heavily influenced by the church; on the other, churchmen themselves were important actors in Carolingian politics and in practice, notably in the organization of resources to provide military service for themselves and for the kingdom, shared the priorities of other magnates and their followers.[144] Layman and cleric alike operated with and within the relationships and values of kin ties, patronage, and personal service. As Patrick Wormald has reminded us, the audiences of Bede and of *Beowulf* were often one and the same, and the "ancient songs" were appreciated by some inmates of monasteries as well as those of lordly mead-halls.[145] Disputes arose between particular lay and ecclesiastical parties over the exploitation of lands, especially when a church claimed restitution: such a dispute is recorded, for instance, in the *Annals* of St. Bertin for 846, here reflecting a Rheims tradition and a Rheims grievance.[146] But it is wrong to generalize this into a great divide between "episcopate" and "lay aristocracy" in the

[141] MGH Capit 300, 2:450–53.

[142] See Ferdinand Lot, "Une année du règne de Charles le Chauve, année 866," *Le moyen âge* 15 (1902), 393–438 at 407–21 (reprinted in *Recueil . . . Lot,* 2:429–43); Devisse, *Hincmar,* 2:600–628, and interesting information on Wulfad's earlier career ibid., 1:98–99.

[143] Lay members of Lothar II's entourage seem to have participated actively in these: see Hincmar, *De divortio Lotharii et Tetbergae,* PL 125:746, 754, 756.

[144] Notably apparent in ecclesiastical nepotism and in the mobilizing of kinsmen in the military service of churches: see "The Church's Military Service", above, p. 124.. Among recent works pioneering a sociology of the ninth-century West Frankish church are Oexle, "Ebroin," and *Forschungen zu monastischen und geistlichen Gemeinschaften im Westfrankischen Bereich* (Munich, 1978); and Michel Sot, "Historiographie épiscopale et modèle familiale en occident au IXe siècle," *Annales* 33 (1978), 433–49.

[145] See above, n. 33.

[146] AB, p. 52. This passage looks to me like a Hincmarian interpolation in Prudentius's text. It should be linked with the note prefacing the capitula of the Council of Epernay (MGH Capit 2:261), another Rheims production. I hope to discuss this text more fully elsewhere. Lot and Halphen, *Règne de Charles le Chauve,* pp. 162–66, saw in this episode a conflict between "les évêques" and "les grands." For a similar view see Walter Ullmann, *The Carolingian Renaissance and the Idea of Kingship* (London, 1969), p. 112, and, carefully nuanced and with due account of the complex issues involved in restitutions, J. M. Wallace-Hadrill, *The Frankish Church,* p. 271.

West Frankish kingdom. In terms of ninth-century practice, each successive political crisis showed that two such separate and rival elites did not exist.

But what is true of practical politics may also be true at an ideological level. Nithard was a Christian layman who believed in miracles and appreciated the ritual services of bishops. He held principles about political morality: it was wrong to put private before public interest. There is no reason to think Nithard unrepresentative in these respects. Yet, paradoxically, it is through a selective reliance on Nithard's testimony that historians have sought to justify some very harsh judgments on the greed and egoism of the ninth-century aristocracy.[147] Those historians have taken insufficient account of the role of precisely such accusations in ninth-century polemic: it was as much standard practice then to accuse your political opponents, ecclesiastical or lay, of egoism[148] as it is nowadays to accuse them of defending class rather than national interests. I do not believe that Nithard was unique in caring for what he saw as the common good in 842–43 and he himself makes no claim to have been so in 841. Book 4's sour grapes should not be allowed to spoil our palates: there is much in the *Histories*, especially in book 3, to support the view that for many if not all Frankish nobles the experience of participation in the politics of Carolingian courts and assemblies had indeed fostered an awareness of "public utility" and that the language of the capitularies, like that of the Strasbourg oaths, reflected that reality in addition to clerical ideals. In terms of values and expectations, then, there is no sharp distinction to be drawn between Nithard's private history and his public *Histories*.

The second main area on which Nithard's work throws welcome light is the actual workings of Carolingian politics. Here many major points have already been picked up by historians, some indeed almost exclusively documented by the *Histories* (such is the extent of our dependence on Nithard). A good example is Nithard's indication of the political importance of the fisc in Francia. (An explanation for his lack of interest in fisc lands elsewhere has been suggested above.) We are shown why the *regnum*, that is, the Frankish heartland between the Seine and the Rhine, was the real object of conflict between Carolingians, both in Nithard's own time and long after (when other rivals were also involved), and why the practice of dividing the fisc in Francia persisted despite some attractions of the unitary alternative. Nithard shows, too, how Frankish nobles were able to exploit the Carolingians' conflicts, how for each king the provision of honors to satisfy faithful men was an imperative made only more pressing by divisions of the *regnum Francorum*, and how these divisions were the product of complex transactions

[147] See, for instance, the comments à propos Nithard, *Histoire* 4.6–7, pp. 142–43, of James W. Thompson, *The Dissolution of the Carolingian Fisc* (Berkeley, Calif., 1935), p. 44 with n. 63; or Devisse, *Hincmar*, 1:287.

[148] So, Paschasius on Bernard, Thegan on Ebbo, Lupus on Odulf, Hincmar on Rothad, etc.

between nobles as well as between nobles and kings and between kings themselves.[149] Carolingian "solicitings," on which no source is more informative than Nithard, reveal a dependence of kings on aristocratic support that was certainly one, and perhaps the most conspicuous, side of Carolingian consensus politics.

But Nithard also invites us to look at the other side of the coin, showing us nobles dependent on the collaboration and favor of the king.[150] If consensus could be a cloak for aristocractic pressure, it could also be an instrument of royal control; and if honors could be granted, they could also be withheld. I have suggested that Nithard's own career illustrates some forms of this aristocratic dependence. Other cases are explicitly described in the *Histories*. Nithard shows how dangerous it was for Bernard of Septimania to be the object of Charles the Bald's ill will, and he makes it clear that Bernard's son William could gain possession of some lands in Burgundy only with the permission of the king.[151] These cases may be untypical insofar as Bernard had rebelled against Charles's father and later supported Charles's rival Pippin II. Yet what is remarkable is that Nithard presents Bernard as an isolated and almost rootless figure in the latter part of his career when he lacked strong or consistent royal support,[152] for this picture is curiously at odds with that given by most modern historians who stress, instead, Bernard's membership of the Burgundy-based family of the "historic Nibelungen"[153] — the allegedly archetypical Frankish noble clan. Any assessment of the dependence of the West Frankish aristocracy on the king will be conditioned by our view of how that aristocracy was organized and functioned, in other words, by the extent of our willingness to generalize, or even retain, the "Nibelungen model."[154] Does Nithard offer any guidance here?

[149] On the above points much light has been thrown by Ganshof, "Zur Entstehungsgeschichte"; Classen, "Verträge"; Schlesinger, "Auflösung"; Tellenbach, "Die geistigen und politischen Grundlagen."

[150] On *Königsnähe* (closeness to the king) in general, see Schmid, "Zur Problematik" (cited above, n. 3), and "Über die Struktur des Adels im frühen Mittelalter," *Jahrbuch für fränkische Landesforschung* 19 (1959), 1–23, translated in *The Medieval Nobility*, ed. Reuter, pp. 37–59, especially 39–40.

[151] Nithard, *Histoire* 2.5, pp. 50–52; 3.2, p. 84. (On the latter passage, see above, n. 116.)

[152] Compare the reflections of Wollasch, "Eine adlige Familie," pp. 170–77.

[153] Levillain, "Nibelungen historiques," 1, pp. 361–63, and 2, pp. 11–12.

[154] See the interesting historiographical survey by Jane Martindale, "The French Aristocracy in the Early Middle Ages: A Reappraisal," *Past and Present* 75 (1977), 5–45, especially 18–20; and Constance B. Bouchard, "The Origins of the French Nobility: A Reassessment," *American Historical Review* 86 (1981), 501–32. The politics of Charles the Bald's reign were long ago depicted in terms of rivalries between aristocratic clans; see Joseph Calmette, *La diplomatie carolingienne* (Paris, 1901), pp. 42–47. More recent commentators have tended to follow this account, especially with reference to the events of 858: for instance, Devisse, *Hincmar*, 1:305; Rosamond McKitterick, *The Frankish Kingdoms under the Carolingians, 751–987* (London, 1983), p. 184. See also Brunner, *Oppositionelle Gruppen*, pp. 120–36.

Régine Hennebicque in a recent paper has argued that "a fundamental element" of the structure of the aristocracy in the ninth century was "a familial group comprising several large families"; as an example of the latter category of large cognatic family she has cited "the Nithards-Richharts-Engilberts." Further, she has proposed a model in which such "infrastructural" families at the level of the region were bonded into the edifice of the Carolingian Empire by a "superstructure" of "great personages" operating at supraregional level, instanced in the case of "the Nithards" by Eberhard of Friuli, son-in-law of Louis the Pious.[155] Hennebicque documents her "Nithards" exclusively from charters and memorial books, but it may be worth asking if our Nithard gives any evidence for familial structures on Hennebicque's model. At first glance the *Histories* seems quite uninformative: none of "the Nithards-Richharts-Engilberts" identified by Hennebicque in the Rhineland, Alsace, and Alamannia is mentioned by Nithard while Eberhard, who according to Hennebicque was the "chef de file" of Nithard's familial group, is mentioned only once, without comment, as one of *Lothar's* envoys in 842.[156] Should we infer that Nithard had chosen in 840 to act outside a "normal structure" or that other factors conditioned his choice? When we find Nithard in book 4 placing himself very positively in what looks like a "small family,"[157] should we begin to doubt whether "large familial groups" were "fundamental" political structures at all?

Such skepticism might be premature. We cannot be quite sure that Nithard does not also refer to a "large family" in book 4 and, more impor-

[155] Régine Hennebicque, "Structures familiales et politiques au IXe siècle: Un groupe familial de l'aristocratie franque," *Revue historique* 265 (1981), 289–333, especially 298–99, 309–10. This fine paper represents a long overdue attempt to examine the workings of kin groupings through ninth-century politics. Changes over time are sensitively observed. But it is probably also necessary to differentiate between the regions covered in the blanket term "Carolingian society." See below, n. 157. To the Nithards mentioned by Hennebicque may be added a *miles* of Lothar II: AB, p. 120; and a monk of Prüm in the 840s: Lupus, *Correspondance*, ep. 68, 2:2.

[156] Nithard, *Histoire* 4.3, p. 124.

[157] Ibid. 4.5, p. 138: "Angilbert was a man sprung from a family (*familia*) well known at that time, while Madhelgaud, Richard, and he were of one progeny (*progenies*) and were held deservedly in great regard by the great Charles." (Note the way in which *Königsnähe* complements genealogical distinction.) In my translation "while" renders "autem," a conjunction habitually used by Nithard to indicate a degree of separation, if not quite of contrast, between two statements (for examples, see 1.3, p. 8; 2.6, p. 54; 3.5, p. 108; 4.2, p. 122). Thus a distinction is implied between the meanings of *familia* and *progenies,* the latter indicating a more restricted group. For *progenies* in other contemporary contexts, see Oexle, "Ebroin," pp. 159–61, 196 with n. 296. But Oexle finds difficulty in defining the dimensions of this group, and even in deciding whether or not it was agnatic: ibid., p. 161, n. 110. The use of the term *Verwandtenkreis* enables Oexle to bypass the problem, though on p. 193 he seems to distinguish between the *Verwandtenkreis* of the Rorgonides and Ebroin's *progenies.* Aware of the artificiality of such "clan" names (p. 149: "the so-called 'Rorgonides' "), Oexle does not discuss the implications of the fact that the only contemporary designation which may possibly refer to such a "clan" in the West Frankish kingdom, the *cognatio Gozberti,* occurs in an East Frankish text: the *Annals* of Fulda, s.a. 854, p. 44.

tantly, we have to recall that his situation when he wrote this last book had changed in ways that could explain a new emphasis on his father's kin. At various points in his work Nithard mentions his connection with a series of powerful persons: first, the two Carolingians, Louis the Pious and Charles the Bald; at the end, his dead (but still powerful) saint-father, Angilbert; and in the crucial period 841 to mid-842, Adalard. The third of these connections, which I have argued played an important part in the shaping of Nithard's work, probably had a kinship component, but Nithard himself never hints at this: what he seems to want his audience to grasp is his service to Adalard, implying that what matters (or matters most) to him here is a patron-client relationship. One of the attractions of Hennebicque's model is that it accommodates such relationships within familial structures, on the assumption that great personages dispensed patronage to clients who were also their kinsmen. It would be going far beyond some rather tenuous evidence to claim that all patron-client ties were also kin ties, but it seems a plausible enough suggestion that kinship provided a basic pattern for this and other types of social and political bonding. As it happens we can trace in a little more detail the connections of Adalard with a man named Nithad, who may have been a kinsman of our Nithard but who is not identified in any document as a kinsman of Adalard. Clearly a much less important person than Adalard, Nithad can be shown to have had links with him over a period of about ten years (until his own death). During this time the two men's political allegiances seem to have moved in parallel from the West Frankish to the Middle Kingdom.[158] It is impossible to tell whether kinship

[158] Nithad first appears in 842 as a witness to a land judgment in favor of Prüm: *Urkundenbuch zur Geschichte der Mittelrheinischen Territorien,* ed. Heinrich Beyer (Koblenz, 1860), no. 103, p. 107. The land was part of a bequest by Count Richard, formerly an important court official of Louis the Pious. (An identification with the Richard of Nithard, *Histoire* 4.5, p. 138, is unlikely for these two Richards seem to have belonged to different generations. But they may have been kinsmen.) One of the executors was Adalard's brother Gerard (above, n. 22): MGH Diplomata Lothar I, no. 68, pp. 181–82. Nithad received a benefice from Charles the Bald in the Laonnois which was regranted him in propriety on 18 April 845: Tessier, *Recueil,* no. 69, 1:197–98. Tessier here expressed puzzlement to find Charles calling Nithad *fidelis noster* when he was "the count of Trier," that is, holder of a countship in Lothar's kingdom; but the evidence connecting Nithad with Trier dates only from 853, while he is called "count" only in a document of 960: Beyer, *Urkundenbuch,* nos. 83, p. 88, and 207, p. 287. Therefore there seems no reason to doubt that Nithad was Charles's *fidelis* in 845. On 7 March 845 Charles was at St. Quentin where Adalard was lay abbot: Tessier, *Recueil,* no. 68, pp. 195–96. Both Nithad and Adalard can be shown to have had connections subsequently with Prüm: Lupus, *Correspondance,* ep. 58, 1:224; MGH Diplomata Lothar I, nos. 127, 128, and Lothar II, no. 5. Finally Nithad's widow made a grant to St. Maximin, Trier, on 1 April 853 "presente Alardo comite," of lands near Verdun which she had been given by her husband. Nithad was perhaps an *amicus* or client of Adalard, who went with him to West Francia while retaining, like him, ties with Prüm and lands in what became Lothar's kingdom in 843. When in 849 Adalard became Lothar's *fidelis* and thereafter, presumably, normally resident on lands in the Middle Kingdom, Nithad seems to have followed suit. Werner, "Untersuchungen," 4, pp. 155–56, n. 39, argues convincingly that Adalard's move should be seen not as a "defection" from Charles but as part of the rapprochement between

or the political friendship of patron and client bound these careers; both may well have done so, and the modes of personal interaction in either case were closely similar. It seems likely that the link between Adalard and Nithard was comparable to this. Perhaps Adalard rather than Eberhard should be regarded as Nithard's "chef de file."

But if so, what is significant is the absence of any other indication in Nithard's case, by contrast with Nithad's, of membership in anything like a "familial group" focused on Adalard. When he felt that Adalard had failed him as a patron, Nithard's mind turned to his close paternal kin. Rather than exploit putative connections with "the Nithards" in the Rhineland or Alamannia, Nithard withdrew to his father's monastery, which Richbod's presence had probably made something less than a comfortable home-base. When both the king and the patron he had served seemed indifferent to his plight, Nithard, it seems, was left with few resources and no alternative means of realizing his own best interests. As in the case of Bernard of Septimania, we are left with the impression of a rather lonely figure and perhaps with a more general awareness that the social support available to a noble in the Carolingian world could be more conditional, more limited, than serried ranks of charter witnesses and memorial book entries might have led us to suppose. A man might not be constrained in his political alignments either by a vast familial group or by the framework of a "small family"; he might be free to claim "his law and justice," to seek a patron and honors where he would. But if he miscalculated or overplayed his hand, kin ties might offer little protection from "the blasts of fortune." We have seen that fraternal solidarity was often more honored in the breach than in the observance, and if the "small family" could be riven with conflict, there is little to suggest that loyalties within "clans" transcended competing private interests any more effectively. From the standpoint of Carolingian kings noble familial structures might be as useful in their weaknesses as in their strengths, for they would offer only limited resistance to royal "rule and wrath" directed against an unfaithful man. But from the standpoint of a noble individual, as Nithard's case shows, those weaknesses could be an additional source of vulnerability. Systems of kinship and lordship alike generated expectations whose fulfillment could never be guaranteed: hence behind the public *Histories* a private history that is, if not quite a tragedy, at least a cautionary tale.

Charles and Lothar in February 849. If the move appealed to Adalard because of his landholdings in the Middle Kingdom, similar considerations probably applied to Nithad.

APPENDIX 1

The *participes secretorum* (Nithard, *Histoire* 2.5, p. 52) of Charles the Bald in 840–41

The following may be regarded as likely members of this group:

(1) Adalgar: Nithard, *Histoire* 2.2, p. 40, and 3.4, p. 96. Possibly to be identified with the count mentioned in AB, s.a. 838, p. 25, and probably (as Stuart Airlie kindly suggests to me) with Charles's envoy sent to negotiate with rebels in 856: MGH Capit 262, 2:279. Perhaps the same man as the *missus* in the Thérouanne area in 854: MGH Capit 260, 2:275.

(2) Hugh: Nithard, *Histoire* 2.3, p. 44. An identification with Abbot Hugh of St. Quentin (above, n. 23) is unconvincing, as has been shown by Grierson, "Hugues de Saint-Bertin" (cited above, n. 23), pp. 246–48. But this man could be the Hugh mentioned by Lupus, *Correspondance,* ep. 17, 1:100. From the context here, Hugh sounds like an Aquitanian magnate. Perhaps he is the same man as the addressee of Lupus, *Correspondance,* ep. 131, 2:212–14. The identification of the latter as count of Sens, though frequently met with in the secondary literature, is hypothetical.

(3) Adalard: Nithard, *Histoire* 2.3, p. 44. See above, n. 22.

(4) Gerard: Nithard, *Histoire* 2.3, p. 44. Probably identifiable as another Aquitanian magnate mentioned by Lupus, *Correspondance,* ep. 17, 1:98, and perhaps ep. 26, 1:122. Levillain dates the latter to 842 but it could just as well belong to February 841. According to Ademar of Chabannes, *Chronique,* ed. Jules Chavanon (Paris, 1897), p. 132, a son of "Count Gerard of the Auvergne" was made count of Poitou in 839. The Astronomer, *Vita Hludovici* 61, MGH SS 2:645, says Count Gerard was the *gener* of Pippin I of Aquitaine. In the light of Ademar's statement, implying that Gerard's marriage should be dated to the early 820s at the latest, the term *gener* has been translated as "brother-in-law" by Werner, "Nachkommen," pp. 450–51. But Ademar's unreliability for this period has been demonstrated by John B. Gillingham, "Ademar of Chabannes and the History of Aquitaine in the Reign of Charles the Bald," in *Charles the Bald,* ed. Gibson and Nelson, pp. 3–14. Discounting Ademar's statement about Gerard's son, the most natural interpretation of the Astronomer's *gener* would be "son-in-law," this (and not brother-in-law) being its usual meaning in classical and Carolingian Latin. A daughter of Pippin I could have been of marriageable age by 835/36, and her marriage to a prominent Aquitanian a politic move on Pippin's part. In the revised version (C text) of his chronicle Ademar says that Gerard was killed (along with the other *gener* of Pippin, Count Rather) at Fontenoy: Lot and Halphen, *Règne de Charles le Chauve,* p. 35, n. 4. If this statement is also discounted, then the Count Gerard of Lupus, ep. 26, could still be identified as the Aquitanian count even if this letter is dated to 842. The Gerard mentioned in Nithard, *Histoire* 2.3, p. 44, immediately after Adalard, is identified by Lauer, n. 3, as Adalard's brother, Count Gerard of Paris. But Nithard mentions the latter by name and title a few lines further on, by implication distinguishing him from this other Gerard.

(5) Egilo: Nithard, *Histoire* 2.3, p. 44. Perhaps the count mentioned in AB, s.a. 838, p. 25.

(6) Warin: Nithard, *Histoire* 2.5, p. 50. Burgundian count who joined Charles in January 841. See further ibid. 2.6, p. 56; 4.4, p. 132, and for his earlier career, 1.5, p. 22.

(7) Theutbald: Nithard, *Histoire* 2.5, p. 50. Joined Charles (with Warin) from Burgundy. Assumed by previous commentators to have been a count. I suggest

identifying as bishop of Langres (see Louis Duchesne, *Fastes épiscopaux de l'ancienne Gaule,* 3 vols. [Paris, 1907–15], 1:189).

(8) Louis: Lupus, *Correspondance,* epp. 14–16 and 25, 1:90–96, 120–22. A son of Charlemagne's daughter Rotrud. Charles the Bald's archchancellor. I see no reason to think he had been chosen for Charles in 839 by Louis the Pious, as suggested by Grierson, "Hugues de Saint-Bertin," p. 251. On Louis's career, see Tessier, *Recueil,* 3:38–42. Nithard, curiously, does not mention him, but Lupus shows him to have been influential in Charles's entourage in 840–41.

(9) Ebroin: Lupus, *Correspondance,* ep. 23, 1:114. Bishop of Poitiers. Charles's archchaplain. Also unmentioned by Nithard. But for his political importance, see Oexle, "Ebroin," pp. 161–68.

(10) Wenilo: Lupus, *Correspondance,* ep. 26, 1:122–28. Archbishop of Sens, apparently Charles's own appointee as early as 837: *Libellus contra Wenilonem,* MGH Capit 300.1, 2:451.

(11) Rainald: Lupus, *Correspondance,* ep. 17, 1:98. Probably identifiable with the duke of Nantes mentioned in AB, s.a. 843, p. 44. Perhaps among the men from Aquitaine who came with the empress Judith to join Charles shortly before Fontenoy: Nithard, *Histoire* 2.9, p. 66.

(12) Lupus: his presence with Charles on 10 May 841 is implicit in Tessier, *Recueil,* 1, no. 3. Hence he was probably still with Charles at Fontenoy (25 June). But his letters, *Correspondance,* epp. 14–25, 1:90–122, show that he had not been with Charles continuously over the preceding nine months. The composition of Charles's entourage naturally fluctuated.

(13) Nithard himself.

To these may perhaps be added Modoin, bishop of Autun (Lupus, *Correspondance,* ep. 17, 1:98), but he may have died before the end of 840; and Jonas, bishop of Orléans, but his death date is also uncertain (see Levillain's note to Lupus, *Correspondance,* ep. 20, 1:106–7).

The following are only documented as receiving patronage from Charles after Fontenoy, but may have been in his camp before the battle: Ingelbert, abbot of Fosses (Tessier, *Recueil,* 1, no. 4, dated 1 September 841); Nibelung (ibid., no. 16, dated 13 January 843); Vivian (ibid., no. 19, dated 18 February 843, where Vivian appears as *impetrator* and, for the first time, as chamberlain); Rabano (Nithard, *Histoire* 3.3, p. 90).

Appendix 2

The date of Nithard's death

The form of the date given in Nithard's epitaph (see above, n. 120), "the eighteenth Kalends of June," could be understood as meaning 15 May, but does not exist in strict Latinity. The learned author is unlikely to have made a slip. Therefore, either a common scribal error was made in the unique manuscript giving "Iunii" by mistake for "Iulii" or the author used the curious dating form for reasons of poetic meter. The emendation entailed by the former assumption was made by Ludwig Traube, MGH Poet 3:311, and by both Müller and Lauer in their editions of Nithard (Müller, pp. vi–vii; Lauer, p. vi and n. 1). It produces a "true" date of 14 June — the date of the battle of the Angoumois: Lot and Halphen, *Règne de Charles le Chauve,* p. 113, n. 1.

F. L. Ganshof, "Note critique sur la biographie de Nithard," *Mélanges Paul Thomas* (Bruges, 1930), pp. 335–44, argued against emending the text of the epitaph and preferred to read "15 May." He rejected the association of Nithard's death with the battle of the Angoumois for two main reasons. First, Nithard's name does not appear on the casualty list in the *Annals* of St. Bertin. Second, Nithard could not have held the office of *rector,* that is, abbot, of St. Riquier, as the epitaph states he did, until after the battle, since according to the *Annals* of St. Bertin, Richbod the previous abbot was still in office when killed in that battle. Ganshof's argument was accepted by Löwe, *Deutschlands Geschichtsquellen,* 3:356. But both objections can in fact be answered.

First, Ganshof presupposed that "a personage of Nithard's importance" would have been mentioned in the *Annals* of St. Bertin. But in 844 Nithard may no longer have been "important" in the sense of being influential at Charles's court. The fact that his death (whenever it occurred) was recorded only at St. Riquier could be seen as a consequence of his retirement there from late 842 onwards. Further, the *Annals* of St. Bertin should not be regarded any longer in 844 as a quasiofficial source; instead it reflects the personal concerns of its authors, Prudentius, now bishop of Troyes (see Nelson, "The Annals of St. Bertin"). The *Annals* mentions by name only four of those killed in the Angoumois, one of these a son of Charlemagne (Hugh), another a grandson (Richbod). But Prudentius may have mentioned them and not Nithard because of some personal connection; compare his mention of a third casualty, Count Rabanus: Werner, "Untersuchungen," 4, pp. 160 and 165 with n. 79. Prudentius may also have found the deaths in battle of the churchmen Hugh and Richbod especially shocking. Since the battle resulted from a surprise attack, they may have been noncombatants (as implied in Hugh's case by his epitaph, MGH Poet 2:139).

Ganshof's second argument turned on Richbod's tenure of the abbacy of St. Riquier until 14 June 844. Charles the Bald's archchancellor Louis was abbot on 27 September 844 (Tessier, *Recueil,* 1, no. 58) and on 29 March 845 (Ganshof, "Note critique," p. 343, n. 1). Charles's maternal uncle Rudolf became abbot later in 845 or early in 846 and remained so until his death in 866 (MGH Poet 106, 3:337–38, with Traube's comments at p. 269). So if Nithard died on a 15 May before 853 (when his epitaph was written), where could his abbacy fit in? Ganshof suggested that it should be fitted into a three- or four-week period in April–May 845 and that Nithard was killed in battle against the Vikings in Ponthieu on 15 May 845. In support of this suggestion, Ganshof, "Note critique," p. 343 with n. 4, cited the *Chronicle* of Hariulf, ed. Lot, p. 102, where Nithard was said to have held office only "paucissimis diebus." But Hariulf, writing in the eleventh century, probably based his words on the epitaph's "nomen rectoris qui modico tenuit" and should not therefore be treated as reflecting any kind of independent "monastic tradition," as surmised by Ganshof.

An alternative solution had been proposed by Lauer, *Histoire,* p. v: he suggested that Nithard could have functioned as lay abbot alongside Richbod as regular abbot, between 842 and 844. Ganshof rejected this solution as anachronistic, claiming that such a double abbacy was virtually unknown before the tenth century and was quite distinct from the traditional Carolingian phenomenon of the lay abbacy. But it is now known that lay abbacies were in effect an innovation of the 830s and 840s: Franz Felten, "Laienäbte in der Karolingerzeit," in *Mönchtum, Episkopat und Adel zur Gründungszeit des Klosters Reichenau,* ed. Arno Borst (Sigmaringen, 1974), pp. 397–431. The institutional arrangements made to cope with them are rarely attested in the ninth century, not least because of ecclesiastical writers' reticence on such uncanonical practices. But there are two likely cases in the 840s: at St. Colombe, Sens (Tessier, *Recueil,* 1, no. 102, and see Emile Lesne, *L'origine des menses dans le temporel des églises et des monastères de France au IXe siècle* [Lille, 1910], p. 75), and at Cormêry, daughterhouse of St. Martin, Tours (Tessier, *Recueil,* 1, nos. 20, 60–63, and especially 131). The further case of St. Germain, Auxerre, cited but considered doubtful by Ganshof, "Note critique," p. 341 with n. 3, seems more likely in the light of the evidence discussed by Joachim Wollasch, "Das Patrimonium Beati Germani in Auxerre," in *Studien und Vorarbeiten,* ed. Tellenbach, p. 209 with nn. 114 and 115. Lauer's guess in the case of St. Riquier is therefore more attractive than Ganshof allowed. And it becomes still more so in the light of the possibility (above, p. 224 and n. 123) that Richbod was Lothar's appointee as abbot. The coexistence of a (lay) abbot appointed by Charles with a (regular) abbot appointed by Lothar seems a likely enough situation in this region at this time. The claims of both incumbents would have been strengthened by their being Charlemagne's grandsons: neither would be easy to oust. But given Nithard's special position as Angilbert's son, it would be naive to suppose that the coexistence was happy. That Richbod and Nithard died in the same battle has a certain poignancy.

10

NATIONAL SYNODS, KINGSHIP AS OFFICE, AND ROYAL ANOINTING: AN EARLY MEDIEVAL SYNDROME

PROFESSOR Gabriel Le Bras, a great pioneer in the field of historical sociology, has spoken of the early medieval Church in a bizarre but effective metaphor as 'a dismembered body striving to reunite itself'.[1] The essential task of the hierarchy within each national Church[2] was one of co-ordination—by means of law, doctrine, and the standardization of worship. In the fragmented world of the barbarian kingdoms, the distinctive feature of each episcopate was its ideology of cohesion, the more ardently propounded when social crisis was particularly acute, as in the seventh-century Visigothic kingdom, or the war-torn West Francia of the 830s and 840s. This ideology was, moreover, often intimately associated with movements of monastic reform. Its influence penetrated down into the rural base of society through episcopal visitations, preaching, and provincial councils. To trace all the elements in these complex processes of interaction and change would encompass that much-needed sociology of the early medieval Church which Max Weber did not live to write and no scholar has yet produced.[3] In this paper, as its title

[1] 'Sociologie de l'Église dans le Haut Moyen Âge', in *Settimana Spoleto*, 7, II (1960), 598.

[2] On the early medieval *Landeskirchen*, see H. von Schubert, *Grundzüge der Kirchengeschichte*, 10th edn. rev. E. Dinkler, Tübingen 1937, 130 ff.; H. F. Feine, *Kirchliche Rechtsgeschichte*, 4th edn., Weimar 1964, 147 ff.; and W. Schlesinger, *Beitrage zur deutschen Verfassungsgeschichte des Mittelalters*, Göttingen 1963, 259, pointing out their character as *Gentilkirchen*. For the term 'national church', see the sensible remarks of T. Schieffer and F. L. Ganshof in *Settimana Spoleto*, 7, I (1960), 312 f.

[3] Cf. the Introduction by T. Parsons to Weber's *The Sociology of Religion*, London 1965, xiv; and suggestions scattered throughout Weber's work: e.g. *Max Weber on Law in Economy and Society*, ed. and trans. E. Shils and M. Rheinstein,

implies, my very limited objective is to isolate and examine certain recurrent phenomena and to point to some hitherto unnoticed connections.

Some historians have depicted the bishops of the early Middle Ages as secular magnates wearing different hats, and thus have seen their activities as one among other forms of *Adelsherrschaft*.[1] It is true that bishops were drawn very largely from noble families. But equally significant is the fact that they were royal nominees, and in the periods I shall be considering, kings preferred to seek their bishops in the monasteries.[2] If such promotions can hardly be termed channels of social mobility, they nevertheless created one important precondition for a separation of episcopal from secular interests.

Within each kingdom, the bishops shared in government, usually at the local level, but they also had specialized functions as exponents of ritual and setters of norms in a Christian society. The main limitation on the effectiveness of their performance of these integrative roles was imposed by the incomplete substitution of Christian for pagan beliefs and values:[3] it was this *ignorantia*, the

Cambridge, Mass., 1954, 250 ff., and *From Max Weber: Essays in Sociology*, ed. and trans. H. H. Gerth and C. W. Mills, London 1947, 245 ff., 295 ff. See now also the masterly survey of Le Bras, 'Sociologie de l'Église'; E. Troeltsch, *The Social Teaching of the Christian Churches*, trans. O. Wyon, London 1931, I, 214 ff., and W. Stark, *The Sociology of Religion: A Study of Christendom*, London 1966, are stimulating, but deal only sketchily with the early medieval period.

1 This approach, first developed by A. Schulte, *Der Adel und die deutsche Kirche*, Stuttgart 1910 (mainly with reference to the later Middle Ages), has, however, corrected a tendency to divorce ecclesiastical history from its social environment. See also H. Mitteis, 'Formen der Adelsherrschaft im Mittelalter', in *Festschrift F. Schulz*, Weimar 1951, 226 ff. esp. 237; K. Bosl, *Frühformen der Gesellschaft*, Munich 1964, 93, 459; K. F. Werner, 'Bedeutende Adelsfamilien...', in *Karl der Grosse*, ed. H. Beumann, Düsseldorf 1965, I, 91 f.

2 Or among the clergy of the royal chapel: see H. Wieruzowski, 'Die Zusammensetzung des gallischen und fränkischen Episkopats bis zum Vertrag von Verdun (843)', in *Bonner Jahrbücher*, 127 (1922), 1–83. Werner, 'Bedeutende Adelsfamilien', 94, notes the break between Merovingian and Carolingian practice. For further evidence from Spain, Germany, and England, see the works of Thompson, Johnson, and Darlington cited below.

3 Copious evidence is adduced by E. A. Thompson, *The Goths in Spain*, Oxford 1969, 308 ff.; J. A. Cabaniss, *Agobard of Lyons*, Syracuse 1953, 20 ff.; K. Hauck, 'Geblütsheiligkeit', in *Liber Floridus. Festschrift P. Lehmann*, St Ottilien 1950, 187 ff.; with special reference to kingship, F. Heiler, 'Fortleben und Wand-

cultural barrier to social cohesion, which bishops explicitly set out to combat by means of the *lux conciliorum*.[1] In the national synods of the early Middle Ages, the bishops went into action. These assemblies, in which, despite the presence in some cases of lay participants, the higher clergy formed the overwhelming majority, were convoked by kings to deliberate and act on problems of nation-wide importance. By their very existence, they provided a definite organization for the whole episcopal group: the hierarchy in this respect presents a striking contrast to the lay magnates, who could never be said to have formed anything so precise as an élite.[2] Repeated meetings over time, collective action, and the

lungen des antiken Gottkönigtums im Christentum', in *The Sacral Kingship*, Leiden 1959, 543 ff.; and W. A. Chaney, 'Paganism to Christianity in Anglo-Saxon England', in *Early Medieval Society*, ed. S. Thrupp, New York 1967, 67 ff. See now also J. Le Goff, 'Culture cléricale et traditions folkloriques dans la civilisation mérovingienne', in *Annales ESC*, 22 (1967), 780 ff. On integration and pattern-maintenance in social systems, see T. Parsons, *Societies*, Englewood Cliffs 1966, 11 and 24 ff. It seems to me that the early medieval Church performed both these functions, and that the Parsonian paradigm involves a certain over-schematization which actually diminishes its analytic usefulness for the historian.

1 Conc. Tol. XI (a provincial synod), prologue, in *PL* 84, 451: 'annosa series temporum subtracta luce conciliorum non tam vitia auxerat quam matrem omnium errorum ignorantiam otiosis mentibus ingerebat'. Cf. Tol. IV, *ibid.* 366: 'de qualitate conciliorum'. See also the Anglo-Saxon *Polity* of *c.* 1000, ed. and trans. B. Thorpe, *Ancient Laws*, I, 428, c. x. '*Incipit de synodo:* It is incumbent on bishops in the synod first of all to consider about unanimity and true concord among themselves, and how they may before all things exalt Christianity and most effectually suppress heathenism.' For synods as 'charismatic assemblies', see N. Baynes, *Byzantine Studies and Other Essays*, London 1955, 111; cf. H. Barion, *Das fränkisch-deutsche Synodalrecht des Frühmittelalters*, Bonn 1931, 110 ff.: 'nur Organe der Kirchenleitung...nicht Versammlungen der Christen, ...sie (i.e. Synods) hierarchischen Charakter trugen und keine Zugeständnisse an demokratische Wünsche ihrer Untergebenen gemacht hätten'. On synods in general, see P. Hinschius, *Das Kirchenrecht der Katholiken und Protestanten in Deutschland*, Berlin 1869 etc., III, 539 ff.

2 On the distinction between an élite and a wider (unorganized) ruling class, see R. Sereno, *The Rulers*, Leiden 1962, 99 ff., and the penetrating study of T. B. Bottomore, *Elites and Society*, London 1966, esp. 41 f. The fluidity of the ruling stratum and the various possibilities for achieving social status in early medieval kingdoms have been discussed by R. Boutruche, *Seigneurie et Féodalité*, Paris 1959, 147 ff.; Bosl, *Frühformen der Gesellschaft*, 156 ff.; F. Graus, *Volk, Herrscher und Heiliger im Reich der Merowinger*, Prague 1965, 200 ff. A clearly defined aristocracy with its own characteristic ethos and system of status-stratification

articulation of common concerns fostered a conscious solidarity on the part of the bishops, and a sense of responsibility for the leadership of their whole society within the wider Church of Christendom. We have to thank Professor Ullmann for showing the full significance of this episcopal deployment of the 'hierocratic theme'.[1]

It has rightly been said that no-one in the Middle Ages wanted a weak king;[2] but it might be fair to add that the lay magnates wanted non-interfering kings, who could give a strong lead in time of crisis but would leave local control in noble hands. The bishops, by contrast, needed a strong and continuously active central power to establish Christian norms and habits of worship, and to protect the rural economic basis of the clergy's livelihood. In view of these divergent interests, it seems to me superficial to see the struggles of the bishops against the feudal laity as 'like against like'.[3] Bishops, especially if they had been monks, had interests *qua* bishops which cut them loose from their anchorage in the aristocracy.[4] In two of the four kingdoms which I shall be

came into existence only with the decline of the Carolingian Empire, and matured in the eleventh and twelfth centuries: see G. Tellenbach, 'Zur Erforschung des mittelalterlichen Adels (9–12 Jhdt.)', in *XII Congrès International des Sciences Historiques*, 1965, Rapports 1,318 ff., and G. Duby, 'The Diffusion of Cultural Patterns in Feudal Society', in *Past and Present*, 39 (1968), 3 ff. The distinction between ranking and stratification is stressed by M. Fried, *The Evolution of Political Society*, New York 1967, and by R. Wenskus, *Stammesbildung und Verfassung*, Köln-Graz 1961, 314 and n. 273: the social anthropologist and the historian, from quite different starting-points, reach similar conclusions. The methodological problem of dealing with periods for which no statistics are available has been ably discussed by M. K. Hopkins, 'Elite Mobility in the Roman Empire', in *Past and Present*, 32 (1965), 12 ff. His structural approach seems very useful also for medieval material.

1 See esp. his *The Growth of Papal Government in the Middle Ages*, 2nd edn., London 1962, 125 ff.

2 J. M. Wallace-Hadrill, *The Barbarian West, 400–1000*, London 1964, 144. Cf. Schlesinger, *Beitrage zur deutschen Verfassungsgeschichte*, 242, and *idem*, 'Die Auflösung des Karlsreiches', in *Karl der Grosse*, I, 833 ff.

3 So E. N. Johnson, *The Secular Activities of the German Episcopate*, Chicago 1932, 23.

4 See Barion, *Das fränkisch-deutsche Synodalrecht*, 332. I would rate very highly the importance of the episcopal ordination rite in aggregating individual to role. The idea of personal regeneration is central to this as to other status-changing rituals: hence the ease of liturgical transpositions from one initiation rite to another. See P. Oppenheim, 'Mönchsweihe und Taufritus', in *Miscellanea Liturgica in honorem L. C. Mohlberg*, Rome 1948, I, esp. 265 ff., and the suggestive remarks of G. H. Williams, *The Norman Anonymous*, Harvard 1951,

considering, the development through national synods of an episcopal group-identity led to the replacement of mixed lay and ecclesiastical councils by two separate assemblies;[1] while in the other two kingdoms, clergy alone deliberated and promoted legislation on doctrinal and ecclesiastical matters (which of course covered a very wide range).[2] If it was the king who, in the first instance, mobilized the episcopate as an instrument of royal government, national synods could nevertheless, like the sorcerer's broom, take on a life and character of their own. The bishops might seek to wield a more direct and extensive control by shifting the balance underlying their alliance with the monarchy: when kings were weak, bishops rallied to their support—but with their own idea of how kings should function. National synods provided the organization and operational means, synodal statements the ideology, which underpinned episcopal attempts to capture the commanding heights of the political structure.

I shall survey briefly the national synods of four areas: Visigothic Spain in the time of Isidore and Julian, West Francia in the time of Jonas and Hincmar, the East Francia of Salomo III and Hatto, and the England of Dunstan and Æthelwold. The crucial role played by leaders both in decision-making and propaganda was hardly a surprising feature of such sustained collective action. This leadership was often formalized as a metropolitan dignity,[3] but it was rooted in the consent and support of the episcopate as a

77 ff. and 158 f. Relevant and valuable in this context are M. Fortes, 'Ritual and Office', in *Essays in the Ritual of Social Relations*, ed. M. Gluckman, Manchester 1962, 53 ff., and the fundamental work of A. van Gennep, *The Rites of Passage*, ed. and trans. M. Vizedom and G. L. Caffee, Chicago 1960, esp. 93 ff.

[1] See Barion, *Das fränkisch-deutsche Synodalrecht*, 163 f. and 267 ff.; Hinschius, *Das Kirchenrecht*, III, 554.

[2] Cf. the ninth-century forger, Benedictus Levita, iii, 444: 'Ne laici intersint quando canonica iura ventilantur.' See on the Spanish councils, Thompson, *The Goths in Spain*, 278 ff., and on Anglo-Saxon clerical legislation, R. Darlington, 'Ecclesiastical Reform in the Late Old English Period', in *EHR*, 51 (1936), 385 ff.

[3] Thompson, *The Goths in Spain*, 275; E. Lesne, *La Hiérarchie Épiscopale*, Paris 1905, 95 ff. Metropolitan rivalries could later come to centre on the right to perform royal consecrations: cf. P. E. Schramm, *Der König von Frankreich*, 2nd edn., Weimar 1960, 113 ff., and U. Stutz, 'Die rheinischen Erzbischöfe und die deutsche Königswahl', in *Festchrift H. Brunner*, Weimar 1910, 57 ff.

whole: witness the lists of episcopal subscriptions to synodal decrees, or the collective episcopal conduct of royal consecrations. Professor Darlington has said of the late Old English episcopate: 'It is unlikely that all the members...were equally zealous in the pursuit of reform, but the more active prelates could influence their colleagues in synods.'[1]

Royal control over the seventh-century synods of Toledo was extensive, but not exclusive: the Church has been called 'the main stabilizing element in Visigothic society',[2] and in view of recurrent dynastic crises, the bishops were themselves vitally concerned to establish constitutional norms determining the nature and scope of royal power and the ways in which it might legitimately be acquired. These preoccupations are to be found in the writings of Isidore, and in the deliberations of the synod of 633 over which he presided.[3] The impact of monasticism on the episcopate at this time was strong, and the bishops were much concerned with the maintenance of standards of clerical discipline.[4] They were fully aware of the importance of synods, and criticized King Recceswinth for his failure to summon one during the last seventeen years of his reign[5]—a fact which speaks as tellingly for the extent of royal control as the criticism itself does for the existence of a distinctively hierarchical standpoint. The bishops, even when they could claim a major voice in elections, had reservations about elective kingship.[6] They wanted a stable monarchy which should be the Church's bulwark: hence their support of Wamba, 'offering himself', so the synodists of 675 believed, 'as a new

1 Darlington, 'Ecclesiastical Reform', 414.

2 J. N. Hillgarth, A Critical Edition of the *Prognosticum futuri saeculi* of St Julian of Toledo, Ph.D. Thesis, Cambridge 1956 (unpublished), XXVII. See also C. Sanchez Albornoz, 'El Aula Regia', in *Cuadernos de Historia de España*, 5 (1946), esp. 85 ff.

3 See M. Reydellet, 'La Conception du Souverain chez Isidore de Séville', in *Isidoriana*, ed. M. Diaz y Diaz, Leon 1961, 457 ff.

4 See E. Perez Pujol, *Historia de las Instituciones Sociales de la España Goda*, Valencia 1896, 106 ff., 143 ff.

5 Conc. Tol. XI, in *PL* 84, 451: the bishops complain of the ills of society 'quia ecclesiastici conventus non aderat disciplina...et quia non erat adunandorum pontificum ulla praeceptio'.

6 See J. Orlandis Rovira, 'La iglesia Visigoda y los problemas de la sucesion al trono en el siglo VII', in *Settimana Spoleto*, 7, 1 (1960), 333–51.

restorer of the Church's discipline in these our times'.[1] The many decrees of Visigothic councils aimed at protecting the Church's economic welfare show the bishops in direct and frequent conflict with the ambitions of secular magnates.[2]

As in seventh-century Spain, the West Frankish synods of the reign of Louis the Pious and the early years of Charles the Bald formed a coherent series: repeated meetings of the same bishops gave rise in time to what Hincmar would call *episcopalis unanimitas*.[3] At Paris in 829, the synodists gave lengthy consideration to the respective functions in Christian government of the king, as *minister*, and the bishops, as 'those who make known the will of God' (divinae voluntatis indices).[4] They were inspired by the ideals of Charlemagne's 'renovation' of society, and by the monastic reform to which Louis had lent his patronage:[5] his penance at Attigny in 822 was a demonstration of faith in personal renewal.[6] The synodists of the 840s attacked lay magnates who violated canon law in appropriating the Church's property. In face of the consistent development of episcopal policy, both royal reservations and lay reaction became more marked, and with the rebuff at Épernay in 847 when the king rejected much

1 *PL* 84, 465: 'ecclesiasticae disciplinae his nostris saeculis novus reparator occurrens'. It was thanks to Wamba that 'lux conciliorum renovata resplenduit', *ibid.* 451.

2 Cf. Thompson, *The Goths in Spain*, 308: 'On no single subject did the bishops spend more time than on the safeguarding of their churches' property.'

3 *De Divortio*, Quaest. 6, in *PL* 125, 757, apropos the reinstatement by the bishops of Louis the Pious in 834.

4 *MGH, Conc.*, II, 605 ff. See also J. Reviron, *Les idées politico-religieuses d'un evêque du IXe siècle: Jonas d'Orléans et son 'De institutione regia'*, Paris 1930, esp. 94 ff. and 113 ff. (Jonas' treatise was a restatement of the Paris decrees), and E. Delaruelle, 'En relisant le *De Institutione regia*...', in *Mélanges Halphen*, Paris 1951, 185 ff., esp. 187: 'C'est l'entrée en scène de l'épiscopat... organisé en corps constitué...se prononçant sur les grands interêts de l'État et de la chrétienté.' The conciliar activities of this period are discussed by Ullmann, *Growth*, 125 ff.

5 See H. Fichtenau, *Das karolingische Imperium*, Zurich 1949, 209 ff.; and the perceptive remarks of J. Winandy, 'L'Oeuvre de S. Benoît d'Aniane', in *Mélanges Bénédictins*, St Wandrille 1947, 235 ff. J. Semmler, 'Die monastische Gesetzgebung Ludwigs des Frommen', in *Deutsches Archiv*, 16 (1960), esp. 384 ff., links the *unitas* of monastic observance with the whole idea of a 'renovatio regni Francorum'.

6 Cf. Isidore, *De Offic.* II, xvii, 6, in *PL* 83, 803: 'Lacrymae enim poenitentium apud deum pro baptismate reputantur.'

of the synodists' programme,[1] the bishops were forced to recognize the inadequacy of synodal action without royal co-operation.

In East Francia half a century later, the synodal development was telescoped. Its beginnings can be seen in the 880s, when the synodists at Mainz promulgated almost verbatim the decrees issued at Paris in 829.[2] Again, a major preoccupation centred on the royal function within the Church: at Tribur in 895, the assembled bishops hailed King Arnulf as 'our pious and gentle comforter and energetic assistant',[3] while a chronicler summed up their work as directed 'against many laymen who were trying to weaken episcopal authority'.[4] During the minority of Arnulf's successor, bishops led by Hatto of Mainz were the real rulers of the kingdom.[5] At the Synod of Hohenaltheim in 916, episcopal interests emerged more clearly than ever opposed to those of the lay aristocracy.[6] In legislating 'for the strength of our kings' (de robore nostrorum regum), these bishops viewed the monarchy as a defence against both encroachments on ecclesiastical property and a more general fragmentation of authority.

Because of the difficulty of distinguishing between royal council and ecclesiastical synod in tenth-century England, it seems justifiable to regard the meetings of that council as analogous to

1 See F. Lot and L. Halphen, *Le Règne de Charles le Chauve*, Paris 1909, 74 ff.; P. Fournier and G. Le Bras, *Histoire des Collections Canoniques en Occident*, Paris 1931, i, 130 ff.; Barion, *Das fränkish-deutsche Synodalrecht*, 297 f.; now also C. De Clercq, 'La législation religieuse franque depuis l'avènement de Louis le Pieux jusqu'aux Fausses Décrétales', in *Revue du Droit Canonique*, 5 (1955), 280 ff. and 390 ff., and continued *ibid.* 6 (1966), 340 f.

2 Mansi, 18, 61 ff.; cf. *MGH Conc.* II, 649 ff.

3 *MGH Capit.* II, 213: 'pius et mitis consolator tamque strenuus adiutor'.

4 Regino, *Chron.*, ed. Kurze, *MGH, SS. rer. Germ.*, I, 606: 'contra plerosque seculares qui auctoritatem episcopalem imminuere tentabant'.

5 See A. Hauck, *Kirchengeschichte Deutschlands*, 3rd edn. Leipzig 1904, III, 7 ff.; R. Holtzmann, *Geschichte der sächsischen Kaiserzeit*, Munich 1943, 42 ff.; Schlesinger, *Beiträge*, 137 f. and 139 ff., and *idem*, 'Auflösung', 841 f.

6 The importance of this synod was ably shown by M. Hellmann, 'Die Synode von Hohenaltheim (916)', in *Die Entstehung des deutschen Reiches*, ed. H. Kampf, Darmstadt 1956, 289 ff. Significantly, the synodists of 916 drew heavily on Visigothic conciliar legislation transmitted by Pseudo-Isidore: see Ullmann, *The Carolingian Renaissance and the Idea of Kingship*, London 1969, 130.

the earlier Continental synods, which were, after all, in some cases also *concilia mixta*.[1] From the time of Athelstan (924–39),[2] at the core of the king's council was a group of bishops, whom the documents, especially those of Edgar's reign, show to have been constantly together around the king, active in legislation and administration, and most notably of all, in the promotion of monastic reform[3]—which since it involved the expropriation of laymen and the communalization of monks' property, brought them into sharp conflict with what Æthelwold castigated as *secularium prioratus*.[4] These bishops assigned a precise and crucial role to the king in the fulfilment of their aims, rightly seeing in royal *dominium* the one effective safeguard against the magnates' local lordship.

I would now like to draw attention to the fact that the rite of royal anointing made its appearance in each of these four national churches at the same period as the upsurge of synodal activity, and even more precisely, at a fairly advanced stage in the synodal sequence in each case. This is not the place to discuss the evidence in detail, but I have elsewhere tried to establish good grounds for pinpointing the date at which the rite was introduced in Spain to

1 See Darlington, *Ecclesiastical Reform*, 414 ff., and D. Whitelock, *English Historical Documents*, vol. I, London 1955, 68 f., as against C. J. Godfrey, *The Church in Anglo-Saxon England*, Cambridge 1962, 390.

2 Synod of Gratley, 928, Mansi, 18, 351. Cf. the evidence of conciliar activity (canons and charters) printed in D. Wilkins, *Concilia Magnae Britanniae et Hiberniae*, London 1737, 212 ff.

3 Surviving monastic charters are especially revealing: see e.g. those printed in W. Birch, *Cartularium Saxonicum*, III, nos. 1047, 1067, 1073, 1283. See also the legislation of Edgar in A. J. Robertson, *The Laws of the Kings of England*, Cambridge 1925, 20 ff., esp. the Code of 962–3 (IV Edgar), probably written by Dunstan: cf. Whitelock, *Documents*, 41.

4 *Reg. Concordia*, ed. T. Symons, 7. See now the valuable study of E. John, 'The king and the monks in the tenth century reformation', in *Bulletin of the John Rylands Library*, 42 (1959), 61–87. An interesting sidelight on the social issues involved may be found in a Canon of Edgar, ed. Thorpe, *Ancient Laws*, I, 396, c. 13: 'that no high-born priest despise the lower born; because if it be rightly considered, then are all men of one birth'. W. Stubbs, *Memorials of Saint Dunstan, RS*, London 1874, cvii, saw Dunstan's influence here. Cf. also the same idea of natural equality enshrined in the conciliar decrees of Paris (829): *MGH, Conc.*, II, 654.

672, in West Francia to 848, in East Francia to 911, and in England to 973.[1]

In each case, anointing almost immediately came to be regarded, not only by clerics but also by the candidates themselves, as indispensable to king-making. The Visigothic bishops declared in 681 that King Erwig 'regnandi per sacrosanctam unctionem suscepit potestatem'. Charles the Bald asserted in 859 that the archbishop of Sens, together with his episcopal colleagues, 'me...in regni regimine...perunxit'. For the East Frankish clergy, Henry I who had refused to be anointed in 918 was 'a sword without a handle'; in the rubrics of the 'Early German' *Ordo* (produced in East Francia in the first half of the tenth century) the *princeps designatus* only after his anointing is termed *rex*. The Anglo-Saxon Ælfric, writing at the close of the tenth century, used the unequivocal word *smyrað* (instead of the vague *gehalgod*) in reference to royal consecration, and stated that 'the king, after he is consecrated, then has dominion over his people'.[2] After Wamba (672), Charles the Bald (848), Otto I (936), and Edgar (973), no unanointed Christian king ruled in any of the four kingdoms.

Royal anointing has usually been interpreted as purely and simply a Christian substitute for the magical sanctions of pagan kingship:[3] its purpose has been seen as the conferment of a sacred character on the king, and thus the protection of monarchy from the attacks of unruly subjects: 'Thou shalt not touch the Lord's

1 For details, see my unpublished Ph.D. dissertation, Rituals of Royal Inauguration in Early Medieval Europe, Cambridge 1967, esp. 52 ff., 150 ff., 370 ff., and 393 ff.

2 Conc. Tol. XII, c. 1, in *PL* 84, 471; Charles' *Libellus...contra Wenilonem* (probably written at Hincmar's instigation), in *MGH Capit.* II, 451; the early tenth-century *Vita Udalrici*, in *MGH, SS*, IV, 389; the 'Frühdeutsch' *Ordo*, ed. C. Erdmann, *Forschungen zur politischen Ideenwelt des Frühmittelalters*, Berlin 1951, 83 ff.; Ælfric quoted in Whitelock, *Documents*, 851.

3 E.g. F. Kern, *Gottesgnadentum und Widerstandsrecht im früheren Mittelalter*, 2nd edn. rev. R. Buchner, Münster 1954, 66 ff.; Schramm, *Herrschaftszeichen und Staatssymbolik*, vol. I, Stuttgart 1954, 127; L. Rougier, 'Le Caractère Sacré de la royauté en France', in *The Sacral Kingship*, 609 ff.; the revealing discussion in *Settimana Spoleto*, 7, I (1960), 385 ff. Henry I, refusing the proffered anointing, and satisfied with a more familiar mundane title, saw the debit side of the bargain; cf. Widukind, *Rer. Gest. Saxon.*, I, 26, ed. Lohmann-Hirsch, 39: 'Satis michi est ut...*rex dicar et designer*.'

Anointed'. This interpretation, though partially accurate, by no means exhausts the meaning of the rite, and indeed overlooks the original essential purpose in the minds of those who designed and performed it. Consideration must be given to the position not only of the consecrated, but also of the consecrators. Kings, even when made rather than born, had hitherto received power through either designation or election; the handing over of insignia by predecessor or electors was the characteristic ritual form of succession. (We saw in the recent Investiture of the Prince of Wales a good example of such an entirely secular transference of power, with clerical blessings tacked on to the royal *fait accompli.*) But anointing meant that the candidate became dependent on the ecclesiastical hierarchy: dependent in what sense?

The idea was certainly not to make a bishop of the king, or to suggest a fusion of kingship with priesthood. It has too often been forgotten that episcopal ordination anointings were unknown at the period when royal anointing was introduced. There is no evidence of ordination anointing in Visigothic Spain and the rite was certainly not practised in Rome before the tenth century. The hands of priests may have been anointed in some parts of Gaul before 751, but the practice seems to have been discontinued, and then revived in West Francia when episcopal head-anointing was introduced in the ninth century.[1] To this day ordination anointing remains foreign to the Eastern Church.

The 'Anointed Ones' of the Old Testament were models for *all* Christians.[2] Although ideas of kingship as such might be strongly influenced by the prototypes of David and Solomon,[3] the

1 See G. Ellard, *Ordination Anointings in the Western Church before 1000 A.D.*, Cambridge, Mass., 1933; M. Andrieu, 'Le sacre épiscopal d'après Hincmar de Reims', in *Revue d'Histoire Ecclésiastique*, 48 (1953), 22–73, esp. 40 ff. Liturgical parallels naturally came to exist between royal and episcopal consecration-rites, but influence worked in both directions, and there is evidence that Hincmar manipulated liturgy very subtly in order to maintain and even to underline the fundamental distinction between the two rites. If the later rite of papal coronation represented an *imitatio imperii* (see Ullmann, *Growth*, 311 ff.), the anointing of the Frankish bishop might be seen as an analogous *imitatio regni*.

2 So Augustine in *PL* 34, 1355; Isidore in *PL* 83, 823; Bede in *PL* 91, 561, 606. See also P. Dabin, *Le Sacerdoce royal des fidèles*, Brussels 1950.

3 See E. H. Kantorowicz, *Laudes Regiae*, Berkeley 1946, esp. 56 ff.

association with a physical anointing was clearly not relevant to Merovingian or Byzantine use of these *exempla*: kings themselves, especially the Visigoths, were more attracted by Byzantine models.[1] An explanation of early medieval anointings as a revival of Scriptural practice is neither self-evident nor wholly satisfactory.

It was in the oil rituals of the Church that the memory of that practice was kept most intensely and constantly alive. The *liturgical* affinity of royal anointing was with the rite of Christian initiation,[2] and specifically with the post-baptismal chrismation of the initiate's head performed by the bishop. At least from the fourth century onwards, this post-baptismal unction was characterized as a royal investiture[3] of which the anointings of Scripture represented the mystic type. It is not hard to see how the liturgical transference could suggest itself: the purpose of royal anointing too was to 'make a new man' of the unworthy candidate,[4] and to qualify him for the burdensome tasks inseparable from the dignity conferred. Here were re-echoed those ideals of personal and social regeneration which animated monastic and synodal reformers. The link with the Old Testament was thus indirect, and was transmitted through the baptismal liturgy with its reference to 'the oil wherewith thou hast anointed priests, kings, and prophets'.[5]

Royal anointing, then, was no mere surrogate for long hair, for the aim of the anointers was not simply to exalt the king, but at the

[1] See E. Ewig, 'Zum christlichen Königsgedanken im Frühmittelalter', in *Das Königtum. Vortrage und Forschungen*, III, Konstanz 1956, 36 f.

[2] Cf. the stimulating, but often unreliable, study of J. de Pange, *Le Roi très chrétien*, Paris 1949, esp. 79 ff. and 98 ff., who wrongly postulates a confusion of rites. See also B. Welte, *Die Postbaptismale Salbung*, Freiburg 1939, and J. D. C. Fisher, *Christian Initiation*, London 1965, for discussion of doctrine and liturgy.

[3] See T. Michels, 'Die Akklamation in der Taufliturgie', in *Jahrbuch für Liturgiewissenschaft*, 8 (1928), 76 ff., for the early development of this idea, especially in the Eastern liturgies. Cf. the Merovingian *Missale Gothicum*, ed. L. C. Mohlberg, Rome 1961, 67, where the newly anointed are referred to as 'baptizati et in Christo coronati'; Pope Leo I, *PL* 54, 149: 'omnes enim in Christo regeneratos crucis signum efficit reges'.

[4] Cf. I *Reg*. x, 6.

[5] *Liber Sacramentorum Romanae Ecclesiae Ordinis Anni Circuli. (Sacramentarium Gelasianum)*, ed. Mohlberg, Rome 1958, 73; *The Gregorian Sacramentary*, ed. H. A. Wilson, *Henry Bradshaw Society*, 49, London 1915, 50. Cf. already the third-century *Apostolic Tradition*, ed. B. Botte, Münster 1963, 18 f.

same time to condition and, when necessary, to control his action. At the VIII Council of Toledo in 653, the bishops declared: 'Regem...iura faciunt non persona (It is the laws, not the individual, which make the king).'[1] The synodists at Paris in 829 posed the question: 'Quid sit proprie ministerium regis? (What really is the king's job?)'[2] The achievement of the Synod of Hohenaltheim has been epitomized as 'a re-interpretation of kingship in the sense of a theocratic office'.[3] King Edgar himself, addressing an Anglo-Saxon synod in 967, expressed his readiness to take up 'the sword of Constantine', and to obey episcopal commands.[4] The notion of kingship as office, whether implied or made explicit, was the remarkable common feature of the synodists' statements in all four areas. An office presupposes clearly defined functions, for the officer, as Weber has pointed out, 'is subject to an impersonal order to which his actions are oriented'.[5] As guardians of that higher order in early medieval Christendom, the bishops saw the royal office as an executive post, themselves as the directors of the corporation.

The bishops were also the ritual specialists in a Christian society, and therefore were uniquely qualified to manipulate ritual to express and to implement their own ideas. It is hardly surprising that the rite of royal anointing, both in a creative and a demonstrative sense, made precisely those points which were of prime importance in the view of the hierarchy: first, the auxiliary role of the chosen king, incorporated into his office and actually made capable of assuming it, through the dynamic rite of anointing, and secondly, the episcopal monopoly of king-making —the *sacerdos* being the unique channel of supernatural power

1 *PL* 84, 431. The significance of this statement is stressed by De Pange, *Le roi*, 120 ff., and by H. Beumann, 'Zur Entwicklung transpersonaler Staatsvorstellungen', in *Das Königtum*, ed. Ewig, 215 ff.

2 *MGH*, *Conc.*, II, 651–2.

3 Hellmann, 'Die Synode', 303.

4 *PL* 138, 515. Cf. IV Edg. 1, 8, ed. Robertson, *Laws*, 32 f.: 'the obedience which we show (the bishops) as representatives of God'.

5 *The Theory of Social and Economic Organisation*, Oxford 1947, 330. See also Fortes, 'Ritual and Office', 57 ff.; and the penetrating analysis of comparative institutions, and of terminology, by J. Goody, *Succession to High Office*, Cambridge 1966, 1–56, and 170–2, stressing the special characteristics of *royal* office as a 'scarce resource'.

conceived of as *gratia divina*. Here is the central passage of the anointing prayer which appeared in almost all the medieval *ordines* for royal consecration:

Almighty eternal God,...we ask thee to attend to the prayers of our humility and to establish this thy servant in the high rulership of the kingdom, and anoint him with the oil of the grace of thy Holy Spirit wherewith thou hast anointed those priests, kings, prophets, and martyrs who through faith conquered kingdoms, worked justice, and obtained thy promises.

This text, *Omnipotens sempiterne deus*, composed by Hincmar for the consecration of Louis the Stammerer in 877, was used by the author of the 'Seven Forms' *Ordo* (early tenth century), when it passed into the *Ordo* of 'Mainz' in the *Pontificale Romano-Germanicum* (*c.* 960) and from there into the mainstream of the medieval *ordines* tradition.[1]

Moreover, Hincmar would show that anointing, unlike penance, provided a basis for episcopal jurisdiction over the king: Charles the Bald, having been consecrated by the bishops, could be deposed *only* by their decision, and was subject to their 'fatherly correction'. This subordination paralleled that of the bishop to his consecrators, for, as Hincmar succinctly told his erring nephew the bishop of Laon: 'You can be judged by those who had the power to ordain you.' Likewise, in demanding a *professio* or solemn undertaking from the king, Hincmar extended to the royal office the penalty which canon law prescribed for a broken *professio* in the case of a bishop: *privatio honoris* or deposition.[2]

[1] The *Ordo* of 877 in *MGH, Capit.*, II, 461–2; the 'Seven Forms', ed. Erdmann, *op. cit.*, 87 ff.; the 'Mainz' Pontifical, ed. C. Vogel and R. Elze, Rome 1963, 246 ff.

Episcopal mediation was most heavily stressed in the 'Seven Forms' texts for the delivery of crown and sword, *ed. cit.*, 88: the kingdom is committed to the royal 'regimen, per officium nostrae benedictionis', the sword is handed over 'per manus episcoporum licet indignas vice tamen et auctoritate sanctorum apostolorum consecratas'.

[2] Cf. the *Libellus* of 859, in *Capit.*, II, 451: 'a qua consecratione (i.e. Charles's anointing in 848)...proici a nullo debueram, saltem sine audientia et iudicio episcoporum, quorum ministerio in regem sum consecratus...quorum paternis

At the last synod over which Hincmar presided, in 881, the Gelasian doctrine of responsibility was given a new and pregnant meaning when the consecration of kings was seen as the concrete application of episcopal *auctoritas*:

so much greater is the responsibility of the priesthood in that they must render account in God's judgement even for the very kings of men, and by so much greater are the rank and prestige of bishops than of kings 'quia reges in culmen regium sacrantur a pontificibus, pontifices autem a regibus consecrari non possunt (because kings are consecrated to their kingship by bishops, but bishops cannot be consecrated by kings)'.[1]

The candidate received from his consecrators not only symbols—crown or spear or sceptre—though these too were soon transferred from secular ritual to ecclesiastical rite, but royal power itself together with the qualities required for its exercise. The king was now the bishops' creature, and in a quite literal sense their right-hand man. This implication of anointing distinguishes it clearly from other ritual forms of king-making which were taken over by the Church. In Byzantium from the fifth century onwards, the imperial accession ritual became increasingly an ecclesiastical affair, but the coronation, whether performed by the senior Basileus or by the Patriarch of Constantinople, was never regarded as dynamic or constitutive.[2]

It is worth noting, in this context, that the bishops of the Western Churches were not initially interested in crowning their kings. There is no evidence for an ecclesiastical rite of coronation in Visigothic Spain, although Byzantine influence may well have brought crown-wearing into royal ceremonial, and perhaps even into a secular accession ritual. Coronation was introduced into the

correptionibus et castigatoriis iudiciis...sum subditus'; Hincmar to his nephew, in *PL* 126, 378: 'ab his potes iudicari a quibus potuisti ordinari'; *idem*, *PL* 125, 1040 f. and Mansi, 16, 601.

[1] *PL* 125, 1071, in the *acta* of the Synod of St Macre-de-Fismes.

[2] See O. Treitinger, *Die Oströmische Kaiser- und Reichsidee nach ihrer Gestaltung im höfischen Zeremoniell*, Jena 1938, 7 ff., 27 ff., and F. Dölger's effective refutation of the contrary opinion of P. Charanis, in *Byzantinische Zeitschrift*, 43 (1950), 146–7.

Frankish royal consecration by the papacy, again probably through a modelling on Byzantine practice. In 848, the deliveries of both crown and sceptre seem to have remained within the framework of a secular ritual of enthronement. Even much later, the actual coronation was of secondary importance in the full rite of inauguration: in the 'Edgar' *Ordo* as performed in 973, three antiphons were prescribed for reasons of emphasis at the entrance of the *electus*, at the anointing, and at the girding-on of the sword.[1]

Of course, ideas of sacral kingship did not die: and in the context of *that* tradition, especially when its pagan origins had been concealed by a Christian theocratic gloss, royal anointing from the later tenth century onwards, when ordination anointings had become widely practised, could be cited as evidence of the king's priestly powers: the 'rex ex nobilitate' engendered 'le roi thaumaturge'.[2] But the ideas of the Norman Anonymous[3] were *not* those of the men who first devised and performed the rite of royal anointing. I suggest that there was in the early medieval period a connection between sustained synodal activity and the introduction of this rite. The link was made by the bishops'

[1] Isidore, *Hist. Goth.*, 48, 51, 52, in *MGH, AA*, XI, 286 f.; P. Classen, 'Karl der Grosse, das Papsttum und Byzanz', in *Karl der Grosse*, I, 557 f.; *Ann. Bertin.*, ed. F. Grat, 55 and cf. *ibid.* 71; the 'Edgar' *Ordo*, ed. L. G. Wickham Legg, *English Coronation Records*, Westminster 1901, 15 ff.

[2] See M. Bloch, *Les Rois Thaumaturges*, Strasbourg 1924; H. Beumann, 'Die sakrale Legitimierung des Herrschers im Denken der ottonischen Zeit', in *Zeitschrift für Rechtsgeschichte, Germ. Abt.*, 66 (1948), 1–45; H. Wolfram, *Splendor Imperii*, Graz-Köln 1963, 126 ff. and 137, calling the replacement of the king's *splendor fortunae* by a *splendor fidei* 'ein echt mitteralterlich Kompromiss'.

[3] See Williams, *The Norman Anonymous*, esp. 167 ff. The Anonymous regarded the king's anointing as superior to that of the bishop: *MGH, L de L*, III, tract. IV, 669: 'Nam unctio et sanctificatio sacerdotum ad exemplum Aaron instituta est...et...ad exemplum apostolorum...regis vero unctio instituta est ad exemplum illius quem Deus pater unxit ante saecula.' On these ideas, which drew heavily on expressions contained in the royal *ordines*, see the perceptive remarks of Kantorowicz, *The King's Two Bodies*, Princeton 1957, 42 ff. But both he, and the equally perceptive R. W. Southern, *The Making of the Middle Ages*, London 1953, 97 ff., somewhat misleadingly suggest that the Anonymous was really representative of early medieval attitudes. Stark, *Sociology of Religion*, 58 f., mischievously juxtaposes the Anonymous and the Vicar of Bray, the former's argument being 'a near-perfect reflection of the sentiments which, when the time came, produced the Anglican establishment'.

preoccupation with the function of secular power *intra ecclesiam*,[1] and the problem of controlling its exercise. These series of synods at once manifested and promoted the group-consciousness and ideological maturity of the episcopates, while at the same time, they revealed the dependence of the hierarchy on royal support. The result was a crystallization of the clergy's needs and expectations of kingship. The transmission of rulership by secular and autonomous means now appeared clearly for what it was: an anomaly in the Christian society. Theology and practical need coalesced to suggest a ritual expression for a new social reality.

By way of contrast, one might glance for a moment at Ireland and Byzantium in this period. In both cases, the Church accommodated itself to the wider society in ways quite different from those which evolved in the barbarian kingdoms. No theories emerged of kingship as office, or of the hierarchy as supervisor of the ruler's usefulness. Not the bishop but the charismatic figure of monk or abbot appeared to castigate royal or imperial sin: such interventions were individual, intermittent, and never institutionalized or formalized in law. The absence here of synodal movements comparable to those outlined above may be linked with the fact that the practice of royal or imperial anointing was never introduced by the indigenous episcopates.[2] This is not to postulate a

[1] Cf. Isidore, *Sent.* III, 51, 4, in *PL* 83, 723: 'Principes saeculi *nonnumquam* intra ecclesiam potestatis adeptae culmina tenent, *ut* per eandem potestatem disciplinam ecclesiasticam *muniant*.'

[2] On Irish conditions, see P. Fournier, 'Le *Liber ex lege Moysi* et les tendances bibliques du droit canonique irlandais', in *Revue Celtique*, 30 (1909), esp. 228: 'Les conciles n'y tiennent qu'une place secondaire, comme les evêques dont le rôle est singulièrement effacé.' Also valuable are J. Ryan's observations in *Settimana Spoleto*, 7, II (1960), 554 ff. and 584 f., and K. Hughes, *The Church in Early Irish Society*, London 1966. On synods in the Eastern Church, see H. G. Beck, *Kirche und Theologische Literatur im Byzantinischen Reich*, Munich 1959, 38 ff., esp. 55 ff.: only ten local synods are recorded for the whole Empire in four centuries (from 600 to 1000), and nearly all were exclusively concerned with the doctrinal problems of monothelitism or iconoclasm, rather than with administrative or legislative matters, which were in any case looked after by the imperial government. On imperial control, see A. Michel, 'Die Kaisermacht in der Ostkirche', in *Ostkirchliche Studien*, 3 (1954), 1 ff.; for monastic criticisms, see the lively essay of H. Grégoire in N. H. Baynes and H. B. Moss, eds., *Byzantium*, Oxford 1948, 86 ff. On royal inaugurations in Ireland, which

simple causal relationship between institution and rite: rather that these are best seen as interrelated features of specific social and political conditions.

There is time only for a brief mention of the anointings of Pippin in 751 and 754. I have tried to show elsewhere that these were the results of papal initiative,[1] and therefore not cases of the syndrome I have been examining here, though obviously relevant to it. It was no coincidence that the Frankish bishops allowed the practice of royal anointing to fall into abeyance after 751, and did not resume it on their own initiative until the mid-ninth century. Seen in this perspective, the so-called 'delayed anointings' of Charles the Bald and, in the tenth century, of the Anglo-Saxon Edgar, lose their aura of mystery.[2]

I have said that two key ideas lay behind the anointing rite: the executive function of Christian kingship and the mediatory role of the bishops in conferring and legitimizing secular power. These ideas were nowhere more clearly apparent than at a synod; and it is significant that prayers 'pro rege in tempore sinodi' were incorporated into the earliest *ordines* for royal consecration. Two of Alcuin's collects for this purpose were used by Hincmar in the anointing prayer of the *ordo* which he composed for the consecration of Charles the Bald as king of Lotharingia in 869.[3] The reference of one of these texts to the royal *ministerium* was no doubt its chief recommendation; while the whole meaning of the rite was epitomized in its opening prayer, that God's servant 'in

remained entirely secular even in the later Middle Ages, see M. Dillon and N. Chadwick, *The Celtic Realms*, London 1967, 93 ff. G. Ostrogorsky, 'Zur Kaisersalbung und Schilderhebung im Spätbyzantinischen Krönungszeremoniell', in *Historia*, 4 (1955), 246 ff., resumes the evidence, and shows that an imperial anointing was not practised in Byzantium before the thirteenth century, when the rite was imported from the West.

1 For details, see my unpublished dissertation, ch. III.

2 Cf. *Settimana Spoleto*, 7, 1 (1960), 397 f. and 403 f.

3 *MGH, Capit.*, II, 457: 'Et qui te voluit'. Cf. Alcuin's *Benedictio* in the Gregorian Sacramentary, *ed. cit.*, 351. The same collect was employed quite independently by the East Frankish author of the 'Early German' *Ordo*, ed. Erdmann, *op. cit.*, 86. In this form (which differed slightly from Hincmar's text) the prayer passed into 'Mainz', and thus into the later *ordines*. Cf. also the echo in Hincmar's opening benediction, 'Deus qui populis', of two Alcuinian Mass prayers *pro rege in tempore synodi*: Gregorian, *ed. cit.*, 188 and 189.

regni regimine maneat semper idoneus'. Between the two great liturgists Alcuin and Hincmar lies the distance from the monarch acting in synod to the suitable king consecrated by the synodists.*

* I should like to take this opportunity of acknowledging the help and encouragement of Professor W. Ullmann and of my husband, H. G. H. Nelson, both of whom have discussed with me some ideas contained in this paper.

11

SYMBOLS IN CONTEXT: RULERS' INAUGURATION RITUALS IN BYZANTIUM AND THE WEST IN THE EARLY MIDDLE AGES[1]

HOBSBAWM[2] recently reminded young historians prone to methodologising that they would be well advised always to begin with a problem. He meant to imply—and very properly—that experimentation with methods becomes vapid and useless unless it is seen clearly for what it is: a means to an end. I propose to experiment with a method, so I want first to emphasise that I do have a problem. It is this: why, within a common framework of Christian theology, belief and practice, did the rituals for the inauguration of rulers, in early Byzantium on the one hand, and in the early medieval western kingdoms on the other, diverge as they did? What has this divergence to tell us about the differences not just between types of political power but between the two societies? These questions relate, of course, to a mere subsection of the whole vast subject of 'liturgies eastern and western' which Brightman long ago promised to survey.[3] Unfortunately, even his work was left only half-complete: the further task of systematic comparative analysis seems hardly to have been begun. But that would surely be a lifetime's work. In this paper, I confine myself to a small though significant area of the field, a single type of ritual; and I cover a limited time-span, the period down to about 1000 AD.

First, to define the size and shape of the problem, I sketch two ritual models, eastern and western, and examine what were the historical contexts in which the critical phases of their respective developments

[1] I am grateful for their help to my friends and colleagues Averil and Alan Cameron, who kindly let me see work in advance of publication, Johnny Parry, who advised me on the anthropological literature, and John Gillingham, who discussed with me some of the ideas in this paper.

[2] In a contribution to the discussion at the conference of the Past and Present Society at University College, London, 2 July 1975.

[3] F. E. Brightman, *Liturgies* [*Eastern and Western*] (Oxford 1896), a revised version of the work of C. E. Hammond (1878). Only volume 1 ever appeared.

took place. Second, and this is where the experiment comes in, I offer a provisional answer to the question: why?—both in the sense of how come? and also of what for?[4]

First then: the rituals themselves. I begin with the east. How was a Byzantine emperor made? A distinction has to be made at the outset between two sorts of emperor: the co-emperor raised as colleague by an existing senior emperor,[5] and what may be termed the 'new' emperor—a category which will include not only a usurper, would-be founder of a new dynasty, but also an emperor who did in fact succeed a member of his own family but whose succession was not formally transacted during his predecessor's lifetime. An obvious distinction between the two categories is thus that a 'new' emperor's inauguration was generally preceded by an imperial funeral, a co-emperor's never.

The inauguration of the co-emperor (and incidentally there are considerably more of these in our period than of the other kind of accession)[6] consisted basically of a coronation of the junior by the senior colleague,[7] followed by acclamations from those witnessing the ritual. The coronation of a co-emperor was final in the sense that no

[4] Compare E. R. Leach, 'Ritualization in man in relation to conceptual and social development.', in *P*[*hilosophical*] *T*[*ransactions of the*] *R*[*oyal*] *S*[*ociety of*] *L*[*ondon* Series B. Biological Sciences], no 772, vol 251 (London 1966) pp 403 *seq*. Distinguishing the 'philo-genetic question "how come?" from the functional question "what for?",' Leach comments (p 404): 'The enormous complexity of the ritual sequences which anthropologists have to study makes any guesses of the "How come" type more or less absurd.' To a historian, the anthropologist's self-limitation appears a result, less of the complexity of his material, than of its usual lack of diachronic depth. Philogenetic questions are the historian's stock-in-trade: for him, the complexity of ritual sequences must invite rather than preclude historical investigation.

[5] For the characteristics of pre-mortem succession, see J. Goody, [*Succession to High Office*] (Cambridge 1966) pp 8 *seq*.

[6] Between 450 and 1000, there were, on my calculations, thirty-six inaugurations of co-emperors, as against twenty-seven of 'new' emperors.

[7] The dynastic element of pre-mortem succession was observed by the sixth-century chronicler Malalas, *Chronographia*, ed L. Dindorf (Bonn 1831) p 439: 'τὰ τέκνα αὐτῶν ἐκ παιδόθεν ἔστεφον.' For the role of the senior emperor, see the *B*[*ook of*] *C*[*eremonies*] of Constantine Porphyrogenitus, ed J. Reiske (Bonn 1829) I, 94, p 431. On this indispensable source, see J. B. Bury, 'The Book of Ceremonies', in *EHR*, 22 (1907) pp 209 *seq*, 418 *seq*. The role of crowner was sometimes delegated to the patriarch: [W.] Sickel, ['Das byzantinische Krönungsrecht bis zum 10 Jht.'], in *BZ*, 7 (1898) pp 511 *seq*, at 520, and O. Treitinger in *BZ*, 39 (1939) p 200, stressing that in any event the senior emperor always remained 'der auctor der Krönung.' See also P. Classen, 'Karl der Grosse, das Papsttum und Byzanz', in *Karl der Grosse*, 1, ed H. Beumann (Düsseldorf 1965) pp 580, 595. [Ai.] Christophilopoulou, ['Ἐκλογή, ἀναγόρευσις καὶ στέψις τοῦ βυζαντινοῦ αὐτοκράτορος] (Athens 1956) pp 80 *seq*, is needlessly over-schematic in insisting that the senior emperor always personally performed the coronation of a colleague. The events of 641 show public opinion preferring this, but

further ritual was required to legitimise him as sole or senior emperor when the existing senior colleague died.[8] The inauguration of a co-emperor until the early ninth century would regularly take place in the Hippodrome[9] or in the palace, rather than, as in the ninth and tenth centuries, in Hagia Sophia.[10]

The inauguration of a 'new' emperor was more complicated. Christophilopoulou has suggested that the procedures should be seen in terms of two originally distinct blocs,[11] and her approach is useful so long as the integration of these blocs is stressed, rather than any contradiction between them.[12] First came the *anagoreusis*, the formal proclamation of the new emperor, with ritual acclamations signifying the divinely-inspired election. All this often occurred in a military camp, and in the early period was accompanied by the shield-raising and torques-crowning appropriate to the elevation of a war-chief. Then the emperor was crowned by the patriarch and acclaimed again with laudatory hails signifying recognition of the legitimacy of the

---

equally show the possibility of delegation to the patriarch: Nicephorus, *Historia*, ed C. de Boor (Leipzig 1880) p 30. For a good instance of delegation, with the senior emperor the subject of the action, see Theophanes, *Chronographia*, ed C. de Boor (Leipzig 1883) p 426 (for the year 748): '"Εστεψε Κωνσταντῖνος ὁ δυσσεβὴς βασιλεὺς τὸν ἑαυτοῦ υἱὸν Λέοντα εἰς βασιλέα δι' Ἀναστασίου τοῦ . . . . πατριάρχου.' For some further evidence, see now the important and wide-ranging article of [C.] Walter, ['Raising on a shield in Byzantine iconography'], in *REB* 33 (1975) pp 133 *seq*, especially pp 134–5. Professor D. M. Nicol very kindly drew my attention to this article.

8 This seems true of the seventh century and later. Gregory of Tours, *Historia Francorum*, V, 30, on the accession of Tiberius II (578) seems to imply that an acclamation in the Hippodrome was 'customary' then, as it certainly was in the case of a 'new' emperor. Averil Cameron, in a forthcoming article, shows that Gregory depended on good Byzantine sources. If he can be trusted here, despite his mistaken reference to Tiberius as Caesar instead of Augustus (this Byzantine distinction may no longer have been appreciated in the west), the two forms of inauguration were not yet as clearly differentiated as they soon became. Since a senior emperor was often forced to appoint a colleague under external pressure, the difference between the political implications of the two forms should not be exaggerated.

9 For these and other public occasions in this setting, R. Guilland, 'Études sur l'Hippodrome [de Byzance]', in *BS*, 28 (1967) pp 262 *seq*.

10 Full references to the data on which this and subsequent generalizations are based can be found in Christophilopoulou—a very rich collection of material.

11 Christophilopoulou pp 58 *seq*.

12 Christophilopoulou's exaggeration of the discreteness of the two phases is most misleading in regard to the early period. Still more misleading is her interpretation of the first phase as secular and constitutive, the second as religious and ancillary. For some criticisms, see below, 267. The identification of two ritual blocs is useful for analytic purposes, but remains an artificial construct: the variability of practice, especially in the early period, needs to be remembered even when, as in the present paper, a high degree of generality is aimed at.

newly-invested ruler. From the early seventh century, the coronation was performed inside a church.

It is probably due to something more than a coincidental loss of evidence that there is so little indication of rituals associated with Roman imperial inauguration during the period from Augustus to the fourth century. At least part of the explanation lies in the persistently republican ideology of the principate, expressed in the continuing importance of the paradoxical ideal of imperial *civilitas*, the emperor being expected to act as a holder of republican office, a 'citizen amongst his fellows.'[13] The waning of the western empire fostered the revival of a very different tradition in the east, that of hellenistic monarchy.[14] The continuous history of the Byzantine imperial inauguration ritual begins in the mid-fifth century,[15] and from the outset that ritual was set in a religious, and specifically Christian, framework. What might look at first glance like a purely military affair with the shield-raising, torques-crowning and raising of the standards by the acclaiming troops was punctuated by acts of religious observance which must be treated as part of the ritual process.[16] The evolution of the Byzantine ritual down to the early seventh century was characterised by an increasingly overt religious symbolism which affected every part of the inauguration and shaped its basic structure for the whole early medieval period, as the ninth- and tenth-century sections of the *Book of Ceremonies* show.[17] The importance of a single source, Corippus, in

[13] So, Alan Cameron, 'Bread and circuses: the Roman emperor and his people', an inaugural lecture in the chair of Latin language and literature, delivered at King's College, London, 21 May 1973, p 10. Compare also A. Alföldi, 'Die Ausgestaltung des monarchischen Zeremoniells am römischen Kaiserhofe', in *Mitteilungen des deutschen archäologischen Instituts, Röm,* Abt 49 (Munich 1934), and 'Insignien und Tracht der römischen Kaiser', *ibid* 50 (1935), both now reprinted as *Die monarchische Repräsentation im römischen Kaiserreiche* (Darmstadt 1970) especially pp 25 *seq*, 45 and 127 *seq*.

[14] N. H. Baynes, 'Eusebius and the Christian Empire', in *Annuaire de l'Institut de Philologie et d'Histoire orientales,* 2 (Brussels 1934) pp 13 *seq*, reprinted in Baynes, [*Byzantine Studies and Other Essays*] (London 1955) pp 168 *seq*; [F,] Dvornik, [*Early Christian and Byzantine Political Philosophy*], 2 vols, (Washington, D.C. 1966) 2, pp 706 *seq*. On the replacement of *civilitas* by an autocratic ideal by the close of the fifth century, see cap 8 of Alan Cameron, *Circus Factions* (Oxford 1977).

[15] It is no coincidence that the first of the series of protocols in *BC*, that covering Leo I's inauguration, dates from this period. See Brightman, '[Byzantine imperial] coronations', in *JTS*, 2 (1901) pp 359 *seq*; G. Ostrogorsky and E. Stein, 'Die Krönungsurkunden des Zeremonienbuches', in *B* 7 (1932) pp 185 *seq*, and the important review of this by F. Dölger in *BZ*, 36 (1936) pp 145 *seq*. *BC* here draws on materials collected in the mid-sixth century by Peter the Patrician. See below, n 18.

[16] This is evident already with Leo I: *BC* I, 91, p 413. See also p 425 (Anastasius) and p 430 (Justin I.)

[17] *BC* I 38, pp 191 *seq*. For the dating of the two sections of this chapter, see Dölger in

illuminating the formative developments of the later sixth century has now been brilliantly demonstrated by Averil Cameron,[18] who has noted too a second critical element: the role of the demes or factions of Constantinople[19] who intervened, sometimes decisively, in the making of several emperors in the sixth and seventh centuries and came to perform various ritual functions on state occasions, most particularly that of acclaiming both 'new' emperors and co-emperors immediately after their coronations.[20] What needs to be stressed is the contemporaneity of the two main trends. The 'liturgification'[21] of the imperial inauguration, its climax the diadem-crowning by the patriarch in

---

BZ, 36 (1936) pp 149 *seq*. The originally military rituals of shield-raising and torques-crowning went out of use from the seventh century: Christophilopoulou pp 60 *seq*. Less convincing is her explanation in terms of a 'demilitarization' of ritual corresponding to the seventh-century hellenisation of Byzantine society: so also, following her almost verbatim, A. N. Stratos, *Byzantium in the Seventh Century* (Amsterdam 1968) I, pp 7, 49. But a ritual could be 'demilitarized', yet survive with other symbolic associations, as had already happened in the case of shield-raising in the sixth century and again, with its revival, in the late Byzantine period: see H. P. L'Orange, *Studies on the Iconography of Cosmic Kingship* (Oslo 1953) pp 87 *seq*; [E. H.] Kantorowicz, ['Oriens Augusti: Lever du Roi'], in *DOP*, 17 (1963) pp 152 *seq*; Ostrogorsky, 'Zur Kaisersalbung und Schilderhebung [im spätbyzantinischen Krönungszeremoniell]', in *Historia* 4 (Wiesbaden 1955) esp pp 254 *seq*. I prefer to attribute its disappearance less to conscious abandonment than to long disuse: there were no 'new' emperors between 610 and 695. For the iconographic tradition, its earliest form dating 'possibly' from the sixth century, see Walter, 'Raising on a shield', p 167 and *passim*. As for the torques-crowning, the growing importance of the diadem and the practical need to avoid an awkward 'double coronation' sufficiently account for its omission from the inauguration ritual: see [W.] Ensslin, 'Zur Torqueskrönung [und Schilderhebung bei der Kaiserwahl]', in *Klio*, 35 (Leipzig 1942) p 292.

18 In A. Cameron's edition of Corippus, [*In laudem Iustini Augusti minoris*] (London 1976), especially in section 7 of her introduction and the notes to II, lines 84 *seq* and 159 *seq*. For the increasing interest, in precisely this period, both in ritual and in the imperial ideology behind it, evidence can be found in the work of Peter the Patrician: see [A.] Pertusi, ['I principi fondamentali della concezione del potere a Bisancio. Per un commento al dialogo "Sulla scienza politica" attributo a Pietro Patrizio (secolo VI)'] in *Bulletino del Istituto Storico Italiano per il Medio Evo*, 80 (Rome 1968) pp 1 *seq*.

19 Corippus, notes to II, lines 308 *seq*. Alan Cameron, *Circus Factions*, offers a major reassessment of the role of the demes in politics and ritual. See also, A. Maricq, 'La durée du régime des partis populaires à Constantinople', in *Bulletin de l'Académie Royale de Belgique*, Cl. des Lettres, 35 (Brussels 1949) pp 64 *seq*, and [H.-G.] Beck, 'Konstantinopel. [Zur Sozialgeschichte einer frühmittelalterlichen Hauptstadt'], in *BZ*, 63 (1965) pp 35 *seq*.

20 *BC* I 38 especially section b: 'Ακτολογία τῶν δήμων ἐπὶ στεψίμῳ βασιλέως.'

21 For this process, see Treitinger, [*Die oströmische Kaiser- und Reichsidee nach ihrer Gestaltung im höfischen Zeremoniell*] (2 ed Darmstadt 1956) pp 27–8. Treitinger presents rich illustrative material, but his analysis of the critical sixth-century development includes an identification of *Liturgisierung* with *Verkirchlichung* which, in my view, is misconceived because it presupposes a radical discontinuity between the categories 'secular'

Hagia Sophia, proceeded along with, not at the expense of, the growing involvement of the groups representative of the people of Constantinople and so of the whole empire.[22] I leave for my final section a discussion of the significance of this twofold development.

Let us turn now to the west. There is very little evidence concerning royal inauguration rituals among Germanic peoples before the church became involved here. It is possible that in many cases, regular ritual procedures did not exist, in the absence either of permanent political communities or of permanent kingships.[23] The merovingian dynasty, as Grierson has pointed out,[24] was atypical in its relative stability, and yet, sacral features notwithstanding, it seems to have lacked a fixed ritual for the transmission of royal power.[25] More relevant is the absence of any barbarian inauguration ritual exclusive to kingship: rather, the *rex* was a household-lord writ large, whose succession to his inheritance was thus aptly signified when he took his place on the high-seat in the paternal hall or beat the bounds of the paternal property. Similarly, the

---

and 'ecclesiastical'. The term 'ritualization', accommodating religious action both inside and outside the physical location of a church, seems more apt here: *BC* is concerned as much with the one as the other. Treitinger's misconception generated the conclusion that *Liturgisierung* was operative 'only' in the realm of ideas. See p 28, n 84: 'Trotz alledem bleibt . . . der Gedankengehalt der verkirchlichten Riten und Zeremonien *nur gedankliche Haltung* . . ."Verkirchlichung" bedeutet also *nicht praktisch und rechtlich* grösseren Einfluss der Kirche auf den Kaiser.' (my stress.)

22 See Beck, 'Senat und Volk [von Konstantinopel]', in *SBAW* PhK (1966) pp 18–19.

23 See E. A. Thompson, *The Early Germans* (Oxford 1965) pp 32 *seq*; [J. M.] Wallace-Hadrill, [*Early Germanic Kingship in England and on the Continent*] (Oxford 1971) pp 7–8. A primitive Indo-European inauguration ritual persisted for Irish kings: see D. A. Binchy, *Celtic and Anglo-Saxon Kingship* (Oxford 1970) pp 11 *seq*; F. J. Byrne, *Irish Kings and High Kings* (London 1973) pp 15 *seq*. The relative scarcity of Germanic evidence is apparent in O. Höfler, 'Der Sakralcharakter des germanischen Königtums', in *Das Königtum. [Seine geistigen und rechtlichen Grundlagen,]* Vorträge und Forschungen 3 (Lindau-Konstanz 1956) pp 85 *seq*, and R. Wenskus, *Stammesbildung und Verfassung* (Cologne/Graz 1961) pp 482 *seq*. Compare W. Baetke, 'Zur Frage des altnordischen Sakralkönigtums', in *Kleine Schriften* (Weimar 1973) pp 146–7.

24 'Election and inheritance in early Germanic Kingship', in *CHJ*, 7 (1941) pp 1–22.

25 [R.] Schneider, [*Königswahl und Königserhebung im Frühmittelalter*] (Stuttgart 1972) pp 190 *seq*, deals very fully with this problem, rejecting the extreme view of K. Hauck, 'Von einer spätantiken Randkultur zum karolingischen Europa', in *Frühmittelalterliche Studien*, 1 (Berlin 1967) pp 30 *seq*, and recognising, p 260, that no *fest verbindliche Schema* existed, though the merovingians clearly had some kind of *Erhebungszeremoniell*. [K.-U.] Jäschke, ['Frühmittelalterliche Festkrönungen?'], in *HZ*, 211 (1970) pp 580 *seq*, argues persuasively against merovingian crown-wearing or (by implication, *a fortiori*) coronation. Enthronement may have been the norm in the seventh century. Schneider, pp 226–7 and 259, discusses possible clerical influence on late merovingian and Lombard *Königszeremoniell* but the relevance of this to inauguration practices remains problematical.

dux was set up through rituals of shield-raising and investiture with weapons which were common to all lords of military followings.[26] As our concern is with the inauguration of medieval kings as such, we should concentrate on the period when the characteristics of *rex* and *dux* were becoming fused. The transformative role of the Christian church in the production of this synthesis was critical: what D. H. Green has shown of the linguistic evidence on the origins of kingship[27] seems equally true of royal ritual. Just as Christian clergy were responsible for the formulation of a clearly-defined ideology of kingship as office, so they created (in part, from ingredients ready to hand) rituals to inaugurate the officers.[28] Conversion to Christianity in itself did not immediately bring about these consequences. If the delay in the ritualisation of ruler-making in the empire was caused by the persistence of a rival ideology, in the post-Roman west a similar and more prolonged delay occurred for other reasons. One was the barbarians' consciousness of inhabiting, in Hauck's phrase, 'late antique marginal cultures'; another was the existence of an ideological vacuum, filled only, I suggest, when barbarian élites had fully appropriated (and in so doing remoulded) Christianity. This happened in Visigothic Spain precociously in the seventh century, in England and Gaul in the eighth and ninth centuries, and in east Francia in the tenth century. The outcome so far as royal inaugurations were concerned was broadly common to all these realms: the local hierarchy took over the essential procedures of king-making, made of them a liturgical rite whose central act was the anointing, preceded by the acceptance of conditions by the new office-holder (a foreshadowing, this, of the later coronation oath) and followed by an investiture with weapons and other insignia, usually including a crown.[29]

[26] [W.] Schlesinger, 'Herrschaft und Gefolgschaft', in *HZ*, 176 (1953) pp 225–75, and 'Über germanisches Heerkönigtum', in *Das Königtum*, pp 105–41, both now reprinted in *Beiträge* [*zur deutschen Verfassungsgeschichte des Mittelalters*] (Göttingen 1963) especially pp 26, 35 and 80–1. On the usefulness and the limitations of the typological distinction between *rex* and *dux*, see the sensible remarks of Wallace-Hadrill, pp 14 *seq*.

[27] *The Carolingian Lord* (Cambridge 1965) especially pp 223 *seq*, 378 *seq*. Green does not refer to the work of F. Graus, who, from a different standpoint, reaches similar conclusions in 'Über die sogenannte germanische Treue', in *Historica*, 1 (Prague 1959) pp 71–121 and 'Herrschaft und Treue', *ibid* 12 (1966) pp 5–44.

[28] F. Kern, *Gottesgnadentum und Widerstandsrecht im früheren Mittelalter*, rev ed R. Buchner (Münster 1954) pp 46 *seq*; Wallace-Hadrill, 'The Via Regia of the Carolingian Age', in *Trends in Medieval Political Thought*, ed B. Smalley (Oxford 1965) pp 27 *seq*; [W.] Ullmann, '[Der] Souveränitätsgedanke [in den mittelalterlichen Krönungsordines]', in *Festschrift P. E. Schramm* (Wiesbaden 1964) pp 81–2.

[29] E. Müller, 'Die Anfänge der Königssalbung im Mittelalter', in *HJch* 58 (1938) pp 322

This necessarily brief introduction has served to throw into relief the contrast between the inauguration rituals of east and west. For, although the attention of students of western *Staatssymbolik* in this early period has been focussed on eastern influences, on Byzantium as 'school-mistress' of the west,[30] more fundamental than any east-west borrowings, it seems to me, is the difference between the inauguration rituals practised in the two main areas of Christendom. Here, again, is our problem. But before offering a possible explanation, it is necessary to clear the ground of a misconception according to which a contrast is seen in terms of Byzantine secular ceremonial on the one hand, western ecclesiastical rite on the other. (I prefer to use the term 'ritual'[31] to transcend what seems to me a false distinction in the context of medieval Christendom, western *and* eastern.) The misconception arises from a widely-held interpretation of the Byzantine inauguration as essentially 'secular'. The original constitutive moment, it is held, was the extra-ecclesiastical elective *Augustus*-acclamation at the beginning of the ritual. The Byzantine emperor, on this view, 'never stood in any need of coronation.'[32] And, in any case, this allegedly unnecessary

---

seq; [C. A.] Bouman, [*Sacring and Crowning*] (Groningen 1957); Schneider pp 190 *seq*, and also pp 52 *seq* for developments in the Lombard kingdom cut short in the eighth century. I have attempted a comparative survey in 'National synods, [kingship as office, and royal anointing: an early medieval syndrome]', above, ch. 10, p 239 *seq*, though I should now take a different view of the English evidence. The best analysis of the structure of these rituals remains A. M. Hocart, *Kingship* (Oxford 1927) pp 70 *seq*. See now also the fine paper of M. Fortes, 'Of Installation Ceremonies', in *Proceedings of the Royal Anthropological Institute for 1967* (London 1968) pp 5 *seq*.

30 P. E. Schramm, *Herrschaftszeichen und Staatssymbolik*, 3 vols (Stuttgart 1954–6) I pp 30 *seq*, and *passim*; J. Deér, 'Byzanz und die Herrschaftszeichen des Abendlandes', in *BZ*, 50 (1957) pp 405 *seq*, and in *BZ*, 54 (1961) pp 58 *seq*; Jäschke, pp 571 *seq*; Schneider pp 232–3, 260. For Schramm's fundamental contribution here, see the interesting historiographical survey of J. Bak, 'Medieval Symbology of the State', in *Viator*, 4 (Berkeley 1973) pp 33 *seq*, especially 59–60.

31 I distinguish the term 'ritual' from 'ceremonial' along lines suggested by Goody, 'Religion and Ritual: the Definitional Problem', in *British Journal of Sociology*, 12 (London 1961) pp 142 *seq*. The behaviour we are presently concerned with has the public and collective characteristics of ceremonial, but it also has the religious and, from the actors' standpoint, the purposive characteristics of ritual. Compare the careful distinction drawn by S. MacCormack, ['Change and Continuity in Late Antiquity: the Ceremony of Adventus'], in *Historia*, 21 (1972) p 722. [S.] Tambiah, [*Buddhism and the Spirit-cults in North-East Thailand*] (Cambridge 1970) p 35 and *passim*, is an exemplary study of ritual as 'cosmology in action' in the context of another world-religion.

32 So Treitinger pp 27–8. For similar views, see Sickel pp 524–5; Dölger, *Byzanz* [*und die europäische Staatenwelt*] (Ettal 1953) pp 292–3; [A.] Michel, [*Die Kaisermacht in der Ostkirche*] (Darmstadt 1959) pp 166 *seq*.

coronation was itself a piece of secular ceremonial, the patriarch acting as the 'foremost Byzantine citizen',[33] or 'the representative of the state'.[34] More recently, Christophilopoulou has advanced a rather different view: she has claimed that the removal of the coronation from such locations as the palace or the Hippodrome to the inside of a church created 'a new constitutional situation'. The coronation now 'assumed a religious character and became remote from legal consequences'.[35] Which interpretation is correct? Both—and neither. The coronation was a constitutive in the sense that it was part of the process which *as a whole* legitimised co-emperor and 'new' emperor alike, a part which, since in practice throughout Byzantine history it was never dispensed with, can be labelled 'dispensable' only at the risk of some artificiality, not to say anachronism.[36] Further, the reality of Byzantine belief and practice (in contrast to illusions which some modern scholars have cherished), and never more so than in the sixth century, makes nonsense of any interpretation that depends on isolating religious and secular ritual components. Might these categories, along with the implicit assumption of their institutionalisation in 'Church' and 'State', represent unconscious imports from later medieval western history? They have little meaning in the contest of early medieval Byzantium.

Of course, the clerical hierarchy existed as a specialist institution in eastern as in western christendom. But in Byzantium it produced no hierocratic theory, laid no claim to monopolise active participation in the church—which in a sociological sense was coterminous with the

[33] Treitinger p 30.

[34] Bury, [*The*] *Constitution* [*of the Later Roman Empire*] (Cambridge 1910) p 12. Compare Ensslin, 'The Emperor and Imperial Administration', in *Byzantium*, ed Baynes and H. St. L. B. Moss (Oxford 1948) p 270; 'The Patriarch officiated . . . not as representative of the Church but as representative of the electors.'

[35] Christophilopoulou pp 61–2. But this view rests on questionable assumptions.

[36] For the coronation as in some sense 'essential', see Ostrogorsky, in *BZ*, 41 (1941) pp 213 *seq*; L. Bréhier, *Les Institutions de l'Empire Byzantin* (2 ed Paris 1970) p 17; J. M. Hussey, *The Byzantine World* (4 ed London 1970) p 83. Compare also the cautious remarks of Baynes pp 34–5, and Guilland, *Études Byzantines* (Paris 1959) p 210. Still valuable are the comments of Bury, *Constitution*, pp 9 *seq*, 35–6. The extreme argument of [P.] Charanis, 'Coronation [and its constitutional significance in the later Roman Empire]', in *B* 15 (1940/1) pp 49 *seq*, claiming a 'constitutive' role for 'the Church', was effectively rebutted by Dölger, in *BZ*, 43 (1950) pp 146–7. C. Tsirpanlis, ['The Imperial Coronation and Theory in "De Cerimoniis"'], in Κληρονομία, 4 (Thessaloniki 1972) pp 63 *seq*, criticises Charanis without using all the recent literature on the subject. He also wrongly asserts that 'the British' have followed 'the German scholars' in accepting Sickel's opinion. This is hardly true of Bury, Baynes or Hussey. But Tsirpanlis here cites only A. E. R. Boak—an American!

community of Christian believers. The divine will was believed to operate directly through all members of this community. Thus sixth-century theorists focussed not on the coronation (which they did not even mention) but on election and consent as the crucial elements in imperial inauguration. And in election and consent, leading officials, senators and people (Aristotle's πολῖται live on in our sixth-century source) are all involved in the expression of the divine choice, and precisely their coincidence generates a 'lawful succession' (ἔννομος ἀνάρρησις).[37] In such an inclusive cosmology, the patriarch took his place without friction alongside other channels of divine communication.

But whence his special qualification to crown 'new' emperors? It is worth stressing the uniqueness of his role here. The physical performance of the coronation in the ambo of Hagia Sophia underlines the fact that there was room for only two real actors in this drama.[38] Other clergy had no active share in the ritual,[39] nor did the priesthood have any collective role either as electors or as guardians of the regalia, which were kept not in a church but in the palace by imperial chamberlains.[40] The patriarch acted alone, and his position here corresponded to that of the emperor himself in relation to the inauguration of a co-emperor. Just as the senior emperor normally occupied a transcendent composite status at the head of both clerical and political hierarchies—an anomalous status expressed, for instance, in

[37] Pertusi pp 12 *seq.*

[38] The ambo of Hagia Sophia (from 563 to 1204) was described in detail by Paul the Silentiary, Ἔκφρασις τοῦ Ἄμβωνος τῆς Ἁγίας Σωφίας ed P. Friedlander (Leipzig/Berlin 1912) pp 257 *seq*, especially 297–8. J. J. Kreutzer, *Paulus des Silentiarers Beschreibung der Hagia Sophia* (Leipzig 1875) p 71–2, estimates the base-diameter of the ambo at 12 feet. The rather smaller elevated platform had also to accommodate the chamberlains who invested the 'new' emperor with the chlamys, and the portable table (ἀντιμίσιον) on which the insignia were placed: *BC* I 38, p 194. Compare the eighth- and twelfth-century *ordines* printed by [J.] Goar, [Εὐχολόγιον] (2 ed Venice 1730) pp 726 *seq.* On the manuscripts, see Brightman, *Liturgies*, pp lxxxvii *seq*, and 'Coronations' p 378, with the interesting conclusion that the rite itself remained constant 'from at least the end of the eighth century down to the twelfth.'

[39] The only other cleric mentioned in the *ordines* is the deacon, who recited the collect and summoned to prayer. *BC* I 38 makes no specific mention of the clergy, but assigns, on the other hand, a major role to the acclaimers: 'ὁ λαός' and 'τὰ μέρη'.

[40] *BC* I 38, p 194: 'οἱ τοῦ κουβουκλείου' Compare their role at Justin I's inauguration, *BC* I 93, p 428; and at Justin II's, similarly, *fidi ministri*, Corippus, II, lines 86–7. *BC* I oo p 466 shows how the insignia were looked after in the 'οἰκειακὸν βασιλικὸν βεστιάριον'. See [R. J. H.] Jenkins, *Commentary* (London 1962) pp 64 *seq*, [to the *De Administrando Imperii* of Constantine Porphyrogenitus], ed Jenkins and G. Moravcsik (Washington, D.C., 1967).

the Melchisedech mosaics of Justinian's Ravenna,[41] or in the emperor's performance of certain liturgical functions and participation in certain liturgical privileges of the priesthood[42]—so, if there were no emperor, the patriarch as head of the clerical hierarchy, and at the same time a senior political dignitary, came to occupy for the time being the highest rank in the system.[43] In the act of coronation, the patriarch was not therefore priest as such, but, like the emperor himself, transcended the distinction between empire and priesthood. Bury and Treitinger were right then to regard him as 'representative of' a collectivity of citizens, but wrong in implying that that collectivity was anything less than a total society, religiously – as well as politically – defined. Thus the coronation was a religious act without being essentially ecclesiastical. The patriarch prayed: so did the demes through their acclamations. The Hippodrome no less than Hagia Sophia was a religious location.[44] Both were centres of the cult of the emperor, and through him, of the whole society. If imperial triumph was celebrated in the success of the charioteer, this was because all victory, like the empire itself, was believed to be divinely-authorised: (ἔνθεος βασιλεία, ἔνθεα ὅπλα).[45]

If then the coronation of a Byzantine emperor was a religious act, the contrast between eastern and western practice should no longer be

[41] E. R. Leach, 'Melchisedech and the emperor: icons of subversion and orthodoxy', in *Proceedings of the Royal Anthropological Institute for 1972* (London 1973) pp 5 *seq*, especially 12–13.

[42] Treitinger pp 139–40; Tsirpanlis p 86, n 8.

[43] For the position of the emperor, see B. Sinogowicz, ['Die Begriffe Reich, Macht und Herrschaft im byzantinischen Kulturbereich'], in *Saeculum*, 4 (Freiburg 1956) pp 450 *seq*; Dvornik pp 815 *seq*; D. A. Miller, 'Royauté et ambiguité sexuelle: symbolique de la monarchie à Byzance', in *Annales*, 26 (1971) pp 639 *seq*. The patriarch was of course ineligible for this position. For the role of ineligibles as 'stand-ins and stake-holders', see Goody pp 10–2: 'The stand-in serves as temporary deputy . . . It is as if the kingship cannot be allowed to lie vacant.' I am suggesting that the patriarch's role was analogous to that of the 'neutrals' cited by Goody.

[44] I cannot agree with the suggestion of Guilland,'Études sur l'Hippodrome', p 264, that a patriarch would have to hurry away from the Hippodrome embarrassed. For the inauguration of a co-emperor here as late as 776, with the patriarch present, blessing the insignia on a portable altar set up in the kathisma, see Theophanes p 450. For the demes in Hagia Sophia, compare n 20 above. *BC* offers many examples of rituals flowing naturally from one location to another, all of them, and not only churches, having religious significance.

[45] *BC* I 63, p 281, and I 68 and 69, pp 303 *seq*, especially 321–2, show the Hippodrome ritual and acclamations. See J. Gagé, 'Σταυρὸς νικοποιός. La victoire impériale dans l'empire chrétien', in *Revue d'Histoire et de Philosophie Religieuses*, 13 (Strasbourg 1933) pp 370 *seq*, esp p 400 on the fusion of 'deux mystiques triomphales.' See now Alan Cameron, *Porphyrius the Charioteer* (Oxford 1973) pp 250 *seq*.

sought in a crude distinction between religious and secular, but rather, in differing conceptions of the sacred and the profane.[46]

I approach the problem now from the opposite side, taking as my entry-point the central feature of western inaugurations lacking in those of the east: the anointing.[47] In the rest of this paper, I consider three levels of meaning in the anointing ritual and try, through these, to explore the contrast between east and west.

1 Anointing in relation to its recipient, as a *rite de passage*.[48] Both western commentators, notably Hincmar of Rheims, and the western *ordines* themselves made clear that the anointing of a king was constitutive.[49] It incorporated the candidate into his office, changing his status. But it also changed the man, transmitting the divine grace by which alone he was enabled to fulfil his royal *ministerium*.[50] In the belief-system of the west therefore, the anointing was conceived in this as in other ritual contexts as dynamic. It performed a specific function, making the *electus* into a *rex*.[51] The coronation in the east, on the other hand, while it demonstrated an emperor's legitimacy in his right to the universally-recognised symbol of monarchy, the diadem,[52] did not confer qualification to rule. It constituted, instead, a recognition that the chosen emperor was already so qualified. For the absence in early medieval Byzantium of any theory of hereditary emperorship, and the continuing adherence to the principle of election, meant that an emperor, like the Dalai Lama, was strictly

[46] Compare M. Douglas, *Purity and Danger* (London 1966) and ed, *Rules and Meanings* (Harmondsworth 1973).

[47] Ostrogorsky, 'Zur Kaisersalbung und Schilderhebung', pp 246–9, has argued that Byzantine imperial anointing was a thirteenth-century import from the west. But this was a Comnenian innovation of the twelfth century: see Christophilopoulou pp 142–4, 210–1; Walter, 'Raising on a shield', pp 162, 171. For information on this matter, I am grateful to professor D. M. Nicol, who revises Ostrogorsky's opinion in an article in *Byzantine and Modern Greek Studies*, 2 (Oxford 1976).

[48] A. Van Gennep, *The Rites of Passage*, ed and trans M. Vizedom and G. L. Caffee (London 1960).

[49] Ullmann,'Souveränitätsgedanke', p 77; and [*The*] *Carolingian Renaissance* [*and the Idea of Kingship*] (London 1969) pp 71 *seq*; Wallace-Hadrill pp 133 *seq*.

[50] J. Funkenstein, 'Unction of the Ruler', in *Adel und Kirche. Festschrift G. Tellenbach* (Freiburg 1968) pp 6 *seq*. For the gifts conferred through anointing, see the *consecratio*-prayer of Hincmar's *ordo* for Louis the Stammerer in 877, *MGH Cap* 2, p 461.

[51] Ullmann,'Souveränitätsgedanke', p 77 n 24.

[52] H.-W. Ritter, *Diadem und Königsherrschaft* (Munich 1965); Alföldi pp 263 *seq*; Jäschke pp 572 *seq*.

speaking found rather than made.[53] The electors were channels through whom a divine predetermination was manifested. Where a western king prostrated himself before his inauguration[54] a Byzantine emperor remained standing throughout his acclamation and coronation alike[55]. Thus the coronation, unlike the western anointing, effected no symbolic rebirth, was not dynamic: it was a static representation of a pre-existing fact, an articulated icon. In asserting the timelessness of the empire,[56] it precluded the possibility of true interregna. Hence the exercise of full governmental powers by a 'new' emperor during the time-lag between *anagoreusis* and coronation;[57] and hence also, I suggest, the absence in Byzantium of anything equivalent to the western 'coronation'-oath.[58]

2 Anointing as a liturgical rite, in relation to the performers. In the west, royal inaugurations were taken over by the national élites of ritual specialists, without whose interaction no ruler could thereafter be made. Some members of these élites used their indispensable ritual function to buttress claims to superiority over the secular power: *quod minus est a meliore benedicitur.*[59] The consecration of a king was regarded as a collective act performed by the episcopate as clerical

[53] Guilland, *Études Byzantines*, pp 207 *seq*: 'Le Droit Divin à Byzance', esp p 221. Compare Goody pp 21–2.

[54] 'Frühdeutsch' *Ordo*, ed C. Erdmann, *Forschungen zur politischen Ideenwelt des Frühmittelalters* (Berlin 1951) pp 83–7; 'Edgar' *Ordo*, ed Schramm, *Kaiser, Könige und Päpste*, 4 vols (Stuttgart 1968) 2, pp 233–41. Compare my comments above, ch. 10, p. 244. The idea of rebirth was intimately linked with western conceptions of royal anointing: P. Oppenheim, 'Die sakralen Momente in der deutschen Herrscherweihe', in *Ephemerides Liturgicae*, 58 (Rome 1944) pp 42 *seq*; Ullmann, *Carolingian Renaissance*, pp 71 *seq*.

[55] Goar p 727. At the beginning of the *ordo*, the emperor bows his head in prayer. On the iconographical evidence, see A. Grabar, *L'Empereur dans l'art byzantin* (Paris 1936) pp 112 *seq*, and plate XXVII, 2. It is noteworthy that the theme of royal inauguration/coronation, though not entirely absent from western baptismal liturgies, is particularly stressed in those of the eastern churches: every Christian becomes 'royal.' See T. Michels, 'Die Akklamation in der Taufliturgie', in *Jahrbuch für Liturgiewissenschaft*, 8 (1928) pp 76 *seq*. On the other hand, the Byzantine conception of imperial coronation as a mystic anointing did not essentially involve the idea of rebirth: see A. Michel pp 10 *seq*.

[56] H. U. Instinsky, 'Kaiser und Ewigkeit', in *Hermes*, 77 (Wiesbaden 1942) pp 313 *seq*.

[57] Dölger and J. Karayannopoulos, *Byzantinische Urkundenlehre* (Munich 1968) pp 51–2.

[58] The contrary view of Charanis, 'Coronation', pp 56 *seq*, must be rejected. Compare Treitinger p 30, on the 'obvious difference' between eastern and western practices.

[59] Heb. 7:7. For the claim that the pope was superior to the emperor whom he anointed, see, for example, Innocent III, *Das Register Papst Innozenz III über den deutschen Thronstreit*, ed W. Holtzmann (Bonn 1947) p 29, n 18. For a similar claim by Hincmar, see my paper, 'Kingship, law and liturgy in the political thought of Hincmar of Rheims' , above, chapter 7, pp. 133-71.

mediators of grace:[60] any laymen present had a relatively passive role as witnesses only. It can hardly be coincidental that the same period which saw the clergy assume this new function, with such notable long-term implications for medieval politics and society in the west, saw them also asserting their status as a corporate élite of *oratores*, increasingly separated from the laity by their own law, their own education-system, their monopoly of the language of learning and, above all, of liturgy.[61]

Coronation, by contrast, could be performed by non-specialists. In the east senior emperors themselves crowned their junior colleagues, while in the west, before the crucial addition of anointing to the emperor-making ritual as practised by the papacy, Charlemagne could himself make his son co-emperor.[62] But senior emperors were not the only lay crowners in Byzantium: in the very early period, 'new' emperors were crowned by a military commander and a dowager empress, and subsequently there is sporadic evidence down to the late tenth century of coronations of would-be usurpers by demesmen and soldiers.[63]

The Byzantine inauguration ritual was never devised and managed exclusively by clerics. Its details were revised by the emperors themselves, according to Constantine Porphyrogenitus, 'in whatever way each thinks fit.'[64] It was shaped by a range of participants including the acclaimers[65]—officials, senators, demesmen, soldiers: in this context, all were ritual specialists now. The absence of any clerical monopoly may be related to the general position of the clergy in Byzantine society.[66] The eastern priesthood never conceived of itself as a discrete

[60] See the rubrics of the early medieval ordines in Bouman pp 165 *seq*.

[61] J. Le Goff, 'Note sur société tripartite, idéologie monarchique et renouveau économique dans la chrétienté du IXe au XIIe siècle', in *L'Europe au IXe au XIe Siècle*, ed T. Manteuffel and A. Gieysztor (Warsaw 1968) pp 63 *seq*; D. B. Loomis, '*Regnum* and *sacerdotium* in the early eleventh century', in *England before the Conquest. Studies presented to D. Whitelock*, ed P. Clemoes and K. Hughes (Cambridge 1971) pp 129 *seq*; and, for further references, my paper, see above, ch. 10, 242-7. See also M. Richter, 'A socio-linguistic approach to the Latin Middle Ages', in *Studies in Church History*, 11 (1975) pp 69-82.

[62] The sources are discussed by [C.-R.] Brühl, ['Fränkischer Krönungsbrauch'], in *HZ*, 194 (1962) pp 276–7.

[63] Ensslin, 'Zur Torqueskrönung', pp 271 *seq*, gives evidence on the early cases; for Hypatius (532), see Malalas p 475; for Basil-Tiberius (717), see Nicephorus p 54; for Bardas-Phocas (987), see Skylitzes-Kedrenos, *Historiarum Compendium*, ed I. Bekker (Bonn 1839) 2, p 438. See also Jenkins, *Commentary*, p. 66.

[64] *BC* I 91, p 417.

[65] Treitinger pp 71 *seq*; Kantorowicz pp 156 *seq*.

[66] For much of what follows in this paragraph, I have relied on Michel, pp 27 *seq*, 56 *seq*,

juristic corporation. A clear distinction was maintained between the canons, governing internal ecclesiastical organisations, and the laws, made and enforced by the emperor and covering a wide range of ecclesiastical affairs, including the formulation of doctrine. The emperor as law-maker directly implemented God's will[67]. There was no notion of the priesthood as unique mouthpiece of the divine law to which earthly law conformed. The Gelasian distinction between *potestas* and *auctoritas* could not even find linguistic equivalents in Greek.[68] In such imperial characteristics as philanthropy and providence, for the Byzantines as for their hellenistic forebears, power and authority were concentrated.[69] Politically, the institutional church revolved in the imperial orbit. The patriarch, who owed his position to 'the divine grace and our empire [derived] from it' (ἡ θεία χάρις καὶ ἡ ἐξ αὐτῆς βασιλεία ἡμῶν),[70] joined the *archontes* as a leading figure at court; and the synods summoned *by* the emperor engendered like-mindedness *with* the emperor rather than a specifically *episcopalis unanimitas* as in the west. Socially, the maintenance of cultural traditions through education remained to a considerable extent in lay hands.[71] Law in particular was laymen's business. The language of the eastern liturgies was intelligible to lay congregations.[72] The parish-priest, like the layman, could be married in law as in fact.[73] In all these

etc, and Beck pp 36 *seq*, 62 *seq*. See also D. Savramis, *Zur Soziologie des byzantinischen Mönchtums* (Leiden 1962) pp 81 *seq*, for some interesting perspectives, though important aspects of the subject are left untouched.

[67] For a clear statement, see the prologue to Justinian's Nov. lxxiii: "Επειδὴ τοίνυν βασιλείαν διὰ τοῦτο ὁ θεὸς ἐξ οὐρανοῦ καθῆκεν ἵνα . . . τοὺς νόμους ἁρμόζῃ πρὸς τὴν τῆς φύσεως ποικιλίαν, διὰ τοῦτο ᾠήθημεν χρῆναι καὶ τοῦτον γράψαι τὸν νόμον καὶ δοῦναι ἐν κοινῷ τοῖς ὑπηκόοις.'

[68] There was no translation for *auctoritas* which conveyed the etymological link with *auctor*, or the legal-constitutional overtones of the Latin term. It was translated ἀξίωμα (dignity) in the Greek version of the *Res Gestae Divi Augusti*. In the sixth-century eastern law-schools, *auctoritate* seems simply to have been transliterated as αὐκτορίτατε, etc. See A. Dain, 'La transcription des mots latins dans les gloses nomiques', in *Revue des Études Latines*, 8 (Paris 1930) pp 96, 111.

[69] For φιλανθρωπία, εὐεργεσία, etc, see now D. J. Constantelos, *Byzantine Philanthropy and Social Welfare* (New Brunswick 1968) pp 43 *seq*; [H.] Hunger, *Prooimion. [Elemente der byzantinischen Kaiseridee in den Arengen der Urkunden]* (Vienna 1964) pp 84 *seq*, 143 *seq*.

[70] *BC* II 14, p 565.

[71] Beck, 'Konstantinopel', pp 24 *seq*; and 'Bildung und Theologie im frühmittalelterlichen Byzanz', in *Polychronion. Festschrift F. Dölger* (Heidelberg 1966) pp 69 *seq*, esp p 77.

[72] This feature is unusual among the great world-religions: see Tambiah 197–8. Byzantinists hardly seem to have recognised its significance. But for the neglect of Byzantine history by sociologists of religion see the critical remarks of Savramis p 5.

[73] For the social position of the lower clergy, see Beck, 'Konstantinopel', pp 28–9; and 'Kirche und Klerus im stattlichen Leben von Byzanz', in *REB*, 24 (1966) pp 22–3.

ways, the continuity and homogeneity of eastern society produced a firm integration within it of the institutional church which contrasts significantly with the tension endemic in the western situation. The absence of Byzantine imperial anointing should be seen in relation to the range of performers involved in the inauguration: among these, the clergy were naturally included, yet would hardly seek predominance as a sharply-differentiated élite, still less exploit any such role in a political contest. Where anointing presupposed a restricted group of clerical consecrators, coronation and acclamation, in manifesting 'him who reigned with God',[74] affirmed the divine inspiration operating through all the electors, and so expressed the complementarity of theocratic and democratic principles in Byzantine political thought.[75]

3 Anointing as a symbol. The meaning of the western ritual of royal (and imperial) anointing cannot be understood in isolation. Yet there has been a tendency for ecclesiastical historians simply to acknowledge parallels with one or another anointing ritual, for example those of baptism or episcopal ordination,[76] without attempting any kind of comprehensive systematic analysis of their interrelations[77] or social referents. As for the liturgiologists, they have confined themselves to the invaluable, but from this standpoint preliminary, work of collecting and describing the various rituals involving the use of anointing.[78] What has been neglected is the 'positional dimension' in

[74] Goar p 726: 'ὁ μέλλων σὺν θεῷ βασιλεύειν.' For the conception of the emperor as 'θεόστεπτος', see Treitinger p 37; Guilland *Études Byzantines*, pp 216 *seq*; Hunger, *Prooimion*, p 56.

[75] On the integration of the two principles, see Pertusi p 13. See also Guilland, *Études Byzantines*, pp 207 *seq*, and the important reassessments of Beck, 'Senat und Volk', esp pp 40–2, 51–2, and 'Res Publica Romana. Vom Staatsdenken der Byzantiner', in *SBAW* (1970) pp 7 *seq*. Compare the parallel duality in linguistic developments perceived by G. Dagron, 'Aux origines de la civilisation byzantine: langue de culture et langue d'état', in *RH*, 241 (1969) pp 23 *seq*, esp pp 49–50 on two tendencies: 'l'une conduisant à une Église hierarchisée et hellenophone, l'autre à une Église moins imperiale, plus diversifiée, cosmopolite et polyglotte.'

[76] [E.] Eichmann, [Königs-und Bischofsweihe'], in *SBAW* (1928); K. Hoffmann, *Taufsymbolik im mittelalterlichen Herrscherbild* (Düsseldorf 1968) pp 9 *seq*, with rich bibliography. The need for a comprehensive approach had already been suggested by Kantorowicz, *The King's Two Bodies* (Princeton 1957) p 52, n 22, and by Bouman, 'De oorsprong van de rituele zalving der koningen. De stand van een probleem', in *Dancwerc, opstellen aangeboden aan D. T. Enklaar* (Groningen 1959) pp 64 *seq*.

[77] But see the valuable, though brief, section, 'Die Personensalbung', in [R.] Kottje, [*Studien zum Einfluss des Alten Testaments auf Recht und Liturgie des frühen Mittelalters*] (Bonn 1964) pp 94 *seq*.

[78] See, for example, the rich material in [P.] Hofmeister, [*Die heiligen Öle in der morgen- und abendländischen Kirche*] (Würzburg 1948); [L. L.] Mitchell, [*Baptismal Anointing*] (London 1966); [G.] Ellard, [*Ordination Anointings in the Western Church*] (Cambridge,

which, as V. W. Turner has said, 'we see the meaning of a symbol as deriving from its relation to other symbols in a specific cluster or gestalt of symbols whose elements acquire much of their significance from their position in its structure.'[79] Such a cluster of symbols confronts us in the oil-rituals of the Christian church. Fully to explore the positional dimension of one such ritual is a task far beyond the scope of this paper. I want merely to suggest some lines along which we might start, lines relevant to our present problem in that they etch still more deeply the contrast between eastern and western Christendom.

In the world of antiquity, and especially in the near east, ritual anointing whether applied to things or persons transferred from the category of the profane to that of the sacred,[80] and in so doing defined boundaries. Here our concern is with rituals of personal anointing, and with the social boundaries these define. The prime function of personal anointing in the eastern church in the early medieval period was to initiate Christians.[81] The oil used for the post-baptismal anointing was made and used especially for this purpose. The chrism, a mixture of aromatics and olive oil, made the Christian: *christi dicti a chrismate.*[82] To a Greek-speaker, the linguistic association

---

Mass., 1933); [H. B.] Porter, '[The] Origin [of the Medieval Rite for Anointing the Sick or Dying]' in *JTS*, ns 7 (1956) pp 211 *seq.* [P.] Menevizoglou, [Τὸ Ἅγιον Μύρον ἐν τῇ ὀρθοδόξῳ ἀνατολικῇ ἐκκλησίᾳ] (Thessaloniki 1972), presents useful material on liturgical and doctrinal aspects, but is relatively weak on the early medieval period and neglects nearly all the major work done on this subject by such 'westerners' as Hofmeister and Mitchell.

[79] 'The syntax of symbolism in an African religion', in *PTRSL* no 772, vol 251 (London 1966) p 295. Turner's concept should prove useful to all students of symbolism. For insights into 'the concordance between symbolic and social experience', see M. Douglas, *Natural Symbols* (London 1970) p 64 and *passim*. J. C. Faris, 'Validation in ethnographical description', in *Man*, ns 3 (London 1968) pp 112 *seq*, implies that many anthropologists have yet to be converted to a recognition of the need to set symbols in a total cultural context. Faris also pleads for a diachronic approach.

[80] E. Kutsch, G. Delling and C. A. Bouman, art. 'Salbung', in *RGG* 5, cols 1330–6; [A. S.] Pease, [art. 'Oleum'], in *PW*, 34, cols 2454 *seq*, at 2466–8.

[81] Mitchell pp 37–8, 44, 53–4, 63–4; Menevizoglou pp 41 *seq*, 188 *seq*. Typically, in both eastern and western churches, simple oil was used for the pre-baptismal anointing associated with exorcism, and chrism (μύρον) for the post-baptismal anointing, associated with the gift of the holy spirit: see B. Welte, *Die Postbaptismale Salbung* (Freiburg 1939). An exception was the Syrian rite, which probably down to the fifth century had had only one, pre-baptismal, anointing.

[82] Tertullian, *De Baptismo*, 7, in *CC* 1, p 282. Compare Isidore, *Etymologiae*, VI, 50 in *PL* 82, col 256: 'Chrisma graece, latine unctio nominatur, ex cuius nomine et christus dicitur et homo post lavacrum sanctificatur.' For other liturgical uses of chrism, see [P.] Bernard, [art. 'Chrême'], in *DTC* 2, cols 2395 *seq*. For its composition, in the west from oil and balsam, in the east from these and a long list of additional ingredients, see Menevizoglou pp 29 *seq*. A basic recipe appears in Exod. 30: 23–5.

was immediately obvious: anointing was the essential ritual of incorporation in Christian initiation. It, if not baptism, had to be repeated when a lapsed member was being readmitted.[83] When the empire became Christian and the *oikoumene* synonymous with Christendom[84] (in thought if not in fact) it was natural for Christian initiation to be identified with membership of the Christian Roman empire. Ullmann has shown how the equation Roman = Christian operated in the carolingian west.[85] Was it not equally basic in a rather different sense, to the Byzantine world-view? The one boundary which that world-view required lay between the Christian and non-Christian worlds.[86] The Christian world participated actively in the *basileia*, ruled by an emperor whom, according to the opening prayer of the Byzantine *ordo* of *c*800, 'the Lord has been pleased to establish as king over the holy race bought by the blood of his son.[87] The non-Christian world passively acknowledged the superiority of Byzantium. The crucial threshold lay between the non-Christian, un-anointed, profane, barbarian outside, and the Christian, anointed, 'holy race' within. By means of chrism, Christian Byzantine society separated itself off from the external world of non-*christi*.

Conversely, the anointed, the Christian Romans, formed a single community, within which the emphasis was not on boundaries but on communications. Characteristic of Byzantine society were rituals of mass participation:[88] the processions of the emperor or of relics or images through the great cities, the *adventus*, the acclamations in the vernacular of the crowds in the hippodromes, and in the great churches the elaborate preparation of chrism by the patriarch 'before all the people.'[89] To the pure, all things are holy. This was a centripetal

[83] Council of Constantinople (381), cap 7, Mansi, 3, cols 563–4; Council *in Trullo* (692), cap 95, Mansi 11, cols 983–4; the Visigothic *Liber Ordinum*, ed M. Férotin (Paris 1904) cols 100 *seq*.

[84] Sinogowitz pp 452-3, Beck 'Christliche Mission und politische Propaganda im byzantinischen Reich', in *Settimane di studio del Centro italiano di studi sull'alto medioevo*, 14 (Spoleto 1967) pp 650 *seq*.

[85] [*The*] *Growth* [*of Papal Government in the Middle Ages*] (2 ed London 1962) pp 105 *seq*. For this equation in an eighth-century Frankish source, see M. Andrieu, *Les Ordines Romani du haut Moyen Age*, 3 (Louvain 1951) p 187 (*Ordo* XVII): 'romani devoti vel boni cristiani.'

[86] Baynes pp 19-20; Dölger, *Byzanz*, pp 70 *seq*.

[87] Goar p. 726: 'ὃν εὐδόκησας καταστῆσαι βασιλέα ἐπὶ τὸ ἔθνος σου τὸ ἅγιον, ὃ περιεποιήσω τῷ τιμίῳ αἵματι τοῦ μονογενοῦς σου υἱοῦ'.

[88] For what follows, compare n 45 above. See also Treitinger pp 71–2, 172 *seq*; Hunger, *Reich* [*der Neuen Mitte*] (Graz/Cologne 1965) pp 184–5; MacCormack pp 746–8.

[89] Theodore Lector, cited in *PG* 86, col 208, describes the practice 'τὸ μυστήριον (=μύρον) ἐν τῇ ἐκκλησίᾳ ἐπὶ παντὸς τοῦ λαοῦ ἁγιάζεσθαι', attributing its origin

society,[90] integrated without being rigidly stratified, in which some careers at least were open to talent, emperorship remained elective, diverse lines of access, both institutional and personal, linked provinces and centre, and spiritual power was accessible to persons, monks and holy men especially, outside the institutional priesthood. As it came into being in the fifth and sixth centuries, as it evolved from the later sixth century with the 'democratisation' of culture, the growing importance of Constantinople itself, and the more pressing consciousness of struggling against an upsurge of surrounding pagan enemies along its boundaries, this society shaped new symbols. The liturgification of Byzantine public life, centred on the capital, reflected a new-found and increasing confidence, yes, but also and in the long run more fundamentally, a new inclusive social structure cemented by common religious belief and practice. Within this structure, it was relatively unimportant to demarcate individual functionaries or specialist groups as monopolists of spiritual power: hence the absence in the Byzantine world of personal anointings defining exclusive status, such as those of emperor or priest. All children born into this society qualified for anointing with chrism. Other personal anointings in the eastern churches had a similarly universal application. This was obviously so in the case of the anointing of the sick,[91] but such later practices in some eastern churches[92] as the anointing of every member of the congregation on great feastdays, of brides and grooms, of newly-delivered mothers and babies, all exemplify the use of anointing as an inclusive symbol, available to all Christians as such in their natural life-crises.

Turning now to the west, we find a different picture. There too, anointing during the early Christian centuries was associated with

---

to a fifth-century patriarch of Antioch. Theodore wrote in Constantinople in the early sixth century. For this and other evidence, see Menevizoglou pp 45–6.

[90] For the following sketch, I have drawn on the works of Guilland and Beck already cited; also Beck, 'Byzantinisches Gefolgschaftswesen', in *SBAW* (1965); and for the critical formative period, D. Claude, *Die Byzantinische Stadt im 6 Jht.* (Munich 1969) pp 121 *seq*, 156 *seq*; P. Brown, *The World of Late Antiquity* (London 1971) esp cap 14, and 'The Rise and Function of the Holy Man in Late Antiquity', in *JRS* 61 (1971) pp 80 *seq*. Hunger, *Reich*, pp 262 *seq*, gives evidence for the continuing significance of holy men throughout the early Byzantine period. Useful comparative perspectives on aspects of Byzantine society can be found in S. Eisenstadt, *The Political Systems of Empires* (New York 1967) esp pp 238 *seq*.

[91] F. W. Puller, *The Anointing of the Sick in Scripture and Tradition* (London 1904) especially appendix II. In these anointings only blessed oil, not chrism, was used.

[92] For details, see Hofmeister pp 226 *seq*.

Christian baptism, and, by extension, with curative functions.[93] The critical change came in the various western realms between the seventh and tenth centuries, when anointing began to be used in the initiation of two specialised classes of people: clergy and kings.[94] Rome, it is clear, had nothing to do with the origins of these practices, although many popes from Stephen II onwards were quick to perceive the implications of anointing rulers in terms of increased papal leverage.[95] The origins lie north of the Alps. Scholars have long debated precisely where, and contemporary fashion seems to be veering again towards identifying a penchant for anointings of various sorts as a typically bizarre Celtic symptom.[96] (Douglas's 'bog Irish' have a long pedigree!) But the evidence is very slim, and the whole question needs re-examining in a broader context. In general, two explanations of these ritual innovations have been offered. One is that the influence of the old testament model proved irresistible—an especially popular interpretation of Pippin's royal anointing in 751.[97] The other is epitomised in Andrieu's comment à propos the addition of a physical anointing to the episcopal ordination just at the point where the prayer-text reads, *Eum caelestis unguenti flore sanctifica*: 'Prendre ces expressions au sens materiel et les traduire en acte dut paraitre naturel,' especially when kings were already being anointed.[98] To become chary of these explanations, we only have to look at the Byzantine imperial *ordo* with its reference to David's anointing by Samuel and its request to the Lord to 'anoint thy faithful servant with the oil of exultation',[99] and then to recall that the Byzantines never

[93] For western baptismal anointings, see J. D. C. Fisher, *Christian Initiation: Baptism in the Medieval West* (London 1965) pp 18 *seq*, 64 *seq*; Mitchell pp 80 *seq*. For the anointing of the sick, Porter, 'Origin'; and for the magical properties assigned to chrism by the laity in the west, Bernard col 2413.

[94] For ordination anointings, see Ellard; Andrieu, '[Le] Sacre [épiscopale d'après Hincmar de Reims]' in *RHE*, 48 (1953) pp 22 *seq*; D. H. Turner, *The Claudius Pontificals, HBS* 97 for 1964 (1971) pp xxiv–vi. For royal anointings, see the works cited above, n 29, and Kottje pp 94 *seq*.

[95] Ullmann, *Growth*, pp 67 *seq*, 143 *seq*.

[96] So, Porter, 'Origin'; Bouman pp xi–xii; Kottje pp 98–100; Schneider pp 197–8. Earlier upholders of this view were Eichmann, pp 24 *seq*, and T. Klauser, reviewing Ellard, in *JLW*, 13 (1933) pp 350–1.

[97] So, Brühl, p 304 with n 2, giving details of earlier literature.

[98] Andrieu, 'Sacre', p 41, n 5.

[99] Goar, p 726: 'τὸν πιστόν σου δοῦλον . . . χρῖσαι καταξίωσον τῷ ἐλαίῳ τῆς ἀγαλλιάσεως'. For the influence of the old testament on Byzantine ideology, see Baynes, pp 33 *seq*, and, especially relevant to the present context, Walter pp 168–72. See also above, n 55, for the Byzantine conception of mystical anointing—in Walter's terms, an 'ideological' rather than a 'historical' theme.

drew the allegedly 'natural' conclusion, any more than western christians had before the seventh century. It remains legitimate to ask why western kings and priests began to be anointed as and when they did. The question can be posed in terms of the interpretation I have already suggested for the anointing-ritual itself: why were these categories of person specially and now so emphatically marked off from other members of the *populus christianus*? Why were they alone now the 'twice-born'?[100] Why did the chrism, in the west as in the east long since the symbol of incorporation—*illud unde christo incorporemur et unde omnes fideles sanctificantur*[101]—now acquire the further function of marking off internal boundaries within a Christian society? In the various western realms, this development followed closely, indeed presupposed, the achievement of a permanent political and cultural synthesis between Christian (with all that implied in terms of Roman survivals) and barbarian elements: in Visigothic Spain, in late merovingian Gaul, in eighth-century England, and in Ottonian Germany.[102] The barbarians asserted not only their political independence with the creation of their kingdoms of *gentes*, but also their cultural autonomy within Christendom in the sense that, as well as assimilating something of Roman christianity, they imposed new demands and new interpretations on the religion that was now their own. Barbarian clergy innovated. Rome spoke—and also adapted. For the differentiation of hierarchical grades and functions was congenial enough to the Roman church itself. If the anointing of kings made difficulties for the papacy in the age of the Gregorian reform, the anointing of members of the *sacerdotium*, which Rome had finally imported from the north, was found to provide a very practical instrument of demarcation.[103]

For this, surely, was the significance of anointing: the reinforcement

[100] For this conception in Hinduism, see Van Gennep pp 104–6, and L. Dumont, *Homo Hierarchicus*, English trans (London 1970) pp 106–7. The analogous linkage of the ideas of rebirth and hierarchy in western Christendom would repay further investigation.

[101] Council of Tours (461), *Mansi* 7, col 949.

[102] For very perceptive comments on this synthesis, see H. Löwe, 'Von Theoderich der Grossen zu Karl dem Grossen. Das Werden des Abendlandes im Geschichtsbild des frühen Mittelalters', in *DA*, 9 (1952) pp 353 *seq*, and, from a different standpoint, the fine analysis of P. Anderson, *Passages from Antiquity to Feudalism* (London 1974) pp 120 *seq*.

[103] For the imperialist interpretation of the anointings of kings and emperors, see *MGH, Li*, 1, p 467; 1, p 566; 2, p 538. But for sacerdotal anointing as helping to define functional boundaries, compare the argument of cardinal Humbert, *ibid* 1, p 234, on the workings of the holy spirit: 'Ipse sanctum chrisma instituit, ipse clericorum vel ministrorum diversos gradus et officia in ecclesia disposuit'.

of stratification, the sharp delineation of restricted channels of access to supernatural power, the specification of those offices which guaranteed the identity and continuity of new political communities. Ritual, in the hands of barbarian priests, defined the holders of theocratic power. For justification the old testament, for clarification the church's law, lay ready to hand. But these *auctoritates* were servants whose utility depended on their relevance to the makers of ritual. The western societies within which and for which the new rituals were designed differed profoundly from the society of Byzantium. They were at once simpler and more highly stratified, they were self-consciously dynamic, assertive. The anointing of their power-holders on the one hand marked off the dominators from the dominated within, and on the other, through the exegesis of divine grace, legitimised that dominance both within, challenging the pagan ideology of *Adelsherrschaft*,[104] and without, asserting political independence in a world of *regna*.

But, finally, why should this one ritual rather than any other have been used for the purposes I have attributed to it? Why specifically anointing? We must expand the positional dimension. In the mediterranean world, olive oil was (and is) a basic commodity. Like corn and wine it was an essential foodstuff (nearly everything was cooked in it); it was fuel for lamps; and it was also soap, shampoo, cosmetic and every sort of patent remedy for ordinary men and women.[105] Outside the mediterranean zone, in temperate Europe, where even the agriculture of corn and vine was an alien imposition (and Duby has shown the implications of that revolution),[106] the olive simply cannot be cultivated.[107] Here, and so in the heartland of the

[104] For the persistent tension between kingship and nobility, see Hauck, 'Die geschichtliche Bedeutung der germanisch Auffassung von Königtum und Adel', in *XI International Congress of Historical Sciences* (Stockholm 1960) Rapports 3, pp 96 *seq*; Schlesinger, *Beiträge*, pp 28 *seq*. H. Hoffmann, 'Französische Fürstenweihen des Hochmittelalters', in *DA*, 18 (1962) pp 92 *seq*, discusses aristocratic imitations of royal insignia and ritual, but stresses that anointing was the one ritual never thus appropriated.

[105] Pease, 'Oleum', and art. 'Ölbaum', in *PW* 34, cols 1998 *seq*. P. D. King, *Law and Society in the Visigothic Kingdom* (Cambridge 1970) pp 212–24, draws attention to the particularly high penalty for damage to olive trees (as compared with other trees) in Visigothic legislation.

[106] G. Duby, 'Le monachisme et l'économie rurale', in *Il monachismo e la riforma ecclesiastica, 1049–1122*, Atti della IV Settimana internazionale di Studio, Mendola 1968 (Milan 1971) pp 336 *seq*, and *Guerriers et Paysans* (Paris 1973) pp 26–7, on the essential place of the olive also in the new *type d'alimentation 'civilisée'*.

[107] For the frequent use by geographers of the criterion of olive-cultivation in defining the mediterranean zone, see [F.] Braudel, [*La Méditerranée et le Monde Méditerranéen*

new medieval society of the west, there was a permanent oil-crisis. Flesh-renouncing monks had to have special permission to cook their vegetables in lard.[108] The ecclesiastical authorities had to proscribe the substitution of nut-oil, or butter.[109] For north-western Europe olive-oil was like pepper or spice, a luxury item. But it was one that northern churchmen insisted upon,[110] and that northern society was willing to pay for. The barbarians conquered the cultivators of the olive; their adoption of Christianity assimilated them to the oil-users. Their power-holders sealed their and their peoples' God-given domination by claiming an extra share of the oil which was both so potent and so scarce.

Within a single Christendom, a single liturgical tradition, personal anointings thus came to have contrasting significance in east and west. In Byzantium, they were inclusive, universally available; in the west they became, additionally, exclusive, defining internal as well as external boundaries. In each case the oil functioned through ritual as, in Douglas's sense, a natural symbol. The divergent social contexts which, for medieval participants, supplied the symbol's divergent meanings may, for the modern ecclesiastical historian, explain them.

à l'Époque de Philippe II] (Paris 1949) pp 139–41. See further R. Grand and R. Delatouche, *L'Agriculture au Moyen Age* (Paris 1951) pp 315, 365.

108 *Fragmentum historicum* about the council of Aix-la-Chapelle (816), in *MGH Conc, aevi karolini*, I, pp 831–5, at 833: 'Et quia oleum olivarum *non habent Franci*, voluerunt episcopi, ut oleo lardivo utantur.' Compare *ibid*, n 2, for the same problem in the eleventh century. In the present context, it is irrelevant whether this passage of the *Fragmentum* genuinely represents what happened in 816, or belongs with some eleventh-century special pleading: the ecological exigency was constant.

109 Bede, *PL* 91, col 1097; Gregory VII, *Register* VII, I. To natives of the mediterranean world, the use of butter appeared a very salient sign of barbarism: see Sidonius Apollinaris, *Carmina* XII, 7, and Braudel p 201, with n 4, for similar expressions of disgust in the sixteenth century. The symbolism of 'inside' and 'outside' arising from such divergent culinary practices deserves further study: in some ascetic traditions, dairy products are classed with flesh as 'impure', while olive-oil belongs unequivocally to the 'pure' vegetable category.

110 R. Doehaerd, *Le Haut Moyen Age Occidental. Economies et Sociétés* (Paris 1971) pp 270–1, 274 with n 7. Compare also the indignant western rebuttals of ninth-century Greek accusations that Latins made chrism with river-water: Nicholas I, writing to the Frankish bishops, in *PL* 119, col 1155, and Ratramnus of Corbie, in *PL* 121, col 334. Were the accusations mere Photian canards, or did the Franks protest too much?

12

INAUGURATION RITUALS *

If I'd been addressing an audience of anthropologists, I'd have felt no need to begin by justifying my contribution to this series of lectures. Anthropologists have long been convinced of the importance of inauguration rituals. One of them who has contributed much on this subject, Meyer Fortes, said ten years ago: 'The mysterious quality of continuity through time in its organisation and values, which is basic to the self-image of every society, modern, archaic, or primitive, is in some way congealed in these installation ceremonies. . . . Politics and law, rank and kinship, religious and philosophical concepts and values, the economics of display and hospitality, the aesthetics and symbolism of institutional representation, and last but not least the social psychology of popular participation, all are concentrated in them'.[1] With such a lively appreciation of what they can convey, the anthropologist will expect to be able to 'read' from inauguration rituals a good deal about the nature of power, the structure, beliefs and values in this or that society at a given time.[2]

But are inauguration rituals equally useful to historians of early medieval kingship? For us the answer is not so simple. The time-dimension we work in raises two problems. First that of fossilisation: the congealing of ritual forms over time makes them suspect as historical documents. Some of the forms used at the coronation of Elizabeth II in 1953,[3] for instance, go back at least a thousand years; but who would claim that the 'politics and law' or 'religious or philosophical concepts and values' of post-war Britain were in any very real sense represented in that inauguration ritual. Already in the sixteenth century, Thomas Cranmer, himself ex officio a king's consecrator, said of royal anointing that it was 'but a ceremony', having 'its ends and utility yet neither direct force nor necessity'.[4] What did such rituals mean in the early Middle Ages?

Here we broach the second problem: that of origins. Another eminent anthropologist, Edmund Leach, recognised the existence of 'the philogenetic question "how come?"' as distinct from 'the functional question "what for?"'. But, he claimed, 'the enormous complexity of the ritual sequences which anthropologists

* For full references to notes in this chapter, *see* pp. 305-7 below.

[1] Fortes 1968, pp. 5–20.

[2] See, for example Balandier, 1972, esp. ch. 5.

[3] Ratcliff 1953.

[4] Strype 1848, vol. 1, bk. 2, p. 206.

have to study makes any guesses of the "how come" type more or less absurd'.[5] And what about the ritual sequences which historians have to study? Well, as a mere historian, I claim the right to be absurd in my own philo-genetic way. Despite enormous difficulties, enough material survives if handled correctly to allow some kind of history of royal inauguration rituals to be reconstructed, including answers to some 'how come' questions. The liturgical rites of royal consecration, the *Ordines*, present special problems,[6] and we need the expert help of liturgists in their interpretation; but for the early Middle Ages, they do constitute contemporary evidence, becoming more or less stereotyped only from the eleventh century onwards. But *Ordinesforschung* should be only a part of our repertoire: we need to bear in mind the diversity of other available evidence and thus of the varieties of treatment required. Perhaps because of a certain tendency towards an 'abstract-legal' or *ideengeschichtlich* approach on the part of such scholars as E. Eichmann and P. E. Schramm who pioneered our subject,[7] many more sociologically-minded medievalists have as yet hardly cast more than side-glances at royal inauguration rituals or appreciated the potential contribution which they offer, so the anthropologists assure us. for our general understanding of early medieval society and not just of the political theory of some of its clerical elite. Yet it is half a century since Marc Bloch in his early masterpiece *Les Rois Thaumaturges*[8] blazed the broadest of trails for us to follow.

There is one point to stress at the outset: the significance, political and symbolic, of inauguration rituals arose largely from the fact that no early medieval king ever simply succeeded to his kingdom as a matter of course. A man might be born king-worthy, but he had to be made a king. In no kingdom of the early medieval West was there quickly established a very restrictive norm of royal succession. Sometimes a king was succeeded by a son or brother, sometimes by a distant kinsman, and sometimes by one who was no kin at all. Interregna happened: the Anglo-Saxon evidence is predictably clear, but clear also is that from Merovingian Gaul although, as Ian Wood reminds us,[9] dynastic continuity has tended to obscure historians' sense of the contingent in Frankish royal accessions. Kenneth Harrison, has recently written, tongue in cheek: 'much is known about the legal and "sacral" aspects of Germanic kingship. Far less is known of the events which could and sometimes did follow when personal power was extinguished by the death of a king, and the hungry athelings began to prowl'.[10] The inauguration of a new king, when it ended such a time of prowling, publicly indicated the victor of a political struggle: by no means

[5] Leach 1966, pp. 403 sqq., at 404.

[6] I indicated some of these below, chapter 14, pp. 329-39.

[7] See Bak 1973 with full references to the work of Eichmann and Schramm.

[8] Originally published 1924, now translated into English as *The Royal Touch. Sacred Monarchy and Scrofula in England and France* (London, 1973).

[9] See above.

[10] Harrison 1976, p. 92.

'but a ceremony', it must have reminded all who participated in it of the powers and functions of kingship.

Having convinced you, I hope, that an interest in early medieval inauguration rituals is legitimate, I don't propose now to embark on a potted history of them. It would be all too easy to get bogged down at the beginning. For during the period before churchmen got closely involved in king-makings, the evidence all over the barbarian West is very sketchy indeed; and any case for which it's more than sketchy is more likely to be odd than typical. Of early Anglo-Saxon accessions, for instance, the Anglo-Saxon Chronicle will simply say that so-and-so 'took the realm';[11] and neither Eddius nor even Bede is much more helpful. Then suddenly the Chronicle for the year 787 reports that Ecgferth, son of Offa of Mercia, was 'hallowed to king'.[12] Caution has impelled some scholars to write in terms only of some kind of consecration;[13] but most interpret this as the first case of royal anointing in England.[14] Certainly this is the Chronicle's earliest use of the word 'hallowed' for a royal, as distinct from an episcopal, inauguration. But it is also its last, for almost a century and a half during which we know that royal anointings were practised in England. It seems possible that the Chronicle uses 'hallowed' for Ecgferth, simply because in his case the normal 'took the realm' was inapposite;[15] and that what was thought special was the pre-mortem character of Ecgferth's succession, not any novelty in its ritual form. It could be that kings had been anointed in England — perhaps were regularly anointed — before 787. In any case, the Chronicle is not the place we should expect to find such an innovation registered at the date it was introduced. For Scotland there is a similar general lack of evidence with information on a single case which could be the exception that proves the rule: St. Columba, according to Adamnan writing over a century later, 'ordained' a king in Scottish Dalriada as early as 574 by laying hands on him and blessing him.[16] But this obviously special case, cited by the hagiographer to show Columba's prophetic vision, need not imply that any sixth-century Celtic 'ritual' or 'ceremony' for ordaining kings existed, let alone that this was its normal form.[17] Historians seem sometimes to have forgotten that a saint's life demands different treatment from a chronicle. When Adamnan recounts Columba's vision of an angel bearing a glass book 'of the ordinations of kings' and then

[11] 'Feng to rice': on this, and on Bede's terminology, see Chadwick 1905, p. 355 sqq., esp. 360.

[12] Anglo-Saxon Chronicle s.a. 785 (recte 787), ed. B. Thorpe (Rolls Series, 1861), pp. 96–7.

[13] E.g. D. Whitelock in her translation of the *Anglo-Saxon Chronicle* (Cambridge, 1961), p. 35, n. 2.

[14] See e.g., Levison 1946, p. 119; Stenton 1971, pp. 218–9; Wallace-Hadrill 1971, pp. 113–5. On the possibility of earlier insular anointings see Kottje 1964, pp. 94–106. Bloch 1924, Appendix III: 'les débuts de l'onction royale', remains well worth reading.

[15] Compare the similarly exceptional case of the one-year reign of Cenwalh's widow, queen Seaxburh in Wessex, *Anglo-Saxon Chronicle* Preface to MS 'A', p. 1: 'þa heold Seaxburg . . . þaet rice æfter him'.

[16] *Adomnan's Life of Columba*, edd. A. O. and M. O. Anderson (Edinburgh, 1961), pp. 473–5.

[17] As inferred by Martène 1736, II, 10 col. 212; Ellard 1933, p. 13; Ratcliff 1953, p. 2. But see now Kottje 1964, p. 97.

describes the saint prophesying 'between the words of the ordination', we get a blend of scriptural reminiscence, liturgical phraseology and legendary motif.

For the historian, one saint's life may have very different evidential value from another: there is one remarkable passage in the late seventh-century Passion of St. Leudegarius which to my mind strongly suggests that a fixed inauguration ritual existed in at any rate later Merovingian times. This text is all the more credible here because the hagiographer, who is a contemporary of the events he describes, mentions king-making procedures en passant, in an unforced, unselfconscious way. He is out to blacken Ebroin, the enemy of Leudegarius, but he gives an essentially historical account of the background to Ebroin's fall. The date is 673:

> King Clothar (III) died . . . But while Ebroin should have summoned the optimates together and should have raised Clothar's full brother, Theuderic by name, to the kingdom with due solemnity as is the custom, puffed up with the spirit of pride he refused to summon them. So they began to be very fearful, because Ebroin would be able to do harm to whomever he wished with impunity, so long as he could keep under his control, and exploit the name of, the king whom he should have elevated for the glory of the public fatherland.[18]

Here we have the technical phrase *sublimare in regnum* (we shall meet it again presently) with a clear reference to a traditional ritual procedure: *solemniter, ut mos est,* which should be performed in the presence of the *optimates*, subsequently termed a *multitudo nobilium.* There is also a very significant indication that these same *optimates*, whose views the hagiographer is expressing at this point, saw the *gloria patriae publicae* as at stake in king-making: because they had not been rightfully summoned to play their part, they rejected Ebroin and his puppet-king and invited in instead another Merovingian from Austrasia. Clearly a power-struggle was fought out in 673, and the inauguration ritual became the focus of the political conflict. If only the hagiographer had stopped to say in detail what the customary procedures — the *mos* — consisted of. But that was no part of his concern.

That *mos*, from the sixth century onwards, seems to have centred on an enthronement.[19] I think it very unlikely that, as Levison claimed, 'the accession to the throne of the Merovingians was a secular act devoid of any ecclesiastical ingredient'[20] — unlikely, I mean, either that it was ever not religious (there is a difference between religious and christian) or that it did not also come under clerical influence before the mid-eighth century. The regal benedictions that survive in late eighth- and ninth-century manuscripts for use 'when the king is elevated into the kingdom'[21] seem to me to be of Merovingian origin; and the *pontifices et proceres* who appear together so often in late Merovingian sources would surely all have attended the inauguration of

18 *Passio Leudegarii* I, c. 5, ed. B. Krusch, MGH SS rer. merov. V, p. 287.

19 For a full discussion and references, see Schneider 1972, p. 213.

20 Levison 1946, p. 116.

21 See Bouman, 1957, pp. 163, 175 and pp. 91 and 189–90, for the texts of the regal benedictions 'Prospice' and 'Deus inenarrabilis'.

a king. The liturgist C. A. Bouman's remark about Carolingian inaugurations seems equally apposite in a Merovingian context: 'Whenever bishops were present at an official function, it was in the nature of things that they accentuated the religious aspects of a long-standing usage by giving it a ritual turn'[22] — though in the case of king-making what was new was not the ritual turn but the ecclesiastical twist.

As long as ecclesiastical blessings remained relatively subordinate adjuncts to such inauguration rituals as enthronement, investiture with weapons or regalia, symbolic marriage with an earth-goddess, or the mounting of an ancestral burial-mound, clerical writers would naturally tend to say little about procedures of king-making. They began to say more when their colleagues in the ecclesiastical hierarchies of the barbarian kingdoms took over, clericalised, 'liturgified' the conduct of a major part of the ritual. This happened at different times in the various kingdoms, but it had happened in the main ones by the mid-tenth century. This take-over centred on the introduction of royal anointing and came to involve the elaboration of a full ecclesiastical rite for the king's consecration, an *Ordo*, analogous to the other personal status-changing rites already provided for in liturgical books. Thus where an eighth-century Sacramentary might contain some regal blessings, a tenth-century Pontifical might well include — after ordination-forms for the seven ecclesiastical grades and for abbot and abbess, and consecrations for monk, nun and widow — *Ordines* also for the king and queen. The royal rite was thus regularised and recorded. But such a record by no means included the total process of a king's inauguration. Clerics rarely cared to document non-clerical procedures; yet when we happen to have evidence of these, we can see how partial a picture the *Ordines* give. Widukind, for instance, gives an account of Otto I's inauguration which begins with an enthronement ritual outside the church performed by the *duces et milites* making Otto king *more suo* — 'in their own traditional way'[23] — and ends with a description of the clearly very important feast that followed after the ecclesiastical rite was over.[24] The early Anglo-Saxon *Ordines* open with tantalising references to the immediately preceding election and a *conventus seniorum*, presumably the Witan, but we know nothing of what ritual procedures were enacted. One of these *Ordines* ends with a mention of the feast to follow, but it is an anecdote in the earliest life of St. Dunstan which happens to reveal how important this feast was felt to be by tenth-century participants.[25] The *Ordines*, then, though often our only evidence for the inauguration rituals of the ninth and tenth centuries, have to be married up with other types of evidence if we are to begin to appreciate their context, function and meaning for contemporaries.

If we have to think in terms of a whole process, consisting of extra- and intra-ecclesiastical ritual, constitutive only in its totality,[26] we also have to distinguish

[22] Op. cit., p. 127.

[23] *Rerum Gestarum Saxonicarum Libri Tres*, ed. H. E. Lohmann, rev. P. Hirsch (Hanover 1935), pp. 64–5.

[24] Hauck 1950, pp. 620–1. For other kinds of *mos*, see Schmidt 1961, pp. 97–233.

[25] Further details below, chapter 14, pp. 330-1.

[26] See Mitteis 1944, pp. 47–60.

different observers and different periods in the rituals' evolution. Let's consider the rite of anointing — which historians seem to agree is very important but which has been too rarely considered in the context of a particular place and time, or studied comparatively in different kingdoms. There may be no point in asking who borrowed the rite from whom, if in fact it was not, or not always, diffused but 'invented' autonomously in various places: but if so, the question must become, under what conditions? It is probably equally pointless to ask what was the purpose of royal anointing, or to whose advantage did it operate, or was it indispensable:[27] I doubt if there is a single, generally-applicable answer to any of these questions. As to the constitutive character of anointing, for instance, the cleric who composed the 'Frühdeutsch' *Ordo* seems to distinguish between the *princeps*, or *electus*, before the anointing, and the *rex* after it.[28] But Widukind's terminology suggests nothing of the kind: he doesn't even distinguish consistently between *rex* and *dux*, Otto being termed now one, now the other. Hincmar of Rheims, when it suited him, stressed the constitutive character of Charles the Bald's anointing in 848;[29] but he certainly never questioned the fulness of Charles' kingly powers before that date (Rheims, after all, had benefited a good deal from their exercise)[30] nor did he cast doubt on the title of unanointed kings as such. The historical situation of the ninth century was too varied and too fluid for even a political theorist of Hincmar's stature to attempt to produce a clearcut or consistently-presented theory of royal anointing. What does seem to have happened is that once anointings had come to be regularly performed by the local hierarchy of a given realm, within a couple of generations or so anointing would tend to be regarded as indispensable. It joined, or rather was added to, the series of ritual acts which together made a king. For some kind of formal election, possibly culminating in procedures of elevation or enthronement, had invariably preceded it. The time-lag between these two main phases of the inauguration might be minimised, as in Otto I's case. But they remained distinct. In tenth-century England, for example, there is some evidence for the reckoning of reign years from the formal election rather than from the consecration. When practical difficulties enforced a longish delay between the two events, as in Athelstan's case (with Edgar's I deal in some detail below) we might hope to find some evidence, notably in charters, which might enable to test whether the royal powers of a *rex electus* before his consecration were less than complete in fact. But the results of such an enquiry are disappointing: whereas two of Athelstan's charters do clearly show reckoning of reign years in Wessex from a date before Christmas 924,[31] his earliest genuine one that is securely datable was issued on the day of his

[27] For these and other questions, see the discussion in *Settimane di studio del centro italiano di studi sull' alto medioevo*, VII, i (Spoleto, 1960), pp. 385–403.

[28] Ed. Erdmann 1951, pp. 83–7.

[29] Details above, chapter 7, pp. 137-42.

[30] See Tessier 1943, I, pp. 210ff., and 262ff.

[31] Birch, nos. 691, 692.

consecration 4 September, 925,[32] but the charter evidence as a whole is too scarce to warrant any suggestion that Athelstan was reluctant (or unable) to issue charters before he was consecrated. Edgar, as we shall see, certainly did just that. It is a commonplace that medieval men saw no incompatibility between the principles of election and heredity which to modern eyes tend to appear mutually exclusive:[33] we must also accept that a ninth- or tenth-century king exercised his royal powers from the time of his formal acceptance — *electio* or *acclamatio* — by some or all of his leading subjects, but still needed to be anointed as soon as possible thereafter for the king-making to be thought complete. Neither of the general statements in the preceding sentence will be found explicit in an early medieval text, but both are to be inferred from the evidence of what kings and others actually did.

In the light of all this, and especially of the need for more detailed preliminary work to be done before that general history of medieval inauguration rituals can be written (as, begging Leach's patience, one day it surely will be), I shall now examine three particular cases of inauguration rituals, including anointing, in practice in Francia and England in the eighth, ninth and tenth centuries. All three are problem cases, but they're perhaps more interesting, and certainly more instructive than so-called 'normal' ones. Together they reveal the dimensions of our subject. Firstly then, and inevitably: the case of Pippin. For only here do we have fairly good evidence as to the date and circumstances of the introduction of royal anointing in one realm. The background is well-known: Pippin's patronage of the Bonifacian reforms in the 740s, his sending of envoys to Rome, 'with the advice and consent of the Franks',[34] to ask Pope Zacharias 'about kings in Francia',[35] the receiving of the papal response that the name of king should be brought back into line with the reality of who held royal power, and that Pippin should therefore replace the last Merovingian. You did not make this *non*-Merovingian king of the Franks by letting his hair grow long and then enthroning him, but by anointing and enthroning him. Now medievalists have been all too eager to stress the revolutionary effect of 751: I say 'too eager' because the effect of this anointing on the nature of medieval kingship seems to me to have been sometimes exaggerated. Pirenne,[36] for instance, following Fustel de Coulanges,[37] drew rather too heavy a line between the allegedly quite 'secular' Merovingian rex crinitus and the Carolingian rex dei gratia. I would see a more continuous evolution of Frankish kingship starting with Clovis himself who, long-haired warrior-king though he remained, had a 'salvation-giving helmet of holy anointing'[38] put on his head when he received christian baptism. The royal

[32] Birch, no. 641 (strictly speaking, a memorandum based on a charter).

[33] A point best made by Kern 1954, pp. 13ff., 248ff.

[34] Continuator Fredegarii, ed. Wallace-Hadrill 1960, p. 102.

[35] *Annales regni Francorum*, ed. F. Kurze (Hanover 1895), SS rer. Germ. in usum schol., p. 8.

[36] Pirenne, trans. Miall 1939, pp. 136, 268ff.

[37] de Coulanges, 1888–92, vol. VI, 'Les transformations de la royauté pendant l'époque carolingienne', pp. 206–8, 226ff.

[38] Avitus of Vienne, Ep. 46, ed. R. Peiper (Berlin 1883), MGH AA VI(2), p. 75.

anointings of the Carolingians represent a quantitative rather than a qualitative change in the degree of integration between political power and ecclesiastical authority in Francia, and, underlying both, the development of the Franks' own self-image as a chosen people with a mission. Between Dagobert and Pippin — or even Charlemagne — is a difference more of style than substance.

But to return to 751: how do we explain the fact of Pippin's anointing? Fritz Kern in *Kingship and Law* had a crisp answer: 'Secular politics were the effective reason for the introduction of anointing into the constitutional law of the Frankish state'.[39] Underlying such an implicit assumption of royal initiative lies a rationalist view of politics as calculation operating in an autonomous secular sphere. This view, though apparently surviving in some of our contemporary practitioners of *Realpolitik*, is really an eighteenth-century one. Voltaire in his article, 'Roi' in the *Dictionnaire Philosophique*[40] imagined the following early medieval conversation: 'Le prince disait au pretre: Tiens, voici de l'or, mais il faut que tu affermisses mon pouvoir . . . Je serais oint, tu seras oint' ('I'll be greased — and so will you!') In similar vein Gibbon wrote of Pippin's royal unction as 'dexterously applied . . . and' (Gibbon could not refrain from adding) 'this Jewish rite has been diffused and maintained by the superstition and vanity of modern Europe'.[41] We should beware of projecting the cynicism of the Enlightenment back into the eighth century.

Now Pippin had been brought up in the monastery of St. Denis and may well have been literate. But how should a layman have understood how to operate in the clerical preserve of oil-rituals? Just what his own anointing may have meant to him we cannot know: one of his diplomas may mention it,[42] but that was of course drawn up by a cleric. We have some evidence, however, that the Frankish aristocracy, in the short run anyway, was little impressed by the new rite. The Continuation of Fredegar's Chronicle, written at this point by Pippin's uncle, does allude to the anointing of 751, but without enthusiasm:

> Pippin, by the election of all the Franks to the throne of the kingdom, by the consecration of bishops and by the subjection of the lay magnates, together with the queen Bertrada, as the rules of ancient tradition require was elevated into the kingdom.[43]

The use of the 'consecration' *(consecratio)* may be deliberately vague, for this could refer in the eighth century to any status-changing rite — the profession of a nun, for instance — without at all implying an anointing. But the chronicler's emphasis is not on the consecration anyway, but on the election and elevation of the Frankish king

[39] Kern 1954, pp. 77. I quote here from the English translation by S. B. Chrimes (Oxford, 1939), p. 41.

[40] Quoted by de Pange 1951, p. 557.

[41] *Decline and Fall of the Roman Empire*, abridged D. Low (Harmondsworth 1960), p. 636.

[42] MGH Diplomata Karolinorum, ed. E. Mühlbacher (Hanover 1906), no. 16, p. 22.

[43] Wallace-Hadrill 1960, p. 102. Rather than using Professor Wallace-Hadrill's elegant translation, I have translated this passage myself to reproduce the clumsiness and ambiguity of the original. The Continuator here is Count Childebrand, son of Charles Martel.

by the Franks — *ut antiquitus ordo deposcit.* Whatever the term *ordo* may mean in other documents or contexts of this period (and Pope Zacharias' desire 'that *ordo* be not disturbed', as reported in the *Annales regni Francorum* under the year 749, may well have Augustinian undertones[44]) here in the Continuation of Fredegar the *ordo antiquitus* is surely to be identified with the *mos* of Leudegarius' hagiographer.[45] The inauguration ritual of 751 accorded with that of Frankish tradition — which also happened to be Merovingian. In the eyes of contemporary Frankish laymen, and probably therefore of Pippin himself, this was what mattered most.

But the ritual of 751 also included the novelty of anointing. Its instigators should be sought, as von Ranke long ago surmised, in Pippin's clerical entourage, among such men as Fulrad of St. Denis and the enthusiastic reformer Chrodegang of Metz. Such men were on their home ground in the royal monastery of St. Médard at Soissons where the anointing took place. No doubt they acted under the influence of an Old Testament model, but why should a literal imitation now have been thought appropriate? Thanks to the lucky survival of the Missale Francorum, written somewhere in the Paris-Corbie-Soissons triangle in the first half of the eighth century,[46] we can be fairly sure that ordination anointings of priests were already being practised in precisely this region. If a literal interpretation of Scripture dictated the anointing of the priest's hands (the Vulgate rendering of Leviticus 16: 32 gave the erroneous translation: '*sacerdos . . . cuius manus initiatae sunt ut sacerdotio fungatur* . . .') it becomes understandable why priests thus anointed might then have found in Old Testament history their warrant for anointing the head of a king. I doubt if a special parallel was seen between Saul and David on the one hand, Childeric and Pippin on the other: David, after all, unlike Pippin, had observed the precept: 'Touch not the Lord's anointed', and had waited for Saul to be killed in battle. It was not a precise situational model, but a more general one that the Frankish clergy found in the Old Testament. The typological link existed not only between Carolingian and Davidic kingship and between reformed Frankish and Levite priesthood, but between the whole Frankish *gens* and the people of Israel. The 'inventors' of Frankish royal anointing belong in the same milieux that produced the Second Prologue to Lex Salica and the also contemporary Frankish *Laudes* with their invocations of divine blessings on the *iudices* and the *exercitus* as well as the king and princes of the Franks.[47]

A glance at Frankish inaugurations in the century after 751 shows no case in which royal anointing can be ascribed to a ruler's initiative. If anointings were performed in 768 or 771 (and the evidence is not clear-cut[48]) then Frankish clergy must again have

[44] As suggested by Büttner 1952, pp. 77–90.

[45] Compare the sense of *antiquitus* in *Passio Leudegarii* I, c. 7, SS rer. merov. V., p. 289.

[46] Ed. L. C. Mohlberg, Rerum Ecclesiasticarum Documenta, Series Maior, Fontes I (Rome, 1957), p. 10, with comments, pp. 64–7, and B. Bischoff's views on place and date, p. xvi.

[47] Kantorowicz 1946, pp. 41ff. See also Ewig 1956, pp. 16f., 47ff.

[48] See Brühl 1962, pp. 314ff.

been responsible. The Carolingians' own practice when they made their sons sub-kings reveals a remarkable lack of interest in the new rite: Charlemagne's second son Charles was made sub-king of Neustria in 790 without receiving any anointing,[49] and when Louis the Pious made his son Charles a sub-king in 838, he invested him with the weapons of manhood and with a crown, and, keeping abreast of the times, had all the magnates commend themselves with oaths of fidelity to the young man, but in neither of the two quite full accounts of this occasion is there any hint of an ecclesiastical rite.[50] I can't now go into the complicating factor of eighth-century papal involvement in Frankish royal anointings. But it may be worth noting that the anointings of Pippin and his two sons performed by Stephen II in 754 don't seem to have cut much ice with contemporary Franks: the Continuation of Fredegar (now being kept up to date by Pippin's cousin) simply does not mention these anointings, and the Frankish bishops implicitly ignored them if they indeed reconsecrated Pippin's sons in 768 and 771. Only at St. Denis was the memory of these anointings kept green,[51] and that was because they'd taken place at St. Denis and redounded therefore to *its* glory. It's surely a significant (and rather neglected) fact that not a single one of Charlemagne's court poets, panegyrists or correspondents, especially the prolific Alcuin, ever mentions that Charlemagne or his sons had been anointed. Don't courtiers write what kings want to hear?

One or two general points emerge from the obscure history of early Carolingian inaugurations. First, while anointing might operate at one level as a rival christian brand of sacral magic, a substitute for long hair, functionally it was bound to have some different implications, if only because it required artifice, clerical artifice, in addition to nature. It did not just grow; it had to be conferred at a point in time, specifically through an inauguration ritual, and this meant that churchmen became involved in the procedure of king-making in a new and prominent way. If relatively many reigning Merovingians and no Carolingians were assassinated, this can hardly be explained simply in terms of the protective effect of anointing for the latter dynasty, at least in its earlier period. More relevant here are such factors as the maintenance of a fairly restrictive form of royal succession[52] (and the Carolingians' abandonment of polygamy must soon have narrowed the circle of royals) and the growth of a clerically-fostered ideology of christian kingship.[53] Anointing in fact caught on slowly with the Carolingians — not because of its hierocratic undertones (can you imagine Pippin or Charlemagne afraid of being 'captured' by the Church?) but because Pippin, Charlemagne and, in this respect,

[49] See Eiten 1907, pp. 46ff.

[50] Astronomus, *Vita Hludovici Pii,* ed. W. Pertz, MGH SS II, p. 643; Nithard, *Historiarum libri quattuor,* ed. E. Mueller, MGH SS rer. Germ. in usum schol., p. 10.

[51] This is well brought out, in reference both to the Chronicle of Moissac and to the *Clausula de unctione Pippini*, by Levillain 1933, pp. 225–95.

[52] Cf. I. Wood, in P. Sawyer and I. Wood ed., *Early Medieval Kingship* (Leeds, 1977), p. 10.

[53] For some consequences in terms of juristic means of dealing with bad rulers, see Ullmann 1969, pp. 66f.

even Louis the Pious were traditionalists, making their sons sub-kings simply according to the pattern of the Frankish past, not deliberately by-passing clerical consecrators. And in practice the appointment of sub-kings, given a series of long-lived fathers, became a kind of pre-mortem succession, which meant in the end that no Carolingian between Pippin and Lothar II in 855 had to wait for a predecessor's death in order to become king. This effectively limited the extent of possible clerical intervention in, and ritual elaboration of, king-making procedures, and helps explain the absence of a developed liturgical tradition of Frankish *Ordines* before the mid-ninth century. It also accounts for the problem at the outset of my second case-study.

The consecration of Charles the Bald at Orleans is problematical because of when it occurred: how, if anointing had become — as it's often alleged — well-established in Frankish practice from the mid-eighth century, could Charles the Bald reign *un*anointed as king of the West Franks from 840, when his father died, until 848? Ganshof has concluded that for a Frankish king in the 840s, anointing, 'though something important, was not something indispensable'.[54] Well, it was dispensable, evidently. But what evidence is there that anointing was thought 'something important' by Franks, lay or clerical, before 848? It's likely that no Frankish king had been anointed since 800, and none anointed except by the pope since 771[55] (or possibly, even, since Pippin himself in 751). There *was* no real indigenous Frankish tradition of royal anointing. Not only Charles the Bald but his elder half-brother Louis in Bavaria and his nephew Pippin II in Aquitaine ruled unanointed after 840.

The problem therefore is to explain not how Charles reigned for eight years without receiving anointing, but why he ever was anointed at all. We must look at the situation in Aquitaine, which though it had been assigned to Charles in 843 had been held on to by Pippin II at first illegally, then from 845 under Charles' nominal overlordship. Early in 848 the Vikings burned Bordeaux. Pippin had offered no resistance: Charles had at least tried. So the Aquitainians, 'constrained by Pippin's inertia', deserted him and 'sought Charles'. But why was the decision then made to 'anoint him with sacred chrism and solemnly consecrate him with episcopal benediction'?[56] Why anointing? Alternative explanations have been offered: one is that Charles' position in 848 was so weak that he 'had himself anointed' as a last resort to protect himself with a 'sacred character' against his unruly subjects;[57] the other is that since Charles' position was looking healthier in 848 than at any time since his accession he could now assert his authority by 'having himself anointed'.[58] Well, oil may be versatile stuff, but both these explanations can't be right — and I doubt if

54 *Settimane Spoleto,* VII, i (1960), p. 397.

55 Brühl 1962, pp. 321f.

56 *Annales Bertiniani*, edd. F. Grat, J. Viellard and S. Clemencet (Paris, 1964), p. 55.

57 Levillain 1903, pp. 31ff. at 51.

58 Lot and Halphen (part 1: 840–53; no other parts appeared) 1909, pp. 193f. Lot's suggestion, p. 194, n. 2, that the Aquitainian clergy had waited until Charles reached the Roman age of majority at 25, is not borne out by the consecration of Charles' son as king of Aquitaine at Limoges in 855 when the boy cannot have been more than 8.

either is. I see no reason to assume Charles' initiative. The idea, as in 751, was surely a clerical one, and the developing situation of the 840s with the increasing pretensions of the episcopate in general to a governmental role and the influence of Hincmar of Rheims in particular, supplies a credible context.[59]

If the object of Charles' anointing was to protect him from the infidelity of his *fideles*, it was not a success: the Aquitainians were not deterred from revolting in 853, and that was just the first in a series of stabs in Charles' back. But we ought not to apply such a crude yardstick to the question of whether anointing 'worked', for a ritual does not create a political situation. We need to ask, rather, what in 848 anointing signified, and to whom? Here, again as in 751, the broader ritual context is relevant: just around the 840s, the anointing of bishops, with chrism on the head, was coming into practice in north-western Frankish ordinations. This fact, and the importance attached to it, we know from a letter written by Hincmar himself giving details of an episcopal consecration in 845.[60] Some of the prescriptions in the rite for Charles the Bald's next anointing in 869 as king of Lotharingia show deliberate parallels with the episcopal anointing described in Hincmar's letter.[61] Though details are lacking for 848, I suggest that the bishops who devised and performed the Orleans rite were following the same model, making the king, like themselves, in a special way consecrated to God,[62] emphasising the gap between the man and the office and thus the responsibilities the office involved. If anointing was, as Arquillière wrote, 'la traduction liturgique du *ministerium regis*',[63] it became so explicity only in the ninth century: before that, kings might have been seen, in Scriptural terms, as *ministri* of God's kingdom, but not until the reign of Louis the Pious was the concept of royal office worked out and publicised.[64] The churchmen who did this had their feet firmly on the ground of contemporary politics. In the *Annales Bertiniani*, written at this point by Prudentius, bishop of Troyes, the 848 consecration is represented as the act of all the Aquitainians, lay *nobiliores* as well as bishops;[65] and in a subsequent reference to what came to be seen in retrospect as an anointing to his whole West Frankish realm, Charles under Hincmar's guidance stressed the *consensus* and *voluntas* of all his *fideles*.[66] If an enthronement also took place

59 See Lot and Halphen 1909, pp. 130ff., and above, ch. 7, 137, n. 4. Devisse 1976 I, pp. 291f., seems rather to underestimate Hincmar's influence on Charles in the 840s.

60 Andrieu 1953, pp. 22–73.

61 MGH Capit II, pp. 456–7. This text, strictly speaking a protocol, not an *Ordo*, describes the *modus* and *materia* of the anointing in some detail.

62 As stated explicitly in Hincmar's *adnuntiatio* preceding the 869 rite, MGH Capit. II, p. 341: '. . . ut in obtentu regni . . . sacerdotali ministreio ante altare hoc coronetur et sacra unctione Domino consecretur'. Compare I Paral. xxix: 22, describing the anointing of Solomon: 'Unxerunt autem eum Domino in principem'.

63 Arquillière 1955, p. 43.

64 Anton 1968, pp. 208ff.

65 *Ann. Bertin.*, p. 55. Compare ibid., p. 71 on the elevation of the younger Charles in 855: 'Aquitani . . . Karlum puerum . . . regem generaliter constituunt, unctoque per pontifices coronam regni imponunt . . .'

66 *Libellus adversus Wenilonem*, MGH Capit. II, p. 451.

in 848, laymen no doubt participated. Certainly West Frankish bishops were staking a claim to an indispensable role in the king-making ritual; and it then became possible for Hincmar, at any rate, to construct a theory of the king's accountability to his episcopal consecrators. But the bishops in their new role acted, in turn, as guarantors of the law and justice of all the king's subjects, as guardians of the christian people and thus as representatives, in some sense, of the realm as a whole. This became clear when something like a 'coronation-oath' was demanded of the king by the bishops as part of the ritual proceedings inside the church.[67]

I have stressed that anointing was by its very nature a clerical monopoly. This was not true of coronation, attested for the first time as part of a royal inauguration in Francia only in 838.[68] Before that popes had crowned Frankish sub-kings and Frankish emperors, and Carolingian kings themselves had experimented with the wearing of crowns and various other insignia on important liturgical occasions. But crown-wearing and *Festkrönungen* need to be kept distinct from coronation as part of the royal inauguration ritual.[69] 848 seems again to have marked an innovation in Francia, in that the archbishop crowned, as well as anointed, Charles.[70] This association of rituals was confirmed in the *Ordines* of Hincmar, who even used coronation as a metaphor for anointing itself in the anointing prayer, *'Coronet te dominus corona gloriae . . .'*,[71] and when Charles was inaugurated to a new kingdom in 869, the scriptural model to which Hincmar appealed was not David, reanointed at successive inaugurations, but the Hellenistic king Ptolemy who when he acquired a second kingdom placed 'two diadems on his head, those of Egypt and Asia'.[72] Hincmar made coronation, alongside anointing, permanently part of the ecclesiastical procedures of king-making. In West Francia the 'liturgification' of enthronement had followed by about 900.[73]

Clearly the ninth century was a seminal period in the history of royal inaugurations in western christendom. Before leaving it, I'd like to make just one more general point about anointing rituals in the time of Charles the Bald. Personal anointing was conceived as one very special, peculiarly intense form of benediction whereby the recipient was exposed in a unique way to the outpouring of divine grace. The common factor was the fullness of the benediction, but the application varied with the context. The addition of anointing to episcopal ordination did not alter the character of the rite — the central blessing-prayer indeed remained unchanged — but it translated into visible, sensible terms what had hitherto been a metaphor: 'the flower of heavenly ointment'.[74] The sorts of grace requested for the

[67] See above, chapter 7, pp. 133-71 passim.

[68] Brühl 1962, p. 301.

[69] A point rightly stressed by Jäschke 1970, pp. 556–88, esp. 565ff., 584ff.

[70] MGH Capit. II, p. 451; for coronation in 855, see n.65 above.

[71] MGH Capit. II, p. 457.

[72] MGH Capit. II, p. 340, with reference to I Macc. xi: 13.

[73] In the 'Seven Forms' *Ordo*, ed. Erdmann 1951, p. 89. See further Bouman 1957, pp. 136–40.

[74] Andrieu 1953, pp. 40–53.

bishop were specific to his office: 'constancy of faith, purity of love, sincerity of faith' and so on. The king's anointing, similarly, was intended to secure blessings needful for the carrying-out of royal functions — in particular the blessings of victory over visible as well as invisible enemies.[75] The point was that only God could provide the qualities a mere man needed to fulfil great public responsibilities. If an inauguration ritual as such presupposed a gulf separating the office from its incumbent, anointing focussed attention precisely here; for it was associated in the western liturgies with *rites de passage* covering the most drastic kinds of change in status, namely baptism and last unction, both involving a transition from 'death' to 'life'.[76] The anointings of bishops, priests and kings did not imply any functional likeness in the offices concerned, beyond their public governmental character and general importance (expressed in terms of divine foundation): anointing did not make the king into any sort of priest (any more than it made the priest a sort of king! Such a combination of functions was precisely a part of Christ's uniqueness.) If it had implied anything of the kind, what could we make of the anointing of queens, introduced in the time of Charles the Bald (another mid-ninth century innovation) and a feature thereafter of West Frankish ritual practice?[77] Priest, bishop and king each had his own specific function on whose performance the welfare of the christian people depended and for which special grace had to be acquired. The queen too had her function — one of the utmost public concern; and she too had specific needs: 'may she perceive through this anointing', prayed Hincmar over Charles' wife Ermentrude, 'cleanness of mind, safety of body. Crown her, Lord, with holy fruits . . . make her bear such offspring as may obtain the inheritance of your paradise'.[78] Though surely proving a lack of any necessary connection with priesthood, to use anointing as a fertility charm[79] was not to devalue it: rather to affirm the faith of Hincmar, Charles and their contemporaries in the sacramental outward and visible sign as guarantor of inward and spiritual grace.

And so to the tenth century: my third and last case-study is Edgar, king of the Mercians and, probably, Northumbrians from 957, and of the West Saxons from 959, to 975.[80] If there's one famous thing about Edgar, it's his 'delayed' or 'deferred' consecration at Bath in 973. 'One of the most puzzling things in our

[75] See Sprengler 1950/1, pp. 245–67, esp. 252ff.

[76] See above, chapter 11, pp. 270 ff.

[77] The *Ordines* of Judith (856) and Ermentrude (866): MGH Capit. II, pp. 425–7, 453–5; the *Ordo ad ordinandam reginam* associated with the 'Erdmann' *Ordo* of *c.*900, ed. Schramm, 1968, II, pp. 220–1; the *Ordo ad reginam benedicendam* associated with the *Ordo* of 'Ratoldus' (=Schramm's 'Fulrad'), ed. Ward, 1942, pp. 358–9 (in use in France in the twelfth and thirteenth centuries). I do not think that Cont. Fred. as quoted above, 290, implies that Pippin's queen Bertrada was anointed, and the *Clausula* makes no such claim for her.

[78] MGH Capit. II, p. 455. Quoting the episcopal *adlocutio*, ibid. p. 454, Wintersig 1925, pp. 150–3, at p. 152 speaks of 'eine Weihe der Thronfolgermutter'.

[79] So, Kantorowicz 1955, p. 293.

[80] Stenton 1971, pp. 366–7.

history', E. A. Freeman called it,[81] just a century ago. Historians have been puzzling over it since the twelfth century. Osbern in his Life of Dunstan[82] told a story about Edgar's having run off with a nun whereupon Dunstan imposed a seven-year penance on him 'that he should not wear the crown of his realm during this whole period'. 973 thus became a spectacular crown-wearing when the seven years were up: *redeunte quasi jubileo termino.* William of Malmesbury[83] was clearly sceptical about this tale (which he nevertheless recounted with relish!) but still asserted that Edgar ruled 'from the sixteenth year of his age, when he was constituted king' until 973 'without any regal symbol' *(sine regio insigne).* These twelfth-century writers seem to be invoking popular legend to explain the mystery of 973;[84] but a seven-year penance would take us back only to 966 and not to the beginning of Edgar's reign at all. In fact Osbern, in depicting 973 as a *Festkrönung*, a *coronatio* or festal coronation such as was familiar to him from the practice of his own day, thereby implied that Edgar *had* been normally consecrated already at his accession. Similar interpretations seem to be offered in the thirteenth century by Roger of Wendover[85] and Matthew Paris.[85a] On the other hand, William's contemporary Nicholas of Worcester[86] thought that Edgar himself had delayed his consecration out of 'piety . . . until he might be capable of controlling and overcoming the lustful urges of youth'. Well, if that took Edgar until he was nearly thirty, he must have been — for those days — a late developer! The two most recent attempts to solve the mystery are elaborations or revised versions of these medieval hypotheses: H. R. Richardson and G. O. Sayles[87] follow Osbern with their *Festkrönung* theory, while Eric John[88] thinks there's a kernel of truth in William's and Nicholas's belief that Edgar's consecration was delayed. Let's go back to the tenth-century evidence.

A first question: did Edgar really reign for over thirteen years without being consecrated as king? We have to start from the fact that no contemporary or near-contemporary witness actually states that Edgar received consecration when he became king either of the Mercians in 957 or of the West Saxons in 959.[89] But there is no valid argument from silence here, because literary or chronicle or charter evidence for *any* pre-Conquest royal inauguration is very rare. It's true that the Anglo-Saxon Chronicle's entry for 973 describing with uncharacteristic fullness the

[81] Freeman, 1887, p. 639.

[82] Ed. Stubbs, 1874, pp. 111–2.

[83] *Gesta Regum*, ed. W. Stubbs (Rolls Series, 1887–9), I, pp. 179–80.

[84] Note the comments of Stubbs, 1874, pp. xcix–ci.

[85] *Chronica sive Flores Historiarum*, ed. H. O. Coxe (London, 1841), I, p. 414.

[85a] *Chronica Majora*, ed. H. R. Luard (Rolls Series, 1872), I, p. 466.

[86] Stubbs, 1874, p. 423.

[87] Richardson & Sayles, 1963, Appen. 1, pp. 397–412.

[88] John, 1966, pp. 276–89.

[89] But no abnormality in the form of his accession is implied in the earliest Life of Dunstan, Stubbs, 1874, p. 36, or by Æthelweard, *Chronicon*, ed. A. Campbell (London, 1962), p. 55.

occasion at Bath gives no hint of any previous consecration,[90] though Æthelweard can be construed as doing so; but as I said earlier there was a tendency for only those inaugurations that were in some way odd to get written up. It is more remarkable, though even Eric John neglects this, that the regnal list '*β*' reckons Edgar's reign in Wessex from 11 May, 959, which since Edgar's brother Eadwig only died on 1 October, 959, is obviously a mistake:[91] in fact 11 May is the day and month of the Bath consecration in 973. Did the list's compiler get into difficulties because he simply assumed that the day and month supplied by his source must relate to the outset of Edgar's reign? He doesn't seem to have taken any multiple consecrations into account — and he was writing during the brief reign of Edgar's successor. Yet it would be hasty to infer that no consecration occurred before 973.

What historians medieval and modern alike have too rarely appreciated is the extraordinarily complex circumstances surrounding *both* Edgar's successive successions, in 957 and in 959. In both cases, it was actually impossible for Edgar to be consecrated king for some time after he had been chosen king. In 957, Canterbury was still in the hands of the elder brother against whom Edgar was in revolt, and the archbishop of Canterbury, Oda, until his death on 2 June, 958 remained loyal to Eadwig.[92] As for York, the new archbishop Oskytel, appointed in the 'unusual' situation following the less-than-complete reinstatement of the traitorous Wulfstan I, only attests charters as 'bishop' throughout 957 and 958 and therefore probably did not return from Rome with his pallium until 959.[93] His attestations before this date, as well as other evidence, suggest that English archbishops already at this period as later did not exercise full archiepisopal powers until after receiving the pallium, and again from just about this period, pressures seem to have been brought on these archbishops to go to Rome to fetch their pallia in person. In 957 then, since consecration by a mere bishop would hardly have done, Edgar had to wait. Some of his charters show reign-years being reckoned in the northern kingdoms from his election by the Mercians and Northumbrians.[94] His uncle Athelstan had experienced similar difficulties, and as we saw, seems sometimes, anyway, to have reckoned his reign-years from his election, not his belated consecration.

The situation in 959 was more 'unusual' still: the archbishop of Canterbury at the time of Eadwig's death on 1 October was Brihthelm, a recent appointee who had

[90] A point stressed by John, 1966, p. 278. The 'D' version of the *Anglo-Saxon Chronicle*, p. 225, after terming Edgar 'king' in annals for the earlier part of his reign, calls him 'Ætheling' in 973. But I cannot follow Mr. John in assigning great significance to this word, especially as it does not appear in versions 'A', 'B' or 'C': since, as I hope to show below, 973 was indeed an inauguration-rite, 'ætheling' could well represent a pendantic reflex on the part of the 'D' chronicler.

[91] *The Anglo-Saxon Chronicle*, trans. D. Whitelock (Cambridge, 1961), p. 5, with Professor Whitelock's comments, pp. 3 and 5, n. 2.

[92] As indicated by his attestation of Birch, no. 1032.

[93] For details, see Whitelock, 1973, pp. 232–47, at 240f. I am much indebted also to earlier correspondence with Professor Whitelock on this topic.

[94] Birch, nos. 1112, 1119, 1270.

not yet received his pallium. Edgar lost little time in, as the first biographer of Dunstan so frankly puts it, 'sending [Brihthelm] back where he came from'[95] — to make way for Dunstan at Canterbury. Then Dunstan had to go to Rome to square all this with the venial pope John XII (no doubt a good deal of grease was needed) and also to receive his pallium, on 21 September, 960. Dunstan therefore couldn't have been available to perform Edgar's consecration until the very end of 960, or more probably, allowing time for invitations to be issued, early 961 — which gives a delay of at least 13 or 14 months between Edgar's accession in Wessex and any possible consecration. Now it just so happens that all versions of the Anglo-Saxon Chronicle fail completely for the years 960 and 961; and the irregularity of Dunstan's appointment could account for a discrete silence of the part of other sources for these crucial years.

But arguments from silence are never entirely satisfactory. So I want now to offer two sorts of positive, if indirect, evidence that Edgar did indeed receive a royal consecration as soon as possible, at least, after his coming to power in Wessex. The first is composite, consisting of liturgical documents whose significance has only very recently been brought to light by liturgists.[96] Successive recensions of West Saxon *Ordines* contained in manuscripts of the tenth century and later can be shown to demonstrate the likelihood of a tradition of West Saxon royal consecration-rites, including anointing, continuous from the first half of the ninth century (and probably older still).[97] It is very likely that from 900 the same basic rite, the so-called Second Anglo-Saxon *Ordo*, remained in use until the Conquest, with relatively minor alterations being made sometimes, for specific consecrations, in the course of that period.[98] If then probably for more than a century before Edgar and certainly from 900 West Saxon kings had been consecrated according to a fixed rite as soon as possible after election,[99] I can't see Edgar suddenly breaking with that tradition for any of the reasons that have been alleged. Not only would such a breach have no known parallel either English or Continental (the difference between Edgar's case and that of Charles the Bald is clear), but Edgar, having been trained at Abingdon by

[95] Stubbs 1874, p. 38. Professor Whitelock, 1973, has recently shed light on this obscure episode.

[96] See Turner 1971, pp. xxx–xxxiii; Hohler, 1975, pp. 60–83; 217–27.

[97] I have argued this in 'The earliest surviving royal *Ordo*: some liturgical and historical aspects', below, chapter 15, pp. 341-60.

[98] Turner 1971, p. xxxiii, associates this *Ordo* with Athelstan (925) but leaves open the possibility of an earlier date. I hope to show elsewhere that the earliest form of this Second *Ordo* was very probably used for the consecration of Edward the Elder at Pentecost, 900.

[99] Edward the Elder: Pentecost (8 June) 900: Æthelweard, *Chron.*, p. 51, with xxxf.; Athelstan: *Mercian Register* in *Anglo-Saxon Chronicle*, *s.a.* 924; Birch no. 641, with regnal list '*β*' (giving date, 4 Sept. 925); Edmund: '*β*' calculates from '*c*29 Nov. 939', according to Whitelock, *Anglo-Saxon Chronicle*, p. 4, no. 13, making an interregnum of just over a month from Athelstan's death on 27 Oct. (might Edmund's consecration have been on Advent Sunday, 1 Dec. 939?); Eadred: Birch nos. 815, 909, but the date, 16 Aug. 946, given by Florence of Worcester, *Chronicon*, ed. B. Thorpe (London, 1848), p. 134, does not fit with that implied by '*β*' (see Whitelock, *Anglo-Saxon Chronicle*, p. 4, no. 14); Eadwig: '*β*' suggests 27 Jan. 956, the third Sunday after Epiphany, Florence, p. 136, says archbishop Oda officiated, and the first Life of Dunstan, Stubbs 1874, p. 32, gives further details.

Æthelwold and come under the influence of Dunstan, was just the man to appreciate the divine gifts anointing was believed to convey. For their part Æthelwold and Dunstan needed Edgar to help realise their ambitions for reform: recent experience of royal mortality could hardly encourage confidence that Edgar would reach his thirtieth year,[100] and in my view it seems highly unlikely that they would have taken the dangerous risk of impairing Edgar's legitimacy as king by any such deliberate deferment of the consecration as Sir Frank Stenton postulated. And legitimacy was precisely what was involved — which is where my second bit of evidence comes in. On Edgar's death, supporters of his younger son Æthelred challenged the succession of his elder son Edward, Æthelred's half-brother: their main arguments were that Edgar had not himself been anointed at the time when he begot Edward, i.e. 959 or 960, and that Edward's mother had never been anointed at all.[101] Now obviously Æthelred's partisans would not have used these arguments against Edward if the same objections had applied to Æthelred too:[102] the two inferences must be, surely, that Æthelred's mother *was* anointed queen, something which we know from other evidence anyway, and that Edgar *had* been anointed at the time when he begot Æthelred, i.e. 966 or 967 — an anointing which can only be identified with the one which I have argued took place as early as possible after Edgar succeeded in Wessex. And there is the further point that if Edgar's anointing was credited with such retrospective significance, so to speak, for his heir, its significance for the reigning king himself surely follows *a fortiori*.

If Edgar was consecrated already at the end of 960 or early 961, whatever happened in 973 was not a 'delayed' or 'deferred' consecration. But what then was it? Clearly the rite at Bath was not just a *Festkrönung* but an inauguration, because Edgar was certainly anointed then (and no *Festkrönung* ever involved a repeated anointing). But an inauguration to what? On my argument, Edgar had already been ritually inaugurated to his Anglo-Saxon realm. Continental parallels show, however, that new inaugurations, including anointing, were perfectly in order — didn't the Old Testament offer the precedent of David? — when a king acquired new realms.[104] Charles the Bald in 869 is a case in point. What then was the new realm in 973? The

[100] Edmund was only about 25 when he was killed in 946, and Eadwig died aged about 15.

[101] Eadmer, *Vita Dunstani*, Stubbs 1874, p. 214: '. . . quia matrem eius (i.e. Edward's) Licet legaliter nuptam in regnum tamen *non magis quam patrem eius dum eum genuit* sacratam fuisse sciebant'. The accuracy of Eadmer's information about the two queens is confirmed by Nicholas of Worcester, who had made a special study of the subject: Stubbs 1874, pp. 422–4, and sent Eadmer his results. Though Eadmer is a late source, it is hard to see how the above intricate argument could be a later fabrication.

[102] Those historians who believe that Edgar was consecrated only once, in 973, have had difficulty explaining away this passage of Eadmer's: see, e.g., Freeman 1887, p. 639.

[103] Despite the objections of Richardson and Sayles 1963, pp. 397ff., I still regard the *Vita Oswaldi*, ed. J. Raine 1879, pp. 436–8, as a reliable witness to the use of the Second Anglo-Saxon *Ordo* in 973. A further and hitherto unrecognised pointer in this direction is the associated queen's *Ordo* prefaced by a very curious rubric which, in my view, can only relate to Edgar's wife Ælfthryth. I intend to argue this fully elsewhere.

[104] See Brühl 1962, p. 306 with no. 5.

key lies in the choice of ritual-site: whereas the royal vill of Kingston-upon-Thames was the place of all West Saxon royal consecrations whose site is known,[105] the 973 consecration took place in Bath — an ancient city whose Roman buildings and walls still stood impressively in the tenth century.[106] Then even more than now, this place must have conjured up the shades of Britannia, of the Roman and imperial past.[107] Here we enter a world of political ideas that have much to do with insular traditions but also with the tenth-century Continental present.[108] Henry, father of Otto I, like Charlemagne before him, was 'king and emperor of many peoples': Otto's great great diets were attended by 'a multitude of diverse peoples'.[109] The English kings of the tenth century, in touch fairly continuously with the Ottonian court through kindred, diplomatic and ecclesiastical links, could hardly have failed to be impressed by this contemporary imperial power. The West Frankish kings of the later tenth century, more alienated than impressed, were beginning to claim, or have claimed for them, an imperial status of their own, as 'lords of many sceptres'. If Abbo of Fleury, like Widukind in the East Frankish realm a generation earlier, used *regalis* and *imperialis* virtually as interchangeable concepts,[110] this was because the 'regal' now included a strong 'imperial' component, a real king, as distinct from a mere kinglet, being one who ruled over a plurality of realms or peoples. There are many signs that the Anglo-Saxon monarchy around the middle of the tenth century was coming to be regarded, anyway by those clerical authors whose work survives, in a similar light. Already in the 940s, Archbishop Oda hailed the *regalis imperium* of Edgar's father Edmund, to which 'all peoples *(gentes)* are subject'.[111] For Æthelwold, Edgar himself was a *rex egregius* to whom it was appropriate to apply the text of Jeremiah 1:10: 'Behold I have set you over the peoples and over the nations *(super gentes et super nationes)*'.[112] The biographer of St. Oswald, whose detailed information about 973 should in my view be taken very seriously, stresses the size and scale of the great assembly at Bath — suitable to 'the dignity of so far-flung a realm', adding, with an obvious reminiscence of Luke's Gospel (2:1): 'a decree went out from the emperor that all should flow together to him from east and west, north and

[105] Plummer 1899, II, pp. 133, 145, 149, 163.

[106] Biddle and Hill 1971, pp. 81–2.

[107] The Old English poem *The Ruin*, ed. Krapp and Dobbie 1936, pp. 227–9, with its reference (line 37) to 'the crowning city of a far-flung kingdom', is usually thought to relate to Bath. For the impact of Roman ruins on the Anglo-Saxons as reflected in their poetry, see Frankis 1973, pp. 253–69, esp. 257f.

[108] Stengel 1965, pp. 287ff. (England); 56ff. (tenth-century East Francia); Vollrath-Reichelt 1971, pp. 87ff. Despite the reservations of H. Hoffmann 1972, pp. 42–73, at 66ff., rightly noting that not every 'imperialis' means 'imperial', the existence of a non-Roman imperial idea of overlordship of other kings and peoples has been established beyond doubt: see esp. Erdmann 1951, and Löwe 1963, pp. 529–62.

[109] Widukind, *Rer. Gest. Saxon.* iii, pp. 38, 75. See Brackmann 1967, pp. 150ff.

[110] Werner 1965, pp. 1–60, esp. 16ff.

[111] PL CXXXIII, col. 952.

[112] Birch no. 1190.

south'.[113] These are, I think, the authentic voices of a hegemonial imperialism, an idea of empire smacking more of confederation than autocracy, and harking back, therefore, to an earlier Anglo-Saxon tradition of *ducatus* — leadership of allied peoples based on consent and common defence interests, as distinct from *regnum* based on conquest and military domination.[114] Edgar's revival (whether consciously or not) of this *ducatus* was in line with much previous West Saxon policy[115] but also showed his own sureness of touch. The need for collective defence was again being forced on the peoples of the British Isles from the later 960s onwards by the reappearance of the Vikings. That some of Edgar's closest advisers responded very quickly to the renewed threat just might be suggested by the appearance in charters from the late 960s of proems warning that the end of the world may be nigh.[116]

There is further evidence that imperial ideas of this kind were finding expression precisely in the early 970s. First, on the numismatic side, there is the special 973 'Circumscription' issue at Bath, which could have been produced partly for the purpose of an imperial *sparsio* following the consecration;[117] and the impact of the great coinage reform, later in the same year, must have been felt directly or indirectly throughout the British Isles.[118] Second, there is Edgar's fourth code of laws — that is, if we can accept the code's recently-proposed redating to this period of the reign.[119] One provision in this code is to be 'common to all the nations, whether Englishmen, Danes or Britons, in every province of my dominion'; another is to apply to 'all who inhabit these islands'.[120] Such phrases are unprecedented in earlier laws. Third, there is the submission to Edgar, very probably also in 973, of Kenneth king of the Scots, and the cession to him of Lothian under Edgar's overlordship.[121] Fourth, there is the ritual at Chester which followed the inauguration at Bath: eight 'sub-kings' rowed Edgar along the river Dee, including five Scots and Welsh and two sea-kings of the western and northern isles[122] — all members of a pan-Britannic

113 *Vita Oswaldi*, pp. 436–7, compare ibid., p. 425–6.

114 Vollrath-Reichelt 1971, pp. 182ff.

115 See *Anglo-Saxon Chronicle*, s.a. 926, p. 199; s.a. 945, p. 212; compare the attestations of *reguli* in Birch nos. 815, 883, 909. For contemporary and later interpretations of Edgar's reign on hegemonial lines, see Æthelwold's account of Edgar's establishment of monasteries, in Whitelock 1955, I, pp. 846f., the 'D' version of the *Chronicle*, s.a. 959; Ælfric's *Life of St. Swithin* in Whitelock 1955, p. 853; Nicholas of Worcester, Stubbs 1874, p. 423; Florence of Worcester, *Chron.*, pp. 139, 143.

116 See Whitelock 1955, I, p. 345.

117 My suggestion is based on the evidence presented by Dolley 1973, pp. 156–9, that the Bath mint was uniquely productive in 973. Professor Dolley himself comments, p. 159: 'The need for largesse apart, the ceremony would have brought together a quite exceptional concourse of dignitaries . . .' whose board and lodging would have to be paid for from royal resources.

118 Dolley and Metcalf 1961, pp. 136-68.

119 Hart 1973, pp. 115–44, at p. 133, n. 6.

120 Trans. Whitelock 1955, I, pp. 397–401: IV Edgar, 2,2; 14,2.

121 Roger of Wendover, *Flores* I, p. 416. For the date, see Stenton 1971, p. 370; Freeman 1887, pp. 582–8.

122 Ælfric, *Life of St. Swithin*, trans. Whitelock 1955, p. 853. Only six kings are mentioned in the *Anglo-Saxon Chronicle*, versions 'D' and 'E', p. 225. Florence, *Chron.*, pp. 142–3, using both these sources, gives the names of eight kings. For the substantial accuracy of his account, see Stenton 1971, p. 369.

alliance who presumably were also participants in Edgar's annual naval exercises around the coasts of Britain.[123] Fifth, there are the imperial styles in charters which, though not new, become now very prominent.[124] In one case Edgar is termed *'basileos anglorum et rex atque imperator . . . regum et nationum infra fines brittanniae commorantium'*.[125] Such political ideas did not grow in a vacuum. Sixth, there is the architectural innovation (for England) of westworks in several later tenth-century churches, notably Winchester, where the extension was begun in 971 but not completed until 994.[126] It has recently been suggested that the new church at Bath had a westwork already by 973.[127] Carolingian and Ottonian westworks, on which these English ones were modelled, were the settings for special kinds of imperial liturgical performance: were the English westworks designed, or could they have been used, for similar purposes? Seventh, there is the Benedictional of Æthelwold, now plausibly dated to 971–5, which displays a new and specifically imperial iconography of Christ, with a deliberate paralleling of Christ and the English monarch in the role of 'imperial king of kings', a model of tenth-century 'ruler theology' which may have gone from England to Germany, not vice versa.[128] Eighth and finally, there is a small piece of liturgical evidence from the royal *Ordo* which, despite some recent objections, I remain convinced was the one used in 973. Amongst the few changes made in the existing royal *Ordo* (and I should explain that in terms of the injection of imperial content into a pre-existing royal model) one makes perfect sense in the context of an imperial rite: in the prayer following the investiture with the sceptre, a prime symbol of Anglo-Saxon rulership, the word *Britannia* was substituted for the colourless *terra* of the scriptural model in the phrase, 'Honour him above *all kings of Britain*'.[129] None of these bits of evidence in isolation might mean much; but cumulatively they show that a case can be made (not a new case, certainly,[130] but stronger than previously realised) for seeing in 973 an imperial inauguration rite and Edgar in his later years as ruler of a British Empire, tenth-century style.

[123] Williams of Malmesbury, *Gesta Regum*, pp. 177–8.

[124] Stengel 1965, pp. 325ff; John 1966, p. 58f.

[125] Birch no. 1201 (original grant probably 967, assignment to St. Mary's Worcester, 973; dated 'anno . . . regno (sic) mei xiii'). Compare also Birch nos. 1266, 1268, 1270, 1307, 1316, and possibly 1302. In the light of Chaplais 1965, pp. 48–61, the specific connexions of these and earlier charters with 'imperial titles' are worth noting: Abingdon and Winchester, and, later, such houses as Ely influenced by Æthelwold and his circle, seem to be centres of imperial terminology.

[126] Cherry 1976, pp. 186–7; Biddle 1975, p. 138.

[127] C. A. Ralegh Radford, 'The architecture and sculpture of the tenth century with particular reference to the Bath area', unpublished lecture given at Bath in June, 1973. I am very grateful to Dr. Ralegh Radford for allowing me to use this citation.

[128] Deshman 1976, pp. 367–405, esp. 390ff. with 399–400, very pertinent comments on Edgar's imperial position.

[129] Turner 1971, p. 93, for the text in British Library, Cotton MS. Claudius A. iii, f. 14; for a list of the MSS. of this 973 recension of the Second English *Ordo*, see ibid. p. xxx, under (1), to which should be added the recently discovered BL Additional MS 57337.

[130] For an early fine exposition, see Robertson 1872, pp. 203–15. Compare Robinson 1918, p. 72.

I am not sure that my three case-studies will lend themselves to any summary generalisations. Instead, by way of conclusion I shall pose two very basic philogenetic questions. One: why anointing? Two: why kings? I recently suggested elsewhere that it was the existence of a permanent oil-crisis in the early medieval West which helped to make anointing with oil — a commodity potent and scarce — a 'natural symbol' to designate the power-holders in barbarian christian society. A first anointing made the christian; a second anointing identified the 'twice-born'.[131] But in glibly borrowing from India that notion of the twice-born as two specialist classes of men — priests and warriors — I evaded an important difference between India and the early medieval West. Within each barbarian kingdom while the priesthood did indeed constitute a class, only one individual was king. If the Indian analogy had been complete, there should have been anointing also of warrior lords, of dukes and counts for instance, in this age of 'guerriers et paysans'. The peculiar discrimination with which anointing was in fact applied mirrored, therefore, not simply an actual political situation but an ideal. Where aristocratic interests constantly threatened to tear apart society, kingship represented force contained, harnessed, institutionalised so as to unify each people in fact as well as in name. The very survival of kingship, under the later Merovingians for example, itself suggests that such an ideology was not just something ecclesiastically conceived and purveyed but represents lay sentiments too: how else could we explain those popular beliefs in the sacral powers of kings embodied in the royal touch? I will end where I began, with Fortes' comment about 'the mysterious quality of continuity through time . . . basic to the self-image of every society' and expressed in inauguration rituals. Since in the early medieval West 'society' was a kingdom or accumulation of kingdoms, to consecrate a king was to assert a society's identity. And its continuity through time? Here, finally, is where the queen's anointing came in; for it was through the provision of heirs to the royal house and the implied confining of those heirs to a single line, that the queen's divinely-blessed fertility helped assure the integrity and the continuance of society itself.*

131 See above, pp. 279-81.

*I should like to acknowledge a long-standing debt to Professor Walter Ullmann. Especially in relation to the last part of this paper, I must thank, for help on various points, Dr. Michael Lapidge, Professor Michael Dolley and most of all Professor Dorothy Whitelock. Harald Kleinschmidt generously allowed me to read his unpublished Göttingen dissertation on Edgar's consecration in 973: I benefited much from our discussions of many problems. The friendly advice and criticism of Ian Wood and John Gillingham have been, as usual, invaluable.

List of works cited in Nelson, 'Inauguration Rituals'.

ANDRIEU, M., 1953: 'Le sacre épiscopal d'après Hincmar de Reims', *Revue d'Histoire Ecclésiastique*, 48, pp.22–73.

ANTON, H. H., 1968: *Fürstenspiegel und Herrscherethos in der Karolingerzeit* (Bonn).

ARQUILLIÈRE, H. X., 1955: *L'Augustinisme politique* (2nd edn, Paris).

BAK, J. M., 1973: 'Medieval Symbology of the State: Percy E. Schramm's contribution', *Viator*, 4, pp.33–63.

BALANDIER, G., 1972: *Political Anthropology* (Harmondsworth).

BIDDLE, M., 1975: 'Felix Urbs Winthonia; Winchester in the age of monastic reform', in D. Parsons, ed., *Tenth-Century Studies* (Chichester), pp. 123–40.

BIDDLE, M., and HILL, D., 1971: 'Late Saxon planned towns', *Antiquaries Journal*, 51, pp.70–85.

BIRCH, W. G.: *Cartularium Saxonicum* (3 vols. 1885–93).

BLOCH, M., 1924: *Les Rois Thaumaturges* (Paris).

BOUMAN, C. A., 1957: *Sacring and Crowning* (Groningen).

BRACKMANN, A., 1967: *Gesammelte Aufsätze* (Darmstadt).

BRÜHL, C. R., 1962: 'Fränkischer Krönungsbrauch', *Historische Zeitschrift*, 194, pp.265–326.

BÜTTNER, H., 1952: 'Aus den Anfängen des abendlandischen Staatsdenkens', *Historisches Jahrbuch*, 71 pp.77–90.

CAPITULARIA: A. Boretius ed., *Capitularia Regum Francorum, Monumenta Germaniae Historica, Legum Secto* II, vol. 1 (1883), vol 2 (1890–1901).

CHADWICK, H. M., 1905: *Studies in Anglo-Saxon Institutions* (Cambridge).

CHERRY, B., 1976: 'Ecclesiastical Architecture', in D. M. Wilson, ed., *The Archaeology of Anglo-Saxon England* (London), pp.151–200.

de COULANGES, F., 1888–92: *Histoire des Institutions politiques de l'ancienne France* (6 vols. Paris).

DESHMAN, R., 1976: '*Christus rex et magi reges*: Kingship and Christology in Ottonian and Anglo-Saxon Art', *Frühmittelalterliche Studien*, 10, pp.367–405.

DEVISSE, J., 1976: *Hincmar, archevêque de Reims 845–882* (3 vols. Geneva).

DOLLEY, M., 1973: 'The Eadgar Millenary – a note on the Bath Mint', *Seaby's Coin and Medal Bulletin*, pp.156–9.

DOLLEY, M., and METCALF, D. M., 1961: 'The reform of the English coinage under Eadgar', in M. Dolley, ed., *Anglo-Saxon Coins* (London), pp.136–68.

EITEN, G., 1907: *Das Unterkönigtum im Reiche der Merovinger und Karolinger* (Heidelberg).

ELLARD, G., 1933: *Ordination Anointings in the Western Church before 1000 A.D.* (Cambridge, Mass.).

ERDMANN, C., 1951: *Forschungen zur politischen Ideenwelt des Frühmittelalters* (Berlin).

EWIG, C., 1956: 'Zum christlichen Königsgedanken im Frühmittelalter', in *Das Königtum*, ed. T. Mayer, *Vorträge und Forschungen*, 3, pp.7–73.

FORTES, E., 1968: 'Of Installation Ceremonies', *Proceedings of the Royal Anthropological Institute for 1967*, pp.5–20.

FRANKIS, P. J., 1973: 'The thematic significance of "enta geweorc" in *The Wanderer*', *Anglo-Saxon England*, 2, pp.253–69.

FREEMAN, E. A., 1887: *The History of the Norman Conquest of England*, vol. 1 (3rd edn. Oxford).

GIBBON, E., 1960: *Decline and Fall of the Roman Empire*, abridged D. Low (Harmondsworth).

HARRISON, K., 1976: *The Framework of Anglo-Saxon History to A.D. 900* (Cambridge).

HART, C., 1973: 'Athelstan "Half-King" and his family', *Anglo-Saxon England*, 2, pp.115–44.

HAUCK, K., 1950: 'Rituelle Speisegemeinschaft im 10 und 11 Jht', *Studium Generale*, 3.

HAUCK, K., 1967: 'Von einer spätantiken Randkulter zum karolingischen Europa', *Frühmittelalterliche Studien*, 1, pp.1–91.
HOFFMAN, H., 1972: 'Zur Geschichte Ottos des Grossen', *Deutsches Archiv*, 28, pp.42–73.
HOHLER, C., 1975: 'Some service books of the later Saxon Church', in D. Parsons, ed., *Tenth-Century Studies* (Chichester), pp.60–83.
JÄSCHKE, K.-U., 1970: 'Frühmittelalterliche Festkrönungen?', *Historische Zeitschrift*, 211, pp.556–88.
JOHN, E., 1966: *Orbis Britanniae* (Leicester).
KANTOROWICZ, E. H., 1946: *Laudes Regiae* (Berkeley, Calif.).
KANTOROWICZ, E. H., 1955: 'The Carolingian King in the Bible of San Paolo fuori le Mura', in *Late Classical and Medieval Studies in Honour of A. M. Friend* (Princeton).
KERN, F., 1954: *Gottesgnadentum und Widerstandsrecht*, 2nd ed. by R. Buchner (Darmstadt).
KOTTJE, R., 1964: *Studien sum Einfluss des alten Testament auf Recht und Liturgie des frühen Mittelalters* (Bonn).
LEACH, E., 1966: 'Ritualisation in man in relation to conceptual and social development', *Philosophical Transactions of the Royal Society of London*, series B, Biological Sciences, no. 772, vol. 251, pp.403–8.
LEVILLAIN, L., 1903: 'Le Sacre de Charles le Chauve à Orléans, *Bibliothèque de l'Ecole des Chartes*, 64, pp.31–53.
LEVILLAIN, L., 1933: 'L'avènement de la dynastie carolingienne, *Bibliothèque de l'Ecole des Chartes*, 94, pp.225–95.
LÖWE, H. 1963: 'Kaisertum und Abendland in ottonischer und frühsalischer Zeit', *Historische Zeitschift*, 196, pp.529–62.
MITTEIS, H., 1944: *Die Deutsche Königswahl*, 2nd edn. (Brunn).
NELSON, J. L. 1975: 'Ritual and reality in the early medieval *ordines*', *Studies in Church History*, 11, pp.41–51 ; below, chapter 14, pp. 329-39.
NELSON, J. L., 1976: 'Symbols in context: rulers' inauguration rituals in Byzantium and the West in the early Middle Ages', *SCH*, 13, pp. 97-119; above, chapter 11, pp.259-81.
NELSON, J. L., 1977a 'Kingship, law and liturgy in the political thought of Hincmar of Rheims', *English Historical Review*, 92, pp.241–79 ; above, chapter 7, pp. 133-71.
NELSON, J. L., 1977b: 'On the limits of the Carolingian Renaissance', *Studies in Church History*, 14, pp.51–69 ; above, chapter 2, pp. 49-67.
de PANGE, J., 1951: 'Doutes sur la certitude de cette opinion que le sacre de Pépin est la première époque du sacre des rois de France', *Mélanges Halphen* (Paris), pp.557–64.
PIRENNE, H., 1939: *Mohammed and Charlemagne*, trans. B. Miall (London).
PLUMMER, C., 1899: *Two of the Saxon Chronicles Parallel* (Oxford).
RATCLIFFE, E. C., 1953: *The coronation service of Queen Elizabeth II* (Cambridge).
RICHARDSON, H. G., and SAYLES, G. O., 1963: *The Governance of Medieval England* (Edinburgh).
ROBERTSON, E. W., 1872: *Historical Essays* (Edinburgh).
ROBINSON, J. A., 1918: 'The Coronation Order in the tenth century', *Journal of Theological Studies*, 19, pp.56–72.
SCHMIDT, R., 1961: 'Königsumritt und Huldigung in ottonisch-salischer Zeit', *Vorträge und Forschungen*, 6, ed. T. Mayer, pp.97–233.
SCHNEIDER, R., 1967: *Königswahl und Königserhebung im Frühmittelalter* (Stuttgart).
SCHRAMM, P. E., 1968: *Kaiser, Könige und Päpste*, 4 vols. (Stuttgart).
SPRENGLER, A., 1950–1: 'Die Gebete der Krönungsordines Hinkmars von Reims für Karl den Kahlen als König von Lothringen und für Ludwig den Stammler', *Zeitschrift für Kirchengeschichte*, 63, pp.245–67.
STENGEL, E. E., 1965: *Abhandlungen und Untersuchungen zur Geschichte des Kaisertums im Mittelalter* (Köln-Graz).
STENTON, F. M., 1971: *Anglo-Saxon England*, 3rd edn. (Oxford).

STRYPE, J., 1848: *Memorials of Archbishop Cranmer* (Oxford).
TESSIER, G. 1943: *Receuil des Actes de Charles II le Chauve* (Paris).
TURNER, D. H., 1971: *The Claudius Pontificals* (Henry Bradshaw Society, vol. 97 issued for the year 1964, publ. 1971).
ULLMANN, W., 1969: *The Carolingian Renaissance and the Idea of Kingship* (London).
VOLLRATH-REICHELT, H., 1971: *Königsgedanke und Königtum bei den Angelsachsen* (Köln-Wien).
WALLACE-HADRILL, J. M., 1960: ed. and trans., *The Fourth Book of the Chronicle of Fredegar* (London).
WALLACE-HADRILL, J. M., 1971: *Early Germanic Kingship in England and on the Continent* (Oxford).
WARD, P. L., 1942: 'An early version of the Anglo-Saxon coronation ceremony', *English Historical Review*, 57, pp.345–61.
WERNER, K. F., 1965: 'Das hochmittelalterliche Imperium im politischen Bewüsstsein Frankreichs (10–12 Jhdts)', *Historische Zeitschrift*, 200, pp.1–60.
WHITELOCK, D., 1955: *English Historical Documents c.500–1042* (London).
WHITELOCK, D., 1973: 'The Appointment of Dunstan as Archbishop of Canterbury', in *Otium et Negotium. Studies in Onomatology and Library Science presented to Olof von Feilitzen*, ed. F. Sandgren (Stockholm), pp.232–47.
WINTERSIG, A., 1925: 'Zur Königinnenweihe', *Jahrbuch für Liturgiewissenschaft*, 5, pp.150–3.

13

THE PROBLEM OF KING ALFRED'S ROYAL ANOINTING

Alfred's royal anointing by Leo IV has long been one of the puzzles of Alfredian scholarship.[1] Despite the ingenuity of the greatest Anglo-Saxon specialists, no really satisfactory explanation has yet been given of the strange story retailed by the *Anglo-Saxon Chronicle* under the year 853,[2] and repeated in Latin translation by Asser in his *Vita Alfredi.*[3] Such near-contemporary evidence demands careful attention, especially since it has important implications for the authorship of the *Chronicle* itself.

The English evidence might have seemed less convincing, however, had it not been supported by an apparently independent witness: a fragment from the letter of Leo IV to Æthelwulf, describing the reception at Rome of 'your son Alfred'.[4] But a detailed comparison makes it clear that the two accounts are by no means in complete agreement:

English sources		*Roman source*
Chronicle (A, B, C.)	Asser.	Ep. Leonis IV.
þa was domne Leo papa on Rome 7 he hine to cyninge gehalgode 7 hiene him to biscep suna nam.	Leo papa . . . Alfredum oppido ordinans unxit in regem et in filium adoptionis sibimet accipiens confirmavit.	Filium vestrum Erfred . . . benigne suscepimus, et quasi spiritalem filium consulatus cingulo honore vestimentisque, ut mos est Romanis consulibus decoravimus eo quod in nostris se tradidit manibus.

[1] The problem was recognised already by Sir J. Spelman, *Life of Alfred the Great*, written in 1643, ed. T. Hearne, Oxford 1709, 19 f. Bishop Stubbs, in his edition of William of Malmesbury's *Gesta Regum*, Rolls Series, London 1887–9, ii. xli, classed the anointing story among 'obscure points' in the life of Alfred. W. Stevenson devoted six pages of notes to the problem in his edition of Asser's *Life of King Alfred*, Oxford 1904, 179–85. See also the modern authorities cited below.

[2] On the *Anglo-Saxon Chronicles*, see C. Plummer, *Two of the Saxon Chronicles Parallel*, Oxford 1892, 1899, especially the introduction to vol. ii; and now also Professor D. Whitelock's edition and translation, *The Anglo-Saxon Chronicle*, Cambridge 1961, with an introduction on the various MSS. and full bibliography. I quote below from the Parker MS. (*Chronicle*, version A) in the facsimile edition of R. Flower and A. H. Smith, *The Parker Chronicle and Laws* (Early English Text Society), London 1941, where the 853 entry appears on folio 13a.

[3] Cap. viii: ed. cit., 7.

[4] Ed. A. de Hirsch-Gereuth, in *Monumenta Germaniae Historica, Epistolae Karolini Aevi*, iii. 602.

Bishop Stubbs, who first sought to reconcile these different versions, seems to have felt that the Roman evidence actually raised more questions than it answered.[1] From the English sources alone, it had been possible to construct the hypothesis that an original confirmation anointing had later been confused with royal anointing. This suggestion was tentatively restated by Stubbs, although Sir John Spelman had effectively challenged it already in 1643.[2] But the evidence of Leo's letter inspired a new theory of a confusion between consular investiture and royal inauguration. The problem at this point became enmeshed in the wider controversy over the authorship of the *Anglo-Saxon Chronicle*: the Roman anointing was seized on as ammunition by both the defenders and the assailants of Alfredian authorship.[3] It was argued, on the one hand, that Alfred, having made an honest mistake as to what had happened in 853, must himself have written or inspired that curious entry in the *Chronicle*; but, on the other hand, that if such confusion were impossible, then the *Chronicle* must have originated outside court circles, where, either through ignorance or from a deliberate desire to falsify the record, the anointing story was concocted. These various considerations, while they serve to show the complexity of the problem, have not brought about its resolution. The state of the controversy at present is highly inconclusive, and expert opinion remains divided.[4]

The Anglo-Saxon specialists have naturally centred their interest upon the English evidence, taking for granted the fragment of Leo's letter as corroboration of it and explaining away any divergences. Perhaps it is time to approach the whole problem by the alternative route of the Roman evidence, and to concentrate not on trying to reconcile the conflicting accounts, but on elucidating the causes of discrepancy. For the discovery of Leo's letter in a sense confused and obscured the real issue: what is to be made of the evidence of the *Chronicle* itself? Only when the Roman account has been placed in its true perspective can the story of Alfred's anointing reveal its full significance in the history of English royal consecrations. We, therefore, begin this study with an attempt at something which no Anglo-Saxon specialist seems to have thought worthwhile—a critical re-examination of the letter of Leo IV to Æthelwulf.

[1] Stubbs (op. cit., xlii) gives Leo's letter in translation, adding 'whatever that may mean'.

[2] Stubbs, loc. cit. See also P. E. Schramm, *A History of the English Coronation*, trans. L. G. W. Legg, Oxford 1937, 16 and n., echoing Stubb's opinion. But cf. Spelman, op. cit., 20, quoted below, 157.

[3] See C. Plummer, *The Life and Times of Alfred the Great*, Oxford 1902, 70 ff.; Stevenson, op. cit., 183 f.; R. H. Hodgkin, *History of the Anglo-Saxons*, 3rd. ed., Oxford 1952, ii, 624 f.; and 746. And, opposing Alfredian authorship, Sir F. M. Stenton, *Anglo-Saxon England*, 2nd ed., Oxford 1947, 269 n.2, and 683; also D. Whitelock, *English Historical Documents*, London 1955, i. no. 219, 810.

[4] The conflicting views will be discussed more fully below. That the recent argument of Stenton and Professor Whitelock has not entirely prevailed must be inferred from a comment of H. Löwe in Wattenbach-Levison, *Deutschlands Geschichtsquellen im Mittelalter*, Hft. iii, *Die Karolinger*, Weimar 1957, 373: 'Es wird auch zu fragen sein ob diese Umdeutung des Ehrenkonsulats wirklich . . . die Verfasserschaft oder Initiative Alfreds bei der sog. *Chronik* auszuschliessen geeignet ist'.

It has not been sufficiently emphasised that the sole source of this fragment is an Italian canon law collection of c. 1100, probably based on material compiled in the latter half of the eleventh century.[1] The importance of this *Collectio Britannica*—so called from its present location in the British Museum[2]—was first realised by Edmund Bishop, whose transcript was analysed and published by Ewald.[3] Thence the various papal letters and fragments found their way into the solidly respectable volumes of the *Monumenta Germaniae Historica*, and their authenticity thereafter was generally accepted, as Ewald accepted it, without question.[4]

But objections have been raised to several entries in the CB. and, significantly for the purpose of the present discussion, to letters of Leo IV in particular.[5] These objections collectively form good grounds for treating any CB. fragment ascribed to Leo IV with rather more critical caution than Ewald used. There is no need to repeat here the shrewd and forceful arguments of Parisot and Ullmann. But it is worth noting that Fournier, who in his major work on canonical collections gives no hint of these suspicions, had written to Parisot before 1899: 'We must conceive the composition of the *Britannica* quite otherwise than Ewald did', and agreed that the letters of Leo IV at any rate needed re-examination.[6] The judgement of Ullmann, in a recent study, was that while the CB., following an earlier source, contained some genuine register-fragments of Leo IV, 'this basis was tampered with by falsifying certain entries or inserting some new ones. . . . It seems an urgent task to subject the register-fragments of Leo IV to a very close scrutiny'.[7]

In view of all this, and while no further study of the CB. has yet been undertaken, there is some justification for a sceptical attitude towards the

[1] P. Ewald ('Die Papstbriefe der Brittischen Sammlung', in *Neues Archiv*, v (1879), 275–414, 505–96) could find this fragment in no other canonical collection. It is not even in the *Tripartita*, which contains a number of letters ascribed to Leo IV; cf. Ewald, art. cit., 595. Nor do the *M.G.H. Libelli de Lite* contain any references to the story of Alfred's anointing.

[2] Add. MS. 8873, acquired by the BM. in 1831. The earlier history of the MS. is apparently unknown.

[3] Art. cit. The letter 'Edeluulfo regi anglorum', which is the 31st entry 'ex registro Leonis IIII' in the MS., appears on fol. 168r, not fol. 167, as stated by Ewald and in the *M.G.H.* edition cited above. The dating, and the 'Italian, probably Roman' origin of the MS. are affirmed by P. Fournier and G. le Bras, *Histoire des Collections Canoniques*, ii. Paris 1932, 162. The *Collectio Britannica* will hereafter be referred to as the CB.

[4] Cf. Stubbs, op. cit., xliii; Plummer, *Alfred*, 70 ff.; Stevenson, op. cit., 180: and more recently, Schramm, op. cit., 16 n.1, and Whitelock, *Documents*, 572. The *M.G.H.* editor, Hirsch-Gereuth, closely followed Ewald's conclusions; see *Epp. Kar. Aevi*, iii. 581.

[5] The basic critical study is that of W. Ullmann, 'Nos si aliquid incompetenter . . .', in *Ephemerides Iuris Canonici*, ix (1953), 279 ff., suggesting that one letter-fragment ascribed to Leo IV is a later forgery. Objections to other CB. fragments of Leo IV were made earlier by R. Parisot, *Le Royaume de Lorraine sous les Carolingiens*, Paris 1899, 739 f. F. Dvornik (*The Photian Schism*, Cambridge 1948, 324–6) criticised other parts of the CB. Ullmann rightly called attention to the 'intricate problems presented by the CB.': see art. cit., 281.

[6] Fournier's letter is quoted by Parisot, op. cit., 741 n.8. But cf. his later stance in *Histoire des Collections*, ii. 157: 'Nous adhérons aux conclusions d'Ewald . . . '.

[7] Art. cit., 286–7.

fragment headed in the MS., 'Edeluulfo regi Anglorum'. At first sight, its contents suggest that it is genuine, for it seems neatly to confirm the English sources for 853. But a closer inspection lays bare the essential incongruity of the two accounts: while a confirmation is, indeed, stated or implied by both, there is flat disagreement as to the ceremony which accompanied it. The peculiarities of Leo's version merit detailed analysis.

(a) 'Consulatus cingulo honore vestimentisque, ut mos est Romanis consulibus, decoravimus'.

Schramm first pointed out the significance of this passage in the context of the papal *imitatio imperii*. Accepting the ascription of this letter to Leo IV, he linked the papal conferment of the consulate with the Donation of Constantine[1]; the Frankish patriciate in the eighth century might seem an obvious parallel.[2] Now Leo was, it is true, the renovator of Rome, the consecrator and adopter of the emperor Louis II.[3] But Laehr's observations on the papal neglect of the Donation in this period must be allowed due weight: although it was known to the popes of the mid-ninth century, there is no real evidence that the Donation was used by them as a blueprint for action.[4] There is, moreover, no parallel for the papal conferment of a consulship,[5] a title which had by now reached a nadir of debasement, being assumed at will not only by members of the Roman nobility, but also, it seems, by secretaries and merchants.[6] Gregorovius's assumption that the pope conferred the title in these cases is quite unfounded,[7] and, even had this been possible, it is hard to see why Alfred should have been given so tawdry a rank if, as Schramm surmised, the pope's aim was to flatter Æthelwulf.[8] The parallel with the Frankish patriciate is merely superficial. That conferment served an immediate practical purpose; its implications were clear and far-reaching.[9] But none

[1] Schramm, *Kaiser, Rom, und Renovatio*, Leipzig 1929, i. 26 f.; and *History of English Coronation*, 16.

[2] Cf. the suggestion of F. L. Ganshof, 'Note sur les origines byzantines du titre "Patricius Romanorum"', in *Annuaire de l'Institut de Philologie et d'Histoire Orientales*, x (1950), esp. 282, relating the patriciate conferred on Pippin to cap. 15 of the Donation.

[3] On all this see Schramm, *Kaiser*, i. 57.

[4] G. Laehr, *Die konstantinische Schenkung*, Berlin 1926, 15–18, 181–3.

[5] This was admitted by Schramm, *History of English Coronation*, 16: 'There is on record no parallel for such an act'. Stevenson (op. cit., 184) suggested as a parallel the 'consulship' offered by Gregory III to Charles Martel, but this story is now rejected as resting on a wrong emendation of the text of Pseudo-Fredegar: see K. Heldmann, *Das Kaisertum Karls der Grosse*, Weimar 1928, 152 n.5, and Ganshof, art. cit., 271 f., with full references.

[6] F. Gregorovius, *Geschichte der Stadt Rom im Mittelalter*, 5th ed., Stuttgart 1903, ii. 420.

[7] Ibid., accepted by Stevenson solely on the evidence of the CB. fragment. Cf. also, B. A. Lees, *Alfred the Great, the Truth-teller*, London 1915, 85.

[8] *History of English Coronation*, 16. But Æthelwulf would find out when he visited Rome how little the consulate was now worth, and his intended pilgrimage had evidently been known about at Rome for some time: cf. *Annales Bertiniani*, sub anno 839.

[9] On the Frankish patriciate, see Ganshof, art. cit., passim; also W. Ullmann, *The Growth of Papal Government in the Middle Ages*, 2nd ed., London 1962, 66 ff.

of this was true of Alfred's consulship. Had Leo wished to assert his imperial powers derived from the Donation, he would surely have chosen to confer a more valuable dignity on a more distinguished recipient. Precisely because of the Donation's unique value, the papacy could not afford to debase it by wanton exploitation.

It was in the eleventh century, in fact, that greater use was made than ever before of the papal *imitatio imperii*,[1] and it was, therefore, no coincidence that a notable revival in the use of the Donation took place under the Reform papacy.[2] It seems probable that the influence of imperial models affected also the conception of the consulship current in Rome at this time, so that the title regained something of its ancient status. Some evidence may be found in the statement of the early eleventh-century *Graphia Libellus*: 'Consules in unaquaque provincia ab imperatoribus constituti sunt, ut subditos suos consilio regant'. The idea that the emperor appointed a consul 'in each province' has a certain relevance to Alfred's investiture. It is, therefore, interesting that this idea is not found in any of the sources used by the author of the *Libellus*.[3] This apparently new conception was doubtless known to the reforming popes.

The *cingulum* mentioned as part of Alfred's investiture is probably to be understood as a sword: the term certainly carries a military connotation.[4] Stevenson had already observed that while a sword never formed part of the consul's official equipment, Sergius II in 844 invested Louis II as king of Lombardy with the '*regalis* gladius'.[5] But if the sword as a royal symbol was already familiar to the mid-ninth century papacy, it was only in the course of the two centuries which followed that the sword assumed the full significance of symbolising, and thus defining, the function of secular power divinely conceded through priestly mediators.[6] This

[1] See E. H. Kantorowicz, *Laudes Regiae*, Berkeley 1946, 136 ff.; also Schramm, 'Sacerdotium und Regnum im Austausch ihrer Vorrechte', in *Studi Gregoriani*, ii (1947), esp. 436 ff., and 446, where he comments about the period after 1046: 'Gewarhen wir nun eine konsequent durchgeführte Gegenoffensive auf einen Papst-Kaiser zu, die einsetzt, sowie das Reformpapsttum die Lenkung der Kirche übernommen hat'; and Ullmann, op. cit., 310 ff.

[2] Laehr, op. cit., 34 f.

[3] For all this see Schramm, *Kaiser*, i. 196 f., and his edition of the *Libellus de caeremoniis aulae imperatoris*, in op. cit., ii. 90–104. The passage about consuls is at p. 91. Schramm shows clearly the extent to which the *Libellus* is dependent on its sources, especially Isidore; cf. i. 197. In the passage quoted here, only the words 'consilio regant' are taken from an earlier source—Isidore's *Etymologies*, ix. 3, 6.

[4] Cf. Stevenson, op. cit., 183 n.5. A good instance of 'cingulum' used synonymously with 'gladius' may be found in the parallel accounts of Louis II's investiture in 844 given by *Ann. Bertin.*, sub anno, and the *Vita* of Sergius II, cap. 13 in the *Liber Pontificalis*, ed. L. Duchesne, Paris 1886–, ii. 89. See also Ducange, *Glossarium mediae et infimae Latinitatis*, s.v. 'cingulum', for evidence of the word's military connotation.

[5] Op. cit., 183, n.3; see also the previous note.

[6] This appears most clearly in the royal coronation *ordines* of the tenth and eleventh centuries: cf. the rubric of the 'Frühdeutsche Ordo' edited by C. Erdmann, *Forschungen zur politischen Ideenwelt des Frühmittelalters*, Berlin 1951, 86, section 12; and also the sword-prayer of the 'Ordo der Sieben Formeln', ibid., 89. On this, see the comments of Ullmann, 'Der Souveränitätsgedanke in den Krönungsordines', in *Festschrift P. E. Schramm*, i., Wiesbaden 1964, 72–89, esp. 82.

association of the sword with conceded, and therefore revocable, power emerged clearly in the thought of Gregory VII.[1]

(b) 'Eo quod in nostris se tradidit manibus'.

This expression has, to my knowledge, aroused no comment, still less suspicion, in the secondary authorities; and yet it is strangely out of place in a ninth-century papal letter. Although at first glance the clause might seem to refer to the reception of the child from the baptismal font by his confirmer and spiritual father, this is not the terminology of the confirmation rite.[2] It sounds, in fact, more like a feudal commendation: the expression used is characteristic of the homage ceremony, whose essence was 'the self-surrender (*traditio*) of one person to another'.[3] Brunner, moreover, observed that: 'Im Kreise der fränkisch-italischen Quellen wird die Wendung *manibus se tradere* gelegentlich für die Ergebung in die Hörigkeit . . . gebraucht'.[4] Such an interpretation of the words of the CB. fragment is in accordance with the curial policy, not indeed of the ninth, but of the eleventh century. The reformers and most of all Gregory VII used the feudal nexus as just one means of extending and tightening their control of secular princes and their resources, both human and material. It has been shrewdly noted that this was itself an imperial feature of the reformist programme.[5]

The attempts of Alexander II and Gregory VII to establish this feudal relationship with England have deservedly attracted attention.[6] Gregory's letter to William the Conqueror is unfortunately lost, but the surviving evidence allows the bases of the papal claim to be inferred:[7]

[1] A. M. Stickler ('Il gladius nel Registro di Gregorio VII', in *Studi Gregoriani*, iii (1948), 89–103) gives some evidence for this conclusion. See also Ullmann, *Growth of Papal Government*, 304 ff.

[2] The liturgical evidence offers no parallel for such an expression; it is rather the idea of transmission and reception by the officiant, or by the godparents, which predominates in confirmation. The active role is that of the bishop, while the person received, at this period normally an infant, naturally remains passive during this rite of incorporation. See P. de Puniet, art. 'Confirmation', in *Dictionnaire d'Archéologie Chrétienne et de Liturgie*, iii. pt. 2. cols. 2575 ff., esp. the passages there cited from Western liturgies. Cf. also the Roman rite of *Ordo Romanus* XI, cap. 100, ed. M. Andrieu in *Les Ordines Romani du haut Moyen Age*, Louvain 1949, ii. 446.

[3] F. L. Ganshof, *Feudalism*, trans. P. Grierson, London 1952, 67, cf. 27, 74. See also H. Mitteis, *Lehnrecht und Staatsgewalt*, Weimar 1933, 70 f., 479 f. For further examples of terminology see Ducange, *Glossarium*, s.v. 'Manus', 'Hominium', 'Investitura'.

[4] H. Brunner, *Deutsche Rechtsgeschichte*, 2nd ed. revised by C. F. von Schwerin, Munich 1928, ii. 364 and nn. cf. 66 nn.

[5] K. Jordan, 'Das Eindringen des Lehnwesens in das Rechtsleben der römischen Kurie', in *Archiv für Urkundenforschung*, xii (1932), 64–5; and, for the feudal activities of the Reform papacy in general, ibid., 71–83.

[6] See Z. N. Brooke, 'Pope Gregory VII's Demand for Fealty from William the Conqueror', in *English Historical Review*, xxvi (1911), 225–38; and also, partially revising the views there put forward, *The English Church and the Papacy*, Cambridge 1931, 140 ff. Also L. Weckmann, *Las Bulas Alejandrinas*, Mexico 1949, 80–90.

[7] The evidence of papal claims is to be found in (1) the letter of Alexander II to William, preserved in the *Collectio Canonum* of Deusdedit, iii. cap. 269, ed. Wolf von Glanvell, Paderborn 1905, 378; and (2) William's reply to Gregory VII's revival of his predecessor's claims, printed in *Lanfranci Opera*, (Ep. x.), ed. J. A. Giles, Oxford 1844, 32. I quote this passage below, 315, n.4.

first, the payment of tribute, and secondly, the performance of homage by earlier English kings to the Holy See. The second argument was rejected out of hand by William, and apparently the papacy thereafter abandoned it. The claim is so remarkable, however, that it may be asked if the curia put forward any justification for it, beyond the fact that gifts and payments to Rome had been made by several English kings from Offa onwards.[1] The comparison with papal claims to feudal rights over other lands is instructive. There were two main grounds for asserting papal overlordship, both of which were put forward whenever possible: first, that 'tribute' had been paid, and second, that the kingdom or duchy has been 'handed over' to St. Peter sometime in the past.[2] Now, in the case of England, there was no historical evidence of a 'handing-over' by any reigning monarch; and it may be noted that Rome did not allege the Donation as the basis for its claims here, as was apparently done in the case of Spain.[3] There was every reason, then, to try to find some evidence to suggest the feudal submission of an English prince, even if that evidence had to be twisted, and even if the transference of the kingdom itself to St. Peter could not be adduced. A precedent was needed to buttress the demand for fealty from William I, and it may be inferred from William's indignant denial that a bogus precedent had actually been alleged by Gregory VII.[4] Is it possible that Alfred's 'self-surrender' to Leo IV was put forward at this time as an argument in favour of William's following suit?

A significant pointer towards this conclusion is to be found in the words '*eo quod*' which introduce the statement of Alfred's submission in the CB. fragment, and which have a definitely causal sense. Leo's meaning is, therefore, clear: 'We have received your son, and decorated him . . . *because* he has given himself into our hands'. It is difficult to see why this point has hitherto been neglected, for the inference to be drawn from it is surely unambiguous: Leo's decoration of Alfred is presented as conditional on the prince's submission. The choice of expression thus seems to reflect

[1] See Weckmann, op. cit., 74 ff.; also Stenton, op. cit., 215–16 n.1, and 460–1. Payments by Alfred are recorded in the *Anglo-Saxon Chronicle*, sub anno 883, 887, 888 and 890. *A propos* papal claims in general, note the observation of B. A. Pocquet du Haut-Jussé, 'La Bretagne a-t-elle été vassalle du Saint-Siège?', in *Studi Gregoriani*, i (1947) 189: 'Il est exceptionnel que le Saint-Siège ait fait les premières démarches en vue d'obtenir la soumission d'un état. Nous ne pensons pas qu'il se soit jamais risqué à en lancer l'idée sans s'appuyer sur un titre sérieux ou supposé tel'.

[2] Cf. the relations of the Reform papacy with Denmark, as revealed in Alexander II's letter quoted by Deusdedit, *Collectio*, iii. cap. 268, and Gregory VII's *Register*, ii. 51 and 75 (ed. E. Caspar). On papal claims to Brittany, see B. A. Pocquet du Haut-Jussé, art. cit. Cf. also Gregory's claims to Spain, *Reg.*, iv. 28; Hungary, *Reg.*, ii. 13; and even France, *Reg.*, viii. 23.

[3] See Weckmann, op. cit., 90, also referring to the 'omni-insular theory' of the papacy. The suggestion (ibid.) that this was perhaps relevant in the English case finds no support in the sources.

[4] Note the tone of indignant refutation in William's reply; Giles ed. cit., 32: 'Fidelitatem facere nolui nec volo, quia nec ego promisi, *nec antecessores meos antecessoribus tuis id fecisse comperio*'. Stenton (op. cit., 667) comments: 'No statesman has ever settled a major issue in fewer words, or more conclusively'.

feudal influence in the outlook of the curia; and the 1060s and 1070s were, in fact, the very decades in which this influence began to affect papal practice on a wide scale.[1]

More specifically, the attempt to present Alfred's submission to the pope as the precondition of his investiture could be directly related to the actual history of William's earlier intercourse with Rome. Although no evidence has survived that the papacy used this argument, it seems not unreasonable to suppose, with Z. N. Brooke and Sir Frank Stenton, that William's application for papal support in 1066 might later have been regarded at Rome as tantamount to a proffer of fealty, and hence used as a basis for further claims.[2] From the papal standpoint, the case of Alfred would provide a useful parallel.

The military connotation of the word *cingulum* has already been stressed and it is interesting to note that the term came to be linked with the service of knighthood.[3] This implication is, perhaps, present in the fragment under discussion; if so, it lends a typically feudal tone to the 'Roman' investiture there described. Such an interpretation would, in any case, readily suggest itself to so practised an exponent of feudal government as William I.[4]

Certain analogies to the fragmentary letter 'to Æthelwulf' may be found in those documents of the later eleventh century which describe the feudal submission of princes to the Holy See. A phrase curiously reminiscent of the first part of the fragment occurs at the beginning of Gregory VII's letter to Isjaslaw of Russia, reporting his reception of the latter's son at Rome,[5] while comparable passages appear, for instance, in the letter of an Aragonese prince to Urban II, referring to the events of 1068, and contained, significantly, in the CB. itself[6]; and in the report of the Synod

[1] Jordan, art. cit., 71–83; and C. Erdmann, *Die Entstehung des Kreuzzugsgedankens*, Stuttgart 1953, 202 ff.

[2] On this suggestion, see Brooke, op. cit., 140–5, and Stenton, op cit., 667; also, cautiously inclined to accept this view, Weckmann, op. cit., 81 ff., and Erdmann, *Entstehung*, 172 f.

[3] Cf. Ducange, *Glossarium*, s.v. 'Cingulum', and the evidence of the dubbing liturgies cited by M. Bloch, *Feudal Society*, trans. L. A. Manyon, London 1961, 315, noting, *à propos* the permeation of the dubbing ceremony by the liturgy: 'This process was completed by the eleventh century'. See also following note.

[4] For the more usual view of the rapid feudalisation of England under William, see D. C. Douglas and G. W. Greenaway, *English Historical Documents*, London 1953, ii. 24–8, and 894 ff. But see also on William's feudal methods even critics of this view: H. G. Richardson and G. O. Sayles, *The Governance of Medieval England*, Edinburgh 1963, 77. It is interesting to note the account by Ordericus Vitalis, *Historia Ecclesiastica*, viii. 1 (P.L., lxxxviii. 560) of the knighting of William's son Henry: 'Hunc Lanfrancus Dorobernensis episcopus . . . ad arma pro defensione regni sustulit . . . eique . . . *militiae cingulum* in nomine Domini cinxit'. For a brief but very favourable judgement on the value of this early twelfth-century source, see Douglas and Greenaway, op. cit., 98.

[5] *Reg.*, ii. 74: 'Filius vester limina apostolorum visitans ad nos venit, et quod regnum illud dono sancti Petri *per manus nostras* vellet obtinere . . .'. Cf. Leo IV to Æthelwulf: 'Filium vestrum Erfred quem hoc in tempore ad sanctorum apostolorum limina destinare curastis benigne suscepimus . . .' (etc. as cited above, 309).

[6] The letter of Sancho Ramirez is on fol. 146 of the CB., and is cited by P. Kehr, 'Wie und wann wurde das Reich Aragon ein Lehen der römischen Kirche?' in *Sitzungs-*

of Spalato (1076) preserved in the collection of Deusdedit.[1] If the first of these parallels may be merely coincidental, one is left, nevertheless, with the impression that the fragment 'to Æthelwulf' has, to say the least, strong affinities with an eleventh-century genre.

It may be as well to recall here the nature and purpose of the CB. itself. Classed by Fournier among 'collections which have undergone Gregorian influence', it probably dates, in its original form, from Gregory VII's pontificate. It is especially important in the history of canon law as the sole survivor of the *Excerpta*, the first-fruits of the Reformers' search for precedents.[2] The common feature of the eleventh-century collections is, as Ullmann has observed,[3] their tendency 'to give documentary and justificatory evidence in favour of the hierocratic theme', and their main purpose is to demonstrate the authority of the Roman pontiff: hence their extreme selectivity, and a proneness to include any evidence, even from dubious sources, which is conducive to this end. The letter-fragment under discussion fits perfectly, needless to say, into such a body of material.

If the fragment 'to Æthelwulf' may indeed be, as I am suggesting, a Roman forgery of the 1060s or 1070s, the question of transmission must be considered. The CB. letter, despite its idiosyncracies, so coincides, and tallies so neatly in date, with the English sources as to suggest that these (or one of them) were known to its author. Do the facts justify the assumption that the story of Alfred's anointing could have reached Rome at this period? The evidence is only circumstantial, but it does not, I think, exclude this possibility. In the first place, the assiduity of the Roman researchers should not be underestimated[4]; in the second, the papal claims to English fealty, partly based on the historical facts of earlier payments to Rome, may well have stimulated interest in the origins of those payments,[5] and thus in the dutiful conduct of Alfred towards the Holy See. Intercourse between England and Italy was lively at this time: possible transmitters of information were the English archbishops who came to Rome for their *pallia*; the English representatives at papal councils in Rome and elsewhere; and, from the other side, the legates who visited Worcester (1060) and Winchester (1070).[6] Asser's work, being

---

berichte der preussischen Akademie der Wissenschaften, (1928) at 218: 'Beati Petri limina adii, *meque regnumque meum Deo et eius potestati tradidi* . . .'.

[1] *Collectio*, iii. cap. 278; ed. cit., 383–5: King Zvonimir of Dalmatia and Croatia after his investiture 'per vexillum, ensem, sceptrum et coronam' becomes a papal vassal: 'Me *tuis manibus* committo . . .'.

[2] Fournier-Le Bras, op. cit., ii. 155 ff.

[3] *Growth of Papal Government*, 363.

[4] Cf. Fournier, 'Un tournant de l'histoire du droit', in *Revue historique du Droit français et étranger*, xli (1917), 141 f.; and *Histoire des Collections Canoniques*, ii. 7–14. Fournier mentions 'Italian libraries', but there seems no reason to limit the researchers' field of operations too narrowly: if the arguments of Parisot (op. cit., 739 ff.) are accepted, as I believe they should be, then at least one forged CB. fragment may well have depended on a northern French source.

[5] See references above, 315 n. 1.

[6] Stenton, op. cit., 461–2, and 651.

written in Latin, was perhaps a more likely source than the *Anglo-Saxon Chronicle*,[1] and MSS. of the *Vita Alfredi* were more widespread in the early twelfth century, at least, than they later became.[2] The *Chronicon* of Æthelweard and the *Vita Grimbaldi* were possible sources for the story of Alfred's visit to Rome; and continental MSS. of both may well have existed in the later eleventh century.[3]

Thus there were various ways by which the story of Alfred's Roman anointing could have reached Rome from England. Papal apologists would readily grasp its potential usefulness, and the task of recasting it in a feudal mould could soon be completed. The question must be faced however, why, if the fragment of Leo's letter was a forgery based on English sources, the royal anointing of the insular account was replaced by a conferment of the consulship. The explanation might lie partly in the idea that only emperors were consecrated by the pope; the consulship was, as the forger was concerned to stress, a peculiarly Roman dignity, and the creation of a consul appeared as an emanation of the pope's own Roman-imperial status.[4] But the main reason for the change would more probably have been the need for emphasis on the conditional nature of the dignity conferred: the consulship, because it was unfamiliar beyond the Alps, could more easily be presented as depending on a previous personal submission to the pope than could royal anointing, which was by now a traditional prerogative of English kings.

That the forgery would have been grounded on English material is suggested also by the omission of this episode from other Roman sources. The author of Leo IV's *Vita* in the *Liber Pontificalis* makes no mention at all of Alfred's visit, although he is a contemporary witness[5]; the *Vita* of Benedict III, by contrast, gives a fairly long account of Æthelwulf's pilgrimage two years later.[6] The CB. is the only canon law collection to include Leo's letter; had it been genuine, one might have expected to find it elsewhere, especially for instance in the collection of Deusdedit, who devotes a whole section to evidence of feudal subjections to St. Peter.[7]

[1] The bilingual (Latin and Anglo-Saxon) version F cannot be dated earlier than the first half of the twelfth century; cf. F. P. Magoun in *Modern Language Review*, vi (1945), 371 f.

[2] Stevenson, op. cit., xi, lv ff.

[3] Æthelweard's *Chronicon*, a late tenth-century work, has recently been re-edited by A. Campbell, London 1962. See his Introduction, xii. The original MS., now lost, was sent to Essen, where the author's relative was abbess; see L. Whitbread in *Eng. Hist. Rev.*, lxxiv (1959), 581. On the *Vita Grimbaldi*, see P. Grierson, 'Grimbald of St. Bertin's', in *Eng. Hist. Rev.*, lv (1940), 541 ff. Grimbald's English *Vita*, whose information on Alfred's visit to Rome was very probably derived from Asser, was certainly known at St. Omer by the early twelfth century.

[4] This is evident from the deliberate and imposing phrase: 'Ut mos est Romanis consulibus'.

[5] Ed. cit., ii. 106–34: and an unusually long *Vita*. The significance of this omission should not be overstressed, however, for there are one or two other surprising omissions from this *Vita*. Cf. Duchesne, ibid., v.

[6] Ibid., 148.

[7] *Collectio*, iii. esp. caps. 185–289; ed. cit., 350–96. Alexander II's letter to William the Conqueror is naturally included in this section. Brooke (op. cit., 141) described this part of the *Collectio* as a 'a sort of early *Liber Censuum*'.

It had, of course, failed in its immediate polemecial purpose after Gregory's acceptance of the Conqueror's checkmate. The canonists may have felt that there was no further use for this strangely twisted version of an old tale; or, perhaps, they recognised that it was unlikely ever to supplant the aboriginal story of royal anointing—without strings—in England itself.[1]

Enough has now been said to suggest that Leo's letter to Æthelwulf should no longer be unquestionably admitted as an independent and genuine witness to the anointing/investiture of 853. Like the reference to Alfred's Roman journey in the *Vita Grimbaldi*, it could depend on English sources. It seems, moreover, to reflect more accurately the conditions of the eleventh than of the ninth century. But whether or not the hypothesis is accepted that this fragment is a Gregorian forgery, the arguments set out above, and, in particular, the doubtful nature of certain parts of the CB., make it impossible to base firm conclusions on evidence from this source. The whole problem must be thrown back upon the *Anglo-Saxon Chronicle* itself: will its evidence stand alone?

Since Asser took his account of 853, like so much else, *en bloc* from the *Chronicle*,[2] the English evidence, in fact, derives from only one source—the A version of the *Chronicle*. But Asser's testimony is of crucial importance, because he translates the Anglo-Saxon *gehalgode* by the unequivocal *unxit*. Without doubt, then, what is being claimed is anointing and not merely a blessing.[3] The full significance of this fact will appear later; meanwhile, it can be noted that this immediately suggests Frankish rather than Byzantine liturgical influence, for the consecration of the Eastern emperor was built around the coronation ceremony and did not at this period include unction.[4] The anointing, on the other hand, is the essential feature of contemporary West Frankish *Ordines*.[5]

[1] The *Chronicle* version of the story, of course, maintained its popularity with English writers throughout the Middle Ages: cf. the sources named by Plummer, *Alfred*, 73, n.

[2] On Asser's 'remarkable' form of composition, see Stevenson, op. cit., lxxix ff.

[3] On the Anglo-Saxon 'gehalgian', see P. Hunter Blair, *An Introduction to Anglo-Saxon England*, Cambridge 1959, 205. The word was certainly 'normally used of the consecration of bishops' in Anglo-Saxon texts, but this was the case long before anointing formed part of episcopal consecration. Cf. G. Ellard. *Ordination Anointings in the Western Church*, Cambridge, Mass. 1933, chs. 1 and 2; and Andrieu, 'Le sacre épiscopal d'après Hincmar', in *Revue d'Histoire Ecclésiastique*, xlvii (1953), 22 ff. It is, therefore, hazardous to assume, without further evidence, that terms like 'gehalgod' or 'gebletsod' used of eighth or ninth century royal consecrations imply that unction was performed.

[4] See O. Treitinger, *Die oströmische Kaiser- und Reichsidee*, Jena 1938, 29, 194 f.; and F. Dölger, *Byzanz und die europäische Staatenwelt*, Ettal 1953, 296, both decisively against the view that imperial anointing was practised in the East at this period. In general, however, Byzantine influence pervaded the ceremonial of Western Europe and, perhaps, lay behind the adoption of the practice of co-rulership by Offa of Mercia (787) and later by the Capetians; it might also have lead Æthelweard to stress the 'stemma' or 'stefos' in describing early tenth-century royal inaugurations. Cf. *Chronicon*, ed. cit., 51, 54, though note Campbell ibid., xlv, on the 'hermeneutic tradition'. On the possibility of more general Anglo-Byzantine contacts in the pre-Conquest period see R. S. Lopez, 'Le Problème des Relations Anglo-Byzantines . . .', in *Byzantion*, xviii (1948), 139–62.

[5] Schramm, 'Die Krönung bei den Westfranken und Angelsachsen', in *Zeitschrift für Rechtsgeschichte*, liv, *Kan. Abt.* 23 (1934), 117–242; and C. A. Bouman, *Sacring and Crowning*, Gröningen 1957, 9–27, 107–26.

Three main points can be made at the outset of the inquiry: first, that whatever happened in 853 (or 855), it was not royal anointing; second, that a confirmation could not have been mistaken for such by anyone present at, or informed of, the event; third, that the story of the anointing could not have got into both the *Chronicle* (A) and Asser's *Vita* without the knowledge and, one must presume, the approval of Alfred himself.

For the first point, the most obvious objection to accepting the account in the *Chronicle* at face value is the fact that Alfred had three elder brothers alive in 853[1]; his eventual succession to the throne could have been foreseen at this time only by a prophet. Thus, a later medieval writer, recounting the story, was actually impelled to endow Leo IV with the vision of Samuel.[2] The difficulty seems to have been appreciated by the authors of recensions D, E, and F of the *Chronicle*, none of whom adopted a mystical explanation: D and E omit that part of the 853 entry which reports Alfred's Roman adventure, while F puts it after the death of Æthelwulf.[3] The problem was hardly disposed of by Plummer's suggestion that Æthelwulf wanted the special honour of a papal anointing to be bestowed on his favourite son, and that a 'titular . . . subordinate royalty' had previously been 'conferred on him by his father for this very object'.[4] There is, of course, no evidence at all for this highly artificial account of the 'kingship' of 853.

The second point calls for some explanation. The brilliant but wayward thesis of de Pange should have been sufficiently refuted elsewhere to dispose of the idea that the confirmation-anointing of a prince and his royal anointing could ever have been identified[5]; liturgically, these were quite separate, though not unrelated rites.[6] Now, whether or not Alfred directly influenced the compilation of the *Chronicle*, the main tasks of advising and writing must have been carried out by clerics, since the Church virtually monopolised literacy. But the *literati* of early medieval

[1] There was, further, no West Saxon precedent for a co-rulership, although the Chronicle, sub anno 836, relates the establishment of a sub-kingship for Alfred's elder brother; but there is no evidence of any such arrangement in the case of Alfred himself. See below for a discussion of Plummer's hypothesis.

[2] Ailred of Rievaulx, in his *Genealogy of English Kings;* P.L., cxcv. 718.

[3] For D and E, see the edition of D. Whitelock cited above. F must be compared from the edition of B. Thorpe, *The Anglo-Saxon Chronicle* (Rolls Series), London 1861, i., Texts.

[4] *Alfred*, 74.

[5] J. de Pange, *Le Roi très chrétien*, Paris 1949. The Alfred story was, on his own admission, one of his strongest arguments. Cf. 218: 'La confirmation reçue a cinq ans aurait donc rétrospectivement été regardée comme une consécration à la royauté'; and n. 83, where Stubbs's agreement is adduced. For a short but cogent refutation of de Pange's theory, see now Bouman, op. cit., x n.3. This provides a basis for the reappraisal of the Alfred story itself.

[6] This relationship is too complex to be discussed here; but cf. the perceptive, though not always reliable analysis of de Pange, op. cit., 98–128. The crucial New Testament text is I Peter, ii. 9: 'Vos autem genus electum, *regale sacerdotium*. . .'. See also the important article of T. Michels, 'Die Akklamation in der Taufliturgie', in *Jahrbuch für Liturgiewissenschaft*, viii (1928), 79 f., and 85 n.1.

society were at the same time its ritual specialists and, thus, the guardians of liturgical order. The theory of an unconscious confusion in the contemporary sources between two quite distinct types of unction should be discarded. Sir John Spelman long ago summed up the case against it with inimitable force and clarity: 'I must so far oppose [that theory]', he wrote, 'as offer it to Judgement, whether likely the Religious that have writ that passage could be so far mistaken, as not to distinguish betwixt Regal Unction and the Chrisme, a Ceremony of the Church at that time common and in frequent use? especially Asser, a learned Bishop then living . . .'.[1]

Discussion of the third point involves trespassing on the thorny field of *Chronicle* studies, for the originally quite separate problem of the Roman anointing has long been entangled, as remarked above, in the briars of the authorship controversy. Plummer, Stevenson and Hodgkin assumed, on stylistic and other grounds, that Alfred either wrote or directly influenced the compilation of the *Chronicle* in the early 890s. This view was strongly supported, in Stevenson's opinion, by the account of the Roman anointing, which he was sure smacked of Alfredian influence.[2] Sir Frank Stenton, on the other hand, used the 853 as a major argument against the older view: 'It is incredible', he wrote, 'that Alfred himself should have confused decoration, or even the rite of confirmation at the pope's hands with an anointing to kingship'.[3] Hodgkin tried to counter this argument by suggesting that the story was inspired by Franks at Alfred's court[4]; while by no means adequate as a full explanation, the suggestion provides a useful clue which will be followed up below. But, meanwhile, the most recent expert opinion, that of Professor D. Whitelock, has endorsed that of Stenton.[5]

To pronounce on the question of *Chronicle* authorship is not, however, the purpose of this study. Only the entry for 853 is of concern here, and the question of its wider implications will be left open. It will be possible, I think, to deal with this limited problem more successfully once it is cleared of a smoke-screen of subjective opinion.

Stevenson, Plummer and Hodgkin maintained that the entry for 853 was so significant, and of such personal importance for Alfred, that the king himself must have composed it. But, since it was more or less explicitly recognised that a royal anointing could not really have been performed, Alfred was held to have been under a 'misapprehension'.[6] It has become clear, however, that Alfred and his circle (for the Franks at his

[1] *Life of Alfred*, 22.

[2] Cf. the works cited above, esp. Stevenson, ed. cit., 181: 'It is difficult to reject the theory that we can detect his [Alfred's] influence in this strange entry'.

[3] Op. cit., 683.

[4] Op. cit., 624.

[5] *Anglo-Saxon Chronicle*, xxii-iii; cf. her statement in 'Recent work on Asser's *Life*', a survey added to the reprint of the 1904 ed., Oxford 1959, cxxxvii: 'Stevenson's opinion . . has not won general acceptance'. Note, however, the comment of H. Löwe quoted above, 310 n. 4.

[6] Thus Stevenson, ed. cit., 181; cf. Plummer, *Alfred*, 71.

court were clerics) could not have confused confirmation with royal anointing; and I have further suggested that the story of a consular conferment which is given in the 'Roman' version of events should, perhaps, be regarded as neither sound nor contemporary evidence. A confusion, postulated by Stevenson and Plummer, of consular investiture with royal investiture can, therefore, also be discounted.

Stenton's view, though, might seem to accord better with the conclusions which have emerged from the earlier part of this study: for he denies the possibility of confusion on Alfred's part as to what happened at Rome in 853. But his (unstated) arguments were evidently quite different from those developed above, since he goes on to foist exactly that confusion on to the anonymous 'compiler of the *Chronicle*'.[1] His views turns out to rest on the rather subjective assumption that Alfred who was there—although in fact aged only four at the time—could not have mistaken consular investiture for 'ordination to kingship', whereas a contemporary author reporting the event at second hand could have and did: hence the 853 entry. But, if the conclusions so far reached in this study are accepted, all hypotheses which ascribe misunderstanding to the author of this entry, whoever he is assumed to have been, must be disallowed.

There remains, however, another and quite obvious possibility: one may grant Stenton's point that Alfred could not have confused another ceremony with royal anointing; but he could deliberately have transformed the one into the other. Had Leo IV (or, as I shall suggest, his successor), only even said blessings over Alfred, as he might well have done in the case of a foreign prince visiting Rome, this could have been quietly converted forty years later into a royal consecration, and publicised as such; and a transformation of this kind would be all the more easily effected if what had actually happened was a confirmation. Hincmar's contemporary treatment of the story of Clovis's baptism-confirmation offers an interesting comparison.[2]

This amounts, admittedly, to crediting Alfred and his circle of advisers with the deliberate falsification of events; but this seems the most plausible explanation of the *Chronicle* entry for 853,[3] and so of Asser's account too.

[1] Op. cit., 269 n.2; it was the 'consular investiture' which the compiler 'afterwards confused (!) with ordination to kingship'. Stenton's view on the authorship question is fully set out in his study, 'The South-western Element in the Old English Chronicle', in *Essays . . . presented to T. F. Tout*, Manchester 1925, 15–24.

[2] See de Pange, op. cit., 206 ff.; and F. Oppenheimer, *The Legend of the Ste. Ampoule*, London 1953, 173 f. The crucial text is Hincmar's *Adnuntiatio* preceding the consecration of Charles the Bald as king of Lorraine in 869, printed in *M.G.H. Capit*, ii. 340.

[3] I am aware of the attempts that have been made to prove that Alfred himself confused the terms 'consul' and 'king'. The evidence from his works has been discussed by B. A. Lees, op. cit., 85 n.; and by H. R. Loyn in *Eng. Hist. Rev.*, lxviii (1953), 519. Alfred's usage is far from consistent; but there is only one case where his translation of Bede's *consul* by *consul 7 cyning* could be read as evidence of confusion. In fact, this reveals his awareness of the problem of translating this alien constitutional term, and his grasp of the distinctive element of the consulship—its kingly quality. Another perceptive foreign observer, Polybius, had found a problem of definition here, and had come to a similar conclusion; cf. *Hist.*, vi. 11.

That no Anglo-Saxon specialist has considered the possibility of an Alfredian forgery is really rather surprising. I would tentatively suggest that this neglect has been due, not to oversight, but, perhaps, to an unconscious desire to preserve the image of Alfred the 'truth-teller'.[1] Liebermann, in a relatively little-known piece, made a very revealing observation about the story of the Roman anointing. After giving reasons for rejecting Plummer's belief in Alfred's authorship of the *Chronicle*, he added: 'Ferner möchte ich eine Fälschung (*sic*), vielleicht bloss die erwünschte Konfusion eines nach 871 schreibenden Royalisten, dem *rex veridicus* nicht zutrauen'.[2] So far as I know, Liebermann was the only scholar to admit the possibility that the anointing was a deliberate fabrication and not just the result of error; but the further possibility that Alfred was its author was clearly too much for him. Perhaps this was at the back of Stenton's mind when he so vehemently denied Alfred's authorship of the 853 entry. It may be significant too, that Liebermann's point has never been revived in more recent literature.

But the reasoning behind it should be clearly appreciated. It seems to be based on an assumption of incongruity in the idea of a forgery committed by one who was, by ninth-century standards, 'truthful'. The antithesis implied here is, however, meaningless in an early medieval context. On the forgeries of this period, Marc Bloch made the perceptive observation that 'many pious and indisputably high-minded persons . . . had a hand in such dealings'.[3] Asser's idea of truth is, then, a far cry from that of scientific rationalism.

The anointing story is, I believe, too significant to have got into the 'official' sources simply through the well-meaning invention of a 'royalist' scribe or compiler. Is it perhaps more likely that, so far from being a chance accretion, this entry was deliberately inserted into the records by an interested party, fully aware of its implications? This part, at any rate, of the entry for 853 must have been written after 871, when Alfred acceded. Now versions D and E of the *Chronicle* omit *only* this part of the entry, while for the rest giving the events of the A version. Perhaps they present here the kernel of the original contemporary annal, before the Alfredian addition. It is interesting, at all events, that the anointing story is already present in the A version: the first part of this MS., the annals down to 891, is in a hand of c. 900, and represents the revision of the annals possibly undertaken at Alfred's instigation, and circulated quite widely from 892 onwards.[4] The MS. evidence, then, is by no means incompatible with the

[1] 'Veredicus'; *Vita*, cap. 13: ed. cit., 12. It should, perhaps, be noted that Asser seems to use the term here in the rather narrow sense of 'accurate informant', for he goes on to mention the 'multi veredici' from whom Alfred got his information.

[2] *Archiv für das Studium der Neueren Sprachen*, civ (1900), 193. (A review of Plummer, *Two of the Saxon Chronicles Parallel*, cited above.)

[3] Op. cit., 92. The 'psychological implications' of this fact are, as Bloch insists, 'well worth pondering'.

[4] Stenton himself (op. cit., 682–3) refers to the 'Alfredian section' of the MS., for the revision of the annals in the 890s certainly reflected the revival of learning which Alfred inspired.

hypothesis that Alfred, or one close to him, inserted the anointing story into the *Chronicle* entry for 853.[1]

The crucial problem is that of motivation: why might Alfred have wished to reconstruct his childhood confirmation in order to appear as a king who had been papally anointed? This question can only be answered in the wider context of the history and development of royal anointing in England—a subject still in need of further study. The unfortunate influence of the misdating of the 'Egbert' *Ordo* was surprisingly persistent: Stevenson, following Maskell, still believed in 1904 on the basis of that evidence alone that Alfred was 'crowned' in 871,[2] and it was not until 1918 that J. A. Robinson gave sound reasons for challenging the eighth-century dating of 'Egbert'.[3] This is not the place to go into the questions of Ecgfrith's 'hallowing' in 787, and of Eardwulf's 'blessing' in 796. It is enough to say that although the use of these terms is evidence of ecclesiastical participation in the ceremonies of king-making, there is no indication that anointing was involved.[4] The raising of Offa's son to the throne during his father's lifetime might even suggest Byzantine rather than Frankish influence.[5]

In the ninth century, the *Chronicle* speaks uniformly of kings 'succeeding to the kingdom', and the expression *feng to rice* has purely secular implications. The rather surprising inference is that ecclesiastical influence, which had seemed to be growing dominant in the later eighth century, had disappeared again from Mercian and Northumbrian inauguration rites without affecting those of Wessex[6]: surprising, that is, by comparison with the steady progress made by the ninth-century West Frankish hierarchy towards complete control of royal consecrations. Perhaps because of its greater dependence on Rome, and because it was relatively weak and divided, the English hierarchy was evidently far less concerned to impose itself in this area.[7] None of the sources gives the least hint that

[1] This view would be supported if the two big marginal crosses which flank the 853 entry in the Parker MS. (A) are contemporary with the section down to 891. See fol. 13[a] in the facsimile edition cited above. But the crosses are more probably an addition of the second half of the tenth century. I am indebted to Professor F. Wormald and Mr. N. Ker for their help on this point. [2] Ed. cit., 182.

[3] 'The Coronation Order in the Tenth Century', in *J.T.S.*, xix (1917), 56 f., esp. 66.

[4] See above, 319 n.3. The theory that the Anglo-Saxons practised royal anointing before its introduction among the Franks has recently been revived by several scholars of distinction: cf. T. Klauser, in *Jahrbuch fur Liturgiewissenschaft*, xiii (1933), 350; and now Bouman, op. cit., xi; also Richardson and Sayles, op. cit., 397 f. But cf., too, the arguments of Ellard, op. cit., ch. i, which seem to me convincing. The verdict on Anglo-Saxon priority must remain 'unproven'. [5] See above, 319 n.4.

[6] Richardson and Sayles argue (loc. cit.) that royal anointings were too familiar to attract contemporary comment. A comparison with the copious references to anointing in Frankish sources might suggest otherwise.

[7] Until 848, Frankish anointings had, of course, been performed by the pope. The 'take-over' of royal consecrations by the Frankish hierarchy might be seen from one angle as part of their general opposition to Roman centralisation; in this Hincmar was a leading figure. Cf. Ullmann, *Growth of Papal Government*, 119 ff., 153. No comparable movement existed in England, for fairly obvious reasons. On the maintainance of links with Rome and on the ever-growing problems of the English Church in the ninth century, see Stenton, op. cit., 427 f.

any of the ninth-century Anglo-Saxon kings, down to and including Alfred himself,[1] (*feng to rice*, 871), received any kind of priest-given consecration at their accessions. Asser implies that an election took place in 871, and that is all.[2]

Throughout his reign, Alfred faced serious problems in imposing his rule beyond the borders of Wessex. But English solidarity was necessary if the Danes were to be effectively resisted.[3] Alfred maintained fairly close relations with the Continent,[4] yet, as he must have realised, he lacked the *charisma* of Frankish princes. Of his piety there can be no doubt, but it has been pointed out above that the pious man did not scruple in those times to perpetrate falsehoods if God's or the Church's interests could be furthered thereby: one has only to consider the mentality of a Stephen II or a Hincmar. Alfred was also a shrewd leader, who could hardly fail to see the advantages of a religious consecration[5]; far better to popularise the story of his papal anointing in 853, than to undergo some analogous, though less imposing rite, in his mid-forties.

If the motive behind the myth of the 853 anointing would have been Alfred's desire for a powerful spiritual, and, moreover, papal sanction for his authority, the inspiritation was provided by the memory of the infant Alfred's visit to Rome. The myth was credible, in fact, precisely because it rested on a factual basis. It may be doubted if Alfred could successfully have inserted the story of the papal anointing into the *Chronicle*, unless it had been widely known that he had indeed visited Rome in his infancy. But few would remember much about the actual event forty years later; nor would they wish to question the truth of a story which cast such an aura of divine approval around their king.

Although Alfred is mentioned neither in the papal nor in the Frankish sources which describe Æthelwulf's visit to Rome,[6] there is nothing improbable in the idea that the son accompanied his father. The *Chronicle*, however, ascribes Alfred's visit not to 855, the year of Æthelwulf's pilgrimage, but to 853. It is Asser who, after faithfully copying the account of the 853 visit, adds that Alfred went again to Rome with his father two years later.[7] On the face of it, this double journey seems highly unlikely. The route was at this period made more hazardous than ever by Saracen raids[8]; would a child of four have been sent off to Italy only to be taken

[1] As Schramm rightly points out: *History of English Coronation*, 16.

[2] Cf. *Vita*, cap. 42; ed. cit., 32.

[3] Stenton, op. cit., 256 ff.

[4] Hodgkin, op. cit., 647 ff.

[5] On the implications of becoming a 'christus', see F. Kern, *Gottesgnadentum und Widerstandrecht*, 2nd ed., R. Buchner, Munster 1954, 46 ff.; also Schramm, *Herrschaftszeichen und Staatssymbolik*, Stuttgart 1954, i. 127.

[6] Cf. *Vita* of Benedict III cited above, 318 n. 6, and *Annales Bertiniani*, sub anno 855. The silence of these sources bears out the view that the English princeling, seemingly without hope of the crown, was not unnaturally regarded at this time as of little account. Benedict III, it may be noted, became pope only in 855.

[7] *Vita*, cap 11; ed. cit., 9: 'Roman perrexit, praefatumque filium suum Alfredum *iterum in eandem viam* secum ducens, eo quod illum plus ceteris filiis diligebat. . . .'

[8] On the dangers of pilgrimage to Rome at this time and for long after, see Plummer, *Alfred*, 76 ff., and Bloch, op. cit., 6.

again at the still tender age of six? Asser says that Alfred suffered from illness 'ab infantia'.[1] All things considered, the imposition of a double journey across Europe could hardly be taken, as Asser interprets it, for evidence of Æthelwulf's special love for his youngest son. On the other hand, the *Chronicle*, where I am suggesting the entry for 853 was interpolated at the instance of Alfred himself, makes no mention of his second visit. How are the two sources to be reconciled? Asser perhaps gives a clue to what really happened: Alfred made only one journey, accompanying his father. The separate visit of 853 was a later invention, and because a double visit was implausible, the real one had to be deleted from the records. Asser, however, whose *Vita* was not subject to the same scrutiny as the 'official' account of the *Chronicle*, preserved the fact of the 853 visit alongside the Alfredian myth. His failure to observe the incongruity of the two statements accords with the often clumsy and ill-organised nature of his work.[2] This explanation of a long-standing problem presupposes that Alfred himself concocted the anointing story, but it does not conflict with the dictates of common sense.

But why was the Roman expedition pre-dated to 853 in the *Chronicle*? The reason for this may be sought in the Frankish model of the royal anointing. Stubbs had already noted the parallel between the *Chronicle's* account of 853 and the Frankish sources for 781, when Charlemagne's sons were papally confirmed and anointed as kings.[3] Hodgkin suggested that Frankish influence was behind the 'official' revision of the *Chronicle* at Alfred's court,[4] and it is well-known that Asser took Einhard's *Vita Karoli* as his model.[5] The story of Alfred's Roman anointing, then, was conceived under the shadow of Charlemagne. The name of pope Leo fitted into the scheme suggested by the Frankish sources: the anointing of Alfred thus echoed the imperial coronation of his prototype by another Leo. It is interesting that several forged decretals were later ascribed to 'Pope Leo'[6]: this was a name to conjure with. But what mystique was there after all in the name of Benedict III who had, in fact, received Æthelwulf and, it may now be assumed, his son in 855?

If, finally, the hypothesis set out above is correct, one might expect to find evidence, perhaps of royal anointing, or at any rate of markedly increased ecclesiastical influence on accession rites in England during the period immediately following Alfred's death. Despite the deficiencies of the sources, some indications of a new development in this direction can, I

[1] *Vita*, cap. 74; ed. cit., 55.

[2] See Stevenson, ed. cit., lxxix ff.; also the criticisms of V. H. Galbraith, *Historical Research . . .*, London 1951, 13 ff.

[3] For Stubbs's observation, see his ed. of William of Malmesbury's *Gesta Regum* cited above, 145 n.1; also Stevenson, ed. cit., 180. It should be noted, however, that the *Annales Regni Francorum*, sub anno 781 distinguish very carefully between baptism/confirmation and royal anointing.

[4] Op. cit., 624.

[5] Cf. Galbraith, loc. cit., and Stevenson, ed. cit., lxxxi f.

[6] Ullmann, *Ephem. Iuris Canon.*, ix (1953), 287 n.3: 'The papal name of Leo seems to play a crucial role in forgeries and falsifications of the tenth and eleventh centuries'.

think, be discerned. In the case of Edward the Elder, the *Chronicle* offers no clues, but Æthelweard, a specially well-informed source for this obscure reign, states that Pentecost was the day of his coronation.[1] This fact implies both the intrusion of clerical influence, and probably also a desire to conform to Frankish practice.[2] For the inaguration of his successor, Athelstan, the evidence is clearer: the contemporary *Mercian Register* says he was *gehalgod*,[3] while the near-contemporary Latin panegyric quoted by William of Malmesbury apparently referred to a *consecratio*, and certainly noted that the new king was in his thirtieth year, and also spoke of 'pontifices' pronouncing an anathema on disloyal subjects.[4] If it is not yet quite certain that anointing took place, then one can at least say that all had been gradually prepared for an English Hincmar to take the final step towards complete control by the local hierarchy over royal consecrations. Alfred the myth-maker had helped to pave the way for Dunstan.

[1] *Chronicon*, sub anno 900; ed. cit., 51, xxx f.

[2] Cf. Schramm, 'Die Krönung bei den Westfranken', 194, 198; also Bouman, op. cit., 125 n.3. It may not be without significance that Pentecost was traditionally the day of confirmation. Byzantine emperors were also often crowned on this day; cf. Treitinger, op. cit., 37. King Edgar, too, was crowned at Pentecost; see *Chronicle*, sub anno 973.

[3] The *Mercian Register* was incorporated in versions B and C of the *Chronicle*. See ed. cit., sub anno 924 for Athelstan's consecration. The true date was 925: see M. L. R. Beaven in *Eng. Hist. Rev.*, xxxii (1917), 521 ff., and J. A. Robinson, *The Times of St. Dunstan*, Oxford 1923, 27–36.

[4] See Stubbs's edition, i. 145. For an excellent discussion of the Latin poem used by William, see now L. K. Loomis, 'The Holy Relics of Charlemagne and King Athelstan', in *Speculum*, xxv (1950), 437–9, stressing the value of this source. The fact that Athelstan was in his thirtieth year affords a remarkable parallel, hitherto unnoticed, with the case of Edgar. On the significance of this age *à propos* Edgar's deferred coronation, see the illuminating suggestion of Stenton, op. cit., 363.

14

RITUAL AND REALITY IN THE EARLY MEDIEVAL *ORDINES*

'TO know what was generally believed in all ages, the way is to consult the liturgies, not any private man's writings.' John Selden's maxim, which surely owed much to his own pioneering work as a liturgist, shows a shrewd appreciation of the significance of the medieval *ordines* for the consecration of kings.[1] Thanks to the more recent efforts of Waitz, Eichmann, Schramm[2] and others, this material now forms part of the medievalist's stock in trade; and much has been written on the evidence which the *ordines* provide concerning the nature of kingship, and the interaction of church and state, in the middle ages.[3] The usefulness of the *ordines* to the historian might therefore seem to need no further demonstration or qualification. But there is another

I am grateful to professor Walter Ullmann for first showing me the importance of the *ordines*, to professor Dorothy Whitelock for her generous help on several points relating to tenth-century England, and to John Gillingham for his always stimulating criticism.

[1] The quotation is from Selden's *Table-Talk* (London 1689) under 'Liturgy'. His great work on liturgy, *Titles of Honor*, was first published in 1614. I have used the third edition of 1672.

[2] G. Waitz, 'Die Formeln der deutschen Königs-und der Römischen Kaiser-Krönung vom zehnten bis zum zwölften Jahrhundert', in *Abhandlungen der Königlichen Gesellschaft der Wissenschaften zu Göttingen*, 18 (1873); [E.] Eichmann, 'Königs—und Bischofsweihe', in *Sitzungsberichte der bayrischen Akademie der Wissenschaften. Phil. Hist. Klasse*, Abh. 6 (Munich 1928), and many other articles; P. E. Schramm, *A History of the English Coronation* (Oxford 1937), *Der König von Frankreich* (2 ed Weimar 1960), *Herrschaftszeichen und Staatssymbolik* (3 vols Stuttgart 1954–6), various articles on the west frankish, anglo-saxon, and german *ordines*, originally published during the 1930s, now conveniently reprinted in vols II and III of his collected papers, *K[aiser,] K[önige und] P[äpste]* (Stuttgart 1968). The imperial *ordines* have been edited by R. Elze, *Ordines Coronationis Imperialis, MGH Fontes Iuris Germanici Antiqui*, 9 (Hanover 1960). But only royal *ordines* will come under consideration below.

[3] See, for example, R. W. Southern, *The Making of the Middle Ages* (London 1953) pp 97 *et seq*; W. Ullmann, *P[rinciples of] G[overnment and] P[olitics in the Middle Ages]* (London 1961) pp 129 *et seq*; *The Carolingian Renaissance and the Idea of Kingship* (London 1969) pp 101 *et seq*; B. Tierney, *The Crisis of Church and State* (Englewood Cliffs 1964) pp 25 *et seq*; J. M. Wallace-Hadrill, *Early Germanic Kingship in England and on the Continent* (Oxford 1971) pp 133 *et seq*.

side to the coin. The value of the early medieval *ordines* can be, not perhaps overestimated, but misconstrued. 'The liturgies' may indeed tell us 'what was generally believed'—but we must first be sure that we know how they were perceived and understood by their participants, as well as by their designers. They need to be correlated with other sources, and as often as possible with 'private writings' too, before the full picture becomes intelligible.

Amongst the various materials for early medieval king-makings, such as laws, charters, chronicles, and sometimes literature or hagiography, the *ordines* occupy a singular position. As liturgical texts, they belong to a type of historical record not normally used by general historians: thus their limitations, and the special problems of interpretation which they present, have not always been clearly recognised. If we are to 'consult' them with profit, we should consult liturgical scholarship also. With this in mind, I want briefly to consider certain aspects of the *ordines* which seem to bear on their value as historical material. I shall select most of my illustrations from the anglo-saxon *ordines*, because these texts are most easily available, and probably most familiar, in this country.[4]

The *ordines*, by their very nature, are far from providing complete or accurate records of specific actual king makings. They are incomplete because they cover only the intra-ecclesiastical part of the process of installation. Sometimes, fortunately, some other source survives to fill in details of the ritual procedures outside the church. Perhaps the best-known example is Widukind's account of Otto I's inauguration in 936.[5] But for some tenth-century anglo-saxon cases comparable information can be pieced together. We can be fairly sure, for instance, in the light of a charter apparently issued by king Eadred just after his consecration in 946, that the liturgical rite was then preceded by a formal election in which magnates from all over the realm took part.[6]

[4] Thanks especially to the publications of the *H[enry] B[radshaw] S[ociety]*. For the anglo-saxon *ordines* discussed below, the relevant editions are those of *The Lanalet Pontifical*, by G. H. Doble *HBS* 74 (for 1937); *The Benedictional of Archbishop Robert*, by H. Wilson, *HBS* 24 (for 1903); *Three Coronation Orders*, by J. Wickham Legg, *HBS* 19 (for 1900); *The Claudius Pontificals*, by D. H. Turner, *HBS* 97 (for 1964, publ 1971). Other editions will be cited below. As yet, unfortunately, there is no complete edition of the english *ordines*.

[5] Widukind, *Rerum Gestarum Saxonicarum Libri Tres*, ed H. E. Lohmann, rev P. Hirsch (Hanover 1935) pp 64 *et seq*.

[6] W. G. Birch, *Cartularium Saxonicum*, 3 vols (London 1885–93) no 815. This charter, dated 946, is translated with an excellent commentary by D. Whitelock, *English Historical Documents*, I (London 1955) pp 508 *et seq*. The presence

Again, two pieces of hagiography, the *Vita Dunstani* for 956, and the *Vita Oswaldi* for 973, show that the feast which followed the consecration had major significance in the series of legitimating acts.[7] Yet the *ordo* used in mid tenth-century England says nothing of the prior election outside the church, and mentions the feast only in the laconic concluding line: *Post pergant ad mensam.*[8] The *ordo* used in 973 opens with the king leaving the *conventus seniorum*, but does not elucidate the significance of this meeting, which I take to have involved a formal election by the Witan; and it says nothing at all about the feast.[9]

Many of the earliest *ordines* are scarcely more than lists of prayers. The king's consecration in the early tenth-century *Leofric Missal*, for example, which may well represent the earliest *ordo* to be used for a west saxon king, consists of seven prayers linked by rubrics which in most cases are no more explicit than *Benedictio* or *Alia*.[10] This layout represents an early phase in the development of such major rites as royal consecration or episcopal ordination. Only the broad structure was fixed, the details being left to the clerics who stage-managed each individual occasion. In the case of the bishop's rite, a letter written by Hincmar of Rheims provides details of an actual performance, and we can see how the bare bones of the texts in a ninth-century pontifical

---

of northumbrian magnates and welsh princes at Eadred's inauguration may be inferred from the witness-list.

[7] *Vita Dunstani* (Auctore 'B') ed W. Stubbs in *Memorials of St Dunstan RS* (1874) p 32; *Vita Oswaldi* ed J. Raine in *Historians of the Church of York*, RS (1879) I, pp 437 *et seq*, this passage reprinted in Schramm, *KKP*, II, pp 241 *et seq*. On the significance of the feast, see K. Hauck, 'Rituelle Speisegemeinschaft im 10. und 11. Jht.', in *Studium Generale*, III (Heidelberg 1950) pp 611 *et seq.*

[8] See P. L. Ward, 'An early version [of the Anglo-Saxon coronation ceremony'], in *EHR*, 57 (1942) pp 345 *et seq*, at p 358. I hope to show elsewhere that this *ordo* represents mid-tenth-century usage. For the priority of this *ordo* over that of 973, see Ward, 'The coronation ceremony in medieval England', in *Speculum*, 14 (1939) pp 160 *et seq*, at pp 169 *et seq*. Compare the earlier view of J. A. Robinson, 'The coronation order in the tenth century', in *JTS*, 19 (1917) pp 56 *et seq.*

[9] The text is most conveniently consulted in Schramm, *KKP*, II, pp 233 *et seq*, at p 239, showing manuscript variants. See also the text of BM Cotton Claudius Aiii, in Turner's edition, pp 89 and 94. For the association of this *ordo* with 973, see Schramm, *KKP*, II, pp 180 *et seq*; and the more convincing arguments of C. A. Bouman, *S[acring and] C[rowning]* (Groningen 1957) p 18 and n 1. Some of the objections raised by H. C. Richardson and G. Sayles, *The Governance of Medieval England* (Edinburgh 1963) pp 397 *et seq* have been answered by E. John, *Orbis Britanniae* (Leicester 1966) pp 276 *et seq.*

[10] Ed F. E. Warren (Oxford 1883) pp 230 *et seq*, the *ordo* reprinted in Schramm, *KKP*, II, pp 223 *et seq*. See also Bouman, *SC*, pp 167 *et seq.*

would be fleshed out in liturgical practice.[11] As for the 'Leofric' *ordo*, fortunately later manuscripts give fuller rubrical directions which seem to represent the way the rite was originally performed.[12] In the later middle ages, the *ordines* have increasingly detailed rubrics, prescribing, for example, the king's behaviour during the period preceding his consecration, the procession from palace to church, and the concluding feast.[13] But no *ordo* before the thirteenth century gives anything like an account of the ritual procedures as a whole.

In view of these severe limitations, the early medieval *ordines* might seem far less useful as historical sources than the later elaborate and explicit texts. But a further important consideration partly redresses the balance: it was in the early middle ages, particularly in the ninth and tenth centuries, that the first royal *ordines*, which decisively shaped all their successors, were actually composed. For this period alone, therefore, they are contemporary witnesses in the strict sense. The conservatism of scribes, and the universal, timeless and normative character of liturgy in general, ensured that an *ordo* would go on being copied out and used at times and places often far removed from those of its original composition.[14] Indeed only quite rarely is it possible to date precisely the genesis of a prayer-text, or even a complete *ordo*. The clergy designing a rite for a specific royal consecration usually preferred to follow the main lines of a received indigenous tradition. But sometimes, as for instance when the practice of royal consecration itself was being introduced in a given realm, an imported *ordo* might

[11] Hincmar's letter to Adventius of Metz has been edited and well-discussed by M. Andrieu, 'Le sacre épiscopal d'après Hincmar de Reims', in *RHE*, 48 (1953) pp 22 *et seq*. The best general introduction to this subject is to be found in Bouman, *SC*, part II, esp pp 70 *et seq*.

[12] See Schramm, *KKP*, II, pp 223 *et seq*. I have argued for a ninth-century dating for the whole *ordo* in my unpublished Cambridge dissertation, *Rituals of Royal Inauguration in Early Medieval Europe* (Cambridge 1967) cap 5.

[13] See, for example, the *ordo* of Burgundy, ed E. Eichmann, 'Die sogenannte römische Königskrönungsformel', in *Historisches Jahrbuch*, 45 *Jahrbuch*, 45 (Cologne 1925) pp 518 *et seq*. I cannot agree with L. Böhm, 'Rechtsformen und Rechtstitel der burgundischen Konigserhebungen im 9.Jht.', in *Historisches Jahrbuch*, 80 (1961) pp 27 *et seq*, that the text of this *ordo* as it survives in manuscripts of the thirteenth and fourteenth centuries represents ninth-century practice. Two later medieval english *ordines* may be found in the fourteenth-century *Liber Regalis*, ed L. G. Wickham Legg, *English Coronation Records* (Westminster 1901) pp 81 *et seq*, and in the fifteenth-century *Liber Regie Capelle*, ed W. Ullmann (*HBS*, 92 for 1959, publ 1961) pp 74 *et seq* and introduction, pp 22 *et seq*.

[14] See A. Baumstark, *Comparative Liturgy*, rev B. Botte, new ed and trans F. L. Cross (Oxford 1958); and Bouman, *SC*, pp 55 *et seq*, 79 *et seq*.

be used; or partial revisions might be made in a traditional text. In such a case, the *ordo* clearly would not reveal 'what was generally believed' in quite the same sense as it would in its original context of time and place.

The point is illustrated by an *ordo* which survives in more than a dozen french pontificals copied during the central and later middle ages, including the splendid *Coronation Book* of Charles V (1365). Here, in the anointing prayer itself, is a reference to the 'sceptres of the Saxons, Mercians and Northumbrians.'[15] John Selden was moved to indignation: 'The negligence or forgetfulness that left these names in were almost incredible if we saw it not'.[16] Perhaps he asked himself in what conceivable sense these words in a fourteenth-century French liturgy revealed anything of 'what was generally believed' in fourteenth-century France! What they do reveal is, first that they were added to the anointing prayer originally in England, in the mid tenth century (though not a single anglo-saxon manuscript has survived to witness this), and second, that for the french scribes who copied them, and for the archbishops of Rheims who pronounced them, contemporary political relevance mattered not a straw. For the mention of the Saxons, Mercians and Northumbrians had nothing to do with french dynastic claims to the realms of the english king:[17] the names appear already in french manuscripts of the eleventh and twelfth centuries, and I doubt whether even then their original meaning was understood in France. Nevertheless they are not without meaning. Long after the topical reference to anglo-saxon hegemonial rulership had been forgotten, the solemn copying out of these time honoured words in french manuscripts signified the profound respect of the later middle ages for ritual tradition, precisely observed. The medium itself had become the message.

Similar questions of meaning are raised by the formal similarities which by the close of the tenth century had come to exist between royal and episcopal consecration-rites.[18] It may seem tempting to

[15] The manuscripts are listed by Ward, 'An early version', pp 347 *et seq*, with the 'SMN' variant at p 352 (and n 6). The *Coronation Book* of Charles V has been edited by E. S. Dewick (*HBS*, 16 for 1899), with the variant at p 27.

[16] *Titles of Honor* Bk I, c 8, p 177. Selden quite rightly saw that the names must have been 'without question taken out of some Saxon ceremonial'.

[17] As used to be surmised: see the note by Dewick in his edition, p 80. These names seem to have reappeared at french royal consecrations for as long as the ancien régime lasted.

[18] See Eichmann, 'Königs-und Bischofsweihe'.

regard these as expressions of an ideology which drew constant parallels between the offices of king and bishop and in which kingship was delineated, in terms of a hierocratic doctrine, as the church's executive arm. While not wishing to deny that such significance may perhaps be discerned in some cases, I suggest that many of these parallels manifest 'laws' of liturgical development which governed the elaboration of major rites. For instance, the practice of beginning rites of personal consecration with the prostration of the initiate before the altar affected monastic profession and, later, the wedding service, as well as royal and episcopal consecrations.[19] Not surprisingly, status-changing rites were felt to have a common character in as much as they were the means by which an individual assumed a new social personality. As the preliminary to such a transformation prostration was surely more than 'a gesture of deepest humility and contrition'[20] or 'a supplication;'[21] it symbolised the annihilation of the initiate's former personality in preparation for 'rebirth' into a new status. If, therefore, we find prostration specified before the consecrations of both king and bishop in the tenth century, this might be attributed to a trend in liturgical technique rather than to some ideologically motivated direct borrowing from the episcopal to the royal rite. Other kinds of elaboration can also be referred to the exigencies of actual performance, and as C. A. Bouman observed, 'the *horror vacui* has always been an active factor in the development of the liturgy.'[22]

As a final example of the difficulty of interpreting the texts of the *ordines*, the prayer, *Sta et retine* is worth considering. It seems to have been composed in west Francia early in the tenth century as part of a complete series of seven prayers. Ever since it was brilliantly identified by Carl Erdmann, this 'Seven-Forms' *ordo* has been regarded as unusually rich in political ideas.[23] *Sta et retine*, in particular, refers to the

[19] See E. H. Kantorowicz, *Laudes Regiae* (Berkeley 1946) p 36, n 89, and p 90, n 84; Bouman, *SC*, pp 147 *et seq*; K. Ritzer, *Formen, Riten und religiöses Brauchtum der Eheschliessung in den christlichen Kirchen des ersten Jahrtausends* (Münster 1962) p 258. The similarities between status changing rites were first pointed out by A. van Gennep, *The Rites of Passage*, trans M. Vizedom and G. L. Caffee (Chicago 1960).

[20] Kantorowicz, *Laudes Regiae*, p. 91

[21] Bouman, *SC*, p 148.

[22] *Ibid* p 147.

[23] C. Erdmann, *Forschungen zur politischen Ideenwelt des Frühmittelaters* (Berlin) 1951 pp 56 *et seq*, and his edition of the *ordo*, pp 87 *et seq*. See also Schramm's interpretation: 'die Auffassung des Königtums in die Otto I hineingewachsen ist' (—still believing the *ordo* to be a German composition of *c* 960) in his article of

king as *mediator cleri et plebis* in an explicit analogy with Christ's function as *mediator Dei et hominum*, but at the same time, the ritually-superior status of the clergy is emphasised: . . . *quanto clerum sacris altaribus propinquiorem prospicis, tanto ei potiorem in locis congruis honorem impendere memineris*. It seems to me misleading, however, to interpret this prayer solely by reference to its *verbal* content, as an exposition of 'pure' ideology, hincmarian, ottonian, theocratic or what you will. This, after all, is a prayer with a precise ritual function: it is, as Bouman recognised, the sole surviving text specifically designed for the enthronement of the king. Now enthronement may well have been the central act in royal inaugurations before these came under ecclesiastical influence;[24] and it seems likely that, even as late as the tenth century, lay *principes* as well as the officiating bishops continued to take part in this ritual, as they undoubtedly did in the acclamations which followed.[25] In the *ordo* used in tenth-century England, *Sta et retine* appears at the enthronement, immediately after which the king exercises his newly assumed powers in the issue of a three point 'programme' of good government aimed at the welfare of 'the church and the whole Christian people.' Appropriately, therefore, the next and final act of the liturgical drama is the people's three-fold shout, *vivat rex*, in recognition of the new king.[26] The significance assigned to the prayer *Sta et retine* must be compatible with this ritual corollary. From the standpoint of the lay subjects who witnessed it, the enthronement clearly signified the king's installation as holder of an office defined by tradition, in the interests of the 'christian people', and with duties more in evidence than rights and powers. We need constantly to recall that the consecration-rite involved more than the merely verbal component which we can read on the manuscript or printed page: it was replete with audio-visual, and even olfactory,[27] aids, by means of which communication extended to the illiterate lay participants.

1935, now reprinted in *KKP*, III, pp 81 *et seq*. Compare the views of Kantorowicz, [*The*] *K*[*ing's*] *T*[*wo*] *B*[*odies*] (Princeton 1957) p 88; Ullmann, *PGP*, pp 130, 142 *et seq*, and 'Der Souveränitätsgedanke in den mittelalterlichen Krönungsordines', in *Festschrift P. E. Schramm* (Wiesbaden 1964) pp 81 *et seq*; Bouman, SC, pp 137 *et seq*.

[24] See R. Schmidt, 'Zur Geschichte des fränkischen Königsthrons', in *Frühmittelalterliche Studien*, II (Berlin 1968) pp 45 *et seq*.

[25] This is the arrangement envisaged in the 'Leofric', and related, *ordines*. See above 331 n 10.

[26] For the text, see Ward, 'An early version', p 357.

[27] For the aromatic ingredients in chrism, see P. Hofmeister, *Die heiligen Öle in der morgen-und abendlandischen Kirche* (Würzburg 1948) pp 25 *et seq*.

Once the church performed such essential symbolic acts as investiture and enthronement, the whole king making ritual assumed a strongly clerical colouring. But to view this as a kind of hierocratic take over bid, to term it a 'clericalisation' of kingship,[28] is to risk misrepresenting early medieval reality. In support of a rather different view. I should like to relate the process of *Liturgiesierung*[29] to the general problem of the *ordines*' significance in terms of political ideas.

The clerical performance of the intra-ecclesiastical rites of king making, in particular of the anointing patterned after the biblical *unctio in regem*,[30] certainly resulted from a differentiation of roles within christian society. The clergy were now believed to be uniquely qualified to operate with the symbols that bridged the gulf between the material world of time and flux and the celestial world of the unseen, unchanging, eternal. The practical manifestation of this belief was that the laity confided, and the clergy willingly assumed, specialist ritual functions. The anglo-saxon evidence, at least, suggests no conflict of interests here. The aspect of tenth-century king makings which seems to be of paramount importance is the expression, and presumably the reinforcement, of solidarity between officiants and witnesses, between ruler and ruled. The clearest indication of this is the presence within the *ordo* of a royal commitment to certain recognised norms of right government. We have already noticed the three point 'programme' of one tenth-century rite. In the *ordo* of 973, the formulation shifts from that of a three part command issued by the newly enthroned king, to that of a three fold promise made by the king as the preliminary, and condition, of his consecration.[31] The constitutional implications of this change have been stressed often enough.[32] But perhaps just as

[28] Kantorowicz, *KTB*, p 89. Compare the penetrating comments of R. Nineham, 'The so-called Anonymous of York', in *JEH* 14 (1963) pp 31 *et seq* at p 41 *et seq.*

[29] This term was used by O. Treitinger, *Die Oströmische Kaiser-und Reichsidee nach ihrer Gestaltung im höfischen Zeremoniell* (Jena 1938) pp 233 *et seq*, with reference to developments in Byzantium. It is hard to think of an elegant english translation.

[30] See J. De Pange, *Le Roi très chrétien* (Paris 1949); Kantorowicz, *Laudes Regiae*, pp 56 *et seq*; A. R. Johnson, *Sacral Kingship in Ancient Israel* (Cardiff 1955) pp 12 *et seq.*

[31] For the text, see Schramm, *KKP*, II, p 235.

[32] See Schramm, *History of the English Coronation*, pp 179 *et seq*; M. David, 'Le serment du sacre du IXe au XVe siècle. Contribution a l'étude des limites juridiques de la souveraineté', in *Revue du Moyen Age Latin*, 6 (Lyons 1950), p 144 *et seq.* F. Kern, *Gottesgnadentum und Widerstandsrecht im früheren Mittelalter*, rev R. Buchner (2 ed Münster 1954), anhang 14, pp 304 *et seq*, tried (in my view unsuccessfully) to obliterate the distinction between precept and promise. See also Bouman, *SC*, pp 144 *et seq.*

striking as the difference of form is the identity of content between the earlier *mandatum* and the later *promissio*. If the king is the subject of both acts, the recipient of both is also identical: the *populus christianus*.

But the full significance of the introduction of a fully fledged oath in the later tenth century is not apparent in the *ordines* texts themselves. Other evidence fortunately survives. The king was given a copy of the oath in anglo-saxon from which, presumably, he read out its provisions so that all the 'christian folk' present – to whom after all the commitment was given – could understand.[33] This text was then laid on the altar before which the consecration was performed. The manuscript evidence shows that the vernacular oath was linked with an address, also in anglo-saxon,[34] to the new king, exhorting him to keep his promises:

> The christian king who keeps these engagements earns for himself wordly honour, and the eternal God also is merciful to him. . . . But if he violate that which was promised to God, then shall it forthwith right soon grow worse among his people . . .

The king is reminded of his responsibility for 'the flock of which thou hast been made the shepherd in this life'. It is he who, on judgement day, will have to 'give account how thou heldest that which Christ afore purchased with his own blood'. The king's obligations are then spelt out in far more detailed and specific terms than in the *ordo* itself:

> The duty of a hallowed king is that he judge no man unrighteously, and that he defend and protect widows and orphans and strangers, that he forbid thefts . . . feed the needy with alms, and have old and wise men for counsellors, and set righteous men for stewards . . .

That an address of this type was a feature of late saxon consecrations is supported by the *Anglo-Saxon Chronicle*, MSS C and E, in its account of Edward the Confessor's inauguration in 1043:

[33] For the text, see Schramm, KKP, II pp 243 *et seq*, with references to other editions. This oath is explicitly linked with Dunstan. It was given 'at Kingston', and could relate to 975 (Edward) or 978 (Aethelred).

[34] BM Cotton Cleopatra B xiii is dated to the third quarter of the eleventh century. BM Cotton Vitellius A vii, of the first half of the eleventh century, was damaged in the fire of 1731, but a copy of it survives: Oxford Bodleian, Junius 60. In both manuscripts the address followed the oath. I quote below from the translation by Stubbs, *Memorials of St Dunstan*, pp 356 *et seq*. Professor D. Whitelock kindly drew my attention to this text.

Archbishop Eadsige consecrated him and gave him
good instructions before all the people,
and admonished him well for his own sake and for
the sake of all the people.[35]

Here the archbishop fulfils a representative function: he administers the oath, admonishes the king, and performs the consecration, but he acts on behalf of the whole people. They are the recipients of the oath, the beneficiaries of its terms, the witnesses to the consecration. However passive they might appear, their participation is vital. In their name divine sanctions are invoked to constrain the king; and the ritual process of election, consecration and installation reaffirms the collective interests of king, church and 'christian folk', claiming divine authorisation for the political society thus constituted.[36]

One last point can be made concerning the interpretation of the early medieval *ordines*: they are better approached as patterns of symbols expressing the continuity and integration of society through the kingship, than as juristic texts in which conflicting hierocratic or theocratic claims are clearly spelled out. Later, it is true, lawyers and polemicists could, and did, interpret the *ordines* in this latter sense. Much was made, on the papalist side, of the superiority of those who blessed over those who received blessing. On the royalist side, the norman Anonymous, finding in an ancient but still current regal benediction (probably of merovingian origin) the prayer, *Benedic domine hunc presulem principem*, exploited the apparent conflation of episcopal and royal functions to argue that if the king was *presul, et summus presul est, quia super alios presules principatum habet*.[37] The frankish and anglo-saxon clerics who continued to copy and use this prayer-text in the tenth century, when *presul* had long since come to be used exclusively of episcopal office,

[35] *The Anglo-Saxon Chronicle: a Revised Translation*, ed D. Whitelock with D. C. Douglas and S. I. Tucker (London 1961) p 107.

[36] Compare O. Gierke, *Political Theories of the Middle Age*, trans F. W. Maitland (Cambridge 1900) p 34: 'Lordship was never merely a right; primarily it was a duty; it was divine, but for that very reason an all the more onerous calling; it was a public office.' M. Douglas, *Natural Symbols* (London 1970) pp 55 *et seq* recalling Durkheim's premise 'that society and God can be equated', suggests a correlation between the development of ritual as 'a system of control as well as a system of communication' and the value placed on 'effective social coherence' within a given society. See also *ibid* pp 73 *et seq*, where professor Douglas outlines the social conditions in which ritual is likely to be emphasised.

[37] All the treatises of the Anonymous, including the *De consecratione pontificum et regum et de regimine eorum in ecclesia sancta*, are now edited by K. Pellens (Wiesbaden 1966). The quotation is from p 160 of his edition; *ibid* pp 166 *et seq*, is the

were slow to react against what should by then have appeared a solecism: not until 973 was the wording altered to ... *hunc praeelectum principem*, with a neat double reference to divine and human preselection. We must conclude that the *ordines* of the tenth century were neither conceived nor understood in precise legalistic terms, even by clerical specialists. E. H. Kantorowicz contrasted the political ideas of the early middle ages, 'still hedged in by a general framework of liturgical language and theological thought', with the law-centred kingship of the succeeding period: there was an 'evolutionary change'– 'from liturgy to legal science'.[38] Pursuing the implications of this subtle contrast, we might observe that where the lawyer deals in conflicts, operating with logic through nice verbal distinctions, the liturgist deals in communications, operating with faith through a symbolic code. In view of these differences, he who consults the early medieval *ordines* should be wary of imposing on the age of liturgy the preoccupations of an age of law.

---

royal *ordo* quoted in extenso. The Anonymous was using an earlier version of the anglo-saxon ordo of 973: see Nineham, 'The so-called Anonymous of York', pp 34 *et seq*. The prayer *Benedic domine hos presules principes* appears in the *Sacramentary* of Angoulême of *c* 800, ed P. Cagin, *Le sacramentair gélasien d'Angoulême* (Angoulême 1919) fol 168v. I believe that its content shows it to be a late Merovingian composition: see my unpublished dissertation, pp 44 *et seq*. For the later role of this prayer (referring now only to a single ruler) as part of 'the stock of "regal texts" ', see Bouman, *SC*, pp 75 *et seq*. In some tenth-century manuscripts, its *incipit* is recast to read, *Benedic domine hunc principem*, or *hunc regem*, compare Bouman, SC, pp 174 and 180, but *presul* remains in the 'Leofric' *ordo*, ed Warren, p 251, in the *ordo* of the Benedictional of Archbishop Robert, ed Wilson, p 146, and in the *ordo* of the Sacramentary of Ratold of Corbie, ed Ward, 'An early version ', p 357. Compare above 331 n 10.

[38] Kantorowicz, *KTB*, pp 87 *et seq*.

15

THE EARLIEST ROYAL *ORDO*: SOME LITURGICAL AND HISTORICAL ASPECTS*

IN HIS OWN CONTRIBUTION to the *Festschrift* for P. E. Schramm, Walter Ullmann wrote with characteristic generosity of Schramm's 'brilliant accomplishments' in the field of *Ordinesforschung*, and modestly offered his own remarkable paper as 'only a note' thereto.[1] I now offer the following further note, which consists in part of a revision of some of Schramm's work but would have been inconceivable without it, as a tribute to the no less brilliant accomplishments of Walter Ullmann himself. He will know just how much it owes to his inspiration.

Schramm began his study of the Anglo-Saxon *Ordines*[2] by distinguishing between, on the one hand, the date at which royal anointing was introduced and the king-making ritual in part assumed a liturgical form, and, on the other, the date at which a fixed rite was established and written down as an *Ordo*. While acknowledging the relevance of this distinction (in this paper I confine myself to the *Ordines*) and the possibility of such a time-lag, I would stress a further distinction between the date at which a fixed rite was used and the date of its earliest surviving manuscripts. That these may differ widely is the first and fundamental lesson that historians have to learn from liturgists. The *Ordo* Schramm identified as the earliest English one survives today in three manuscripts: Oxford, Bodleian MS 579 (the so-called Leofric Missal), Paris, Bibliothèque Nationale MS lat.10575 (the so-called Egbert Pontifical), and Rouen, Bibliothèque Municipale MS A.27 (the

* I am very grateful to Herr Josef Kirschner for kindly allowing me to draw on his work before it was published; to Mr Christopher Hohler for commenting on an earlier draft of this paper; and especially to Professor Dorothy Whitelock for her usual unstinting help.

[1] 'Der Souveränitätsgedanke in den mittelalterlichen Krönungsordines', in *Festschrift Schramm*, ed. P. Classen and P. Scheibert (2 vols., Wiesbaden, 1964), I, p. 72.

[2] 'Die Krönung bei den Westfranken und Angelsachsen von 878 bis um 1000', *ZRG* Kan., XXIII (1934), pp. 117–242, now reprinted with some additional references in Schramm's collected papers, *Kaiser, Könige und Päpste* (4 vols., Stuttgart, 1968), II, pp. 140–248. All my references below are to the latter reprint of the 1934 article.

Lanalet Pontifical).[3] In the case of the Egbert Pontifical, liturgists had long since pointed to a time-lag between the date of the manuscript, *c.*1000, and the date of its contents, allegedly the mid-eighth century; but because the arguments adduced in this case were unsound,[4] Schramm was able to ignore not only them but also their methodological implications for the treatment of liturgical materials in general. The Lanalet Pontifical is now usually assigned to the later tenth or early eleventh century. As for the Leofric Missal, Schramm followed its editor in believing this manuscript to have been written in Lotharingia *c.*900 but claimed, idiosyncratically, that its royal *Ordo* was among the additions made to the book in England *c.*969.[5]

Schramm's conclusions, which he emphasised were based on a manuscript tradition going back to 'the tenth century and no earlier', were first, that although royal anointing was practised in England 'from 787 onwards' no fixed rite existed until the 960s, and second, that the *Ordo* of the Leofric Missal (hereafter 'Leofric') represented a 'first draft' and the *Ordo* of the other two manuscripts (hereafter 'Egbert'/'Lanalet') a revised and amplified version of a royal *Ordo* drawn up by St Dunstan 'between 960 and 973' but never actually used. These two main conclusions, repeated in Schramm's *History of the English Coronation*

[3] The Leofric Missal was edited by F. E. Warren (Oxford, 1883), the *Benedictiones super regem noviter electum* there pp. 230–2 (I hope to justify below my application of the term *Ordo* to this series of benedictions, which form a full rite of royal inauguration including anointing); the Pontifical of Egbert by W. Greenwell, Surtees Society vol. XXVII (Durham, 1853), the consecration-rite (*Benedictio*) there pp. 100–5; the Lanalet Pontifical by G. H. Doble, Henry Bradshaw Society vol. LXXIV (London, 1937), the rite there (with only the *incipits* of the prayers appearing also in the *Benedictional of Archbishop Robert*, ed. H. A. Wilson, Henry Bradshaw Society vol. XXIV (London, 1903)) pp. 59–63. Schramm, *Kaiser*, pp. 223–33, gives further details and prints the *Ordo*, giving some (not all) variants of these three texts and of a fourth, the royal consecration-rite in the eleventh-century Pontifical of Milan, ed. M. Magistretti (Milan, 1897), pp. 112–19, in which a rite of the above type is spliced in with the West Frankish 'Seven-Forms'. C. A. Bouman, *Sacring and Crowning* (Groningen, 1957), pp. 9–15, 23–4, gives further details and supplies some corrections to Warren's and Greenwell's editions. Clearly, a new edition of the *Ordo* is urgently needed. I have been able to consult the Paris MS and photographs of the Oxford one. I dealt with this *Ordo* at length in my unpublished dissertation, 'Rituals of Royal Inauguration in Early Medieval Europe' (Cambridge, 1967), ch. 5, for which the inspiration and careful supervision of Walter Ullmann must here be gratefully acknowledged. I wish to make clear, however, that some of the views expressed therein, especially on the early English *Ordines* (briefly indicated in my paper [ch. 10 above, pp. 247-8]), were wrong, and that I have thoroughly revised them in what follows.

[4] At the beginning of the Paris MS appears material from penitential canons once attributed to Archbishop Egbert of York (734–66). But the attribution is very questionable and, as Schramm saw, need have no bearing on the date of the Pontifical proper.

[5] For the most recent opinions on the date and character of all three books, see D. H. Turner, *The Claudius Pontificals*, Henry Bradshaw Society vol. XCVII (1971, issued for the year 1964), pp. xvi–xxviii, xxxiii; and C. Hohler, 'Some Service Books of the Later Saxon Church', in D. Parsons, ed., *Tenth-Century Studies* (London, 1975), pp. 60–83, 217–27 (notes).

(Oxford, 1937) and more recently in his collected papers, *Kaiser, Könige und Päpste*, continue to be accepted by leading historians of Anglo-Saxon England.[6] Yet work already published before 1934 (some of it then unknown to Schramm) as well as subsequent critical studies show both Schramm's conclusions to be untenable. They have survived partly through a regrettable lack of contact between liturgists and general historians, partly through the magic of Schramm's name reinforced, notably, by the magic of Sir Frank Stenton's, and partly through the coincidence that Schramm's two liturgist-critics, P. E. Ward[7] and C. A. Bouman (the latter unfortunately writing in ignorance of Ward's work), both abandoned academic life after publishing relatively little. It is now clear that the methods of *Diplomforschung*, which Schramm quite explicitly applied to the medieval *Ordines*, are simply not appropriate for liturgical documents.[8] In what follows, taking up some problems where Ward and Bouman left off and drawing on more recent liturgists' work, I attempt a long-overdue revision of Schramm's views and offer an alternative hypothesis which, whatever historical questionmarks it leaves, at least does no violence to the liturgical evidence.

I. THE 'LEOFRIC' 'ORDO' AND ITS RELATIONSHIP TO THE 'ORDO' OF JUDITH

Ward already observed against Schramm that the royal *Ordo* belongs to that part of the Leofric Missal which was written *c.*900.[9] 'Leofric' therefore could not have been Dunstan's work. But how much earlier than *c.*900 was such an *Ordo* in existence? The earliest securely dated royal *Ordo* is that used for Judith, Charles the Bald's daughter, as queen of the West Saxons when she married Æthelwulf in 856.[10] Schramm classed this *Ordo* as West Frankish,[11] not Anglo-Saxon,

6 See F. M. Stenton, *Anglo-Saxon England*, 3rd edn (Oxford, 1971), p. 368; C. J. Godfrey, *The Church in Anglo-Saxon England* (Cambridge, 1962), p. 382; H. G. Richardson and G. O. Sayles, *The Governance of Medieval England* (Edinburgh, 1963), pp. 398–9.

7 'The Coronation Ceremony in Medieval England', *Speculum*, XIV (1939), pp. 160–78; 'An Early Version of the Anglo-Saxon Coronation Ceremony', *EHR*, LVII (1942), pp. 345–61.

8 For excellent suggestions on method, see Bouman, *Sacring*, pp. 50–89; R. Elze, ed., *Ordines Coronationis Imperialis*, MGH, Fontes Iuris Germanici Antiqui, IX (Hanover, 1960), pp. xxiv–xxxv.

9 Ward, 'Coronation Ceremony', pp. 162–3.

10 *Benedictio super reginam quam Edelulfus rex accepit in uxorem*, ed. from a now lost Liège MS by J. Sirmond, *Hincmari archiepiscopi remensis opera* (Paris, 1645), I, pp. 741–4; reprinted in MGH, Capit. II, no. 296, pp. 425–7. (The couple were married at Verberie).

11 'Ordines-Studien II: die Krönung in Frankreich', *Archiv für Urkundenforschung*, XV (1938), p. 8

attributing not only its structure but also its prayer-forms to Hincmar's authorship and ignoring the question of what sources Hincmar might have drawn on in existing regal liturgies, whether Frankish or English. Scholars have long been aware that 'Leofric' and 'Judith' are related. Schramm, asserting the priority of 'Judith', neglected the important article of Armitage Robinson, where the case for the priority of the king's *Ordo* was soundly based on careful comparison of the prayer-texts, showing the 'Judith' forms to be adaptations, those of 'Leofric' original.[12] Bouman produced some additional evidence pointing the same way, but he was very cautious about attributing a date pre-856 to 'the "Leofric" formulary as a whole', insisting only that some of the regal blessing-formulae which compose it were available in 856.[13]

As I hope to show, Robinson was substantially correct. But neither he nor Bouman really disposed of Schramm's main argument for the priority of a queen's *Ordo* over the king's: namely, the appearance in 'Leofric' of two passages which Schramm diagnosed as borrowings from the *Consecratio virginum* of the Gelasian Sacramentary[14] – proof enough, he claimed, of the dependence of 'Leofric' upon 'Judith', 'for how could anyone in the case of a king have conceived the idea of putting a prayer over virgins at the base of the *Ordo*?'[15] What are these alleged borrowings? First, Schramm observed that the *incipit* of the opening prayer of 'Leofric', 'Te invocamus domine sancte pater omnipotens aeterne deus', is paralleled in the Gelasian and Gregorian Sacramentaries only in the *Oratio super ancillas Dei*. Second, in the prayer 'Benedic domine hunc presulem principem', there are three clauses almost identical with a passage in the *Consecratio virginum*. (It was because these clauses do not in fact appear in 'Judith', as we have it, that Schramm felt forced to hypothesise a lost 'fuller version' – for whose existence there is otherwise no evidence at all.) Schramm's argument has, at first sight, considerable force: even if another possible source for *either* of the two passages in question could be found,

[12] J. A. Robinson, 'The Coronation Order in the Tenth Century', *JTS*, XIX (1918), pp. 56–72, esp. pp. 62–3. Schramm had discovered this article by 1938 when he listed it, without comment, in a bibliography in 'Ordines-Studien III: die Krönung in England', *Archiv für Urkundenforschung*, XV (1938), p. 308. It is important to stress that in reprinting his 1934 paper in 1968, Schramm did not take the opportunity for any serious revision, merely citing Robinson's article, *Kaiser*, p. 169, n. 1, with the comment: 'seine Feststellungen sind – wie ich hoffe – durch meine Feststellungen überholt'(!).

[13] *Sacring*, pp. 100–3, 110–11, 153.

[14] Ed. L. C. Mohlberg, *Liber Sacramentorum Romanae Ecclesiae Ordinis Anni Circuli.* (*Sacramentarium Gelasianum*), Rerum Ecclesiasticarum Documenta, Series maior, Fontes IV (Rome, 1958), p. 126.

[15] 'Ordines-Studien III', p. 9, n. 3.

Schramm's explanation, relying on a single source as the model for *both*, would remain the most parsimonious one. But close examination of the liturgical sources shows Schramm's to be a false economy. In the borrowed clauses of 'Benedic domine', there are two critical variant readings, one of which occurs in the Gelasian *Consecratio virginum* but not in the Gregorian, the other in the Gregorian but not the Gelasian.[16] Only in the Leonine Sacramentary (*Veronense*) do both these variants occur: yet the *incipit* 'Te invocamus' does not appear in the Leonine virgins' prayer.[17] Thus, since we cannot in any event manage with fewer than two sources for these borrowings, we do better to deal separately with them.

'Te invocamus' is an *incipit* rare but not unparalleled in the Visigothic *Liber Ordinum*,[18] where it occurs, for instance, in the *Oratio ad barbas tondendas*, part of what in the Spanish book is still a coming-of-age rite adopted by the early church from pagan Rome.[19] In the Gelasian Sacramentary, a similar prayer has become associated with clerical orders. A comparison of these prayers with the opening benediction of 'Leofric' is suggestive:

Lib. Ord.	Gel.	'Leofric'
Te invocamus, aeterne omnipotens deus, ut abundantia fontis tuae benedicas hunc famulum tuum illum . . . Postea: Oratio . . . respice propitius . . . ut per huius benedictionis copiam ad iuvenilem se etatem pervenire congaudeat letabundus . . . ut . . . gratiam per manus inpositionem accipiat, sicut David per manus Samuelis accepit quod in apostolorum tuorum tipo prefiguratum est.	Deus cuius providentia creatura omnes crementes adulta congaudet, propitius super hunc famulum tuum iuvenilia aetatis decorem laetantem et florem primis auspiciis adtundentem . . .[20]	Te invocamus, d.s.p.o.a.d., ut hunc famulum tuum quem tuae divine dispensationis providentia . . . usque ad hunc presentem diem iuvenili flore laetantem crescere concessisti . . .

[16] Gregorian, ed. J. Deshusses, *Le Sacramentaire Grégorien*, Spicilegium Friburgense, XVI (Freiburg, 1971), p. 420: 'tu in merore solatium', where the Gelasian reads 'consolatio'. But the words 'In te habeat omnia' in the Gelasian have disappeared from the Gregorian version.

[17] Ed. C. Mohlberg, *Sacramentarium Veronense*, R.E.D., Fontes I (Rome, 1956), pp. 139–40.

[18] Ed. M. Férotin, *Monumenta Ecclesiae Liturgica*, V (Paris, 1904), p. 294. On such related expressions as 'Te rogamus', etc., see E. Bishop, 'Liturgical Note' to *The Book of Cerne*, ed. A. B. Kuypers (Cambridge, 1902), p. 258. See also Bouman, *Sacring*, p. 58, n. 1, for 'domine sancte pater . . .' etc. as 'a commonplace of euchology'.

[19] Ed. Férotin, p. 37. See A. Chavasse, *Le Sacramentaire Gélasien* (Tournai, 1958), pp. 451–2.

[20] Ed. Mohlberg, p. 229.

Regrettably, no comparable Leonine *Oratio* exists: if it did, we might have found here further evidence for the link which Coebergh traced between the sixth-century Roman liturgy and early Spanish texts.[21] In any case, it seems just as plausible to suggest that the author of the regal blessing drew on a coming-of-age rite as on a nun's consecration, especially if he were writing at a time and place in which Spanish texts could well have been available.

In fact the Spanish and insular affinities of the first two 'Leofric' prayers ('Te invocamus' and 'In diebus', Bouman suggests, were originally one)[22] are so obvious as to strike any open-minded reader. Spanish and insular 'symptoms' abound: *plasmatum*; *de die in diem . . . ad meliora proficere*; *pax et securitas*; the antithesis *cor–corpus*.[23] Relevant also are those Leonine affinities which C. Hohler now shows to be characteristic of insular as well as Spanish liturgies.[24] Schramm preferred to see 'In diebus' as a *Virtuosenstück* of a kind 'beloved by the age of Charles the Bald',[25] but he adduced no evidence in support of this statement, and the *liturgical* sources of that period will not, I think, afford any. Bouman was equally disinclined to see the obvious: noting the pronounced use of alliteration in these two prayers, he admitted that 'we might be tempted to regard the phenomenon . . . as an indication of their insular origin', but he resisted temptation by stalwartly concentrating on a literary tradition that linked Sidonius and Venantius with ninth-century Frankish writers, and finally by appealing to Schramm's comment on 'the age of Charles the Bald'. But Bouman, on his own admission, started from the assumption that these prayers were West Frankish of the mid-ninth century, and then proceeded to find an 'argument of style . . . entirely consistent with that conclusion'. Thus again, he described 'Te invocamus' as 'a wordy *oratio* of the Frankish–German pattern', and 'In diebus' as possibly designed to be pronounced 'as a "Gallican" benediction'.[26] What neither Schramm nor Bouman recognised is that not a literary but a *liturgical* context is of primary

[21] C. Coebergh, 'Sacramentaire léonien et liturgie mozarabe', in *Miscellanea liturgica in honorem L. C. Mohlberg* (2 vols., Rome, 1948–9), II, pp. 295–304.

[22] *Sacring*, p. 102.

[23] See F. E. Warren, *The Liturgy and Ritual of the Celtic Church* (Oxford, 1881), p. 168, n. 1; Bishop, 'Liturgical Note', pp. 252–3; G. Manz, *Ausdrucksformen der lateinischen Liturgiesprachen bis ins 11 Jht.* (Beuron, 1941), pp. 23–9; A. Dold and L. Eizenhoefer, eds., *Das Irische Palimpsestsakramentar im Clm. 14429* (Beuron, 1964), p. 88; H. Porter, 'The Origin of the Medieval Rite for Anointing the Sick', *JTS*, n.s. VII (1956), p. 219.

[24] 'Service Books', pp. 79–80. Compare *idem*, 'The Type of Sacramentary used by St Boniface', in *Sankt Bonifatius Gedenkgabe* (Fulda, 1964), pp. 89–93.

[25] *Kaiser*, p. 174.

[26] *Sacring*, pp. 60–1, 102.

relevance here. In relation to that context, Bouman's mention only of Frankish and Gallican parallels is dangerously misleading when in fact extended alliteration, rhymed cola and rhythmic cursus are all well-known stylistic features of Spanish and insular liturgies par excellence.[27] There is one further piece of evidence for the insular origin of 'In diebus': the prayer 'Deus qui sub tuae maiestatis arbitrio', which appears in the rite for an abbot's consecration and which is clearly modelled on the king's prayer 'In diebus', is present in no fewer than seven liturgical books of English origin, and *only* in these.[28] Though none of them predates the tenth century, the fact that the abbot's prayer was then so widely used in England implies its considerably earlier adaptation, also in England, from the regal text.

The second alleged 'borrowing' by the 'Leofric' redactor from the *Consecratio virginum* consists of three clauses in the series of benedictions beginning 'Benedic domine hunc presulem principem'.[29] If, as the variants here suggest, the source of these clauses was a Leonine rather than a Gelasian or Gregorian Sacramentary, this would itself imply early date and the possibility of insular provenance.[30] Further, the whole passage beginning 'Sit in eis' (including all our borrowed clauses) in the Leonine virgins' prayer may originally have existed separately as 'a traditional form of blessing on solemn occasions',[31] and thus lacked any specific connection with virgins only. Certainly its wider suitability is shown by its use for the blessings of widows, kings and abbots. Thus we need not follow Schramm in regarding the presence of these clauses as proof of the dependence of the 'Leofric' king's *Ordo* on 'Judith'. Study of early Christian rites of passage as a group shows, not surprisingly, that these were felt to contain a common

[27] The fundamental work remains Bishop, *Liturgica Historica* (Oxford, 1918), esp. pp. 163–202. See also W. Meyer, *Gesammelte Abhandlungen zur mittellateinischen Rhythmik* (2 vols., Berlin, 1905), I, pp. 178, 192–3; K. Polheim, *Die lateinische Reimprosa* (Berlin, 1925), pp. 309–11; L. Brou, 'Problèmes liturgiques chez Saint Isidore', in *Isidoriana* (León, 1961), pp. 193–209; Dold and Eizenhoefer, *Palimpsestsakramentar*, pp. 87–9. For the background, see J. N. Hillgarth, 'The East, Visigothic Spain and the Irish', *Studia Patristica*, IV (1961), pp. 442–56; *idem*, 'Visigothic Spain and Early Christian Ireland', *Proceedings of the Royal Irish Academy*, CXII (1962), pp. 167–94.

[28] Turner, *Claudius Pontificals*, pp. xxxvi–xxxvii. V. Leroquais, *Les Pontificaux Manuscrits des bibliothèques publiques de France* (4 vols., Paris, 1937), notes no further instance of this prayer.

[29] Schramm, *Kaiser*, p. 229: clauses l., m., n. and the beginning of o. ('amore te timeat et timore diligat. Tu ei honor sis, tu gaudium, tu voluntas . . .' etc.).

[30] Above, p. 346.

[31] O. G. Harrison, 'The Formulas "Ad virgines sacras". A Study of the Sources', *Ephemerides Liturgicae*, LXVI (1952), pp. 260–1. But R. Metz, *La Consécration des vierges dans l'église romaine* (Paris, 1954), p. 160, n. 81, remains sceptical.

quality, such that borrowings from one to another were thought apt: from baptism to monastic profession, from the bishop's consecration to the king's to the abbot's, from the abbess's to the queen's, and so forth.[32]

If Schramm's case for the priority of 'Judith' must be rejected, can the priority of the 'Leofric' *Ordo* as such be affirmed? Bouman thought it 'easier to date some of the formulas ... than the formulary as a whole'.[33] But he was needlessly cautious. The near-identical ordering of the prayers in 'Leofric' and 'Judith' cannot be coincidental. The model which Hincmar had before him in 856 opened with 'Te invocamus', which needed relatively little adaptation for a queen; and if, on Bouman's own showing, this prayer and 'In diebus' which follows it in 'Leofric' originally 'belong together', Hincmar could have had both available but bypassed the second because he was using 'Te invocamus' as a *prooemium* to the consecration prayer which he was now casting as a Preface on the pattern of other major rites.[34] Then the model gave the 'Leofric' anointing-prayer, 'Deus electorum', which had to be adapted, in a characteristically Hincmarian style, for a royal lady.[35] It seems likely that the model next included the 'Leofric' benediction-series beginning 'Benedic domine hunc presulem principem': Hincmar adapted its first clause for Judith – a fact unnoticed by Bouman.[36] Next in the model came the blessings 'Omnipotens deus det tibi' and 'Benedic domine fortitudinem': in these prayers, which in 'Leofric' consist wholly of scriptural quotations, the adaptation for Judith is especially obvious. The only 'Leofric' prayer which cannot be shown to have influenced 'Judith' is the last, 'Deus perpetuitatis', but it was associated with an enthronement-ritual which would not have been required at Verberie.[37] Otherwise, the content and structure of

32 For some detailed references, see above, chapter 10, p. 242, n. 4 and chapter 14, p. 334, n. 19.

33 *Sacring*, p. 153.

34 *Ibid.*, pp. 100–3.

35 Compare the Old Testament paradigms introduced here with those of the *consecratio* in Hincmar's *Ordo* of 877. Of the two 'quaint words' in the adapted section noted by Bouman, *Sacring*, pp. 60, n. 1, and 111, as 'not in keeping with the sober and traditional vocabulary of the rest of the formula', *lucifluam* was used by Hincmar in the *Annales Bertiniani*, *s.a.* 868, while *efferatum* is biblical.

36 The 'Leofric' series is largely borrowed from two eighth-century Gelasian regal benedictions. A further argument for the priority of 'Leofric' is thus the improbability of Hincmar's having drawn directly on the eighth-century Gelasian source for just one clause of 'Judith'.

37 It was also used as an *Oratio super militantes*, which might have been thought inappropriate for Judith. The prayer's earliest appearance under this rubric was not, as Schramm and, surprisingly, Bouman (*Sacring*, p. 67) seem to have believed, in the Sacramentary of Fulda (*c.*950), but in the Leofric Missal on the very same folio as the royal *Ordo* itself: its last three

'Judith' implies not only, as Bouman suggested, that Hincmar's sources in 856 included some regal benedictions like those of 'Leofric', but that Hincmar had before him a series in precisely 'Leofric's' order and with the anointing-prayer occupying the same central place. If we add the negative evidence that Hincmar had to compose a coronation-prayer for Judith presumably because his model lacked one, we need no longer leave open Bouman's possibility that 'the Order [of 'Leofric'] as such may have been composed at a later date than 856'. In other words, a full king's *Ordo* of 'Leofric' type was in existence by the mid-ninth century.

II. WHERE DOES THE 'LEOFRIC' 'ORDO' COME FROM?

The editor of the Leofric Missal, F. E. Warren, was convinced that this was a Lotharingian manuscript. More recently, Ward has claimed on 'paleographical grounds' that the 'Leofric' *Ordo* was evidence for 'Flanders *ca.*900'. Bouman, independently, inferred that the regal benedictions in the Leofric book 'are undoubtedly of West Frankish origin' though remaining 'no more than an "outsider"' on the continental side of the Channel, while Robinson having established the dependence of 'Judith' on 'Leofric' thought that this showed the latter to have been 'current in Rheims before 856'.[38] Now since the material in a liturgical (or any other) manuscript may originate in a different location from that in which the manuscript itself was written, it may seem odd that none of these three scholars seriously considered the possibility that 'Leofric' was English. Perhaps embarrassed or irritated by the chauvinism (real or imagined) of earlier and insular writers,[39] Robinson, Ward and Bouman, and I myself until recently, were very ready to accept indications of a continental origin for the earliest extant royal *Ordo*. Fortunately Hohler has now addressed the

lines immediately precede the *Ordo*'s opening rubric on fo.302v. The prayer reappears, along with the two benedictions preceding it in 'Leofric', to form a *Benedictio principis*, following blessings of banner and weapons, in a twelfth-century Cracow Pontifical, ed. W. Abraham, in *Polska Akademja: Umiejetuosci Hist.-Fil. Rozprawy*. Ser. II, 41, no. I (Cracow, 1927), pp. 1–17; but according to Ward, 'Anglo-Saxon Coronation', p. 346, n. 3, this pontifical was written in Lotharingia. The quite large variants in the texts of 'Deus perpetuitatis' suggest wide currency, but its history, whether English or continental, before *c.* 900 remains unknown: the Leofric Missal shows it in use for both warrior and king, but who borrowed from whom?

38 Ward, 'Coronation Ceremony', p. 163; Bouman, *Sacring*, pp. 10; 154; Robinson, 'Coronation Order', p. 63.

39 E.g. W. Maskell, *Monumenta ritualia ecclesiae Anglicanae*, 2nd edn (3 vols., Oxford, 1882), II, pp. x–xi; H. A. Wilson, 'The English Coronation Orders', *JTS*, II (1901), pp. 481–504.

problem without inhibitions: after demonstrating the extreme complexity of the make-up of early liturgical books, he has argued that the Leofric Missal, though it contains Lotharingian and West Frankish material and is written in a continental hand, is in fact an English book, and that parts of it, especially in its 'pontifical' section, may be as old as the 'sixth or seventh century'.[40] Although Hohler himself has been concerned with the book as a whole rather than with the royal *Ordo* as such, his conclusions at once require and enable us to take a fresh look at 'Leofric' and the problem of origins.[41]

Certain features of the 'Leofric' prayer-texts are suggestive of early date and/or insular provenance. First, 'Omnipotens deus det tibi' and 'Benedic fortitudinem', composed of quotations from the Old Testament, have only early parallels in regal liturgies, and they centre on the linked concepts of divine favour and the blessings of nature – identifiable themes of insular *Fürstenspiegel*.[42] Second, the Frankish benediction, 'Benedic domine hunc presulem principem', in my view of Merovingian origin, is adopted unchanged: since the use of the term *presul* for the king[43] was barely acceptable to ninth- and tenth-century clerics,[44] it had probably got into the English *Ordo* early enough to have become traditional by the end of the ninth century. Thirdly, the ideological content of 'Te invocamus', of 'In diebus' and of the

[40] 'Service Books', pp. 69–70, 78–80. The assertion, p. 80, that Bouman 'accepted' that 'the ['Leofric'] *Ordo* is English' is a little misleading, however: this may be, as Mr Hohler implies, the only reasonable inference from Bouman's work, but Bouman himself in fact repeatedly affirmed (*Sacring*, pp. 10, 61, 102, 144, 153–4) the West Frankish origin of both 'the formulary' and its component prayers and procedures. That is why the present paper still needed to be written.

[41] Since completing this paper, I have learned through the kindness of Professor Julian Brown of Mrs Elaine Drage's unpublished Oxford D.Phil. dissertation (1978), 'Bishop Leofric and Exeter Cathedral Chapter: a reassessment of the Manuscript Evidence'. Mrs Drage has produced very strong paleographical reasons for believing that the Leofric Missal was written in Lotharingia, at St Vaast, Arras, *c.*880. Nevertheless, in view of St Vaast's geographical position in the Rheims archdiocese, of ninth-century contacts between England and Flanders, and of the diverse origins of the liturgical material in the Leofric Missal, my arguments for the Anglo-Saxon origin of the king's *Ordo* itself will I hope stand independently of the MS's provenance. I am very grateful to Mrs Drage for discussion of all these points.

[42] H. H. Anton, *Fürstenspiegel und Herrscherethos in der Karolingerzeit* (Bonn, 1968), pp. 66–79.

[43] Aurelian of Arles addressed Theudebert as *praesul*: MGH, Epp. III, p. 124. For the late antique context, see J. Straub, 'Zur Ordination von Bischofen und Beamten in der christlichen Spätantike', in *Mullus. Festschrift T. Klauser* (Münster, 1964), pp. 336–45, at p. 342. Compare Isidore, *Sententiae*, PL LXXXIII. 721: 'Dedit deus principibus praesulatum.'

[44] See Bouman, *Sacring*, p. 164, for the original reading ('hos praesules principes') in the Sacramentary of Angoulême, and pp. 174 and 180, for alterations in West and East Frankish *Ordines* of the later ninth and tenth centuries. For 'hunc praeelectum principem' in the mature version of the Second English *Ordo*, see *Claudius Pontificals* II, ed. Turner, p. 94.

additional material in 'Deus electorum' and 'Benedic domine hunc presulem principem'[45] is reminiscent of such Spanish and insular texts as the Visigothic regal Mass,[46] the eighth-century Gelasian regal prayers 'Deus pater gloriae' and 'Christe deus oriens'[47] (both of these showing 'Spanish symptoms'), of Pseudo-Cyprian and the Irish *Collectio Canonum*, and of the letters of Boniface, Cathwulf and Alcuin.[48] In all these, the emphasis tends to be on the king as judge rather than as war-leader, on the king's protective function in relation to his people in general rather than to the Church and its ministers in particular, and on royal rights rather than royal duties.

It seems plausible for several reasons that an English *Ordo* should have provided the basis for Hincmar's *Ordo* of 856. The historical context is right. Charles the Bald had himself been anointed in 848, and his second son was anointed sub-king of Aquitaine in 855.[49] Charles and Hincmar would have planned the consecration of the thirteen-year-old Judith with a view to enhancing her status amongst the West Saxons, a people notorious in the ninth century for the scant respect they accorded kings' wives.[50] There was obviously no West Saxon queen's *Ordo* for Hincmar to borrow,[51] and neither, it seems, was there any West Frankish one: hence the need to adapt a king's *Ordo*, as in 856, or to compose a new rite, as for Ermentrude in 866.[52] But why should Hincmar not have adapted a West Frankish king's *ordo* in 856? It is possible that an English rite would in any case have been thought more apt for someone

[45] The material in these prayers for which no source has been identified amounts in 'Deus electorum' to the phrase: 'regnique fastigia in consiliis scientiae et aequitate iudicii semper assequi', and a reference to 'plebs commissa'; in 'Benedic domine' to nearly all of clause o. and all of p.: 'per tuam discat commissa sapientiam regni gubernacula moderari, ut semper felix, semper a te gaudens, de tuis mereatur beneficiis gratulari, et aeternis valeat commerciis copulari. Ut quem tu nobis hodie tua misericordia iucundum presentare dignatus es, tua facias multorum annorum curriculis protectione securum.' The stylistic similarities here are with eighth-century regal benedictions.

[46] *Liber Ordinum*, pp. 295–6.

[47] Ed. Bouman, p. 190, from the Sacramentary of Gellone. On the components and dating of the eighth-century Gelasian, see C. Vogel, *Introduction aux sources de l'histoire du culte chrétien* (Spoleto, 1966), pp. 58–67.

[48] For details of these insular texts, see Anton, *Fürstenspiegel*, pp. 67–131.

[49] *Annales Bertiniani*, *s.a.* 848, 855, ed. F. Grat *et al.*, pp. 55, 71.

[50] *Ann. Bertin.*, p. 73; Asser, *Vita Alfredi*, ed. W. Stevenson (repr. with introduction by D. Whitelock, Oxford, 1959), p. 11, with Stevenson's comments, pp. 200–2.

[51] It is just possible that a Mercian queen's *Ordo* existed: Professor Whitelock reminds me that in a charter of 869, W. G. Birch, *Cartularium Saxonicum* (3 vols., London, 1885–9) (hereafter cited as *BCS*), no. 524, Burgred's queen Æthelswith appears as 'pari coronata stemma regali', which could imply a consecration-rite for her, paralleling her husband's. But how could Hincmar have got hold of such an *Ordo*? Æthelwulf would be an unlikely middleman. In any event, Hincmar in 856 clearly adapted a *king*'s rite.

[52] MGH, Capit., II, pp. 453–5.

becoming an English queen. But it is also likely that no fixed rite as yet existed in West Francia: there the *continuous* history of royal consecrations only begins in 848 and the *Ordines* tradition can be traced back no further than 869.[53] For England the picture is rather different. It is not so much that the virtual absence of liturgical evidence here,[54] as compared with the dozen or so surviving Frankish sacramentaries and pontificals of the later eighth and earlier ninth centuries,[55] precludes any argument from silence; for royal *Ordines* do not quickly become regular features of such books. (Equally, for the later tenth century when the English evidence becomes more plentiful, it would be easy to misinterpret the contrast between the regular appearance of a royal *Ordo* in Anglo-Saxon pontificals with the continuing rarity of such appearances in contemporary French books: the contrast is a symptom of varying degrees of royal power and ecclesiastical centralisation in the two realms.) It is rather that there is actually more English than Frankish evidence for the indigenous practice of royal consecration in the late eighth and early ninth centuries. Certainly the English evidence comes from Northumbria and Mercia,[56] not Wessex. But in view of the relations between the three kingdoms at this period, it seems unlikely that West Saxon kings would have neglected their

[53] See my comments above, chapter 7, p. 137., with nn. 3 and 4, for full bibliographical references. The consecration of 869 was a Lotharingian affair but the *Ordo* used, because of its influence on that of 877, is the fount of a West Frankish liturgical tradition. The Supplemented Gregorian, of course, unlike the eighth-century Gelasian, contained no formulas for royal consecration. Such formulae, and full *Ordines*, begin to reappear in sacramentaries and pontificals from the later ninth and tenth centuries onwards. For the *Ordo secundum occidentales*, see below, 354 , n. 66.

[54] For the few mere fragments surviving, see K. Gamber, *Codices Liturgici Latini Antiquiores*, 2nd edn (Freiburg, 1968), pp. 150–1, 227–32.

[55] Vogel, *Introduction aux sources*, pp. 81–2, 185–6. For ninth-century MSS of the Gregorian, see now the edn of Deshusses, pp. 34–47.

[56] Northumbria: *Anglo-Saxon Chronicle, s.a.* 795 in the 'Northern' recension, ed. B. Thorpe, R.S. (London, 1861), p. 103, trans. D. Whitelock, *English Historical Documents* (London, 1955), p. 168; and Symeon of Durham, *Historia Regum*, ed. T. Arnold, R.S. (London, 1885), p. 58: both these draw on a lost set of Northumbrian annals nearly contemporary with the events they describe. Mercia: *Anglo-Saxon Chronicle, s.a.* 785 (for 787), ed. Thorpe, pp. 96–7, trans. Whitelock, *Documents*, p. 166 (the 'A' text here drawing on lost Mercian annals); *BCS* no. 370 (Ceolwulf I referring to his *consecratio* by the archbishop of Canterbury), on which see now K. Harrison, *The Framework of Anglo-Saxon History* (Cambridge, 1976), p. 115. J. M. Wallace-Hadrill, *Early Medieval History* (Oxford, 1976), pp. 158–9, is helpful, but in my view overestimates Frankish influence. Of the decrees issued by the Synod of Chelsea (787), A. W. Haddan and W. Stubbs, eds., *Councils and Ecclesiastical Documents* (3 vols., Oxford, 1869–73), III, pp. 453f., c. 12, 'De ordinatione et honore regum', refers to the king as *christus domini*, but this need not imply *per se* a Mercian royal consecration-rite, as has sometimes been alleged. The novelty in 787, however, may well have lain in the pre-mortem succession, rather than the 'hallowing', of Offa's son: see my comment in 'Inauguration Rituals', in P. H. Sawyer and I. N. Wood, eds., *Early Medieval Kingship* (Leeds, 1977); above, p. 285.

neighbours' practice,[57] or that Æthelwulf and his advisers would have exported in 856 anything other than a West Saxon rite; unlikely too that Æthelwulf would have agreed to Judith's being anointed had he not been so himself, which could well mean taking the West Saxon fixed rite back at least to his accession in 839, if not to Egbert's in 802 or even Beorhtric's in 786.

How much older could 'Leofric' be? All its datable sources are considerably older than the mid-ninth century. The *Benedictio chrismatis* which forms the basis of 'Deus electorum' is Gelasian, and, like the Spanish sources discussed above, could have been available in England as early as the seventh century.[58] 'Benedic domine hunc presulem principem' is largely composed from two series of regal benedictions whose earliest extant source is eighth-century Gelasian but which themselves could fit very well in a Merovingian context. The origins of royal anointing in England cannot be explored here; nor can the further intriguing problem of possible Celtic precedents.[59] But if 'Leofric' represents an English fixed rite dating from the first half of the ninth century *at the latest*, then the search for origins could take us back a century or more before that.

III. 'LEOFRIC' IN RELATION TO 'EGBERT'/'LANALET'

If the 'Leofric' *Ordo* preserves the West Saxon usage of pre-856, what of its brother-*Ordo*, 'Egbert'/'Lanalet'? Here Schramm's view, that 'Egbert'/'Lanalet' is an 'amplification' of 'Leofric', has retained the assent of all subsequent scholars. Apart from the setting of the *Ordo* within the Mass, which even if a late feature[60] need not affect our view of the *Ordo* itself, the two characteristics of this alleged 'longer version'

[57] Compare the evidence for the elaboration of the West Saxon royal genealogy during the first half of the ninth century, probably to emulate that of the Mercian kings: see K. Sisam, 'Anglo-Saxon Royal Genealogies', *Proceedings of the British Academy*, XXXIX (1953), pp. 287–348. D. Dumville, 'Kingship, Genealogies and Regnal Lists', in Sawyer and Wood, *Early Medieval Kingship*, pp. 72–104, at p. 73, cites some later Scottish and Irish evidence for a link between genealogies and inauguration rituals (the recitation of the new king's genealogy is part of the king-making), and, pp. 74–5, shows the legitimising function of genealogies and king-lists on the continent.

[58] H. Mayr-Harting, *The Coming of Christianity to Anglo-Saxon England* (London, 1972), pp. 168–82, 272–5.

[59] For references, see my papers above, chapter 13, p. 312 and chapter 11, p. 278. See now J. Prelog, 'Sind die Weihesalbungen insularen Ursprungs?', *Frühmittelalterliche Studien*, XIII (1979), pp. 303–56.

[60] See T. Klauser in *Jahrbuch für Liturgiewissenschaft*, XIV (1938), p. 461, though on pp. 289–91 of my dissertation, I adduced some evidence that early ninth-century Frankish inaugurations might have been set within the Mass.

are first, the insertion of the prayer 'Deus qui populis' between the first and second prayers of 'Leofric', and second, the presence of 'much more explicit rubrics'. But 'Deus qui populis' is clearly a late interpolation in an existing *Ordo*,[61] and therefore irrelevant to our dating problem. Neither do the 'more explicit rubrics' constitute in themselves an indication of later date by comparison with 'Leofric', any more than short or non-existent rubrics necessarily imply early date. We know that in the ninth century, the prayer texts for a major rite would be copied out in a *rotula*, while the detailed instructions on movement, gesture and so on would be set out separately in an *ordo*.[62] Although it was only from the tenth century onwards that it became normal practice to work from a single text, there are plenty of earlier examples, especially in baptismal and ordination rites, of detailed indications already being inserted in rubrics between the prayers. The very fact that the final, rather full rubrical direction of 'Egbert'/'Lanalet' actually appears in 'Leofric' too,[63] shows that the presence or absence of full rubrics will provide no sure criterion for relative datings. 'Leofric' may, indeed, have been intended for performance in just the same way as 'Egbert' or 'Lanalet', but with its officiants using a separate guidebook of ritual instructions.

'Archaic traits' were long since recognised in the 'Egbert'/'Lanalet' rubrics.[64] My own somewhat extended list runs as follows:

(i) In three rubrics, all the participating bishops are termed *pontifices*. Though this usage is extremely rare in early medieval liturgical sources, the word *pontifex* for 'bishop' does occur twice in rubrics in the Visigothic *Liber Ordinum*.[65] In the probably ninth-century *Ordo secundum occidentales*, the term will refer to an *arch*bishop,[66] but in other liturgical sources of this period it always denotes the pope. In the sixth and seventh centuries, writers used *pontifex* and *episcopus* interchange-

[61] The 'Egbert' scribe had no space to copy out the whole prayer, but seems to have been clumsily copying the rubric of his model (*req. in agapite libri*). See Bouman, *Sacring*, pp. 100–5.

[62] See Hincmar's letter to Adventius of Metz, and the excellent discussion of this evidence in M. Andrieu, 'Le Sacre épiscopal d'après Hincmar de Reims', *RHE*, XLVIII (1953), pp. 22–73.

[63] See below, pp. 358-9.

[64] G. Waitz, 'Die Formeln der deutschen Königs- und der römischen Kaiser-Krönung vom 10. bis zum 12. Jht.', *Abhandlungen der königlichen Gesellschaft der Wissenschaften zu Göttingen*, XVIII (1873), p. 21; E. Eichmann, 'Königs- und Bischofsweihe', *Sitzungsberichte der bayerischen Akademie der Wissenschaften, Phil.-Hist. Klasse*, VI (1928), p. 26.

[65] Ed. Férotin, pp. 61, 543.

[66] Ed. Elze, *Ordines*, pp. 3–5. I see no reason to link this *Ordo* with 816 and thus to interpret its *pontifex* as 'the pope'.

ably;[67] but thereafter there is a tendency (in Bede, for instance) for the latter term to be used for 'bishop', the former for 'archbishop' or 'pope'. The unspecialised sense of *pontifices* in our *Ordo* could thus be an indication of early date; and it may be worth noting that both *pontifex* and *episcopus* were translated by Anglo-Saxon *bisceop*.[68] The absence of early English liturgical material for comparison is very unfortunate.

(ii) The anointing-rubric shows the literal application of an Old Testament model: oil is to be poured out from a horn over the king's head, with the antiphon 'Uncserunt Salomonem'. As in contemporary rites of episcopal consecration, the emphasis is on the collective nature of the central act: one bishop pours the oil, the rest anoint.[69] There is no need to postulate a special link here with the circumstances of 751: the Solomon-model, well-attested in Merovingian sources, remained potent in the ninth century.[70] With Hincmar, the *modus* of royal anointing seems to have taken on new affinities with contemporary rites of baptism and of episcopal consecration. The very explicit Old Testament symbolism, which distinguishes 'Egbert'/'Lanalet' from all other western *Ordines* (and which finds parallels in the prayer texts too, as 'Leofric' showed) seems likely to be old.[71] It could also be insular, for Old Testament typology is at least as prominent in Anglo-Saxon historical and hagiographical writings of the seventh and eighth centuries as in contemporary Frankish products, and Fournier long ago drew attention to 'les tendances bibliques' in the Irish canons.[72]

[67] This is also true of 'Egbert'/'Lanalet', where in the final section the officiants are termed *episcopi*. See below, p. 358.

[68] Eddi, *Vita Wilfrithi*, ed. B. Colgrave (Cambridge, 1927) nearly always keeps *pontifex* for his hero Wilfrid (whom he occasionally also calls *episcopus*), and renders 'archbishop' by *archiepiscopus*, never *pontifex*. In M. Richter, ed., *The Canterbury Professions* (Torquay, 1973), there seems to be no case of *pontifex* for 'bishop', though nos. 1 and 19 contain rare appearances of *pontifex* for 'archbishop' in the late eighth and ninth centuries.

[69] The 'Egbert' rubric is perfectly clear: 'Unus ex pontificibus' is the subject of 'verget oleum'. I cannot see why Schramm and Bouman follow Greenwell in seeking to emend the text, and their punctuation has no manuscript support. The collective nature of Old Testament public king-makings was rightly stressed by J. De Pange, *Le Roi très chrétien* (Paris, 1949), pp. 49–50.

[70] Anton, *Fürstenspiegel*, pp. 51, with n. 31, 430–2, gives references.

[71] Eichmann, 'Die rechtliche und kirchenpolitische Bedeutung der Kaisersalbung im Mittelalter', *Festschrift G. Hertling* (Kempten, 1913), p. 264. For the possible modelling of the final section of the *Ordo* on Solomon's inauguration, see below, p. 359.

[72] P. Fournier, 'Le *Liber ex lege Moysi* et les tendances bibliques du droit canonique irlandais', *Revue Celtique*, XXX (1909), pp. 221–34; on Anglo-Saxon material, Mayr-Harting, *Coming of Christianity*, pp. 139–41, 204–19.

(iii) The *principes* join with the *pontifices* in handing over the sceptre. This surely represents a transitional phase in the evolution of a part of the inauguration ritual which, by the tenth century, would be monopolised by clergy. This is the only extant *Ordo* to prescribe the active participation of laymen within the liturgical rite proper[73] – in striking contrast with the West Frankish *Ordines* tradition from Hincmar onwards. Linking the appearance of the *principes* at this point with their and the people's role in the acclamation and enthronement which conclude the *Ordo*, I am tempted to compare the evidence for lay participation in the *deportatio ad cathedram* in Frankish episcopal consecration rituals.[74] Clearly, the sceptre is the central *Herrschaftszeichen* in our *Ordo* (there is, we recall, no coronation). This short sceptre has Old Testament and specifically Davidic connotations, signifying law as equity (as against the long *virga* – law as chastisement), but it also has Germanic ones.[75] Did early English kings have sceptres? Even if we leave the Sutton Hoo whetstone aside, we should perhaps treat the reference of Boniface to *sceptra imperii Anglorum* when writing to an English king[76] as more than rhetorical metonymy. The absence of any special tradition-prayer for the sceptre in the *Ordo* (compare Hincmar's 'Accipe sceptrum' and later similar formulae) is a further sign of early date.

(iv) The use of a helmet (*galea*)[77] rather than a crown has often been noted as archaic. While coronation was practised from at least the mid-ninth century in West Francia and the early tenth century in England, evidence for the helmet as a royal *Herrschaftszeichen* among Germanic peoples is considerably earlier.[78] Whether any regular

[73] That is, apart from their role in ritualised election procedures within the church.

[74] Bishops alone performed this at Wilfrid's ordination: Eddius, *Vita Wilfridi*, c. xii, ed. B. Colgrave (Cambridge, 1927), p. 26. But for lay participation, see Gregory of Tours, *Historiae Francorum*, III, 2, ed. B. Krusch and W. Levison, MGH, SS rer. Merov., I, i, p. 99; and the sources cited by E. Martène, *De Antiquis Ecclesiae Ritibus* (4 vols., Antwerp, 1736), II, pp. 80–1. Andrieu, 'Le Sacre épiscopal', p. 63, infers continuity in this usage from Merovingian times, though it is attested in liturgical books only from *c.*900.

[75] A. Gauert, 'Das "Szepter" von Sutton Hoo', in P. E. Schramm, *Herrschaftszeichen und Staatssymbolik* (3 vols., Stuttgart, 1954–6), I, pp. 260–80; and K. Hauck, 'Halsring und Ahnenstab als herrscherliche Würdezeichen', *ibid.*, pp. 145–212; S. L. Cohen, 'The Sutton Hoo Whetstone', *Speculum*, XLI (1966), pp. 466–70; R. L. S. Bruce-Mitford, *Aspects of Anglo-Saxon Archaeology* (London, 1974), pp. 6–7, 76–7.

[76] Boniface to Æthelbald of Mercia, ed. M. Tangl, MGH, Epp. sel., I, no. 73, p. 146.

[77] 'Egbert' gives: 'Hic omnes pontifices sumunt gal*eum* [*sic*] et ponant super caput ipsius.'

[78] Paulus Diaconus, *Historia Langobardorum*, ed. G. Waitz, MGH, SS. rer. Lang., p. 59. See also H. Jankuhn, 'Herrschaftszeichen aus vor- und frühgeschichtlichen Funden Nordeuropas', in Schramm, *Herrschaftszeichen*, I, pp. 113–14.

Anglo-Saxon practice may be inferred from the Sutton Hoo helmet,[79] or from the dying Beowulf's handing-over of his gold-mounted helmet to his successor,[80] is debatable. But that a helmet did remain the prime royal headgear in ninth-century England is suggested by linguistic evidence which Josef Kirschner has expertly assembled.[81] Until about 900, the Latin *corona* was almost invariably translated by the Anglo-Saxon *beag*; but thereafter, West Saxon writers nearly always used *helm* and *cynehelm* instead to convey the concrete meaning of 'royal crown', *beag* being then restricted to religious contexts ('crown of glory', and so on). This change in linguistic usage may be seen as the outcome of a search for a more precise terminology, which itself reflected the reality of an Anglo-Saxon practice persisting throughout the ninth century: in other words, still around 900, the chief royal headgear actually was a *cynehelm* and not an open circlet (*beag*). We know, however, that precisely in the early tenth century a royal *Ordo* became current in England in which the use of a crown was prescribed[82] (though the crown did not necessarily immediately oust the helmet as an alternative *Herrschaftszeichen*); and it may also be relevant that the earliest numismatic portrayal of a crowned head in England dates from the reign of Athelstan.[83] It is possible that the *galea* of the Egbert and Lanalet books simply reflected the standard West Saxon terminology of the period when they were written, *corona* and *galea* being then perhaps treated as interchangeable (just as *cynehelm*, and even *helm*, were used to render 'crown of thorns'!).[84] But it seems more likely, in view of the 'Lanalet' scribe's possible difficulty with the word,[85] that *galea* in these two manuscripts faithfully reproduces a model dating from the period, that is, pre-900, when the helmet was

[79] Bruce-Mitford, *Anglo-Saxon Archaeology*, pp. 198–252.

[80] *Beowulf*, lines 2809–15.

[81] Herr Kirschner generously informed me of this material in a series of personal communications in 1973. I should stress that I alone am responsible for the historical inferences I have drawn from it. See now J. Kirschner, *Die Bezeichnungen für Kranz und Krone im Altenglischen*, Inaugural dissertation, Munich, 1975, esp. pp. 144ff., 177ff., 253ff.

[82] I accept the dating of the Second English *Ordo* by Turner, *Claudius Pontificals*, pp. xxxii–xxxiii. I hope to deal more fully with this *Ordo* in a forthcoming study.

[83] See C. E. Blunt, 'The Coinage of Athelstan', in *British Numismatic Journal*, XLII (1974), pp. 35–160. Hitherto kings had normally been shown wearing diadems. Mr Blunt interestingly notes (p. 47) the comparison with the similar crown worn by Athelstan in the frontispiece to the *Life of Cuthbert* in Corpus Christi College, Cambridge, MS 183, fo.1v (a contemporary picture). I am very grateful to Mr Blunt for kindly confirming this point.

[84] For instance by Ælfric: Herr Kirschner comments that this would seem 'an unlikely translator's choice, if not motivated by a rather old, strong and finally lexically "petrified" role of the Teutonic royal helmet'. See *Die Bezeichnungen*, pp. 187–8, 208–9, 252.

[85] According to Doble, p. 62, this word in the 'Lanalet' rubric is 'much blurred'.

the royal headgear. The rubric probably preserves the memory of a practice long outmoded by the time it was recorded: *galea* betokens both Englishness and antiquity.

The last and perhaps the most significant point in a comparison of 'Leofric' with 'Egbert'/'Lanalet' is the near-identity of their final sections, full rubrics and all. 'Leofric' in fact preserves in one passage what is evidently the original reading:

'Leofric'	*'Egbert'*	*'Lanalet'*
Tunc dicat omnis populus cum episcopis[86]. iii. vicibus	Et dicat omnis populus tribus vicibus cum episcopis et presbyteris	Et dicat omnis populus tribus vicibus cum episcopis et presbiteris
Vivat rex ill. in sempiternum. R. Amen.	Vivat rex .N. in sempiternum.	Vivat rex .N. in sempiternum. R.Amen. et venit omnis populus ad osculandum principem sempiternum.
Et confirmabitur cum benedictione omni populo in solio regni, et osculant principes in sempiternum dicentes Amen. Amen. Amen.	Tunc confirmabitur cum benedictione omnis populus et osculandum principem in sempiternum dicit. Amen. Amen. Amen. Tunc dicunt orationem septimam supra regem.	Tunc confirmabitur cum benedictione ista.
Deus perpetuitatis . . . . . . et defendas. Per.	Deus perpetuitatis . . . Per. [Mass prayers] Primum mandatum regis ad populum hic videre potes.	Deus perpet . . . [Mass prayers]
Rectitudo regis est noviter ordinati et in solium sublimati populo tria precepta sibi subdito precipere.	Rectitudo regis est noviter ordinati et in solium sublimati haec tria precepta populo christiano sibi subdito precipere.	

In primis ut ecclesia dei et omnis populus christianus veram pacem servent in omni tempore. R.Amen.[87]

Aliud est ut rapacitates et omnes iniquitates omnibus gradibus interdicat. R.Amen.

Tertium est ut in omnibus iudiciis aequitatem et misericordiam praecipiat ut per hoc[88] nobis indulgeat misericordiam suam[89] clemens et misericors deus. R.Amen.

Here is a discrete ritual bloc composed of acclamation and enthronement. Again the active participation of the *principes* here, and the

86 Bouman, *Sacring*, p. 168, wrongly gives: 'cum episcop*o*'.

87 'Lanalet' omits 'R.Amen' here and after the second and third clauses. See Doble, p. 63.

88 'Lanalet' gives, instead of 'per hoc', 'sibi et'.

89 'Lanalet' gives 'suam misericordiam'; 'Leofric' omits 'suam'.

direct drawing on Old Testament models,[90] might indicate an early date: in later *Ordines*, clerically performed chants would take the place of this *collaudatio*.[91] That 'Leofric' preserves the correct technical sense of *confirmatio* = enthronement is borne out by the subsequent reference to the king as *in solium sublimatus*. The term *principes* reappears, evidently denoting a more restricted group than the whole acclaiming *populus*: those who took a hand in the tradition of the sceptre now come forward to kiss the new king in a ritual of recognition, not (as Schramm supposed) an act of feudal homage. The issuing of governmental *precepta* by the *rex noviter ordinatus* to his subjects was a natural corollary. The content of these *precepta* can be paralleled in insular sources – not only, as Schramm implied, in mid-tenth-century Anglo-Saxon laws, but in earlier laws,[92] and most notably in earlier Latin prose-writers: Pseudo-Cyprian, Boniface and Alcuin.[93] The programmatic formulation: 'rectitudo regis est . . . haec tria precipere' is reminiscent of the Irish canon-collection's: 'justitia regis justi haec est . . .' or 'sunt septem quae omni regi conveniunt . . .', Pseudo-Cyprian's 'Justitia regis est', and Alcuin's 'regis bonitas est . . .' and 'regis est'.[94]

CONCLUSION

Leaving open the problem of where royal anointings may first have been practised, I have tried merely to show good reasons for admitting Wilson's claim of 1901 that 'perhaps the earliest of all known western coronation [*sic*] orders is one contained in an English servicebook',[95] and for regarding that *Ordo* itself as English. I have also suggested that the *Ordo* is represented not only by 'Leofric' but by 'Egbert'/'Lanalet' too. Is it fortuitous that the earliest surviving *Ordo* should be an

[90] Schramm, *Kaiser*, p. 218, notes III Reg., 1. 39 and Dan., 2. 4 as models for the acclamation 'Vivat rex ill. in sempiternum'. But he neglected the much more significant I Paral. 29. 22–4, where the role of the *principes* is set out: 'Unxerunt . . . Salomonem . . . Seditque Salomon super solium Domini in regem pro David, patre suo; et cunctis placuit, et paruit illi omnis Israel. Sed et universi principes et potentes . . . dederunt manum, et subjecti fuerunt Salomoni regi.' Compare also II Paral. 23. 20.

[91] E. H. Kantorowicz, *Laudes Regiae* (Berkeley, 1946), pp. 78–80.

[92] Compare the preface and cap.1 of Ine's laws, ed. F. Liebermann, *Die Gesetze der Angelsachsen* (Halle, 1903–16), I, p. 88; also Alfred, cap.4,2, *ibid.*, p. 50, ('Swa we éac settað be eallum hadum' corresponding to the 'omnibus gradibus' of the *precepta*).

[93] Pseudo-Cyprian, ed. S. Hellmann, p. 51; Boniface, MGH, Epp. sel., I, p. 147; Alcuin, MGH, Epp., IV, pp. 51, 172, 293, etc.

[94] F. W. H. Wasserschleben, *Die Irische Kanonensammlung*, 2nd edn (Leipzig, 1885), pp. 77, 81; Pseudo-Cyprian and Alcuin as cited in preceding note.

[95] *JTS*, II (1901), p. 482.

English one? Perhaps – if a seventh-century Visigothic or Celtic rite ever existed. But in any case, this particular survival may have its own significance. Whatever the gap between the introduction of royal anointing in England, in the eighth century at the latest, and the establishment of a fixed rite, the liturgical tradition here seems to have been remarkably stable: if I am right, the same *Ordo* was used for West Saxon kings through most (if not all) the ninth century, and it was then very largely incorporated in the new *Ordo* current from the early tenth century until the close of the Anglo-Saxon period. In West Francia, by contrast, if a fixed rite existed before the mid-ninth century (and the evidence implies, rather, the continued use of Merovingian regal benedictions for early Carolingian king-makings) it was wholly abandoned by Hincmar whose *Ordines* seem to be quite original compositions; then a Sens tradition distinct from that of Rheims developed in the later ninth century; and a further break came in the tenth century with the importation of the English rite into West Francia.[96] If the relatively early introduction of a fixed rite in England may be explained in terms of the precocious political and ecclesiastical centralisation already achieved by the eighth century (had more evidence survived, Æthelheard of Canterbury might have appeared a figure comparable to Julian of Toledo or Hincmar of Rheims), the subsequent persistence of that rite through the ninth, tenth and most of the eleventh centuries reflects the continuity of English kingship and of the independent liturgical traditions of the English Church. As a witness to some of the political realities, as well as the political ideas, linking pre-Viking England with the age of the Conqueror, the first Anglo-Saxon *Ordo* can claim the attention of historians as well as liturgists. 'Leofric' and 'Egbert' have their origins in the world of *Beowulf*: they survive in the consecration-rite of 1066.[97]

[96] Turner, *Claudius Pontificals*, p. xxxiii.

[97] Corpus Christi College, Cambridge, MS 44, ed. J. Wickham Legg, *Three Coronation Orders*, Henry Bradshaw Society vol. XIX (London, 1900), pp. 53–61. For the association with William the Conqueror, see Schramm, *Archiv für Urkundenforschung*, XV (1938), pp. 317–18; and *idem*, *Kaiser*, pp. 180–2 – a characteristically brilliant and, in this case, plausible interpretation of textual variants in a liturgical document.

16

THE SECOND ENGLISH *ORDO**

It is more than usually appropriate to begin this paper with a tribute to previous scholars, and especially to John Brückmann. His own work was of course on the Third English *Ordo* in the twelfth century.[1] But his perception of the importance of queens' *ordines* for understanding those of kings is just as relevant to the First English *Ordo*, which I think was in use in Wessex at least by the mid-ninth century, and to the Second English *Ordo* which is my present subject.[2] The sources of the Second *Ordo* are indicated on Table 1. The First *Ordo* is an obvious component. Otherwise the sources are West Frankish: Hincmar of Rheims' *Ordo* for Charles the Bald in 869; the so-called 'Erdmann' *Ordo*; and the 'Seven Forms' *Ordo*.[3] These last two sources are both post-877. They have been dated *c.*900, but I suggest were produced in the 880s or 890s, evoked by the then rapid turn-over of West Frankish kings.[4] Table 1 also shows the existence of two distinct versions of the Second *Ordo*. For the moment I shall call them A and B. A's best-known MS exemplar is the Sacramentary of Ratold (BN lat.12052) dating to 973/986.[5] Some

* This paper was presented to the International Conference on Medieval Coronations held in Toronto in February, 1985, in memory of Professor John Brückmann. My thanks are due to Professors Janos Bak, Jane Couchman and Patricia Brückmann for their help and hospitality. I must also record a longstanding debt to Simon Keynes for sustaining my interest in the Anglo-Saxon *Ordines* and for much advice and criticism.

[1] J. Brückmann, 'The *Ordines* of the Third Recension of the Medieval English Coronation Order', in T. A. Sandquist and M. R. Powicke (eds.), *Essays in Medieval History presented to Bertie Wilkinson* (Toronto, 1969), pp.99–115.

[2] J. L. Nelson, 'The earliest surviving royal *Ordo*', in B. Tierney and P. Linehan (eds.) *Authority and Power. Studies on Medieval Law and Government presented to Walter Ullmann* (Cambridge, 1980); above, chapter 15, pp. 341-60.

[3] See Notes to Table 1.

[4] There were six royal inaugurations in the West Frankish kingdom between 877 and 893, five of them certainly involving anointing-rites; see C. R. Brühl, 'Fränkischer Krönungsbrauch und das Problem der Festkrönungen', *Historische Zeitschrift*, 194 (1962), 205–326, at 325–6. All three of the Second *Ordo*'s West Frankish sources may have come separately to England; but it seems likelier that some combination, at least of 869 prayers with 'Erdmann', had been done already in West Francia. The process of blending may have gone further: a lost West Frankish *Ordo*, combining 'Erdmann' and the 'Seven Forms', is surmised by George Garnett in an unpublished paper on the Second English *Ordo*. I am very grateful to him for letting me read this paper in advance of publication.

[5] See P. L. Ward, 'An early version of the Anglo-Saxon coronation ceremony', *English Historical Review*, 57 (1942), 345–58. For this Sacramentary as a whole, and for English elements within it, see C. Hohler, 'Some service books of the later Saxon church', in D. Parsons (ed.), *Tenth-Century Studies* (Chichester, 1975), pp.60–83, at 64–7.

	First English Ordo(b)	*Hincmar's Ordo of 869*(c)	*'Erdmann' Ordo*(d)	*'Seven forms' Ordo*(e)	*Second English Ordo* 'A'	*Second English Ordo* 'B'
PRELIMINARIES		*Adnuntiatio* of Bishop Response of King Enquiry of Bishops to people [Acclamation](f) *Te deum*	Petition of Bishops Response of King Enquiry of Bishops to people [Acclamation](f) *Te deum*		Petition of Bishops Response of King Enquiry of Bishops to people [Acclamation](f) *Te deum* – King's prostration	Antiphon: *Firmetur* *Te deum* Three-fold promise
	Benedictions *Te invocamus* *In diebus*	Benedictions including *Extendat*	Benedictions *Deus qui populis*		Benedictions *Te invocamus* *Deus qui populis* *In diebus*	Benedictions *Te invocamus* *Deus qui populis* *In diebus*
ANOINTING	Anointing Antiphon: *Unxerunt* *Deus electorum*	Anointing *Coronet te ... in misericordia*	Anointing *Omnipotens ... deus creator*	*Omnipotens eterne Deus creator* Anointing *Deus dei filius*	Anointing Antiphon: *Unxerunt* *Omnipotens ... deus creator* *Deus electorum* *Deus dei filius*	Anointing Antiphon: *Unxerunt* *Omnipotens ... deus creator* *Christe perunge* *Deus electorum* *Deus dei filius*
INVESTITURES	Sceptre *Benedic domine* Staff *(baculus)* *Omnipotens ... det* Helmet *Benedic .... fortitudinem*	Crowning *Coronet te ... ut cum fide* Palm and sceptre *Det tibi Dominus*	Ring *Accipe 1*(g) *Deus cuius* Sword *Accipe 1*(h) Crowning *Coronet te* *Omnium domine fons* Sceptre *Accipe sceptrum* Staff *(baculus)* *Accipe*	Crowning *Accipe coronam regni* Sceptre *Accipe virgam* Ring *Accipe regie dignitatis anulum* Sword *Accipe gladium*	Ring *Accipe 2*(g) *Deus cuius* Sword *Accipe 1*(h) Crowning *Coronet te* *Deus perpetuitatis* Sceptre *Accipe sceptrum* *Omnium domine fons* Rod *(virga)* *Accipe virgam*(i) Benedictions *Extendat*	Ring *Accipe 2*(g) *Deus cuius* Sword Antiphon: *Confortare* *Accipe 1*(h) Crowning *Coronet te* *Deus perpetuitatis* Sceptre *Accipe sceptrum* *Omnium domine fons* Rod *(virga)* *Accipe virgam* Benedictions *Extendat*
ENTHRONEMENT	Acclamation Enthronement *Deus perpetuitatis* Three precepts			Enthronement *Sta et retine*	Enthronement *Sta et retine* Three precepts Acclamation	Enthronement *Sta et retine* Benedictions *Omnipotens ... det* *Benedic ... fortitudinem*

TABLE 1

(a) This table shows only the main features of the *ordines*, and excludes the *ordines* for queens.
(b) See chapter 15, pp. 341-60 above.
(c) MGH Capitularia, vol. II, nos. 276 and 302, pp. 337-41, 456-8.
(d) See P.E. Schramm, 'Die Krönung bei den Westfranken und Angelsachsen', *Zeitschrift für Rechtsgeschichte, Kanonistische Abteilung*, xxiii (1934), pp. 201-5 (reprinted in his *Kaiser, Könige und Päpste* [Stuttgart, 1968], vol. II, pp. 216-19).
(e) See C. Erdmann, *Forschungen zur politischen Ideenwelt des Frühmittelalters* (Berlin, 1951), pp. 87-9.
(f) I have put this acclamation in square brackets because it is implicit in the rubric here.
(g) The various ring formulae are discussed by Bouman, *Sacring*, pp. 129-31.
(h) For the sword-formulae, see Schramm, 'Krönung', p. 204 (*Kaiser, Könige und Päpste*, p. 218) and Erdmann, *Forschungen*, p. 89.
(i) This prayer is that of the 'Seven-Forms' *Ordo*.

seventeen other manuscripts were identified over forty years ago by P. L. Ward.[6] All of these dates are from the eleventh century or later, all are of West Frankish/French or Lotharingian origin, and most are characterised by the mention in the consecration-prayer of 'the sceptres of the Saxons, Mercians and Northumbrians' – hence the label: 'SMN' *Ordo*. B appears in six manuscripts written in England in the later tenth or first half of the eleventh century. They are, in likely chronological order:

The Benedictional of Archbishop Robert (Rouen Bibl.Mun. Y 7)[7]
The Sherborne Pontifical (Paris BN lat.943)[8]
The Anderson Pontifical (London BL Addit. 57337)[9]
The Sampson Pontifical (Cambridge Corpus Christi College 146)[10]
Claudius Pontifical II (London BL Cotton Claudius A.iii)[11]
Fragments of a pontifical probably from Ramsey Abbey (London BL Cotton Vitellius A.vii)[12]

Table 1 shows that Version A consists of almost the whole of the 'Erdmann' *Ordo*, with a final section taken, virtually unaltered, from the First English *Ordo*. Version B by contrast omits the preliminary section of A (as derived from 'Erdmann') and substitutes a three-fold promise remodelled from the final *tria precepta* section of the First English *Ordo*.[13]

[6] Ward, 'Early version', pp.347–9. See further E. A. R. Brown, *'Franks, Burgundians, and Aquitanians' and the Royal Coronation Ceremony in France: the Ordo of Paris, Bibliothèque Nationale, manuscrit latin 1419*, Appendix 1 (forthcoming).

[7] Ed. H. A. Wilson, Henry Bradshaw Society, vol. 24 (London, 1903), with the king's *ordo* at pp.140–7. See also J. Backhouse, D. H. Turner and L. Webster (eds.), *The Golden Age of Anglo-Saxon Art, 966–1066* (London, 1984), p.60.

[8] Also known as the Pontifical of St. Dunstan. See V. Leroquais, *Les Pontificaux Manuscrits des Bibliothèques de France*, 3 vols. (Paris, 1937), vol. 2, pp.160–4; Backhouse, Turner and Webster, *Golden Age*, p.55. I am indebted to the late Mr. Derek Turner for allowing me to consult his microfilm of this manuscript, and for his expert advice.

[9] This recently-found manuscript was written *c.*1000, at Canterbury, or perhaps at Winchester. (D. Turner, personal communication.)

[10] The royal *ordo* was printed, with English translation, by L. G. Wickham Legg, *English Coronation Records* (Westminster, 1901), pp.15–21). The manuscript, written at Winchester early in the eleventh century, later belonged to Bishop Sampson of Worcester (1096–1112).

[11] Ed. D. H. Turner, *The Claudius Pontificals*, Henry Bradshaw Society, vol. 97 (Chichester, 1971, issued for the year 1964), with the king's *ordo* of Claudius Pontifical II at pp.89 –95.

[12] This MS was very badly damaged in the fire of 1731, and only parts of the *ordines* for king and queen are legible. They were clearly very similar to those of Cambridge, Corpus Christi College MS 44, written in the second half of the eleventh century: ed. J. Wickham Legg, *Three Coronation Orders*, Henry Bradshaw Society, vol. 19 (London, 1900). pp.53–63. The king's *ordo* in these MSS is a slightly elaborated form of the B version. See below, chapter 17, pp. 375-402.

[13] For the 'threefold commands' concluding the First *Ordo*, see above, chapter 15, pp. 358-9.

Seven-Forms	*SMN*	*Ratold*	*B*
Omnipotens eterne deus	Omnipotens sempiterne deus creator ...	O.s.d.c.	O.s.d.c.
super hunc famulum tuum N. quem supplici devotione in regem eligimus .... ecclesiamque tuam deinceps .... enutriat .... virtutis regimen administret et ad vere fidei pacisque concordiam eorum animos te opitulante reformet, ut horum populorum debita subiectione fultus, condigno amore glorificatus, ad paternum decenter solium tua miseratione conscendere mereatur.	quem supplici devotione in regnum *pariter* eligimus ... administret ut regale solium *videlicet saxonum merciorum nordhanhimbrorum* sceptra non deserat sed ad pristine fidei ... reformet, ut *utrorumque horum populorum* .... glorificatus, per longum vite spatium paterne apicem glorie tua miseratione *unatim* stabilire et gubernare mereatur.	in regnum N. *Albionis totius videlicet francorum pariter* eligimus ... totius *Albionis* ecclesiam ... solium *videlicet francorum* sceptra ... ut utrorumque horum populorum ... unatim stabilire ...	in regnum *Anglorum vel Saxonum pariter* eligimus totius regni N. ecclesiam ... solium *videlicet anglorum vel saxonum* sceptra ... ut populorum debita subiectione ... unatim stabilire ...

TABLE 2

Since B is therefore substantially further removed from it sources than A, it looks as if A is the prior version of the Second *Ordo*. C. A. Bouman's analysis of the structure of the consecration-prayer in the two versions powerfully supported the argument for A's priority.[14]

A clue to A's date may emerge from an examination of verbal variants in the same prayer. Table 2 compares the relevant passages in the original source (the 'Seven Forms' *Ordo*), in the two sub-versions of A, and in B. The 'Ratold' redactor has clearly tried to adapt the text to a West Frankish situation. But the 'SMN' form cannot have been A's original one, for the mention of 'both peoples' (*utrique populi*) suggests a reference to two peoples, and two only, earlier in the prayer. Again the word *pariter* seems linked to two peoples, not the 'SMN' text's three or 'Ratold''s one. The B text, however, while specifying two peoples by name in the earlier passage, lacks the *utrique* of the later one. Hence the original readings of the Second English *Ordo* revision seem to survive in no extant text but can be reconstructed: two references to two peoples supported by the additions *pariter*, *utrique*, and finally the passage referring to 'the apex of paternal glory' and 'stablishing and governing [it] unitedly'. This last passage seems to refer to the making permanent of a political union, and – if we press a literal reading – one achieved by the father of the king for whose consecration the new passage was designed. Given the frequency of fraternal succession in the ninth and tenth centuries in England, the allusion would have more point if the king in question were succeeding directly to his father: two of the only three cases in the whole period from 860 to 1000 are Edward the Elder and Athelstan.[15] Both at first glance seem equally good candidates for association with the redaction of the Second *Ordo*. In the early 880s Alfred had annexed Anglian Mercia to his West Saxon kingdom, and thereafter he and his two next successors Edward and Athelstan, sometimes used titles referring to two peoples, and Angles and Saxons.[16] Further, the relevant West Frankish materials could well have been available in Wessex at any point from 886 onwards when Grimbald came from Rheims to Alfred's court expecting, it seems, promotion to the see of Canterbury.[17] The Second *Ordo*'s *terminus post*

[14] C. A. Bouman, *Sacring and Crowing* (Groningen, Djakarta, 1957), pp.112–9.

[15] Edward succeeded his father Alfred in 899, and was succeeded by his son Athelstan in 924. The third case, Edward the Martyr, who succeeded Edgar in 975 is too late for consideration here: see below, 368-74. The frequency of fraternal succession in Wessex is perceptively discussed by P. Stafford, 'The King's Wife in Wessex, 800–1066', *Past and Present*, 91 (1981), 3–27, at 10, 19–20.

[16] See S. Keynes and M. Lapidge, *Alfred the Great. Asser's Life of King Alfred and other contemporary sources* (Harmondsworth, 1983), pp.227–8; H. Kleinschmidt, *Untersuchungen über das englische Königtum im 10.Jahrhundert* (Göttingen, 1979), pp.40–1, 52–65.

[17] P. Grierson, 'Grimbald of St. Bertin's', *English Historical Review*, 55 (1940), 529–61; M. B. Parkes, 'The Palaeography of the Parker Manuscript', *Anglo-Saxon England*, 5 (1976), 149–71, at 163–6. I am not convinced by Keynes and Lapidge, *Alfred the Great*,

quem therefore predates the accession of Edward as well as that of Athelstan.

But there are two reasons for thinking Edward's consecration a more likely occasion than Athelstan's for the first use of the Second English *Ordo*. First the emphasis on the unity of the two peoples (echoed in the ring-prayer's *subditos coadunare*) is better attributed to Alfred's last years, or even the months immediately following his death, than to the reign of his successor.[18] Several texts produced in the 890s show Alfred claiming rule over Mercians as well as West Saxons and asserting the oneness of 'Englishkind' (*Angelcynn*).[19] Asser's information on the different kinds of education given to Alfred's elder and younger sons hints at a plan to hand on an undivided Wessex-Mercia to Edward, and perhaps put Aethelweard into the church. Alfred's Will points the same way.[20] Edward the Elder himself, by contrast, seems to have envisaged a redivision between his eldest but illegitimate son Athelstan and his second, legitimate son, Aelfweard – a plan frustrated in the event by Aelfweard's death within days of his father's.[21]

The second reason has to with what I will call the Brückmann factor –

pp.332–3, that Grimbald did not expect a bishopric when he came to Wessex. If Canterbury was the see envisaged, it is relevant to note that archbishops of Canterbury had probably consecrated kings earlier in the ninth century: N. Brooks, *The Early History of the Church of Canterbury* (Leicester University Press, 1984), pp.146–7. Cf. Nelson, 'Earliest surviving royal *Ordo*', above, pp. 352-3.

[18] For the rebellion of Alfred's nephew Aethelwold immediately after Alfred's death, see *Anglo-Saxon Chronicle*, s.a.900, ed. C. Plummer, *Two of the Saxon Chronicles Parallel*, 2 vols. (Oxford, 1892–9), vol. 1, p.92. See also Keynes and Lapidge, *Alfred the Great*, p.173. Aethelwold was presumably bidding for a share in the enlarged inheritance of Alfred's kingdom.

[19] Keynes and Lapidge, *Alfred the Great*, pp.124–5 (preface to translation of Gregory the Great's *Pastoral Care*), 163–4 (prologue to Laws). Cf. *Anglo-Saxon Chronicle*, s.a.886, 896, vol. 1, pp.80, 89. One further hint of a link between the Second English *Ordo* and Alfred may be its insertion in the benediction 'Extendat', derived from Hincmar's 869 *Ordo*, of a reference to 'Sanctus Gregorius anglorum apostolicus' (so, all the Version B MSS; 'Ratold' gives *angelorum* (!), while the other A MSS omit this phrase altogether). Alfred's devotion to Gregory is well-known; and Gregory's relevance to the fostering of English unity has recently been stressed by P. Wormald, 'Bede, the *Bretwaldas* and the origins of the *gens Anglorum*', in Wormald (ed.), *Ideal and Reality in Frankish and Anglo-Saxon Society* (Oxford, 1983), pp.99–129.

[20] Asser, *De Rebus Gestis Aelfredi*, *c.*75, ed. W. H. Stevenson (Oxford, 1904), p.58; Keynes and Lapidge, *Alfred the Great*, pp.90, 173–6. See further M. Lapidge, 'Some Latin Poems as Evidence for the Reign of Athelstan', *Anglo-Saxon England*, 9 (1981), 61–98, at 80–1; Nelson, '"A king across the sea": Alfred in Continental perspective', *Transactions of the Royal Historical Society*, 5th series, 31 (1986) (forthcoming).

[21] Edward had Athelstan brought up in Mercia: William of Malmesbury, *Gesta Regum*, ed. W. Stubbs, Rolls Series, 2 vols. (London, 1887–9), vol. 1, p.145. The evidence for events following Edward's death is set out by Plummer, *Two of the Saxon Chronicles Parallel*, vol. 2, pp.132–3. Even after Aelfweard's death in July 924, Athelstan was not consecrated to the reunited kingdom until September 925.

the need to take into account the queen's *ordo* that goes with the king's. The A version of the Second English *Ordo* is accompanied in all the manuscripts by a queen's *ordo* that does not simply replicate its model, the 'Erdmann' queen's *ordo*, but slightly modifies it at two points, and hence must surely have been produced with the possibility of use in mind.[22] We know that West Saxon kings' wives in the ninth century received no consecration, or even recognition as queen.[23] Whether under Mercian or Carolingian influence, or both, change was clearly envisaged by the redactor of the Second *Ordo*. Who was the beneficiary? Athelstan never married. The philoprogenitive Edward, on the other hand, married Aelfweard's mother Aelfflaed probably very soon after his father Alfred's death and possibly before his own consecration on 8 June 900.[24] Was Aelfflaed in fact consecrated? No surviving charter bears her subscription as queen, and she is nowhere accorded that title.[25] Yet her daughter Edith, bride of Otto I, does seem to have been consecrated with him in 936 – an innovation in the East Frankish kingdom.[26] Was Edith perhaps following in her mother's footsteps? A consecration for Aelfflaed would have aptly signified Edward's intention of keeping the succession in his own line, thereby excluding his cousins, one of whom still posed a serious threat to Edward in 900, and was not defeated and killed in battle until 902.[27] I suggest that Aelfflaed's existence, in the circumstances of 900, inspired the preparation of a West Saxon queen's *ordo*, evidently for the first time, and by someone capable of identifying, and returning to, his source's model: the rite for consecrating an abbess.[28]

So far I have tried to date the Second *Ordo* mainly on internal grounds. But there is another approach. A survives only in Continental manuscripts, and it is worth posing again the question asked many years

[22] Both of these occur in the prayer immediately following the queen's anointing. Here 'Erdmann''s model was the prayer for the consecration of an abbess as found in such Frankish Gelasian sacramentaries as *Liber Sacramentorum Gellonensis*, ed. A. Dumas, Corpus Christianorum, Series Latina CLIX (Turnholdt, 1982), no. 2578, p.400; cf. *Pontificale Romano-Germanicum*, ed. C. Vogel and R. Elze, 2 vols. Vatican City, (1963), vol. 1, pp.80–1. The redactor of the Second English *Ordo* used the abbess's prayer to reinsert the word 'affluentem' at the opening of the queen's benediction, and the phrase 'ut numquam postmodum de tua gratia separetur indigna' at the end.

[23] Stafford, 'King's Wife in Wessex' pp.3–4, 16–7.

[24] If we can trust the witness list of a Malmesbury charter dated 901, P. Sawyer, *Anglo-Saxon Charters. An Annotated List and Bibliography* (London, 1968), no. 363, Aelfflaed was then Edward's wife. Cf. William of Malmesbury, *Gesta Regum*, vol. 1, p.137.

[25] She subscribed Sawyer, no. 363 simply as *conjux regis*. For the title *regina* assigned to Edward's third wife Eadgifu in a German source, see Stafford, 'King's Wife in Wessex', p.17, n.44.

[26] K. Leyser, 'Die Ottonen und Wessex', *Frühmittelalterliche Studien*, 17 (1983), 73–97, at 81–2.

[27] Cf. above, n.18.

[28] Above, n.22.

ago by Edmund Bishop, of 'when such orders "got" across the water and into France'.[29] P. E. Schramm, who telescoped the First and Second *Ordines* into the years from 957 to 973, and regarded Dunstan as the author of both, believed that the B version of the Second *Ordo* was its original form and that A was a Continental derivative resulting from Dunstan's sending of a copy of B to a friend at Arras.[30] More recently, Derek Turner has pointed out that the Second *Ordo* 'lies behind actual French usage, which does suggest that it was originally imported [into France] for practical rather than literary purposes'. Those practical purposes Turner linked with the situation in 936 when Louis IV d'Outremer returned from years of exile in Wessex to be consecrated king at Laon by the archbishop of Rheims. 'This, if any', wrote Turner, 'seems to be the occasion in the tenth century when an English Coronation rite might have been employed [in France]'.[31] The importance of Turner's suggestion lies in his clear recognition of the priority, and antiquity, of A. The Second *Ordo*'s composition can be detached from Edgar's consecration at Bath in 973 – where even Schramm's critics had left it.[32] But even if Turner is right about 936, that cannot be the whole story. According to Schramm, the 'SMN' *Ordo* did not become 'French usage' until the twelfth century.[33] In any case, Ward's identification of distinct sub-groups among the Continental 'SMN' manuscripts means that we have to account for the 'getting across the water' of more than one version of A quite apart from that of the Ratold Sacramentary.[34] The amount of evidence for contacts between England and the Continent in Athelstan's reign and later leaves no difficulty in supposing that several copies of the Second *Ordo* were

[29] Quoted in N. J. Abercrombie, *The Life and Work of Edmund Bishop* (London, 1959), Appendix: 'E. B. on Coronation' (1914), p.520.

[30] P. E. Schramm, 'Die Krönung bei den Westfranken und Angelsachsen', *Zeitschrift für Rechtsgeschichte*, 54, Kanonistische Abteilung 23 (1934), 117–242, at 151–90, reprinted in his *Kaiser, Könige und Päpste*, 4 vols. (Stuttgart, 1968), vol. 2, pp.140–248, at pp.169–98.

[31] *Claudius Pontificals*, p.xxxiii.

[32] Ward, 'The Coronation Ceremony in Medieval England', *Speculum*, 14 (1939), 160–78, at 166–70; Bouman, *Sacring and Crowning*, pp.106, 157.

[33] Schramm, *Der König von Frankreich*, revised ed., 2 vols. (Weimar, 1960), p.100, inferred from the archbishop of Rheims' Memorial on Philip I's consecration in 1069 that the 'West Frankish' ('Erdmann') *Ordo* was still in use; and, ibid., pp. 119–20, from Suger's account of the consecration of the next king, Louis VI in 1108, *Vie de Louis VI le Gros*, ed. H. Waquet (Paris, 1929), p.86, that the 'Fulrad' ('SMN') *Ordo* was then followed. Brown, *'Franks, Burgundians and Aquitanians'*, section III, notes that Suger wrote over thirty years after the event, perhaps with a text of the 'SMN' *Ordo* at his elbow. She observes, however, that the large number of French twelfth- and thirteenth-century MSS suggest the use of the 'SMN' *Ordo* probably in 1108 and for some time thereafter.

[34] Ward, 'Early version', p.349.

transmitted in liturgical books.[35] The 'SMN' and 'Albion' variants in the consecration prayer would thus represent attempts at updating the A *Ordo* made in England after *c.*930 and *c.*950 respectively.[36]

It is time now to turn to the B version of the Second English *Ordo*. There are two distinct sub-versions, one contained in the Benedictional of Archbishop Robert, the other in the remaining B manuscripts. The differences between these sub-versions are verbal, not structural, but they clearly show that 'Robert' is closer to A than is the other sub-version.[37] 'Robert' has sometimes been depicted as intermediate between A and B, or as 'outside the main line of development'.[38] In fact it represents the one major revision of A, a revision to which only minor verbal changes were subsequently made. As such 'Robert' deserves more attention than it has so far received. The Benedictional itself is one of the earliest products of the Winchester school. Against the suggestion that it was made for a bishop of Selsey, the presence of benedictions for the feast of Grimbald, *tantus patronus*, points to the New Minster Winchester as the book's destination.[39] There seems good reason to date it to *c.*975, quite well on in the pontificate of Aethelwold (963-84).[40] In fact, the obvious explanation for the inclusion of the revised Second *Ordo* is that a copy was available at Winchester through Aethelwold's initiative.

The single significant innovation in this revision is what would later be known as the Coronation Oath. Its substance was derived from the three-fold precept, originally the concluding section of the First English *Ordo* and taken from it into the A version of the Second *Ordo*. But the change in place meant a change in function: what had been a royal declaration of intent, a kind of programmatic statement issued literally from the throne by the newly-installed king, was turned by the reviser into a promise that was implicitly a pre-condition of the ensuing consecration. Schramm was right to insist on the crucial ideological difference between *Vorschrift* (prescription) and *Verpflichtung*

[35] See Turner, Introduction to the *Claudius Pontificals*, passim; D. Bullough, 'The Continental Background of the Reform', in D. Parsons (ed.), *Tenth-Century Studies* (Chichester, 1975), pp.20–36; S. Keynes, 'King Athelstan's books', in M. Lapidge and H. Gneuss (eds.), *Learning and Literature in Anglo-Saxon England* (Cambridge, 1985), pp.143–201.

[36] I assume that these can be correlated, partly with political developments, partly with royal styles used in charters; Kleinschmidt, *Untersuchungen*, pp.40–1, 64–89; Keynes, 'King Athelstan's books', pp.157–8, 190.

[37] J. A. Robinson, 'The Coronation Order in the Tenth Century', *Journal of Theological Studies*, 19 (1917–8), 56–72. Ward, 'Coronation Ceremony', p.170, n.3.

[38] Robinson, 'Coronation Order', pp.56–62; Ward, 'Coronation Ceremony', p.170, n.3.

[39] *Benedictional of Archbishop Robert*, p.39.

[40] This dating can be established on iconographical grounds. I am very grateful to Robert Deshman for this information, and for helpful discussion: cf. below, n.45.

(commitment).[41] It was not that the reviser wished to imply a diminution of royal authority: rather he intended to highlight far more clearly than A's opening section had allowed, the functional requirements of christian kingship as an office.

The inclusion of a promise of some kind in royal *ordines* went back at least to the ninth century. Hincmar of Rheims drew on the model of the profession of the bishop elect.[42] The same parallel may have inspired the reviser of the Second English *Ordo*.[43] But he was also influenced, perhaps, by the model of the abbot's profession, and, more generally, by the parallel between abbatial and royal office. The Benedictional of Robert contains in its rite for the blessing of an abbot the prayer, 'Deus qui sub tuae maiestatis arbitrio', which is largely derived from the royal blessing, 'In diebus' of the First and Second English *Ordines*.[44] Since the Benedictional of Robert is perhaps the earliest book in which this abbot's prayer appears, the prayer could well have been available at Winchester because it reflected the views of Aethelwold as evidenced in the *Regularis Concordia* and in Winchester iconography of the period.[45] Had Aethelwold himself composed the new abbot's prayer while he occupied the abbatial office?

It seems unlikely that the reviser produced the B-*Ordo* as a mere *jeu d'esprit*. If however he had a particular king-making in mind, whose was it? Edgar is an obvious candidate, 973 the occasion. But (as I have argued elsewhere) 973 was not Edgar's only consecration: he was very probably also consecrated at the beginning of his reign in Wessex, *c.*960, and I am tempted to link the producton of B version with this occasion.[46] Aethelwold as abbot of Abingdon had been closely associated with Edgar since the aetheling had sought his guidance there in the mid-950s; looking back on these years, Aethelwold recalled teacher and student planning monastic reform together. From Abingdon, Aethelwold sent to Fleury and Corbie for help in modernising and beautifying the

41 Schramm, 'Krönung bei den Westfranken', p.166 (=*Kaiser, Könige und Päpste*, vol. 2, p.180), against Bouman, *Sacring and Crowning*, pp.144–5.

42 Nelson, 'Kingship, law and liturgy in the political thought of Hincmar of Rheims', above, chapter 7, pp. 143-66.

43 Compare the opening rubrics in the rites for the consecrations of bishop and king in the *Benedictional of Archbishop Robert*, pp.125, 140. A parallel was evidently seen between the two rites.

44 *Benedictional of Archbishop Robert*, pp.130–1.

45 The views of the tenth-century reformers, especially Aethelwold, will be examined by Robert Deshman in a forthcoming paper on the iconography of St. Benedict, a version of which was read to the University of London Palaeography Seminar in 1985. The abbot's prayer also appears in the so-called Pontifical of Egbert of *c.*1000, the Lanalet Pontifical of the early eleventh century, and the Sherborne Pontifical which Ward, 'Coronation Ceremony', p.167, n.5 dated *c.*1000, though Turner, *Claudius Pontificals*, p.xvi, thought possibly mid-tenth-century.

46 See above, chapter 12, pp. 297-300.

monastic litury.[47] If, as I have suggested, he was capable of revising the rite for abbatial inauguration, might he not have thought the production of a new king's *ordo* desirable, to express his and Edgar's conception of kingship as office? If so, Aethelwold could have taken a copy of this *ordo* to Winchester with him when he became bishop in 963: this would have been the model of the scribe of the 'Robert' book.

Though the connexion of the 'Robert' *Ordo* with Edgar's consecration *c.*960, is plausible, it is not the only possibility. Edgar's elder brother Eadwig may also have been taught by Aethelwold at Abingdon, and the new *Ordo* could have been produced with Eadwig's consecration in mind.[48] But that hypothesis leaves little time between Aethelwold's assumption of the abbacy in 954 and Eadwig's consecration on 27 January 956. In Edgar's case, by contrast, the time-span involved is more comfortable; and there was a probable further delay of up to 18 months between Edgar's succession and his consecration.[49] Moreover, it could have been the experience of Eadwig's lukewarm support for monastic reform which impelled our enterprising liturgist to revise the king's *ordo* as he did, for Eadwig's successor. There is a further difficulty about linking the 'Robert' *Ordo* with Eadwig in 956 which applies equally to the Edgar hypothesis. No queen was consecrated along with either Eadwig in 956 or with Edgar at the outset of his reign, yet the 'Robert' *Ordo* does have an *ordo* for a queen to go with it.[50] However this queen's *ordo* is simply a copy of the existing A queen's *ordo*: hence its presence in the Benedictional of Robert could be attributed to the scribe's desire for completeness, or even to the conservatism of liturgical manuscripts in general.[51] There is an obvious distinction, anyway, between copying, and composing or adapting, a liturgical text. The 'Robert' queen's *ordo*, as a straight copy, contrasts strikingly with the restructured king's *ordo*, and therefore throws no light on the circumstances of the latter's composition. The changes within the king's *ordo* itself seem to me to point to the beginning of Edgar's reign, and to Aethelwold who (far more than Dunstan) was the ideological force behind that king's

[47] Aethelwold's close relations with the young Edgar: Old English account of King Edgar's establishment of the monasteries, in D. Whitelock ed., *English Historical Documents*, vol. 1, rev. ed. (London, 1979) no. 238, p.921; influence of reformed Frankish liturgy: Aelfric, *Life of St. Ethelwold*, c.10, and Wulfstan, *Life of St. Ethelwold* c.14, both ed. M. Winterbottom, *Three Lives of English Saints* (Toronto, 1972), pp. 21, 42; *Historia Monasterii Abingdon*, ed. J. Stevenson, Rolls Series 2,i (London, 1858), p.129.

[48] Sue Mathews kindly drew my attention to the possibility that Eadwig too stayed at Abingdon. See C. Hart, 'Athelston Half-King and his family', *Anglo-Saxon England*, 2 (1973), 115–44, at 126, n.4.

[49] See above, pp. 298-9.

[50] *Benedictional of Archbishop Robert,* p.148. Did the 'Robert' composer envisage the possibility that a queen's *ordo* might be needed, perhaps for Edgar's first wife, Aethelflaed? In fact she was never consecrated: see above, p. 300.

[51] Bouman, *Sacring and Crowning*, pp.55–7, 79–80; Nelson, 'Ritual and reality in the early medieval *Ordines*', above, chapter 14, pp. 329-39.

engagement with ecclesiastical reform.[52]

If we turn, finally, to the remaining sub-version of B, that is, the *ordo* contained in the Sherborne Pontifical and the other four English manuscripts listed above, we find the Brückmann factor again significant. For although the queen's *ordo* that appears in these manuscripts is also a straight copy of the A queen's *ordo*, it is prefaced by a new rubric that surely pins it down to an occasion when immediate use was envisaged:

The king's consecration ends. The queen's consecration follows. To do her honour, she is anointed on the crown of her head by the bishop with the oil of sacred unction. And let her be blessed and consecrated in church, in the presence of the magnates, to consortship of the royal bed, as it is shown on the following page. We further decree that she be adorned with a ring for the integrity of the faith, and a crown for the glory of eternity.[53]

The references to 'the following page' and to a 'decree' are incongruous in a liturgical book, and, interestingly, were dropped in eleventh-century copies of the Second *Ordo*.[54] They seem to echo a decision of the witan relating to the consecration, perhaps controversial, of a particular queen. Who could this have been? The likeliest possibility is Aelfthryth, consecrated along with her husband Edgar in 973.[55] The only statement to this effect occurs in the *Vita Oswaldi*, and doubt has been cast on the accuracy of this account on the grounds that the hagiographer was clearly writing with a copy of the Second *Ordo* at his elbow.[56] He was also writing, however, for an audience at Oswald's own house of Ramsey,

[52] Aethelwold's role is highlighted by E. John, *Orbis Britanniae* (Leicester, 1966), pp.159–60, and Dunstan's relatively low profile by N. Brooks, *The Early History of the Church of Canterbury* (Leicester, 1984), pp.245–53. Aethelwold's stress on the significance of royal consecration rites may be reflected in the marginal crosses added at Winchester, possibly during his pontificate, to the Parker MS ('A') of the Anglo-Saxon Chronicle at the annal for 853: see Nelson, 'The Problem of King Alfred's Royal Anointing, *Journal of Ecclesiastical History*, 18 ; above, ch. 13, p. 324, n.1, and the facsimile edition by R. Flower and A. H. Smith, *The Parker Chronicle and Laws*, Early English Text Society, (London, 1941), fol. 13a. But see further Parkes, 'The Palaeography of the Parker Manuscript', pp.168–70, suggesting a mid-tenth century dating for the marginal crosses.

[53] This rubric appears before the queen's *ordo* in the Sherborne Pontifical, fol.74; the Sampson Pontifical, ed. Wickham Legg, *English Coronation Records*, p.21; and the Anderson Pontifical, fols. 63r–63v.

[54] *Claudius Pontificals*, ed. Turner, p.95; Corpus 44, ed. Wickham Legg, *Three Coronation Orders*, p.61; perhaps also Cotton Vitellius A.vii, though this passage has unfortunately been totally obliterated.

[55] No previous tenth-century king's wife is known to have been consecrated, or to have used the title of queen during her husband's lifetime: Stafford, 'King's Wife in Wessex', p.17, with nn.42, 44.

[56] *Vita Oswaldi*, ed. J. Raine, *Historians of the Church of York*, 2 vols., Rolls Series (London, 1879), vol. 1, pp.436–8, reprinted Schramm, 'Krönung bei den Westfranken', pp.231–3 (=*Kaiser, Könige und Päpste*, pp.241–3). See H. G. Richardson and G. O. Sayles, *The Governance of Medieval England* (Edinburgh, 1963), Appendix 1, pp.397–412, at 400.

hence for men who knew at first hand what had happened at Bath in 973; and he is in fact quite explicit about his use of an *ordo* text, presumably because it was known at Ramsey to have been the rite used on that occasion.[57] H. G. Richardson and G. O. Sayles spotted a difficulty in the *Vita*'s account, which, in their view, rendered it 'useless' as evidence for 973. The *Vita* author, near the end of his account of the consecrations of king and queen, wrote the words: 'peractis egregiis nuptiis regalis thori' ('when the distinguished nuptials of the royal bed had been completed'). Richardson and Sayles saw here a reference to the marriage of Edgar and Aelfthryth, which happened in 964, and not to 973 at all.[58] I suggest that the rubric introducing the queen's *ordo* helps account for the *Vita*'s curious expression: the phrase 'consortium regalis thori', which I take to refer to Aelfthryth's queenship, could have inspired what was in effect a synonym in 'nuptiae'. It is clear, anyway, that the *Vita* author, as Eric John pointed out, 'cannot have taken the reference to the nuptials literally'.[59] He described what he thought were royal inauguration rites of the king and queen, and these were of interest precisely because of the role of Oswald as archbishop of York, an office he assumed in 972.

I should like to end with some further arguments linking a rather special queen's consecration, hence the revised version of the B *Ordo*, with 973. First, there is evidence that while Aelfthryth was consecrated queen her predecessor, Edgar's previous wife Aethelflaed, was not, and that this contrast was exploited by the partisans of Aelfthryth's son against Aethelflaed's son in the succession dispute that followed Edgar's death in 975.[60] Second, Aelfthryth subscribed charters as queen in the 960s and early 970s, indicating heightened aspirations to status on her part as compared with her predecessors.[61] Third, Aelfthryth had associated herself closely with the monastic reformers patronised by her husband and especially with Aethelwold who, perhaps in consequence, assigned the queen an important role in the *Regularis Concordia*.[62] Those who designed Edgar's consecration in 973 were well-disposed to Aelfthryth. Fourth, the Byzantine princess Theophano was crowned and probably anointed empress in Rome when she married Otto II on 14 April 972.[63] It just happened that Oswald, archbishop-elect of York, visited Rome for his pallium sometime in 972 and so either witnessed

[57] *Vita Oswaldi*, p.437: '. . . stetit archipraesul [Dunstanus] et oravit pro eo orationes, quae in illorum libris scriptae sunt. Deinde secundum dixit Oswaldus . . .'

[58] Richardson and Sayles, *Governance*, pp.401–2.

[59] E. John, *Orbis Britanniae*, pp.276–89, at 286.

[60] See above, p. 300.

[61] Sawyer, nos. 757, 771, 794, 795, 801, 805; and the possibly authentic 731, 779, 785, 806 and 1449.

[62] Stafford, 'King's Wife in Wessex', pp.23–4.

[63] Benedict of Monte Soracte, *Chronicon*, in Monumenta Germaniae Historica, Scriptores vol. III, p.718. See *Regesten des Kaiserreiches unter Otto II*, ed. J. F. Böhmer, rev. H. L. Mikoletzky (Berlin, 1950), p. 270.

Theophano's consecration or heard about it very soon afterwards.[64] That could have provided an authoritative precedent for Aelfthryth's consecration the following year.

Finally, while the sequence of versions of the Second *Ordo* seems fairly clear, one remaining difficulty should be acknowledged in the chronology of use I have suggested. The date of the 'Robert' manuscript is almost certainly slightly later than 973: this means that a scribe at Aethelwold's Winchester copied out the 'Robert' *Ordo* when it had been, so to speak, superseded by the revised version of the other B manuscripts. Is this credible? I think it is, for three reasons. One: all the other bits of evidence (the date of the manuscripts of the Sherborne, Anderson, and Sampson Pontificals; the queen's *ordo* rubric; the *Vita Oswaldi*; the emphasis of the *Anglo-Saxon Chronicle*) point towards the use of the revised B version in 973.[65] Two: it may be inappropriate to assign criteria of 'up-to-dateness' overriding importance for the scribe of a tenth-century liturgical book. The compiler of the Pontifical section of the Benedictional of Archbishop Robert presumably incorporated the texts he found to hand at Winchester. How much supervision was exercised by Bishop Aethelwold over these texts (as distinct from the iconography of the illuminations) is hard to say. If, as I have suggested, Aethelwold took a personal interest in some rituals, it would follow that the texts that lay to hand for the scribe of the Robert book might tend to be 'up-to-date' in any case. Turner showed that the rituals for the consecration of a church and for the ordinations of priests and deacons were 'more advanced' in the Robert book than in any of the other near-contemporary English Pontificals with which he compared it; on the other hand, however, this was not true of the rites of monastic profession or the blessing of an abbot.[66] Three: the leading roles in Edgar's consecration at Bath in 973 were played, not by Aethelwold, but by Archbishops Dunstan and Oswald. In other words, while Aethelwold was a key figure, I believe, in the planning of that occasion, he may not have been so closely involved in the detailed revision of the *ordo* used for it. After all, those details were relatively insignificant compared with the major revision which I have argued was done a few years earlier, and probably by Aethelwold himself. It is even possible that Aethelwold himself in 975 did not possess one of the 'books', that is *ordo*-texts, used, acording to the *Vita Oswaldi*, by the officiants in 973.[67] Even if he did (and a copy does seem to have been at Winchester by the close of the tenth century), it could have been an understandable pride in his own work that led the bishop to allow 'his' *ordo* to be included in one of the most beautiful books produced in Winchester's 'golden age'.

[64] *Vita Oswaldi*, pp. 435–6.
[65] See above, pp. 297-8, 302-3.
[66] Turner, *Claudius Pontificals*, Introduction, pp.xx–xxviii, xxxiii–xxxix.
[67] Cf. above, n.57.

17

THE RITES OF THE CONQUEROR[1]

The two months between mid-October and mid-December, 1066, were a liminal period during which, despite Hastings, a state of 'public war'[2] continued, and the political consequences of Harold's death had to be painfully worked out. Two crucial events in this period were enacted through ritual. First came the submission of 'the metropolitan bishop Stigand' at Wallingford: 'he gave himself into [Duke William's] hands', wrote William of Poitiers, 'and confirmed his faith with an oath'.[3] The second set of actions was performed soon after, at Little Berkhamstead, by the chief men of London, together with Archbishop Ealdred of York, the Ætheling Edgar and Earls Edwin and Morcar: 'they bowed', according to the 'D' text of the Anglo-Saxon Chronicle, '. . . and they swore oaths [to Duke William] and he promised them that he would be a true lord to them.'[4] The similarities between Norman and Anglo-Saxon versions of commendation are obvious: though the terminology of each source derives from a distinct tradition, both present the essential acts as the oath and the gesture of self-abasement, and both imply that the resultant personal relationship was modelled on that between lord and retainer. So if we cannot be sure that in either Norman or Anglo-Saxon practice personalised rituals of subordination were always – or even normally – used to constitute a formal relationship between duke or king on the one hand, and noble on the other,[5] it does seem that such a relationship was perceived in terms of the vassalage model[6] – *as if* such oaths and gestures had been performed. Furthermore, Anglo-Saxon and

1 I am most grateful to H. E. J. Cowdrey for his criticisms of a draft of this paper, and to both him and Michael Lapidge for valuable advice. Any remaining errors of fact or interpretation are of course my own. I should also like to thank Simon Keynes and John Gillingham for their help, many other members of the Fourth Battle Conference for useful suggestions, and especially my friend and colleague Allen Brown for encouraging me to enlist.

2 See the Penitential Ordinance issued after Hastings, ed. C. Morton, 'Pope Alexander II and the Norman Conquest', *Latomus* xxxiv, 1975, 382.

3 *Gesta Guillelmi*, 216. Translations of primary sources in this paper are my own.

4 *ASC**edd. J. Earle and C. Plummer, *Two of the Saxon Chronicles Parallel*, i, Oxford 1892, 'D', s.a. 1066, 200. All my *ASC* references are to this edition.

5 For eleventh-century Normandy, the evidence is scarce. In the *Gesta Guillelmi*, such rituals are mentioned only in exceptional cases concerning unusually asymmetrical relationships between Duke William and non-Norman magnates: 78-9, 88, 96, 104. The broader political context of such relations is well described by E. M. Hallam, 'The King and the Princes in Eleventh-Century France', *Bulletin of the Institute of Historical Research* liii, 1980, 143-56. For Anglo-Saxon England, the *Vita Eadwardi*, 22 and 27-8, is suggestive, as is the text printed by F. Liebermann, *Gesetze der Angelsachsen* i, Halle 1903, 396.

6 J. Le Goff, 'The Symbolic Ritual of Vassalage', in *Time, Work and Culture in the Middle Ages*, Chicago 1980, 237-87, offers many insights, though some of his conclusions are, in my view, questionable.

* *Anglo-Saxon Chronicle* (hereafter *ASC*).

Norman rituals were mutually intelligible: Duke William in 1051 took Edward the Confessor as his lord,[7] while Harold in 1064 took William as his.[8] The sacred character of these procedures was obviously crucial. William of Poitiers describes Harold giving his oath to the duke as his retainer (*satelles*) 'according to the holy rite of the Christians'; and hence, appropriately, the duke at Hastings wore around his neck 'the relics whose favour Harold had alienated from himself by violating the faith he had pledged by swearing on them'. Duke William was no cynical manipulator of the holy, but a pious man in contemporary terms, who 'frequently bought the prayers of the servants of Christ, especially when war or some other difficult assignment was looming'.[10] But he was also aware of the propaganda-value of ritual, and that awareness was heightened by his situation as Conqueror of the English kingdom.

The English magnates who bowed and swore to Duke William in 1066 saw these acts as more than tokens of personal submission: their collective public recognition of him as lord amounted, under the circumstances of an interregnum, to an acceptance of him as king.[11] This is stated explicitly by William of Poitiers: '[After the oaths] they begged him to take the crown, asserting that they were accustomed to serve a king and therefore wished to have their lord as king'.[12] The 'D' text of the Anglo-Saxon Chronicle makes the same point implicitly in its comment on the magnates' bowings: 'It was a great folly that they did not do so sooner'[13] – that is, instead of having publicly recognised the claims of the Ætheling Edgar in the aftermath of Hastings and hence provoked the Norman harrying of the Home Counties. Duke William surely knew quite well the meaning of the Englishmen's oaths and bowings.[14] But they were not the only men he had to reckon with. To his Norman followers, according to William of Poitiers, he gave three reasons for his reluctance to proceed immediately to consecration as king: the uncertain political situation, the wish for his wife to be consecrated alongside him, and the need to avoid haste when climbing a high peak.[15] William of Poitiers is clearly deploying the topos of modest hesitation, but, interestingly, he does not depict the duke's Norman retainers as responding with an instant counterblast of encouragement to accede to the English request, but only with milder advice. They suggested, instead, that the whole army be consulted. This was an army consisting of many besides Normans, and it was not a Norman but an 'Aquitanian', a Poitevin, who urged his comrades to follow the Englishmen's example and wish their lord to become a king. Even with this prompting, the army came round to the Poitevin's view only after deciding 'that their advantage and lands would be increased by the duke's elevation'. When the duke finally yielded to 'the

7 *ASC* 'D', s.a. 1051, 176. The historicity of Duke William's visit to England is accepted by M. Campbell, 'A pre-Conquest occupation of England?' *Speculum* xlvi, 1971, 28-9. See also the important discussion by E. John, 'Edward the Confessor and the Norman Conquest', *English Historical Review* (hereafter *EHR*) xciv, 1979, 253-4.

8 *Gesta Guillelmi*, 104.

9 *Gesta Guillelmi*, 180-2.

10 *Gesta Guillelmi*, 128.

11 H. M. Chadwick, *Studies in Anglo-Saxon Institutions*, Cambridge 1905, 355-66, remains the fundamental account of such procedures in Anglo-Saxon England.

12 *Gesta Guillelmi*, 216, where Stigand's oath is also linked with his abandonment of Edgar Ætheling.

13 *ASC*, 'D', s.a. 1066, 200.

14 Cf. above, n. 7.

15 *Gesta Guillelmi*, 216-18.

requests and pressure of so many', he too acted on the prudential grounds that it would be easier as king to crush English opponents of his regime. Both these calculations, the duke's and his followers', were thus presented by William of Poitiers as based on awareness of English sentiment: the Conqueror as king could hope for a large gain in English support; from the Conqueror as king his men could hope for access to English wealth. To become king, in short, was to acquire legitimacy and therefore increased effectiveness in the exercise of power in England. William of Poitiers' story thus suggests a contrast between Norman and Anglo-Saxon attitudes. The Conqueror's Norman followers were initially unenthusiastic, even wary, about his elevation to a royalty which was not only unfamiliar to them[16] but also threatened more regular, institutionalised pressure on their own interests in the longer term. The Anglo-Saxon nobles, by contrast, expected, demanded, that their lord become their king, since to them kingship was the traditional, authoritative centre of power.[17] The consecration of Christmas Day, 1066, was planned and executed to further Norman objectives in England because it conformed to English expectations.

This was the political context, then, in which the Conqueror's royal inauguration was performed. My purpose in the main part of this paper will be to identify the liturgical ordo used on that occasion. What follows might well be sub-titled 'Footnotes to Foreville', because, as Battle veterans will recall, Professor R. Foreville gave a notable paper here in 1978 on Anglo-Norman and Angevin royal consecrations and coronation-oaths.[18] Foreville made it clear in that paper that she did not share the generally-held identification of the ordo of William the Conqueror as a version of the Second English Ordo, that is, of the ordo which had been used, with minor variations, for William's Anglo-Saxon predecessors since the beginning of the tenth

16 For the *de facto* situation in eleventh-century Normandy, see C. W. Hollister, 'Normandy, France and the Anglo-Norman *Regnum*', *Speculum* li, 1976, 202-12; also J. Boussard, 'La notion de royauté sous Guillaume le Conquérant: ses origines et ses prolongements', *Annali della Fondazione Italiana per la Historia Amministrativa* iv, 1967, 47-77, where, however, the strength of ducal jurisdiction in Normandy both before and after 1066 seems rather overestimated.

17 For royal ideology in late Anglo-Saxon England, see Boussard, 'Notion de royauté', 55-64; and the characteristically judicious survey of F. Barlow, *Edward the Confessor*, London 1970, 60-72. Evidence for the reality of royal power is cogently presented by J. Campbell, 'The significance of the Anglo-Norman State in the administrative history of western Europe', *Francia* ix, 1980, 117-34, which should now be supplemented by S. Keynes, *The Diplomas of King Aethelred 'the Unready', 978-1016*, Cambridge 1980, especially 126-53, and P. A. Stafford, 'The "Farm of One Night" and the Organisation of King Edward's Estates in Domesday', *Economic History Review* xxxiii, 1980, 491-502.

18 'Le sacre des rois anglo-normands et angevins et le serment du sacre', *ANS* i,* 1978, 49-62. While acknowledging my debt to Professor Foreville, I must also register my disagreement with some of her views: the arbitrary selection of texts in her n. 31 gives a misleading impression of the pre-Conquest development of the royal consecration-rite; 1066 was certainly not the first occasion on which a 'coronation-oath' was given in England (see above, chapter 14, pp. 329-39 and chapter 12, pp. 283-307); and the *Carmen*'s evidence on the Conqueror's consecration seems to me of questionable value (see below, p. 387).

* *Proceedings of the Battle Conference on Anglo-Norman Studies* (hereafter *ANS*)

Table . *Main western royal ordines up to c.1100*[a]

	First English Ordo[b]	*'Erdmann' Ordo* (W. Frankish, late ninth century)[c]	*Second English Ordo* *Earlier version* (c.900)[d]	*Second English Ordo* *Ordo of 973*[e]	*PRG King's Ordo*[f]	*Third English Ordo*[g]
Preliminaries		Petition of Bishops Response of King Enquiry of Bishops to people [Acclamation[h]] *Te deum*	Petition of Bishops Response of King Enquiry of Bishops to people [Acclamation[h]] *Te deum* – King's prostration	Antiphon: *Firmetur* *Te deum* Three-fold promise	Prayers Responsory Antiphon: *Domine salvum fac.* King's prostration Litany Archbishop's enquiry to King King's promise Archbishop's enquiry to people Acclamation	Antiphon: *Firmetur* King's prostration Litany Three-fold promise Bishop's enquiry to people Acclamation
Anointing	Benedictions *Te invocamus* *In diebus* Anointing Antiphon: *Unxerunt* *Deus electorum*	Benediction *Deus qui populis* Anointing *Omnipotens . . . deus creator*	Benedictions *Te invocamus* *Deus qui populis* *In diebus* Anointing Antiphon: *Unxerunt* *Omnipotens . . . deus creator* *Deus electorum* *Deus dei filius*[j]	Benedictions *Te invocamus* *Deus qui populis* *In diebus* Anointing Antiphon: *Unxerunt* *Omnipotens . . . deus creator* *Christe perunge* *Deus electorum* *Deus dei filius*	Benedictions *Benedic domine hunc regem* *Omnipotens . . . creator* *Deus inenarrabilis auctor* Anointing of Hands *Unguantur manus iste* *Prospice* Anointings of head, breast, shoulders and elbows with blessed oil: *Unguo te.* *Spiritus sancti gratia* *Deus qui es iustorum* *Deus dei filius*[j]	Benedictions *Omnipotens . . . creator* *Benedic domine hunc regem* *Deus ineffabilis auctor* Anointing of Hands *Unguantur manus iste* *Prospice* Anointings of breast, shoulders, elbows and head with blessed oil, then head again with chrism. *Deus dei filius* *Deus qui es iustorum*
Investitures	Sceptre *Benedic domine* Staff (*baculus*) *Omnipotens . . . det* Helmet *Benedic . . . fortitudinem*	Ring *Accipe*[i](1) *Deus cuius* Sword *Accipe*[k](1) Crowning *Coronet te* *Omnium domine fons* Sceptre *Accipe sceptrum* Staff (*baculus*) *Accipe*	Ring *Accipe*[i](2) *Deus cuius* Sword *Accipe*[k](1) Crowning *Coronet te* *Deus perpetuitatis* Sceptre *Accipe sceptrum* *Omnium domine fons* Rod (*virga*) *Accipe virgam*[j]	Ring *Accipe*[i](2) *Deus cuius* Sword Antiphon: *Confortare* *Accipe*[k](1) Crowning *Coronet te* *Deus perpetuitatis* Sceptre *Accipe sceptrum* *Omnium domine fons* Rod (*virga*) *Accipe virgam*	Sword *Accipe*[k](2) Armills and Pall Ring *Accipe*[i](3) Sceptre and staff (*baculus*) *Accipe virgam*[j] Crowning *Accipe coronam*	Sword *Accipe*[k](2) Armills: *Accipe* Pall: *Accipe* Blessing of crown: *Deus tuorum* Crowning *Coronet te* *Deus perpetuitatis* Ring *Accipe*[i](3) Sceptre: *Accipe* *Omnium domine fons* Rod (*virga*) *Accipe virgam*
Enthronement	Acclamation Enthronement *Deus perpetuitatis* Three precepts		Benedictions Enthronement *Sta et retine*[j] Three precepts Acclamation	Benedictions Enthronement *Sta et retine*	Benedictions *Benedicat tibi* Enthronement *Sta et retine*[j] Kiss of peace. *Te deum*	Benedictions *Benedicat tibi* Kiss of peace. *Te deum* Enthronement *Sta et retine*

century.[19] (See Table .) I must say at the outset that I am convinced Foreville was right to dissent from the prevailing consensus. But why then any need to echo her dissenting voice? Well, for one thing, not everyone has read his or her Foreville: for

19 For the basic sequence of the English Ordines, see L. G. Wickham Legg, *English Coronation Records*, London 1901. P. E. Schramm summarised the results of his own researches in *A History of the English Coronation*, Oxford 1937. For further references and some revisions of Schramm's views on the First English Ordo, see above, chapter 15, pp. 341-60. See also, above, chapter 16, pp. 361-74.

Notes to Table

a This table is designed to show the basic structure of the various ordines and to allow comparisons to be made between those discussed in this paper. *Incipits* only of the prayers are given. The table is incomplete because (i) it does not show every detail of the ordines included (ii) it omits ordines for queens, and (iii) it omits some important Continental ordines of the ninth and early tenth centuries: for the ordines of Hincmar, the 'Seven-Forms' Ordo (also known as the 'Stavelot' Ordo) and other West Frankish texts, see C. A. Bouman, *Sacring and Crowning*, Groningen 1957, 163-75, and for full editions of the 'Seven-Forms' Ordo and the 'Early German' Ordo, see C. Erdmann, *Forschungen zur politischen Ideenwelt des Frühmittelalters*, Berlin 1951, 83-9.

b See J. L. Nelson, 'The Earliest Royal *Ordo*', in B. Tierney and P. Linehan edd., *Authority and Power. Studies on Medieval Law and Government presented to Walter Ullmann on his seventieth birthday* (1980); above, chapter 15, pp. 341-60.

c See P. E. Schramm, 'Die Krönung bei den Westfranken und Angelsachsen', *Zeitschrift für Rechtsgeschichte, Kanonistische Abteilung* xxiii, 1934, 201-5, reprinted *Kaiser, Könige und Päpste*, Stuttgart 1968, ii, 216-19.

d See P. L. Ward, 'An early version of the Anglo-Saxon coronation ceremony', *EHR* lvii, 1942, 345-58.

e See Schramm, 'Krönung', 221-8, *Kaiser, Könige und Päpste*, 233-9; Nelson, 'Inauguration Rituals', in P. H. Sawyer and I. N. Wood edd., *Medieval Kingship*, Leeds 1977, 63-70; above, chapter 12, pp. 283-308.

f See C. Vogel and R. Elze, *Le Pontifical romano-germanique du dixième siècle*, i, Rome 1963, 246-59.

g See H. A. Wilson, *The Pontifical of Magdalen College*, Henry Bradshaw Society volume xxxix, 1910, 89-95.

h I have put this acclamation in square brackets because it is implicit in the rubric: 'Alloquantur duo episcopi populum in ecclesia inquirentes eorum voluntatem. *Et si concordes fuerint*, agant deo gratias decantantes, "Te deum laudamus".'

i The various ring-formulae are discussed by Bouman, *Sacring*, 129-31.

j This prayer is taken from the West Frankish 'Seven-Forms' Ordo.

k For the sword-formulae, see Schramm, 'Krönung', 204, *Kaiser, Könige und Päpste*, 218, and Erdmann, *Forschungen*, 89.

instance, in two recent publications, Mr H. E. J. Cowdrey[20] and Ms J. L. Nelson[21] have continued to assert the probability that the Second English Ordo was used for the Conqueror. For another thing, all the best recent studies of the Conqueror and the Conquest seem to repeat or implicitly subscribe to that assertion.[22] It will, I predict, die hard; for it carries the imprimatur of the doyen of ordines-researchers, the late P. E. Schramm. To Schramm's work, historians naturally and rightly turn for information on English ordines, and as naturally (but less rightly) tend to reiterate his views. Foreville is therefore an honourable exception, and the force of her challenge deserves to be fully appreciated. In fact, she modestly concealed quite how exceptional she was by referring to J. Brückmann's work,[23] though he still agreed with Schramm about the ordo used for the Conqueror.[24]

What, then, is this ordo, according to Schramm? It is the ordo in Cambridge, Corpus Christi College MS 44, a Canterbury pontifical of the second half of the eleventh century.[25] Here, Schramm argued, we have a unique version of the Second English Ordo containing several variants which can be linked specifically with the Conqueror's situation. The phrase 'by paternal suggestion' has been removed from one prayer, from another the words 'rejoicing in the flower of youth up to this present day' – words thought by Schramm to be inappropriate for a thirty-nine year old![26] More than merely verbal changes were the substitution of new antiphons for two of the four found in other Second English Ordo manuscripts, and the provision of seven other antiphons at each major stage in the rite.[27] In several of

20 'The Anglo-Norman *Laudes Regiae*', *Viator* xii, 1981, 39-78, at 51, n.47. Cowdrey carefully says only 'probably used'; and the identification of the Conqueror's Ordo was of course peripheral to his theme. My debt to this important paper will be very obvious in what follows.

21 'Earliest Royal Ordo', 48 and n.97. See also Turner, *Claudius Pontificals*, xxxi, noting this view, without adverse comment.

22 It may be enough simply to list the names of D. Douglas, C. N. L. Brooke, D. J. A. Matthew, F. Barlow, and R. A. Brown.

23 'Sacre', 59 and n.41, with reference to J. Brückmann, 'The *Ordines* of the Third Recension of the Medieval English Coronation Order', in T. A. Sandquist and M. R. Powicke edd., *Essays in Medieval History presented to Bertie Wilkinson*, Toronto 1969, 99-115.

24 Brückmann, '*Ordines*', 102, n.7.

25 The royal ordo was edited by J. Wickham Legg, *Three Coronation Orders*, Henry Bradshaw Society, xix, 1900, 54-64, with notes, 162-73. On the pontifical, see Brückmann, 'Latin Manuscript Pontificals and Benedictionals in England and Wales', *Traditio* xxix, 1973, 403-404: 'probably . . . Canterbury, possibly St Augustine's or Christ Church'. Cf. Turner, *Claudius Pontificals*, xxxi-xxxviii, making a good case for Christ Church.

26 'Die Krönung bei den Westfranken und Angelsachsen von 878 bis um 1000', *Zeitschrift für Rechtsgeschichte, Kanonistische Abteilung* xxiii, 1934, 117-242, now reprinted with additional references in Schramm's collected papers, *Kaiser, Könige und Päpste*, 4 volumes, Stuttgart 1968, ii, 140-248, at 181-2. (Here and below, page-references for Schramm's articles are given to the reprinted versions in *Kaiser, Könige und Päpste.*) See also idem, *English Coronation*, 28-9.

27 'Vivat rex' at the enthronement has a tenth-century precedent in the version of the Second English Ordo in the *Benedictional of Archbishop Robert*, ed. H. A. Wilson, Henry Bradshaw Society, xxiv, 1903, 147. Other Second Ordo manuscripts have only three antiphons, of which 'Firmetur manus tua' alone reappears in the Corpus 44 Ordo.

these Schramm noted terms like '*Anglisaxoni*' (so, Schramm; but this should be corrected to *Anglisaxonici*), *populus Anglicus* and *Anglia*, which he contrasted with the phrase *regnum Anglorum vel Saxonum* in earlier versions of the Second Ordo. Schramm commented: 'A phrase highly commendable in the days of Dunstan is relegated to obscurity, for under the pressure of Danes and Normans the old racial units of the heptarchy have been welded into one *English* people'.[28] How a phrase can be said to have been 'relegated to obscurity' when it remains (twice) in the consecration-prayer at the very heart of the ordo,[29] is beyond me. And in any case, *Anglia* and *Anglisaxones* were already quite old terms by the mid-eleventh century.[30] As for the verbal changes in the prayers, these need not refer to William I. Edward the Confessor, oddly enough, was probably also thirty-nine when he was consecrated and he too could hardly be said to have succeeded 'by paternal suggestion'. Indeed, that is true more often than not in English and German royal inaugurations throughout the tenth and eleventh centuries, when successions of brothers, nephews, cousins and others exceeded in total those of sons, yet the ordines in both realms continued to prescribe the enthronement-prayer: 'Stand and hold fast now the place that you have held to this time by paternal suggestion, [the place] delegated to you by hereditary right'.[31] This means, I think, that contemporary relevance was not a consideration in the minds of liturgists and that 'standard' texts usually continued to be copied out, and presumably used, without anyone's worrying about their precise aptness. Occasionally an attempt might be made to iron out a conspicuous discrepancy between ritual prescription and reality, as when a twelfth-century French scribe substituted 'the Franks, Burgundians and Aquitanians' for 'the Saxons, Mercians and Northumbrians' of his exemplar (which derived ultimately, of course, from an English ordo of c.900) – but few copyists baulked even at those![32] It is possible that officiants actually omitted or changed such unapt phrases in performance, but if so, in the nature of things we have no record of this kind of verbal alteration. Schramm's view of the Corpus 44 ordo as an instance of such tailoring to suit a particular individual cannot be disproved, though there are few parallels for it in medieval ordines surviving in liturgical books. But in my view, the peculiarities of that ordo, including the removal of 'paternal suggestion' from the prayer 'Stand and hold fast', are better explained in terms of a competent liturgist's attempt, in line with the timelessness of liturgical texts as such, to generalise the suitability of the Second English Ordo.

28 *English Coronation*, 28-9.

29 Ed. Wickham Legg, *Three Coronation Orders*, 55.

30 See e.g. Asser's *Life of Alfred*, ed. W. Stevenson, 1904, reissued with additions by D. Whitelock, Oxford 1959, and editor's comments at 148-50; Æthelweard's *Chronicle*, ed. A. Campbell, London 1962, 9.

31 'Sta et retine amodo statum quem hucusque paterna suggestione tenuisti hereditario iure tibi delegatum.' This is the text of other Second English Ordo manuscripts. Corpus 44 gives: 'Sta et retine regalem statum honoris videlicet et regni solium hereditario iure . . .' (etc.) Continental ordines containing this prayer (see Table I) have *successione* instead of *suggestione*, but this is not significant for my present argument. For the reworkings in some of the other prayers in the Corpus 44 Ordo, see Wickham Legg, *Three Coronation Orders*, xxxix-xl. The most extensive are in 'Accipe virgam', 58. The forms for the vesting with the pall, 59, are peculiar to this manuscript: see below, n.39.

32 See P. L. Ward, 'An early version of the Anglo-Saxon coronation ceremony', *EHR* lvii, 1942, 345-9; **above, chapter 14, p. 333.**

A further argument against Schramm's identification is that a rite very close to that of Corpus 44 survives in a pre-Conquest manuscript: London, British Library MS Cotton Vitellius A.vii, a pontifical probably from Ramsey Abbey.[33] Unfortunately it is hardly possible to check the relevant variants in the prayer-texts, for this is a manuscript that suffered very badly in the fire of 1731 and only fragments of the ordines for king and queen survive.[34] Still, enough can be deciphered to show that the king's ordo contained some (perhaps all?) of the antiphons that appear in Corpus 44[35] – *Angli-saxonici* included.[36]

There seem to be some grounds, then, for questioning the belief that Corpus 44 contains the ordo of the Conqueror. But this raises the further question: was *any* version of the Second English Ordo used on Christmas Day 1066? I turn now to the positive part of Foreville's alternative to Schramm, namely, her suggestion that the Conqueror was consecrated according to the Third English Ordo.[37] Since this means dating the use of the Third Ordo considerably earlier than had previously been done, the argument merits rather fuller exposition than has yet been possible. As the Table shows, the Third English Ordo is a splicing together of forms from the Second English Ordo with forms from the king's ordo in the *Pontificale Romano-Germanicum* compiled at St Alban's, Mainz, c.961, and thereafter diffused throughout western Christendom.[38] The mid tenth century thus provides a firm *terminus post quem* for the Third English Ordo,[39] while the extant manuscripts give a *terminus ante quem*

33 The manuscript was collated by Wickham Legg's son for the edition of the Corpus 44 Ordo in *Three Coronation Orders*, but has since been neglected by Schramm and others. I am very grateful to Simon Keynes for drawing my attention to its possible significance. For its date, see N. Ker, *Catalogue of Manuscripts Containing Anglo-Saxon*, Oxford 1957, 278-9, where, given his dating 's.XI[1]', '1130' is an obvious misprint for '1030' (the date of St Olaf's death) and is included in the list on the corrigenda-slip. Brückmann, 'Pontificals and Benedictionals', 437, unfortunately reproduces the error and gives a dating 'twelfth century'. Cowdrey, '*Laudes Regiae*', 56, correctly dates 's.XI in'.

34 Towards the end of 'Deus electorum', Vitellius A.vii gives the reading: 'te adiuvante', following other Second Ordo manuscripts, against Corpus 44's 'te inspirante', and similarly in the Queen's Ordo prayer 'Deus cuius est omnis potestas', gives 'digna' against Corpus 44's 'firma'. But Wickham Legg's statement, *Three Coronation Orders*, xl, that Vitellius A.vii 'preserves the usual forms of the [Second Ordo] recension in the prayers' is not verifiable, since Corpus 44's most significant variants occur in prayers now illegible in, or totally missing from, Vitellius A. vii.

35 This is true of the antiphons for the deliveries of ring, sword and crown. Apparently Vitellius A.vii had a further antiphon after the (King's Ordo) prayer 'Deus cuius est omnis potestas', but only the rubric is now legible.

36 The ring-antiphon concludes: 'pax . . . sit in nationibus cunctis anglisaxonicae gentis'. In the Queen's Ordo, the post-coronation antiphon, again common to Vitellius A.vii and Corpus 44, contains the phrase: 'hodie coronatur anglisaxonica divine virtutis gloria'.

37 Foreville, 'Sacre', 60. For the manuscripts of the Third English Ordo, see below, n.42.

38 Ed. C. Vogel and R. Elze, *Le Pontifical romano-germanique du dixième siècle*, 3 volumes, Studi e Testi 226, 227 and 269, Rome 1963-72, with the *Ordo ad regem benedicendum* (= Ordo LXXII) at i, 246-59. I refer to the Pontifical hereafter as the *PRG*. On its various forms, see below, nn.42 and 72.

39 Three of its prayers were derived neither from the Second English Ordo nor from the *PRG* but were apparently composed for the Third Ordo itself: the prayers for the delivery of armills and pall, and for the blessing of the crown.

in the early-to-mid twelfth century. Schramm believed he could identify an ideological thrust in the Third English Ordo which placed it in the age of the Investiture Contest and its composer amongst the 'ecclesiastical reformers': hence his label, 'the Ordo of Anselm'.[40] But successive recensions of ordines ought not to be treated like set texts in a Political Ideas course. Liturgy is not the place to look for polemic, and though political ideas can be found in the ordines, they are of the most general, uncontentious and normative kind. To say that many of the prayer-texts are catenae of clichés, scriptural or liturgical, is not perhaps a very helpful observation: nevertheless, the would-be seeker-out of new claims or theories in these formulae will find it disappointingly often true. Anyway, Schramm was wrong, I think, on one important feature of the Third English Ordo. Relying on Wickham Legg's printed edition of what is probably a second, revised version of the ordo, Schramm claimed that anointing-chrism was here replaced by 'the less noble oil . . . of the catechumens'.[41] But the rubric in what I would regard as the ordo's

Though the *PRG* Ordo prescribes for the delivery of armills and pall, like its source the 'Early German' Ordo it gives no special prayers: see C. Erdmann, *Forschungen zur politischen Ideenwelt des Frühmittelalters*, Berlin 1951, 66, 86; and Schramm, 'Die Krönung im Deutschland', *Zeitschrift für Rechtsgeschichte, Kanonistische Abteilung* xxiv, 1935, 184-332, reprinted *Kaiser, Könige und Päpste*, iii, 33-134, at 77. Widukind, *Rerum Gestarum Saxonicarum Libri Tres*, ed. H. E. Lohmann, MGH Scriptores rerum germanicarum in usum scholarum, 66, implies that a prayer accompanied the delivery of the pall to Otto I in 936, but the prayer 'Accipe pallium' in the Third English Ordo is quite different both from this, and from the corresponding text in the Ordo of Corpus 44, *Three Coronation Orders*, 59. The three original prayers in the Third English Ordo do not seem to me to offer any clues as to place or date of composition let alone their author's identity:

> Armillas accipiat dicente metropolitano.
>
> Accipe armillas sinceritatis et sapientiae divinaeque circumdationis indicium quibus intelligas omnes operationes tuas contra hostes visibiles et invisibiles posse esse munitas.
>
> Cum datur pallium.
>
> Accipe pallium quattuor initiis formatum per quod intelligas quattuor mundi partes divinae potestati esse subiectas, nec quenquam posse feliciter regnare in terris nisi cui potestas regnandi fuerit collocata de caelis.
>
> Benedictio coronae regiae.
>
> Deus tuorum corona fidelium, qui in capitibus eorum ponis coronam de lapide pretioso, benedic et sanctifica coronam istam, quatinus sicut ipsa diversis preciosisque lapidibus adornatur, sic famulus tuus gestator ipsius multiplici pretiosarum virtutum munere tua largiente gratia repleatur.

40 *English Coronation*, 37; idem, 'Ordines-Studien III: die Krönung in England vom 10 Jht. bis zur Neuzeit', *Archiv für Urkundenforschung* xv, 1938, (1), 305-91 at 319-24. N. F. Cantor, *Kingship and Lay Investiture in England, 1089-1135*, Princeton 1958, 137-46, despite his polemic stance, makes similar assumptions. Cf. Turner, *Claudius Pontificals*, xli-xlii, with some sensible criticisms of Schramm's interpretation.

41 *English Coronation*, 37, following Wickham Legg's edition of London, BL Cotton Tiberius B.viii in *English Coronation Records*, 30-6, but neglecting the careful survey of all the manuscripts containing the Third Ordo by H. A. Wilson in his preface to *The Pontifical of Magdalen College*, Henry Bradshaw Society, xxxix, 1910, xiii-xxxi.

original version directs a *double* head-anointing:

> et de oleo sanctificato crux fiat super caput eius, et postea de chrismate.[42]

Foreville is in good company in assuming that the Third English Ordo could be considerably older than its earliest extant manuscript. That possibility was noted forty years ago by P. L. Ward,[43] and more recently, Mr Derek Turner has cast Lanfranc in the role of the ordo's composer.[44] But Lanfranc seems to have had no special interest in liturgical innovation, or indeed in liturgy, except in a monastic

42 Oxford, Magdalen College, MS. 226, ed. Wilson, *Pontifical of Magdalen College*, 9; London, BL Cotton Claudius A.iii, ed. Turner, *Claudius Pontificals*, 117. Wilson's arguments for the priority of the version of the Third Ordo contained in these manuscripts have been accepted by P. L. Ward, 'The Coronation Ceremony in Medieval England', *Speculum* xiv, 1939, 160-78, at 174-5, and Turner, *Claudius Pontificals*, xli. A contrary view is expressed by Brückmann, '*Ordines*', 109-10, but he has not so far published any counter-arguments to Wilson's. Brückmann lays some stress on his own 'early twelfth-century' dating of Cambridge, University Library, MS. Ee. 2.3, whose version of the Third Ordo belongs with that of Tiberius B. viii, but himself acknowledges that the relevant part of Claudius A.iii could also be early twelfth-century. Wilson, *Pontifical of Magdalen College*, xxiii-v, dated Cambridge, UL, Ee. 2.3 to 'about 1200', as did Turner, *Claudius Pontificals*, xl. Ward, art. cit., 175, thought that the identification of the *PRG* form behind the Third Ordo would settle the question of which of the latter's two versions is the earlier, but I do not think this is so. The anointing-prescription of neither version is to be found in any *PRG* manuscript. Ward speculated that the 'clumsy' rubric of the Magdalen College version (quoted above) arose from the absence of any head-anointing in the composer's *PRG*-model. But this feature is not found in any extant *PRG* manuscript (though cf. the 'Early German' Ordo, ed. Erdmann, *Forschungen*, 85, and the imperial 'Cencius I' Ordo, ed. Elze, *Die Ordines für die Weihe und Krönung des Kaisers und der Kaiserin*, MGH Fontes Iuris Germanici antiqui in usum scholarum IX, Hannover 1960, 2-3). Since the relevant *PRG* texts (see below, n. 72) all include a head-anointing *de oleo sanctificato*, then an alternative explanation for the clumsiness of the anointing-rubric of the Magdalen College version is the determination of the Third Ordo's composer, confronted with divergent Anglo-Saxon and German liturgical traditions, to preserve, and even stress, the Anglo-Saxon practice of royal chrismation (for which clear evidence can be found in (1) the extensive borrowings from the *Benedictio chrismatis* in the anointing-prayer *Deus electorum* in the First and Second English Ordines and (2) the use of chrism in the West Frankish Ordines drawn on in the Second English Ordo: cf. some details in chapters VI and VII of my unpublished Cambridge Dissertation (1967), *Rituals of Royal Inauguration in Early Medieval Europe*). The Norman Anonymous was using a form of the Second English Ordo but, writing c.1100, insisted on the fact of the king's chrismation: *Die Texte des Normannischen Anonymus*, ed. K. Pellens, Wiesbaden 1966, 140-1. I hope to return in a future paper to the Third English Ordo. A full edition is urgently needed.

43 'Coronation Ceremony', 176.

44 *Claudius Pontificals*, lxi-lxii. M. Gibson, *Lanfranc of Bec*, Oxford 1980, 243 observes: 'The major difficulty in the view that [the Third Ordo] was *composed* with William Rufus in mind is the provision for crowning the Queen'. (Rufus, of course, was unmarried.) But Turner did not suggest that Lanfranc composed the ordo with any specific occasion in mind. It is worth recalling the unspecific, normative character of liturgical texts in general.

context, nor had he any special connexion with the Rhineland home of the *PRG*. From Lanfranc back to 1066 is only a short step. What evidence persuades me to take it? First, the most reliable testimony we have for the events of Christmas Day 1066 makes it clear that the rite included in its opening stages something not to be found in the Second English Ordo, namely, the acclamation shouted by the 'people' (*populus*) inside the church in response to an episcopal inquiry as to the new ruler's acceptability. William of Poitiers recorded the fact that this ritual question-and-answer happened on Christmas Day 1066 because he wanted to describe the famous accident that ensued:

> The armed and mounted men who had been stationed around the abbey to guard it, hearing the tremendous shouting in a language they could not understand, thought that something had gone wrong, and under this misapprehension they set fire to the environs of the city.[45]

Orderic continues and elaborates the story:

> As the fire spread rapidly through the houses, the people who had been rejoicing in the church were thrown into confusion, and a crowd of men and women of every rank and status, impelled by this disaster, rushed out of the church. Only the bishops and a few clergy along with the monks stayed, terrified, in front of the altar, and only just managed to complete the consecration-rite over the king who was trembling violently. Nearly everyone else ran towards the raging fire, some to fight bravely against the force of the flames, but more hoping to grab loot for themselves amid such great confusion. The English, reckoning there was a plot behind something so completely unlooked-for, were extremely angry, and afterwards always held the Normans in suspicion, judging them treacherous . . .[46]

This picture of the trembling Conqueror is an unforgettable one, and to my mind there is no more sensitive comment on it than Professor Allen Brown's:

> For William this must have been the one terrifying moment of his life . . . It must have seemed to him that in spite of all previous signs and portents he was wrong, unworthy, that his God had turned against him and rejected both him and his cause, and it is no wonder that he trembled until the awful moment passed.[47]

The episode probably mattered a good deal to the English too, and if Orderic's suggestion that it had far-reaching effects in alienating English public opinion from

45 *Gesta Guillelmi*, 220. The term *collaudatio* has become current in modern historiography but was not so in contemporary writers or liturgical texts. Though William of Poitiers does not state at what point in the consecration this ritual came, it clearly happened at any early stage as it was a precondition of the anointing. See Table . The opening rubric of the Second English Ordo, as Mr Cowdrey has kindly pointed out to me, certainly does not preclude an acclamation immediately following the 'Te Deum' and before the king's promise. But what does seem specific to the Third Ordo rather than the Second is the procedure of episcopal enquiry-people's response.

46 Orderic, ii, 184.

47 *The Normans and the Norman Conquest*, London 1969, 182.

the Normans is no mere literary embellishment,[48] the ill-omened acclamation would be one part of that consecration likely to survive in contemporary memories.

So it seems clear that this acclamation really took place. Those scholars who have maintained, nevertheless, that the Second English Ordo was the rite in progress have had to postulate a *collaudatio* specially imported for this occasion from the Continent, or else to assume a gap at this point between liturgical prescription and reality. Such gaps did sometimes occur, though rarely if ever at so critical a point in the ritual as we are dealing with here. As for the possibility of a Continental import, the accepted suggestion is of borrowing from the contemporary French rite, the so-called 'Erdmann' Ordo, as used for Philip I in 1059 (and apparently for his Capetian and later-Carolingian predecessors as well:[49] see Table). In the nature of things, this can not be disproved, but it does seem implausible. Why should the *collaudatio* alone have been borrowed if the whole French ordo was in the hands of the designer of the Conqueror's consecration?[50] And can we afford to beg the whole question of who that designer might have been? There is no evidence for the availability of that French ordo in England or in Normandy in the mid eleventh century, though it had of course been one of the components of the Second English Ordo a century and more earlier (see Table). Nor does there seem any good reason to expect liturgical influence from Rheims or Sens in the England of 1066. Lastly, a general objection can be made against needless multiplication of entities – in this case ordines – when one simple alternative explanation of the facts is available: namely, that the Conqueror's ordo, complete with an initial acclamation derived from the royal consecration-rite of the *PRG*, was after all the Third English Ordo.[51]

48 Dr Marjorie Chibnall in discussion at the Fourth Battle Conference suggested that this whole passage was elaborated by Orderic, lacking other evidence than that of the *Gesta Guillelmi*, partly as a foil to his equally dramatic set-piece on William's death (iv, 100-102). Dr Chibnall knows Orderic better than any of us, and her stress on his literary skill and purposes is a just corrective to any simplistic reading of his work as 'straight history'. Moreover, Orderic was writing fifty years or more after the event: Chibnall, Orderic, ii, xv. Nevertheless, he sometimes did draw on 'good oral traditions', Chibnall, Orderic, ii, xxii-xxiv, xxxiv-xxxv; and I think his account of the Conqueror's consecration could well be a case in point. If so, Brown's reconstruction of the Conqueror's reactions seems a useful bit of psycho-history.

49 Schramm, 'Krönung bei den Westfranken', 159-64, with the Ordo-text, 216-21; idem, *Der König von Frankreich*, 2 volumes, 1939, reprinted Weimar 1960, i, 102-3.

50 For instance, the intimate connexion in 'Erdmann' between acclamation and 'Te Deum' might have suggested the latter's shifting to this phase of the rite. 'Erdmann' provides for an enquiry by two bishops of the people's will, but implies they act simultaneously. The *doubling* of the episcopal inquiry on Christmas Day 1066 is a different matter and has an obvious alternative explanation in the need to address two distinct groups of magnates in two different languages. See also following note.

51 Here the rubric prescribes for only *one* bishop to enquire about the people's will. But the generalised nature of the ordines has to be taken into account, as does the obvious modelling on the *PRG* Ordo, 249-50. This is equally true of the reference to 'paternal succession' (rather than the Second English Ordo's 'suggestion') in the enthronement prayer: of course this was as unapt for the Conqueror as 'paternal suggestion' would have been for any of three immediate predecessors, and as either 'paternal suggestion' or 'paternal succession' for several of his twelfth-century successors. But ordines in liturgical books were not designed to take account of such accidents. Cf. above, p. 381.

It needs to be stressed at this point that none of our (admittedly fairly meagre) sources for the Conqueror's consecration conflicts with the hypothesis that the Third English Ordo was used then. None, that is, except the *Carmen de Hastingae Proelio*, and it conflicts with every royal ordo known to have been used during or before this period anywhere in Christendom.[52] But the battle over the *Carmen* – though it seems to be becoming a traditional exercise – is one I have no stomach for here. It is enough to say that as far as the Conqueror's consecration is concerned, the *Carmen*'s account seems to me to fall into Professor Davis's category of 'poetic license'.[53] If I think it very likely that Stigand did attend the Conqueror's consecration, that is not because of the *Carmen*'s 'two metropolitans' but because of what we know from more reliable sources of Stigand's high standing with Normans as well as English in the early years of the Conqueror's reign.[54] I certainly would not claim that the Third English Ordo gives a complete picture of what happened on Christmas Day 1066. The very nature of an ordo is to provide a normative framework of essentials and prayer-texts which can be supplemented ad hoc. For instance, it looks as if at Edward the Confessor's consecration in 1043, the officiating archbishop after receiving the king's oath delivered himself of a little homily, of which no ordo, naturally, preserves any record.[55] I mention this bit of ad hocery because it may help in the interpretation of the Anglo-Saxon Chronicle's account of the Conqueror's consecration:

> [the archbishop] consecrated him king at Westminster. And he pledged himself by his hand with Christ's book and indeed he swore, before [the archbishop] would then set the crown on his head, that he would rule this people as well as any king before him best did, if they would be faithful to him.[56]

Schramm inferred that William took two oaths, the second after the anointing and immediately before the crowning 'to appease the riot'.[57] Again my view is: possible

52 This is acknowledged by C. Morton and H. Muntz, *Carmen*, lvi-lviii; and is very clear from a comparison of the rite described by the *Carmen* as conveniently set out by Barlow, 'The *Carmen de Hastingae proelio*', in *Studies in International History presented to W. Norton Medlicott*, London 1967, 66, with those in Table 1. Foreville in putting a high valuation on the *Carmen*'s account as historical evidence, *ante* i, 58-9 and ii, 18, stressed its concern with liturgical details 'faisant ressortir ainsi sa parenté avec le sacre épiscopal'. Parallels did of course exist between the two rites (cf. Nelson, **above, chapter 14, pp. 333-4)** but I suggest that the *parenté* implied by the *Carmen* is too close for historically-realistic comfort: the ritual sequence it presents – interrogation, prostration and litany, head-anointing, all set within the Mass – is exactly that of episcopal ordinations as generally practised in the eleventh and twelfth centuries: see for instance *PRG*, i, 200-18. The author of the *Carmen* was, I do not doubt, an ecclesiastic who knew how episcopal ordinations were conducted and may indeed have wished to bring out the *parenté* noted by Professor Foreville. But it does not follow that he had special knowledge of what actually went on at the Conqueror's consecration. The critique of R. H. C. Davis, 'The *Carmen de Hastingae proelio*', *EHR* xciii, 1978, 251, seems to me very telling, and is now reinforced by Cowdrey, '*Laudes Regiae*', 50, nn.46 and 47.

53 Davis, *ANS* ii, 2-3.

54 *Carmen*, ll. 803-4; cf. *Gesta Guillelmi*, 214, and evidence cited below, n.98.

55 **See above, 337.**

56 *ASC* 'D', s.a. 1066, 200.

57 *English Coronation*, 185-6.

but unlikely. What I think the Chronicler is doing is, first, making the general statement that the consecration took place, and then, going on to give the details that seem to him most significant, stressing the oath as the precondition of the subsequent inauguration-rite. As for his terminology, he uses 'coronation' in the second place to refer (as we might) to the ritual as a whole.[58] The phrase 'before [the archbishop] would then set the crown on his head' could be an allusion to a brief homily expanding on the obligations incurred in the oath, along the lines of 1043. And the conditional clause 'if they would be faithful to him', following the mention of William's oath, could be a reference to the people's assent as conveyed in the acclamation which immediately follows the king's three-fold promise in the Third English Ordo. The alleged 'discordance'[59] between the accounts of the oath in this Chronicler and in Florence of Worcester I think reflects only the difference between more or less reproducing the text of the oath as given in the ordo, which is what Florence does,[60] and giving a more impressionistic version of the oath's underlying significance, as expounded, perhaps, in the archbishop's homily, which is what the Chronicler does. It is certainly interesting that Howden in his report of Richard I's inauguration mentions a second promise given immediately before the crowning.[61] But I do not think that such a double promise could have persisted in the consecration-rite continuously from 1066 to 1189 without leaving any trace in the relatively numerous Third Ordo manuscripts of the twelfth century. In other words, like Brückmann,[62] I see no reason to doubt that twelfth-century consecrations were conducted substantially according to the Third Ordo; but, unlike Brückmann, I think that is also true of Christmas Day 1066.

But was that the *first* occasion on which the Third Ordo was used? The question seems relevant, because historians are agreed that the Conqueror's consecration gave legitimacy to his rule precisely by identifying it as continuous with Anglo-Saxon tradition, affirming William's claim to succeed *iure hereditario*.[63] If continuity and tradition formed, so to speak, the rite's basic message, was a new ordo an appropriate medium? Now it can certainly be argued that few lay persons, or indeed ecclesiastics, present at Westminster on Christmas Day 1066, and perhaps not William himself,

58 As for instance in the Second English Ordo heading in Claudius A.iii, *Claudius Pontificals*, 89, and *Gesta Guillelmi*, 220. The synecdoche was naturally encouraged by the liturgical presentation of the anointing itself as a spiritual 'coronation' (see Nelson, above, chapter 12, p. 295), and my impression is that it was becoming commoner (substituting for *consecratio* or *ordinatio*) in the eleventh and twelfth centuries, though there are Carolingian precedents. The prayer for the blessing of the crown in the Third English Ordo might be seen as highlighting the importance of the coronation proper: Ward, 'Coronation Ceremony', 175 with n.1, noting the parallel with Byzantine practice. See further, Nelson, 'Symbols in context: rulers' inauguration rituals in Byzantium and the West in the early Middle Ages', *Studies in Church History* xiii; above, 259-81. For the crown-kingdom synecdoche in the twelfth century and later, see K. F. Werner, 'Königtum und Fürstentum im französischen 12. Jht.', *Vorträge und Forschungen* xii, 1968, 218 with n.108 (translated as 'Kingdom and principality in 12th-century France', in T. Reuter ed., *The Medieval Nobility*, Amsterdam 1978, 270 with n.73).

59 Foreville, 'Sacre', 56.

60 Worcester, 229.

61 Howden, *Chronica*, ed. W. Stubbs, *RS* 1868-71, iii, 11.

62 '*Ordines*', 112-15, against H. G. Richardson, 'The Coronation in Medieval England', *Traditio* xvi, 1960, 181-89.

63 See Douglas, *William the Conqueror*, 250-1.

would appreciate the finer points of liturgical usage or realise whether or not the rite contained innovation so long as it presented the essential acts of oath, anointing, crowning, investiture and enthronement. Royal consecrations were not rites that were frequently performed, and were therefore, it might be thought, less liable than, say, priestly ordination-rites, to be fixed by the inherent conservatism of liturgy. But in fact, after an initial period of experimentation in the ninth and tenth centuries, royal ordines in the realms of the Christian West (like the imperial ordo in Byzantium) tended to remain in use over long periods.[64] This tendency was promoted by the monopoly over royal consecrations established relatively early in each realm by one metropolitan. When that monopoly was breached because of special political circumstances, as for instance in France in 1108,[65] the chance of a break in liturgical tradition too might be increased: much could then depend on what ordo the 'alternative' archbishop had to hand.

From these general considerations, let us turn to the particular: the fact was that many, even most, Englishmen who participated in William's king-making had probably witnessed Harold's on 6 January of that same eventful year. In view of later attempts to present William as the rightful direct heir to Edward the Confessor and therefore to subject Harold's reign to a kind of *damnatio memoriae*, it is possible that William's consecration was designed completely to supersede Harold's, replacing it by, so to speak, a carbon copy, performed in the same church[66] and by the same consecrator. However it was perceived by the Normans, William's king-making presumably seemed to the English participants more acceptable, more correct, more legitimate and hence legitimising the more closely it resembled his predecessor's. All this prompts the suggestion that if the Third English Ordo was used for William, it may also have been used for Harold. To test this possibility, we need first to check the liturgical evidence, and here the crucial factor is the *PRG*: could this have been available to an English composer before the Conquest? The manuscripts relevant to tracing the *PRG*'s early influence in England are four in number. The first, London, British Library MS Cotton Tiberius C.i, a composite Salisbury pontifical dated to the mid eleventh century, consists in part of extracts from the *PRG* written in two German hands.[67] Professor Barlow has suggested that the import of these *PRG* texts into England might be linked with Bishop Herman of Ramsbury (Wilts).[68] The second, Cambridge, Corpus Christi College MS 265, is from Worcester and dated to the mid eleventh century.[69] It contains various *PRG* texts, copied from an exemplar, dated between 1022 and 1035, of a Roman version of the *PRG*.[70] The third and fourth manuscripts are still more significant, and what I said about them at the Fourth Battle Conference has needed some elaboration and

64 See above, chapter 14, 332-3.

65 Schramm, *König von Frankreich*, i, 112-13. The political context emerges from Suger, *Vita Ludovici Grossi*, chapter xiv, ed. H. Waquet, Paris 1929, 84-8.

66 The location of Harold's consecration is not certain: E. A. Freeman, *The History of the Norman Conquest of England* 3rd revised edition, Oxford 1877, iii, 623-6, discusses the alternatives of St Paul's or Westminster Abbey. Douglas, *William the Conqueror*, 182, plumps for the latter.

67 Ker, 'Three Old English Texts in a Salisbury Pontifical, Cotton Tiberius C.i', in P. Clemoes ed., *The Anglo-Saxons. Studies . . . presented to Bruce Dickins*, Cambridge, 1959, 262-79.

68 *The English Church, 1000-1066*, London 1963, 82, n.4.

69 Ker, *Catalogue*, 92; Brückmann, 'Pontificals and Benedictionals', 407.

70 M. Andrieu, *Les Ordines Romani du haut moyen âge*, 5 volumes, i, Spicilegium Sacrum Lovaniense xi, 1931, 99.

revision in the light of a forthcoming study by Dr Michael Lapidge.[71] On the basis of far more detailed examination of the contents of Cambridge, Corpus Christi College MS 163 than ever previously made, Lapidge has concluded that this manuscript, dated to the mid eleventh century, is 'the most complete of [the] surviving copies of the Romano-German Pontifical which were written in Anglo-Saxon England'. Further, he has shown its close affinity with a *PRG* manuscript copied from one very probably made at Cologne between 1036 and 1056 for Archbishop Hermann II.[72] As for the last of the four manuscripts in our group, London, British Library MS Cotton Vitellius E.xii: it contains texts which Lapidge argues are so closely related to those in CCCC 163 that 'one must be a copy of the other, or both must be copied from a common exemplar'.[73]

There can be no doubt, then, that the *PRG* was known in England before the Conquest, and in at least two versions, one of them having particular associations with Cologne. What historical context can be given to these data? Edward the Confessor had a well-known liking for foreign clerks, and one of them, the Lotharingian Herman (d.1075) has already been mentioned as a possible conveyor of the *PRG* to England. Herman was sent by Edward to Rome in 1050, and may well

71 'The Origin of CCCC 163', in *Transactions of the Cambridge Bibliographical Society* viii, 1982., 18-28. I am grateful to Dr Lapidge for sharing his insights and generously allowing me to make use of his conclusions in advance of publication. We arrived independently at similar views about Ealdred's role in the diffusion of the *PRG* in England, but Dr Lapidge based his arguments far more solidly by showing (1) the liturgical and paleographical indications of a Cologne connexion and (2) the extent and specificity of Ealdred's liturgical interests. My thanks are due also to Simon Keynes who showed Dr Lapidge a copy of my original paper as delivered to the Fourth Battle Conference.

72 London, BL Addit. MS. 17004. Brückmann, '*Ordines*', 108-9, states that the *PRG* version used in the composition of the Third English Ordo is that found in the manuscripts designated *R* and *T* by Elze and Vogel. But a comparison of the relevant variants shows that more often than not those peculiar to *RT* are absent from the rubrics and prayers of the Third English Ordo in both its versions (cf. above n.42). Elze and Vogel did not collate the readings of Addit. MS.17004 in their edition of *PRG* Ordo LXXII, the king's ordo. Dr Lapidge has kindly informed me that the *PRG* texts in general in Addit. MS. 17004 show more common readings than *RT* with those of English *PRG* manuscripts. My own comparison of the king's ordo in Addit. MS. 17004, ff. 140r-146r with the relevant readings in the Third English Ordo has borne out Lapidge's conclusion. It will be noted, however, that the arrangement of the various anointings in the Third English Ordo differs from that in Addit. MS. 17004: see Table . But in this section of the Ordo, Addit. MS. 17004 coincides with *RT*, and the *PRG* manuscripts which in fact show the Third English Ordo's sequence of hand-anointing followed by anointings of head, breast, etc. are those designated *C* and *D* by Vogel and Elze, and regarded by them as 'preserving most faithfully the primitive arrangement' of the *PRG*: *Pontifical romano-germanique* I, xiii. Yet in other respects, the Third English Ordo diverges from the comparable parts of the *CD* king's ordo. I infer that the composer of the Third English Ordo either had more than one *PRG* version of the king's ordo at his disposal, or used a version slightly different from any now extant. (The third possibility, that he arrived independently at *CD*'s sequence of anointings, seems less likely.)

73 'Origin of CCCC 163', 21.

have travelled via the Rhineland.[74] Others of Edward's foreign clerks, Lotharingian or Norman, are known to have been interested in liturgy, but cannot be linked either with the *PRG* or with its Rhineland area of origin.[75] There is one man, however, for whom precisely those links can be shown, or plausibly surmised: Ealdred, archbishop of York from 1060 to 1069.[76] I would like now to make a case for associating Ealdred with the bringing of the *PRG* into England and with the composition of the Third English Ordo.[77] Happily, his career is exceptionally well-documented because of his connexions with two churches where historical records were kept: Worcester and York.[78] After being a monk at Winchester[79] (he was presumably of West Saxon origin), he became bishop of Worcester in 1046.[80] With his colleague Herman, he attended the Easter Synod at Rome in 1050 'on the king's errand'.[81] In 1054, Edward used him on another errand, this time to the Emperor Henry III. According to Florence of Worcester:

> He was received by the emperor and by Archbishop Hermann of Cologne with great honour, and he stayed [at Cologne] for a whole year. He suggested to the emperor on the king's i.e. Edward's behalf that envoys should be sent to Hungary and that he [Ealdred] should bring back from there the king's nephew Edward son of Edmund Ironside and get him to come to England.

Some lines further on, Florence adds à propos this royal nephew:

74 *ASC* 'C' s.a. 1049, 171. Herman's route is unknown, but cf. *Vita Eadwardi* 34 for Englishmen travelling to Rome via the Rhineland in 1060-1.

75 For Herman, Goscelin, Giso, Leofric and Robert, see Barlow, *English Church*, 82-6. Lapidge, 'Origin of CCCC 163', 26, n.8 notes that *PRG* texts were copied into the so-called Leofric Missal, ed. F. Warren, Oxford 1883, 256-62. Warren, lvii-lviii, linked their inclusion with Leofric bishop of Exeter (1050-72) but did not discuss the problem of their transmission.

76 Still fundamental is Freeman, *Norman Conquest*, ii, Appendix GG, 668-73. See also Barlow, *Vita Eadwardi*, 34, n.4 and idem, *English Church*, 86-90; J. M. Cooper, *The Last Four Anglo-Saxon Archbishops of York*, Borthwick Papers no. 38, University of York Borthwick Institute of Historical Research 1970, 23-9.

77 Note again the cue given by Foreville, 'Sacre', 60.

78 The Worcester evidence is discussed by S. Korner, *The Battle of Hastings, England, and Europe 1035-1066*, Bibliotheca Historica Lundensis xiv, Lund 1964, 43-6. Ealdred himself commissioned a *Life* of St John of Beverley from Folcard of St Bertin, ed. J. Raine, *Historians of the Church of York*, RS London 1879, i, 242. The dedicatory preface gives information on Ealdred's work as archbishop. (For the date of the *Life*, 'shortly before 1066', see Barlow, *English Church*, 89, and idem, *Vita Eadwardi*, lvi-lvii.) More details are given in the twelfth-century *Chronicle of the Archbishops of York*, ed. Raine, *Historians of the Church of York* ii, 344-54. Lapidge, 'Origin of CCCC 163', 21-2 and n.32, has drawn attention to further evidence hitherto neglected in this context: the *Miracula S. Swithuni*, 'apparently composed at Sherborne c.1100' and still unprinted. An edition is included in Lapidge's forthcoming *The Cult of St Swithun*.

79 Worcester, 199: testimony supported apparently independently by the *Miracula S. Swithuni*, London, BL Arundel 169, f.59r: '. . . venerande memorie Aldredus ex monacho Wintoniensi Eboracensis archiepiscopus . . .'

80 *ASC* 'D' s.a. 1047, 165. See Cooper, *Archbishops of York*, 23-4.

81 Cf. n.74 above.

> The king had decided to establish him as the heir to the kingdom after him.[82]

So Ealdred spent a year at Cologne, and with a king-making in view. The anonymous Chronicle of the Archbishops of York shows us Ealdred putting his time in the great ecclesiastical centre to good use:

> He heard, saw and committed to memory many things that pertain to the dignity of ecclesiastical observance and many to the rigour of ecclesiastical discipline – things which he subsequently caused to be observed in the churches of England.[83]

Barlow rightly sees a reference here to Ealdred's reforming of secular chapters as archbishop of York;[84] but *honestas ecclesiasticae observantiae*, as distinct from *disciplina*, could have a more specific connexion with liturgical improvements, and Folcard in his *Life* of John of Beverley gives independent and strictly contemporary evidence of Ealdred's interest in liturgy.[85] One event that Ealdred may well have witnessed and must certainly have heard all about during his Rhineland stay was the royal consecration at Aachen of the child-king Henry (the future Henry IV) on 17 July 1054, for the consecrator on this occasion was, exceptionally, by a special imperial decision to by-pass the claims of Mainz, the archbishop of Cologne, none other than Ealdred's host Hermann.[86] I suggest that among the things Ealdred read at Cologne was the royal ordo in the *PRG* and among the things he may have done with a view to increasing 'the dignity of ecclesiastical observance' back home was to compose or plan a new consecration-rite: the Third English Ordo. If he did this during his stay in Cologne or soon after returning to England,[87] he could well have

82 Worcester, 212, 215. Cf. *Miracula S. Swithuni*, Arundel 169, f. 59r: 'gloriosi regis Eadwardi legatione (sic) ad regem Almannie tulit, a quo honorifice susceptus et multorum munerum liberali largitione donatus, negotio gratia cuius erat per iussione (sic) mittentis sapienter et bene composito . . . in Angliam remeabat . . .'

83 *Historians of the Church of York*, ii, 345.

84 *English Church*, 90.

85 *Historians of the Church of York*, i, 239-42, especially 241. For further evidence, see below, p. 130. On Folcard's career, see Barlow, *Vita Eadwardi*, li-lix.

86 Lampert of Hersfeld, *Annales* s.a. 1054, *Lamperti Opera*, ed. O. Holder-Egger, Monumenta Germaniae Historica. Scriptores rerum germanicarum in usum scholarum, Hannover and Leipzig 1894, 66: 'Imperatoris filius Heinricus consecratus est in regem Aquisgrani ab Herimanno Colonensi archiepiscopo, vix et aegre super hoc impetrato consensu Liupoldi archiepiscopi ad quem propter primatum Mogontinae sedis consecratio regis et caetera negociorum regni dispositio potissimum pertinebat. Sed imperator pocius Herimanno archiepiscopo hoc privilegium vendicabat propter claritatem generis eius, et quia intra diocesim ipsius consecratio haec celebranda contigisset'. For the date, see D. von Gladiss ed., *Die Urkunden Heinrichs IV*, Monumenta Germaniae Historica, Diplomata regum et imperatorum Germaniae vi, part 2, Weimar 1959, 639-41, no. 471; H. Bresslau and P. Kehr edd., *Die Urkunden Heinrichs III*, Monumenta Germaniae Historica, Diplomata regum et imperatorum Germaniae v, Berlin 1931, 442, no. 324; E. Steindorff, *Jahrbücher des deutschen Reichs unter Heinrich III*, 2 volumes, Leipzig 1874-81, ii, 279 with n. 3. Unfortunately, the exact date of Ealdred's arrival in Germany is unknown.

87 Two other liturgical books known to have been brought back to England by Ealdred had been presented to him by Henry III. For the full story, see William of Malmesbury's *Vita Wulfstani*, ed. R. Darlington, London 1928, 5, 15-16.

had in mind the consecrations of Edward Ætheling and his wife Agatha (she was a kinswoman of Henry III);[88] if he completed it after the Ætheling's death in 1057, he may have been thinking of a specific alternative successor to the Confessor for, as Barlow suggests, he was perhaps in search of another English prince when he travelled to Hungary himself in 1058 en route for Jerusalem.[89] But in any event, Ealdred could have composed his new ordo with the more general purpose of liturgical improvement and modernisation in line with the German practice which had so impressed him. The details of Ealdred's biography so far could account for the presence of two *PRG* versions in England (one from Rome, the other from Cologne) in the 1050s, and for the subsequent presence of *PRG* manuscripts in Ealdred's own see of Worcester, in Salisbury, successor-see to Ramsbury where Ealdred's travel-companion was bishop, and perhaps in Winchester, where had begun his career and with which he kept up connexions.[90]

But even if Ealdred had already composed the Third English Ordo in the 1050s, it might never have entered English practice, remaining instead in the limbo of Schramm's 'non-received' ordines,[91] but for two further historical accidents: first Ealdred's own promotion to York in 1060,[92] and second the hardening of opinion against Stigand's intrusion at Canterbury. It was because of the question-mark over Stigand's position that Earl Harold asked Ealdred's predecessor at York to consecrate his foundation at Waltham probably in 1060,[93] but it is also relevant to recall the longstanding association of Ealdred with Harold and his family.[94] So, despite Stigand's presence at the Confessor's deathbed,[95] it was Ealdred whom Harold wanted to officiate at his consecration. On this point, I am convinced we should prefer the evidence of Florence and the York Chronicle,[96] well-informed as they were on Ealdred's career, to that of William of Poitiers whose claim that Stigand consecrated Harold should be assessed in the light of his obvious wish to contrast Harold's wrongful inauguration *non sancta consecratione* with the Conqueror's thoroughly correct one by the admirable Ealdred.[97] Writing after Lanfranc's

Lapidge, 'Origin of CCCC 163', 20, comments that this episode 'provides a plausible context for the advent of the exemplar of CCCC 163 in England'. Cf. also n.82 above.

88 *ASC* 'D', s.a. 1057, 188.

89 Barlow, *English Church*, 87-8.

90 *Miracula S. Swithuni*, Arundel 169, f.59r, records his donation of funds to the Old Minster in (or soon after) 1055. Lapidge, 'Origin of CCCC 163', 18, 21, points out, however, that the conventional attributions of CCCC 163 and Vitellius E.xii to Winchester rest on no conclusive arguments, and he suggests alternative possibilities.

91 'Krönung bei den Westfranken', in *Kaiser, Könige und Päpste*, ii, 160-1.

92 *ASC* 'D', s.a. 1060, 189.

93 *De Inventione Sanctae Crucis*, ed. W. Stubbs, *The Foundation of Waltham Abbey*, Oxford 1861, 21. This twelfth-century work can probably be trusted on this point: Cooper, *Archbishops of York*, 20-1.

94 *ASC* 'D', s.a. 1051, 176; *ASC* 'C', s.a. 1056, 186; Worcester, 215; *Vita Eadwardi*, 34-6. See also Barlow, *English Church*, 87; Cooper, *Archbishops of York*, 23-6; John, 'Edward the Confessor', *EHR* xciv, 1979, 257.

95 *Vita Eadwardi*, 76-7.

96 Worcester, 224; *Chronicle of the Archbishops of York*, *Historians of the Church of York* ii, 348. Cooper, *Archbishops of York*, 26, discusses evidence for Ealdred's relations with Harold during 1066.

97 *Gesta Guillelmi*, 146, 220. See Freeman, *Norman Conquest*, iii, Appendix Note E, 616-26. In discussion at Battle, Chibnall and Brown questioned whether

appointment to Canterbury, William of Poitiers was embarrassed at the degree of favour Stigand actually enjoyed in the early years of the Conqueror's reign,[98] and so had to underline the refusal of his ministrations on Christmas Day 1066 by an alleged contrast with Harold's acceptance of them only months before. As for the other sources claiming that Stigand consecrated Harold: Orderic of course simply copies William of Poitiers here,[99] and the Bayeux Tapestry, if it is not based directly on that same text,[100] surely reflects similar Norman propaganda at this point. Its depiction of *Stigant archiepiscopus* apparently displaying the king to his new subjects after his enthronement[101] might, I suppose, reflect the final rubric and prayer of the Third English Ordo: 'Tunc dicat metropolitanus, "Sta et retine . . ."'.[102] But I am not really convinced that the Tapestry-designer, as Dr Brooks has claimed,

William of Poitiers, writing within a few years of the event, could have misrepresented so well-known a fact as the identity of Harold's consecrator. But the character of his work is clearly crucial: it was written for the Conqueror, just as Asser's *Life of Alfred*, with an equally clear misrepresentation of (admittedly less recent) reality was almost certainly written for Alfred (see above, chapter 13, pp. 309-27). In both cases the very slim manuscript tradition supports the view that circulation was always limited, essentially to a court audience, and that widespread 'publication' was never intended. In such circumstances, some tampering with historical fact is hardly surprising, given medieval notions of 'truth-telling'. See also the critique of William of Poitiers by Morton, 'Pope Alexander II', 378-80. John Palmer pointed out that a similar, and still more blatant, misrepresentation may have occurred in the official record of Richard II's surrender at Conway in 1399: the *Rolls of Parliament* state that the Archbishop of Canterbury was there, thus lending legitimacy to the Lancastrian case, but what Palmer argues is that our best source says nothing of the archbishop's presence. See J. J. N. Palmer, 'The authorship, date and historical value of the French Chronicles on the Lancastrian Revolution', *Bulletin of the John Rylands Library* lxi, no. 1, 1978, 1-37, and lxi, no. 2, 1979, 38-61, especially 57-9. I am very grateful to Dr Palmer for bringing this case to my notice. Twentieth-century experience should have ensured our willingness to entertain the possibility of lying in official documents even when the truth can readily be ascertained from external or unofficial sources: the possibility surely increases when, as in the Middle Ages, there were few or no written records to set against those produced by, or for, the powers that were. The processes whereby ideology was formed and disseminated have not yet received enough attention from medievalists: merely to nod in the direction of the Church is to beg too many interesting questions.

98 *Gesta Guillelmi*, 244, 252. Bishop Remigius of Dorchester was consecrated by Stigand in 1067: this caused him some embarrassment after Lanfranc's appointment. See M. Richter ed., *Canterbury Professions*, Torquay 1973, no. 32, with Richter's comments, lvi, lxi. Stigand took precedence over Ealdred in several charter-attestations in 1068 and 1069: Cowdrey, '*Laudes Regiae*', 52, n.52 and 54, n.55.

99 Orderic, ii, 136-8, with Chibnall's comments, 138, n.1.

100 Foreville, Introduction to *Gesta Guillelmi*, xxii, supposes that *BT** was a source for William of Poitiers. Other writers have argued for the inverse relationship: see N. P. Brooks, 'The authority and interpretation of the Bayeux Tapestry', *ANS* i, 1978, 5 with nn. 17 and 18.

101 *BT*, pl.34.

102 *Pontifical of Magdalen College*, 95; *Claudius Pontificals*, 120.

* The Bayeux Tapestry (hereafter *BT*).

'clearly . . . knew the coronation ordo',[103] for neither the laymen's presentation of the sword nor the king's holding an orb have any liturgical counterparts at this period, but are presumably based on iconographic models.[104] The scene may, incidentally, be another instance of the kind of *double-entendre* noticed by Brooks elsewhere in the Tapestry, where there seems to be 'one message for its Norman audience' yet at the same time 'a hint' of an English, indeed a Canterbury, version of events.[105] For if Brooks is right in seeing St Augustine's Canterbury as the likely home of the Tapestry's designer(s), then it is tempting to explain Stigand's prominence in this scene by its double reference – for Normans, to the unholiness of Harold's consecration, for Englishmen (especially those at Canterbury), to Stigand's patronage of St Augustine's at the expense of Christ Church.[106] Brooks rightly says that St Augustine's had reason to remember Odo with gratitude, but this was hardly less true of Stigand.

When the magnates gathered at Westminster at Christmas 1065, they were aware that the Confessor was dying. Under the circumstances, it is reasonable to suppose that Ealdred of York might have provided himself for the eventuality of a new king-making. Given the shortage of time for lengthy discussion, Ealdred would have been free to use the ordo he had ready. Thus, I suggest, the Third English Ordo fortuitously entered English usage. It was because it had been used by Ealdred already on 6 January 1066 that the same consecrator used it again on 25 December. In other words, the rite of Harold was also, and precisely because it had been Harold's, the rite of the Conqueror.

William's king-making was aimed primarily at English public opinion, an act of reconciliation marking the end of a time of harrying and war, and inaugurating

103 'Bayeux Tapestry', 20.

104 In *BT*, pl.34, the two laymen presenting the sword on Harold's right seem to be descended from similar soldierly figures in Carolingian and later ruler-portraits, all of which in turn go back ultimately to late-classical models: see e.g. Lothar I's picture in his Gospel-book, Paris, Bibliothèque nationale MS. lat. 266, reproduced in Schramm, *Kaiser, Könige und Päpste* ii, Abb. 12, with Schramm's comments, 102. For other examples, see Schramm, *Die Deutschen Kaiser und Könige in Bildern ihrer Zeit*, Leipzig 1928, Abb. 29, 41, 85, 99, and Schramm and F. Mütterich, *Die Denkmale der deutschen Könige und Kaiser*, Munich 1962, pl.56, 108, 111. The iconography of the sword presented to Harold, quite distinct from that of Carolingian models, may be another *BT double-entendre*: in late Anglo-Saxon illustrations of the Old Testament such as those of London, BL Claudius B.iv, ff.22, 34, 48, 60b, 68b, 71, 76 and 84, the 'unguarded' sword (unsheathed and raised, point upwards) indicates impending conflict. For this information, I am very grateful to Jenny Kiff who is preparing a study of the Anglo-Saxon iconographical background to the *BT*. On Harold's orb, see Schramm, *Sphaira-Globus-Reichsapfel*, Stuttgart 1958, 116-17, relating this to the iconography of late Anglo-Saxon royal seals, and this in turn to contemporary German models. For illustrations of Ottonian and Salian seals showing orbs similar to Harold's in *BT*, pl.34, see Schramm, *Kaiser und Könige in Bildern*, Abb. 59, 62, 68 etc., and for a similar seal-image of Robert the Pious, see J. R. Johnson, 'The Tree of Jesse window of Chartres: *Laudes Regiae*', *Speculum* xxxvi 1961, fig. 3. It is possible that Harold really had an orb among his regalia though it had no place in the inauguration-ordo; orbs have been found in the graves of contemporary German rulers: see e.g. Henry III's, Schramm and Mütterich, *Denkmale*, Abb. 158.

105 Brooks, 'Bayeux Tapestry', 11-13.

106 Cf. Gibson, *Lanfranc*, 168.

peace between conquerors and conquered.[107] Three months later there took place in Normandy a further series of rituals that confirmed the meaning of the consecration yet gave it a new, Norman, dimension. William's return was a triumphant *adventus* where he paraded not captives but new companions and followers[108] in his vastly expanded retinue. The two high-points were a *joyeuse entrée* into Rouen, the ducal 'metropolis', and the splendid Easter celebrations at Fécamp, the ducal house-monastery. William of Poitiers says of the former occasion:

> Nothing was left out that was customarily performed for the purpose of such doing of honour to the duke. Furthermore, if something new could be devised, it was added too.[109]

If a specific meaning can be given to that 'something new', I would propose the singing of *laudes regiae* such as those of Rouen origin preserved in an early twelfth-century manuscript[110] and including the acclamation:

> .N. Normannorum duci invictissimo pax salus et victoria.

William in 1067 seems a good candidate for identification as the *dux invictissimus*.[111] It is commonly assumed that *laudes regiae* had been sung in Normandy before 1066, and Cowdrey in his recent fine survey of the evidence thinks this 'a reasonable supposition' in the light of the fact that a Norman *laudes regiae* text originating from Fécamp got over to England not long after the Conquest.[112] But Cowdrey goes on to stress that 'the absence of any reference to William as *rex* has no significance for the date, since [the Rouen text just quoted] indicates that the Norman king-dukes were never acclaimed as *rex* in texts that were sung within the *regnum Francorum*'.[113] If it is possible that *laudes regiae* were the novelty in the Rouen *adventus*, it may be worth floating the further suggestion that the Fécamp community, not to be outdone by the cathedral clergy, devised its own form of *laudes regiae* and sang them for William on Easter Day 1067. William of Poitiers says that the duke took special care that 'the crowds of soldiers and people' should

107 The consecration carries this significance of a temporal demarcator in the Penitential Ordinance: cf. n.2 above. See also Cowdrey, 'Bishop Ermenfrid of Sion and the Penitential Ordinance following the Battle of Hastings', *Journal of Ecclesiastical History* xx, 1969, 234-5, and for the date of the Ordinance, idem, '*Laudes Regiae*', 59, n.68.

108 *Gesta Guillelmi*, 242-4, and 256 where the term *adventus*, used to describe the Conqueror's entry into Rouen, may well have ritual connotations: see E. H. Kantorowicz, *Laudes Regiae*, Berkeley 1946, 71-6.

109 *Gesta Guillelmi*, 256.

110 Rouen, Bibliothèque municipale MS 537, f.90r-v, now edited by Cowdrey, '*Laudes Regiae*', 76-8.

111 This suggestion might be thought incompatible with the presence in the text of an acclamation: 'Regi Francorum .N. pax salus et victoria'. But this is standard form in French *laudes regiae*. What is remarkable, indeed 'virtually unknown outside Normandy' (Cowdrey, '*Laudes Regiae*', 49) is the acclamation to a non-royal layman. Cf. Kantorowicz, *Laudes Regiae*, 168-9, inferring 'the curious sovereignlike position' of Duke William.

112 '*Laudes Regiae*', 48, with references at n.43 to other writers. The Fécamp *laudes regiae* present in Rouen, Bibl. munic. MS. 489, f.71 and in Salisbury, Cathedral Library MS 89, recto of title page, are edited by Cowdrey, '*Laudes Regiae*', 68-9. They contain an acclamation: 'Guillelmo Normannorum duci salus et pax continua'.

113 '*Laudes Regiae*', 48.

participate in that liturgical celebration, forcing them to 'break off for a while from their frivolous pastimes and hasten together to things divine'.[114]

So, whether or not Norman *laudes regiae* had been sung before, they very probably were sung in the Spring of 1067. Why should they have been thought so apt? First and foremost, they expressed the sharing of the Norman Church, and especially the cathedral and monastery that had closest links with the ducal dynasty, in William's triumph – and in its rewards. The initiative in devising an elaborate liturgical performance would have been ecclesiastical rather than ducal. But the Norman Church knew what was expected of it, and the duke's behaviour at Fécamp suggests that he appreciated the usefulness of rituals that proffered 'an unparalleled blazoning of ducal power'.[115] The stress on peace in the Fécamp *laudes regiae* may be linked with another important suggestion of Cowdrey's: that the Fécamp Easter assembly of 1067 may have been the occasion of the promulgating of the Penitential Ordinance with its reference back to Hastings and to the months of continuing 'public war' up to the consecration on Christmas Day.[116] If this association is correct – and it fits with William's preoccupation in 1067 with issuing peace-edicts in Normandy and perhaps deciding to found Battle Abbey as an 'act of reparation' in England[117] – this might explain the omission from the Fécamp *laudes regiae* of the usual acclamation for 'the whole army' and the attachment of the soldier-saints Maurice and Sebastian to William instead.

There is no doubt, I think, that the message that William wanted to convey to his Norman followers was that of his own increased power, his own authority as arbiter of war and peace. Whether the *laudes regiae* were a very useful teaching aid in Normandy is more open to question. For there the *laudes regiae* were, it seems, usually performed in the duke's absence, their hearers largely consisting of clergy or monks.[118] This was preaching to the converted. In England, by contrast, the *laudes regiae* in the Conqueror's reign seem to have been particularly associated with great public occasions attended by important laymen. The first was Matilda's consecration as queen on 11 May (Pentecost) 1068.[119] Cowdrey argues powerfully that this was probably the first time *laudes regiae* were sung in England, for such evidence as has been adduced for pre-Conquest *laudes regiae*, and indeed crown-wearings, is either too late or too flimsy to convince, while the *laudes* mentioned in the *Carmen*'s account of William's consecration whatever they are can hardly be *laudes regiae*.[120]

114 *Gesta Guillelmi*, 260.

115 '*Laudes Regiae*', 49.

116 '*Laudes Regiae*', 59. Cf. above, n. 107.

117 *Gesta Guillelmi*, 262; Orderic, ii, 198, 208. Cowdrey, '*Laudes Regiae*', 60, notes a contemporary German parallel, and suggests the link with the decision to found Battle. Eleanor Searle, 'The Abbey of the Conquerors', *ANS*, ii, 1979, 156, puts the foundation in 'the 1070s', but one of her main arguments is its association with the Penitential Ordinance which she dates similarly. On the dating of the Ordinance, I have been persuaded by Cowdrey's arguments: see above n. 107.

118 Kantorowicz, *Laudes Regiae*, 169; Cowdrey, '*Laudes Regiae*', 46-7.

119 Like her husband, in Westminster Abbey: *ASC* 'D', s.a. 1067 (for 1068), 202. Cowdrey, '*Laudes Regiae*', 52 with n. 52, cites charter evidence to show that the occasion coincided with a well-attended Pentecost court.

120 Cowdrey, '*Laudes Regiae*', 50, n. 46, to my mind effectively refutes the arguments of H. G. Richardson and G. O. Sayles, *The Governance of Medieval England*, Edinburgh 1963, Appendix 1, 403-11; and 50-1, n. 47, shows the difficulty of accepting ll. 805-8 of the *Carmen* as evidence of *laudes regiae*.

The 1068 text has now been edited and discussed in detail by Cowdrey[121] and shown to be a remarkable and unique composition. But I must confess to being rather less impressed than Cowdrey by a 'symmetry' which, as he himself notes, is achieved at the cost of some curious, if not inept, pairings of heavenly and earthly personages – notably when Mary Magdalen and three holy virgins are assigned as intercessors for 'the chief men of the English and the whole army'.[122] More seriously, I am not entirely convinced that this text 'expressed to perfection the "political theory" of the Norman Conquest': not even when 'political theory' is put in inverted commas![123] *Laudes regiae* always carried one basic ideological message of hierarchical order in heaven as the template for an earthly hierarchy headed by the pope with the king (or more rarely the local bishop) second and the various ecclesiastical and secular powers ranked beneath. For all its peculiarities, the 1068 text seems to me to have no more complicated message than that; and so it is only in this general sense that the formula can be said to have been 'well suited to William's purposes in the immediate aftermath of the Conquest of England'.[124] If it did have a 'theory' to present, then whatever purposes we discern should be attributed to a clerical composer rather than directly to William himself.

In discussing the sources of the 1068 text, Cowdrey has shown that a first and major one was a distinctively English Litany of the Saints, but has also suggested that another possible source may have been German *laudes regiae* texts, especially those associated with the Emperor Henry III.[125] This second suggested source could tally, in the most general way, with 'an attempt on William's part to display his newly-won regality upon a German, rather than a Capetian model',[126] since from William's standpoint, the far more prestigeous German monarchy was the obvious one to imitate. But, as Cowdrey has observed, German liturgical influence could give a clue to the composer of the 1068 text. After considering several possible candidates, Cowdrey plumps for Bishop Ermenfrid of Sion, who may have visited Normandy in 1067 and 'may have advised William about his ecclesiastical plans in England including the queen's coronation'.[127] Certainly, Ermenfrid, as a confidant of German kings, is likely to have been familiar with German *laudes regiae*. But is not a likelier candidate one whose career could account as well for the English as for the German component in the 1068 text? My own hunch is that the composer was Ealdred of York, who was also Matilda's consecrator; and the likelihood of some kind of connection, at least, with Ealdred is much strengthened by Lapidge's analysis of the other contents of Vitellius E.xii[128] and his demonstration that their

121 '*Laudes Regiae*', 52-5, with the text edited at 70-1, from Vitellius E. xii.

122 '*Laudes Regiae*', 61.

123 '*Laudes Regiae*', 53.

124 '*Laudes Regiae*', 53, and cf. 55: 'The *Laudes regiae* of 1068 were drafted . . . to express William I's view of divine and human affairs as he at that time wished to communicate it to his subjects both French and English . . .' It is true that the *principes* attending the Pentecost court of 1068 would have heard sung *laudes regiae* which included the acclamation: 'Omnibus principibus Anglorum . . . vita et victoria'; but were they themselves aware of that liturgical detail, or did they simply receive a general impression of ritual splendour and refinement? This again raises the problem referred to at the end of n. 97, above.

125 '*Laudes Regiae*', 55-8.

126 '*Laudes Regiae*', 58.

127 '*Laudes Regiae*', 60.

128 Cf. above, **390.**

special features are best explicable by reference to the known interests and doings of Ealdred.[129] There may be a parallel between 1068 and Edgar's consecration in 973: on both occasions, perhaps, a crucial factor was that one of the officiants had become familiar with German ritual and sought to transplant some of it to England.[130] The *laudes regiae* of 1068 could thus be seen as a post-Conquest import but in no sense a Norman one. The use of the imperial epithet *serenissimus*[131] should be seen in the context of Anglo-Saxon ideas of imperial kingship and of a persistent English admiration for German imperial models. As for the 'political theory' to be read in this text, it is entirely in line with Anglo-Saxon tradition.

I cannot end this paper without saying something about the festal crown-wearings[132] with which performances of the *laudes regiae* were often associated.[133] There is indirect evidence for these from the early years of William's reign. A *sublimatio* was staged at London for Christmas 1067, when the king, apparently in seasonal spirit, 'sweetly invited all to kisses' – kisses of peace, as Orderic's translator has assumed, or kisses associated with renewed oaths of fidelity?[134] It seems likely that William wore his crown for Matilda's consecration at Pentecost 1068,[135] and this may well have been the occasion for a true *Festkrönung*. Before Christmas 1069, William, *inter bella*, sent from the North to Winchester for 'his crowns, royal insignia and plate', so that a crown-wearing could be held at York.[136] In the 1070s, the evidence fails: we have little more than occasional references to the king's spending Easter at Winchester (1070, 1072, 1076), Pentecost at Windsor (1070) and Christmas at Westminster (1075). Perhaps regular crown-wearings continued. Mr Gillingham has pointed out to me that a Pentecost assembly at Clarendon (or possibly Salisbury) is implied for 1072(?) by the famous Evesham writ which also seems to suggest that those summoned were expected to be 'prepared' to take an

129 Lapidge, 'CCCC 163', 21-2. Lapidge thinks it even possible that Vitellius E. xii could be a remnant of Ealdred's own manuscript, compiled over a period from 1054 to 1068, though he also notes some difficulties in this hypothesis. Against my suggestion that Ealdred himself composed the *laudes regiae*, Lapidge, n. 28, drawing attention to the fact that the text is heavily-neumed, proposes Folcard, whose musicianship was praised by Orderic, vi, 150. Perhaps client and patron collaborated? Lapidge promises a full discussion of Folcard's possible authorship in a forthcoming article in the *Yorkshire Archaeological Journal*.

130 *Vita Oswaldi*, ed. Raine, *Historians of the Church of York* i, 435-6, describes Oswald's visit to Rome in 972. While there, he may have witnessed, or would surely have heard about, the coronation by the pope of Otto II's bride Theophano: J. F. Böhmer, *Die Regesten des Kaiserreiches unter Otto II*, revised edition by H. L. Mikoletzky, Graz 1950, 270. *Vita Oswaldi*, 435, mentions Edgar's contacts with the Ottonian court in the 960s. On the imperial connotations of 973, see above, chapter 12, 300-3.

131 *Laudes regiae* of 1068, ed. Cowdrey, '*Laudes Regiae*', 70: 'Wilhelmo serenissimo a deo coronato magno et pacifico regi vita et victoria'.

132 See K.-U. Jäschke, 'Frühmittelalterliche Festkrönungen?', *Historische Zeitschrift* ccxi, 1970, 556-88.

133 Cowdrey, '*Laudes Regiae*', 47-8.

134 Orderic, ii, 210: 'Adventui regis Angli occurrerunt: ipsumque tam honorificentia monasteriali quam saecularibus officiis sullimaverunt. Rex . . . dulciter ad oscula invitabat . . .'

135 Cf. above, n. 119.

136 Orderic, ii, 232.

oath to the king.[137] We have more information towards the close of William's reign, notably the statement in the Anglo-Saxon Chronicle's epitaph on the Conqueror:

> He was very dignified. He wore his royal crown three times a year as often as he was in England at Easter at Winchester, at Whitsuntide (Pentecost) at Westminster, at Christmas at Gloucester. On these occasions all the great men of England were assembled about him: archbishops, bishops, abbots, earls, thegns and knights.

But there is no break in the Chronicle's text there; it continues:

> He was so stern and relentless a man that no-one dared to do anything against his will . . .

And the Chronicler goes on to speak of 'earls imprisoned' and 'bishops deprived of their sees and abbots their abbacies'.[138] We recall that it was at the 1075 Christmas court at Westminster that the king wreaked vengeance on those who had joined the great revolt of that year.[139] Given their political context, it was hardly surprising that William's crown-wearings made such an impression, anyway towards the end of the reign when perhaps their staging assumed greater regularity. It was in these last years that William may have felt a still greater need than before for impressive rituals that demonstrated the Anglo-Norman Church's support for his régime and presented the king to his great men and their vassals as the divinely appointed ruler exalted over them all. A similarly increased need for new oaths and bowings[140] was the natural corollary. The Domesday Survey belongs here too: ordered at the Gloucester Christmas court of 1085[141] and conducted as a kind of vicarious royal progress, it had a purpose, so Dr Clanchy has observed, not only practical but also symbolic. The name 'Domesday' is contemporary, and must have evoked 'the tremendous image of Christ in majesty seated as judge . . .'[142] The crown-wearing king intended to project an earthly version of just that tremendous image.

And there I might have chosen to leave the rites of the Conqueror. But instead I will end by looking briefly at the image from another perspective. The Chronicler qualified his account of William's crown-wearings with the phrase, 'as often as he was in England'. What about Normandy? Was it that the Chronicler simply did not know about crown-wearings there, or was he implying a real contrast? In view of William's continuing care to preserve formal Capetian precedence in Normandy and to assert for himself no more than ducal status there, it seems fairly clear that he staged no crown-wearings in the duchy.[143] There was also the matter of Norman

137 *EHD** ii, 895. The date 'before the Octave of Easter' is mistakenly given in *Regesta*, i, 17. (John Gillingham also kindly drew my attention to this error.) Possible parallels between this occasion and the Salisbury Oaths of 1086 have been noted by Matthew, *The Norman Conquest*, London 1966, 117-20.

138 *ASC* 'E', s.a. 1086, 219-20.

139 *ASC* 'D', s.a. 1076 (for 1075), 212.

140 *ASC* 'E', s.a. 1085 (for 1086), 217: '⁊ ealle hi bugon to him. ⁊ weron his menn. ⁊ him hold aðas sworon þ hi woldon ongean ealle oðre men him holde beon.' Earle and Plummer, 362, treat *holde* here as a nominative plural – the product of a semantic evolution paralleling that of Latin *fidelis*, *fideles*.

141 *ASC* 'E', s.a. 1085, 216.

142 M. T. Clanchy, *From Memory to Written Record*, London 1979, 18 and 121-2.

143 See the canons of the Council of Lillebonne (1080) as cited by J. Le Patourel, *The Norman Empire*, Oxford 1976, 239 n.2. I am grateful to Mr Cowdrey for help on this point.

* *English Historical Documents*.

attitudes to royalty, and here it is relevant to recall one more well-known story, told in the anonymous *Life* of Lanfranc attributed to Milo Crispin:

> It was one of those three great festivals on which the king, wearing his crown, is accustomed to hold his court. On the day of the festival, when the king was seated at table adorned in crown and royal robes, and Lanfranc beside him, a certain jester (*scurra*), seeing the king resplendent in gold and jewels, cried out in the hall in great tones of adulation: 'Behold, I see God! Behold, I see God!' Lanfranc turning to the king said: 'Don't allow such things to be said of you . . . Order that fellow to be severely flogged, so that he never dares to say such things again'.[144]

This story has been cited by some historians to illustrate the tremendous image of the *rex coronatus* and the propaganda impact of crown-wearings on the Conqueror's subjects.[145] But is this really what it implies? Ought we to take as seriously as Lanfranc reportedly did the exclamations of the fool? If this *scurra* was a Norman (and William would hardly have had an English jester) he may have been expressing a more than merely personal reaction to William's ritual efforts. And since high ideological solemnity is not what we expect from a fool, that reaction, I suggest, was something less than reverential. We can remember the Conqueror's wariness about using his royal title in relation to his Norman subjects, his care to maintain some kind of distinction (if not a logical one) between his roles in kingdom and duchy.[146] Kingship of any sort can have meant little in Normandy before 1066: Dudo's story of Rollo's refusal to kiss the foot of Charles the Simple, and of Rollo's man lifting the royal foot and throwing the king backwards,[147] was more than a Norman banana-skin joke: it reflected a sturdy scepticism about royal claims, which presumably appealed to a Norman audience. By 1086, the cult of kingship had made so little headway amongst laymen in Normandy that the Conqueror's corpse was abandoned and left 'almost naked' by those who had attended his deathbed, and when the clergy arranged his burial at Caen, one of the locals popped up with a claim to the burial ground.[148] The response of the fool, confronted with the most imposing spectacle majesty could offer, was parody. Did he not expect the duke to share the joke (he was at table, after all) with his old *contubernales*?[149] And might not the Conqueror have done so too? But the shocked Lanfranc intervened, and the king, self-consciously playing out his theocratic role, presumably had the blasphemer whipped. The crown-wearing Conqueror, God's anointed, *serenissimus*, knew much about the uses of royal rites, but knew at the same time, and never more so than in his latter years, the limits imposed by the political realities of Norman sentiment and power. To eleventh-century Normans, even the most angelic royal image had feet of clay. We should leave the last word – *magna adulationis voce* – with the Conqueror's fool: *Ecce deum video. Ecce deum video*.

144 *Vita Lanfranci*, cap. 13, PL 150, 53-4. On the attribution of this work, see Gibson, *Lanfranc*, 196-8. For the meaning of *scurra*, see J. D. A. Ogilvy, '*Mimi, scurrae, histriones*', *Speculum* xxxviii, 1963, 603-19. Cf. Gibson, *Lanfranc*, 140 with n.2. Douglas, *William the Conqueror*, 258, writes of Lanfranc 'reproving' a 'clerk' (!)

145 See Douglas and Gibson in works cited in previous note; also Cowdrey, '*Laudes Regiae*', 52.

146 Hollister, 'Anglo-Norman *Regnum*', *Speculum* li, 1976, 207-8.

147 Dudo, 169.

148 Orderic, iv, 100-106. But cf. n.48 above.

149 I echo the term used in *Gesta Guillelmi*, 104.

INDEX